Lecture Notes in Computer Science 8566

Commenced Publication in 1973
Founding and Former Series Editors:
Gerhard Goos, Juris Hartmanis, and Jan van Leeuwe

Vijay Atluri   Günther Pernul (Eds.)

Data and Applications Security and Privacy XXVIII

28th Annual IFIP WG 11.3 Working Conference, DBSec 2014
Vienna, Austria, July 14-16, 2014
Proceedings

 Springer

Volume Editors

Vijay Atluri
Rutgers University
1 Washington Park, Newark, NJ 07102, USA
E-mail: atluri@rutgers.edu

Günther Pernul
Universität Regensburg
Universitätsstraße 31, 93053 Regensburg, Germany
E-mail: guenther.pernul@wiwi.uni-regensburg.de

ISSN 0302-9743   e-ISSN 1611-3349
ISBN 978-3-662-43935-7   e-ISBN 978-3-662-43936-4
DOI 10.1007/978-3-662-43936-4
Springer Heidelberg New York Dordrecht London

Library of Congress Control Number: 2014941798

LNCS Sublibrary: SL 3 – Information Systems and Application, incl. Internet/Web and HCI

Typesetting: Camera-ready by author, data conversion by Scientific Publishing Services, Chennai, India

Printed on acid-free paper

Springer is part of Springer Science+Business Media (www.springer.com)

Preface

This volume contains the papers presented at the 28th Annual IFIP WG 11.3 Working Conference on Data and Applications Security and Privacy (DBSEC) held in Vienna, Austria, July 14–16, 2014. This year's conference continued its tradition of being a forum for disseminating original research results and practical experiences in data and applications security and privacy.

This year we had an excellent program that consisted of 8 regular research paper sessions with 22 regular research papers, and 4 short papers, which were selected from a total of 63 submissions after a rigorous reviewing process by the Program Committee members and external reviewers. These sessions included such topics as access control, privacy, networked and mobile environments, data access, cloud databases and private retrieval. In addition, the program included two keynote talks by Chris Clifton and Reinhard Posch.

The success of this conference was a result of the efforts of many people. We would like to extend our appreciation to the Program Committee members and external reviewers for their hard work. We would like to thank the general chairs, Pierangela Samarati, and Edgar Weippl, for taking care of the organization aspects of the conference. We would also like to thank Yvonne Poul for serving as the local arrangement chair and for promptly updating the conference web page, and Giovanni Livraga for serving as the publication chair. Special thanks go to Alfred Hofmann, Editorial Director of Springer, for agreeing to include these conference proceedings in the Lecture Notes in Computer Science series.

Last but not least, my thanks go to all of the authors who submitted papers and to all of the attendees. We hope you find the program stimulating and beneficial for your research. Welcome and enjoy the conference.

July 2014

Vijay Atluri
Günther Pernul

Organization

Program Committee

Gail-Joon Ahn	Arizona State University, USA
Claudio Agostino Ardagna	Universita' degli Studi di Milano, Italy
Vijay Atluri	Rutgers University, USA
Joachim Biskup	Technische Universität Dortmund, Germany
Marina Blanton	University of Notre Dame, USA
David Chadwick	University of Kent, UK
Soon Ae Chun	CUNY, USA
Frédéric Cuppens	Télécom Bretagne, France
Nora Cuppens-Boulahia	Télécom Bretagne, France
Sabrina De Capitani Di Vimercati	Universita' degli Studi di Milano, Italy
Mourad Debbabi	Concordia University, Canada
Josep Domingo-Ferrer	Universitat Rovira i Virgili, Spain
Eduardo B. Fernandez	Florida Atlantic University, USA
Simone Fischer-Hübner	Karlstad University, Sweden
Sara Foresti	Universita' degli Studi di Milano, Italy
Ehud Gudes	Ben-Gurion University, Israel
Ragib Hasan	University of Alabama at Birmingham, USA
Yuan Hong	University at Albany, SUNY, USA
Sushil Jajodia	George Mason University, USA
Sokratis Katsikas	University of Piraeus, Greece
Adam J. Lee	University of Pittsburgh, USA
Haibing Lu	Santa Clara University, USA
Emil Lupu	Imperial College, UK
Martin Olivier	ICSA, University of Pretoria, South Africa
Sylvia Osborn	The University of Western Ontario, Canada
Stefano Paraboschi	Universita di Bergamo, Italy
Guenther Pernul	
Indrajit Ray	Colorado State University, USA
Indrakshi Ray	Colorado State University, USA
Kui Ren	State University of New York at Buffalo, USA
Kouichi Sakurai	Kyushu University, Japan
Pierangela Samarati	Universita' degli Studi di Milano, Italy
Andreas Schaad	SAP AG, Germany
Basit Shafiq	Lahore University of Management Sciences, Pakistan
Heechang Shin	Iona College, USA
Shamik Sural	IIT, Kharagpur, India

Traian Marius Truta	Northern Kentucky University, USA
Jaideep Vaidya	Rutgers University, USA
Lingyu Wang	Concordia University, Canada
Meng Yu	Virginia Commonwealth University, USA
Zutao Zhu	Google Inc., USA

Additional Reviewers

Alrabaee, Saed	Mukherjee, Subhojeet
Blanco-Justicia, Alberto	Mulamba, Dieudonne
Boukhtouta, Amine	Ohtaki, Yasuhiro
Centonze, Paolina	Preda, Stere
Gaspar, Jaime	Pujol, Marta
Hahn, Florian	Ray, Sujoy
Hang, Isabelle	Romero, Cristina
Haque, Md	Rufian-Torrell, Guillem
Huo, Wei	Sabaté-Pla, Albert
Jarraya, Yosr	Servos, Daniel
Jhanwar, Mahabir Prasad	Sgandurra, Daniele
Kawamoto, Junpei	Shirani, Paria
Khalili, Mina	Soeanu, Andrei
Khan, Rasib	Sun, Kun
Le, Meixing	Wang, Guan
Livraga, Giovanni	Zang, Wanyu
Madi, Leila	Zawoad, Shams
Matsumoto, Shinichi	Zhang, Lei
Moataz, Tarik	Zhang, Mengyuan
Mueller, Tobias	Zhang, Yihua

Abstracts of Invited Talks

Privacy without Encrypting: Protect Your Data and Use It Too

Chris Clifton

Purdue University, West Lafayette, IN 47907, USA
clifton@cs.purdue.edu
http://www.cs.purdue.edu/people/clifton

There has been ongoing work in encrypted database as a means to protect privacy, but this comes at a high price. An alternative is separating sensitive and identifying information, through models such as fragmentation[2], anatomization[6], and slicing[3]. In our DBSec'11 paper, we presented a query processor over such a data separation model, where the server cannot violate privacy constraints, but still does most of the work before sending final results to be joined by the client (who is allowed access to private data.)[4] A follow-on paper extended this to updates.[5] In DBSec'13 we showed how to ensure privacy constraints are satisfied when storing transactional data under such a model.[1]

This talk will look at using such data: How do we learn (and what can't we learn) when data is stored under a data separation approach. This involves both server-only approaches (what value can the server get in return for storing privacy-protected data), and client/server cooperation (pushing as much work to the server as possible, with the client doing only what is needed to ensure quality results.) We will look at anonymization techniques that support learning while providing privacy, as well as data mining techniques adapted to this model.

This talk presents work that was made possible by NPRP grant 02-256-1-046 from the Qatar National Research Fund. The statements made herein are solely the responsibility of the author.

References

1. Al Bouna, B., Clifton, C., Malluhi, Q.: Using safety constraint for transactional dataset anonymization. In: Wang, L., Shafiq, B. (eds.) DBSec 2013. LNCS, vol. 7964, pp. 164–178. Springer, Heidelberg (2013)
2. Ciriani, V., Vimercati, S.D.C.D., Foresti, S., Jajodia, S., Paraboschi, S., Samarati, P.: Combining fragmentation and encryption to protect privacy in data storage. ACM Trans. Inf. Syst. Secur. 13, 22:1–22:33 (2010), http://doi.acm.org/10.1145/1805974.1805978
3. Li, T., Li, N., Zhang, J., Molloy, I.: Slicing: A new approach for privacy preserving data publishing. IEEE Transactions on Knowledge and Data Engineering 24(3), 561–574 (2012), http://doi.ieeecomputersociety.org/10.1109/TKDE.2010.236

4. Nergiz, A.E., Clifton, C.: Query processing in private data outsourcing using anonymization. In: Li, Y. (ed.) DBSec. LNCS, vol. 6818, pp. 138–153. Springer, Heidelberg (2011)
5. Nergiz, A.E., Clifton, C., Malluhi, Q.: Updating outsourced anatomized private databases. In: 16th International Conference on Extending Database Technology (EDBT), Genoa, Italy, March 18-22, pp. 179–190 (2013),
   http://doi.acm.org/10.1145/2452376.2452399
6. Xiao, X., Tao, Y.: Anatomy: Simple and effective privacy preservation. In: Proceedings of 32nd International Conference on Very Large Data Bases (VLDB 2006), Seoul, Korea, September 12-15 (2006),
   http://www.vldb.org/conf/2006/p139-xiao.pdf

Getting Ready for the Next Privacy and Security Challenges

Reinhard Posch

CIO, Federal Government Austria
reinhard.posch@cio.gv.at

Cloud, Bring your own Device, Big Data, what have you . . . unless people comply with these Buzzwords they feel to be old-fashioned. Indeed these are often synonyms for big money – but can we understand at all what security and privacy means in this context.

Thanks to Edward Snowden basically everyone talks about privacy. However, unfortunately the impact of the "Snowden effect" on security and privacy might be equally sustainable as the oil crisis was on the global climate change.

Even if this sounds pessimistic the keynote will try to paint a view about what it needs to advance privacy and security at this very point in time where mobile devices, Cloud and collaboration is changing the IT-world dramatically both in dimension and in concept. It is about Europe to take the situation and advance and to sell its leadership in these areas. "eIDaS" the new identity and signature regulation, the new data protection regulation and the NIS directive might be helpful legal instruments helping for European ICT to grow from 28 Member States to a 500 Mio society. Large scale projects arching from examples like STORK to implementation and procurement like Cloud for Europe have a fair chance to be the cornerstones of this development.

Europe has for a long time made profit from its excellence in cryptography and security in academia. Algorithms, concepts and protocols still need to bridge the gap to practical use. While full holomorphic encryption is far from being practical and needing big efforts in research, there are other advances that might be of great help. Privacy preserving authentication and proxy reencryption are just examples helping to close some gaps today in real life.

Given a holistic view of this domain it needs more than just a few algorithmic advances. Pushing up dimension and complexity will not work unless we replace trust by provable trustworthiness and complement this with enabling infrastructures. One such enabling infrastructure will be jurisdiction-aware communication. We must head versus infrastructures that are not limiting communication but identifying jurisdictions data have passed. Then applications and users will be empowered to decide in what environments and jurisdictions they will allow data to flow into and to be received from.

Taking advantage from the momentum NSA and Snowden provide, we need to create environments and infrastructures that allow sustainability and there is ample of challenges ahead. Privacy preserving sharing and collaboration of is one of these big next challenges already emerging.

Table of Contents

Integrity Assurance for Outsourced Databases without DBMS Modification

Wei Wei[1] and Ting Yu[1,2]

[1] North Carolina State University, Raleigh NC 27606, USA
wwei5@ncsu.edu, yu@csc.ncsu.edu
[2] Qatar Computing Research Institute, Tornado Tower, 18th floor, Doha, Qatar

Abstract. Database outsourcing has become increasingly popular as a cost-effective solution to provide database services to clients. Previous work proposed different approaches to ensuring data integrity, one of the most important security concerns in database outsourcing. However, to the best of our knowledge, existing approaches require modification of DBMSs to facilitate data authentication, which greatly hampers their adoption in practice. In this paper, we present the design and implementation of an efficient and practical integrity assurance scheme *without requiring any modification to the DBMS at the server side*. We develop novel schemes to serialize Merkle B-tree based authentication structures into a relational database that allows efficient data retrieval for integrity verification. We design efficient algorithms to accelerate query processing with integrity protection. We further build a proof-of-concept prototype and conduct extensive experiments to evaluate the performance overhead of the proposed schemes. The experimental results show that our scheme imposes a low overhead for queries and a reasonable overhead for updates while ensuring integrity of an outsourced database without special support from server-side DBMSs.

Keywords: Data Integrity, Database Outsourcing, Radix-Path Identifier.

1 Introduction

Database outsourcing has become increasingly popular as a cost-effective solution to provide database services to clients. In this model, a *data owner* (DO) outsources data to a third-party *database service provider* (DSP), which maintains the data in a DBMS and answers queries from *clients* on behalf of the data owner. However, it introduces one of the most important security concerns, data integrity. Usually, DSPs are not fully trusted by data owners. Thus, data owners have to protect the integrity of their own data when outsourcing data to DSPs. Specifically, when clients retrieve data from a DSP, they should be able to verify that the returned data is what should be returned for their requests on behalf of data owners, i.e., no data is maliciously modified by DSPs and DSPs return all data clients request.

There are many techniques proposed to address integrity issues, including correctness, completeness and freshness. These techniques can be divided into two categories. Approaches belonging to the first category are based on *authenticated data structures* (ADSs) such as Merkle hash tree (MHT) [4, 9, 12] and Signature Aggregation

V. Atluri and G. Pernul (Eds.): DBSec 2014, LNCS 8566, pp. 1–16, 2014.

[9, 14, 16, 18]. Existing ADS-based approaches require modifying a DBMS so that it can generate a *verification object* (VO) when executing a query and return the VO along with the actual result to clients, so that clients can verify the integrity of the query result. Such modification is usually costly and hard to be deployed in a third-party service provider, which hampers the adoption of database outsourcing [24]. The second category uses a probabilistic approach [20, 24, 25], which injects some fake data into outsourced databases. Although the probabilistic approach does not require the modification of DBMSs, its integrity guarantee is significantly weaker than that of those based on ADSs.

In this paper, we explore the feasibility of utilizing approaches of the first category to provide integrity assurance *without requiring any modification of DBMSs*. In existing approaches, DBMSs are modified to be ADS-aware. That is, they are enhanced with special modules that efficiently manage ADSs and facilitate the generation of VOs. Unfortunately, it is often hard to convince database service providers to make such modifications to their DBMSs. In fact, up to today, to the best of our knowledge, no existing cloud database services support integrity checking [19]. Thus, for clients who care about query integrity, it is desirable to have integrity assurance techniques over "vanilla" DBMSs (i.e., without any special features for outsourced data integrity). The general approach is straightforward: the data owner would have to store authenticated data structures along with their own data in relations, and retrieve appropriate integrity verification data besides issuing queries. And all these have to be done through the generic query interface (usually SQL) of the DBMS. Though the basic idea is simple, the challenge is to make it practical: we need to design appropriate schemes to convert ADSs into relations and form efficient queries to retrieve and update authentication information, *without imposing significant overhead*.

In this paper, we present an efficient and practical scheme based on Merkle B-tree, which provides strong integrity assurance without requiring special support from database service providers. Our scheme serializes a Merkle B-tree based ADS into relations in a way, such that the data in the ADS can be retrieved and updated directly and efficiently using existing functionality provided by DBMSs, that is, SQL statements. Our major contributions are summarized as follows:

- We propose a novel scheme called Radix-Path Identifier to identify each piece of authentication data in a Merkle B-tree based ADS so that the MBT can be serialized into and de-serialized from a database, and design an efficient and practical mechanism to store all authentication data of a Merkle B-tree in a database, where the authentication data in the MBT can be retrieved and updated efficiently.

- We explore the efficiency of different methods such as Multi-Join, Single-Join, Zero-Join and Range-Condition, to retrieve authentication data from a serialized MBT stored in a database, create appropriate indexes to accelerate the retrieval of authentication data, and optimize the update process for authentication data.

- We build a proof-of-concept prototype and conduct extensive experiments to evaluate the performance overhead and efficiency of our proposed scheme. The results show that our scheme imposes a low overhead for queries and a reasonable overhead for updates while providing integrity assurance. Note that although we describe our scheme based on relational DBMSs, it is not hard to see that our scheme can also be applied to Non-SQL databases such as Bigtable [3], Hbase [1].

We note that many modern relational databases also have built-in support for XML. One seemingly promising approach is to represent Merkle B-tree as XML, store the XML representation into the DBMSs, and utilize their built-in XML support to retrieve authentication data for integrity verification. However, as can be seen from the performance result presented in Section 6, the XML-based solutions do not provide a good performance compared with our scheme, which is mainly because the XML features are not targeting at providing efficient operations of MHT-based integrity verification.

The rest of the paper is organized as follows. We discuss related work in Section 2. In Section 3, we describe the data outsourcing model we target, state assumptions, attack models and our goals. Section 4 explains the major design of our scheme in details, and section 5 illustrate how our scheme provides integrity assurance for different data operations such as *select, update, insert and delete*. Section 6 discusses the experimental results. Finally, the paper concludes in Section 7.

2   Related Work

Researchers have investigated on data integrity issues for years in the area of database outsourcing [5, 8, 9, 13, 16, 17, 20, 24, 25]. Pang et. al. [16] proposed a signature aggregation based scheme that enables a user to verify the completeness of a query result by assuming an order of the records according to one attribute. Devanbu et. al. [5] uses Merkle hash tree based methods to verify the completeness of query results. But they do not consider the freshness aspect of data integrity. Xie et al. [24] proposed a probabilistic approach by inserting a small amount of fake records into outsourced databases so that integrity can be effectively audited by analyzing the inserted records in the query results, which only protects integrity probabilistically.

Li et. al. [9] first brought forward the freshness issue as an aspect of data integrity. It verifies if data updates are correctly executed by DSPs so that queries will be executed over the up-to-date data instead of old data. Xie et al. [25] analyzed different approaches to ensuring query freshness. The aggregated signature based approaches [14, 16] require to modify signatures of all the records, which renders it impractical considering the number of signatures.

Miklau et. al. [11] designed a scheme based on interval tree to guarantee data integrity when interacting with a vulnerable or untrusted database server. However, several disadvantages are mentioned in Di's work [6], which dealt with a similar issue based on authenticated skip list [7]. Di Battista's work [6] does not explain clearly how authentication data is retrieved. It claims that only one query is required for integrity verification while it also mentions that multiple queries are necessary to retrieve all authentication data. Palazzi et. al. [15] proposed approaches to support range queries based on multiple attributes with integrity guarantee, complementary to our work.

Compared with previous work, our scheme is able to provide integrity assurance for database outsourcing, including all three aspects: correctness, completeness and freshness. More importantly, one significant advantage of our scheme is that existing approaches need to modify the implementation of DBMSs in order to maintain an appropriate authenticated data structure and generate VOs. This requirement often make these approaches hard to be deployed in real-world applications [24]. Our work provides a strong integrity guarantee (instead of probabilistic guarantee [24]) without requiring DBMSs to be modified to perform any special function beyond query processing.

3   System Model

3.1   Database Outsourcing Model

Figure 1 shows our database outsourcing model with integrity protection. There are three types of entities: *data owner*, *database service provider* (DSP) and *clients*. A data owner uploads a database with data and authentication data to a DSP, which provides database functionality on behalf of the data owner. Clients send to the DSP queries to retrieve data and a *verification object* (VO).

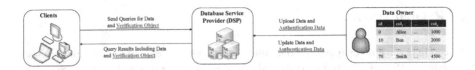

Fig. 1. Non-Intrusive Database Outsourcing Model

In our outsourcing model, we assume that the DSP is oblivious to integrity protection. In fact, the DSP does not even know where and how to store authentication data and when and how to return authentication data to clients for integrity verification. Everything related to data integrity verification is done at the client side through an integrity-aware DBMS driver and is transparent to applications running in the client side, and data and authentication data updates are done by the data owner. In this way, data owners can provide integrity assurance for their outsourced databases without any special support from DSPs. Therefore, the adoption of database outsourcing with integrity assurance is completely decided by data owners themselves.

3.2   Assumptions and Attack Models

First, we assume that data owners and clients do not fully trust the services provided by DSPs. Second, since our scheme relies on digital signatures to provide integrity protection, we assume that the data owner has a pair of private and public keys for signature generation and verification. The public key is known to all clients. Moreover, like in many existing work [8, 9, 14, 18], we assume that the data owner is the only entity who can update its data. In addition, we assume that communications between DSPs and clients are through a secure channel (e.g., through SSL). Thus, DSPs and clients can detect any tampered communication.

Regarding attack models, we focus ourselves on the malicious behavior from a DSP since it is the only untrusted party in our target database outsourcing model. We do not have any assumption about what kind of attacks or malicious behavior a DSP may take. A DSP can behave arbitrarily to compromise data integrity. Typical malicious behaviors include, but not limited to, modifying a data owner's data without the data owner's authorization, returning partial data queried to clients and reporting non-existence of data even if data does exist. Further, it could return stale data to clients instead of executing queries over the latest data updated by the data owner [23].

3.3 Security Goals

We aim at providing integrity protection for all three aspects in data integrity: correctness, completeness, and freshness. First, the correctness checks if all records returned in a query result come from the original data set without being maliciously modified, which is usually achieved using digital signatures that authenticate the authenticity of records. Second, the completeness checks if all records satisfying conditions in a query are completely returned to clients. Third, the freshness checks if all records in a query result are the up-to-date data instead of some stale data.

Regarding freshness, we propose mechanisms for data owners to efficiently compute signatures of updated data and guarantee the correctness of the signatures, which is the key to provide freshness guarantee. The security guarantee we provide is as strong as Merkle B-tree (MBT) [9]. In the paper, we do not focus on how the latest signatures are propagated to clients for integrity verification purpose, as it can be easily achieved by applying existing techniques [10, 25].

4   System Design

4.1   Running Example

We first present an example that will be referred to throughout the paper to illustrate our schemes. Without loss of generality, we assume that a data owner has a database with a table called "data", as shown in the left side of Figure 2. The table has several columns. The id column is a unique key or indexed. Besides, there are n columns $\{col_1, ..., col_n\}$ containing arbitrary data.

4.2   Authenticated Data Structure

Regarding Authenticated Data Structure (ADS), there are two options: signature aggregation based ADS and Merkle hash tree based ADS. We observe that there are several disadvantages of developing a scheme based on signature aggregation based ADS. First, to minimize communication cost, signature aggregation operation needs to be done dynamically in DBMSs, which unfortunately is not supported. Moreover, it is unknown how to efficiently guarantee freshness using signature aggregation based approaches [9]. Additionally, techniques based on signature aggregation incur significant computation cost in client side and much larger storage cost in the server side.

Thus, we choose to adapt MHT-based ADS, in particular, Merkle B-tree (MBT) [9]. MHT-based ADS can not only guarantee correctness and completeness, but also provide efficient freshness protection since only one root hash needs to be maintained correctly. Figure 2 shows a Merkle B-tree created based on the table introduced in Section 4.1. The values in the *id* column are used as keys in the MBT. A hash h_i is associated with a pointer in an internal node or a record in a leaf node. For simplicity, the hashes associated with pointers and records in nodes of the MBT are not shown in the figure. The hash of a record in a leaf node is the hash value of the data record in the data table. The hash associated with a pointer in an internal node is the hash of concatenating all hashes in the node pointed by the pointer.

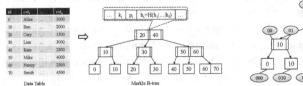

Fig. 2. Data table to Merkle B-tree   **Fig. 3.** Radix-path identifier

4.3 Identify Authentication Data

The first thing is to identify pointers in internal nodes and records in leaf nodes of a MBT since each pointer or record is associated with a piece of authentication data, that is, a hash. And also we need to capture their parent-child and sibling relationships. Besides, we need to preserve the ordering of pointers or records in a node of a MBT.

Existing Approaches. There are a few widely-used models such as adjacency list, path enumeration, nested set and closure table to store tree-like hierarchical data into a database [2, 21]. Each of them has its own advantages and disadvantages. For example, with an adjacency list, it is easy to find the parent of a pointer or a record since it captures the parent-child relationship directly. But to find its ancestor, we have to traverse the parent-child relationship step by step, which could make the process of retrieving VO inefficient. The path enumeration model uses a string to store the path of each pointer or record, which is used to track the parent-child relationship. Unlike the adjacency list model, it is easy to find an ancestor of a pointer or record in a node. But same as the adjacency list, path enumeration does not capture the order of pointers or records in a node.

Radix-Path Identifier. To address the disadvantages of existing approaches, we propose a novel and efficient scheme called *Radix-Path Identifier*. The basic idea is to use numbers based on a certain radix to identify each pointer or record in a MBT. Figure 3 shows all identifiers as base-4 numbers for pointers or records in the tree based on a radix equal to 4. Given a MBT, the *Radix-Path Identifier* of a pointer or record depends on its level and position in the MBT. To illustrate this scheme, suppose that the fanout of a MBT is f. The radix base r_b could be any number larger than or equal to f. l denotes the level where a node resides in the MBT. The level of the root node is 0. i denotes the index of a pointer or record in a node, ranging from 0 to f. The *Radix-Path Identifier* $rpid$ of a pointer or record can be computed using the following equation:

$$rpid = \begin{cases} i & \text{if } l == 0, \\ rpid_{parent} * r_b + i & \text{if } l > 0. \end{cases} \tag{1}$$

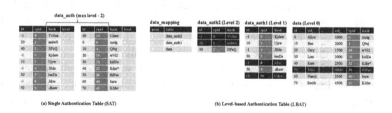

(a) Single Authentication Table (SAT)   (b) Level-based Authentication Table (LBAT)

Fig. 4. Authentication Data Organization

Note that $rpid_{parent}$ is the *Radix-Path Identifier* of its parent pointer in the tree. Equation 1 captures not only the ordering among pointers or records in one node, but also the parent-child and sibling relationships among nodes. The identifier of each pointer or record in the root node is i. With identifiers in the root node, we can use the second part of Equation 1 to compute identifiers of pointers or records in their child nodes. In this way, all identifiers can be computed starting from the root node to the leaf nodes. The proposed *Radix-Path Identifier* scheme has several important properties: 1) Identifiers of pointers or records in a node are continuous, but not continuous between that of those in two sibling nodes. For example, the base-4 numbers $20, 21, 22$ are continuous and $200, 210$ are not continuous, shown in Figure 3; 2) From an identifier of a pointer or record in a node, we can easily find the identifier of its parent pointer based on the fact that $rpid_{parent}$ equals to $\lfloor rpid/r_b \rfloor$; 3) From the identifier of a pointer or record in a node, we can easily calculate the min and max identifiers in the node, which are $(\lfloor rpid/r_b \rfloor) * r_b$ and $(\lfloor rpid/r_b \rfloor) * r_b + (r_b - 1)$; 4) From an identifier of a pointer or record in a node, we can easily compute the index i of the pointer or record in the node, which is $rpid$ mod r_b. These properties will be utilized for efficient VO retrieval and authentication data updates.

4.4 Store Authentication Data

Once we identify each pointer or record in nodes of a MBT, the next step is how we can store the authentication data associated with them into a database. In the following, we propose two different designs - Single Authentication Table (SAT) and Level-based Authentication Table (LBAT), and discuss their advantages and disadvantages.

SAT: Single Authentication Table. A straightforward way is to store all authentication data as data records called *Authentication Data Record* (ADR) into one table in a database, where its corresponding data table is stored. Figure 4(a) shows all authentication data records in a single table for the data table described in the running example.

The name of the authentication table adds a suffix "_auth" to the original table name "data". The authentication table has 4 columns: *id*, *rpid*, *hash* and *level*. *id* column stores values from *id* column of the data table, which are keys in the B+ tree except "-1". Note that since the number of keys is less than the number of pointers in the internal nodes in a B+ tree node, we use "-1" as the *id* for the left-most pointers in the internal nodes. *rpid* records identifiers for pointers or records in the B+ tree. *hash* column stores the hash values of pointers or records in the B+ tree, which is essential for integrity verification. *level* stores values indicating the level of a pointer or record in the B+ tree. The *level* value is necessary for searching the *rpid* for a data record given an *id* of the data record because the *rpid* values could be the same in different levels. The level of a leaf node is 0, and the level of the root node is the maximum level.

Although SAT is simple and straightforward, it has several disadvantages, which makes it an inefficient scheme. First, updates could be inefficient since one data record update usually requires updating ADRs in different levels. With table level locks, it is not allowed to concurrently execute ADR updates since all ADR updates have to be executed over the only one table. Although concurrent updates can be enabled with row level locks, it may consume much more database server resources, which may not be desired. Second, it may require join queries to find the *rpid* of a data record since the data table is separated from the authentication data table. Third, updates to a data record and its ADR in the leaf level cannot be merged into a single query to improve the performance since they go to different tables.

LBAT: Level-Based Authentication Table. To resolve the above issues, we propose a Level-based Authentication Table (LBAT). In this scheme, instead of storing all ADRs into one table, we store ADRs in different levels to different tables. We create one table per level for an MBT except the leaf level (for reasons given below) along with a mapping table to indicate which table corresponds to which level. For nodes in the leaf level of the MBT, since each data record corresponds to an ADR in leaf nodes, we extend the data table by adding two columns - *rpid* and *hash* to store ADRs instead of creating a new table, which reduces the redundancy of *id* values as well as the update cost to some extent. Figure 4(b) shows all tables created or extended to store ADRs and the mapping table for the data table described in the running example. Tables for different levels have different number of records. For the root level, it may only contain a few records. Also, the number of records in the mapping table is equal to the number of levels in the MBT. We name those tables by adding a suffix such as "_mapping", "_auth0", etc, based on table types and levels.

The proposed LBAT scheme presents several advantages. First, since ADRs in different levels are stored in different authentication tables, it makes concurrent updates possible with table level lock, which also allows to design efficient concurrent update mechanisms. Second, since we store ADRs in the leaf level along with data, it makes it straightforward to retrieve the *rpid* of a data record. Third, due to the same advantage, it is easy to merge updates for a data records and its ADR in the leaf level for performance improvement.

4.5 Extract Authentication Data

To extract the ADRs for the record based on LBAT, we make the best use of the properties of our *Radix-Path Identifier*. Once we receive all related ADRs, we can compute the root hash since we can infer the tree structure from the *rpid* values, which conveniently captures the relationship among pointers, records and nodes in the MBT.

Since the DSP is only assumed to provide standard DBMS functionalities, all the above operations have to be realized by SQL queries issued by the client. We explore four different ways - Multi-Join, Single-Join, Zero-Join and Range-Condition, to find the authentication data records based on LBAT. We use specific examples to show how they work. All examples are based on the data presented in the running example. Suppose that we want to verify the integrity of the data record with the *id* 50. The ADRs needs to be returned shown as the black parts in Figure 3, which is also highlighted with a black background in Figure 4(b). Multi-join uses one query joining all related tables to retrieve authentication data records, which returns a lot of redundant data, and Single-Join uses multiple queries, each of which joins two tables to avoid returning redundant data. Due to space limit, we only illustrate Zero-Join and Range-Condition in details below. More details about Multi-join and Single-Join can be found at [22].

Zero-Join. In this scheme, we aim at minimizing the redundant data returned in Multi-Join and avoid multiple join queries in Single-Join. In fact, what we actually need is the *rpid* of the record 50. If we know its *rpid*, we can eliminate the "join" completely from the SQL statements. The following shows the SQL statements we use to retrieve the authentication data without joining any table.

```
-- find the rpid of the data record with the id 50
declare @rowrpid AS int;
set @rowrpid=(select top 1 rpid from data where id=50);
-- level 2, 1, 0 (from root level to leaf level)
select rpid,hash from data where rpid/4=@rowrpid/(4);
select rpid,hash from data_auth1 where rpid/4=@rowrpid/(4*4);
select rpid,hash from data_auth2 where rpid/4=@rowrpid/(4*4*4);
```

Compared with Single-Join, the major difference is that we declare a "rowrpid" variable to store the *rpid* of the record, which is retrieved from the first query. After that, we use the "rowrpid" for other queries to retrieve the authentication data for nodes in different levels. Although it needs to execute one more query, it eliminates the "join" clause completely.

Range-Condition. We observe that the execution of the above queries does not utilize the indexes created on the *rpid* field in the authentication tables. Instead of doing an index seek, each of them actually does an index scan, which is inefficient and incurs a high computation cost in the server side. To utilize indexes, we propose a new method called Range-Condition to retrieve authentication data for records. The following shows the SQL statements we use to retrieve the authentication data for the record 50 using Range-Condition.

```
-- find the rpid of the data record with the id 50
declare @rowrpid AS int;
set @rowrpid=(select top 1 rpid from data where id=50);
-- level 2, 1, 0 (from leaf level to root level)
select rpid,hash from data
where rpid>=(@rowrpid/(4))*4 and rpid<(@rowrpid/(4))*4+4;
```

```
select rpid,hash from data_auth1
where rpid>=(@rowrpid/(4*4))*4 and rpid<(@rowrpid/(4*4))*4+4;
select rpid,hash from data_auth2
where rpid>=(@rowrpid/(4*4*4))*4 and rpid<(@rowrpid/(4*4*4))*4+4;
```

As can be seen from the figure, the major difference from Zero-Join is the *where* condition. Instead of using equality, the Range-Condition uses a range query selection based on the *rpid* column. The range query retrieves the same set of ADRs as the equality condition used in Zero-Join. Thus, they both return the same set of authentication data records, and Single-Join does that too. However, with the range query on the *rpid* field, it can utilize indexes built on the *rpid* column, which minimizes the computation cost in the server side.

5   Data Operations

In this section, we illustrate the details of handling basic queries such as *select*, *update*, *insert* and *delete* with integrity protection efficiently based on our design using the running example. Without loss of generality, we assume that clients always have the latest root hash of the table for integrity verification, and we focus on how to retrieve authentication data from DSPs. Due to space limit, we do not discuss *insert* and *delete*. Please refer to [22] for implementation details and experimental results.

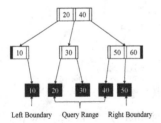

Fig. 5. Range Query with Integrity Protection

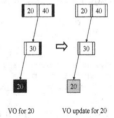

Fig. 6. Update with Integrity Protection

5.1   Select

As discussed in Section 4.5, we can retrieve authentication data for a *Unique Select* query, which returns only one data record based on a unique key selection. Thus, we focus on how to handle a *Range Select* query with integrity protection, which retrieves records within a range.

The verification process for *Range Select* queries is different from *Unique Select* queries. First, we need to find the two boundary keys for a range query. For example, for a range query with a range from 15 to 45, we need to identify its two boundaries, which are 10 and 50 in this case. Although DBMSs do not provide a function to return the boundary records directly, we can use the following two queries to figure out what the left and right boundaries are for a query range:

```
select top 1 id from data where id < 15 order by id desc
select top 1 id from data where id > 45 order by id asc
```

Then, to retrieve the authentication data for the range query, we only need to retrieve the authentication data for both boundaries, which is similar to the way we use to retrieve authentication data object for a data record since the authentication data for records within the range are not necessary and they will be computed by using the returned records. Figure 5 shows the authentication data records and the data records that need to be retrieved for the range query from 15 to 45.

To execute the range query with integrity protection, we need to rewrite the range query by adding SQL statements of retrieving authentication data records. Then, we execute all SQL statements in one database transaction. Once the result with authentication data is returned, we verify the integrity of the query result using the authentication data. If the verification succeeds, the data result is returned to the client as before; otherwise, an integrity violation exception could be thrown to warn the client of the integrity verification failure.

The overhead to provide data integrity for range queries consists of both computation and communication cost. The computation cost in the client side includes two parts: rewriting range query and verifying data integrity. The computation cost in the server side is the execution of additional queries for authentication data retrieval. The communication cost between them includes the text data of additional queries and the authentication data returned along with the data result.

This process can also handle *Unique Select* queries. However, it requires to retrieve authentication data for both left boundary and right boundary, which may not be necessary. If the key does not exist, we have to resort to the process of handling range queries, where we can check left boundary and right boundary to make sure the record with the key does not exist.

5.2 Update

Single Record Update. When a data record is updated, we need to update its authentication data (mainly hash values) accordingly. For updating a record, we assume that the record to be updated already exists in the client side and the VO for the updated record is cached in the client too. Otherwise, we retrieve the data record and its VO first, then update it and its authentication data.

Figure 6 shows the VO in black for the record 20 in the left side and the hash values in gray to be updated once the record is updated. Each data update requires an update on all authentication data tables. It means if the MBT tree's height is h, then the total Number of update queries is $h + 1$. In this case, we need to actually update 4 records. One of them is to update the data record and three of them is to update the authentication data records. The generation of update queries for authentication data is simple since we know the *rpid* of the data record to be updated, and then we can easily compute its parent *rpid* and generate update queries.

Since the authentication data table for the leaf level of a MBT is combined with the data table, we can combine two update queries into one to improve the performance. Thus, in this case we only need 3 update queries instead of 4. All update queries are executed within one transaction. So, consistency of data records and authentication data is guaranteed by the ACID properties of DBMSs, and data integrity is also guaranteed since the verification and the root hash update are done directly by the data owner.

Batch Update and Optimization. Suppose that we want to update x records at one time. As the number of records to be updated increases, the total number of update queries we need to generate to update both data and authentication data increases linearly. In this case, the total number of update queries is $x * h$. We observe from those update queries that several update queries try to update the same authentication data record again and again due to the hierarchical structure of a B+ tree. We also notice that each update SQL statement only updates the same authentication record in one table. In fact, we just need to get the latest hash of the authentication data record, and do one update. To do that, we need to track all update queries for each table, find the set of queries to update one authentication data record in an authentication table, and remove all of them except the latest one. In this way, the number of necessary update queries could be much less than the number of update queries we generate before. The process, called *MergeUpdate*, improves the performance of batch update to a great extent.

6   Experimental Evaluation

System Implementation. We have implemented the Merkle B-tree and the query rewrite algorithms for clients, which is the core of generating select, update and insert SQL statements to operate authentication data. We also built a tool to create authentication tables and generate authentication data based on a data table in a database. Data owners can run this tool on all data tables in a database before outsourcing the database to a DSP. Once the authentication data is created for the database, they can upload the database to the DSP. We have also implemented all four different ways - *MultiJoin*, *SingleJoin*, *ZeroJoin* and *RangeCondition* - to retrieve authentication data for performance overhead evaluation. Our implementation is based on .NET and SQL Server 2008. In addition, we implemented two XML-based schemes: OPEN-XML and DT-XML, which utilize built-in XML functionality of SQL Server, for efficiency analysis and comparison. In both OPEN-XML and DT-XML schemes, we use a hierarchical XML structure to represent the authentication data of a Merkle B-tree and store the XML string into a database. The OPEN-XML scheme uses OPENXML function provided in SQL Server to retrieve VO data from the XML string, and the DT-XML uses XPath and nodes() methods to retrieve VO data from an indexed XML data field, where the XML string is stored.

Experiment Setup. We use a synthetic database that consists of one table with $100,000$ records. Each record contains multiple columns, a primary key *id*, and is about 1KB long. For simplicity, we assume that an authenticated index is built on *id* column. We upload the database with authentication data to a third-party cloud service provider, which deploys the SQL Server 2008 R2 as a database service, and run experiments from a client through a home network with 30Mbps download and 4Mbps upload. To evaluate the performance overhead of integrity verification and the efficiency of the proposed mechanisms, we design a set of experiments using the synthetic database.

6.1 Performance Analysis

VO Size. Figure 7 shows how the VO size changes as the fanout of a MBT changes for *Unique Select* and *Range Select*. The results clearly show that as the fanout increases, the VO size increases, and the VO size of *Range Select* is almost twice of that of *Unique Select* since the VO of *Range Select* includes the VO of two boundaries of the range. Note that for *Range Select*, its VO size almost stays the same no matter how many records are returned in a *Range Select*.

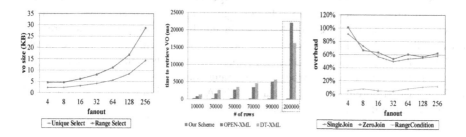

Fig. 7. VO size vs fanout   **Fig. 8.** VO retrieval time   **Fig. 9.** Unique select overhead

VO Retrieval. Figure 8 shows the time to retrieve a VO for our scheme using Range-Condition and two XML-based schemes when the number of rows in the data set changes. As can be seen from the figure, when the data size is small, three schemes show a similar time to retrieve the VO. However, as the data size increases, two XML-based schemes show linear increases in terms of the VO retrieval time. When the data size goes up to 200,000 records, the XML-based schemes take more than 15 seconds to retrieve a VO for one single record. In this case, our scheme is about 100 times faster than the two XML-based schemes. The result indicates that a well-design scheme could be much more efficient than a scheme using built-in XML functionality in DBMSs.

Unique Select. We conduct experiments to see how different fanouts of a MBT and different methods of retrieving VO could affect the performance of *Unique Select* queries, where we vary the fanout of a MBT and compare the performance overhead caused by different VO retrieval methods, shown in Figure 9. The results show that the overhead of SingleJoin and ZeroJoin is much higher than that of RangeCondition. When the fanout is 32, the overhead of SingJoin or ZeroJoin is about 50%, but the overhead of RangeCondition is 4.6%. The communication cost for the three different methods is almost same, and the major performance difference is caused by the computation cost in the server side. As we can see from this figure, when the fanout increases from 4 to 32, the overhead of both SingleJoin and ZeroJoin drops, and when the fanout is larger than 32, their overhead increases. It is because in general the VO size increases and the number of queries to be executed to retrieve authentication data decreases as the fanout increases, and when the fanout is less than 32 the computation cost dominates the overhead and when the fanout is larger than 32 the communication cost dominates the overhead. Based on the current experiment environment, the 32 fantout shows a better performance compared with other fanouts. In the following experiments we use 32 as the default fanout unless specified otherwise.

Range Select. We also run experiments to explore how the overhead changes when the number of records retrieved increases. Figure 10 shows the response time of retrieving different number of records in range queries, where NoVeri denotes range queries without integrity verification support, ZeroJoin and RangeCondition denote rang queries with integrity verification but using VO retrieval method ZeroJoin and RangeCondition respectively. The results show two points: 1) the RangeCondition is much better than ZeroJoin when the number of rows to be retrieved is small, which is because the computation cost dominates the overhead caused by different VO retrieval methods; 2) once the number of records to be retrieved is larger than a certain number, the response time of all three is almost the same. In our algorithm, the overhead caused by different VO retrieval methods does not change as the number of retrieved records increases. Thus, as the number of retrieved records increases, the overhead becomes relatively smaller and smaller. We also conduct experiments to show how the overhead changes as the database size increases, where we run range queries to retrieve 512 rows from databases with different number of data records. As shown in Figure 11, the overhead is about 3% even if the number of data records goes up to 1.6 million.

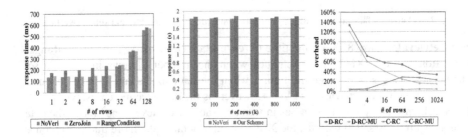

Fig. 10. Range select response time

Fig. 11. Scalability of Range Select

Fig. 12. Direct and cached update overhead comparison

Update. We evaluate the performance overhead caused by two different update cases - Direct Update and Cached Update. For Direct Update, we first retrieve the data to be updated and verify its data integrity, and then we generate update queries for both data and authentication data and send them to the sever for execution. For Cached Update, we assume that the data to be updated is already cached in the memory, we just need to generate update queries and send them to the server for execution. Figure 12 shows the overhead versus the number of rows to be updated. In the figure, 'D' denotes Direct Update, C denotes Cached Update, "RC" denotes RangeCondition, and "MU" denotes MergeUpdate, which indicates if a MergeUpdate process is used to reduce the number of SQL statements generated for updating authentication data records. The results show that when we directly update only a few records with integrity protection, the overhead could go above 100%, but if we update cached records, the overhead is about 2.5%. In this case, the additional round-trip time in Direct Update dominates the response time of the whole update process. As the number of updated rows increases, the overhead percentage of Direct Update decreases because the response time is dominated by the update time in the server side. The major overhead for Cached Update comes from the execution of update statements to update authentication data in the server side. The results also show that the performance of C-RC-MU is comparable to the performance of NoVeri without integrity protection, but without the MergeUpdate optimization, the overhead of C-RC ranges from 3% to 30% shown in the figure.

7 Conclusion

In the paper, we present an efficient and practical Merkle B-tree based scheme that provides integrity assurance without modifying the implementation of existing DBMSs. We have proposed a novel approach called Radix-Path Identifier, which makes it possible to serializes a Merkle B-tree into a database while enabling highly efficient authentication data retrieval and updates. We have explored the efficiency of different methods such as MultiJoin, SingleJoin, ZeroJoin and RangeCondition, to retrieve authentication data from a serialized MBT stored in a database, implemented a proof-of-concept prototype, and conducted extensive experimental evaluation. Our experimental results show that our scheme imposes a small overhead for *Select*, *Update* and *Append* and a reasonable overhead for *Insert* and *Delete*.

Acknowledgments. The authors would like to thank the anonymous reviewers for their helpful suggestions. This work is partially supported by the U.S. Army Research Office under grant W911NF-08-1-0105 managed by NCSU Secure Open Systems Initiative (SOSI), by the NSF under grants CNS-0747247 and CCF-0914946, by NSFC under Grants No. 61170280, and SPRPCAS under Grant No. XDA06010701, and by K.C. Wong Education Foundation. The contents of this paper do not necessarily reflect the position or the policies of the U.S. Government.

References

1. Hbase, http://hbase.apache.org/
2. Celko, J.: Joe Celko's Trees and Hierarchies in SQL for Smarties. Morgan Kaufmann (2004)
3. Chang, F., Dean, J., Ghemawat, S., Hsieh, W.C., Wallach, D.A., Burrows, M., Chandra, T., Fikes, A., Gruber, R.E.: Bigtable: A distributed storage system for structured data. ACM Trans. Comput. Syst. 26, 4:1–4:26 (2008)
4. Devanbu, P., Gertz, M., Martel, C., Stubblebine, S.G.: Authentic data publication over the internet. J. Comput. Secur. 11, 291–314 (2003)
5. Devanbu, P.T., Gertz, M., Martel, C.U., Stubblebine, S.G.: Authentic third-party data publication. In: Thuraisingham, B., van de Riet, R., Dittrich, K.R., Tari, Z. (eds.) Data and Application Security. IFIP, vol. 78, pp. 101–112. Springer, Heidelberg (2001)
6. Di Battista, G., Palazzi, B.: Authenticated relational tables and authenticated skip lists. In: Barker, S., Ahn, G.-J. (eds.) Data and Applications Security 2007. LNCS, vol. 4602, pp. 31–46. Springer, Heidelberg (2007)
7. Goodrich, M.T., Tamassia, R.: Efficient authenticated dictionaries with skip lists and commutative hashing. Technical report. Johns Hopkins Information Security Institute (2001)
8. Goodrich, M.T., Tamassia, R., Triandopoulos, N.: Super-efficient verification of dynamic outsourced databases. In: Malkin, T. (ed.) CT-RSA 2008. LNCS, vol. 4964, pp. 407–424. Springer, Heidelberg (2008)

9. Li, F., Hadjieleftheriou, M., Kollios, G., Reyzin, L.: Dynamic authenticated index structures for outsourced databases. In: Proceedings of the 2006 ACM SIGMOD International Conference on Management of Data, SIGMOD 2006, pp. 121–132. ACM, New York (2006)
10. Micali, S.: Efficient certificate revocation. Technical report, Cambridge, MA, USA (1996)
11. Miklau, G., Suciu, D.: Implementing a tamper-evident database system. In: Grumbach, S., Sui, L., Vianu, V. (eds.) ASIAN 2005. LNCS, vol. 3818, pp. 28–48. Springer, Heidelberg (2005)
12. Mouratidis, K., Sacharidis, D., Pang, H.: Partially materialized digest scheme: an efficient verification method for outsourced databases. The VLDB Journal 18, 363–381 (2009)
13. Mykletun, E., Narasimha, M., Tsudik, G.: Authentication and integrity in outsourced databases. Trans. Storage 2, 107–138 (2006)
14. Narasimha, M., Tsudik, G.: Authentication of outsourced databases using signature aggregation and chaining. In: Li Lee, M., Tan, K.-L., Wuwongse, V. (eds.) DASFAA 2006. LNCS, vol. 3882, pp. 420–436. Springer, Heidelberg (2006)
15. Palazzi, B., Pizzonia, M., Pucacco, S.: Query racing: fast completeness certification of query results. In: Foresti, S., Jajodia, S. (eds.) Data and Applications Security and Privacy XXIV. LNCS, vol. 6166, pp. 177–192. Springer, Heidelberg (2010)
16. Pang, H., Jain, A., Ramamritham, K., Tan, K.-L.: Verifying completeness of relational query results in data publishing. In: Proceedings of the 2005 ACM SIGMOD International Conference on Management of Data, SIGMOD 2005, pp. 407–418. ACM, New York (2005)
17. Pang, H., Tan, K.-L.: Authenticating query results in edge computing. In: Proceedings of the 20th International Conference on Data Engineering, ICDE 2004, pp. 560–571. IEEE Computer Society, Washington, DC (2004)
18. Pang, H., Zhang, J., Mouratidis, K.: Scalable verification for outsourced dynamic databases. Proc. VLDB Endow. 2, 802–813 (2009)
19. Pizzette, L., Cabot, T.: Database as a service: A marketplace assessment (2012)
20. Sion, R.: Query execution assurance for outsourced databases. In: Proceedings of the 31st International Conference on Very Large Data Bases, VLDB 2005, pp. 601–612. VLDB Endowment (2005)
21. Tropashko, V.: Nested intervals tree encoding in sql. SIGMOD Rec. 34(2), 47–52 (2005)
22. Wei, W., Yu, T.: Practical Integrity Assurance for Big Data Processing Deployed over Open Cloud. PhD thesis, North Carolina State University (2013)
23. Wei, W., Yu, T., Xue, R.: ibigtable: Practical data integrity for bigtable in public cloud. In: Proceedings of the Second ACM Conference on Data and Application Security and Privacy, CODASPY 2013. ACM (2013)
24. Xie, M., Wang, H., Yin, J., Meng, X.: Integrity auditing of outsourced data. In: Proceedings of the 33rd International Conference on Very Large Data Bases, VLDB 2007, pp. 782–793. VLDB Endowment (2007)
25. Xie, M., Wang, H., Yin, J., Meng, X.: Providing freshness guarantees for outsourced databases. In: Proceedings of the 11th International Conference on Extending Database Technology: Advances in Database Technology, EDBT 2008, pp. 323–332. ACM, New York (2008)

Specification and Deployment of Integrated Security Policies for Outsourced Data

Anis Bkakria[1], Frédéric Cuppens[1], Nora Cuppens-Boulahia[1],
and David Gross-Amblard[2]

[1] Télécom Bretagne
{anis.bkakria,frederic.cuppens,nora.cuppens}@telecom-bretagne.eu
[2] IRISA,Université de Rennes 1
david.gross_amblard@irisa.fr

Abstract. This paper presents a well-founded language allowing in one hand data owners to easily specify their security and utility requirements over the data to be outsourced and in an another hand to formalize the set of security mechanisms that can be used for the protection of outsourced data. Based on the formalization of security and utility requirements and security mechanisms properties, we formally identify the best mechanisms, and the best way to combine them to get the best trade-off between utility and security.

Keywords: Security policy, data confidentiality, privacy-preserving, data outsourcing, relational databases, temporal logics of knowledge.

1   Introduction

Because of the rapid evolution of communication technologies, data storage and data processing, outsourcing data to a third-party has grown up over the last few years. Information system architecture adopted by public and private companies is changing for mainly two causes. First, it offers several advantages to the client companies, especially for small ones with limited IT budget as it allows them to reduce the cost of maintaining computing infrastructure and data-rich applications. Second, data collected by companies generally contain sensitive information which must be protected.

Data outsourcing gives rise to many security issues, e.g., confidentiality, integrity, authentication, copyright protection, privacy and anonymity, because outsourced data contains often highly sensitive information which will be stored and managed by third parties. These security issues are traditionally addressed by using security and cryptography mechanisms such as encryption, anonymization, watermarking, fragmentation, etc. In our work, we consider that the set of security mechanisms that can be used for the protection of outsourced data are represented as a toolbox giving security administrators the ability to enforce their security requirements. We develop a logic-based language allowing the security administrators to specify their security and utility requirements

V. Atluri and G. Pernul (Eds.): DBSec 2014, LNCS 8566, pp. 17–32, 2014.
© IFIP International Federation for Information Processing 2014

and automatically choose the best mechanisms, and the best way to combine them in order to enforce defined security requirements.

As a case of study, we address the problem of secure data integration in which two data owners storing two private tables having the same set of records on different sets of attributes want to create a joint table containing involved attributes of both private tables. The joint table must satisfy the set of security and utility requirements defined by both data owners. To meet these goals, we first develop a well-founded logic based language allowing to model the used system, the security and utility requirements defined by both data owners, and the security mechanisms that can be used to satisfy them. Second, we show how to use those specifications to choose the best combination of security mechanisms that can satisfy the selected security and utility requirements defined by both data owners.

The reminder of this paper is organized as follows, Section 2 discusses related work. Section 3 describes our approach. Section 4 presents our defined language and the specification of the used system. Section 5 shows the modeling of the policy to be applied over the outsourced information. Section 6 presents the specification of the security mechanisms that can be used to satisfy a defined policy. Section 7 shows how to choose the best combination of security mechanisms that can satisfy a defined policy. Section 8 gives a demonstration of our approach. Finally, Section 9 reports our conclusions.

2   Related Work

Many approaches to protect confidentiality and privacy of outsourced data are based on encryption [5,9,10]. Hacigümüs et al. [9] have proposed the first approach aiming to query encrypted data. The proposed technique is based on the definition of a number of buckets on the attribute domain which allows the server-side evaluation of point queries. Hore et al. [10] improve the bucket-based index methods by presenting an efficient method for partitioning the domain of attributes. Many interesting techniques providing protection of outsourced data are based on order preserving encryption OPE schemes [5]. OPE schemes are symmetric-key deterministic encryption schemes which produce cipher-texts that preserve the order of the plain-texts. However, in all mentioned approaches, authors use only encryption to protect sensitive outsourced data which makes query execution on the outsourced encrypted data much more difficult.

Few research efforts have investigated how to combine security mechanisms to protect sensitive outsourced data. In [6], authors combine data fragmentation together with encryption to ensure confidentiality of outsourced mono-relational database. This approach was improved in [1] by combining the best features of encryption and fragmentation to deal efficiently with multi-relation normalized databases. Popa et al. [15] propose an interesting approach called CryptDB. The proposed system relies on a trusted party containing a proxy server allowing the interception of users queries which will be executed over the protected databases. The proxy stores a set of encryption keys allowing to encrypt and decrypt data and queries. In order to allow the execution of different kind of SQL queries, CryptDB system combines different encryption schemes. For range query, it use an implementation of the Order Preserving Encryption (OPE) [5], computations on numeric data are supported using homomorphic encryption based on the Paillier cryptosystem [14] and matching keywords are supported using searchable encryption [17]. The CryptDB approach offers a solution to the encryption type selection problem by proposing an adaptive scheme that dynamically adjusts encryption strategies. The idea of this approach is to encrypt each data item in many *onions*: onion for equal and order comparison, onion for aggregate operations and onion for word search operations. In each onion, the values is dressed in layers of increasingly stronger encryption, each of these layers provides certain kind of functionality. This approach has two main drawbacks. First, it will significantly increase the size of the encrypted database. Second, in order to enable certain functionality, some encryption layers must be removed by updating the database which can be, for big databases, very expensive in terms of execution time.

Formal verification of security protocols [3,4] has been extensively used to verify security properties such as secrecy [3] and strong secrecy [4]. A security protocol involves two or more principal actors, these actors are classified into honest actors aiming to securely exchange information and dishonest actors (attackers) aiming to subvert the protocol. Therefore, dishonest actors are not constrained to follow the protocol rules. Despite that formal verification-based approaches are efficient in security properties verification, they cannot be used in our case as we consider that the actors are honest-but-curious. They are honest as they are constrained to follow the chosen combination of security mechanisms and they are curious in that they will try to infer protected sensitive information by analyzing the joined table.

3   Proposed Approach

In our approach, we strive to design a support tool allowing, for a given security policy, selection of the best combination of mechanisms to enforce this security policy. To achieve this goal, we suggest the following methodology :

- Using an Epistemic Linear Temporal Logic, we defined an expressive language allowing to formally model a system composed of involved entities and the data on which the security policy should be enforced, and formally express the security policy defined by the security administrators.
- We conducted a formal study of the security mechanisms allowing the achievement of a chosen goal. This formal study enables us to extract the security and utility properties that characterize each security mechanism. These properties are formally expressed using our language.
- Based on the system formalization, the security policy formalization and the security mechanisms properties formalization, we formally identify the relevant combination of mechanisms to efficiently enforce the defined security policy.

4   System Specification Using Epistemic LTL

In this section, we will define and use the language $\mathcal{L}$ to formalize our system. In particular, we will define axioms which describe the basic knowledge of each agent and the formalization of the chosen goal.

4.1   Syntax and Semantics

The first-order temporal epistemic language $\mathcal{L}$ is made up of a set of predicates $\mathcal{P}$, propositional connectives $\vee$, $\wedge$, $\neg$, $\rightarrow$ and $\leftrightarrow$, the quantifiers $\forall$, $\exists$. We take the usual set of future connectives $\bigcirc$ (next), $\Diamond$ (Sometime, or eventually), $\Box$ (always) [8]. For knowledge we assume a set of agents $A_g = \{1, \cdots, m\}$ and use a set of unary modal connectives K_j, for $j \in A_g$, in which a formula $K_j\psi$ is to be read as "agent j knows ψ".

Definition 1. *Let φ and ψ be propositions and P_i be a predicate of arity n in $\mathcal{P}$. The set of well-formed formulas of $\mathcal{L}$ is defined as follows:*

$$\phi := P_i(t_1, \cdots, t_n)| \, K_i\psi| \, \neg\varphi| \, \varphi \vee \psi| \, \varphi \wedge \psi| \, \bigcirc\varphi| \, \Diamond\varphi| \, \Box\varphi|\varphi \rightarrow \psi| \, \varphi \leftrightarrow \psi \mid \exists x\psi \mid \forall x\psi$$

Definition 2. *An interpretation of the language $\mathcal{L}$ is the triple $\mathcal{K} = (\mathcal{W}, \mathcal{I}, \Phi)$ consisting of a sequence of states $\mathcal{W} = \{w_0, w_1, \cdots\}$, a set of classical first-order structures $\mathcal{I}$ that assigns for each states $w_i \in \mathcal{W}$ a predicate $I_{w_i}(P) : |I_{w_i}|^n \rightarrow \{True, False\}$ for each n-places predicate $P \in \mathcal{P}$ and Φ a transition function which defines transitions between states due to the application of mechanisms (actions). $\Phi(w_i, m_k) = w_j$ if the mechanism m_k transits our system from states w_i to state w_j.*

Definition 3. *Let $\mathcal{W}$ be a sequence of states, w_i ($i \geq 0$) denote a state of $\mathcal{W}$ and v an assignment. The satisfaction relation $\models$ for a formula ψ of $\mathcal{L}$ is defined as follows:*

- $(w_i, \mathcal{W}) \models P(t_1, \cdots, t_n) \iff I_{w_i}(P)(v(t_1), \cdots, v(t_n)) = True$
- $(w_i, \mathcal{W}) \models \neg\psi \iff (w_i, \mathcal{W}) \not\models \psi$
- $(w_i, \mathcal{W}) \models \psi \rightarrow \varphi \iff (w_i, \mathcal{W}) \not\models \psi$ or $(w_i, \mathcal{W}) \models \varphi$
- $(w_i, \mathcal{W}) \models \psi \leftrightarrow \varphi \iff (w_i, \mathcal{W}) \models (\psi \rightarrow \varphi) \wedge (\varphi \rightarrow \psi)$
- $(w_i, \mathcal{W}) \models \forall x\psi \iff (w_i, \mathcal{W}) \models \psi[x/c]$ for all $c \in |I_{w_i}|$
- $(w_i, \mathcal{W}) \models \psi \wedge \varphi \iff (w_i, \mathcal{W}) \models \psi$ and $(w_i, \mathcal{W}) \models \varphi$
- $(w_i, \mathcal{W}) \models \psi \vee \varphi \iff (w_i, \mathcal{W}) \models \psi$ or $(w_i, \mathcal{W}) \models \varphi$
- $(w_i, \mathcal{W}) \models \bigcirc\psi \iff (w_{i+1}, \mathcal{W}) \models \psi$
- $(w_i, \mathcal{W}) \models \Diamond\psi \iff (w_k, \mathcal{W}) \models \psi$ for some $k \geq i$
- $(w_i, \mathcal{W}) \models \Box\psi \iff (w_k, \mathcal{W}) \models \psi$ for all $k \geq i$

In our approach, we choose to work with relational databases which are composed of tables, attributes, records and values. We suppose that relational databases schemes are known to all agents in the system. Epistemic operator K is only used to represents the knowledge of relation between objects (attribute and records) and values which represent an instantiations of these objects. These relations are represented using the three-places predicates $valueOf$,

$valueOf(R, A, V)$ is to be read "the value of the attribute A in the record R is V". In order to simplify our language $\mathcal{L}$, we transform the epistemic operator K using the two-places predicate $knows$ as following:

$$K_i \; valueOf(R, A, V) \rightarrow valueOf(R, A, V) \wedge knows(i, V) \qquad (1)$$

$knows(i, v)$ is to be read "the agent i knows V".

4.2   Data Model

A system $\mathcal{S} = \langle \mathcal{O}, \mathcal{T}, \mathcal{A}, \mathcal{R}, \mathcal{V} \rangle$ consists of a finite set of owners $\mathcal{O}$, a finite set of relational tables $\mathcal{T}$, a finite set of attributes $\mathcal{A}$, a finite set of records $\mathcal{R}$ and a finite set of values $\mathcal{V}$. We use the following syntactic conventions. Let $O_1, O_2, \cdots$ be variables over owners $\mathcal{O}$, $T_1, T_2, \cdots$ be variables over relational tables $\mathcal{T}$, $A_1, A_2, \cdots$ be variables over attributes $\mathcal{A}$, $R_1, R_2, \cdots$ be variables over records $\mathcal{R}$ and $V_1, V_2, \cdots$ be variables over the set of values $\mathcal{V}$. We identify the following predicates :

- $belongs(O_1, T_1)$ is satisfied if the owner of the relational table T_1 is O_1.
- $attribute\_of(T_1, A_1)$ is satisfied if A_1 is an attribute of the relational table T_1.
- $recordOf(T_1, R_1)$ is satisfied if R_1 is a record of the relational table T_1.
- $valueOf(R_1, A_1, V_1)$ is satisfied if V_1 is the value of the attribute A_1 in the record R_1.

We denote by Σ the set of formulas representing the formalization of our system using previous predicates. We suppose that the set of formulas Σ are always true in the system (e.g., the table T belongs to the owner O and will belong always to the owner O). This can be formalized as follows:

$$\forall f \in \Sigma. \; (w_0, \mathcal{W}) \models \Box f \qquad (2)$$

4.3   Specifying Basic Knowledge Axioms

In our system, we consider each data owner as an agent. An owner's knowledge is specified using the following axioms:

$$\forall T_1, O_1, A_1, R_1, V_1. \; [\; belongs(O_1, T_1) \; \wedge \; attribute\_of(T_1, A_1) \; \wedge$$
$$recordOf(T_1, R_1) \; \wedge \; valueOf(R_1, A_1, V_1) \rightarrow knows(O_1, V_1) \;] \qquad (3)$$

$$\forall T_1, O_1, A_1, R_1, V_1. \; [\; \neg belongs(O_1, T_1) \; \wedge \; attribute\_of(T_1, A_1) \; \wedge$$
$$recordOf(T_1, R_1) \; \wedge \; valueOf(R_1, A_1, V_1) \rightarrow \neg knows(O_1, V_1) \;] \qquad (4)$$

$$\forall O_1, V_1. \; knows(O_1, V_1) \rightarrow \bigcirc knows(O_1, V_1) \qquad (5)$$

$$\forall O, T_1, R, A, V.\ attribute\_of(T_1, A)\ \wedge\ recordOf(T_1, R)\ \wedge\ valueOf(R, A, V)\wedge$$
$$knows(O, V) \leftrightarrow belongs(O, T_1) \vee \left(\exists T_2, T_3. belongs(O, T_2) \wedge joinOf(T_1, T_2, T_3)\right) \quad (6)$$
$$\wedge join\_involved(T_1, A)\ \wedge\ \neg protected(T_1, A, O))$$

Axiom 3 means that an owner knows all information stored in tables that belong to him while axiom 4 means that an owner has no knowledge about the information stored in tables that do not belong to him. Axiom 5 states that data owners never forget information they know. Axiom 6 means that an owner O knows the values assumed by an attribute A of the table T_1 if and only if the table T_1 belongs to the owner O or there exists a table T_3 representing the join of a table T_2 and the table T_1 in which the attribute A is not protected.

4.4   Goal Representation

According to our scenario, the goal consists in joining two private relational tables. This goal is specified using the axioms 7 and 8 in which we use the following predicates:

- $join(T_1, T_2)$ is satisfied if both owners of T_1 and T_2 want to join their private tables T_1 and T_2.
- $joinAttribute(T_1, T_2, A_1)$ is satisfied if the tables T_1 and T_2 are joined over the attribute A_1.
- $join\_involved(T_1, A_1)$ is satisfied if the attribute A_1 of the table T_1 is involved in join operations. This predicate allows us to specify which are the attributes concerned by the joint.

Axiom 7 states that if the data owners of two tables T_1 and T_2 want to integrate their private data then eventually, there will exist a table T_j representing the join of T_1 and T_2. Axiom 8 states that the set of attributes of the joined table T_j is composed of the union of sets of join-involved attributes of private tables T_1 and T_2.

$$\forall T_1, T_2.\ join(T_1, T_2)\ \rightarrow\ \Diamond \left(\exists T_3\ JoinOf(T_1, T_2, T_3)\right) \quad (7)$$

$$\forall T_1, T_2, T_j, A.\ JoinOf(T_1, T_2, T_j)\ \wedge\ \left(join\_involved(T_1, A) \vee \right.$$
$$\left. join\_involved(T_2, A)\right)\ \rightarrow\ attribute\_of(T_j, A) \quad (8)$$

5   Security Policy Specification

The policy to be deployed is composed of a set of abstract-level constraints. Using these constraints, data owners will be able to model in a quite simple and powerful way, their security and utility requirements. In this section, we present different kinds of constraints: security constraint and utility constraint. We present for each kind of constraint the abstract-level representation and their corresponding transformation to the concrete level.

5.1   Security Constraint

Confidentiality Constraint: Using confidentiality constraint, a data owner will be able to require that the values assumed by some attributes are sensitive and therefore must be protected. For this purpose, we define the two-places predicate $SAttributeOf$. The formula $SAttributeOf(t, a)$ means that "The attribute a of the table t is a sensitive attribute". A confidentiality constraint is transformed to the concrete level using the following rule:

$$\forall A, T.\ SAttributeOf(T, A) \rightarrow \Box\ [\forall O, R, V. recordOf(T, R) \land$$
$$valueOf(R, A, V)\ \land\ \neg belongs(O, T)\ \rightarrow\ \neg knows(O, V)] \tag{9}$$

Anonymization Constraints: Using this kind of constraints, a data owner will be able to require the prevention of identity disclosure by protecting personal identifiers. We define the one-place predicate $withoutIDDisclosure$. Thus, the formula $withoutIDDisclosure(t)$ is to be read "Prevent identity disclosure in the table t". An Anonymization constraint is transformed to the concrete level using the following rule:

$$\forall T.\ withoutIDDisclosure(T) \rightarrow \Box\ \big(\forall A, O, R, V.\ IDAttributeOf(T, A)$$
$$\land\ recordOf(T, R)\ \land valueOf(R, A, V)\ \land\ \neg belongs(O, T)\ \rightarrow\ \neg knows(O, V)\big) \tag{10}$$

5.2   Utility Constraint

Confidentiality and privacy protection is offered at the expense of data utility. Utility constraint gives the ability to a data owner to require that particular properties on data must be respected. The violation of these properties makes the data useless. As we work with relational databases, utility requirements are properties allowing the data owner to execute certain kind of queries over the protected data. These utility requirements can be classified into four classes.

Equality Check Requirements. With this kind of requirements, a data owner wants to be able to perform equality checks, which means that he or she wants to be able to perform selects with equality predicates, equality joins, etc.

Order Check Requirements. A data owner can use this kind of requirement in order to perform order check, which means that he or she wants to have the ability to execute range queries, order joins, ORDER BY, MIN, MAX, etc.

Computational Requirements. With this kind of requirements, a data owner wants to have the ability to perform computation over encrypted data, which means the ability to execute queries with SUM, AVG, etc.

Keyword Search Requirements. Using keyword search requirements, a data owner wants to have the ability to perform keyword based search over the encrypted data (e.g, to check if a word exists in an encrypted text).

To be able to express these different kinds of utility requirements, we define the one place predicate $utility\_requirement()$. Then, an utility constraint defined over the attribute A can be expressed by the axiom 11, which is to be read: "the ability to perform the utility requirement U over the attribute A".

$$utility\_requirement(U) \ \wedge \ provides(U, A) \tag{11}$$

6   Security Mechanisms Specification

Security policies are enforced through the application of security mechanisms which can be methods or approaches for supporting the requirements of the security policies. Each security policy is specified using three groups of formulas: preconditions formulas, effects formulas, and properties formulas.

Preconditions. For each security mechanism, preconditions are represented by a set of formulas which are necessary conditions under which the security mechanism can be applied. We define the two-places predicated $is\_applicable$. The formula $is\_applicable(M, O)$ is to be read "the mechanism M can be applied over the object O", O can be a table, an attribute, or a value. Preconditions of a security mechanism M are specified using a formula of the following form:

$$\square \ (is\_applicable(M, O) \ \rightarrow \ \Delta_M) \tag{12}$$

Where Δ_M represents necessary conditions for the applicability of the mechanism M. A formula of the form 12 is to be read "At any state of the system, M can be applied if the preconditions Δ_M hold".

Effects. Effects of the application of a mechanism M that transits the system from a state w_i to a state w_j are modifications applied to the system during this transition. We use the two-places predicate $apply(M, O)$ to say that the mechanism M is applied over the object O. For a mechanism M, effects are represented by a set of formulas Σ_M such that:

$$\Phi(w_i, \ apply(M, O)) = w_j \ \rightarrow \ (w_j \ \models \ \Sigma_M) \tag{13}$$

Axiom 13 states that if the application of the mechanism M over the object O transits the system from a state w_i to a state w_j, therefore the set of effects Σ_M of the application of the mechanism M is satisfied on the state w_j.

Properties. The set of security and utility properties $P_1, \cdots, P_n$ that can be derived from the effects of the mechanism application.

$$\Sigma_M \rightarrow \bigwedge_{i=1}^{n} P_i \tag{14}$$

In our approach, security policies are composed mainly of confidentiality constraints and anonymization constraints. In the next section, we specify using the three previously presented groups of formulas (preconditions, effects, and properties) the set of security mechanisms that can be used to enforce the security policy. We classify these security mechanisms into encryption-based mechanisms and anonymization-based mechanisms.

6.1   Encryption-Based Mechanism Specification

Encryption-based security mechanism can be classified using two main factors: the security properties they offer and the level of security they provide (e.g, the amount of information revealed about the encrypted data). Encryption-based security mechanisms are to be applied over an attribute A if the following preconditions hold: (1) the attribute A is considered sensitive, (2) the attribute A is involved in the joint table. This can be specified as follows:

$$\square \left[\forall M, A. \enspace enc\_based\_mechanism(M) \wedge is\_applicable(M, A) \rightarrow \right.$$
$$\left. \exists T. \enspace SAttributeOf(T, A) \wedge join\_involved(T, A) \right] \tag{15}$$

The effects of the application of encryption-based mechanisms are specified using the following axiom:

$$\forall M, A, T, K. \enspace enc\_based\_mechanism(M) \wedge attribute\_of(T, A) \wedge$$
$$enc\_key(K) \wedge apply(M, A) \rightarrow encrypted(T, A, K) \tag{16}$$

Once we have defined the above axiom describing the effects of encryption-based mechanisms, we can specify the conditions under which an encryption-based mechanism can protect the values of an attribute. Obliviously, the values of an attribute over which an encryption-based mechanism is applied are protected from unauthorized data owners if those data owners have no knowledge about the used encrypted key (axiom 17). An attribute is protected from an unauthorized data owner means that this data owner has no knowledge about the values of the protected attribute (axiom 18).

$$\forall A, T, K, O. \enspace enc\_key(K) \wedge encrypted(T, A, K) \wedge \neg knows(O, K) \rightarrow$$
$$protected(T, A, O) \tag{17}$$

$$\forall A, T, O, R, V. \enspace protected(T, A, O) \wedge recordOf(T, R) \wedge$$
$$valueOf(R, A, V) \rightarrow \neg knows(O, V) \tag{18}$$

Encryption-based mechanisms can be classified using the security properties they offer into four categories: deterministic encryption based mechanisms, order-preserving encryption based mechanisms, homomorphic encryption based mechanisms, and searchable encryption based mechanisms. For each of these four categories, we formalize the security and utility properties that characterize them.

Deterministic Encryption Based Mechanisms: Deterministic encryption based mechanisms allow logarithmic time equality check over encrypted data. This means that it can perform select queries with equality predicates, equality joins, etc. Deterministic encryption based mechanisms cannot achieve the classical notions of security of probabilistic encryption because it leaks which encrypted values correspond to the same plaintext value. Therefore, each attribute over which a deterministic encryption based mechanism is applied will have the deterministic (det) security level (axiom 19).

$$\forall M, A. \ \ det\_enc\_mechanism(M) \land \ apply(M, A) \rightarrow$$
$$provides(equality\_check, A) \land sec\_level(A, det) \tag{19}$$

Order-preserving Encryption Based Mechanisms: Order preserving symmetric encryption (OPE) mechanisms are based on deterministic symmetric encryption schemes which produce encrypted values that preserve numerical ordering of the plaintext values. OPE mechanisms are weaker than deterministic encryption based mechanisms as they leak the order between plaintext values. Based on this fact, each attribute over which an OPE mechanism is applied will have the order-preserving (ope) security level (axiom 20).

$$\forall M, A. \ \ ope\_mechanism(M) \land \ apply(M, A) \rightarrow \ sec\_level(A, ope) \land$$
$$provides(equality\_check, A) \ \land \ provides(order\_check, A) \tag{20}$$

Homomorphic Encryption Based Mechanisms: Homomorphic encryption mechanisms are based on secure probabilistic encryption schemes which enable to perform computation over encrypted data. For efficiency, we suppose that we will use mechanisms based on partially homomorphic encryption as fully homomorphic encryption schemes have a long way to go before they can be used in practice [13]. In our approach, we will use mechanisms based on Paillier cryptosystem [14] to support summation. Paillier cryptosystem provides indistinguishability under an adaptive chosen-plaintext attack (IND-CPA). Therefore, each attribute over which an Homomorphic encryption based mechanisms is applied will have the probabilistic (prob) security level (axiom 21).

$$\forall M, A. \ \ hom\_mechanism(M) \land \ apply(M, A) \rightarrow$$
$$sec\_level(A, prob) \ \land provides(addition, A) \tag{21}$$

Searchable Encryption Based Mechanisms: Searchable encryption mechanisms allow searching for keywords on an encrypted database without revealing the keyword. Therefore, this kind of mechanisms can be used to perform operations such as SQL's LIKE operator. We suppose that we will use the SEARCH mechanism defined in [18] which is proved to be nearly as secure as a probabilistic encryption. Based on this fact, each attribute over which the SEARCH mechanism is applied will have the probabilistic (prob) security level. Properties of the SEARCH-based mechanism is specified as follows:

$$\forall A. \ \ searchable\_enc\_mechanism(SEARCH) \land \ apply(SEARCH, A) \rightarrow$$
$$sec\_level(A, prob) \ \land \ provides(keywork\_search, A) \tag{22}$$

6.2   Anonymization-Based Mechanism Specification

The anonymization technique aims to prevent identity disclosure by protecting personal identifier. To meet this requirement, we use the existing anonymization approach *k-anonymity* [16] in which identifier attributes values are removed from the private table (axiom 25). However, a *Quasi-identifier* attribute value in the released table may lead to infer the value of removed identifier attributes (axiom 23). Therefore, *Quasi-identifier* attributes values are generalized (axiom 26) in such a way that removed identifier attributes values cannot be recovered.

$$\forall O, T_1, A_1, V_1, R. \ IDAttributeOf(T_1, A_1) \wedge \ recordOf(T_1, R) \wedge$$
$$valueOf(R, A_1, V_1) \ \wedge \ knows(O, V_1) \leftrightarrow belongs(T_1, O) \ \vee$$
$$\Big[\exists T_2, T_3. \ belongs(O, T_2) \ \wedge \ joinOf(T_1, T_2, T_3) \wedge \big(join\_involved(T_1, A_1) \quad (23)$$
$$\vee \ (\exists A_2. \ QIDAttributeOf(T_1, A_2) \ \wedge \ \neg \ anonymized(T_1, A_2)))\Big]$$

Anonymization mechanism is applied over a table T if and only if the table T contains at least an identifier attribute or a quasi-identifier attribute. These preconditions is specified as follows:

$$\Box\big[\forall T. \ is\_applicable(kanonymity, T) \rightarrow \exists A.(IDAttributeOf(T, A) \ \vee$$
$$QIDAttributeOf(T, A)) \wedge \neg \ encrypted(T, A)\big] \qquad (24)$$

Effects of the application of Anonymization mechanism over a table T are specified using the following axioms:

$$\forall A. \ IDAttributeOf(T, A) \rightarrow \neg \ join\_involved(T, A) \qquad (25)$$

$$\forall A.QIDAttributeOf(T, A) \wedge join\_involved(T, A) \rightarrow anonymized(T, A) \quad (26)$$

The use of anonymization mechanisms such as k-anonymity offers the data owner the ability to ensure the prevention of identities disclosure by protecting personal identifiers at the same time supporting data analysis (e.g., data mining). In terms of security, anonymization based mechanisms are weaker than encryption based mechanisms as anonymized data can sometimes be re-identified with particular individuals by using *homogeneity Attack* or *Background Knowledge Attack* [12]. Based on this fact, each protected identifier attribute will have the anonymization (anonym) security level. Properties of anonymization-based mechanism is specified as follows:

$$\forall M, T.anon\_mechanism(M) \wedge apply(M, T) \rightarrow$$
$$provides(data\_analysis, T) \wedge \big(\forall A, O.IDAttributeOf(T, A) \wedge \neg \qquad (27)$$
$$belongs(T, O) \rightarrow protected(T, A, O) \wedge sec\_level(anonym, A)\big)$$

In order to compare different security levels provided by previously presented security mechanisms, we define the transitive predicate *more_secure_than*. The formula *more_secure_than*(l_1, l_2) is to be read: "the level l_1 is more secure than the level l_2". A mechanism M_1 is more secure than a mechanism M_2 if the application of M_1 leaks less information about sensitive data than the application of M_2. Therefore, based on the amount of leaked information, we define a rule (axiom 28) stating that: probabilistic security level *prob* is more secure than deterministic security level *det*, the deterministic security level *det* is more secure than the order-preserving security level *ope*, and the order-preserving security level *ope* is more secure than the anonymization security level *anonym*.

$$more\_secure\_than(prob, det) \land more\_secure\_than(det, ope)$$
$$\land more\_secure\_than(ope, anonym) \tag{28}$$

7   Choosing the Right Mechanisms

The right mechanism or combination of mechanisms is the one that fits in the best way the sets of security and utility constraints. As we have seen in the previous section, each security mechanism offers a different level of protection and a different kind of utility properties. The main challenge then is to choose the best mechanisms allowing the satisfaction of the chosen goal while enforcing the defined security policy. In our scenario, security issues come when data is joined. Before applying the joint operation, security constraints are satisfied. This hypothesis is also suitable in the general case of data outsourcing. As we can consider that, since the data is not outsourced, there is no security issue to worry about. Based on this, we defined several steps allowing the selection of the mechanisms to be applied.

7.1   First Step: Satisfy the Chosen Goal

We look for the mechanisms that satisfy the chosen goal. For instance, in our scenario, we look for the suitable join method that can join the data of the two private tables. Formally speaking, a mechanism M_g satisfies a goal G if from the specification of our system Σ and the effects of the mechanism Σ_{M_g} we are able to deduce the set of formula representing the goal G (29).

$$\Sigma \cup \Sigma_{M_g} \vdash \Sigma_G \tag{29}$$

7.2   Second Step: Violated Security Constraints

After getting the set of mechanisms $\mathcal{M}$ that can be applied to achieve the chosen goal, we start looking for the set of violated security and utility constraints for each mechanism $M_g \in \mathcal{M}$. A constraint C is violated while the chosen goal G is satisfied if from the specification of our system Σ, the effects Σ_{M_g} of the mechanism M_g and the set of formulas Σ_C representing the constraint C we can deduce a logic contradiction. This is can be formally represented as follows:

$$\Sigma \cup \Sigma_{M_G} \cup \Sigma_C \vdash \bot \tag{30}$$

Obviously, our toolbox may contain several mechanisms that can satisfy the chosen goal. In that case, we should be able to choose the best one.

Definition 4 (Best goal satisfier). *Given the set of mechanisms $\mathcal{M} = \{M_1, \cdots , M_n\}$ that can be used to satisfy the defined goal G. Let C_i be the set of violated* constraints while applying the mechanism M_i. A mechanism M_j is a best goal satisfier if the following condition holds:

$$\forall i \in \{1, \cdots, n\}.\ |\mathcal{C}_j| \leq |\mathcal{C}_i|, where\ |\mathcal{C}_i|\ is\ the\ cardinality\ of\ \mathcal{C}_i.$$

7.3   Third Step: Satisfying the Violated Constraints

Once we get the *best goal satisfier* M_{bgs} for a defined goal G and the corresponding set of violated security and utility constraints $\mathcal{C}$, the challenge then is to, for each violated security constraint, looking for the properties that can satisfy that constraint. Formally speaking, a set of l properties $\mathcal{P} = \{P_1, \cdots, P_l\}$ satisfies a security constraint C in a state of the system if from: (1) the sets of formulas $\Sigma_{P_1}, \cdots, \Sigma_{P_l}$ representing respectively the specification of the properties $P_1, \cdots, P_l$, (2) the set of formulas Σ representing the system specification, and (3) the set of formulas $\Sigma_{M_{bgs}}$ representing the effects of M_{bgs}, we are able to deduce the set of formulas Σ_C representing the specification of the constraint C. This is can be formalized as follows:

$$\bigwedge_{i=1}^{l} \Sigma_{P_i} \cup \Sigma \cup \Sigma_{M_{bgs}} \vdash \Sigma_C \tag{31}$$

Informally, 31 means that if the set of security properties $\mathcal{P}$ is provided, the application of the M_{bgs} will not violate the security constraint C.

7.4   Fourth Step: Choosing the Best Security Mechanisms

The previous steps allow us to select the *best goal satisfier* M_{bgs} that can satisfy the goal G, the corresponding set of violated security and utility constraints $\mathcal{C}$, and for each security constraint $C_i \in \mathcal{C}$, we select the set of properties $\mathcal{P}_i$ that can satisfy C_i when applying the M_{bgs}. Now, based on those properties, the main goal is to select from our toolbox, the *best combination of security mechanisms* that can *usefully satisfy* each violated constraint in $\mathcal{C}$.

Definition 5 (Useful satisfaction). *Given a violated security constraint C defined over an object (table or attribute) Ob, the set of security properties $\mathcal{P}$ that satisfy C, and the set of utility constraint $\mathcal{U}_{Ob}$ defined over the object Ob. A combination of mechanisms MC usefully satisfy the constraint C if:*

$$\Sigma \cup \{\bigwedge_{M \in MC} apply(M, Ob)\} \models \left(\bigwedge_{P \in \mathcal{P}} P \bigwedge_{U \in \mathcal{U}_{Ob}} provides(U, Ob)\right) \tag{32}$$

Definition 6. *Given a violated security constraint C, the set of properties $\mathcal{P}$ that satisfy C, and a combination of mechanisms $CM = \{M_1, \cdots, M_n\}$ that usefully satisfy C. The security level l provided by the combination of mechanisms CM is the lowest level provided by the application of set of mechanisms $M_1, \cdots, M_n$.*

$$\Sigma \cup \{\forall Ob. \bigwedge_{i=1}^{n} apply(M, Ob)\} \models$$

$$(\forall l'. \ sec\_level(l, Ob) \wedge sec\_level(l', Ob) \to more\_secure\_than(l', l)) \tag{33}$$

Definition 7 (Best combination of mechanisms). *Given a violated security constraint C and the set of properties $\mathcal{P}$ that can satisfy C. Suppose that we find several combinations of security mechanisms $CM_1, \cdots, CM_n$ that provide the set of properties $\mathcal{P}$. Suppose that the set of combinations of security mechanisms $CM_1, \cdots, CM_n$ provides respectively the set of security levels $l_1, \cdots, l_n$. The combination of mechanisms CM_i is the best combination of mechanisms if it has the highest provided security level. For the combinations of mechanisms that provide the same security level, we choose the one that involves the minimal number of security mechanisms. This is can be specified as follows:*

$$\bigwedge_{i=1}^{n} \left(more\_secure\_than(l_i, l_j) \vee (l_i = l_j \ \wedge \ |CM_i| < |CM_j|) \right) \tag{34}$$

8   Best Mechanisms Selection

In this section, we demonstrate how to to select the best combination of mechanisms to satisfy defined security policies using different steps presented in the previous section. Due to the lack of space, proofs of this demonstration which can be found in [2] will be omitted here. Consider two data owners O_1 and O_2 which store respectively two private tables $T_1(SSN, Age, Adress, Balance)$ and $T_2(SSN, Job, ZIP, Salary)$. They want to integrate data stored in both tables. In one side, O_1 defined a policy P_1 composed of two security constraints $SC_{1,1} = \{withoutIDDisclosure(T_1)\}$ and $SC_{2,1} = \{SAttributeOf(T_1, Balance)\}$ and two utility constraints $UC_{1,1} = \{provides(equality, Balance)\}$ and $UC_{2,1} = \{provides(addition, Balance)\}$. O_1 specifies that the attribute SSN is an *identifier* attribute and that the attributes Age and $Address$ are *quasi-identifier* attributes. In another side, O_2 defines a policy P_2 composed of the security constraint $SC_{1,2} = \{withoutIDDisclosure(T_2)\}$. O_2 specifies that the attribute SSN is an *identifier* attribute and that the attributes Job and Zip are *quasi-identifier* attributes. Suppose that all attributes in T_1 and T_2 are involved in the join and that our toolbox is composed of the set of security mechanisms presented in 6.1 and 6.2, and two other mechanisms, rel_join and tds representing respectively the relational join operation and the *top-down specialization* mechanism [7]. Axiom 36 in [2] specifies the effects Σ_{rel_join} of the application of rel_join mechanism. Axiom 37 in [2] describes the effects Σ_{tds} of the application of the mechanism tds. The first step to select the best combination of mechanisms allowing to satisfy P_1 and P_2 while achieving the chosen goal consists in selecting the set of mechanisms to achieve the chosen goal. According to

29, the mechanism rel_join and tds can be applied to satisfy the jointure of the private tables T_1 and T_2 (See Proof 1 in [2]).

After we select the set of mechanisms to satisfy the goal, we choose the *best goal satisfier* from this set of mechanisms. In this demonstration, according to Definition 4, the tds mechanism represents the *best goal satisfier* to join the private tables T_1 and T_2 as it violates only $SC_{2,1}$ (See Proof 2 in [2]. The next step consists in finding the set of security properties to satisfy the violated security constraints that rose from the application of the *best goal satisfier*. When provided for the attribute *Balance*, the protection property *protected* can satisfy the confidentiality constraint $SC_{2,1}$ even when the tds mechanism is applied (See Proof 3 in [2]. Next, we choose from our toolbox the combination of mechanisms that can *usefully satisfy* the security constraint $SC_{2,1}$. Two combinations of mechanisms can *usefully satisfy* the security constraint $SC_{2,1}$: (1) combines an order-preserving encryption based mechanism and an homomorphic encryption based mechanism, and (2) combines a deterministic encryption based mechanism and an homomorphic encryption based mechanism (See Proof 4 in [2]. The final step consists in choosing the *best combination of mechanisms* that can *usefully satisfy* the security constraint $SC_{2,1}$ which is (2) (See Proof 5 in [2]. In conclusion, we can say that the application of the combination of mechanisms (2) before the application of tds mechanism allows us to enforce defined security policies P_1 and P_2 while joining the two tables T_1 and T_2.

9   Conclusion

We defined a well-founded language to select, from a toolbox containing a set of security mechanisms, the best combination of security mechanisms allowing the enforcement security and utility requirements for outsourced data. Our approach can be improved by detecting the incompatibilities and conflicts between security mechanisms to be able to decide which mechanisms can be applied together without losing provided utility requirements.

Acknowledgments. This work has received a French government support granted to the CominLabs excellence laboratory and managed by the National Research Agency in the "Investing for the Future" program under reference ANR-10-LABX-07-01, and to the Frag&Tag project and managed by the Dual Innovation Support Scheme (RAPID) under convention № 132906023

References

1. Bkakria, A., Cuppens, F., Cuppens-Boulahia, N., Fernandez, J.M., Gross-Amblard, D.: Preserving multi-relational outsourced databases confidentiality using fragmentation and encryption. Journal of Wireless Mobile Networks, Ubiquitous Computing, and Dependable Applications (JoWUA) 4(2), 39–62 (2013)
2. Bkakria, A., Cuppens, F., Cuppens-Boulahia, N., Gross-Amblard, D.:
   https://portail.telecom-bretagne.eu/publi/public/fic_download.jsp?id=30178

3. Blanchet, B.: An efficient cryptographic protocol verifier based on prolog rules. In: CSFW, pp. 82–96. IEEE Computer Society (2001)

4. Blanchet, B.: Automatic proof of strong secrecy for security protocols. In: IEEE Symposium on Security and Privacy, pp. 86–100. IEEE Computer Society (2004)

5. Boldyreva, A., Chenette, N., Lee, Y., O'Neill, A.: Order-preserving symmetric encryption. In: Joux [11], pp. 224–241

6. Ciriani, V., De Capitani di Vimercati, S., Foresti, S., Jajodia, S., Paraboschi, S., Samarati, P.: Fragmentation and encryption to enforce privacy in data storage. In: Biskup, J., López, J. (eds.) ESORICS 2007. LNCS, vol. 4734, pp. 171–186. Springer, Heidelberg (2007)

7. Fung, B.C.M., Wang, K., Yu, P.S.: Top-down specialization for information and privacy preservation. In: Aberer, K., Franklin, M.J., Nishio, S. (eds.) ICDE, pp. 205–216. IEEE Computer Society (2005)

8. Gabbay, D., Pnueli, A., Shelah, S., Stavi, J.: On the temporal analysis of fairness. In: Proceedings of the 7th ACM SIGPLAN-SIGACT Symposium on Principles of Programming Languages, POPL 1980, pp. 163–173. ACM, New York (1980)

9. Hacigümüs, H., Iyer, B.R., Li, C., Mehrotra, S.: Executing sql over encrypted data in the database-service-provider model. In: SIGMOD Conference, pp. 216–227. ACM (2002)

10. Hore, B., Mehrotra, S., Tsudik, G.: A privacy-preserving index for range queries. In: Nascimento, M.A., Özsu, M.T., Kossmann, D., Miller, R.J., Blakeley, J.A., Schiefer, K.B. (eds.) VLDB, pp. 720–731. Morgan Kaufmann (2004)

11. Joux, A. (ed.): EUROCRYPT 2009. LNCS, vol. 5479. Springer, Heidelberg (2009)

12. Machanavajjhala, A., Gehrke, J., Kifer, D., Venkitasubramaniam, M.: l-diversity: Privacy beyond k-anonymity. In: Liu, L., Reuter, A., Whang, K.Y., Zhang, J. (eds.) ICDE, p. 24. IEEE Computer Society (2006)

13. Naehrig, M., Lauter, K., Vaikuntanathan, V.: Can homomorphic encryption be practical? In: Cachin, C., Ristenpart, T. (eds.) CCSW, pp. 113–124. ACM (2011)

14. Paillier, P.: Public-key cryptosystems based on composite degree residuosity classes. In: Stern, J. (ed.) EUROCRYPT 1999. LNCS, vol. 1592, pp. 223–238. Springer, Heidelberg (1999)

15. Popa, R.A., Redfield, C.M.S., Zeldovich, N., Balakrishnan, H.: Cryptdb: Protecting confidentiality with encrypted query processing. In: SOSP (2011)

16. Samarati, P., Sweeney, L.: Generalizing data to provide anonymity when disclosing information (abstract). In: Proceedings of the Seventeenth ACM SIGACT-SIGMOD-SIGART Symposium on Principles of Database Systems, PODS 1998, p. 188. ACM, New York (1998)

17. Song, D.X., Wagner, D., Perrig, A.: Practical techniques for searches on encrypted data. In: IEEE Symposium on Security and Privacy, pp. 44–55. IEEE Computer Society (2000)

18. De Capitani di, Vimercati, S., Foresti, S., Jajodia, S., Paraboschi, S., Samarati, P.: A data outsourcing architecture combining cryptography and access control. In: Ning, P., Atluri, V. (eds.) CSAW, pp. 63–69. ACM (2007)

Optimizing Integrity Checks
for Join Queries in the Cloud

Sabrina De Capitani di Vimercati[1], Sara Foresti[1], Sushil Jajodia[2],
Stefano Paraboschi[3], and Pierangela Samarati[1]

[1] Università degli Studi di Milano – 26013 Crema, Italy
{firstname.lastname}@unimi.it
[2] George Mason University – Fairfax, VA 22030-4444
jajodia@gmu.edu
[3] Università di Bergamo – 24044 Dalmine, Italy
parabosc@unibg.it

Abstract. The large adoption of the cloud paradigm is introducing
more and more scenarios where users can access data and services with
an unprecedented convenience, just relying on the storage and computational power offered by external providers. Also, users can enjoy a
diversity and variety of offers, with the possibility of choosing services
by different providers as they best suit their needs. With the growth of
the market, economic factors have become one of the crucial aspects in
the choice of services. However, security remains a major concern and
users will be free to actually benefit from the diversity and variety of
such offers only if they can also have proper security guarantees on the
services. In this paper, we build upon a recent proposal for assessing
integrity of computations performed by potentially untrusted providers
introducing some optimizations, thus limiting the overhead to be paid
for integrity guarantees, and making it suitable to more scenarios.

1 Introduction

The competitive pressures are driving the IT sector away from the classical model
that assumed the processing and storage of an organization data within the internal information system, toward the use of storage and processing capabilities
offered by providers, which can benefit from economies of scale deriving from
the large size of the infrastructure and service catalogue, together with possible
access to less expensive resources. Along this line, we can expect a continuous
increase in the differentiation of the market for cloud services. For instance, in
the area of cloud architectures, interest has emerged on hybrid clouds and on a
distinction between cloud storage and cloud computational services. Storage and
computational services respond in fact to separate requirements, with distinct
profiles. The first should offer reliability for data storage, typically corresponding to providers with high reputation on the market. The second should offer
availability of – possibly cheap – computational power, which can be offered
by unknown providers. Reputation of the provider is, in this case, less critical,

V. Atluri and G. Pernul (Eds.): DBSec 2014, LNCS 8566, pp. 33–48, 2014.

as it is relatively easy to move computation from one provider to another, and the most important parameter becomes the price of the service. An obstacle to a stronger differentiation in the market between storage and computational resources is however represented by the security concerns of users, who can see the involvement of multiple parties in the processing of their information as increasing the risk of confidentiality and integrity violations.

In this paper, we present an approach for users to protect confidentiality of processed data and to assess the integrity of computations performed by potentially untrusted computational providers, operating over data stored at trusted storage providers. Our approach builds upon a recent proposal [5], aimed at controlling the behavior of a computational provider that joins data stored at independent trusted storage servers. We address the problem of optimizing integrity controls so to decrease their performance and economic overheads making them suitable to more scenarios and enabling their application with stronger integrity guarantees. In particular, we introduce two optimization techniques. The first technique (Sect. 3) exploits the execution of the join with a semi-join strategy, hence possibly decreasing data communication and consequent performance/economic costs, while leaving unaltered the offered guarantees. The second technique (Sect. 4) limits the application of the integrity checks to a small portion of the data, producing a considerable saving in terms of performance and economic cost, though at the price of a reduced integrity guarantee. The two optimizations are independent and orthogonal and can be used individually or in combination (Sects. 5 and 6).

2   Scenario and Basic Concepts

We present the basic idea of the approach on which we build our optimization techniques. The scenario is characterized by a client that wishes to evaluate a query involving a join over two relations, B_l and B_r, stored at storage servers S_l and S_r, respectively, by using a computational server C_s. The storage servers are assumed to be trustworthy while the computational server is not. The query is of the form "SELECT A FROM B_l JOIN B_r ON $B_l.I = B_r.I$ WHERE C_l AND C_r AND C_{lr}," where A is a subset of attributes in $B_l \cup B_r$; I is the set of join attributes; and C_l, C_r, and C_{lr} are Boolean formulas of conditions over attributes in B_l, B_r, and $B_l \cup B_r$, respectively. Typically, execution of such a query involves in pushing down, to each of the storage servers, the evaluation of the condition (C_l and C_r) on its own relation. We assume that, regardless of the degree of the original schema, relations L and R resulting from the evaluation of C_l and C_r, respectively, have schema (I, $Attr$), where I and $Attr$ represent the set of join attributes and all the other attributes, respectively, as a unit. Without security concerns, relations L and R are then sent to the computational server, which performs the join, evaluates condition C_{lr} and returns the result to the client. Since the computational server is not trusted, the proposal in [5]: *i)* provides data confidentiality by encrypting on the fly the relations sent to the computational server, with a key communicated by the client to the storage servers, *ii)* provides integrity guarantees by using a combination of controls as follows:

- *markers*: each of the storage servers inserts fake control tuples (markers), not recognizable by the computational server, in the relation to be sent to the computational server. Markers are inserted so to join (i.e., belong to the result) and to not collide with real join attribute values (to not create spurious joined tuples).
- *twins*: each of the storage servers duplicates (twins) some of the tuples in its relation before sending it to the computational server. The creation of twins is easily controlled by the client by specifying a percentage of tuples to be twinned and a condition for twinning.
- *salts/buckets*: used in alternative or in combination to destroy recognizable frequencies of combinations in one-to-many joins. Salts consist in salting the encryption at side "many" of the join so that occurrences of a same value become distinct; at the same time salted replicas are created at side "one" of the join so to create the corresponding matching. Bucketization consists in allowing multiple occurrences of the same (encrypted) value at the side many of the join, but in such a way that all the values have the same number of occurrences. Bucketization can help in reducing the number of salts to be inserted, while possibly requiring insertion of dummy tuples (to fill otherwise not complete buckets).

Join computation, illustrated in Fig. 1(a), works now as follows. Each storage server receives in encrypted form its sub-query, together with the key to be used to encrypt the sub-query result, and the needed information to regulate the use of markers, twins, salts and buckets. It then executes the received sub-query (as before), and applies over the resulting relation L (R, resp.) markers, twins, salts and buckets as appropriate, producing a relation L^* (R^*, resp.). Relation L^* (R^*, resp.) is then encrypted producing relation L_k^* (R_k^*, resp) to be sent to the computational server. Encrypted relation L_k^* (R_k^*, resp.) contains two encrypted chunks for each tuple: $L_k^*.I_k$ ($R_k^*.I_k$, resp.) for the join attribute, and $L_k^*.Tuple_k$ ($R_k^*.Tuple_k$, resp.) for all the other attributes (including the join attribute). The computational server receives the encrypted relations from the storage servers and performs the join returning the result J_k^* to the client. The client receives the join result, decrypts it, checks whether the tuples have been correctly joined (i.e., $L^*.I$ obtained decrypting $L_k^*.Tuple_k$ is equal to $R^*.I$ obtained decrypting $R_k^*.Tuple_k$), and discards possible tuples with dummy content. Then, it checks integrity by analyzing markers and twins: an integrity violation is detected if an expected marker is missing or a twinned tuple appears solo. Note that the combined use of markers and twins offers strong protection guarantees. In fact, when omitting a large number of tuples in query results, the probability that the omission goes undetected increases with respect to twins, and decreases with respect to markers (e.g., one marker is sufficient to detect that an empty result is not correct), and vice versa. Figure 1(b) illustrates an example of relations L and R and of their extensions obtained by assuming: the presences of one marker (with value x for the join attribute), twinning tuples with join attribute equal to b, and adopting 2 salts and buckets with 2 tuples each. Figure 1(c) reports

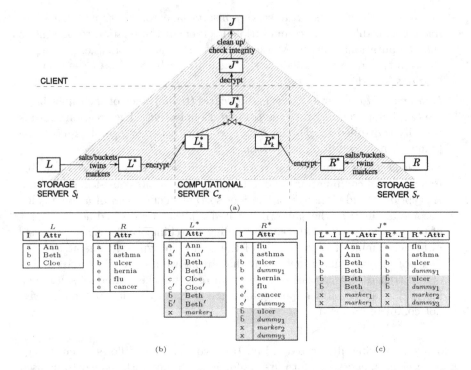

Fig. 1. Join computation as a regular join (a) and an example of relations L and R and their extensions with markers, twins, salts and buckets (b) along with the join computed over them (c)

the join result J^* obtained by the client decrypting relation J_k^* received from the computational server.

3   Semi-join

The first optimization we illustrate consists in performing the join according to a semi-join strategy. Without security concerns, a semi-join simply implements a join operation by first considering only the projection of the join attribute over the stored relations. Only after the join is computed, the join attribute is extended with the other attributes from the source relations to produce the final result. In our distributed setting, semi-joins – while requiring additional data flows – avoid communication of unnecessary tuples to the client and of non-join attributes to the computational server, producing a saving of the total communication costs for selective joins and/or relations with tuples of considerable size (see Sect. 6). Our approach for executing a semi-join in conjunction with the security techniques illustrated in the previous section works as follows. The execution of the join at the computational server basically works as before: it again receives from the storage servers encrypted relations on which markers, twins,

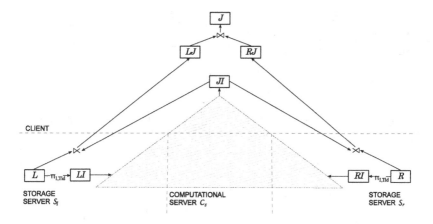

Fig. 2. Join execution as a semi-join

salts and buckets have been applied; it computes the join between them; and it sends the result to the client. However, in this case:

- the storage servers do not communicate to the computational server their entire tuples (relation L) but rather much slimmer tuples (relation LI) with only the join attribute and the tuple identifier (both in encrypted form). The tuple identifier (Tid) is needed to keep tuples with the same value for the join attribute distinct.
- after checking/cleaning the result of the join (relation JI), the client asks the storage servers to complete the tuples in the join with the attributes in $Attr$ in their relations (obtaining relations LJ and RJ), and combines their results.

The join process is illustrated in Fig. 2, where the striped triangle corresponds to the process in Fig. 1(a).

Note that, while entailing more flows (the previous process is a part of this), the semi-join execution limits the transfer of non-join attributes, thus reducing the amount of data transferred. Note also that while the storage servers and the client are involved in the execution of some computation to combine tuples, this computation does not entail an actual join execution but rather a simple scan/merging of ordered tuples that then requires limited cost.

Figure 3 illustrates an example of join computation over relations L and R in Fig. 1(b) according to the semi-join strategy. The semi-join execution strategy leaves unchanged the integrity guarantees offered by our protection techniques. In fact, the join computed by the computational server relies on the same protection techniques used for the computation of a regular join, and the storage servers are assumed to correctly evaluate the queries received from the client. The probability $\wp$ that the computational server omits o tuples without being

JI^*_k			JI^*				JI		RJ			LJ			J		
I_k	$L.Tuple_k$	$R.Tuple_k$	$L^*.I$	$L^*.Tid$	$R^*.I$	$R^*.Tid$	$L.Tid$	$R.Tid$	Tid	I	Dis	Tid	I	$Name$	I	$Name$	Dis
α	λ_1	ρ_1	a	l_1	a	r_1	l_1	r_1	r_1	a	flu	l_1	a	Ann	a	Ann	flu
α	λ_1	ρ_2	a	l_1	a	r_2	l_1	r_2	r_2	a	asthma	l_2	b	Beth	a	Ann	asthma
β	λ_2	ρ_3	b	l_2	b	r_3	l_2	r_3	r_3	b	ulcer				b	Beth	ulcer
β	λ_2	δ_1	b	l_2	b	d_1											
$\bar\beta$	λ_2	ρ_3	$\bar b$	l_2	$\bar b$	r_3											
$\bar\beta$	λ_2	δ_1	$\bar b$	l_2	$\bar b$	d_1											
χ	μ_1	μ_2	x	m_1	x	m_2											
χ	μ_1	δ_3	x	m_1	x	d_3											

L			LI		LI^*		LI^*_k		RI^*_k		RI^*		RI		R		
Tid	I	$Name$	I	Tid	I	Tid	I_k	$L.Tuple_k$	I_k	$R.Tuple_k$	I	Tid	I	Tid	Tid	I	Dis
l_1	a	Ann	a	l_1	a	l_1	α	λ_1	α	ρ_1	a	r_1	a	r_1	r_1	a	flu
l_2	b	Beth	b	l_2	a'	l'_1	α'	λ'_1	α	ρ_2	a	r_2	a	r_2	r_2	a	asthma
l_3	c	Cloe	c	l_3	b	l_2	β	λ_2	β	ρ_3	b	r_3	b	r_3	r_3	b	ulcer
					b'	l'_2	β'	λ'_2	β	δ_1	b	d_1	e	r_4	r_4	e	hernia
					c	l_3	γ	λ_3	ϵ	ρ_4	e	r_4	e	r_5	r_5	e	flu
					c'	l'_3	γ'	λ'_3	ϵ	ρ_5	e	r_5	e	r_6	r_6	e	cancer
					b	l_2	$\bar\beta$	λ_2	ϵ'	ρ_6	e'	r_6					
					$\bar b'$	l'_2	$\bar\beta'$	λ'_2	ϵ'	δ_2	e'	d_2					
					x	m_1	χ	μ_1	$\bar\beta$	ρ_3	$\bar b$	r_3					
									$\bar\beta$	δ_1	$\bar b$	d_1					
									χ	μ_2	x	m_2					
									χ	δ_3	x	d_3					

Fig. 3. An example of query evaluation process with twins on b, one marker, two salts, and buckets of size two

detected is then the same of regular joins, that is, $\wp = (1-\frac{o}{f})^m \cdot (1-2\frac{o}{f}+2(\frac{o}{f})^2)^t \approx e^{-2\frac{t}{f}o}$, where f is the cardinality of relation J^* with t twin pairs and m markers [5]. In fact, the probability that no marker is omitted is $(1-\frac{o}{f})^m$, while the probability that, for each twin pair, either both tuples are omitted or both are preserved is $(1-2\frac{o}{f}+2(\frac{o}{f})^2)^t$. This probabilistic analysis has also been confirmed by experimental analysis [5].

4   Limiting Salts and Buckets to Twins and Markers

The overhead caused by the adoption of our protection techniques is mainly due to salts and buckets [5], which are used to protect the frequency distribution of the values of the join attribute in case of one-to-many joins. In the following discussion, we refer to the execution of the join according to the process described in Sect. 2. Let s be the number of salts and b be the size of buckets defined by the client. Relation L^* includes s copies of each original tuple in L and of each twin. Relation R^* instead includes b tuples for each marker (one marker and $(b-1)$ dummy tuples) and between 0 and $(b-1)$ dummy tuples for each value of the join attribute appearing in R and in the twinned tuples. Hence, also the join result J^* will have b tuples for each marker and between 0 and $(b-1)$ dummy tuples for each original and twinned value of the join attribute. For instance, with respect to the example in Fig. 1(b), the adoption of our protection techniques causes the presence of six additional tuples in L^* and R^*, and five additional tuples in J^*.

The second optimization we propose aims at limiting the overhead caused by the adoption of salts and buckets by applying them only to twins and markers rather than to the whole relations. Twins and markers (properly bucketized

L^*

I	Attr
a	Ann
b	Beth
c	Cloe
ƀ	Beth
ƀ'	Beth'
x	$marker_1$

R^*

I	Attr
a	flu
a	asthma
b	ulcer
e	hernia
e	flu
e	cancer
ƀ	ulcer
ƀ	$dummy_1$
x	$marker_2$
x	$dummy_2$

J^*

L^*.I	L^*.Attr	R^*.I	R^*.Attr
a	Ann	a	flu
a	Ann	a	asthma
b	Beth	b	ulcer
ƀ	Beth	ƀ	ulcer
ƀ	Beth	ƀ	$dummy_1$
x	$marker_1$	x	$marker_2$
x	$marker_1$	x	$dummy_2$

Fig. 4. An example of extensions of relations L and R in Fig. 1(b) and their join when salts and buckets are limited to twins and markers

and salted) would form a *Verification Object* (VO) that can be attached to the original (encrypted) relation. As an example, Fig. 4 illustrates the extended version of relations L and R in Fig. 1(b) where salts and buckets operate only on twins and markers. It is immediate to see that this optimization saves three tuples in L^*, two in R^*, and one in J^*. The strategy of limiting salts and buckets to twins and markers can be adopted in combination with both the regular and the semi-join strategies, reducing the computational overhead in both cases. While providing performance advantages, this strategy may reduce the integrity guarantee provided to the client. Let us consider a relation J^*, with f original tuples, t twin pairs, and m markers. We examine the probability $\wp$ that the computational server omits o original tuples without being detected. We build a probabilistic model considering the worst case scenario, assuming that the computational server: *i)* is able to recognize the tuples in VO (only the tuples in VO have a flat frequency distribution), *ii)* knows the number m of markers in VO, *iii)* but cannot recognize which tuples in VO are twins and which are markers, or which of the original tuples have been twinned. We also consider all the tuples in a bucket as a single tuple. In fact, the computational server either preserves or omits buckets of tuples in their entirety as omissions of subsets of tuples in a bucket can always be detected. If the server omits o tuples out of f, the probability for each twin to be omitted will be $\frac{o}{f}$. To go undetected, the server should provide a configuration of VO consistent with the $f - o$ returned tuples. There is only one such configuration, which contains a number of tuples between m and $(m+t)$. The goal of the computational server is to maximize the probability of being undetected. We can model the behavior of the server considering two phases. In the first phase, the server determines the number of tuples that should belong to VO after the omission. Since there is a uniform and independent probability for the omission of twins, the number of expected tuples in VO follows a binomial distribution. This means that the probability that VO contains $(m+t) - k$ tuples is $\wp_{omit} = \binom{t}{k}(1-\frac{o}{f})^{t-k}(\frac{o}{f})^k$ (e.g., the probability that VO does not miss any tuple, $k = 0$, is $\wp_{omit} = (1 - \frac{o}{f})^t$). In the second phase, the server tries to guess the correct configuration including $(m + t) - k$ tuples. The number of such configurations depends on the number of missing tuples: if the server knows that k of the $(m+t)$ tuples in VO are missing, the number of possible configurations is $\binom{m+t}{k}$, and the probability $\wp_{guess}$ of guessing it right

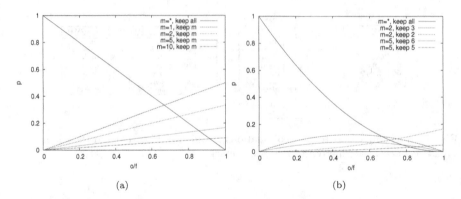

Fig. 5. Probability $\wp$ that the server omits a fraction $\frac{o}{f}$ of the tuples without being detected, considering several strategies, assuming $t = 1$ (a) and $t = 2$ (b)

is the inverse of this quantity. For instance, if no tuple is omitted ($k = 0$), the server is certain of guessing the right configuration, whereas if all the twins have been omitted, the probability of randomly guessing the right configuration with exactly m tuples is $1/\binom{m+t}{m}$, that is, $m! \cdot t!/(m + t)!$. The server can estimate the probability of a correct guess for each strategy by multiplying the first term with the second term, that is, $\wp = \wp_{omit} \cdot \wp_{guess}$. The server, to maximize the chance of not being detected, will have to choose the strategy that exhibits the greatest value. Since the second term exhibits an exponential growth with the increase in k, the server will typically prefer the strategy where no tuple in VO is omitted.

Figure 5 shows the result of the analysis for configurations with 1 or 2 twins and a variable number of markers. For the configuration with 1 twin in Fig. 5(a), we can see that the strategy that keeps all the elements in VO (independently from the number of markers) is preferable for a large range of omissions. When the number of markers increases, the cutoff between the selection of the strategy that tries to guess the tuple to omit from VO moves progressively to the right. A similar behavior characterizes the configuration with 2 twins described in Fig. 5(b), which shows that there is a range of values for $\frac{o}{f}$ where each configuration is preferable, but as the number of markers increases, the "keep all" strategy extends its benefit. The ability to avoid detection when omitting tuples becomes negligible when we consider configurations with the number of twins and markers that we expect to use in real systems.

As said above, it is convenient for the server to keep all the tuples in VO. In this case, the omission goes undetected if the server does not omit any original tuple that has been twinned. The probability $\wp$ for the server to go undetected is then equal to $\wp = (1 - \frac{o}{f})^t \approx e^{-\frac{t}{f} \cdot o}$. Figure 6 compares the results obtained when salts and buckets protect the whole relations ("full salts and buckets" in the figure) with the case where salts and buckets protect only VO ("VO-only salts and buckets" in the figure), assuming $\frac{t}{f}$=15%. We note that limiting salts and buckets to twins and markers offers roughly half the protection of applying salts and buckets to the whole relation. Intuitively, the client can obtain the

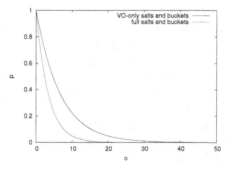

Fig. 6. Probability of the omission of o tuples to go undetected when applying salts and buckets on the whole relations and on twins and markers only

same protection guarantee by doubling the ratio $\frac{t}{f}$ of twins. We note however that, even limiting salts and buckets to VO, the probability that the server is not detected when omitting more than 30 tuples is negligible and is independent from the number f of tuples in the original relation. Since the computational server cannot selectively omit tuples from the join result (i.e., it cannot recognize tuples that have a twin), the advantage obtained from the omission of less than 30 tuples does not justify the risk of being detected in its omission.

5   Performance Analysis

We now evaluate the performance benefits obtained with the introduction of the semi-join strategy and the use of salts and buckets only on twins and markers. The performance costs depend on both the computational and communication costs. The computational costs are however dominated by the communication costs. In fact, the computational costs at the client and at the storage servers can be considered limited with respect to the computational costs at the computational server, which however can rely on a high amount of computational resources and on traditional techniques for optimizing join evaluation. In the following, we then focus our analysis first on the communication costs when evaluating a join as a regular join (*RegJ*) [5] or as a semi-join (*SemiJ*), according to the process described in Sect. 3. We then analyze the communication costs obtained when limiting salts and buckets to twins and markers.

Semi-join vs Regular Join. This analysis focuses on the amount of data exchanged among the involved parties (i.e., number of tuples transferred multiplied by their size). We first note that both the regular join and the semi-join require a common phase (Phase 1) where there is an exchange of data (tuples) between the storage servers and the computational server and between the computational server and the client. In this phase, regular join and semi-join differ in the size of the tuples transferred among the parties. The semi-join then requires an additional phase (Phase 2) where the client and the storage servers interact to compute the final join result. We analyze each of these two phases in details.

Phase 1 $[\mathcal{S}_l, \mathcal{S}_r \rightarrow \mathcal{C}_s; \mathcal{C}_s \rightarrow$ Client]. As already discussed, the only difference between *SemiJ* and *RegJ* is the size of the tuples communicated, while the number of tuples in the join operands and in its result is the same for both strategies. *SemiJ* requires the transmission of the join attribute and of the tuple identifiers only, which are the two attributes forming the schema of relations *LI* and *RI*. *RegJ* requires instead the transmission of all the attributes in *L* and *R*. If the size of the tuples in *L* and *R* is higher than the size of the tuples in *LI* and *RI*, *SemiJ* implies a lower communication cost than *RegJ*. Formally, the amount of data transmitted during this phase is:

SemiJ: $|L^*| \cdot size_L + |R^*| \cdot size_R + |J^*| \cdot (size_L + size_R)$

RegJ: $|LI^*| \cdot size_{IT} + |RI^*| \cdot size_{IT} + |JI^*| \cdot 2size_{IT}$

where $size_L$ is the size of the tuples in *L*, $size_R$ is the size of the tuples in *R*, $size_{IT}$ is the sum $size_I + size_{Tid}$, with $size_I$ the size of the join attribute *I* and $size_{Tid}$ the size of the tuple identifier *Tid*. Since LI^* (RI^* and JI^*, resp.) has the same number of tuples as L^* (R^* and J^*, resp.), the difference in the communication cost is:

$$|L^*| \cdot (size_L - size_{IT}) + |R^*| \cdot (size_R - size_{IT}) + |J^*| \cdot (size_L + size_R - 2size_{IT}).$$

Phase 2 [Client $\rightarrow \mathcal{S}_l, \mathcal{S}_r; \mathcal{S}_l, \mathcal{S}_r \rightarrow$ Client]. The number of tuples exchanged between the client and $\mathcal{S}_r$ is equal to the number of tuples resulting from the join computed by the computational server in the previous phase, after the removal of markers, twins, and dummies (i.e., $|JI|=|RJ|$). The number of tuples exchanged between the client and $\mathcal{S}_l$ depends on the type of join. In case of one-to-one joins, the number of tuples coincides with the number of tuples transmitted from the client to $\mathcal{S}_r$ (i.e., $|JI|=|LI|$). In case of one-to-many joins, the number of tuples is lower since the same tuple in *LI* (*L*, resp.) may appear many times in the join result *JI* (*J*, resp.). Assuming a uniform distribution of values, the number of different values for the join attribute in *RI* is $\frac{2|RI|}{nmax}$. Given the selectivity σ of the join operation, the number of different values for the join attribute in *JI* is $\sigma \cdot \frac{2|RI|}{nmax}$, which corresponds to the number of tuples exchanged between the client and $\mathcal{S}_l$. The size of the tuples transmitted from the client to each storage server is $size_{Tid}$ since the client transmits only the values of the tuple identifier *Tid*. The size of the tuples transmitted from the storage servers to the client is equal to the size of the tuples in the original relations *L* and *R* (i.e., $size_L$ and $size_R$, resp.). Formally, the amount of data exchanged during this phase is:

one-to-one join: $2|JI| \cdot size_{Tid} + |JI| \cdot size_L + |JI| \cdot size_R;$

one-to-many join: $(|JI| + \sigma \cdot \frac{2|RI|}{nmax}) \cdot size_{Tid} + \sigma \cdot \frac{2|RI|}{nmax} \cdot size_L + |JI| \cdot size_R.$

By comparing the amount of data transmitted in Phase 2 with the additional amount of data transmitted in Phase 1 caused by the regular join, we note that the semi-join is convenient for relations with large tuples (i.e., $size_{IT} << size_L$ and $size_{IT} << size_R$), as also shown by our experimental analysis (Sect. 6). The advantage of the semi-join with respect to the regular join appears also more evident in case of one-to-many joins where a tuple in the left operand can appear many times in the join result (i.e., $|LJ| \approx \sigma \cdot \frac{2|RI|}{nmax} << |JI|$). In fact, with the semi-join strategy the client receives each tuple in *L* that belongs to the final result only once, while it receives many copies of the same tuple when adopting the regular join approach.

Limiting Salts and Buckets to Twins and Markers. The saving, in terms of communication cost, provided applying salts and buckets to markers and twins rather than to the whole relation can be computed by analyzing the difference in the number of tuples in L^*, R^*, and J^*. We analyze each relation in detail.

- L^*. Since only twin tuples are salted, we save the salted copies of the tuples in L, that is, $(s-1) \cdot |L|$ tuples.
- R^*. Since buckets operate only on twins and markers, we save the dummy tuples of the buckets formed with the tuples in R. Since for each value of the join attribute, there is at most one bucket with dummy tuples with, on average, $\frac{b-1}{2}$ dummy tuples, and there are $\frac{2|R|}{nmax}$ distinct values for the join attribute (again assuming a uniform distribution of values), we save $\frac{b-1}{nmax} \cdot |R|$ tuples.
- J^*. The join result contains the subset of the tuples in R^* that combine with the tuples in L^*. The number of tuples saved in J^* is then a fraction of the number of tuples saved in R^*, that is, $\sigma \cdot \frac{b-1}{nmax} \cdot |R|$.

The overall advantage provided by limiting salts and buckets to twins and markers is: $(s-1) \cdot |L| \cdot size_L + \frac{b-1}{nmax} \cdot |R| \cdot size_R + \sigma \cdot \frac{b-1}{nmax} \cdot |R| \cdot (size_L + size_R)$.

6   Experimental Results

To assess the performance advantage of the semi-join strategy with respect to the regular join and of limiting salts and buckets to twins and markets, we implemented a prototype enforcing our protection techniques, and run a set of experiments. We used for the computational server a machine with 2 Intel Xeon Quad 2.0GHz, 12GB RAM. The client machine and the storage servers were standard PCs running an Intel Core 2 Duo CPU at 2.4 GHz, with 4GB RAM, connected to the computational server through a WAN connection with a 4 Mbps throughput. The values reported are the average over six runs.

Regular Join vs Semi-join. A first set of experiments was dedicated to the comparison between the regular join and the semi-join. The experiments also evaluated the impact of latency on the computation, comparing the response times for queries over local networks (local client configuration) with those obtained with a client residing on a PC at a distance of 1,000 Km connected through a shared channel that in tests demonstrated to offer a sustained throughput near to 80 Mbit/s (remote client configuration). The experiments used a synthetic database with two tables, each with between 10^4 and 10^6 tuples, with size equal to 30 and 2,000 bytes. We computed one-to-one joins between these tables, using 500 markers and 10% of twins. The results of these experiments are reported in Fig. 7.

The results confirm that the use of semi-join (*SemiJ* in the figure) gives an advantage with respect to regular join (*RegJ* in the figure) when the tuples

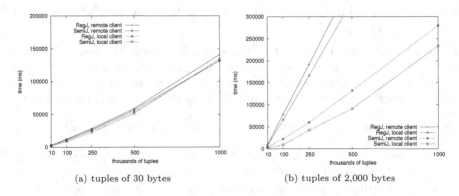

(a) tuples of 30 bytes   (b) tuples of 2,000 bytes

Fig. 7. Response time for regular join and semi-join

have a large size, whereas the advantage becomes negligible when executing a join over compact tuples. This is consistent with the structure of the semi-join computation, which increases the number of exchanges between the different parties, but limits the number of transfers of non-join attributes. When the tuples are large, the benefit from the reduced transfer of the additional attributes compensates the increased number of operations, whereas for compact tuples this benefit is limited. The experiments also show that the impact of latency is modest, as the comparison between local client and remote client configurations of the response times for the same query shows a limited advantage for the local client scenario, consistent with the limited difference in available bandwidth. The results obtained also confirm the scalability of the technique, which can be applied over large tables (up to 2 GB in each table in our experiments) with millions of tuples without a significant overhead.

Limiting Salts and Buckets to Twins and Markers. A second set of experiments was dedicated to the analysis of the use of salts and buckets. The experiments considered a one-to-many join, evaluated as a regular join, over a synthetic database containing 1,000 tuples in both join operands. We tested configurations with at most 50 occurrences of each value, and used a number of salts s varying between 1 and 100 and buckets of size $b = \lceil \frac{50}{s} \rceil$. The experiments evaluating the overhead of the protection techniques when salts and buckets are used only on markers and twins show that the overhead due to salts and buckets is proportional to the fraction of tuples that are twinned. For instance, if we add a 10% of twins, the overhead for salts and buckets will be one tenth of what we would have observed if applying the protection to all the tuples. Figure 8 compares the response time observed when executing the query without using our protection techniques ("base" in the figure), when using 50 markers and 15% of twins with salts and buckets on the whole table ("full salts and buckets" in the figure), and a configuration with 50 markers and 30% of twins with salts and buckets only on markers and twins ("VO-only salts and buckets" in the figure). The experiments confirm that the increase in response time represents a fraction $\frac{t}{f}$ (with t the number of twins and f the cardinality of the join result)

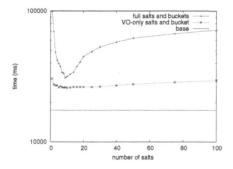

Fig. 8. Response time without adopting protection techniques, with salts and buckets on the whole relation, and with salts and buckets only on markers and twins

of the increase that would otherwise be observed using salts and buckets over all the tuples. The figure also shows that the overhead due to the adoption of our protection techniques is limited.

Economic Analysis. Besides the response time perceived by the user, the choice between regular and semi-join needs to take into consideration also the economic cost of each alternative. We focused on evaluating the economic advantage of the availability of the semi-join, besides regular join, strategy when executing queries [10]. In fact, in many situations the semi-join approach can be less expensive, since it entails smaller flows of information among the parties.

In our analysis, we assumed economic costs varying in line with available solutions (e.g., Amazon S3 and EC2, Windows Azure, GoGrid), number of tuples to reflect realistic query plans, and reasonable numbers for twins and markers. In particular, we considered the following parameters: *i)* cost of transferring data out of each storage server (from 0.00 to 0.30 USD per GB), of the computational server (from 0.00 to 0.10 USD per GB), and of the client (from 0.00 to 1.00 USD per GB); *ii)* cost of transferring data to the client (from 0.00 to 1.00 USD per GB);[1] *iii)* cost of CPU usage for each storage server (from 0.05 to 2.50 USD per hour), for the computational server (from 0.00 to 0.85 USD per hour), and for the client (from 1.00 to 4.00 USD per hour); *iv)* bandwidth of the channel reaching the client (from 4 to 80 Mbit/s); *v)* size $size_{IT} = size_I + size_{Tid}$ of the join attribute and the tuple identifier (from 1 to 100 bytes); *vi)* number of tuples in L (from 10 to 1,000) and the size of the other attributes $size_L - size_{IT}$ (from 1 to 300 bytes); *vii)* number of tuples in R (from 10 to 10,000) and the size of the other attributes $size_R - size_{IT}$ (from 1 to 200 bytes); *viii)* number m of markers (from 0 to 50); *ix)* percentage $\frac{t}{f}$ of twins (from 0 to 0.30); *x)* number s of salts (from 1 to 100); *xi)* maximum number $nmax$ of occurrences of a value in $R.I$ (from 1 to 100); *xii)* selectivity σ of the join operation (from 0.30 to 1.00). Similarly to what is usually done in finance and economics to compare

---

[1] We did not consider the cost of input data for the storage and computational servers since all the price lists we accessed let in-bound traffic be free.

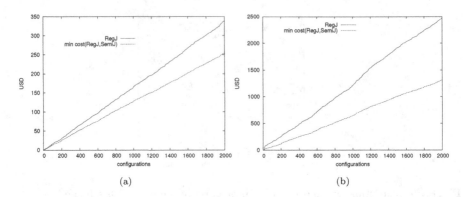

Fig. 9. Total economic cost of executing 2,000 one-to-one (a) and 2,000 one-to-many (b) join queries as a regular join or as the less expensive between regular and semi-join

alternative strategies in systems whose behavior is driven by a large number of parameters assuming values following a probability distribution, we used a Monte Carlo method to generate 2,000 simulations varying the parameters above and, for each simulation, we evaluated the cost of executing a join operation as a regular and as a semi-join.

We compared the cost of evaluating 2,000 one-to-one and 2,000 one-to-many join queries with (and without resp.) the availability of the semi-join technique for query evaluation. We assume that the query optimizer can assess which of the two strategies (i.e., $RegJ$, $SemiJ$) is less expensive for each query. Figures 9(a) and 9(b) illustrate the total costs as the number of query grows for the two scenarios, considering one-to-one and one-to-many queries, respectively. As visible in the figure, if all the queries are evaluated adopting the regular join approach, the total cost (continuous line) reaches higher values than with the availability of the semi-join approach (dotted line). This trend is more visible for one-to-many joins, where the total cost reached when all the queries are evaluated as regular joins is 2,475 USD while with the availability of the semi-join approach it remains at 1,321 USD, with a total saving of 1,160 USD (corresponding to 46,85%). In fact, out of the 2,000 one-to-many queries, 1784 were evaluated as semi-joins, while for the remaining 216 the regular join solution was cheaper. For one-to-one joins, as expected, the total saving is lower (24.77%) since half of the 2,000 queries considered are cheaper when evaluated as regular joins.

7   Related Work

Our work falls in the area of security and privacy in emerging outsourcing and cloud scenarios [2,7]. In this context, researchers have proposed solutions addressing a variety of issues, including data protection, access control, fault tolerance, data and query integrity (e.g., [1,3,4,6,8,9,15]). In particular, current solutions addressing the problem of verifying the integrity (i.e., completeness, correctness, and freshness) of query results are based on the definition of a verification object returned with the query result. Different approaches differ in the definition of the verification object and/or in the kind of guarantees offered, which can be deterministic or probabilistic. For instance, some proposals are based on the definition of an authenticated data structure (e.g., Merkle hash tree or a variation of it [12,19] or of signature-based schemas [13,14]) that allow the verification of the correctness and completeness of query results. These proposals provide deterministic guarantees, that is, they can detect integrity violations with certainty but only for queries involving the attribute(s) on which the authenticated data structure has been created. Some proposals have also addressed the problem of verifying the freshness of query results (e.g., [11,18]). The idea consists in periodically updating a timestamp included in the authenticated data structure or in periodically changing the data generated for integrity verification.

Probabilistic approaches can offer a more general control than deterministic approaches but they can detect an integrity violation only with a given probability (e.g., [5,16,17]). Typically, there is a trade-off between the amount of protection offered and the computational and communication overhead caused. The proposal in [16] consists in replicating a given percentage of tuples and in encrypting them with a key different from the key used for encrypting the original data. Since the replicated tuples are not recognizable as such by the server, the completeness of a query result is guaranteed by the presence of two instances of the tuples that satisfy the query and are among the tuples that have been replicated. The proposal in [17] consists in statically introducing a given number of fake tuples in the data stored at the external server. Fake tuples are generated so that some of them should be part of query results. Consequently, whenever the expected fake tuples are not retrieved in the query result, the completeness of the query result is compromised. In [5] we have introduced the idea of using markers, twins, salts and buckets for assessing the integrity of join queries. This paper extends such a solution proposing two optimizations that limit the overhead introduced by our protection techniques.

8   Conclusions

We presented two variations to markers, twins, salts and buckets proposed for assessing query integrity, offering significant performance benefits. In particular, we illustrated how markers, twins, salts and buckets can be easily adapted when a join query is executed as a semi-join, and how salts and buckets can be limited to twins and markers. The experimental evaluation clearly showed that these two variations limit the computational and communication overhead due to the integrity checks.

Acknowledgements. The authors would like to thank Michele Mangili for support in the implementation of the system and in the experimental evaluation. This work was supported in part by the EC within the 7FP under grant agreement 312797 (ABC4EU) and by the Italian Ministry of Research within PRIN project "GenData 2020" (2010RTFWBH). The work of Sushil Jajodia was partially supported by NSF grant IIP-1266147.

References

1. Basu, A., Vaidya, J., Kikuchi, H., Dimitrakos, T.: Privacy-preserving collaborative filtering on the cloud and practical implementation experiences. In: Proc. of IEEE Cloud, Santa Clara, CA (June-July 2013)
2. Damiani, E., De Capitani di Vimercati, S., Jajodia, S., Paraboschi, S., Samarati, P.: Balancing confidentiality and efficiency in untrusted relational DBMSs. In: Proc. of CCS, Washington, DC (October 2003)
3. De Capitani di Vimercati, S., Foresti, S., Jajodia, S., Livraga, G.: Enforcing subscription-based authorization policies in cloud scenarios. In: Cuppens-Boulahia, N., Cuppens, F., Garcia-Alfaro, J. (eds.) DBSec 2012. LNCS, vol. 7371, pp. 314–329. Springer, Heidelberg (2012)
4. De Capitani di Vimercati, S., Foresti, S., Jajodia, S., Paraboschi, S., Samarati, P.: Encryption policies for regulating access to outsourced data. ACM TODS 35(2), 12:1–12:46 (2010)
5. De Capitani di Vimercati, S., Foresti, S., Jajodia, S., Paraboschi, S., Samarati, P.: Integrity for join queries in the cloud. IEEE TCC 1(2), 187–200 (2013)
6. De Capitani di Vimercati, S., Foresti, S., Samarati, P.: Managing and accessing data in the cloud: Privacy risks and approaches. In: Proc. of CRiSIS, Cork, Ireland (October 2012)
7. Hacigümüş, H., Iyer, B., Mehrotra, S., Li, C.: Executing SQL over encrypted data in the database-service-provider model. In: Proc. of SIGMOD, Madison, WI (June 2002)
8. Jhawar, R., Piuri, V.: Fault tolerance and resilience in cloud computing environments. In: Vacca, J. (ed.) Computer and Information Security Handbook, 2nd edn., pp. 125–142. Morgan Kaufmann (2013)
9. Jhawar, R., Piuri, V., Santambrogio, M.: Fault tolerance management in cloud computing: A system-level perspective. IEEE Systems Journal 7(2), 288–297 (2013)
10. Kossmann, D., Kraska, T., Loesing, S.: An evaluation of alternative architectures for transaction processing in the cloud. In: Proc. of SIGMOD, Indianapolis, IN (June 2010)
11. Li, F., Hadjieleftheriou, M., Kollios, G., Reyzin, L.: Dynamic authenticated index structures for outsourced databases. In: Proc. of SIGMOD, Chicago, IL (June 2006)
12. Li, F., Hadjieleftheriou, M., Kollios, G., Reyzin, L.: Authenticated index structures for aggregation queries. ACM TISSEC 13(4), 32:1–32:35 (2010)
13. Mykletun, E., Narasimha, M., Tsudik, G.: Authentication and integrity in outsourced databases. ACM TOS 2(2), 107–138 (2006)
14. Pang, H., Jain, A., Ramamritham, K., Tan, K.: Verifying completeness of relational query results in data publishing. In: Proc. of SIGMOD, Baltimore, MA (June 2005)
15. Ren, K., Wang, C., Wang, Q.: Security challenges for the public cloud. IEEE Internet Computing 16(1), 69–73 (2012)
16. Wang, H., Yin, J., Perng, C., Yu, P.: Dual encryption for query integrity assurance. In: Proc. of CIKM, Napa Valley, CA (October 2008)
17. Xie, M., Wang, H., Yin, J., Meng, X.: Integrity auditing of outsourced data. In: Proc. of VLDB, Vienna, Austria (September 2007)
18. Xie, M., Wang, H., Yin, J., Meng, X.: Providing freshness guarantees for outsourced databases. In: Proc. of EDBT, Nantes, France (March 2008)
19. Yang, Z., Gao, S., Xu, J., Choi, B.: Authentication of range query results in MapReduce environments. In: Proc. of CloudDB, Glasgow, UK (October 2011)

Privacy-Enhancing Proxy Signatures from Non-interactive Anonymous Credentials*

David Derler, Christian Hanser, and Daniel Slamanig

Institute for Applied Information Processing and Communications (IAIK),
Graz University of Technology (TUG), Inffeldgasse 16a, 8010 Graz, Austria
{david.derler,christian.hanser,daniel.slamanig}@tugraz.at

Abstract. Proxy signatures enable an originator to delegate the signing rights for a restricted set of messages to a proxy. The proxy is then able to produce valid signatures only for messages from this delegated set on behalf of the originator. Recently, two variants of *privacy-enhancing proxy signatures*, namely blank signatures [25] and warrant-hiding proxy signatures [26], have been introduced. In this context, *privacy-enhancing* means that a verifier of a proxy signature does not learn anything about the delegated message set beyond the message being presented for verification.

We observe that this principle bears similarities with functionality provided by anonymous credentials. Inspired by this observation, we examine black-box constructions of the two aforementioned proxy signatures from non-interactive anonymous credentials, i.e., anonymous credentials with a non-interactive showing protocol, and show that the so obtained proxy signatures are secure if the anonymous credential system is secure. Moreover, we present two concrete instantiations using well-known representatives of anonymous credentials, namely Camenisch-Lysyanskaya (CL) and Brands' credentials.

While constructions of anonymous credentials from signature schemes with particular properties, such as CL signatures or structure-preserving signatures, as well as from special variants of signature schemes, such as group signatures, sanitizable and indexed aggregate signatures, are known, this is the first paper that provides constructions of special variants of signature schemes, i.e., privacy-enhancing proxy signatures, from anonymous credentials.

Keywords: Proxy signatures, anonymous credentials, cryptographic protocols, privacy, provable security.

1 Introduction

Proxy signatures allow an *originator* to delegate signing rights to a *proxy*, who is then able to issue signatures on behalf of the originator (cf. [8] for various

---

* The authors have been supported by the European Commission through project FP7-FutureID, grant agreement number 318424. An extended version of this paper can be found at [19].

V. Atluri and G. Pernul (Eds.): DBSec 2014, LNCS 8566, pp. 49–65, 2014.

secure constructions). To restrict the delegation, Mambo et al. [27] introduced the concept of a warrant, which basically encodes a policy describing the delegation of the originator and is signed by the originator using a conventional digital signature scheme as part of the delegation. For instance, such a warrant can be used to restrict the set of messages (message space) a proxy is allowed to sign messages from. In all known constructions, however, the warrant is revealed to every verifier, which could lead to privacy issues. When, for instance, delegating the signing rights for a contract containing multiple choices for a price to a proxy the whole price range would be revealed to any verifier. We call proxy signatures *privacy-preserving*, if they address this issue and do not reveal the warrant upon verification, while still allowing to check whether the message signed by the proxy is covered by the warrant. We note that this concept must not be confused with anonymous proxy signatures [23], which aim at hiding the identity of the delegatee and all intermediate delegators. In this paper, we consider two recently proposed instantiations of privacy-enhancing proxy signature schemes, namely warrant-hiding proxy signatures [26] (WHPS) as well as blank digital signatures [25] (BDS). Roughly speaking, WHPS allow to delegate the signing rights for a set of messages $\mathcal{M}$, e.g., $\mathcal{M} = \{M_1, \ldots, M_4\}$, to a proxy. Given a proxy signature anyone is able to verify the validity of such a signature and the delegation while not learning anything about the remaining delegated message space. Similarly, BDS allow for the delegation of the signing rights for a template $\mathcal{T}$ containing fixed and exchangeable strings (called elements) to a proxy, who is then able to sign a filled in version of such a template on behalf of the originator. Thereby, fixed elements can not be changed by the proxy, while exchangeable elements allow the proxy to choose one message out of a set of predefined messages, e.g., $\mathcal{T} = (M_1, \{M_{2_1}, M_{2_2}, M_{2_3}\}, M_3)$ with M_1 and M_3 being fixed elements. Upon verification, again, anyone is able to verify the validity of the signature and delegation while not learning anything about the unused choices in the exchangeable elements.

We observe, that this principle bears similarities with functionality provided by anonymous credentials. In an anonymous credential system, an organization issues a credential on attributes (which can be viewed as messages in the delegation) and the showing of a credential amounts to selectively opening some of the attributes (messages), while only proving knowledge of the undisclosed attributes. If the showing, thereby, is non-interactive and includes proving knowledge of a secret key, it can be seen as issuing a digital signature. Loosely speaking, for instance, in case of WHPS, one would use the messages in the warrant, i.e., $\mathcal{M} = \{M_1, \ldots, M_n\}$, and the public key of the proxy as attributes of the credential. A proxy signature then amounts to a non-interactive showing of the chosen message and the proxy public key, while only proving knowledge of the remaining message space and the proxy secret key (without revealing it).

1.1   Contribution

In this paper we provide black-box constructions of the two aforementioned privacy-enhancing proxy signature schemes from non-interactive anonymous credentials. Therefore, we provide an explicit encoding of message spaces to attributes of the credential systems. We show that a secure credential system together with this encoding implies the security of the respective privacy-enhancing proxy signature scheme. Furthermore, we present two instantiations based on non-interactive versions of well known Brands' [9] and CL [13] credentials, obtained by applying the Fiat-Shamir heuristic [21] and being secure in the random oracle model. Moreover, we compare the so obtained signature schemes to the originally proposed BDS and WHPS constructions and discuss why they may represent an alternative in specific scenarios. To the best of our knowledge, the presented constructions constitute the first approach to construct special signatures schemes from anonymous credentials, which may be of independent interest and inspiring for the design of other signatures.

1.2   Related Work

In [5], Belenkiy et al. propose a model for practical non-interactive anonymous credentials being secure in the standard model, which uses Groth-Sahai proofs [24]. In [6], Bellare and Fuchsbauer use similar building blocks, i.e., structure preserving signatures [2] and Groth-Sahai proofs, to construct what they call policy based signatures. This approach basically allows for defining policies enforcing certain properties on signed messages. Furthermore, Backes et al. [4] propose a model for delegating the signing rights for messages being derivable from an initial message by applying a particular functionality to the message.

In [22], Fuchsbauer and Pointcheval introduce a generalized model for anonymous proxy signatures and group signatures. The latter concept is conceptually very similar to anonymous credentials and often anonymous credentials are built from group signatures. Though, to the best of our knowledge, no formal implications regarding the security models of the aforementioned concepts exist. Quite recently, two (black-box) constructions for anonymous credentials from aggregate signatures [16], as well as sanitizable signatures [17] were proposed. In a way, this is the opposite of what we are going to show in this paper.

2   Preliminaries

We use additive notation for groups $\mathbb{G}$ which are always of prime order p.

Bilinear Map: A bilinear map (pairing) is a map $e : \mathbb{G}_1 \times \mathbb{G}_2 \to \mathbb{G}_T$, with $\mathbb{G}_1, \mathbb{G}_2$ and $\mathbb{G}_T$ being cyclic groups of prime order p. Let P and P' generate $\mathbb{G}_1$ and $\mathbb{G}_2$. We require e to be efficiently computable and to satisfy:

Bilinearity: $e(aP, bP') = e(P, P')^{ab} = e(bP, aP')$ $\forall a, b \in \mathbb{Z}_p$

Non-degeneracy: $e(P, P') \neq 1_{\mathbb{G}_T}$, i.e., $e(P, P')$ generates $\mathbb{G}_T$.

If $\mathbb{G}_1 = \mathbb{G}_2$, e is called *symmetric* and *asymmetric* otherwise.

Zero-Knowledge Proofs of Knowledge: We use the notation from [14] for denoting the proof of knowledge (PoK) of a discrete logarithm $x = \log_P Y$ to the base P, i.e., $\mathsf{PoK}\{(\alpha) : Y = \alpha P\}$, whereas Greek letters always denote values whose knowledge will be proven. The non-interactive version of such a proof can be obtained using the Fiat-Shamir [21] transform, which is then also called a signature of knowledge (SoK) [18]. When such a proof includes proving knowledge of a secret key, it is a secure digital signature in the random oracle model. Such a signature is interpreted as the signature of the proxy in our setting and is followingly denoted as π.

3   Anonymous Credentials

In an anonymous credential system there is an organization as well as different users. Thereby, the organization issues credentials to users, who can then anonymously demonstrate possession of these credentials to verifiers. Such a system is called *multi-show* when showings carried out by the same user cannot be linked and *one-show* otherwise. A credential cred_i for user i issued by the organization in such a system includes a set $\mathbb{A} = \{(\mathtt{attr}_\ell, dom(\mathtt{attr}_\ell))\}_{\ell=1}^n$ of attribute labels $\mathtt{attr}_\ell$ and corresponding domain $dom(\mathtt{attr}_\ell)$ from which attribute labels can take their values. When we speak of a set $\mathbb{A}_i$ for user i, we mean a subset of $\mathbb{A}$ such that for every $\mathtt{attr}_\ell$ contained in the set, the second element of the tuple takes some concrete value from $dom(\mathtt{attr}_\ell)$. Whenever a user i demonstrates possession of a credential for a subset $\mathbb{A}_i'$ of $\mathbb{A}_i$, we write $\mathbb{A}_i' \sqsubseteq \mathbb{A}_i$ to denote that the showing is compatible with $\mathbb{A}_i$. This means that all selectively disclosed attribute values have been issued for this credential and that all statements proven about attribute values can be proven from the issued attribute values.

3.1   Abstract Model of Anonymous Credentials

Subsequently, we give an abstract definition of an anonymous credential system.

$\mathsf{Setup}(\kappa, t)$: Gets a security parameter κ and an upper bound t for $|\mathbb{A}|$ and returns the global parameters pp.

$\mathsf{OrgKeyGen}(\mathsf{pp})$: Takes pp and produces an organization key pair $(\mathsf{osk}, \mathsf{opk})$.

$\mathsf{UserKeyGen}(\mathsf{pp}, i)$: Takes pp and $i \in \mathbb{N}$ and produces a key pair $(\mathsf{usk}_i, \mathsf{upk}_i)$ for user i.

$(\mathsf{Obtain}(\mathsf{pp}, \mathsf{opk}, \mathsf{usk}_i), \mathsf{Issue}(\mathsf{pp}, \mathsf{osk}, \mathsf{upk}_i, \mathbb{A}_i))$: These algorithms are run by user i and the organization, who interact during execution. Obtain takes input global parameters pp, the user's secret key usk_i and the organization's public key opk. Issue takes input the user's public key upk_i, the organization's secret key osk and a set $\mathbb{A}_i$ of size n. At the end of this protocol, Obtain outputs a credential cred_i for $\mathbb{A}_i$ for user i and the (updated) secret key usk_i'.

$(\mathsf{Show}(\mathsf{pp}, \mathsf{opk}, \mathsf{usk}_i, \mathsf{cred}_i, \mathbb{A}_i, \mathbb{A}_i'), \mathsf{Verify}(\mathsf{pp}, \mathsf{opk}, \mathbb{A}_i'))$: These algorithms are run by user i and a verifier who interact during the execution. Show takes input global parameters pp, the user's secret key usk_i, the organization's public key opk, a credential cred_i with a corresponding set $\mathbb{A}_i$ of size n and a second set $\mathbb{A}_i' \sqsubseteq \mathbb{A}_i$ of size n' with $n' \leq n$. Verify takes input the public parameters pp, the public key opk and a set $\mathbb{A}_i'$. At the end of the protocol, Show outputs an (updated) credential cred'_i and the (updated) user's secret key usk'_i. Verify outputs true upon a valid showing and false otherwise.

We note that in some models the entire key generation is executed by the Setup algorithm. However, we find it more natural to split these algorithms into three algorithms. Furthermore, we note that if there are multiple organizations, then OrgKeyGen is run by every single organization (on potentially distinct pp).

There are various definitions of security for anonymous credential systems [3, 12, 16, 17], which differ in their details as they are sometimes tailored to specific constructions. However, they are essentially only slightly different ways of defining the properties *unforgeability* and *anonymity* in addition to the usual *correctness* property. *Correctness* means that a showing of a credential w.r.t. a set $\mathbb{A}'_i$ of attributes and values must always verify if the credential was issued honestly w.r.t. $\mathbb{A}_i$ such that $\mathbb{A}'_i \sqsubseteq \mathbb{A}_i$. *Unforgeability* means that an adversary can not succeed in showing a credential which is accepted by a verifier, unless a credential w.r.t. to the shown attributes has been issued to it. *Anonymity* means that no adversary, even playing the role of the organization, should be able to identify the user when showing a credential. Furthermore, different showings of a user w.r.t. the same credential must be unlinkable in multi-show anonymous credential systems. Finally, we require a property denoted as *selective disclosure*. This is not covered by the security definition of [3], which we are going to use, but is an informal requirement for all anonymous credential systems. There is a simulation based notion capturing this fact [5], which, however, turns out to be not useful for relating the security properties to our constructions. However, we can assume that any reasonable anonymous credential system satisfies this notion, i.e., even if the user is known, a showing transcript must not reveal any information about attributes beyond the attributes revealed during showing [10]. This is underpinned by the fact that all known anonymous credential systems employ (non-interactive) proofs of knowledge in their showing protocols and such proofs by definition do not reveal anything beyond what is shown. For more formal security definitions, we refer the reader to the extended version [19].

Non-interactive Anonymous Credential Systems: If interaction between the user and the verifier when executing (Show, Verify) algorithms is not required, we call an anonymous credential system non-interactive. These steps can, thus, be executed in isolation and the output of the Show algorithm serves as input for the Verify algorithm. In constructions of credential systems it is straightforward to make the showing non-interactive and the output of the Show algorithm can, thus, be considered as a signature of knowledge.

3.2   Two Concrete Anonymous Credential Systems

Camenisch-Lysyanskaya (CL) credentials [11, 13] are constructed from commitment schemes and efficient protocols for proving the equality of two committed values and a signature scheme with efficient protocols. Latter protocols are for obtaining a signature on a committed value (without revealing the value) and proving the knowledge of it. The used signature schemes support re-randomization, meaning that one can take a signature and compute another signature for the same message without the signing key, such that the signatures are unlinkable. Thus, the resulting credential systems are *multi-show*. Brands' credentials [9] are built from blind signatures which do not support re-randomization and, therefore, represent a one-show credential system.

The two aforementioned approaches are the basis for our instantiations of privacy-enhancing proxy signatures from non-interactive anonymous credential systems. Further details are given in the extended version [19].

3.3   Remarks on Anonymous Credentials in our Constructions

For our black-box constructions, we need to make some clarifications before being able to use an arbitrary anonymous credential system.

First of all, in order to model the delegation, the designated proxy's public key always needs to be encoded within an attribute, being opened upon every non-interactive Show. Therefore, we assume that the user's public key (corresponding to its secret signing key) fits to the system parameters of the anonymous credential scheme. If the proxy's key does not fit to the system parameters of the used scheme, one could include a hash value of the user's public key as an attribute and require the user to sign the output of the non-interactive Show algorithm using the corresponding secret key (latter is not considered here). Moreover, in the case of BDS also a second attribute containing the size of the template needs to be included and always opened during showing. As already mentioned, we require the showing of the anonymous credential scheme to be non-interactive and each non-interactive showing is required to include a proof of knowledge of the secret key corresponding to the public key included in the first attribute. This constitutes a signature of knowledge and is interpreted as the proxy's signature.

Finally, we want to mention that the anonymity property of anonymous credential schemes is stronger than what is required for BDS or WHPS. While we only require the hiding of attributes (selective disclosure) which have not been opened, anonymous credentials also require unlinkability of issuing and showing, which is not necessary for BDS and WHPS, but does not influence our constructions. Similarly, we do not require the multi-show unlinkability, but it does not really influence our constructions as well. One may explicitly enforce breaking the unlinkability by requiring the credential issuer to additionally issue a conventional digital signature on the credential and accepting the credential only if the signature is valid. Conversely, the unlinkability may also be seen as an additional feature for BDS and WHPS, respectively (cf. Section 7).

4   Privacy-Enhancing Proxy-Type Signatures

This section is intended to give a brief overview of the privacy-enhancing proxy signature schemes. Section 4.1 discusses the Blank Digital Signature Scheme (BDSS) proposed in [25], whereas Section 4.2 discusses the Warrant-Hiding Proxy Signature Scheme (WHPSS) proposed in [26].

4.1   Blank Digital Signatures

The BDSS allows an *originator* to delegate the signing rights for a certain *template* to a *proxy*. Based on such a delegation, the *proxy* is able to issue a signature on a so called instance of a template on behalf of the *originator*. A template $\mathcal{T}$ is a sequence of non-empty sets of bitstrings T_i, where these sets are either called *fixed* or *exchangeable*, depending on the cardinality of the respective set. More precisely, exchangeable elements contain more than one bitstring, whereas fixed elements contain exactly one bitstring. Such a template is formally defined as $T_i = \{M_{i_1}, M_{i_2}, \ldots, M_{i_k}\}$, $\mathcal{T} = (T_1, T_2, \ldots, T_n)$.

The template length is defined as the sequence length n of the template, while the template size $|\mathcal{T}|$ is defined as $|\mathcal{T}| = \sum_{i=1}^{n} |T_i|$. An *originator* issues a signature for a template, which also specifies the proxy. Based on this so-called template signature, the designated *proxy* can take the fixed elements, choose concrete values for each exchangeable element, and compute a so-called instance signature for an instance $\mathcal{M}$, which is formally defined as $\mathcal{M} = (M_i)_{i=1}^{n}$. If $\mathcal{M}$ is a correct instantiation of $\mathcal{T}$, we write $\mathcal{M} \preceq \mathcal{T}$.

Given an instance signature, anyone is able to verify its validity, i.e., verify the delegation, whether $\mathcal{M}$ has been signed by the proxy and if $\mathcal{M} \preceq \mathcal{T}$ holds. Thereby, the original template, that is, the unused values of the exchangeable elements of the template, can not be determined (the so called *privacy* property). Formally, a BDSS is defined as follows [25]:

KeyGen(κ, t): On input of a security parameter κ and an upper bound for the template size t the public parameters pp are generated. We assume pp to be an input to all subsequent algorithms.

Sign($\mathcal{T}$, dsk$_O$, dpk$_P$): Given a template $\mathcal{T}$, the secret signing key of the originator dsk$_O$ and the public verification key of the proxy dpk$_P$, this algorithm outputs a template signature $\sigma_\mathcal{T}$ and a secret template signing key for the proxy sk$_P^\mathcal{T}$.

Verify$_\mathsf{T}$($\mathcal{T}, \sigma_\mathcal{T}$, dpk$_O$, dpk$_P$, sk$_P^\mathcal{T}$): Given a template $\mathcal{T}$, a template signature $\sigma_\mathcal{T}$, the public verification keys of originator and proxy (dpk$_O$, dpk$_P$) and the template signing key of the proxy sk$_P^\mathcal{T}$, this algorithm checks whether $\sigma_\mathcal{T}$ is a valid signature for $\mathcal{T}$ and returns true on success and false otherwise.

Inst($\mathcal{T}, \sigma_\mathcal{T}, \mathcal{M}$, dsk$_P$, sk$_P^\mathcal{T}$): On input a template $\mathcal{T}$ with corresponding signature $\sigma_\mathcal{T}$, an instance $\mathcal{M} \preceq \mathcal{T}$, as well as the secret template signing key sk$_P^\mathcal{T}$ and the secret signing key of the proxy dsk$_P$, this algorithm outputs a signature $\sigma_\mathcal{M}$ for $\mathcal{M}$.

Verify$_\mathsf{M}$($\mathcal{M}, \sigma_\mathcal{M}$, dpk$_O$, dpk$_P$): Given an instance $\mathcal{M}$, an instance signature $\sigma_\mathcal{M}$ and the public verification keys of originator and proxy (dpk$_O$, dpk$_P$), this algorithm verifies whether $\sigma_\mathcal{M}$ is a valid signature on $\mathcal{M}$ and $\mathcal{M} \preceq \mathcal{T}$ (for an unknown $\mathcal{T}$). On success, this algorithm outputs true and false otherwise.

The security of a BDSS is defined as follows [25]. *Correctness* states that for all honestly generated parameters and keys it is required that for any template $\mathcal{T}$ and honestly computed template signature $\sigma_\mathcal{T}$ and corresponding sk$_P^\mathcal{T}$, the verification always succeeds and for the originator it is intractable to find a template signature that is valid for different templates (in the sense of non-repudiation of [29]). Furthermore, for any honestly computed instance signature $\sigma_\mathcal{M}$, the verification always succeeds. *Unforgeability* requires that without the knowledge of $\mathsf{dsk_O}, \mathsf{dsk_P}$ and $\mathsf{sk}_P^{\mathcal{T}}$ it is intractable to forge template or message signatures. *Immutability* means that for a proxy (in possession of $\mathsf{sk}_P^{\mathcal{T}}, \mathsf{dsk_P}, \mathcal{T}$ and $\sigma_{\mathcal{T}}$) it is intractable to forge template signatures or instance signatures which are not described in the respective template. *Privacy* captures that no verifier (except for the originator and the proxy) can learn anything about $\mathcal{T}$ besides what is revealed by instance signatures. More formal security definitions are provided in the extended version [19].

4.2 Warrant-Hiding Proxy Signatures

A WHPSS allows an *originator* to delegate the signing rights for a message from a well defined message space $\mathcal{M}$ (sometimes also denoted as ω) to a *proxy*. The message space $\mathcal{M}$ is, thereby, a non-empty set of bitstrings (messages) M_i, i.e., $\mathcal{M} = \{M_1, \ldots, M_n\}$. A proxy is then able to choose one bitstring M_i from the message space $\mathcal{M}$ and issue a proxy signature σ_P on behalf of the originator for M_i. A verifier given M_i and σ_P can verify the validity of the signature and the delegation, while the remaining message space $(\mathcal{M} \setminus M_i)$ stays concealed.

One could argue that the functionality of WHPSS can be easily modeled by the originator by separately signing each message in $\mathcal{M}$ and to let the proxy then countersign a message of its choice. However, using this naive approach would allow the proxy to repudiate that a particular message was contained in the delegated message space. In contrast, one can open the warrant contained in the WHPSS proxy signature in case of a dispute in front of a judge.

The security of a WHPSS is defined as follows [26]. *Correctness* requires that for all honestly computed parameters and for all proxy signing keys obtained by running the delegation algorithm, it holds that for all warrants and proxy signatures for a message M the verification algorithm for proxy signatures accepts a signature for M if M is in the warrant and rejects it otherwise. Furthermore, the proxy-identification algorithm is required to return the correct proxy. *Unforgeability* states that, without the knowledge of the originator's and the proxy's secret key, it is intractable to produce valid delegations and/or proxy signatures which are either inside or outside the warrant. *Privacy* requires that any verifier distinct form the originator and the proxy can not efficiently decide whether a given message (except the ones being revealed by proxy signatures) lies within the warrant when given a proxy signature. More formal definitions are provided in the extended version [19].

5 From Anonymous Credentials to Proxy-Signatures

Subsequently, we show how privacy-enhancing proxy signatures can be built from non-interactive anonymous credential systems. Therefore, we use the abstract notion of an anonymous credential system introduced in Section 3 and map the algorithms to the corresponding algorithms of the respective proxy signature scheme. Furthermore, we introduce an encoding to attributes in order to achieve the same properties as the proxy signature schemes.

The basic idea behind using an anonymous credential system for modeling privacy-enhancing proxy signatures is that we interpret the elements of a template (or the warrant) together with the public key of the designated proxy and the template length as attributes of a credential issued by an originator (organization). On verification, the proxy only reveals the attributes belonging to the instantiation of the template (or reveals one attribute corresponding to a message from the warrant) while hiding all others. We note that the organization's keypair (opk, osk) in the anonymous credential scheme is interpreted as the keypair of the originator in the proxy signature schemes and the user's keypair ($\mathsf{upk}_i, \mathsf{usk}_i$) is the keypair of proxy i. We use this notation of the anonymous credential model henceforth.

5.1 Mapping from Templates and Warrants to Attributes

In both proxy signature approaches, a finite sequence/set of strings needs to be encoded as attributes of a credential, where in the case of BDSS this sequence represents a template and in case of WHPSS the set represents a warrant. The ideas behind the encoding are quite similar, although the BDSS case is a little trickier. Before presenting the encodings, we require some operations on sets and sequences. Firstly, we define an operator $\mathsf{Expand}(\cdot, \cdot)$, which takes an integer k and a set $S = \{s_1, \ldots, s_n\}$ as input and returns a sequence of tuples. This operator assigns a unique position to each element of the set, e.g., by means of their lexicographic order, and encodes the elements together with the integer k in a sequence. More precisely, we define an output sequence a as:

$$a = ((s_1, k), \ldots, (s_n, k)) := \mathsf{Expand}(k, \{s_1, \ldots, s_n\}).$$

When we apply the concatenation operator $||$ to two sequences, e.g., $(x)_{i=1}^n || (y)_{i=1}^m$, the result is a sequence of the form $(x_1, \ldots, x_n, y_1, \ldots, y_m)$. For the concatenation of $\ell \geq 2$ sequences $s_1, \ldots, s_\ell$ we write $||_{i=1}^\ell s_i$. Moreover, we require an operator $\mathsf{Hash}(\cdot)$ which takes a sequence a of tuples as input and returns the sequence a' of corresponding hash values obtained by applying a secure hash function $H : \{0,1\}^* \times \{0,1\}^* \to \mathbb{Z}_p$ to each element in the sequence. The i-th element of such a sequence a' obtained from a is further referred to as $h_i := H(s_i, k)$. Note that we use H to allow for messages/attribute values of arbitrary length.

BDSS: In the original construction of BDSS presented in [25], templates are encoded as polynomials and each template element constitutes a root of the so called encoding polynomial. With such an encoding polynomial at hand, one can not derive anything about the order of the elements within the template and, in further consequence, this property hides the structure of the template. In contrast, anonymous credential systems typically assume an ordering of the attributes within the credential (cf. Section 3.2), and, thus, would leak information about the structure of a template. Let us, for instance, consider a template

$\mathcal{T} = (M_1, \{M_{2_1}, M_{2_2}, M_{2_3}\}, M_3, \{M_{4_1}, M_{4_2}\})$. Here, each element M_i would be encoded within one attribute in the credential. While the unused choices of the exchangeable elements are hidden upon Show, information on the cardinality and position of exchangeable elements can leak due to the order of the attributes.

Template Encoding: In order to map templates $\mathcal{T}$ and instances $\mathcal{M}$, as defined in Section 4.1, the first processing step is to apply the following transformation: $\mathcal{T} \leftarrow \mathsf{Hash}(||_{i=1}^{n}\mathsf{Expand}(i, T_i))$.

Subsequently prefixing $\mathcal{T}$ with the (authentic) public key upk_i of the designated proxy and the template size $|\mathcal{T}|$ would already deliver a suitable encoding for our constructions. However, as mentioned above, such an encoding can leak information about the structure of the template. In order to prevent this kind of leakage, we further apply a random permutation ϕ to the expanded and hashed template, i.e., $\mathcal{T} \leftarrow (\mathsf{upk}_i, |\mathcal{T}|, \phi(\mathcal{T}))$.

In doing so, the order of the attributes becomes independent of their position in the template, and, thus, the template structure is hidden as in the original BDSS construction. Subsequently, this mapping is denoted as $\mathsf{Enc}_{\mathcal{T}}^{\mathsf{BDS}}$.

For example, $\mathcal{T} = \{\{"A", "B"\}, "declares\ to\ pay", \{"50\$", "100\$"\}\}$, would yield a permuted and hashed sequence $(H("100\$.", 3), H("50\$.", 3), H("\ declares\ to\ pay\ ", 2), H("A", 1), H("B", 1))$.

Instance encoding: The encoding of instances $\mathcal{M}$ corresponding to a given template $\mathcal{T}$ does not substantially differ from the encoding of templates. Additionally to the public key upk_i of the proxy and the template size $|\mathcal{T}|$, the following information is included: a sequence $\mathcal{M}'$ containing tuples corresponding to the chosen elements, each containing the element itself, its position in the template and its position in the sequence $\mathcal{T}^{enc}$ according to the permutation ϕ. Furthermore, one includes a signature of knowledge (SoK) π, which represents a proof of knowledge of usk_i and the non-revealed template elements: $\mathcal{M}^{enc} \leftarrow (\mathsf{upk}_i, |\mathcal{T}|, \mathcal{M}', \pi)$.

For our further explanations, this mapping is denoted as $\mathsf{Enc}_{\mathcal{M}}^{\mathsf{BDS}}$. Observe that given $\mathcal{M}'$ in $\mathcal{M}^{enc}$, one can not directly use it in a verification, but for every tuple (s, i, j) in $\mathcal{M}'$ one has to compute $h_j = H(s, i)$, which then represents the value of the j'th attribute. Subsequently, we assume that this step is implicitly computed by a verifier whenever $\mathcal{M}^{enc}$ is provided for verification.

Choosing "B" and "50\$" in the example above, leads to an encoded message $\mathcal{M}^{enc} = (\mathsf{upk}_i, |\mathcal{T}|, (("B", 1, 5), ("\ declares\ to\ pay\ ", 2, 3), ("50\$", 3, 2), \pi)$.

Note that the indices indicating the position in the template sequence according to the permutation ϕ implicitly fix the indices for the sequence of unrevealed values. A more detailed example of the encoding is given in [19].

We also emphasize that both, the encoding function $\mathsf{Enc}_{\mathcal{T}}^{\mathsf{BDS}}$ and the encoding function $\mathsf{Enc}_{\mathcal{M}}^{\mathsf{BDS}}$, take the secret random permutation ϕ (only known to the originator and the proxy) as additional parameter.

WHPSS: The mapping in terms of the WHPSS is a lot easier since, firstly, no explicit order has to be enforced within the messages in the warrant and, secondly, the order of the messages can not leak any useful information.

In order to encode a WHPSS message space for our setting, we redefine the operator $\mathsf{Expand}(\cdot)$ as a unary operator converting a set to a sequence by assigning a unique position to each element from the set. Furthermore, we also redefine H as $H : \{0,1\}^* \to \mathbb{Z}_p$. The encoding of a message space $\mathcal{M}$ then looks as follows: $\mathcal{M}^{enc} \leftarrow (\mathsf{upk}_i, \mathsf{Hash}(\mathsf{Expand}(\mathcal{M})))$.

Similarly, a message chosen by the proxy is encoded by choosing a message $M_k \in \mathcal{M}$ and computing a signature of knowledge (SoK) π of usk_i and the remaining messages in the warrant: $M \leftarrow (\mathsf{upk}_i, M_k, k, \pi)$.

Observe, that M_k cannot be directly used as an attribute value, but needs to be mapped to $H(M_k)$. However, as above we assume that this step is implicitly computed by the verifier whenever M_k is provided for verification. We refer to the encoding defined above as $\mathsf{Enc}_{\mathcal{M}}^{\mathsf{WHPS}}$ and $\mathsf{Enc}_{M}^{\mathsf{WHPS}}$ for our further explanations and note a secret random permutation ϕ is not required.

5.2   Constructing BDS from Anonymous Credentials

We assume that a credential is issued on an encoded template $\mathcal{T}^{enc}$ using the encoding defined above. Upon showing, the proxy chooses a concrete instantiation $\mathcal{M}^{enc}$ for a template by disclosing the elements corresponding to the instance $\mathcal{M}^{enc}$, while providing a signature of knowledge for the elements remaining in $\mathcal{T}^{enc}$. To be more precise, the proxy always discloses the attributes representing the public key and containing the size of the template, as well as at least one element for each position in the template, and provides a signature of knowledge of the secret signing key and the unused choices for the exchangeable elements. We assume that every user (proxy) i has run $\mathsf{AC.UserKeyGen}(\mathsf{pp}, i)$ to obtain $(\mathsf{usk}_i, \mathsf{upk}_i)$ compatible with pp locally. Furthermore, the template secret key $\mathsf{sk}_\mathsf{p}^\mathcal{T}$ is the secret random permutation ϕ. Below, we provide the abstract definition of the construction, where AC denotes an anonymous credential system with non-interactive showing.

$\mathsf{KeyGen}(\kappa, t)$: This algorithm computes the public parameters pp by running $\mathsf{AC.Setup}(\kappa, t)$ and specifies the encodings $\mathsf{Enc}_{\mathcal{T}}^{\mathsf{BDS}}$ and $\mathsf{Enc}_{\mathcal{M}}^{\mathsf{BDS}}$. Then, it runs $\mathsf{AC.OrgKeyGen}(\mathsf{pp})$ to obtain $(\mathsf{osk}, \mathsf{opk})$ and outputs all these parameters. The public parameters pp as well as a description of the encoding functions are assumed to be available to all subsequent algorithms.

$\mathsf{Sign}(\mathcal{T}, (\mathsf{opk}, \mathsf{osk}), \mathsf{upk}_i)$: This algorithm chooses a random permutation ϕ and computes $\mathcal{T}^{enc} \leftarrow \mathsf{Enc}_{\mathcal{T}}^{\mathsf{BDS}}(\mathcal{T}, \phi)$. Then, it locally runs $(\mathsf{AC.Obtain}(\mathsf{pp}, \mathsf{opk}, \mathsf{upk}_i)^1, \mathsf{AC.Issue}(\mathsf{pp}, \mathsf{osk}, \mathsf{upk}_i, \mathcal{T}^{enc}))$ and the results, i.e., the credential cred_i

---

[1] As we assume that the user's key pair fits to the system parameters, we do not require usk_i as an input to the $\mathsf{AC.Obtain}$ algorithm and so the credential is issued using upk_i as public commitment to usk_i. This allows the originator to run both algorithms locally.

as template signature and the template-specific secret key ϕ for the proxy, are returned.

$\mathsf{Verify}_\mathsf{T}(\mathcal{T}, \mathsf{cred}_i, \mathsf{opk}, (\mathsf{upk}_i, \mathsf{usk}_i), \phi)$: This algorithm computes $\mathcal{T}^{enc} \leftarrow \mathsf{Enc}_\mathcal{T}^{\mathsf{BDS}}$ $(\mathcal{T}, \phi)$ and checks the validity of the credential cred_i using usk_i and opk. On success, this algorithm returns $\mathtt{true}$, and $\mathtt{false}$ otherwise.

$\mathsf{Inst}(\mathcal{T}, \mathsf{cred}_i, \mathcal{M}, (\mathsf{opk}, \mathsf{upk}_i, \mathsf{usk}_i), \phi)$: This algorithm computes an encoding $\mathcal{M}^{enc}$ of an instantiation $\mathcal{M}$ of the template $\mathcal{T}$ using ϕ by computing a SoK π including a proof of the user's secret key usk_i and the unused choices of the exchangeable elements, i.e., AC.Show is executed. The instance signature (π, cred_i) and the encoded message $\mathcal{M}^{enc}$ are returned.

$\mathsf{Verify}_\mathsf{M}(\mathcal{M}^{enc}, (\pi, \mathsf{cred}_i), \mathsf{opk}, \mathsf{upk}_i)$: This algorithm verifies whether π is a valid signature of knowledge w.r.t. $\mathcal{M}^{enc}$ and upk_i by executing AC.Verify. On success, this algorithm returns $\mathtt{true}$, and $\mathtt{false}$ otherwise.

5.3 Constructing **WHPS** from Anonymous Credentials

The construction of WHPS from anonymous credentials is very similar to the BDS construction. Due to limited space the reader is referred to the extend version of this paper [19] for a detailed discussion.

5.4 From AC Security to BDS and WHPS Security

In this section, we argue that if we have a secure non-interactive anonymous credential system AC, the constructions of the BDS and WHPS schemes from AC are also secure. Consequently, when building such schemes in the proposed way, these schemes provide adequate security within their respective models.

We note that the anonymity property required from a credential system is much stronger than what is required from BDS and WHPS. Basically, a goal achieved by an anonymous credential system is the indistinguishability of showings of different users, which have credentials to identical attributes, with respect to any verifier (including the issuer). In contrast, the goal of the proxy signature schemes is to hide the non-shown "attributes" from any external verifier, whereas the issuer (the originator) knows all attributes. Consequently, we relate the privacy of the schemes to the selective disclosure of the anonymous credential system. The remaining properties of the schemes are related to the unforgeability of the anonymous credential scheme. In the extended version of this paper [19], we prove the following theorems:

Theorem 1. *If* AC *represents a secure anonymous credential system and the hash function used in the encodings* $\mathsf{Enc}_\mathcal{T}^{\mathsf{BDS}}$ *and* $\mathsf{Enc}_\mathcal{M}^{\mathsf{BDS}}$ *is secure, then the* BDS *from Section 5.2 based on* AC *is secure.*

Theorem 2. *If* AC *represents a secure anonymous credential system and the hash function used in the encoding* $\mathsf{Enc}_\mathcal{M}^{\mathsf{WHPS}}$ *is secure, then the* WHPS *scheme from Section 5.3 based on* AC *is secure.*

6 Instantiations from CL and Brands' Credentials

In this section, we provide two instantiations of BDS making use of CL [13] and Brands' [9] credentials, respectively. We omit the constructions of WHPS as after having seen the construction for BDS, the construction of WHPS is straightforward. In both presented schemes, we assume the keypair of the proxy (upk, usk) to be compatible with the system parameters, i.e., usk is a scalar in $\mathbb{Z}_p$ and upk = usk $\cdot P$, with P being a generator of the respective group.

Furthermore, with hide we denote the elements of $\mathcal{T}^{enc}$ corresponding to the elements in $\mathcal{T}$ without $\mathcal{M}$, whereas with show we denote the elements of $\mathcal{M}^{enc}$ corresponding to elements in $\mathcal{M}$.

In Scheme 1, we present our construction of BDS from CL credentials [13] in detail. Our second instantiation builds up on Brands' one-show credentials, following the *certificates based on Chaum-Pedersen signatures* approach proposed in [9]. In Scheme 2, we present our construction in detail.

Setup(κ, t): Choose an appropriate group $\mathbb{G}$ of large prime order p such that a bilinear map $e : \mathbb{G} \times \mathbb{G} \to \mathbb{G}_T$ exists. Further, choose a generator P of $\mathbb{G}$, as well as $x, y \xleftarrow{R} \mathbb{Z}_p$. With t being the maximal template size, select $z_i \xleftarrow{R} \mathbb{Z}_p$ for $0 \leq i \leq t$ and compute $X \leftarrow xP, Y \leftarrow yP, Z_i \leftarrow z_i P$. The algorithm outputs pp $= (\mathbb{G}, \mathbb{G}_t, e, P, p, \mathsf{Enc}^{\mathsf{BDS}}_{\mathcal{T}}, \mathsf{Enc}^{\mathsf{BDS}}_{\mathcal{M}})$, opk $\leftarrow (X, Y, Z_1, \ldots, Z_t)$ and osk $\leftarrow (x, y, z_1, \ldots, z_t)$.

Sign($\mathcal{T}$, (opk, osk), upk): Choose $\alpha \xleftarrow{R} \mathbb{Z}_p$ and compute $R \leftarrow \alpha P$, $A_i \leftarrow z_i R, B \leftarrow yR, B_i \leftarrow yA_i$. Further, choose a random permutation ϕ and compute $\mathcal{T}^{enc} \leftarrow \mathsf{Enc}^{\mathsf{BDS}}_{\mathcal{T}}(\mathcal{T}, \phi)$. Then, upk$^* \leftarrow \alpha \cdot$ upk $= \alpha \cdot$ usk $\cdot P$. Compute $C \leftarrow x \cdot R + xy \cdot$ upk$^* + xy \cdot |\mathcal{T}| \cdot A_0 + \sum_{h_i \in \mathcal{T}^*} xy \cdot h_i A_i$ and return the credential cred $\leftarrow (R, \{A_i\}, B, \{B_i\}, C)$ and the template-specific proxy secret key ϕ.

Verify$_{\mathsf{T}}$($\mathcal{T}$, cred, opk, (upk, usk), ϕ): Compute $\mathcal{T}^{enc} \leftarrow \mathsf{Enc}^{\mathsf{BDS}}_{\mathcal{T}}(\mathcal{T}, \phi)$ and verify whether cred is a valid signature under opk, i.e., $e(R, Z_i) \overset{?}{=} e(P, A_i) \wedge e(R, Y) \overset{?}{=} e(P, B) \wedge e(A_i, Y) \overset{?}{=} e(P, B_i)$ and $e(X, R) \cdot e(X, B)^{\mathsf{usk}} \cdot e(X, B_0)^{|\mathcal{T}|} \prod_{h_i \in \mathcal{T}^{enc}} e(X, B_i)^{h_i} \overset{?}{=} e(X, C)$ holds and return true on success and false otherwise.

Inst($\mathcal{T}$, cred, $\mathcal{M}$, (opk, upk, usk), ϕ): Using $\mathcal{T}^{enc}$ and $\mathcal{M}^{enc}$, obtained by applying the encoding functions w.r.t. ϕ and compute $\mathsf{v}_x \leftarrow e(X, R), \mathsf{v}_{xy} \leftarrow e(X, B), \mathsf{v}_{(xy,i)} \leftarrow e(X, B_i), \mathsf{v}_s \leftarrow e(P, C)$,

$$\pi \leftarrow \mathsf{SoK}\left\{ (\{(\mu_i)_{m_i \notin \mathcal{M}}, \chi_{\mathsf{usk}}\}) : \begin{array}{c} \mathsf{v}_s = \mathsf{v}_x \mathsf{v}_{xy}^{\chi_{\mathsf{usk}}} \mathsf{v}_{(xy,0)}^{|\mathcal{T}|} \prod\limits_{\mu_i \in \mathsf{hide}} \mathsf{v}_{(xy,i)}^{\mu_i} \prod\limits_{h_i \in \mathsf{show}} \mathsf{v}_{(xy,i)}^{h_i} \\ \wedge \; \chi_{\mathsf{usk}} \cdot P = \mathsf{upk} \end{array} \right\},$$

Return the instance signature (π, cred) and the encoded message $\mathcal{M}^{enc}$.

Verify$_{\mathsf{M}}$($\mathcal{M}^{enc}$, (π, cred), opk, upk): Compute $\mathsf{v}_x \leftarrow e(X, R), \mathsf{v}_{xy} \leftarrow e(X, B), \mathsf{v}_{(xy,i)} \leftarrow e(X, B_i)$ and $\mathsf{v}_s \leftarrow e(P, C)$, check whether $e(R, Z_i) \overset{?}{=} e(P, A_i) \wedge e(R, Y) \overset{?}{=} e(P, B) \wedge e(A_i, Y) \overset{?}{=} e(P, B_i)$ and verify the SoK π w.r.t. $\mathcal{M}^{enc}$, the public key upk and check whether $|\mathcal{T}|$ equals the number of message elements in the proof. On success, return true and false otherwise.

Scheme 1. BDSS from CL credentials

7 Comparison and Discussion

In this section, we compare the instantiations of the proxy signature schemes obtained from non-interactive anonymous credentials with the original instantiations of BDS and WHPS from [25, 26]. Moreover, we discuss the pros and

Setup(κ, t): Let $\mathbb{G}$ be a group of prime order p which is generated by P. Choose $y_0, y_1, \ldots, y_{t+2} \xleftarrow{R} \mathbb{Z}_p$ with t being the maximal template size and compute $H_0 \leftarrow y_0 P, P_1 \leftarrow y_1 P, \ldots, P_{t+2} \leftarrow y_{t+2} P$. The algorithm outputs $\mathsf{pp} \leftarrow (\mathbb{G}, P, p, \mathsf{Enc}_{\mathcal{T}}^{\mathsf{BDS}}, \mathsf{Enc}_{\mathcal{M}}^{\mathsf{BDS}})$, $\mathsf{opk} \leftarrow (H_0, P_1, \ldots, P_{t+2})$ and $\mathsf{osk} \leftarrow (y_0, \ldots, y_{t+2})$.

Sign$(\mathcal{T}, (\mathsf{opk}, \mathsf{osk}), \mathsf{upk})$ The originator and the proxy jointly compute a signature on the template $\mathcal{T}^{enc} \leftarrow \mathsf{Enc}_{\mathcal{T}}^{\mathsf{BDS}}(\mathcal{T}, \phi)$ as follows.

Originator		Proxy
$w_0 \xleftarrow{R} \mathbb{Z}_p, A_0 \leftarrow w_0 P$		$\alpha, \alpha_2, \alpha_3 \xleftarrow{R} \mathbb{Z}_p$
$H \leftarrow y_1 \mathsf{upk} + \lvert\mathcal{T}\rvert P_2 + \sum_{i=1}^{\lvert\mathcal{T}\rvert} h_i P_{i+2}$		
$B_0 \leftarrow w_0(H_0 + H)$	$\xrightarrow{A_0, B_0, H}$	$H' \leftarrow \alpha(H_0 + H)$
		$Z \leftarrow y_0(H_0 + H), \; Z' \leftarrow \alpha Z$
		$A_0' \leftarrow \alpha_2 H_0 + \alpha_3 P + A_0$
		$B_0' \leftarrow \alpha_2 Z' + \alpha_3 H' + \alpha B_0$
		$c_0' \leftarrow H(H' \| Z' \| A_0' \| B_0')$
	$\xleftarrow{c_0}$	$c_0 \leftarrow c_0' + \alpha_2 \pmod{p}$
$r_0 \leftarrow c_0 \cdot y_0 + w_0 \pmod{p}$	$\xrightarrow{r_0}$	$r_0 P - c_0 H_0 \overset{?}{=} A_0$
		$r_0(H_0 + H) - c_0 Z \overset{?}{=} B_0$
		$r_0' \leftarrow r_0 + \alpha_3$

Output the template signature $\mathsf{cred} \leftarrow (H', Z', A_0', B_0', r_0', c_0')$ and the template-specific proxy secret key (ϕ, α).

Verify$_\mathsf{T}$ $(\mathcal{T}, \mathsf{cred}, \mathsf{opk}, (\mathsf{upk}, \mathsf{usk}), (\phi, \alpha))$: Compute $\mathcal{T}^{enc} \leftarrow \mathsf{Enc}_{\mathcal{T}}^{\mathsf{BDS}}(\mathcal{T}, \phi)$ and $H \leftarrow \mathsf{usk} P_1 + \lvert\mathcal{T}\rvert P_2 + \sum_{i=1}^{\lvert\mathcal{T}\rvert} h_i P_{i+2}$ as well as $H' \leftarrow \alpha(H_0 + H)$, and check whether the value H' contained in cred is equal to the the computed value for H'. Check whether $r_0'(P + H') - c_0'(H_0 + Z') \overset{?}{=} A_0' + B_0'$ holds and return $\mathtt{true}$ if all checks hold and $\mathtt{false}$ otherwise.

Inst$(\mathcal{T}, \mathsf{cred}, \mathcal{M}, (\mathsf{opk}, \mathsf{upk}, \mathsf{usk}), (\phi, \alpha))$: Compute $\mathcal{T}^{enc}$ and $\mathcal{M}^{enc}$ from $\mathcal{T}, \mathcal{M}$ and ϕ as well as

$$\pi \leftarrow \mathsf{SoK}\left\{ \left((\mu_i)_{m_i \notin \mathcal{M}}, \alpha, \chi_\mathsf{usk}\right) : \begin{array}{l} H' = \alpha(H_0 + \chi_\mathsf{usk} P_1 + \lvert\mathcal{T}\rvert P_2 + \sum_{\mu_i \in \mathsf{hide}} \mu_i P_{i+2} + \\ \sum_{h_i \in \mathsf{show}} h_i P_{i+2}) \; \wedge \; \chi_\mathsf{usk} P = \mathsf{upk} \end{array} \right\}$$

and return the instance signature (π, cred) as well as the encoded message $\mathcal{M}^{enc}$.

Verify$_\mathsf{M}$ $(\mathcal{M}^{enc}, (\pi, \mathsf{cred}), \mathsf{opk}, \mathsf{upk})$: Verify whether $r_0'(P + H') - c_0'(H_0 + Z') \overset{?}{=} A_0' + B_0'$ holds, verify the SoK π w.r.t. $\mathcal{M}^{enc}$ and the public key upk and check whether $\lvert\mathcal{T}\rvert$ is equal to the number of message elements in the proof. Return $\mathtt{true}$ if all checks hold and $\mathtt{false}$ otherwise.

Scheme 2. BDSS from Brands' credentials

cons of the various approaches and provide an overview regarding computation, bandwidth and parameter sizes in Table 1.

Firstly, we note that for most practical usecases it can be assumed that template sizes are quite small. Consequently, under this assumption, the fact that in some cases the asymptotic computation times and signature sizes are linear in the size of the template does not have a notable influence on the overall performance of the schemes obtained from anonymous credentials. Though, when a usecase requires larger templates, the originally proposed schemes would be preferable.

However, the credential based constructions are flexible regarding the underlying anonymous credential scheme, which, in turn, could be exploited to reach additional properties. For instance, the unlinkability of multiple instances w.r.t. the same template can be realized by using a multi-show anonymous credential system. Furthermore, an anonymity feature, hiding the proxy's identity, could be obtained by skipping the proof part which links usk and upk ($\chi_\mathsf{usk} \cdot P = \mathsf{upk}$).

Table 1. BDSS/WHPSS efficiency comparison

Scheme	Computational effort				Signature size		
	Sign	Verify$_T$	Inst	Verify$_M$	Params	Cert	σ_P
BDSS	$\mathcal{O}(|T|)$	$\mathcal{O}(|T|)$	$\mathcal{O}(|T|)$	$\mathcal{O}(|\mathcal{M}|)$	$\mathcal{O}(|T|)$	$\mathcal{O}(1)$	$\mathcal{O}(1)$
BDSS$_{CL}$	$\mathcal{O}(|T|)$	$\mathcal{O}(|T|)$	$\mathcal{O}(|T|)$	$\mathcal{O}(|T|)$	$\mathcal{O}(|T|)$	$\mathcal{O}(|T|)$	$\mathcal{O}(|T|)$
BDSS$_{Brands}$	$\mathcal{O}(|T|)$	$\mathcal{O}(|T|)$	$\mathcal{O}(|T|)$	$\mathcal{O}(|T|)$	$\mathcal{O}(|T|)$	$\mathcal{O}(1)$	$\mathcal{O}(|T|)$

Scheme	Computational effort					Signature size		
	D	P	PS	PV	ID	Params	Cert	σ_P
WHPSS$_{PolyCommit}$	$\mathcal{O}(|\mathcal{M}|)$	$\mathcal{O}(|\mathcal{M}|)$	$\mathcal{O}(|\mathcal{M}|)$	$\mathcal{O}(1)$	$\mathcal{O}(1)$	$\mathcal{O}(|\mathcal{M}|)$	$\mathcal{O}(1)$	$\mathcal{O}(1)$
WHPSS$_{VectorCommit}$	$\mathcal{O}(|\mathcal{M}|)$	$\mathcal{O}(|\mathcal{M}|)$	$\mathcal{O}(\log(|\mathcal{M}|))$	$\mathcal{O}(\log(|\mathcal{M}|))$	$\mathcal{O}(1)$	$\mathcal{O}(1)$	$\mathcal{O}(1)$	$\mathcal{O}(\log(|\mathcal{M}|))$
WHPSS$_{CL}$	$\mathcal{O}(|\mathcal{M}|)$	$\mathcal{O}(|\mathcal{M}|)$	$\mathcal{O}(|\mathcal{M}|)$	$\mathcal{O}(|\mathcal{M}|)$	$\mathcal{O}(1)$	$\mathcal{O}(|\mathcal{M}|)$	$\mathcal{O}(|\mathcal{M}|)$	$\mathcal{O}(|\mathcal{M}|)$
WHPSS$_{Brands}$	$\mathcal{O}(|\mathcal{M}|)$	$\mathcal{O}(|\mathcal{M}|)$	$\mathcal{O}(|\mathcal{M}|)$	$\mathcal{O}(|\mathcal{M}|)$	$\mathcal{O}(1)$	$\mathcal{O}(|\mathcal{M}|)$	$\mathcal{O}(1)$	$\mathcal{O}(|\mathcal{M}|)$

Moreover, and very important, due to multiple projects such as ABC4Trust [1] building high-level interfaces for credential systems such as IBM's idemix [11,13,15] or Microsoft's U-Prove [9,28], there are quite some implementations of anonymous credential systems available to date. These implementations directly yield a basis for practical implementations of the schemes presented in this paper, which renders them very attractive from a practical point of view.

While the complexities of our instantiations are quite comparable to the originally proposed schemes, our proposed instantiations leave more freedom regarding the choice of groups since there is no pairing friendly elliptic curve group required in Brands' credentials [9] and one could also easily use the RSA based version of CL credentials [11]. This enables implementations on constrained devices such as smart cards (cf. [7, 20]). In contrast, the originally proposed instantiations of BDS as well as one of the instantiation of WHPS require pairing friendly elliptic curve groups.

Finally, we mention that in this paper the first approach for building special signature schemes from anonymous credentials is introduced, which might also be inspiring for other constructions. For instance, one could make use of the proposed encoding to encode finite sets of attribute values into credentials of an anonymous credential systems.

References

1. ABC4Trust Project - Attribute-based Credentials for Trust, http://abc4trust.eu
2. Abe, M., Fuchsbauer, G., Groth, J., Haralambiev, K., Ohkubo, M.: Structure-Preserving Signatures and Commitments to Group Elements. In: Rabin, T. (ed.) CRYPTO 2010. LNCS, vol. 6223, pp. 209–236. Springer, Heidelberg (2010)
3. Akagi, N., Manabe, Y., Okamoto, T.: An Efficient Anonymous Credential System. In: Tsudik, G. (ed.) FC 2008. LNCS, vol. 5143, pp. 272–286. Springer, Heidelberg (2008)
4. Backes, M., Meiser, S., Schröder, D.: Delegatable Functional Signatures. IACR ePrint 2013, 408 (2013)
5. Belenkiy, M., Chase, M., Kohlweiss, M., Lysyanskaya, A.: P-signatures and Noninteractive Anonymous Credentials. In: Canetti, R. (ed.) TCC 2008. LNCS, vol. 4948, pp. 356–374. Springer, Heidelberg (2008)

6. Bellare, M., Fuchsbauer, G.: Policy-Based Signatures. In: Krawczyk, H. (ed.) PKC 2014. LNCS, vol. 8383, pp. 520–537. Springer, Heidelberg (2014)
7. Bichsel, P., Camenisch, J., Groß, T., Shoup, V.: Anonymous credentials on a standard java card. In: ACM CCS 2009, pp. 600–610. ACM (2009)
8. Boldyreva, A., Palacio, A., Warinschi, B.: Secure Proxy Signature Schemes for Delegation of Signing Rights. J. Cryptology 25(1), 57–115 (2012)
9. Brands, S.: Rethinking Public-Key Infrastructures and Digital Certificates: Building in Privacy. MIT Press (2000)
10. Camenisch, J., Groß, T.: Efficient attributes for anonymous credentials. ACM Trans. Inf. Syst. Secur. 15(1), 4 (2012)
11. Camenisch, J., Lysyanskaya, A.: A Signature Scheme with Efficient Protocols. In: Cimato, S., Galdi, C., Persiano, G. (eds.) SCN 2002. LNCS, vol. 2576, pp. 268–289. Springer, Heidelberg (2003)
12. Camenisch, J., Lysyanskaya, A.: An Efficient System for Non-transferable Anonymous Credentials with Optional Anonymity Revocation. In: Pfitzmann, B. (ed.) EUROCRYPT 2001. LNCS, vol. 2045, pp. 93–118. Springer, Heidelberg (2001)
13. Camenisch, J., Lysyanskaya, A.: Signature Schemes and Anonymous Credentials from Bilinear Maps. In: Franklin, M. (ed.) CRYPTO 2004. LNCS, vol. 3152, pp. 56–72. Springer, Heidelberg (2004)
14. Camenisch, J., Stadler, M.: Efficient Group Signature Schemes for Large Groups (Extended Abstract). In: Kaliski Jr., B.S. (ed.) CRYPTO 1997. LNCS, vol. 1294, pp. 410–424. Springer, Heidelberg (1997)
15. Camenisch, J., Van Herreweghen, E.: Design and implementation of the idemix anonymous credential system. In: ACM CCS 2002, pp. 21–30. ACM (2002)
16. Canard, S., Lescuyer, R.: Anonymous credentials from (indexed) aggregate signatures. In: ACM DIM 2011, pp. 53–62. ACM (2011)
17. Canard, S., Lescuyer, R.: Protecting privacy by sanitizing personal data: a new approach to anonymous credentials. In: ASIA CCS 2013, pp. 381–392. ACM (2013)
18. Chase, M., Lysyanskaya, A.: On Signatures of Knowledge. In: Dwork, C. (ed.) CRYPTO 2006. LNCS, vol. 4117, pp. 78–96. Springer, Heidelberg (2006)
19. Derler, D., Hanser, C., Slamanig, D.: Privacy-Enhancing Proxy Signatures from Non-Interactive Anonymous Credentials. IACR ePrint 2014, 285 (2014)
20. Derler, D., Potzmader, K., Winter, J., Dietrich, K.: Anonymous Ticketing for NFC-Enabled Mobile Phones. In: Chen, L., Yung, M., Zhu, L. (eds.) INTRUST 2011. LNCS, vol. 7222, pp. 66–83. Springer, Heidelberg (2012)
21. Fiat, A., Shamir, A.: How to Prove Yourself: Practical Solutions to Identification and Signature Problems. In: Odlyzko, A.M. (ed.) CRYPTO 1986. LNCS, vol. 263, pp. 186–194. Springer, Heidelberg (1987)
22. Fuchsbauer, G., Pointcheval, D.: Anonymous consecutive delegation of signing rights: Unifying group and proxy signatures. In: Cortier, V., Kirchner, C., Okada, M., Sakurada, H. (eds.) Formal to Practical Security. LNCS, vol. 5458, pp. 95–115. Springer, Heidelberg (2009)
23. Fuchsbauer, G., Pointcheval, D.: Anonymous Proxy Signatures. In: Ostrovsky, R., De Prisco, R., Visconti, I. (eds.) SCN 2008. LNCS, vol. 5229, pp. 201–217. Springer, Heidelberg (2008)
24. Groth, J., Sahai, A.: Efficient non-interactive proof systems for bilinear groups. In: Smart, N.P. (ed.) EUROCRYPT 2008. LNCS, vol. 4965, pp. 415–432. Springer, Heidelberg (2008)
25. Hanser, C., Slamanig, D.: Blank Digital Signatures. In: ACM ASIACCS 2013, pp. 95–106. ACM (2013), ext.: IACR ePrint 2013/130

26. Hanser, C., Slamanig, D.: Warrant-Hiding Delegation-by-Certificate Proxy Signature Schemes. In: Paul, G., Vaudenay, S. (eds.) INDOCRYPT 2013. LNCS, vol. 8250, pp. 60–77. Springer, Heidelberg (2013), Ext.: IACR ePrint 2013/544
27. Mambo, M., Usuda, K., Okamoto, E.: Proxy signatures for delegating signing operation. In: ACM CCS 1996, pp. 48–57. ACM (1996)
28. Microsoft: U-Prove, http://research.microsoft.com/en-us/projects/u-prove
29. Stern, J., Pointcheval, D., Malone-Lee, J., Smart, N.P.: Flaws in Applying Proof Methodologies to Signature Schemes. In: Yung, M. (ed.) CRYPTO 2002. LNCS, vol. 2442, pp. 93–110. Springer, Heidelberg (2002)

Privacy-Preserving Multiple Keyword Search on Outsourced Data in the Clouds[*]

Tarik Moataz[1,2], Benjamin Justus[2], Indrakshi Ray[1], Nora Cuppens-Boulahia[2], Frédéric Cuppens[2], and Indrajit Ray[1]

[1] Computer Science Department, Colorado State University, Fort Collins, USA
{tmoataz,indrajit,iray}@cs.colostate.edu
[2] Institut Mines-Télécom, Télécom Bretagne, Cesson Sévigné, France
{benjamin.justus,nora.cuppens,frederic.cuppens}@telecom-bretagne.eu

Abstract. Honest but curious cloud servers can make inferences about the stored encrypted documents and the profile of a user once it knows the keywords queried by her and the keywords contained in the documents. We propose two progressively refined privacy-preserving conjunctive symmetric searchable encryption (PCSSE) schemes that allow cloud servers to perform conjunctive keyword searches on encrypted documents with different privacy assurances. Our scheme generates randomized search queries that prevent the server from detecting if the same set of keywords are being searched by different queries. It is also able to hide the number of keywords in a query as well as the number of keywords contained in an encrypted document. Our searchable encryption scheme is efficient and at the same time it is secure against the adaptive chosen keywords attack.

1 Introduction

Data is often stored in an encrypted form in the clouds for security and privacy reasons. If the volume of the stored data stored is large, it may be infeasible for the client to download the encrypted data, decrypt them locally, and search for the relevant documents. Consequently, researchers have proposed searchable encryption schemes to perform searches on encrypted documents stored in the clouds. Such schemes allow cloud servers to retrieve multiple encrypted documents in response to a client's queries which may be keywords search or numerical range queries. Efficiency of such techniques, which impact the query response time, is critical. Moreover, protecting the privacy of the client against honest but curious servers is also important.

Researchers have proposed schemes that permit exact keyword search on encrypted documents [10,11] as well as conjunctive keyword search (please see Section 2). However, existing conjunctive keyword search schemes do not provide adequate levels of privacy. Often times, the server is aware of the number

---

[*] This work was partially supported by the U.S. National Science Foundation under Grant No. 0905232.

V. Atluri and G. Pernul (Eds.): DBSec 2014, LNCS 8566, pp. 66–81, 2014.

of keywords contained in a document and the number of keywords in a query. Moreover, in these schemes, search on identical set of keywords result in the same encrypted query. An honest but curious cloud server may become aware of the client's search information and gain knowledge about her profile. Such information when correlated with the additional knowledge possessed by the server may constitute a serious privacy leakage. We propose a privacy-preserving approach that protects against such information leakage without increasing the search and storage complexities but at the cost of two rounds of protocol.

We motivate our approach by using a simple example based on exact keyword search. Each document stored in the server is associated with a bit vector whose size depends on the number of keywords in the dictionary. The index i on the vector corresponds to the ith keyword in the dictionary. A value of "1" in index position i signifies that the ith keyword is present in the document. The search query is associated with a similar bit vector. An **and** operation of the bit vectors corresponding to the document and the query reveals the existence or non-existence of the keyword. Such a simple scheme, however, does not provide adequate privacy protection. The server is now aware of the number of keywords in the document and the query. Moreover, it can detect if the user is submitting the same query multiple times. This, together with some background knowledge possessed by the server, can cause serious privacy leakage. We propose a more privacy preserving approach by introducing noise that serves to hide the number and the content of keywords and also is able to randomize the queries. We call this augmented approach Privacy-Preserving Symmetric Searchable Encryption (PCSSE) scheme. We introduce in this article first a rudimentary scheme that we refer to as PCSSE-1 that introduces the concept of noise insertion. However, this scheme is vulnerable to two types of inference attacks. We address these attacks in our second scheme that we refer to as PCSSE-2. One major technical challenge in implementing the PCSSE scheme is how to introduce the noise such that both privacy and correctness of the queries are preserved. The location of noises should be random or else an adaptive adversary can observe the search history and infer the keyword information. The PCSSE-2 scheme is secure against such an adaptive adversary based on the security of the pseudo-random permutation primitives as well as the randomness of the noise generation.

Our approach preserves the privacy of the client. First, the server does not have any information about the number of keywords contained in a document. Second, the scheme hides the number of keywords contained in a query. Last but not the least, PCSSE-2 provides query randomization that generates different encrypted queries even when the client is searching for the same set of keywords. This protects the client against revealing his search pattern to the server. Note that, there are some techniques that have better search complexity and search expressiveness, but they leak the search pattern information.

We have implemented a proof-of-concept for the PCSSE-2 scheme to evaluate its performance. Our approach is efficient with respect to storage and network communication costs. Specifically, the PCSSE-2 scheme has a storage complexity linear in the size of documents and the size of the indexes on the server side. The query phase of the scheme requires two rounds of client-server communication and has a communication complexity linear in the dictionary size. Moreover, the server-client communication during the query verification stage can be carried out efficiently as well since the size of the query, represented in the form of a binary vector, is at most 4 KB.

The rest of the paper is organized as follows. Section 2 discusses the state-of-the-art on searchable encryption. Section 3 presents an overview of our approach and contains the PCSSE algorithm and security definitions. PCSSE-1 construction is carried out in Section 4 while PCSSE-2 is detailed in Section 5. Section 6 evaluates the security and the performance of our scheme. Section 7 concludes the paper.

2   Related Work

Song et al. [20] presented the first symmetric searchable encryption scheme. Subsequently, many works have focused on enhancing the search and storage complexities of the scheme, as well on the strength of the security models [11,8,10,16,15]. The study of asymmetric searchable encryption started with the work of Boneh et al. [4]. Some of the later works focused on providing techniques that improve on the search complexity of Boneh's scheme [1,3,9]. All these constructions deal with exact keyword search, and do not have the capability of performing conjunctive keyword search.

The existing exact keyword searchable encryption schemes are not suitable for a conjunctive search. They disclose sensitive meta-information, and at the same time induce an exponential computation overhead on the server side. Golle et al. [13] introduced the first conjunctive scheme in a symmetric setting. Golle's scheme associates a searchable index with each document. The server performs a matching test on the document index with the client submitted query. Golle presented two constructions: the security of the first construction is based on the hardness of the Decisional Diffie-Hellman (DDH) problem. The first construction has a search complexity linear in the number of stored documents. The second construction has a search complexity linear in the number of dictionary keywords. Both constructions use exponentiations and pairings in the search phase and test phase. Parker et al. [18] presented a similar scheme which handles the asymmetric setting. Ballard et al. [2] later enhanced the scheme's communication and search complexities on the server side. Ryu et al. [19] presented another symmetric solution which additionally reduces the complexity of the encryption phase by diminishing the number of pairing operations. On the other hand, some works deals with multiple keyword search in the cloud by enabling some enhanced privacy preserving techniques [6,21]. Moreover, some works introducing boolean search over encrypted data [17,7] still disclose too many information to the outsourced servers. Specifically, these works fail to hide the search pattern.

Boneh's work [5] extended the search options in a public setting that allow conjunctive subsets, ranges and exact keywords searches. Hwang et al. [14] presented an enhancement for the cipher-text size with a comparable computation complexity. All the above conjunctive searchable encryption schemes leak the following information: the number of keywords contained in each document, and the number of keywords that are in the client's query. These meta-information leakage causes a breach of the client's privacy. Recent work by Wang et al. [22] allows clients to hide this information. Wang's scheme however is not deterministic in the sense that there are false positives associated with each of the client's query. Furthermore in order to minimize the query's false positive rate, the client can store at most 16 keywords in each document, and cannot have more than 4 keywords in a given query.

3   Overview of the Approach

3.1   Problem Statement

Let $\mathcal{D} = \{D_1, ..., D_n\}$ be a collection of documents, and $\mathcal{W} = \{w_1, ..., w_l\}$ be a dictionary of keywords. The collection $\mathcal{D}$ is encrypted using a private-key CPA-secure encryption scheme $\mathcal{E}$. The encrypted collection $\mathcal{E}(\mathcal{D})$ is outsourced and stored on external cloud servers. The dictionary $\mathcal{W}$ is a finite set whose size depends on the underlying language.

Let $\{w_k\}_{k \in I_C}$ be a list of keywords contained in the dictionary $\mathcal{W}$ where I_C contains the keyword indexes. The search query contains a conjunction of keywords, denoted by, $\bigwedge_{k \in I_C} w_k$. The objective of the conjunctive searchable encryption is to retrieve the set of encrypted documents that contain the set of keywords from the encrypted collection $\mathcal{E}(\mathcal{D})$ in an efficient manner, so as to preserve the privacy of the client to the extent possible. In response to the query, the server sends the set of encrypted documents to the client.

3.2   Notations

The notation $x \xleftarrow{R} S$ means uniform sampling the string x from the set S. In this paper, the strings x is a binary string (i.e. $x \xleftarrow{R} \{0,1\}^*$). The size of string x is denoted by $|x|$. Let x and y be two binary strings, then $x \parallel y$ is the concatenation of x and y. Let A be an array, $A[i]$ is the value of the array at i^{th} index. The transpose of array A is represented by A^T. If $\mathcal{AL}$ is an algorithm then $x \leftarrow \mathcal{AL}(...)$ represents the result of applying the algorithm $\mathcal{AL}$ with given arguments. The parameter k is used to denote a security parameter.

Let $\mathcal{D} = \{D_1, ..., D_n\}$ be a set of documents, and $\mathcal{W} = \{w_1, ..., w_l\}$ a dictionary of keywords. Each document D_i is associated a set of keywords. The set of keywords in D_i is represented by the set $M_i = \{r_{i,1}, r_{i,2}, ..., r_{i,|M_i|}\}$, where $|M_i|$ is the number of keywords in D_i and each $r_{i,j}$, where $1 \leq j \leq |M_i|$, gives the position of the keyword in the dictionary, that is, $1 \leq r_{i,j} \leq l$. Moreover, the set of all keywords in all the n documents are given by $\mathcal{M}$, where $\mathcal{M} = \{M_1, ..., M_n\}$. The set of keywords that a client searches for is given by I_C, and the conjunction of these keywords is denoted by $C(W) = \bigwedge_{k \in I_C} w_k$.

Definition 1 *Hamming Weight: The Hamming weight $H(x)$ of a binary vector x is defined to be the number of "1"s in the vector x.*

Consider the inner scalar product ϕ on an inner product space: $\phi : \{0,1\}^n \times \{0,1\}^n \rightarrow [0,n]$. The value $\phi(x,x)$ is a non-negative integer, and it coincides with the Hamming weight of x. Note that, $\phi(x,y) = \sum_{k=1}^{n} x_k y_k$, where x and y are vectors of size n.

Our construction is based on several well known cryptographic primitives. These include private-key CPA-secure encryption scheme (e.g. AES), pseudorandom permutation. We refer the reader to [12] for details.

3.3   PCSSE Protocol

Our PCSSE protocol over a set of documents $\mathcal{D}$ and a dictionary space $\mathcal{W}$ consists of applying five polynomial-time algorithms, namely, *KeyGen, Enc, Query, Response, Dec*, each of which is briefly enumerated below.

Key Generation $(K_1, K_2) \leftarrow KeyGen(k)$: *KeyGen* takes the security parameter k as input and outputs two secret keys K_1 and K_2.

Encryption $(\mathcal{L}, \mathcal{C}) \leftarrow Enc(K_1, K_2, \mathcal{D}, \mathcal{M}, \mathcal{W})$: *Enc* takes as inputs the secret keys K_1, K_2, the collection of documents $\mathcal{D}$, the set of keyword index $\mathcal{M}$, and the dictionary $\mathcal{W}$. It outputs the encrypted collection of documents $\mathcal{C} = \{C_1, ..., C_n\}$ and the associated set of labels $\mathcal{L} = \{L_1, ..., L_n\}$.

Randomized Query Generation $Q \leftarrow Query(K_2, C(\mathsf{W}))$: *Query* is a probabilistic algorithm that takes as inputs the secret key K_2 and the conjunction of keywords $C(\mathsf{W})$. It outputs a randomized query Q .

Query Response $\mathcal{X} \leftarrow Response(Q, \mathcal{L})$: *Response* is a deterministic algorithm that takes as inputs the query Q and the set of labels $\mathcal{L}$ associated with the encrypted documents. The output consists of a set of encrypted documents $\mathcal{X}$ that match the query Q.

Decryption $\mathcal{D}_i \leftarrow Dec(K_1, C_i)$: *Dec* is a deterministic algorithm that takes as inputs the key K_1 and a ciphertext C_i and outputs the unencrypted document D_i.

Definition 2 *Correctness: Let $C(\mathsf{W})$ be a conjunctive keywords query, and $\mathcal{C}$ the set of encrypted documents that match the conjunctive query $C(\mathsf{W})$. Let Q be the result of applying the probabilistic algorithm Query on $C(\mathsf{W})$. We say that PCSSE is correct if:*
$$Response(Q, \mathcal{L}) = \mathcal{C}.$$

3.4   PCSSE Security Definition

In our PCSSE scheme, we are interested in the adaptive security model such as the one introduced in [10], namely, secure against chosen keywords attack CKA-2. In this security model, no pseudorandom polynomial-time adversary, who is given encrypted labels, encrypted documents and encrypted search queries, can learn any information about the content of the documents and the content of search queries other than the *search pattern* and *access pattern*. The access pattern contains information about the identifiers of encrypted documents that match a search query. The search pattern contains the history of all the search queries. We refer the reader to [10] for the formal definitions of search and access patterns. The search pattern, access pattern, the number of documents and the size of documents returned in a query response, are the possible information leakages in an adaptive security model. Note that, the number of keywords in a document is also a possible source of information leakage in existing symmetric searchable encryption schemes; our PCSSE scheme keeps the number of keywords secret (see section 5).

The important characteristic of randomized queries is that no polynomial time adversary is able to discern whether a search query is repeated or not. This is because the query submitted by a client is different each time, even when searching for the same conjunction of keywords. We formally define the notion of randomized query as follows:

Definition 3 *Randomized query:* Let $\{Q_i\}_{1\leq i\leq t}$ be the t queries generated with the $Query(.)$ algorithm with the same key K_2 and the conjunctive keyword expression $\{C(W_i)\}_{1\leq i\leq t}$. Let Q_i and Q_j two queries for the same conjunction of keywords. We say that the scheme satisfies randomized query if no pseudorandom polynomial time adversary can, with high probability, associate these queries to the same conjunction.

As a consequence of using randomized queries, the information leakage is now limited to the access pattern, the number and the size of encrypted documents. However, we want to point out that as we will see later on in the security analysis section, the access pattern is inherently related to the search pattern. In other words, knowing the access pattern can infer as well some information about the user search behavior.

Moreover, with randomized queries the number of keywords sent in each query is completely hidden from the server. Following upon the definition 3, we classify the information leakage into two categories. The *leakage* $\rho_1(\mathcal{L}, \mathcal{C})$ represents a statistical leakage known by the server before receiving any search queries. The second *leakage* $\rho_2(Q_{i\in\{1,\cdots,t\}}, \mathcal{L}, \mathcal{C})$ deals with access patterns disclosed by the search queries results. These are defined below.

Definition 4 *Leakage* $\rho_1(\mathcal{L}, \mathcal{C})$: *The leakage consists of the following information: the number of encrypted documents, the size of each encrypted document, and the identifier of each encrypted document stored on the server.*

Definition 5 *Leakage* $\rho_2(Q_{i\in\{1,\cdots,t\}}, \mathcal{L}, \mathcal{C})$ *(Access pattern): If each Q_i is a randomized query, the leakage caused after submitting Q_i consists of the identifiers of encrypted documents that match the queries $Q_{i\in\{1,\cdots,t\}}$.*

In the following, we define security of our PCSSE scheme using a simulation based definition.

Definition 6 *Adaptive security against chosen keyword attack CKA2:*
Let us consider the five algorithms that defines our PCSSE scheme, namely,
KeyGen, Enc, Query, Response, Dec *as described in Section 3.3. We present*
the following game based on two experiences **Real**$_A$ *and* **Ideal**$_{A,S}$ *where we*
consider a stateful adversary A, *a stateful simulator* S, *the leakages* ρ_1, ρ_2, *and*
the security parameter k:

> **Real**$_A(k)$: *The challenger (user) runs the* $KeyGen(k)$ *algorithm and*
> *outputs the key* (K_1, K_2). A *sends the tuple* $(\mathcal{D}, \mathcal{M}, \mathcal{W})$ *and receives*
> $(\mathcal{L}, \mathcal{C}) \leftarrow Enc(K_1, K_2, \mathcal{D}, \mathcal{M}, \mathcal{W})$ *from the challenger.* A *makes a poly-*
> *nomial number of adaptive queries* $\{C(\mathsf{W}_i)\}_{1 \leq i \leq t}$ *and sends them to*
> *the challenger. The adversary receives the search queries generated by*
> *the challenger such that* $Q_i \leftarrow Query(K_2, C(\mathsf{W}_i))$. A *returns one if his*
> *queries return the expected result, otherwise zero is returned.*
>
> **Ideal**$_{A,S}(k)$: *The adversary outputs the tuple* $(\mathcal{D}, \mathcal{M}, \mathcal{W})$ *and sends it*
> *to the simulator. Given the leakage* ρ_1, S *will generate the labels as well*
> *as the encrypted documents* $(\mathcal{L}, \mathcal{C})$ *and sends them to the adversary.*
> A *makes a polynomial number of adaptive queries* $\{C(\mathsf{W}_i)\}_{1 \leq i \leq t}$ *and*
> *sends them to the simulator. Given the leakage* ρ_2 *(containing the access*
> *pattern or previous queries), the simulator sends the appropriate search*
> *queries to the adversary. Finally,* A *returns a zero or one depending*
> *on whether or not the responses are accurate.*

We say that PCSSE is adaptively secure against chosen keyword attack if
for all polynomial time adversary A, there exists a non-uniform polynomial-size
simulator S such that:

$$|\Pr[\mathbf{Real}_A(k) = 1] - \Pr[\mathbf{Ideal}_{A,S}(k) = 1]| \leq \epsilon(k)$$

4   PCSSE-1 Construction

In this section, we present the construction of the first scheme PCSSE-1. This
scheme represents a fundamental basis for the second scheme where we introduce globally all our techniques. PCSSE-1 suffers as will be described in the
subsequent section 5 from some notable attacks that will lead us to present the
enhancement version of it.

The scheme consists of two phases, namely, the *setup phase* and the *search*
phase. The setup phase is done once by the client when the encrypted documents
and the labels are uploaded on the server. In this phase, the client uses the
algorithms *KeyGen* and *Enc* to construct the labels and create the encrypted
documents. The search phase is performed every time a query is submitted. In
this phase, the client generates the randomized query using the algorithm *Query*
and the the server generates the response using the algorithm *Response*. Since
the PCSSE algorithm is a two-rounds protocol, the *Response* algorithm includes
one additional interaction with the user before outputting the results.

4.1   Setup Phase

The client uses the $KeyGen(k)$ algorithm with the security parameter k to generate the keys K_1, K_2 such that $K_i \in \{0, 1\}^k$.

In the following we will detail the $Enc(.)$ algorithm. In order to encrypt document D_i and generate the label L_i associated with D_i, the client performs the following steps.

[**Step 1:**] Create an array L_i of size $3l$ where l is the size of the dictionary and initialize it with all zeros.

[**Step 2:**] Choose randomly a subset P in $[\![1, 3l]\!]$ such that $|P| = l$. Apply the permutation function $\pi : \{0, 1\}^k \times \{0, 1\}^l \to P$ to the keyword index $M_i = \{r_{i,1}, ..., r_{i,|M_i|}\}$ associated with the document D_i to obtain a permuted index set $\pi_{K_2}(M_i) = \{\pi_{K_2}(r_{i,1}), ..., \pi_{K_2}(r_{i,|M_i|})\}$. For each $\pi_{K_2}(r_{i,j}) \in \pi_{K_2}(M_i)$, where $1 \le j \le |M_i|$, set $L_i[\pi_{K_2}(r_{i,j})] = 1$.

[**Step 3:**] Choose randomly a subset R in $[\![1, 3l]\!] \backslash P$ such that $|R| = l$. Sample randomly two binary vectors a_i and b_i such that $a_i \parallel b_i \xleftarrow{R} \{0, 1\}^{|R|}$. Fill L_i in such a way that L_i restricted to the positions R is $a_i \parallel b_i$, and L_i restricted to the positions $Z = [\![1, 3l]\!] \backslash \{P \bigcup R\}$ is $a_i \parallel \overline{b_i}$.

[**Step 4:**] Client encrypts each document D_i using a private-key CPA-secure encryption scheme $\mathcal{E}_{K_1}$ to produce the encrypted document $\mathcal{E}_{K_1}(D_i)$. Client sends the server the encrypted document along with the label, denoted by $(\mathcal{E}_{K_1}(D_i), L_i)$. The user stores in his side $h(a_i)$, the hamming value of the vector a_i.

4.2   Search Phase

The search step includes both the $Query(.)$ and the $Response(.)$ algorithm.

Let $C(W) = \bigwedge_{k \in I_C} w_k$ be the conjunction of keywords that the client searches for, where I_C is the set of keywords positions in the dictionary such $I_C = \{r_1, ..., r_{|I_C|}\}$. The client performs the three steps of the $Query(.)$ and sends the randomized query to the server such that:

[**Step 1:**] Create an array Q of size $3l$ where l is the size of the dictionary and initialize it with all zeros.

[**Step 2:**] Fill the array Q such that $Q[\pi_{K_2}(r_j)] = 1$ for $1 \le j \le |I_C|$.

[**Step 3:**] Randomly sample two binary vectors c and d such that $c \parallel d \xleftarrow{R} \{0, 1\}^{|R|}$. Fill Q in such a way that Q restricted to the positions R is $c \parallel d$, and Q restricted to the positions Z is $\overline{c} \parallel d$. The user sends the query Q to the server and retains the value $h(d) + |I_C|$.

Once the server receives the query Q, it performs the following steps for the $Response$ algorithm:

[**Step 1:**] The server does the following computation: for each label L_i such that $Token_i = Q.L_i^T$, the server sends the $Token_i$ to the user.

[**Step 2:**] The user performs the following verification: if $Token_i = h(a_i) + h(d) + |I_C|$, the user sends a bit b_i equal to 1, otherwise the bit will be equal to 0.

[**Step 3:**] If the server receives a bit b_i equal to 1, the server sends the encrypted document $\mathcal{E}_{K_1}(D_i)$ to the user.

Finally the user invokes the algorithm $Dec(\cdot)$ in order to decrypt the received documents.

Theorem 1. *The PCSSE-1 construction is correct as per Definition 2.*

5   PCSSE-2 Construction

PCSSE-1 as constructed in the previous section is vulnerable to two critical attacks, referred to as *Attack 1* and *Attack 2*, that can leak the position of the noise and therefore the position of the keywords. We describe first the attacks and then present PCSSE-2 that is going to address these deficiencies.

***Attack 1* description.** The positions of the noise defined by the set R and Z represent a vital information that must be kept secret. Thus, in the PCSSE-1 construction, the hamming values of both binary vectors a_i and d are not shared with the server. Note that if the verification was done in the server side, it can infer directly the value $|I_c|$ (by knowing the values of $h(a_i)$, $h(d)$ and $Token_i$). However, even if the critical part of the verification is done on the client side, the server will finally know all the matching documents (by receiving a bit equal to 1 or 0 for each label). The server then has the knowledge of all labels matching the corresponding query. Let us denote by $(L_1, \cdots, L_q)$ the set of labels matching a query Q. The server knows that all these labels have all the positions of searched for keywords equal to 1. The idea is to reduce the number of ones caused by noise insertions. In fact since the noise is randomly inserted in these fixed positions, some labels will contains '0' and other will contain '1' in the same position. The server then performs a binary 'AND' operation between all these labels such that:

$$L = L_1 \wedge L_2 \wedge \cdots \wedge L_q$$

The resulting L is a binary vector containing fewer 1 values. The most important consequence is that the server now has the certainty that all positions that turn from 1 to 0 are actually a noise position while some of the positions keeping a '1' value correspond to keywords' positions. After executing a number of queries, the server will build an exact knowledge of the noise and keywords' positions.

***Attack 2* description.** The first attack is adaptive in the sense that the adversary needs the result of the search to build an extra-knowledge of the labels' construction. The second attack is more destructive in the sense that the adversary can infer noise positions defined by the sets R and Z *passively*. In fact, the determinism of noise position is the key of this adversary's attack. Even if the noise is randomly inserted independently for each label it does not change anything to its fixed position which is similar to all labels. The noise vector a_i is inserted twice in the label L_i. This redundancy is the origin of the problem (the same for the vector b_i and its complementary). As an instance, if the first bit of a_i is inserted in $R[1]$, then the same bit will be inserted in $Z[1]$, this applies to all labels. Consequently, an attacker can follow this strategy: first select a random bit in the first label and search for a position containing the same bit value. Secondly, check the second label in both positions whether they have the same bits. If so, go to the third label and continue the same test, if not, go back to the first label and choose a different position and go through the process recursively. The attack outputs the noise positions with high probability, which, in turn, reveals the keywords' positions *passively*. Note that, this attack is computationally expensive.

In the following we present PCSSE-2. We detail the noise insertion in the setup phase and the search phase. We generate the keys with the $KeyGen(k)$.

Setup Phase. Steps 1, 2 and 4 are similar to the PCSSE-1 construction. We will detail here the new strategy of noise insertions. Subsequently, we use the term *translation by a nonnegative integer q* applied to a set P. Here we give an example showing this concept. Let us take the ordered set $S = \{2, 5, 10, 20, 35\}$. The translation by a scalar value 2 applied on S will output the new set $\{20, 35, 2, 5, 10\}$. The translation will shift all elements by q modulus the size of the set.

1. Choose randomly a subset R in $[\![1, 3l]\!]\backslash P$ such that $|R| = l$. The positions in R are ordered. The same applies for Z.
2. Sample randomly two binary vectors a_i and b_i such that $a_i, b_i \xleftarrow{R} \{0,1\}^l$.
3. Choose randomly two nonnegative integers l_i^1 and l_i^2 smaller than l.
4. Apply respectively a translation to the positions in R and Z by l_i^1 and l_i^2 and output the new ordered set of positions R_i and Z_i.
5. Fill L_i in such a way that L_i restricted to the positions R_i is $a_i \parallel a_i$, and L_i restricted to the positions Z_i is $b_i \parallel \overline{b_i}$.

Figure 1 describes the process of translation applied to the first label.

Search Phase. For the $Query(.)$ algorithm, Steps 1 and 2 are similar to those of the PCSSE-1 construction. Here we detail the new strategy for the noise insertion in the query:

1. Sample randomly two binary vectors c and d such that $c, d \xleftarrow{R} \{0,1\}^l$.
2. Choose randomly two nonnegative integers[1] l^1 and l^2 smaller than l.
3. Apply respectively a translation to the positions in R and Z by l^1 and l^2 and output the new ordered set of positions R' and Z'.
4. Fill Q in such a way that Q restricted to the positions R' is $c \parallel \overline{c}$, and Q restricted to the positions Z' is $d \parallel d$.

Once the server receives the query Q, it performs the following steps for the *Response* algorithm:

[**Step 1:**] The server performs the following computation: for each label L_i such that: $Token_i = Q.L_i^T$, the server sends the $(Token_1, \cdots, Token_n)$ to the user.

---

[1] These integers are different for each newly generated query.

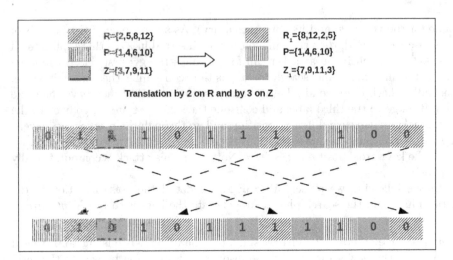

Fig. 1. Translation process applied to a label where $a_i = (1,0)$ and $b_i = (1,1)$ and the size of the dictionary l equal to 4

[**Step 2:**] The user performs the following verification: if $Token_i = h(a_i) + h(d) + |I_C|$, the user outputs a bit b_i equal to 1, otherwise the bit will be equal to 0. Finally the user outputs $\mathbf{b} = (b_1, \cdots, b_n)$.

[**Step 3:**] The user randomly selects r (if available) bits equal to 0 from $\mathbf{b}$ and turns them to 1. The user will then output the new version $\tilde{\mathbf{b}}$.

[**Step 4:**] If the server receives a bit $\tilde{b}_i$ equal to 1, the server sends the encrypted document $\mathcal{E}_{K_1}(D_i)$ to the user.

Finally, the user invokes the algorithm $Dec(\cdot)$ in order to decrypt the received documents. The choice of the value r can be limited such that the exact number of matching labels plus r will not exceed a given value. This will give the user a control on the communication complexity.

Theorem 2. *The PCSSE-2 construction is correct as per Definition 2.*

Discussion. The ideas introduced in PCSSE-2 solve both attacks described earlier. Including false bits in the user answer, will prevent the server from computing the exact value of $L = L_1 \wedge L_2 \wedge \cdots \wedge L_q$ after each query. In fact, this idea will mislead the server by including some noisy labels that do not contain the query. This solution will not create any false positive but will increase the communication complexity (not the number of interactions).

The second countermeasure taken into account in the PCSSE-2 construction phase keeps the position of noise fixed, but introduces a translation to change the position of the noise vector and its redundant value or its complimentary value for each label. This translation is done randomly for each label and is independent from that done to another label. The position of a noise bit and its complement in one label has no relation with the corresponding positions in the second label. The same reasoning applies also to the query since we are changing the scalars of the translations from a query to another.

6   Security Analysis and Evaluation

6.1   Security Analysis

The privacy guarantees of our PCSSE-2 scheme can be expressed in terms of the following lemma and theorem. For lack of space, we omit the proofs but offer an intuition instead.

Lemma 1. *Let Q_i be the outputs of the algorithm $Query(K_2, C(W_i))$ for $1 \leq i \leq t$. The PCSSE-2 primitive has randomized queries such that:*

$$\forall i, j \in [\![1, t]\!] \ s.t. \ i \neq j, \ \Pr(Associate(Q_i, Q_j)) \precsim \frac{1}{\binom{h(Q_i \vee Q_j)}{|I_C|}},$$

where $h(Q_i)$ is the Hamming value of the query Q_i with known number of conjunction I_C.

Theorem 3. *Let $\mathcal{E}$ be a private-key CPA-secure encryption scheme, π a pseudorandom permutation. Then the PCSSE-2 scheme is adaptively secure against chosen keywords attack as defined in Definition 6 where ρ_1 and ρ_2 are the possible leakages, and the queries are randomized in the sense of Definition 3.*

Proof Sketch. The query randomization property is the key to the privacy of our PCSSE-2 scheme. The randomized query gives an attacker negligible chances of discerning the keywords searched by a client or whether the same/similar keyword searches have been performed in the past. As a direct consequence of this property, the adversary (server) cannot find out the number of keywords in a given query. Since the label construction is similar to the query construction, the adversary also cannot infer the number of keywords inside each document.

However, we also need to prove that the indexes and the encrypted documents are indistinguishable from simulated ones based on the leakages previously defined in section 3.4. Note that, the keywords positions are computed using a pseudo-random permutation (PRP) with a key that is secret to the user. The adversary, while in simulation, has to generate randomly a key and use it for the PRP. Consequently the adversary's generated keyword positions and the real positions are indistinguishable. The index is constructed as well by inserting random noise which makes every pair of indexes different even if they contain the same keywords. Thus, an adversary's simulated index and the real index are indistinguishable. The same applies for the generated query since it follows the same index construction. Moreover, the encrypted documents are indistinguishable from the real ones as well since the adversary has to simulate a random key for this purpose. Lastly, during the search phase, the adversary has an additional knowledge about the query results. However with a position of noise different from every two indexes, and a user's answer containing always extra documents, the adversary cannot define the keywords positions. Thus our scheme is secure against adaptive chosen keyword attacks.

6.2 Evaluation

In summary, Table 1 compares our PCSSE-2 scheme with other deterministic conjunctive symmetric schemes with respect to computation complexity, and query privacy properties. The notations n, m and $|C|$ denote respectively the number of documents, the number of keywords and the number of keywords within a given conjunction. We use **exp**, **pr** to designate the operations exponentiation and pairing[2]. p is a 128-bit prime. Finally we use **IP**, **MCG** and **PRF** to designate the inner product, the multiplication in a cyclic group, and a pseudo-random function respectively.

Table 1. Comparison of Conjunctive Symmetric Searchable Encryption Schemes

	Server side computation	Server side storage	Client side computation	Query computation	Query size	Randomized Query	Hide the number of keywords
GSW-1 [13]	n **exp** + n **PRF**	$(m+1)pn + |\mathcal{E}(\mathcal{D})|$	$(m+1)n$ **exp** + nm **PRF**	n **exp** + $(|C| + n)$ **PRF**	$(n+1)p + |C|$	No	No
GSW-2 [13]	$(2|C|+1)n$ **pr**	$(2m+1)pn + |\mathcal{E}(\mathcal{D})|$	$(2m+1)n$ **exp** + nm **PRF**	3 **exp** + $|C|$ **PRF**	$3p + |C|$	No	No
BKM [2]	$2n$ **pr** + $n|C|$ **PRF**	$(m+1)pn + |\mathcal{E}(\mathcal{D})|$	nm **PRF** + $(m+1)n$ **MCG**	$|C|$ **PRF**	$2p + |C|$	No	No
ET [19]	$2n$ **pr**	$(m+2)pn + |\mathcal{E}(\mathcal{D})|$	$(m+1)n$ **exp** + n **pr** + mn **PRF**	2 **exp** + $|C|$ **PRF**	$2p + |C|$	No	No
PCSSE (our approach)	n **IP**	$3ln + |\mathcal{E}(\mathcal{D})|$	nm **PRF**	$|C|$ **PRF**	$3m$	Yes	Yes

We run experiments to evaluate the performance of the search phase of PCSSE-2 as this directly impacts the server's real-time response capabilities. We ignore the time required for query construction as this step can be carried out in constant time; instead, we focus on the query verification that is carried out on the server. Our experiments on the server query-verification stage investigates how PCSSE-2 performs asymptotically taking into account the number of keywords and the number of documents. In the experiment, we have considered up to 1000 file, not taking into account their types. A file can be a document, email, without a specific file type, i.e. it can be a document, email, media etc.). For each scenario, tests are performed on three different dictionary sizes: 1000, 5000, and 10000 keywords. The PCSSE-2 primitive is scripted and tested inside the open-source Scilab environment. The computations are performed on a dell laptop with 2.40GHz processors. The results are plotted in Fig. 2. The plot shows

---

[2] Computing one pairing is equal to 6 to 20 exponentiation.

that the performance is linear with respect to the number of documents n. Furthermore, the label size increase implies only a constant overhead added to the search time. The search time per-document is roughly $30\mu s$ for labels containing 1000 keywords, and $200\mu s$ for labels containing 10000 keywords. The plot gives us a clear idea how PCSSE-2 performs asymptotically.

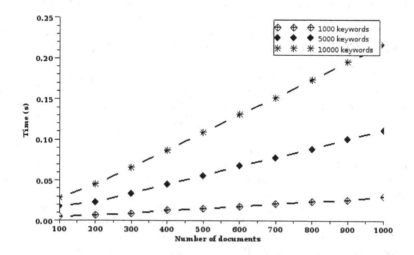

Fig. 2. Performance Evaluation for the Search Phase

7   Conclusion

We have presented a new deterministic privacy-preserving conjunctive symmetric searchable encryption scheme (PCSSE) that allows cloud servers to perform efficient conjunctive keywords searches on encrypted documents while protecting the privacy of clients by hiding the keywords in the query and also the keywords contained in the document.

We plan to extend this work along two dimensions. First, we would extend PCSSE scheme to include sub-match on keywords and also boolean expression searches. Second, we would like to make the scheme more dynamic that will allow efficient and privacy preserving queries even if the documents on the server side are updated.

References

1. Abdalla, M., Bellare, M., Catalano, D., Kiltz, E., Kohno, T., Lange, T., Malone-Lee, J., Neven, G., Paillier, P., Shi, H.: Searchable encryption revisited: Consistency properties, relation to anonymous IBE, and extensions. Journal of Cryptology 21(3), 350–391 (2008)

2. Ballard, L., Kamara, S., Monrose, F.: Achieving efficient conjunctive keyword searches over encrypted data. In: Qing, S., Mao, W., López, J., Wang, G. (eds.) ICICS 2005. LNCS, vol. 3783, pp. 414–426. Springer, Heidelberg (2005)
3. Bellare, M., Boldyreva, A., O'Neill, A.: Deterministic and efficiently searchable encryption. In: Menezes, A. (ed.) CRYPTO 2007. LNCS, vol. 4622, pp. 535–552. Springer, Heidelberg (2007)
4. Boneh, D., Di Crescenzo, G., Ostrovsky, R., Persiano, G.: Public key encryption with keyword search. In: Cachin, C., Camenisch, J.L. (eds.) EUROCRYPT 2004. LNCS, vol. 3027, pp. 506–522. Springer, Heidelberg (2004)
5. Boneh, D., Waters, B.: Conjunctive, subset, and range queries on encrypted data. In: Vadhan, S.P. (ed.) TCC 2007. LNCS, vol. 4392, pp. 535–554. Springer, Heidelberg (2007)
6. Cao, N., Wang, C., Li, M., Ren, K., Lou, W.: Privacy-preserving multi-keyword ranked search over encrypted cloud data. In: Proceedings of the 30th IEEE International Conference on Computer Communications, Joint Conference of the IEEE Computer and Communications Societies, Shanghai, China, pp. 829–837 (April 2011)
7. Cash, D., Jarecki, S., Jutla, C., Krawczyk, H., Roşu, M.-C., Steiner, M.: Highly-scalable searchable symmetric encryption with support for boolean queries. In: Canetti, R., Garay, J.A. (eds.) CRYPTO 2013, Part I. LNCS, vol. 8042, pp. 353–373. Springer, Heidelberg (2013)
8. Chang, Y.-C., Mitzenmacher, M.: Privacy preserving keyword searches on remote encrypted data. In: Ioannidis, J., Keromytis, A.D., Yung, M. (eds.) ACNS 2005. LNCS, vol. 3531, pp. 442–455. Springer, Heidelberg (2005)
9. Di Crescenzo, G., Saraswat, V.: Public key encryption with searchable keywords based on jacobi symbols. In: Srinathan, K., Rangan, C.P., Yung, M. (eds.) INDOCRYPT 2007. LNCS, vol. 4859, pp. 282–296. Springer, Heidelberg (2007)
10. Curtmola, R., Garay, J.A., Kamara, S., Ostrovsky, R.: Searchable symmetric encryption: improved definitions and efficient constructions. In: Proceedings of the 13th ACM Conference on Computer and Communications Security, Alexandria, Virginia, USA, pp. 79–88 (November 2006)
11. Goh, E.J.: Secure indexes. IACR Cryptology ePrint Archive 2003, 216 (2003)
12. Goldreich, O.: Foundations of Cryptography. Basic Applications, vol. 2. Cambridge University Press (2004)
13. Golle, P., Staddon, J., Waters, B.: Secure conjunctive keyword search over encrypted data. In: Jakobsson, M., Yung, M., Zhou, J. (eds.) ACNS 2004. LNCS, vol. 3089, pp. 31–45. Springer, Heidelberg (2004)
14. Hwang, Y.-H., Lee, P.J.: Public key encryption with conjunctive keyword search and its extension to a multi-user system. In: Takagi, T., Okamoto, T., Okamoto, E., Okamoto, T. (eds.) Pairing 2007. LNCS, vol. 4575, pp. 2–22. Springer, Heidelberg (2007)
15. Kamara, S., Papamanthou, C., Roeder, T.: Dynamic searchable symmetric encryption. In: Proceedings of the 19th ACM Conference on Computer and Communications Security, Raleigh, North Carolina, USA, pp. 965–976 (October 2012)
16. van Liesdonk, P., Sedghi, S., Doumen, J., Hartel, P., Jonker, W.: Computationally efficient searchable symmetric encryption. In: Jonker, W., Petković, M. (eds.) SDM 2010. LNCS, vol. 6358, pp. 87–100. Springer, Heidelberg (2010)
17. Moataz, T., Shikfa, A.: Boolean symmetric searchable encryption. In: Proceedings of the 8th ACM Symposium on Information, Computer and Communications Security, Hangzhou, China, pp. 265–276 (May 2013)

18. Park, D.J., Kim, K., Lee, P.J.: Public key encryption with conjunctive field keyword search. In: Lim, C.H., Yung, M. (eds.) WISA 2004. LNCS, vol. 3325, pp. 73–86. Springer, Heidelberg (2005)
19. Ryu, E.K., Takagi, T.: Efficient conjunctive keyword-searchable encryption. In: Proceedings of the 21st International Conference on Advanced Information Networking and Applications, Niagara Falls, Canada, pp. 409–414 (May 2007)
20. Song, D.X., Wagner, D., Perrig, A.: Practical techniques for searches on encrypted data. In: Proceedings of the 21st IEEE Symposium on Security and Privacy, Berkeley, California, USA, pp. 44–55 (May 2000)
21. Sun, W., Wang, B., Cao, N., Li, M., Lou, W., Hou, Y.T., Li, H.: Privacy-preserving multi-keyword text search in the cloud supporting similarity-based ranking. In: Proceedings of the 8th ACM Symposium on Information, Computer and Communications Security, Hangzhou, China, pp. 71–82 (May 2013)
22. Wang, P., Wang, H., Pieprzyk, J.: An efficient scheme of common secure indices for conjunctive keyword-based retrieval on encrypted data. In: Chung, K.-I., Sohn, K., Yung, M. (eds.) WISA 2008. LNCS, vol. 5379, pp. 145–159. Springer, Heidelberg (2009)

Secure and Privacy-Preserving Querying of Personal Health Records in the Cloud

Samira Barouti, Feras Aljumah, Dima Alhadidi, and Mourad Debbabi

Concordia Institute for Information Systems Engineering (CIISE)
Concordia University, Montreal, Canada

Abstract. Personal Health Records (PHR) are user-friendly, online so-lutions that give patients a way of managing their own health informa-tion. Many of the current PHR systems allow storage providers to access patients' data. Recently, architectures of storing PHRs in cloud have been proposed. However, privacy remains a major issue for patients. Conse-quently, it is a promising method to encrypt PHRs before outsourcing. Encrypting PHRs prevents health organizations from analyzing medi-cal data. In this paper, we propose a protocol that would allow health organizations to produce statistical information about encrypted PHRs stored in the cloud. The protocol depends on two threshold homomorphic cryptosystems: Goldwasser-Micali (GM) and Paillier. It executes queries on Kd-trees that are constructed from encrypted health records. It also prevents patients from inferring what health organizations are concerned about. We experimentally evaluate the performance of the proposed pro-tocol and report on the results of implementation.

1 Introduction

Electronic health records are usually managed by different healthcare providers including primary care physicians, therapists, hospitals and pharmacies. Conse-quently, it is difficult to get a single patients history due to the fact that it is spread between multiple providers. It has become a recent trend for patients to take these matters into their own hands by managing their own records using a Personal Health Record (PHR) system. PHRs systems allow patients to man-age their medical data, giving them the ability to create, view, edit, or share their medical records with other users in the system as well as with healthcare providers [1]. In the past few years, many providers have created platforms to manage PHRs with features including flexible access control, mobile access, and complex automated diagnoses that analyze PHRs and alert patients when a pre-ventive checkup is needed. These providers include Microsoft HealthVault [2] and Dossia [3]. Due to the sensitivity nature of health data, security concerns have prevented many patients from using PHR systems. Many of the providers of the current PHR systems have the ability to access all patient records.

Recently, architectures for storing PHRs in the cloud have been proposed [1]. However, this does not solve the privacy problem and the latter remains an issue for many patients. Since these records are stored on cloud servers, it means

V. Atluri and G. Pernul (Eds.): DBSec 2014, LNCS 8566, pp. 82–97, 2014.

that these servers have the ability to read any medical record in the system. In addition, if an attacker is able to compromise a cloud server, then all the PHRs would be exposed. For these reasons, researchers have begun searching for a way to allow patients storing their medical records in the cloud using a Database-as-a-Service (DaaS) model while preserving their privacy. DaaS is a category of cloud computing services that enables IT providers to deliver database functionality as a service. Encrypting PHRs before outsourcing appears to be a promising solution in this domain. However, it prevents health organizations from analyzing medical data for research purposes. To better understand what caused a disease, health organizations and researchers need as much data as possible about the infected patients.

In this paper, we propose a protocol that allows health organizations producing statistical information about encrypted PHRs stored in the cloud. The proposed protocol also does not enable patients to infer about what health organizations are concerned about; not to worry or panic patients targeted by the queries. Intuitively, the proposed protocol works as follows: Patients are organized in small groups. The patients of a given group jointly generate public keys for encryption. They later encrypt their PHRs using their public keys and send the ciphertext to the cloud server. Encrypted records are stored in Kd-trees constructed by the cloud server for each group. To execute SQL queries, Kd-trees are traversed in the cloud server. Finally, the cloud server aggregates the results and sends the final query result to the health organization. However, realizing this seemingly simple system presents a number of significant challenges. First, the search should be performed on encrypted records. To achieve this, our proposed protocol depends on the homomorphic properties of two semantically-secure encryption schemes. Using homomorphic schemes, specific operations can be performed on the encrypted records directly without the need for decryption. More specifically, query predicates are evaluated using the Goldwasser-Micali (GM) cryptosystem [4] and Fischlins protocol [5] whereas query aggregate functions are computed using Paillier cryptosystem [6]. Second, the engagement of the patients in the protocol execution should be minimal. We achieve this by using threshold cryptosystems such that the decryption process is performed by a specific number of patients, namely the threshold k.

The contributions of our paper can be summarized as follows:

- We propose a protocol, which allows health organizations producing statistical information about PHRs stored in the cloud and encrypted using semantically-secure encryption schemes. The main characteristics of the protocol are the following:
  - It preserves the privacy of health organizations and patients.
  - It supports aggregate queries such *count, sum, max* and *min*.
- We design and implement a prototype of the proposed protocol and we also report on the experimental results.

The rest of the paper is organized as follows. Section 2 discusses the execution environment. Section 3 briefly overviews the literature that the proposed solution depends on. Section 4 presents a protocol to find the maximum/minimum value of encrypted inputs without resorting to deterministic encryption schemes. In Section 5, the proposed protocol is presented. The security and complexity analysis of the protocol as well as the experimental results are discussed in Section 6. Section 7 presents the related work. Finally, concluding remarks as well as a discussion of future work are presented in Section 8.

2   Execution Environment

In this section, we first identify the involved entities. Then, we present the assumptions underlying the system design.

2.1   Entities

There are three main entities: (1) *Patients* who own health records and want to store them on a cloud server while keeping them confidential from the cloud server and health organizations. A common way to protect health records stored on cloud servers is through encryption, (2) *Cloud server* that stores the encrypted health records of the patients and executes the queries of the health organization over the encrypted records. The cloud server will assign an assisting server to each group. The assisting server is a cloud computing instance, which will be responsible for storing the encrypted records of the patients and executing the SQL queries of the health organization, (3) *Health organization* that execute queries over the encrypted records of the patients and produce statistical information.

2.2   Assumptions

We assume that there is no fully trusted entity in the environment and all entities are semi-honest. Semi-honest adversaries follow the protocol steps, but they try to extract information about other entities' input or output. This is a common security assumption used in secure multiparty computation literature [7] and it is realistic in our problem scenario since different organizations are collaborating for mutual benefits. Hence, it is reasonable to assume that parties will not

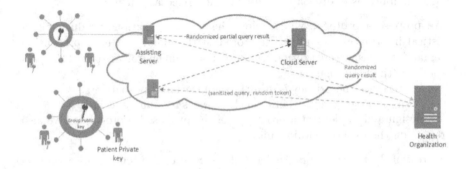

Fig. 1. System Architecture

deviate from the defined protocol. However, they may be curious to learn additional information from the messages they receive during protocol execution. The cloud server and the assisting servers are modeled as "honest but curious" in the sense that they will execute requests correctly, but they are not reliable to maintain data confidentiality. Regarding query privacy, we assume that the shape of SQL queries submitted by health organizations is public whereas the constants contained in the query predicates are private [8, 9]. We also assume that there is no collusion between the different parties and that there are mechanisms that ensure integrity and availability of the remotely stored data. Our scheme focuses only on confidentiality and privacy issues and does not provide protection against attacks such as data tampering and denial of service.

3 Building Blocks

Homomorphic Encryption: It is a form of encryption where a specific algebraic operation performed on the plaintext is equivalent to another (possibly different) algebraic operation performed on the ciphertext. The Paillier's scheme [6] is an additive homomorphic public key encryption. Using Paillier's scheme, given two ciphertexts $E(x)$ and $E(y)$, an encryption of their sum $E(x+y)$ can be efficiently computed by multiplying the ciphertexts modulo a public key N, i.e., $E(x + y) = E(x).E(y) \mod N$. The Goldwasser-Micali (GM) cryptosystem is a semantically-secure scheme based on the quadratic residuosity problem. It has XOR homomorphic properties, in the sense that $E(b) . E(b') = E(b \oplus b') \mod N$ where b and b' are bits and N is the public key. Variations of the homomorphic Paillier and GM cryptosystems are the distributed threshold decryption schemes in which the decryption is performed by a group of participants, rather than one party [10, 11]. In this case, each participant would obtain a share of the secret key by executing the distributed key generation algorithm detailed in [12].

Private Comparison: Yao's classical millionaires' problem [13] involves two millionaires who wish to know who is richer. However, they do not want to find out inadvertently any additional information about each other's wealth. More formally, given two input values x and y, which are held as private inputs by two parties respectively, the problem is to securely evaluate the Greater Than (GT) condition $x > y$ without exposing inputs. In this paper, we employ Fischlin's protocol [5] for the private comparison because it allows us to compare two ciphertexts encrypted with the GM crytosystem using the same public key. Fischlin's protocol takes as input two ciphertexts encrypted using GM cryptosystem and produces ciphertext sequences, namely Δ and c that are encrypted by the same public key. The decryption of these sequences would reveal the result of comparing the private inputs without revealing anything beyond the result of the comparison. Fischlin's protocol utilizes the XOR-homomorphic GM cryptosystem to privately compute:

$$x > y \iff \bigvee_{i=1}^{n} \left(x_i \wedge \neg y_i \wedge \bigwedge_{j=i+1}^{n} (x_j = y_j) \right)$$
$$\iff \bigoplus_{i=1}^{n} \left(x_i \wedge \neg y_i \wedge \bigwedge_{j=i+1}^{n} \neg(x_i \oplus y_i) \right)$$

where $|x| = |y| = n$.

Kd-trees: Kd-trees [14] are binary trees where the keys differs between levels. Kd-trees are used extensively in searching multidimensional data, in particular database records. The normal way of constructing a balanced Kd-tree is to sort the records according to the i-th attribute and split them into left and right parts, with respect to the median element. The process is then repeated recursively on both parts taking into consideration the $(i + 1)$th attribute.

4 Secure Maximum/Minimum Computation

As a major step in our proposed protocol, we need to execute the max/min aggregate queries over encrypted records. In this section, we provide a cloud-based solution that calculates the maximum/minimum of encrypted values owned by some parties. Formally, given n inputs $v_1, \ldots, v_n$ owned by the parties $P_1, \ldots, P_n$ respectively, the cloud server wishes to securely compute $max(v_1, v_2, \ldots, v_n)$ and $min(v_1, v_2, \ldots, v_n)$. We assume that the parties are not malicious and they correctly carry out the prescribed steps. The proposed cloud-based solution relies on Fischlin's protocol [5] and the threshold GM cryptosystem [10]. We explain the technique to find the max but it can be easily modified to find the min.

Parties jointly generate the public key pk for k-out-of-n threshold GM cryptosystem such that at least k patients are required to fully decrypt a ciphertext [10]. Parties then encrypt their values and outsource them to the cloud server. The cloud server initializes the current maximum to the encryption of a small negative value with the threshold GM cryptosystem. Afterwards, the cloud compares the current maximum with the encrypted value of the party P_i using Fischlin's protocol. The outputs of Fischlin's protocol are sequences of λ elements. To decide whether the encrypted value of P_i is greater than the current maximum (If there exists a sequence of λ quadratic residues), the cloud server contacts k other parties and sends the generated sequences for them. Each party performs calculation on the sequences using her share of the factors of the public key [10] using the threshold GM decryption. The results are then submitted to the cloud server. Afterwards, the cloud server combines the results received from k parties and decide if the encrypted value of P_i is greater than the current maximum based on the quadratic residuosity of the combinations. If the output indicates that the current maximum is greater, there is no need to update the current maximum. Otherwise, the cloud server sets the current maximum to the value of P_i and repeats the same process with P_{i+1}. After comparing the current maximum with all the existing values, the cloud server sends the encrypted maximum value to k members for decryption. This idea can be extended to enable a cloud server to sort the encrypted values without knowing the secret key and the plaintexts. In this case, any comparison-based sorting algorithm can be utilized and the comparison is performed on the encrypted values by exploiting Fischlin's protocol.

5   Secure Execution of Health Queries in Cloud

In this section, we present a protocol that enables health organizations to produce statistical information about encrypted personal health records stored in the cloud server. The proposed protocol prevents patients from inferring what health organizations are concerned about. The health organization's input is an aggregate SQL query that consists of exact-matching and interval-matching predicates over multiple attributes combined with logical operators (AND/OR/NOT). The cloud server's input is the encrypted health records of the patients. The naive approach to achieve these objectives is that the health organization communicates with each patient and securely evaluates queries on her record. This can be achieved by exploiting Fischlin's protocol for private comparison. However, this approach incurs excessive communication and computation overhead on the health organization side that is linear to the number of patients.

To reduce this overhead, patients are organized into smaller groups. The patients in each group jointly generate two public keys for Goldwasser-Micali [4] and Paillier [6] encryption schemes. Then, they encrypt their records and outsource them to the cloud server for storage. The cloud server assigns an assisting server to each group. Assisting servers are responsible for securely executing health organization's queries on the database of each group to obtain partial results. Assisting servers then collaborate to combine the partial results into the query result and report it to the health organization. In the following, we elaborate the basic steps of our protocol that protects the data privacy of patients and the query privacy of the health organization.

5.1   Key Generation and Tree Construction

Assuming the total number of N patients, the cloud server defines $L = \lfloor \sqrt{N} \rfloor$ groups. It then randomly maps and assigns each patient into exactly one group. Let $n = \lceil \frac{N}{L} \rceil$ denotes the number of patients in each group. The cloud server assigns an assisting server to each group, which is responsible for executing health organizations' queries over the medical database of patients. Assisting servers collaborate with each other to obtain the query result from the partial results and send it to the health organization. In the i-th group, the patients execute the distributed key generation algorithms for the threshold Paillier and the threshold GM cryptosystems to obtain the public keys pk_i' and pk_i for Paillier and GM cryptosystems. We utilize the protocols explained in [10] and [15] for the threshold GM and the threshold Paillier cryptosystems, respectively. These protocols depend on distributed RSA key-generation protocols [16, 12] without the need to a trusted dealer. Following the execution of the key-generation protocols, each patient obtains a single public key and a share of the secret key. The threshold cryptosystems enable the patients to encrypt their record with a single public key while at least a minimal number of patients are required to decrypt a ciphertext.

Example 1. Consider health records with the attributes *Age* and *Surgery*, where the value of *Surgery* specifies the type of the surgery that a patient undergoes (e.g. 1: Transgender, 2: Plastic, 3:Vascular, 4: Urology). The total number of patients is $N = 10$; therefore, these patients are organized in $L = \lfloor\sqrt{10}\rfloor = 3$ groups, namely, G_1, G_2 and G_3. Assume that patients 1,9 and 10 are assigned to G_1; patients 2, 4, 5 and 8 to G_2 and patients 3, 6 and 7 to G_3, randomly. Furthermore, the patients in the group G_i jointly generate the public key pk_i and pk_i' for the GM and the Paillier cryptosystems, respectively. The members of G_i encrypt their records with pk_i and pk_i' as presented in Fig. 2. The encrypted tables are then outsourced to the cloud server.

To store the shares of a secret key, we assume the secret key is stored on secure hardware such as FPGA [17]. These devices are designed in such a way that after a patient places a key into the on-board key memory on the device, it cannot be read externally. After the secret key of each patient and the group public keys (for Paillier and GM cryptosystems) have been written, the FPGA can be delivered to the cloud operator for installation.

Table 1. Health Records

	Age	Surgery
Patient 1	34	1
Patient 2	39	2
Patient 3	20	1
Patient 4	59	3
Patient 5	63	4
Patient 6	27	2
Patient 7	78	4
Patient 8	11	2
Patient 9	83	3
Patient 10	42	3

	$\mathbf{Age_{GM}}$	$\mathbf{Surgery_{GM}}$	$\mathbf{Age_P}$	$\mathbf{Surgery_P}$
Patient 1	$E_{pk_1}(34)$	$E_{pk_1}(1)$	$E_{pk_1'}(34)$	$E_{pk_1'}(1)$
Patient 9	$E_{pk_1}(83)$	$E_{pk_1}(3)$	$E_{pk_1'}(83)$	$E_{pk_1'}(3)$
Patient 10	$E_{pk_1}(42)$	$E_{pk_1}(3)$	$E_{pk_1'}(42)$	$E_{pk_1'}(3)$

(a) G_1 Data set

	$\mathbf{Age_{GM}}$	$\mathbf{Surgery_{GM}}$	$\mathbf{Age_P}$	$\mathbf{Surgery_P}$
Patient 2	$E_{pk_2}(39)$	$E_{pk_2}(2)$	$E_{pk_2'}(39)$	$E_{pk_2'}(2)$
Patient 4	$E_{pk_2}(59)$	$E_{pk_2}(3)$	$E_{pk_2'}(59)$	$E_{pk_2'}(3)$
Patient 5	$E_{pk_2}(63)$	$E_{pk_2}(4)$	$E_{pk_2'}(63)$	$E_{pk_2'}(4)$
Patient 8	$E_{pk_2}(11)$	$E_{pk_2}(2)$	$E_{pk_2'}(11)$	$E_{pk_2'}(2)$

(b) G_2 Data set

	$\mathbf{Age_{GM}}$	$\mathbf{Surgery_{GM}}$	$\mathbf{Age_P}$	$\mathbf{Surgery_P}$
Patient 3	$E_{pk_3}(20)$	$E_{pk_3}(1)$	$E_{pk_3'}(20)$	$E_{pk_3'}(1)$
Patient 6	$E_{pk_3}(27)$	$E_{pk_3}(2)$	$E_{pk_3'}(27)$	$E_{pk_3'}(2)$
Patient 7	$E_{pk_3}(78)$	$E_{pk_3}(4)$	$E_{pk_3'}(78)$	$E_{pk_3'}(4)$

(c) G_3 Data set

Fig. 2. Outsourced Health Records in Groups

The patients encrypt each record using both Paillier and GM cryptosystems by the group public keys. Therefore, the encrypted record of each patient has two columns for each attribute in the database: one column that contains the encryption of the attribute value using the group public key for the threshold Paillier cryptosystem, and another column that stores the GM encryption of the attribute value using the group public key for the threshold GM cryptosystem. Finally, the cloud server assigns an assisting server to each group. Each assisting server collects the encrypted health records and organizes them as a Kd-tree, as described in Section 3.

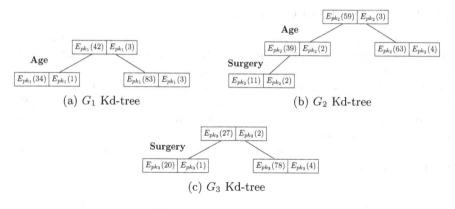

Fig. 3. Generated Kd-trees

Example 2. (Continued from Example 1) The generated Kd-trees for each group are shown in Fig. 3. The partitioning attributes in each group may be different.

5.2 Query Sanitization and Token Generation

The health organization wishes to execute an SQL query such that the constants in the predicates are not revealed to the patients and the cloud server. Therefore, the health organization sanitizes the query by replacing the constants contained in the predicates by their GM encryption using the public key of each group. Furthermore, the health organization uses a token for each group that is encrypted by the group's public key. This token can be manipulated by assisting servers to produce a noisy query result. Generating the token depends on the type of the aggregate function. For *count* and *sum*, the health organization generates L random numbers $R_1, R_2, \ldots, R_L$ such that $R = R_1 + R_2 + \ldots + R_L$. The random share R_i will be the token that is sent to the assisting server of the i-th group. For the *max* and *min*, the health organization generates a random number R as the token for all groups. The health organization then encrypts the token of each group by the Paillier cryptosystem using the group public key. The health organization forwards the sanitized query together with the encrypted token to assisting servers. Therefore, in this step the health organization should create L sanitized queries and L encrypted tokens.

Example 3. Suppose that the health organization's query is:

`SELECT MAX(Age) FROM` D `WHERE Surgery` $= 1$

The sanitized query that will be forwarded to the i-th group would be

`SELECT MAX(Age) FROM` D `WHERE Surgery` $= E_{pk_i}(1)$

In addition, since the function is *max*, the health organization generates a random number R and uses it as the token for all groups. The health organization then encrypts the token using the Paillier encryption by the public key of each group and forwards the encrypted token together with the sanitized query to the corresponding assisting server.

5.3   Tree Traversal and Query Execution

To execute the health organization's query, the assisting servers must traverse the Kd-trees, constructed from the encrypted records of the patients. To do so, the assisting servers follow the tree traversal algorithm. The search begins from the root; the assisting server uses Fischlin's protocol and the threshold GM decryption to evaluate the query predicate on the root record. Based on the result of the query evaluation, the search is continued on the left tree or the right subtree or both. At the end of this step, the assisting servers will end up with the records that satisfy the query predicate. The assisting servers then compute the encrypted query result depending on the type of the aggregate function as follows:

- $count$: The assisting server of the group G_i counts the number of records that are reported as the query result and encrypts this value using the Paillier cryptosystem with the group public key.
- sum: The assisting servers encrypt 0 (as the current sum) by the Paillier encryption using the group public key. While traversing the tree, if at each level the conditions in the query predicate are satisfied, the assisting server projects the record over the Paillier-encrypted column targeted by the aggregate function and multiplies it by the the current sum to update the query result. At the end, the assisting server will end up with the sum that is encrypted with the group public key using the threshold Paillier cryptosystem.
- max, min: Initially, the assisting servers pick up a small negative number (or a large positive in case of min) that denotes the current max/min value and encrypts it by the GM and the Paillier cryptosystems using the group public keys. GM-encrypted ciphertext is utilized for the comparison while Paillier-encrypted ciphertext is used for generating noisy query result. During the tree traversal if a record satisfies the query condition(s), the assisting server projects the record over the columns that contain the GM- and the Paillier-encryption of the record. It then executes Fischlin's protocol using the encrypted current max/min value and the GM-encrypted value, to find out if this record has greater (resp. smaller) value or not. If so, the assisting server initializes the current max/min value to the GM- and the Paillier-encrypted ciphertexts. Otherwise, the current max/min value remains unchanged. At the end, the assisting servers end up with the query result encrypted with the Paillier and GM cryptosystems. For the remaining step of the protocol, the assisting servers only need the Paillier-encrypted ciphertext.

At the end of this step, the assisting servers obtain the partial query result (that has been encrypted using the Paillier scheme by the public key of the group).

Example 4. (Continued from Example 3) Considering the Kd-trees presented in Fig. 3 and the sanitized query

$$\texttt{SELECT MAX(Age) FROM } D \texttt{ WHERE Surgery} = E_{pk'_i}(1)$$

All assisting servers receive an encrypted token $E_{pk'_i}(R)$ from the health organization. The assisting server of the group G_i extracts $E_{pk_i}(1)$ from the query and performs the point search on the Kd-tree constructed by the patients in the group G_i. The assisting servers report the records that satisfy the predicate Surgery $= E_{pk_i}(1)$ by executing Fischlin's protocol and the threshold GM cryptosystem. The record of Patient 1 in G_1 and the record of Patient 3 in G_3 satisfy the predicate. Therefore, the output of the tree traversal for the assisting servers of the groups G_1, G_2 and G_3 will be $\{E_{pk_1}(34), E_{pk'_1}(34)\}$, $\{E_{pk_2}(-1000), E_{pk'_2}(-1000)\}$ and $\{E_{pk_3}(20), E_{pk'_3}(20)\}$, respectively. The resulted outputs will be projected over the column Age_P to obtain $\{E_{pk'_1}(34)\}$, $\{E_{pk'_2}(-1000)\}$ and $\{E_{pk'_3}(20)\}$ as the encrypted query result.

5.4   Query Result Decryption

So far, the assisting servers have obtained the encrypted partial query result, which we will call group results from now on. Therefore, the assisting servers must collaborate with each other to compute the final query result and submit it to the health organization. The group results are encrypted with different keys. Therefore, in order to compute the final query result, the group results must be in plaintext. The assisting servers first obfuscate the group results because they are not willing to reveal these results to each other. The obfuscation is performed by the mean of multiplying the group result by the encrypted token, sent by the health organization (both of them are ciphertexts generated by the same key under the Paillier cryptosystem). The obfuscation allows the assisting servers to collaborate with each other to calculate the noisy query result while hiding the actual group result. In addition, since the noise is generated by the health organization, it allows the health organization to recover the actual query result from the noisy query result. Afterwards, each assisting server decrypts the noisy group result that is encrypted by the Paillier cryptosystem by contacting patients in its group. The assisting servers then need to obtain the final noisy query result by aggregating their group results. In this context, the assisting servers send the noisy group results in plaintext to the cloud server. The cloud server then aggregates the partial noisy query results to obtain the noisy query result. In the case of *count* and *sum*, the cloud server adds up all the group results and submits the summation to the health organization. In the case of max and min aggregate functions, the cloud server executes the *maximum/minimum* algorithm on the plaintexts and sends the resulted value to the health organization. Notice that the noise generated for obfuscating the *maximum/minimum* of all groups is the same, therefore it will not affect the algorithm correctness (i.e., if $a < b$ then $a + R < b + R$). Finally, the health organization in its turn subtracts the noise and obtains the query result.

Example 5. (Continued from Example 4) We have seen that the result of executing the SQL query

SELECT MAX(Age) FROM D WHERE Surgery $= 1$

on the groups G_1, G_2 and G_3 was $\{E_{pk'_1}(34)\}$, $\{E_{pk'_2}(-1000)\}$ and $\{E_{pk'_3}(20)\}$ respectively. Moreover, the token sent by the health organization to the i-th group is $E_{pk'_i}(R)$. The assisting servers multiply the received token $E^R_{pk'_i}$ by all records in the encrypted query result to obtain the encrypted noisy query result, i.e., $\{E_{pk_1'}(34 + R)\}$, $\{E_{pk_2'}(-1000 + R)\}$ and $\{E_{pk_3'}(20 + R)\}$. The assisting servers then decrypt these ciphertexts to obtain $34 + R$, $-1000 + R$ and $20 + R$. They send their noisy plaintexts to the cloud server. The cloud server executes the maximum algorithm on the $34 + R$, $-1000 + R$ and $20 + R$ and eventually ends up with $34 + R$ as the maximum. The cloud server forwards $34 + R$ to the health organization. The health organization subtracts the noise R to obtain 34 as the result of executing the SQL query on the medical database.

6   Security and Efficiency Analysis

6.1   Security Analysis

Assuming the semi-honest adversary model and no collusion between the patients, the security of the protocol depends on the steps where the parties exchange information and it is conducted as follows:

- *Health organization-Cloud server*: The health organization sends the sanitized query and the token that are encrypted by the semantically-secure encryption schemes using patients' public keys. Therefore, the cloud server is not able to decrypt it [4, 6].
- *Patient-Cloud server*. The patients sends their medical records, encrypted using semantically-secure encryption schemes that are secure against semi-honest adversary [4, 6].
- *Cloud server-Patient*. The cloud server communicates with the patients in order to execute Fischlin's protocol, that is proven to be secure in the presence of semi-honest adversaries [5, 10, 11].
- *Assisting servers*. The interactions between assisting servers are required to aggregate the noisy group results and acquire the randomized final query result. Since the query results have been randomized by a number that is generated by the health organization, the assisting servers are not able to extract the actual query results from the noisy results.

Moreover, the output of each subprotocol is the input to another subprototcol. Therefore, according to the Composition Theorem [18], the entire protocol is secure. The main concern with threshold cryptosystems comes from the collusion attack. We address in the following the possible attacks resulted from the collusion between the different parties. The threshold decryption will be compromised if the number of colluding clients under the control of an adversary exceeds the threshold k. Any collusion that contains less than k patients in each group cannot learn any information about the ciphertext sequences Δ and c, generated for comparison as well as constants in the query of the health organization. The most serious collusion attacks are when: (i) the cloud server colludes with more than k patients in each group to recover the encrypted database records, (ii) the cloud server and at least k patients in any group collude to infer constants in the query. In practice, we can increase the threshold k such that attackers will not be able to compromise too many patients. Despite simplicity, this mechanism has

Table 2. Communication and Computation Cost

Health Organization		Assisting Servers	
Communication	Computation	Communication	Computation
$O(\sqrt{N})$	$O(k\sqrt{N})$	$O(kT(N))$	$O(kT(N))$

two disadvantages: First, the number of the required online patients is increased. Second, the communication cost on the assisting servers is increased because they need to communicate with more parties for decryption. Therefore, there should be a trade-off between availability/efficiency and security by choosing a proper value for k.

It should be noted that the proposed protocol does not protect the privacy of patients from being identified through the query result. There is a significant body of works on distributed privacy preserving data mining (e.g. constructing decision trees [19] and differential privacy [20–22]) that provide a rich and useful set of tools to protect the record owner (i.e., patients) from being identified through query results. They allow a trusted server to release obfuscated answers to aggregate queries to avoid leaking information about any specific record in the database. Such works have a different goal and model and can be added as a front end in the proposed protocol to provide privacy-preserving answers to the health organization's queries.

6.2 Complexity Analysis

Let N denotes the number of patients in a PHR system. These patients are organized into L groups and each group contains $n = \frac{N}{L}$ patients. Recall that the execution time of range queries, exact matching queries and partial matching queries on a Kd-tree with $\sqrt{N}$ records, will be $O(N^{0.5-1/2d} + m)$, $O(\log N)$ and $O(N^{0.5-s/2d} + m)$, respectively [23] where d is the number of the attributes in the table, s is the number of attributes in the query predicate and m denotes the number of records, reported as the query result. The communication and the computation cost of the protocol is summarized in Table 2 where $T(N)$ indicates the execution time of different types of queries (e.g., exact-matching, partial matching and range matching). The most communication- and computation-intensive operation on the assisting servers is the tree traversal.

6.3 Performance Evaluation

To evaluate the performance of the proposed protocol, we implement a prototype relying on some existing open source projects [24] in Java 1.6. The secret keys p and q of the GM cryptosystem are 256-bit long. Moreover, we employ the publicly available *Breast Cancer* dataset [25]. It has 286 records with 9 categorical attributes. The patient's and the server's side experiments are conducted on an Intel core i5 2.3GHz notebook with 4GB of RAM. The number of patients in each group is fixed at $L = 286$ leading to approximately $81,800$ patients in the PHR system. The shares of the secret key are stored on FPGAs. Decrypting a ciphertext by the cloud server is performed by sending a ciphertext to the FPGAs. Since the communication is intra-site, we ignore communication delays in the performance evaluation.

To understand the source of the overhead, we measure the query execution time for different types of aggregate SQL queries, but running with only one core enabled. The result is presented in Table 3 and Fig. 4. When k is small, the query time is dominated by Fischlin's protocol, which is independent from the threshold k. Therefore, there is a small difference in the query time when $k = 36$ and $k = 71$. However, as k increases the effect of the threshold decryption becomes more visible and the execution time starts to grow. According to a similar analysis, for small values of k there is a small change in the execution time but as k increases the query time becomes linear with k. Finally, we calculate the execution time of an arbitrary SQL query $k = \frac{n}{4} = 71$. In addition, the execution time of a query heavily depends on the number of comparisons that are performed to traverse the Kd-tree. Therefore, we consider three different scenarios: (1) the worst case scenario is when evaluating predicates targeting a single attribute for interval matching such that all the tree nodes are traversed, (2) the best case scenario is when evaluating predicates targeting all attributes for exact matching, and (3) the real-world scenario is when evaluating predicates targeting multiple attributes for range and exact matching predicates. In the worst case, the time required to evaluate the predicate is 110 seconds (approximately 2 minutes) for each group, whereas in the best case it is 0.3 seconds. In the real-world scenario, we derive the execution time of a SQL query that contains interval matching and exact matching predicates. For each type of predicate, we execute four SQL queries with different number of attributes. The results are presented in Fig. 5. The results indicate that as the number of attributes in the query increases, the execution time decreases due to the smaller search space and the reduction of the number of comparisons. Our experimental results indicate that the proposed protocol would work well with medium size databases (with a total number of 100,000-400,000 patients) and the queries that contain multiple attributes. These results are from a straightforward implementation of the proposed protocol. Further optimizations may lead to a better performance. It is worth to mention that health organizations do not frequently conduct statistical studies on the medical databases (every month or when there is a pandemic). Therefore, the performance of the protocol is acceptable for this type of applications whose goal is to perform search while the absolute privacy of the patients and the health organization is preserved.

Table 3. Assisting server latency for different types of SQL queries ($k = \frac{n}{4} = 71$)

Query	Query Time(ms)
Select by $=$	41.93
Select range	216.14
Select sum	33.02
Select max/min	217.32

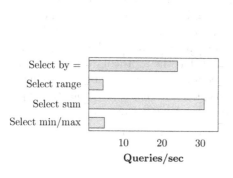

Fig. 4. Query Time

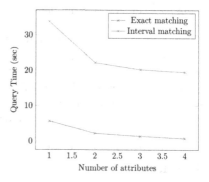

Fig. 5. SQL Query Time (Exact Matching vs Interval Matching)

7 Related Work

Private database outsourcing deals with the problem of hiding database records from an untrusted service provider. To ensure the security and privacy of the data stored in the cloud, most existing approaches rely on encryption [26]. However, using cryptography as a means to protect privacy causes new problems, such as querying the encrypted data. Previous work in querying encrypted data is divided into two categories, one that assumes the existence of a trusted server [27], and another that assumes that the server is semi-trusted [28, 29].Hacigumus *et al.* [28] suggested the addition of secure indexes in each tuple. Although these techniques have been proposed to secure databases hosted in the cloud, they cannot be adopted for this problem for several reasons. First, to evaluate the query on the encrypted data, the health organization must encrypt the query by the same scheme and the same key that are used by the patients and send it to the cloud server. It then forwards the encrypted query to the patients, where the query can be decrypted by the encryption key. Second, a common approach in the existing research proposals is to send a set of encrypted records to the client for filtration and further processing [28, 30]. Therefore, the cloud server may reveal extra information beyond the query result to the client.

Thus, the proposed techniques for secure database outsourcing will not protect the query privacy and the database privacy. Recently, CryptDB [31] has been proposed to execute SQL queries over encrypted data. It depends on a fully trusted component that maintains all the secret and public keys and transforms the users' SQL queries to ones that can be executed over encrypted records. CryptDB has low overhead on query execution time; however, it requires a fully trusted component which is the single point of attack.

8 Conclusion

In this paper, we have presented a protocol that allows executing various types of SQL queries on PHRs stored in the cloud while preserving the privacy of the patients and the health organization as well. The health records are encrypted using probabilistic encryption schemes, which are semantically secure. The protocol supports aggregate, exact matching and range matching queries. It is based on Fischlin's protocol for private comparison and on two threshold cryptosystems. The implementation result has indicated that the protocol works well with medium size databases and the queries that contain multiple attributes. We have shown that we can execute queries over encrypted data using probabilistic cryptosystems. This opens the door for more research for efficiency in this domain.

References

1. Löhr, H., Sadeghi, A., Winandy, M.: Securing the e-health cloud. In: Proceedings of the International Health Informatics Symposium, IHI 2010, pp. 220–229. ACM (2010)
2. Microsoft health vault, http://www.healthvault.com/Personal/index.html (accessed March 2013)
3. Dossia personal health platform, http://www.dossia.org/ (accessed March 2013)
4. Goldwasser, S., Micali, S.: Probabilistic Encryption & How To Play Mental Poker Keeping Secret All Partial Information. In: Proceedings of the 14th Annual ACM Symposium on Theory of Computing, STOC 1982, pp. 365–377 (1982)
5. Fischlin, M.: A cost-effective pay-per-multiplication comparison method for millionaires. In: Naccache, D. (ed.) CT-RSA 2001. LNCS, vol. 2020, pp. 457–472. Springer, Heidelberg (2001)
6. Paillier, P.: Public-Key Cryptosystems Based on Composite Degree Residuosity Classes. In: Stern, J. (ed.) EUROCRYPT 1999. LNCS, vol. 1592, pp. 223–238. Springer, Heidelberg (1999)
7. Jiang, W., Clifton, C.: A Secure Distributed Framework for Achieving k-Anonymity. The VLDB Journal 15(4), 316–333 (2006)
8. Olumofin, F., Goldberg, I.: Privacy-preserving queries over relational databases. In: Atallah, M.J., Hopper, N.J. (eds.) PETS 2010. LNCS, vol. 6205, pp. 75–92. Springer, Heidelberg (2010)
9. Barouti, S., Alhadidi, D., Debbabi, M.: Symmetrically-Private Database Search in Cloud Computing. In: Proceedings of the 5th IEEE International Conference on Cloud Computing Technology and Science, vol. 1, pp. 671–678 (December 2013)
10. Katz, J., Yung, M.: Threshold Cryptosystems Based on Factoring. In: Zheng, Y. (ed.) ASIACRYPT 2002. LNCS, vol. 2501, pp. 192–205. Springer, Heidelberg (2002)
11. Barnett, A., Smart, N.P.: Mental Poker Revisited. In: Paterson, K.G. (ed.) Cryptography and Coding 2003. LNCS, vol. 2898, pp. 370–383. Springer, Heidelberg (2003)
12. Boneh, D., Franklin, M.: Efficient Generation of Shared RSA Keys. J. ACM 48(4), 702–722 (2001)
13. Yao, A.C.: Protocols for Secure Computations. In: Proceedings of the 23rd Annual Symposium on Foundations of Computer Science, SFCS 1982, pp. 160–164. IEEE Computer Society (1982)
14. Bentley, J.L.: Multidimensional binary search trees used for associative searching. Commumications of the ACM 18(9), 509–517 (1975)

15. Nishide, T., Sakurai, K.: Distributed Paillier Cryptosystem without Trusted Dealer. In: Chung, Y., Yung, M. (eds.) WISA 2010. LNCS, vol. 6513, pp. 44–60. Springer, Heidelberg (2011)

16. Frankel, Y., MacKenzie, P.D., Yung, M.: Robust Efficient Distributed RSA-Key Generation. In: Proceedings of the 13th Annual ACM Symposium on Theory of Computing, STOC 1998, pp. 663–672. ACM (1998)

17. Eguro, K., Venkatesan, R.: FPGAs for Trusted Cloud Computing. In: FPL, pp. 63–70 (2012)

18. Goldreich, O.: Foundations of Cryptography, vol. 2. Cambridge University Press (2001)

19. Lindell, Y., Pinkas, B.: Privacy Preserving Data Mining. In: Bellare, M. (ed.) CRYPTO 2000. LNCS, vol. 1880, pp. 36–54. Springer, Heidelberg (2000)

20. Dwork, C.: Differential Privacy: A Survey of Results. In: Agrawal, M., Du, D.-Z., Duan, Z., Li, A. (eds.) TAMC 2008. LNCS, vol. 4978, pp. 1–19. Springer, Heidelberg (2008)

21. McSherry, F.D.: Privacy Integrated Queries: An Extensible Platform for Privacy-Preserving Data Analysis. In: Proceedings of the 2009 SIGMOD International Conference on Management of Data, pp. 19–30. ACM (2009)

22. Roy, I., Setty, S.T.V., Kilzer, A., Shmatikov, V., Witchel, E.: Airavat: Security and Privacy for MapReduce. In: Proceedings of the 7th USENIX Conference on Networked Systems Design and Implementation, NSDI 2010, pp. 297–312. USENIX Association (2010)

23. de Berg, M., Cheong, O., van Kreveld, M., Overmars, M.: Computational Geometry: Algorithms and Applications. Springer-Verlag TELOS (2008)

24. Geisler, M.J.B.: Cryptographic Protocols: Theory and Implementation. PhD thesis, Aarhus Universitet, [Enhedsstruktur før 1.7. 2011] Aarhus University, Det Naturvidenskabelige Fakultet Faculty of Science, Datalogisk InstitutDepartment of Computer Science (2010)

25. UCI Machine Learning Repository: Breast Cancer Data Set (April 2012), http://archive.ics.uci.edu/ml/datasets/Breast+Cancer

26. Sion, R.: Secure data outsourcing. In: Proceedings of the Conference on Very Large Data Bases, VLDB 2007, pp. 1431–1432 (2007)

27. Iyer, B., Mehrotra, S., Mykletun, E., Tsudik, G., Wu, Y.: A framework for efficient storage security in RDBMS. In: Bertino, E., Christodoulakis, S., Plexousakis, D., Christophides, V., Koubarakis, M., Böhm, K. (eds.) EDBT 2004. LNCS, vol. 2992, pp. 147–164. Springer, Heidelberg (2004)

28. Hacıgümüş, H., Iyer, B., Mehrotra, S.: Efficient execution of aggregation queries over encrypted relational databases. In: Lee, Y., Li, J., Whang, K.-Y., Lee, D. (eds.) DASFAA 2004. LNCS, vol. 2973, pp. 125–136. Springer, Heidelberg (2004)

29. Agrawal, R., Kiernan, J., Srikant, R., Xu, Y.: Order preserving encryption for numeric data. In: Proceedings of the 2004 ACM SIGMOD International Conference on Management of Data, SIGMOD 2004, pp. 563–574. ACM, New York (2004)

30. Hore, B., Mehrotra, S., Tsudik, G.: A privacy-preserving index for range queries. In: Proceedings of the International Conference on Very Large Data Bases, VLDB 2004, vol. 30, pp. 720–731. VLDB Endowment (2004)

31. Popa, R.A., Redfield, C.M.S., Zeldovich, N., Balakrishnan, H.: CryptDB: Protecting confidentiality with encrypted query processing. In: Proceedings of the ACM Symposium on Operating Systems Principles, pp. 85–100 (2011)

Data Leakage Quantification*

Sokratis Vavilis[1], Milan Petković[1,2], and Nicola Zannone[1]

[1] Eindhoven University of Technology, The Netherlands
{s.vavilis,m.petkovic,n.zannone}@tue.nl
[2] Philips Research Europe, High Tech Campus, The Netherlands
milan.petkovic@philips.com

Abstract. The detection and handling of data leakages is becoming a critical issue for organizations. To this end, data leakage solutions are usually employed by organizations to monitor network traffic and the use of portable storage devices. These solutions often produce a large number of alerts, whose analysis is time-consuming and costly for organizations. To effectively handle leakage incidents, organizations should be able to focus on the most severe incidents. Therefore, alerts need to be prioritized with respect to their severity. This work presents a novel approach for the quantification of data leakages based on their severity. The approach quantifies leakages with respect to the amount and sensitivity of the leaked information as well as the ability to identify the data subjects of the leaked information. To specify and reason on data sensitivity in an application domain, we propose a data model representing the knowledge in the domain. We validate our approach by analyzing data leakages within a healthcare environment.

Keywords: Data Leakage Detection, Severity Metrics, Data Sensitivity Model.

1 Introduction

In the recent years the number of data breaches reported by public and private organizations has increased sharply. For instance, a study from Ponemon Institute in 2012 showed that 94% of US hospitals suffered serious data breaches [1]. The main cause is that IT systems often implement inadequate measures that allow users to have access on sensitive data, which they are not authorized to access. The problem is that it may not be always possible to specify fine-grained access control policies to protect from the disclosure of data. For example, access control policies in hospitals often do not pose restrictions on the amount of health records that doctors can access. Moreover, access to information should not be restricted under certain circumstances. For instance, doctors should be able to access patient records to face an emergency. Typically, this is addressed using the break-the-glass protocol [2], which allows users to bypass security mechanisms, thus leading to potential data misuse.

Timely detection and management of data leakages is becoming a serious challenge for organizations. According to the newly proposed EU data protection regulation, organizations are obliged to notify privacy authorities within 24 hours after the detection of a data breach [3]. To detect data leakages, organizations usually deploy data leakage

---

* This work has been funded by the Dutch national program COMMIT under the THeCS project.

V. Atluri and G. Pernul (Eds.): DBSec 2014, LNCS 8566, pp. 98–113, 2014.

detection (DLD) solutions. These solutions analyze the disclosed data and raise an alert when a leakage is detected. However, the number of alerts can be huge in certain situations, making difficult their analysis and management. For example, in hospitals a DLD solution might produce a large number of alerts due to the usage of the break-the-glass protocol. Before taking any action (e.g., notifying authorities), organizations typically evaluate a sample of the alerts manually. To effectively manage and mitigate the damage due to security incidents, organizations should be able to focus on the most severe incidents. To this end, data leakages should be quantified based on their severity.

Data leakage quantification, however, has not been properly addressed in the literature. Many proposals [4–6] are founded on quantitative information flow. In particular, they quantify data leakages in terms of the number of "sensitive" bits which have been disclosed. Thereby, they do not consider the semantics of the leaked information in the assessment of data leakages. From our knowledge, only M-Score [7] assesses the severity of data leakages on the basis of the semantics of the leaked information. In particular, M-Score uses the amount and sensitivity of leaked information as well as an identifiability factor to measure the severity of leakages. The amount and sensitivity of leaked information characterize the "quantity" and "quality" aspects of the leakage. These aspects are weighted with respect to the identifiability factor which represents the ability to obtain the identity of the individuals to whom the leaked data refer. However, M-Score requires defining the sensitivity for all pieces of information explicitly. Such a task is time-consuming and error-prone. In addition, M-Score is not able to accurately distinguish data leakages (see Section 7.2).

In this work we propose a novel approach to quantify data leakages on the basis of the content of the leaked information. In particular, we make the following contributions: (i) a new metric that evaluates the severity of data leakages based on the amount and sensitivity of the leaked data and an identifiability factor; (ii) a data model representing the knowledge of an application domain to specify and reason on the sensitivity of the information in the domain. Our metric uses the same factors used by M-Score. However, compared to M-Score, our metric provides a more accurate discrimination of data leakages with respect to their severity. In addition, differently from M-Score, our approach does not require specifying the sensitivity for every piece of information characterizing the application domain explicitly. The data model makes it possible to infer the sensitivity of every piece of information through a sensitivity propagation mechanism based on a small initial sensitivity assignment.

We validate our approach by analyzing a sample scenario in the healthcare domain. Healthcare is indeed an interesting domain to investigate as a large amount of sensitive data, such as patient healthcare records, has to be protected. Based on a given scenario, a group of security experts was asked to evaluate the severity of a number of data leakages. The severity measurements calculated using our metric have been analyzed against the evaluation provided by the security experts.

The remainder of the paper is organized as follows. The next section discusses related work. Section 3 motivates the need of approaches for data leakage quantification using a running example in the healthcare domain. Section 4 presents an overview of our approach. Section 5 defines the data model along with the machinery to reason on data sensitivity, and Section 6 describes how leaked information is mapped to the data model.

Section 7 presents our metric for data leakage quantification along with a comparison with M-Score. A validation of the proposed metric is presented in Section 8. Finally, Section 9 concludes the paper by providing directions for future work.

2   Related Work

Several works aiming at data leakage detection and protection can be found in the literature [8–10]. Data leakage detection (DLD) solutions differ in the approach and technologies used to detect leakages. They are usually rule-based [10], behavior-based [11] or content-based [12–14]. Rule-based approaches set predefined policies (e.g., access control policies, firewall rules) that are used to define which operations are allowed or not. In behavior-based DLD solutions the permitted usage of data is defined by observing users' behavior. For instance, network behavior monitoring technologies, such as anomaly detection and extrusion detection systems [11], can be used to detect unusual behavior. Content-based DLD solutions analyze the values of the disclosed data to detect data leakages. Such approaches include the use of keywords, regular expressions, text classification [14], and information retrieval [12, 13] to detect the presence of sensitive data leaving the organization perimeter. However, most existing DLD solutions only focus on detecting leakages and do not assess their severity.

A number of proposals for the quantification of data breaches exist in the literature [15–17]. These proposals measure the impact of a security incident in financial terms. For instance, security incidents are quantified on the basis of the damage on the reputation of the organization and the losses on the revenue. Another approach for measuring the severity of security incidents is proposed in [2, 18]; this approach evaluates privacy infringements by quantifying deviations from the intended usage of data.

Data leakage quantification is studied in the field of quantitative information flow [4, 6]. These solutions measure the amount of information leaking from a high confidentiality input to a low confidentiality output. Leakages are usually quantified in terms of bits, using metric based on information theory and information entropy. Quantitative information flow has also been applied to quantify leakages at network level [5]. In particular, it has been used to measure the amount of leaked information (measured in bytes) in the hypertext transfer protocol. The major drawback of quantitative information flow methods is that they do not consider the semantics of the leaked information to quantify data leakages. In particular, the sensitivity of leaked data is not considered in the calculation of the severity of a leakage.

To the best of our knowledge, M-Score [7] is the only proposal that uses semantic information to compute the severity of data leakages. In particular, M-Score measures the severity of leakages in database environment on the basis of the amount and sensitivity of the data leaked. However, M-Score is not able to accurately distinguish data leakages. A detailed analysis of M-Score is presented in Section 7.1.

3   Running Example

Consider a local hospital where patients of a small region are treated. The hospital offers treatment for various diseases, ranging from flu to serious cases such as heart attack and infectious diseases. Patient information is stored in a central database at the hospital in the form of electronic health records (EHR). Typically, doctors and nurses can only access EHR of the patients they treat. However, in emergency situations doctors and nurses can bypass access control mechanisms by invoking the break-the-glass protocol. Therefore, they can have access to the EHRs of all patients. The hospital has also administrative personnel for financial management and to make appointments with patients. Moreover, the database is maintained by a database administrator.

To detect data leakages, the hospital employs a DLD solution. In a typical day hospital employees access thousands of patient records. In addition, the number of invocations of the break-the-glass protocol can be huge [2]. Therefore, the DLD system can generate hundreds of alerts, making difficult to evaluate their severity. In particular, the evaluation of a large number of data leakages can be time-consuming for organizations. Below we present three representative alerts of data leakages:

Alert 1. A query is made by a doctor requesting an unusual large number of patient records. In particular, the names and addresses of 10000 patients were retrieved.

Alert 2. A query for patient data is made by a doctor after his regular working hours. He retrieved 200 records containing the names and diseases of patients.

Alert 3. A query for data about patients affected by HIV is made by a medical researcher of the hospital, specialized on cardiovascular diseases. He retrieved 500 anonymized records containing the sex, age and treatment provided to patients.

To assist organizations in the evaluation of data leakages, leakages should be ranked on the basis of their severity. However, the quantification of data leakages is not a trivial task as the leakages may differ on several aspects. The *amount* of leaked information is a main aspect to discriminate data leakages. For instance, the leakage described in Alert 1 contains thousands of patient records, while in Alert 2 only a relatively small amount (200) of records is retrieved. Another difference is the information leaked itself. In particular, the *sensitivity* of the information (i.e., the impact that its disclosure has on the patient) can be different. For instance, disease information (Alert 2) is more sensitive than patient addresses (Alert 1). Finally, data leakages also differ on the extent that an individual related to the data is identifiable. According to the EU Data Protection Directive (95/46/EC), personal data should be protected. However, the principles defined in the directive do not apply to anonymous data. Therefore, the ability to identify the individuals related to the leaked data has an impact on the severity of a leakage. For instance, in Alerts 1 and 2 the leaked data can be directly linked to patients' identity, while in Alert 3 the data are anonymized. Therefore, the first two alerts should be considered more severe than the third alert.

In order to obtain a ranking of alerts we need a method to quantify the severity of data leakages. Such quantification should take into account the amount and sensitivity of leaked information, and the extent to which the identity of the individuals related to the leaked information can be ascertained.

4 Approach

DLD solutions are often deployed to detect data leakages. These solutions analyze the data leaving the system and raise an alert when a data leakage is detected. However, the

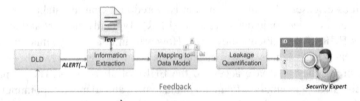

Fig. 1. Data Leakage Quantification Process

number of alerts can be very large, making their analysis costly and time-consuming for organizations. To enable organizations to focus on the most severe incidents, data leakages have to be ranked based on their severity.

To address this issue, we propose a new data leakage quantification system (Fig. 1). The system is connected to a DLD solution. In particular, it receives alerts of data leakages and analyzes the disclosed data to estimate their severity. Since leakages can originate from different sources, data can be structured or unstructured. For instance, data originating from a database are structured, while data in an e-mail are usually unstructured. In this work, we focus on structured data where portions of the database's tables are leaving the database as result of a user query. However, the system can be extended using technologies like natural language processing and information retrieval, to extract information from unstructured data.

The severity of data leakages depends both on the amount of the data leaked and on the data themselves. Therefore, the quantification of data leakages should consider both these factors. In particular, data leakage quantification should reflect the cost of data disclosure according to the data subject/owner or to the organization hosting the data. We represent such a cost in terms of the sensitivity of data. In particular, a sensitivity value should be assigned to every piece of data that may be leaked.

Assigning a sensitivity value to all pieces of data, however, is time-consuming and error prone. We employ a data model representing the knowledge of the application domain to reason on data sensitivity. The data model makes it possible to specify the sensitivity of some pieces of information and infer the sensitivity for the other pieces of information based on this initial assignment (Section 5). To calculate the severity of data leakages, leaked data are mapped to the data model. Intuitively, the attributes and values in the leaked tables are mapped to the corresponding piece of information in the data model (Section 6). The sensitivity of data along with a discrimination factor, which determines to what extent data can be related to an individual, and the amount of leaked data is used to quantify the severity of data leakages (Section 7).

Data leakages are ranked on the basis of their severity. Security experts thus can evaluate data leakages focusing on the more severe incidents. Based on this analysis, organizations can take the appropriate actions to prevent or mitigate the losses. If the analysis reveals that a leakage is a false positive (i.e., wrongly recognized by the DLD solution as a leakage), feedback explaining the assessment is sent to the DLD system to reduce the number of false alerts in the future.

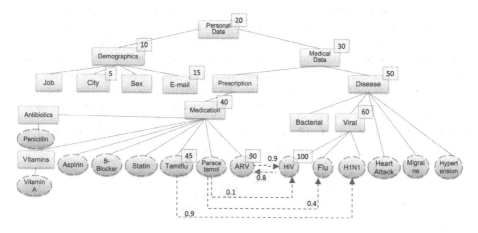

Fig. 2. Data Model Example

5   Modeling and Reasoning on Data Sensitivity

To determine the sensitivity of data we employ a data model. It provides a description of the data within an application domain along with the necessary semantic information.

Definition 1. *A data model is a tuple $DM = (T, I, HR, IR, SL, PL)$, where:*

- *T is a set of data types, and I is a set of data instances.*
- *$HR \subset T \times T \cup I$ is a hierarchy relation representing a specialization relationship.*
- *$IR \subset I \times I$ represents an inference relation on I.*
- *$SL : T \cup I \rightarrow \mathbb{Z}_{\geq 0}$ is a labeling function that assigns a sensitivity value to data types and instances.*
- *$PL : I \times I \rightarrow [0, 1]$ is a labeling function that defines the probability to infer knowledge about a data instance having knowledge about another data instance.*

Fig. 2 shows an example of data model for the healthcare domain. Data types are nodes represented by rectangles, while data instances by ovals. Hierarchy relations are represented with straight edges between two nodes. For instance, the hierarchy relation between Viral diseases and Flu (denoted as $(Viral, Flu)$) nodes indicates that flu is a viral disease. Inference relations are represented by dashed edges. For example, the inference relation between Anti-RetroViral (ARV) and HIV indicates that a patient treated with ARV medication is likely infected with the HIV virus.

Nodes can be annotated with a sensitivity label that indicates the sensitivity of the data represented by the respective node. For instance, the sensitivity label of node HIV is $SL(HIV) = 100$. Inference relations are annotated with probability labels to indicate the probability of the inference. For instance, label $PL(ARV, HIV) = 0.9$ indicates that a patient treated with ARV medication is very likely (90%) infected by HIV.

Both domain and security experts need to be involved in the construction of the data model for a given domain. Domain experts should define data types and instances along with the hierarchy relations between them. Moreover, they should determine the inference relations between instances with the respective probability labels. On the other hand, security experts should annotate the data model with sensitivity labels.

The annotation of the data model with sensitivity labels, however, can be difficult as the number of nodes can be large. Ideally, security experts should assign sensitivity labels to few nodes and the system determines the sensitivity of the other nodes based on this initial assignment. To this end, we introduce the notion of *sensitivity propagation*.

Definition 2. *Let $DM = (T,I,HR,IR,SL,PL)$ be a data model. Sensitivity propagation is a function $SP : T \cup I \rightarrow \mathbb{Z}_{\geq 0}$ such that given a node $x \in T \cup I$*

$$SP(x) = \begin{cases} SL(x) & \text{if } SL(x) \text{ exists} \\ SP(y) & \text{otherwise} \end{cases} \tag{1}$$

with $y \in T$ such that $(y,x) \in HR$.

Sensitivity propagation is used to assign a sensitivity value to the nodes in the data model based on hierarchy relations. Intuitively, if a node does not have a sensitivity label, then its sensitivity is inherited from the node higher in the hierarchy.

Example 1. In Fig. 2 the sensitivity label of Paracetamol is not defined. Therefore, this node inherits the sensitivity value of the parent node (Medication), i.e., $SP(Paracetamol) = SP(Medication) = 40$.

Although sensitivity propagation simplifies the task of assigning sensitivity values to nodes, it may lead to an inaccurate assignment. For instance, a security expert might underestimate the sensitivity of some pieces of information, which is propagated through the data hierarchy. To this end, we use inference relations to validate the propagated values and eventually adjust the sensitivity of the nodes to a higher value.

Definition 3. *Let $DM = (T,I,HR,IR,SL,PL)$ be a data model. Node sensitivity is a function $NS : T \cup I \rightarrow \mathbb{Z}_{\geq 0}$ such that given a node $x \in T \cup I$*

$$NS(x) = \max\{SP(x),IS(x)\} \tag{2}$$

where $SP(x)$ is the sensitivity derived through sensitivity propagation (Definition 2) and the inferred sensitivity $IS(x)$ is computed using function $IS : T \cup I \rightarrow \mathbb{Z}_{\geq 0}$:

$$IS(x) = \begin{cases} \sum_{(x,y)\in IR} PL(x,y) \times NS(y) & \text{if } x \in I \\ 0 & \text{if } x \in T \end{cases} \tag{3}$$

Intuitively, the sensitivity of data types is obtained through sensitivity propagation. On the other hand, the sensitivity of data instances also depends on the sensitivity of the information that can be inferred through the inference relations.

Example 2. Consider the sensitivity value of node Paracetamol calculated in Example 1. The node has an inference relation with nodes HIV and Flu, which have sensitivity 100 and 60 respectively. The inferred sensitivity is 34. As this value is lower than the sensitivity obtained through propagation, the node sensitivity for Paracetamol is 40.

Note that the computation of inferred sensitivity can be problematic as inference relations can form a cyclic graph. This issue can be addressed by representing inference relations as Markov chains. For the lack of space, we omit details of such an approach.

6   Mapping Information on the Data Model

To quantify the severity of data leakages, the leaked data have to be mapped onto the data model in order to determine their sensitivity. Recall that in this work we focus on structured data leaving a database. Thus, the mapping consists in determining, for each entry in the leaked table, the corresponding node in the data model. In this section we first introduce the notation used to represent data; then, we present the mapping.

Let $\mathcal{A}$ be a set of attributes. Attributes can be divided in two types: *quasi-identifiers* and *sensitive* attributes. Quasi-identifiers $Q = \{q_1, \ldots, q_k\} \subseteq \mathcal{A}$ can be used to reveal the identity of an individual, possibly using an external data source (any subset of the quasi-identifiers is a quasi-identifier itself). Sensitive attributes $S = \{s_1, \ldots, s_m\} \subseteq \mathcal{A}$ are the attributes that need to be protected. Certain attributes may belong to both sets. For instance, the sex of a person is a quasi-identifier, as it can be used to partly reveal an individual's identity. Moreover, according to the EU Data Protection Directive (Directive 95/46/EC) the sex of an individual is considered to be sensitive personal information. Note that the distinction between quasi-identifiers and sensitive attributes is related to the purpose and context of use. One may consider all attributes in a table as both quasi-identifiers and sensitive attributes.

A database table $D(a_1, \ldots, a_n)$ is a set of records over a set of attributes $\{a_1, \ldots, a_n\} \subseteq \mathcal{A}$. We denote the records in $D(a_1, \ldots, a_n)$ as $R^{D(a_1, \ldots, a_n)}$. Given a record $r \in R^{D(a_1, \ldots, a_n)}$, $a_i[r]$ represents the value of attribute a_i in r. Attributes take values from a close set of values defined by the domain. Given an attribute $a \in \mathcal{A}$, C_a denotes the domain of a.

Example 3. Consider the scenario in Section 3. The database includes table D(Job, City, Sex, Disease, Medication). Attributes Job and City are quasi-identifiers, while attributes Disease and Medication are sensitive attributes. Attribute Sex belongs to both sets. Each sensitive attribute takes values from a pre-specified domain. For instance, Disease can take a value from {HIV, Heart Attack, Hypertension, Migraine, H1N1, Flu}, and Medication from {ARV, b-Blocker, Tamiflu, Statin, Antibiotics, Aspirin, Paracetamol, Vitamins}. We assume that a doctor can prescribe antibiotics without referring explicitly to a particular medical product, allowing the patient and/or pharmacist to choose an antibiotic from a list of equivalent medication.

In addition to the attributes and values contained in the leaked table, we also consider pre-acquired knowledge as part on the leaked information. In particular, conditional clauses such as WHERE clauses in SQL may leak information. For instance, consider a user query requesting the medication prescribed to patients infected by HIV (i.e., WHERE Disease = 'HIV'). Although the leaked table only contains values concerning attribute Medication, we also assume that value HIV is leaked.

The attributes of a table correspond to data types in the data model presented in Section 5.1. Formally, $\mathcal{A} \subseteq T$. The values of an attribute can correspond either to an instance or a data type node, which is located in the subtree of the data model rooted in the node corresponding to the attribute. Formally, $\{C_a\}_{a \in \mathcal{A}} \subseteq T \cup I$.

To obtain the sensitivity of the leaked data, the values of the attributes in the leaked table need to be mapped onto the data model. For the mapping, search methods can be employed. However, the efficiency of the search methods depends on the size of the data model. To facilitate the search process, the attributes in the leaked table can be first mapped to the corresponding data type node in the data model. The value of the attribute can be then mapped starting the search from the data type node corresponding to the attribute and continuing downward the hierarchy defined by the data model.

Example 4. Consider table D(Job, City, Sex, Disease, Medication) in Example 3 and the data model in Fig. 2. Suppose that a leaked record contains value Hypertension for attribute Disease. First, Disease is mapped by searching from node Personal Data downward the hierarchy until a data type node with the same name is found. Then, value Hypertension is mapped by searching the corresponding node from node Disease.

7   Data Leakage Quantification

The estimation of the severity of data leakages requires metrics that assess the sensitivity and the amount of the data leaked. In this section, we present an overview of M-Score [7] and study its accuracy by applying it to some data leakages. Based on this analysis, we present our proposal for data leakage quantification.

7.1   M-Score

M-Score has been proposed to estimate data misuse in a database environment. It is based on the calculation of the severity of a (portion of) table, which may have been leaked. M-Score evaluates the severity of a data leakage by evaluating three main aspects of the leaked data: the sensitivity, quantity and distinguishing factor (Section 3). The sensitivity of data is defined through a *sensitivity score* function.

Definition 4. *Let $\mathcal{A}$ be a set of attributes and C_{a_i} the domain of an attribute $a_i \in \mathcal{A}$. The sensitivity score function $f : C_{a_i} \rightarrow [0,1]$ assigns a sensitivity value to each value in C_{a_i}.*

Given a record $r \in R^{D(a_1,\dots,a_n)}$, the sensitivity score of a value $a_i[r] \in C_{a_i}$ is denoted by $f(a_i[r])$. The sensitivity of a record is captured by the *raw record score*. In particular, the calculation of the raw record score of a record r, denoted as RRS_r, encompasses the sensitive attributes of a table and their values in r.

Definition 5. *Let $D(a_1,\dots,a_n)$ be a table, $S = \{s_1,\dots,s_m\} \subseteq \mathcal{A}$ the set of sensitive attributes in $D(a_1,\dots,a_n)$, and f the sensitivity score function. Given a record $r \in R^{D(a_1,\dots,a_n)}$, the* raw record score *of r is*

$$RRS_r = \min\left(1, \sum_{s_i \in S} f(s_i[r])\right) \tag{4}$$

Intuitively, the raw record score of a record is obtained by summing the sensitivity score of every piece of sensitive information in the record, with a maximum of 1.

The *distinguishing factor* of a record r with respect to a table, denoted as $DF_r^{D(a_1,\dots,a_n)}$, is the amount of efforts required to identify the individual which r refers to. The distinguishing factor of a record is calculated on the basis of quasi-identifier attributes.

Definition 6. *Let $D(a_1,\dots,a_n)$ be a table, $Q = \{q_1,\dots,q_k\} \subseteq \mathcal{A}$ the set of quasi-identifier attributes in $D(a_1,\dots,a_n)$ and $r \in R^{D(a_1,\dots,a_n)}$ a record in $D(a_1,\dots,a_n)$. Given $\{q_1[r],\dots,q_k[r]\}$ with $q_i[r] \in C_{q_i}$ the set of quasi-identifier values in r, the distinguishing factor of r with respect to $D(a_1,\dots,a_n)$ is*

$$DF_r^{D(a_1,\dots,a_n)} = \frac{1}{|R'|} \qquad (5)$$

where $R' = \{r_i | \forall q_i \in Q \ q_i[r] = q_i[r_i]\}$, i.e. the set of records in $D(a_1,\dots,a_n)$ that have $\{q_1[r],\dots,q_k[r]\}$ as quasi-identifier values and $|R'|$ is the number of such records.

The *final record score* for a leaked table $L(a_1,\dots,a_m)$, denoted as RS_L, is calculated based on the raw record score and distinguishing factor.

Definition 7. *Let $ST(a_1,\dots,a_n)$ be a source table and $L(b_1,\dots,b_m)$ a leaked table with $\{b_1,\dots,b_m\} \subseteq \{a_1,\dots,a_n\}$. Given the raw record score RRS_r and distinguishing factor $DF_r^{ST(a_1,\dots,a_n)}$ for every record $r \in R^{L(b_1,\dots,b_m)}$, the final record score of $L(b_1,\dots,b_m)$ is*

$$RS_L = \max_{r \in R^{L(b_1,\dots,b_m)}} (RRS_r \times DF_r^{ST(a_1,\dots,a_n)}) \qquad (6)$$

It is worth noting that the distinguishing factor is calculated with respect to the source table. To capture the quantity aspect of the leakage, M-Score determines the severity of leakages based on the final record score and the number of records disclosed.

Definition 8. *Let $L(a_1,\dots,a_n)$ be a leaked table. Given the final record score RS_L of $L(b_1,\dots,b_m)$, the M-Score of $L(a_1,\dots,a_n)$ is*

$$M\text{-}Score_L = |R^{L(a_1,\dots,a_n)}|^{\frac{1}{x}} \times RS_L \qquad (7)$$

where $|R^{L(a_1,\dots,a_n)}|$ represents the number of records in $L(a_1,\dots,a_n)$ and $x \in \mathbb{Z}_{>0}$ is a weighting factor for the number of records.

7.2 Application of M-Score

In this section we study the accuracy of M-Score by applying it to a number of leakage examples. The examples are based on table D(Job, City, Sex, Disease, Medication) presented in Section 6. In the examples we analyze the calculation of the severity of leakages with respect to the sensitivity of the leaked data. Therefore, we assume that the amount of records and distinguishing factor are the same for all leakages.

The sensitivity score function used to assess the severity of leakages is shown in Table 1. The sensitivity score assigned to diseases is related to the impact the disclosure

Table 1. Sensitivity score function

Disease		Medication	
$f(HIV) = 1$	$f(Migraine) = 0.3$	$f(ARV) = 1$	$f(Antibiotics) = 0.4$
$f(HeartAttack) = 0.7$	$f(Flu) = 0.1$	$f(b\text{-}Blocker) = 0.8$	$f(Aspirin) = 0.3$
$f(Hypertention) = 0.6$		$f(Statin) = 0.6$	$f(Paracetamol) = 0.1$
$f(H1N1) = 0.4$		$f(Tamiflu) = 0.5$	$f(Vitamins) = 0.1$

of disease information has on the life of an individual. In particular, diseases whose disclosure has a major impact on the life of the patient (e.g., HIV) are assigned a higher sensitivity than diseases with less critical impact (e.g., Flu). The sensitivity of medication is related to its degree of specialization; medication can be general and specialized. General medication is prescribed to treat mild symptoms of different diseases, such as headache. This category includes medication such as Antibiotics, Aspirin and Paracetamol. Specialized medication is prescribed to treat symptoms related to a particular disease. For instance, ARV is usually prescribed to patients infected with HIV. We assume that specialized medication has higher sensitivity than general medication.

We apply M-Score to two cases. We focus on the impact of data sensitivity on the severity of leakages. Thus, we consider the same number of leaked records and set parameter x of M-Score equal to 1. At the end of this section, we discuss the impact of the amount of records and x on the severity of data leakages.

Case 1: Consider the leakages in Tables 2a and 2b. In *Case* 1.1 the records contain general medication prescribed to patients suffering from serious health issues. In *Case* 1.2 the records contain information about specialized medication prescribed to patients suffering from serious health issues. We expect *Case* 1.2 to be more severe than *Case* 1.1 as it contains more sensitive information. However, M-Score calculates the same severity value (2.000) in both cases. The problem lies in the use of the *min* function in the calculation of *RRS*. In particular, this measure has an upper bound equal to 1, which leads to the same *RRS* for all records whose sensitivity is greater than 1.

Case 2: Consider the leakages in Tables 2c and 2d. In *Case* 2.1 the records contain general medication. In contrast, the records in *Case* 2.2 contain information about specialized medication. In both cases we consider only a small percentage of records (1 record) about patients suffering from a serious health issue. Therefore, *Case* 2.2 should be estimated more severe than *Case* 2.1, as it contain more sensitive information. In contrast, M-Score calculates the same severity value (2.000) in both cases. The problem lies in the use of the *max* function in the calculation of *RS*. In particular, *RS* uses the sensitivity value of the record that has the highest sensitivity. Since parameter x is equal to 1, M-Score is the product of *RS* and the number of rows.

As shown above, M-Score may not be able to accurately estimate the severity of leakages. In particular, M-Score is not able to discriminate data leakages that contain at least one highly sensitive record (i.e., $\sum_{s_i \in S} f(s_i[r]) \geq 1$), regardless of the sensitivity of the other records. This is due to the calculation of *RRS* and *RS* and, in particular, to the use of the *min* and *max* functions respectively. The *min* function allows a maximum

Table 2. M-Score evaluation

(a) Case 1.1

Job	City	Sex	Disease	Medication
Lawyer	LA	Male	HIV	Vitamins
Lawyer	LA	Male	Heart Attack	Aspirin
Lawyer	LA	Male	Migraine	Paracetamol
Lawyer	LA	Male	Hypertension	Aspirin
M-Score: 2.000				

(b) Case 1.2

Job	City	Sex	Disease	Medication
Lawyer	LA	Male	HIV	ARV
Lawyer	LA	Male	Hypertension	Statin
Lawyer	LA	Male	Heart Attack	b-Blocker
Lawyer	LA	Male	Migraine	b-Blocker
M-Score: 2.000				

(c) Case 2.1

Job	City	Sex	Disease	Medication
Lawyer	LA	Male	HIV	Vitamins
Lawyer	LA	Male	Flu	Paracetamol
Lawyer	LA	Male	Flu	Aspirin
Lawyer	LA	Male	Migraine	Aspirin
M-Score: 2.000				

(d) Case 2.2

Job	City	Sex	Disease	Medication
Lawyer	LA	Male	HIV	ARV
Lawyer	LA	Male	H1N1	Tamiflu
Lawyer	LA	Male	H1N1	Antibiotics
Lawyer	LA	Male	Flu	Antibiotics
M-Score: 2.000				

sensitivity score of 1 per record; the *max* function leads to consider only the record with the highest *RS* when calculating M-Score. Thus, the discrimination of the severity of leakages relies on the amount of records leaked. The importance of this factor is expresses by parameter x of M-Score. For low values of x (i.e., $x \approx 1$) considerable importance is given to the amount of records. Thus, leakages with a larger number of records result to have a higher severity. Otherwise, for $x \gg 1$, more importance is given to sensitivity. Therefore, M-Score converges to the value of the record with highest *RS*.

7.3   L-Severity

This section presents L-Severity, a new metric for quantifying data leakages that addresses M-Score's drawbacks. Similarly to M-Score, L-Severity assesses the severity of data leakages based on the sensitivity, distinguishing factor and amount of leaked data.

Definition 9. *Let $ST(a_1, \ldots, a_n)$ be a source table, $L(b_1, \ldots, b_m)$ a leaked table with $\{b_1, \ldots, b_m\} \subseteq \{a_1, \ldots, a_n\}$, $S = \{s_l, \ldots, s_m\} \subseteq \mathcal{A}$ the set of sensitive attributes in $L(b_1, \ldots, b_m)$ and $DM = (T, I, HR, IR, SL, PL)$ a data model. Given $r \in R^{L(b_1, \ldots, b_m)}$ a record in $L(b_1, \ldots, b_m)$ and $DF_r^{ST(a_1, \ldots, a_n)}$, the record sensitivity of r is*

$$RSENS_r = DF_r^{ST(a_1, \ldots, a_n)} \times \sum_{s_i \in S} NS(s_i[r]) \tag{8}$$

where NS is the node sensitivity of the node in the data model that corresponds to the value $s_i[r]$ of a sensitive attribute s_i.

In the calculation of record sensitivity we make use of the data model (Section 5). In particular, we use *NS* to calculate the sensitivity of each sensitive attribute value in a record. To calculate the severity of data leakages, we introduce L-Severity metric.

Table 3. Comparison between L-Severity and M-Score

Case	L-Severity	M-Score
Case 1.1	2.050	2.000
Case 1.2	2.900	2.000
Case 2.1	1.150	2.000
Case 2.2	2.100	2.000

Definition 10. *Let $ST(a_1,\ldots,a_n)$ be a source table and $L(b_1,\ldots,b_m)$ a leaked table with $\{b_1,\ldots,b_m\} \subseteq \{a_1,\ldots,a_n\}$. Given the record sensitivity $RSENS_r$ for each record $r \in R^{L(b_1,\ldots,b_n)}$,* the leakage severity (L-Severity) *of $L(b_1,\ldots,b_m)$ is*

$$L\text{-}Severity_L = \sum_{r \in R^{L(b_1,\ldots,b_m)}} RSENS_r \tag{9}$$

To demonstrate L-Severity we applied it to the same cases used to evaluate M-Score (Section 7.2). To make a fair comparison with M-Score we use the sensitivity score function in Table 1 to determine the sensitivity of data. A summary of the severity scores obtained by L-Severity and M-Score is shown in Table 3. Accordingly, the value of L-Severity is 2.050 for *Case* 1.1 and 2.900 for *Case* 1.2. Hence, L-Severity is higher for *Case* 1.2 than for *Case* 1.1. Similarly, the L-Severity value for *Case* 2.2 (2.100) is higher that the value for *Case* 2.1 (1.150). Thus, L-Severity provides values that better characterize the severity of leakages with respect to the intuition (Section 7.2).

8   Validation

In this section we validate L-Severity using a number of representative data leakages in a healthcare environment. First, we discuss the construction of the data model using existing ontologies. Then, we apply L-Severity to assess the severity of the data leakages and validate the results against the evaluation provided by a group of security experts.

8.1   Determining Data Sensitivity

The data model presented in Section 5 provides a description of the data characterizing an application domain along with the necessary semantic information, such as the sensitivity of the data. Ontologies [19] are often adopted to capture the knowledge of a specific domain. The basic elements of ontologies are *Classes, Individuals, Attributes and Relationships*. Classes are abstract groups of objects, while individuals represent instances of classes. Attributes are used to represent properties and characteristics of classes and individuals. Relationships represent ways in which classes and individuals are related to one another. Ontologies can be used as a basis for the definition of a data model. Table 4 shows the correspondence between the elements of the data model and the elements of an ontology.

Several ontologies have been proposed for the healthcare domain [20–25]. In this work we adopted and extended SNOMED-CT [22] as a basis for our data model. In particular, we added an attribute to classes and individuals to represent sensitivity labels and an attribute to relations for the specification of probability labels. SNOMED-CT uses several

Table 4. Correspondence between the Data Model and Ontologies

Data Model	Ontology
Data type	Class
Data instance	Individual
Hierarchy relation	*IS-A* (is-a-subclass-of) relations
Inference relation	Relations between individuals
Sensitivity label	Attribute of classes and individuals
Probability label	Attribute of relations between individuals

relations to relate individuals. For instance, relation *ASSOCIATED WITH* is used to relate an individual of class Disease to an individual of class Substance. Relation *CAUSATIVE AGENT* is used to relate an individual of class Disease to an individual of class Organism. These relations can be seen as instances of our inference relation, as they make it possible to obtain additional information based on the knowledge of a specific instance.

To define the sensitivity of data, we rely on HL7 Healthcare Privacy and Security Classification System (HCS). HL7 HCS provides guidelines and a tagging system for automated labeling and segmentation of protected health care information. Security labels in HL7 HCS are a structured representation of the sensitivity of a piece of information. Relying on HL7 HCS for the definition of data sensitivity has the advantage that the human intervention and judgment is limited and thus the overall outcome of the approach is not affected by the consequent subjectivity. The tagging system provided by HL7 HCS is based on SNOMED-CT (and other code systems). In particular, it provides a partial classification of concepts and individuals in SNOMED-CT. We use this partial classification as the initial assignment and derive the sensitivity for all other classes and individuals using the approach described in Section 5. In particular, *IS-A* relations in SNOMED-CT are used for sensitivity propagation, and the domain relations mentioned above to compute inferred sensitivity.

8.2   Assessing Data Leakage Severity Validation

We evaluated the applicability of L-Severity in a real setting based on the scenario in Section 3. We implemented the hospital database using GNU Health (http://health.gnu.org), a healthcare management system used by several health-care providers worldwide. The system was used to generate a number of data leakages, which have been validated by our industry partner, Roessingh Hospital in the Netherlands.

The generated leakages were manually analyzed by a group of security experts to evaluate the output of L-severity. In particular, we developed a questionnaire describing these leakages; each leakage was described along with its key features. The security experts were invited to answer the questionnaire and evaluate the severity of each data leakage on the basis of the amount and sensitivity of the leaked information as well as the ability to identify the patients to whom the leaked information refers. The security experts assessed the severity of the leakages using a three-valued scale (i.e., low, medium, high severity). Based on this assessment, we built a ground truth data set of leakages along with their severity. For some leakages there was no clear majority in the experts' assessment; thus we considered two additional values namely, low/medium and

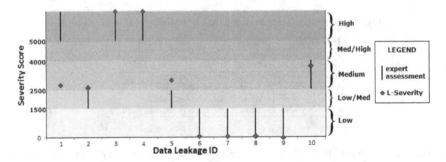

Fig. 3. Evaluation of L-Severity against experts' assessment

medium/high. Low/medium is used to represent the experts' assessment when it ranges in low and medium severity. Similarly, medium/high is used to represent the experts' assessment when it ranges in medium and high severity.

The severity of the same leakages was evaluated using L-Severity. The calculated severity for the leakages is presented in Fig. 3 along with experts' evaluation (in the figure data leakages are identified by an ID). One can observe that the calculated severity matches experts' assessment in nine out of ten cases. Specifically, in seven cases there is a complete match, while in two cases there is a partial match. Therefore, in most cases L-Severity evaluates the data leakages severity correctly. Only one case (#1) presents a notable difference: L-Severity evaluates it to medium severity, whereas the experts evaluated it high. This can be explained by the different weight given to different aspects of the leakage. L-Severity returned medium severity because of the small amount of records leaked. In contrast, the experts weighted more the sensitivity of the leaked information. In cases #2 and #5, the difference between the L-Severity score and experts' assessment is negligible. In both cases L-Severity evaluates it to medium severity, whereas the experts evaluated it low/medium. Therefore, the calculated severity matches the evaluation provided by some experts.

9   Conclusions

In this work we presented a novel approach for the quantification of data leakages with respect to their severity. The assessment of the severity of data leakages considers the amount and sensitivity of the leaked information together with the ability to identify the individuals related to the leaked information. To specify and reason on data sensitivity, we defined a data model representing the knowledge in a given domain. We validated the approach by analyzing data leakages in a typical healthcare environment.

L-Severity as well as M-Score uses a distinguishing factor to determine the level of data anonymization. This factor is based on the number of occurrences of quasi identifiers in the dataset. An interesting direction for future work is to integrate L-Severity with other approaches to data anonymization like differential privacy. Moreover, the alerts generated by a DLD solution may not correspond to data misuses, i.e. alerts may turn out to be false positive. Therefore, the severity of a leakage may not correspond to its risk level (risk is usually defined as the combination of the severity and probability of an event). An interesting direction for further investigation is the integration of our approach with DLD solutions able to determine the probability that an alert is indeed a data breach. This would allow a risk-based ranking of leakages.

References

1. Ponemon Institute: Third annual benchmark study on patient privacy & data security (2012)
2. Banescu, S., Zannone, N.: Measuring privacy compliance with process specifications. In: International Workshop on Security Measurements and Metrics, pp. 41–50. IEEE (2011)
3. Information Age: New EU data laws to include 24hr breach notification (2012)
4. Backes, M., Kopf, B., Rybalchenko, A.: Automatic discovery and quantification of information leaks. In: IEEE Symposium on Security and Privacy, pp. 141–153. IEEE (2009)
5. Borders, K., Prakash, A.: Quantifying information leaks in outbound web traffic. In: IEEE Symposium on Security and Privacy, pp. 129–140. IEEE (2009)
6. Smith, G.: On the foundations of quantitative information flow. In: de Alfaro, L. (ed.) FOS-SACS 2009. LNCS, vol. 5504, pp. 288–302. Springer, Heidelberg (2009)
7. Harel, A., Shabtai, A., Rokach, L., Elovici, Y.: M-score: A misuseability weight measure. IEEE Transactions on Dependable and Secure Computing 9(3), 414–428 (2012)
8. Abbadi, I.M., Alawneh, M.: Preventing insider information leakage for enterprises. In: SE-CURWARE, pp. 99–106. IEEE (2008)
9. Salem, M.B., Hershkop, S., Stolfo, S.J.: A survey of insider attack detection research. In: Insider Attack and Cyber Security. Adv. Inf. Secur., vol. 39, pp. 69–90. Springer (2008)
10. Takebayashi, T., Tsuda, H., Hasebe, T., Masuoka, R.: Data loss prevention technologies. Fujitsu Scientific and Technical Journal 46(1), 47–55 (2010)
11. Koch, R.: Towards next-generation intrusion detection. In: ICCC, pp. 1–18. IEEE (2011)
12. Gessiou, E., Vu, Q.H., Ioannidis, S.: IRILD: an Information Retrieval based method for Information Leak Detection. In: EC2ND, pp. 33–40. IEEE (2011)
13. Gómez-Hidalgo, J., Martın-Abreu, J., Nieves, J., Santos, I., Brezo, F., Bringas, P.: Data leak prevention through named entity recognition. In: SocialCom, pp. 1129–1134. IEEE (2010)
14. Hart, M., Manadhata, P., Johnson, R.: Text classification for data loss prevention. In: Fischer-Hübner, S., Hopper, N. (eds.) PETS 2011. LNCS, vol. 6794, pp. 18–37. Springer, Heidelberg (2011)
15. Farahmand, F., Navathe, S.B., Enslow, P.H., Sharp, G.P.: Managing vulnerabilities of information systems to security incidents. In: ICEC, pp. 348–354. ACM (2003)
16. Garg, A., Curtis, J., Halper, H.: Quantifying the financial impact of it security breaches. Information Management & Computer Security 11(2), 74–83 (2003)
17. Blakley, B., McDermott, E., Geer, D.: Information security is information risk management. In: NSPW, pp. 97–104. ACM (2001)
18. Adriansyah, A., van Dongen, B.F., Zannone, N.: Privacy analysis of user behavior using alignments. it - Information Technology 55(6), 255–260
19. Gruber, T.R.: Toward principles for the design of ontologies used for knowledge sharing? International Journal of Human-Computer Studies 43(5), 907–928 (1995)
20. Doulaverakis, C., Nikolaidis, G., Kleontas, A., Kompatsiaris, I., et al.: GalenOWL: Ontology based drug recommendations discovery. J. Biomedical Semantics 3, 14 (2012)
21. OpenGALEN, http://www.opengalen.org/ (accessed February 24, 2014)
22. SNOMED - CT, http://www.ihtsdo.org/snomed-ct/ (accessed February 24, 2014)
23. The Open Biological and Biomedical Ontologies Foundry, http://www.obofoundry.org/ (accessed February 24, 2014)
24. Open Clinical: Ontologies, http://www.openclinical.org/ontologies.html (accessed February 24, 2014)
25. The Gene ontology, http://www.geneontology.org/ (accessed February 24, 2014)

Toward Software Diversity in Heterogeneous Networked Systems

Chu Huang[1], Sencun Zhu[1,2], and Robert Erbacher[3]

[1] School of Information Science and Technology, Penn State University
[2] Department of Computer Science and Engineering, Penn State University
cuh171@psu.edu, szhu@cse.psu.edu
[3] U.S. Army Research Laboratory(ARL)
robert.f.erbacher.civ@mail.mil

Abstract. When there are either design or implementation flaws, a homogeneous architecture is likely to be disrupted entirely by a single attack (e.g., a worm) that exploits its vulnerability. Following the survivability through heterogeneity philosophy, we present a novel approach to improving survivability of networked systems by adopting the technique of software diversity. Specifically, we design an efficient algorithm to select and deploy a set of off-the-shelf software to hosts in a networked system, such that the number and types of vulnerabilities presented on one host would be different from that on its neighboring nodes. In this way, we are able to contain a worm in an isolated "island". This algorithm addresses software assignment problem in more complex scenarios by taking into consideration practical constraints, e.g., hosts may have diverse requirements based on different system prerequisites. We evaluate the performance of our algorithm through simulations on both simple and complex system models. The results confirm the effectiveness and scalability of our algorithm.

1 Introduction

With the fast advancement of nowadays information technology, organizations are becoming ever more dependent on interconnected systems for carrying on everyday tasks. However, the pervasive interdependence of such infrastructure increases the risk of being attacked and thus poses numerous challenges to system security. One major problem for such networked environments is software monoculture [1,2]–running on the risk of exposing a weakness that is common to all of its components, it facilitates the spread of attacks and enables large-scale exploitations that could easily result in overall crash. Considering the consequences of software monoculture in intensively connected systems, there is an urgent need to control the damage of automated attacks that takes advantage of the connectivity of the networked system.

In contrast to homogeneous systems by software monoculture, heterogeneous architectures are expected to have higher survivability [3–5]. This point is very much like the maintenance of genetic and ecosystem diversity in biology.

V. Atluri and G. Pernul (Eds.): DBSec 2014, LNCS 8566, pp. 114–129, 2014.
© IFIP International Federation for Information Processing 2014

The variability in the biological world allows at least a portion of species to survive an epidemic. Inspired by such phenomena of biodiversity, a good number of techniques have been proposed to improve system resilience and survivability under attacks. However, previous approaches cannot fully meet two highly desired requirements: (R1) *Resistance* against automated attacks in a networked environment; (R2) *Practicability* of the solutions under real-world constraints. To see how existing approaches are limited in meeting these three requirements, we classify them into three main categories: software diversity at the system level, software diversity at network level and N-version programming 1) Diversity at the system level is achieved mainly through randomization techniques, which are limited to individual machines and it is not clear if and how they can be extended to improve the survivability of the networked systems as a whole. 2) Diversification methods at the network level compensate the limitations of the former approach, but it suffers from the problem of only considering assignment of one piece of software. In the real world scenarios, however, a host (i.e., a commodity PC) typically is required to install with more than one software (i.e., operating system, web browser, email client, office suite applications etc.) to perform particular tasks. 3) N-version programming: achieves higher system survivability depending on its underlying multiple-version software units that tolerate software faults. This method has very high computational cost and is not practical enough to be used routinely in real-world organizations. 4) Real world deployment constraints have not been formally incorporated into system design in prior research.

In this study we propose a software diversity-based approach to address the problem of survivability in the complex networked systems under automated attacks, with the goal to meet all the design requirements. First, by assigning appropriate software to hosts considering the network connectivity, our approach enhances the system's resistance to automated attacks. Second, our algorithm considers the real-world constraints on resource allocation, which makes it more practical from implementation point of view. We also demonstrate via simulations that the assignment solution generated by our algorithm is better than previous assigning methods, and very close to the optimal solution. Through experiments we found that the level of heterogeneity in our algorithm depends on the ratio of the number of software installed to the total number of available software, and we also identified critical ratio points for different representative topologies. The capability and possibility of our algorithm in creating moving target defense are also evaluated. Our findings may give some guidelines for choosing appropriate system parameters for balancing the trade-off between survivability and cost.

Take the graph in Fig. 1 as an example. There are 11 machines represented by nodes and 5 distinct software products represented by different colors. We expect diverse software products developed by different people will not have the same vulnerability for the attacker to exploit [6], and an attack can propagate from one node to another by exploring one kind of vulnerabilities residing in a particular software product. By applying our algorithm on this graph, we find that even in the worst-case scenario a successful attack can only compromise four machines (in green) at most. This indicates that by optimally assigning software to connected machines in a non-adjacent manner, our algorithm can effectively reduce the epidemic effect of an attack.

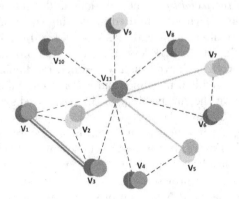

Fig. 1. Network topology utilizing a diverse software distribution. Solid lines connect nodes with the same color and indicate all possible worm-spreading paths; dashed lines connect nodes of different colors and indicate all non-spreading connections.

2   Related Work

Software Diversity. The state-of-the-art approaches on software diversity are classified into three main categories: diversity at the system level and the network level, and N-version programming.

Software diversity at the system level has been researched to address space layout randomization, instruction set randomization and data randomization. Address space layout randomization (ASLR) [7] randomizes the memory address of the program region and has already been implemented in major operating systems [8]. The instruction set randomization (ISR) [9] obfuscates underlying system's instructions in order to defeat code-injection attacks. Data randomization [10] is another randomized-based approach, which applies masks on data in the memory, so that the attacker cannot determine memory regions that are associated with particular objects. Diversity at the network level is achieved by using different applications [4] [5], operating systems, and shuffling techniques within a networked system [11]. N-version programming was introduced in the 1970s which depends on functionally equivalent versions of the same program and monitors the behavior of the variants in order to detect divergence of the results [12].

Graph Coloring. Graph coloring [13] is a famous problem in graph theory, which ensures there is no two adjacent nodes sharing the same color. Its solutions is a natural option in modeling a wide range of real-life problem for making globally optional decision [14] [4]. In most cases, however, the basic graph coloring problem fails to model some real-life problems where additional constraints have to be satisfied. Variants of the basic coloring problem have been introduced and intensively studied which allow one to take into account certain local constraints. List coloring [15], precoloring extension [16] and H-coloring [17] are examples of local constraints. In some cases, these problem can be more difficult algorithmically than traditional vertex coloring [16] [18]. Another widely studied coloring problem is multicoloring problem [19] where more than one color have to be assigned to each vertex. Despite the rich literature, none of the existing coloring algorithms works under our constraints.

3   Problem Formulation

3.1   System Model

In this work, we use an undirected graph as the abstraction of a general finite networked system. Formal definition of the graph is given as follows.

Definition 1. (*Communication Graph*) A communication graph is an undirected graph $G = (V, E)$, where V is a finite set of nodes which represents hosts and devices comprising the networked system, and E as a set of edges represents the communication links (e.g., physically directly connected or can communicate through network e.g. using TCP/UDP) between two nodes.

Example networked systems include intranet, enterprise social networks, tactical mobile ad hoc networks, wireless sensor networks of different network topologies. We show an example of how to model a real-world network using communication graph of nodes and edges (Fig. 2). In this example, we have three servers reside in the DMZ, seven workstations and a database server located in the internal network. The links shown between workstations and servers depict direct communication between them. Corresponding communication graph of the network can then be generated based on their connectivity.

Considering the characteristics of the system model, edges of the communication graph can be classified into two types of links: *defective edge* and *immune edge*. *Defective edge* is a type of connection whose two endpoints have the same type of software installed (hence potentially share the same types of vulnerabilities. Note that our algorithm does not assume the knowledge of vulnerabilities. We discuss this more in Section 6). Otherwise, an edge is an *immune edge*. In this paper, based on the above definitions, we further define formally the concept of common vulnerability graph.

Definition 2. (*Common Vulnerability Graph*): A common vulnerability graph (CVG) S is a subgraph of a communication graph G, inside which all vertices share a common software and are connected through defective edges, whereas all its boundary edges are immune edges.

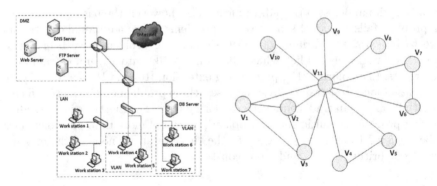

Fig. 2. Example of an enterprise network and its corresponding communication graph

3.2   Graph Multi-coloring Problem with Local Constraints

Using the model described earlier, we model the software assigning problem as a graph multi-coloring problem, where each machine is represented by a vertex and each distinct software product is represented by a color. In the multi-coloring problem each node has a demand $w(v_i)$, which is the number of colors it requires. We further define $G = (V, E, W)$ to be a *weighted communication graph* with a weight vector W which denotes the number of software required for vertices V of the graph. A multi-coloring task of G is an assignment of colors to the vertices such that each vertex v_i is assigned with $w(v_i)$ colors in a way that two connected node cannot be assigned same colors.

However, practical software assignment contains several implicit constraints which basic multi-coloring problem fails to capture. For our work, we specifically consider two types of constraints that give rise to different system requirements, as defined below.

Definition 3. (*Constraint*): If a single host or a pair of hosts is restricted by some pre-defined software assigning rules, we say that the host(s) is/are constrained.

- *Host constraint*: certain hosts must be installed with some specified types of software to perform required functionality (e.g., to deploy a database server it is required to assign DB2);
- *Software constraint*: certain combination of software *must* or *must not* be assigned to specified hosts simultaneously (e.g., PHP, Apache, MySQL and Linux need to be assigned together to implement LAMP on a single node).

We note that these practical requirements could lead to the potential danger that nodes with the same software are neighbors, which violates the coloring rule that adjacent vertices have different colors. To better sketch our problem, we relax the requirement and re-define a less restrictive coloring rule that allows neighboring vertices to receive the same colors. The only thing we require is that the resulting CVG by that color has to be as small as possible. According to the definition, a defective edge indicates that the exploitation of one type of vulnerability on one host could lead to the compromise of its neighboring host following this "path" while immune edge naturally stops propagation of such automated attack. Thus we can use the size of CVG to indicate the infection range of an automated attack (e.g., worm attack). If one can effectively limit the size of the CVG, system survivability can then be improved. Throughout the present paper, we denote the size of the largest size of the CVG as S, indicating the worst-case infection scenario. The ideal case is when every node in the network is isolated as a single CVG with size one (i.e. no defective edge). Hence, our ultimate research question becomes: *given a number of software products and certain constraints, how to load every node with software in a way that the size of the largest CVG is minimized?* One important assumption here is that vulnerabilities are unique for different software packages. Thus diverse software is vulnerable to different exploits and will not be compromised by the same attack. This assumption is confirmed by [6], in which it is found that more than 98.5% software have the substitutes and majority of them do not have the same vulnerabilities.

We are looking for a coloring assignment that satisfies above requirements and serves the goal of minimizing the largest CVG. Let C_h and C_s denote host and software constraints respectively. Next, we give a formal description of our software assignment problem.

Problem. Given a weighted communication graph $G = (V, E, W)$ and a set of colors C, for each $v_i \in V$ assigns a subset $x(v_i) \subseteq C$, such that,

- v_i gets $w(v_i) \in W$ distinct colors, satisfying constraints C_h and C_s;
- for $\forall c \in C$, CVGs $S_i(c) \cap S_j(c) = \emptyset$, for any $i \neq j$;
- the size of the largest CVG is minimized.

The software assignment problem can be solved in either NP-time or P-time, depending on the given constraints. Our problem without considering constraints is a more general problem than ordinary vertex coloring, hence it is NP-hard in those cases where vertex coloring is NP-hard. And polynomial-time algorithms can be expected only in those cases where vertex coloring is polynomial-time solvable. We can expect that in certain situations, the special case of coloring is easier to solve than the general problem. Considering an extreme example when there are sufficient constraints that pre-define all the colors of vertices in G. In this situation, assignment solution can be obtained with $O(1)$. For some cases, however, not only our problem is NP-hard, but the case with constraint(s) is hard as well. In an example where there is only one constraint that pre-assigns a vertex v_1 with color red, the graph $G = (V, E, W)$ can then be updated to $G' = (V, E, W')$ by doing $w'(v_1) = w(v_1) - 1$. The problem then becomes multi-coloring on graph G', which is still NP-hard. It is worthwhile to study some restricted form of coloring with local constraints (e.g., give a bound on the number of constrained vertices), in the hope of finding a polynomial time solvable case. Since our problem can be NP-hard, optimal solutions may only be found when graphs are relatively small. Heuristics are needed to study large graphs. In the next section, we present a greedy algorithm to address the problem of software assignment with arbitrary constraints.

4   Software Assignment Algorithm

In this section, we present our algorithm for software assignment, which will produce an assignment of colors to vertices in a graph, subject to a set of constraints defined in the previous section.

4.1   Formulating Constraints

To incorporate host constraints to the algorithm, we introduce a collection of tuples $CSTR_h = \{(v_i, \varepsilon)\}$ where v_i is a vertex in the communication graph and ε is a (set of) color value(s) indicating that vertex v_i is constrained by color(s) in ε. For example, $C_h = \{(v_1, \{c_1, c_2\}), (v_3, \{c_5\})\}$, means vertices v_1 and v_3 are fixed with colors c_1 and c_2, and color c_5, respectively. Similarly, we denote software constraint using $CSTR_s = (s, \varepsilon)$, where s is the indicator of co-dependent colors and ε is a set of colors. When s equals 0, it states that the set of colors in set ε must not be assigned together to any vertex. In contrast, 1 means that colors in ε must be allocated simultaneously in order to perform certain functionality. For example, assume for an assignment characterized by $C_s = \{(0, \{c_1, c_2, c_4\}), (1, \{c_1, c_3\})\}$ on which c_1, c_2, c_3 represent three distinct software with equivalent functionality, one may prefer not to coloring the single vertex with any combination of c_1, c_2 and c_4, (i.e., assigning them simultaneously) while colors c_1 and c_3 must be assigned together to this vertex.

4.2   Algorithm Description

The algorithm consists two phases: a labeling phase and a coloring phase. In the labeling phase, each vertex is assigned a distinct number as its label and ordered based on that label. Following the labeling phase, the second phase of the algorithm colors vertices in the ordered list sequentially. It works by first scanning the vertices in a graph and load each vertex as many colors as possible while making sure not to create defective edges. It then visits all the vertices that have not been completely colored in order. Upon visiting a particular vertex, the algorithm assigns a color that leads to minimum CVG.

Phase 1–Labeling. We initialize a set UNCOLOR to contain all the ordered, uncolored vertices and we assume that the available colors in the palette C are suitably ordered as $C = \{c_1, c_2, \cdots, c_k\}$, where $k = |C|$. The main process then assigns every vertex a unique number from 1 to n as its label, where n is the total number of vertices in the network graph. Next, based on the numbers assigned, we order the vertices in UNCOLOR so that vertices with smaller labels are listed first. Several ordering heuristics are available to help accomplish the task of labeling: random ordering, increasing degree ordering, and decreasing degree ordering. Here we choose random ordering as the basis of our labelling. The randomness is intentionally designed so that one can run our algorithm once again to get a new color assignment solution by reordering the vertices. Certainly, an important property would be that the qualities of the assignments need to be stable. It means the largest CVGs resulted from different assignments are about the same size. The effect of the ordering will be evaluated in Section 5.

Phase 2–Coloring. The coloring task of phase 2 is done by two procedures: ColorVertexI and ColorVertexII. In the coloring phase, ColorVertexI first applies host constraint and assigns pre-determined colors to certain vertices while satisfying the software constraint. After that, it then successively colors the ordered vertices through the iterative processes. When a current color is determined, the algorithm scans the vertices in UNCOLOR sequentially checking to see if any of them can be colored according to the rules–1) no two adjacent vertices share the same color; 2) software constraints are satisfied by assigning the color. Meanwhile, ColorVertex I also checks the constraint sets to ensure that all the pre-defined constraints are satisfied by assigning the colors. Noted that followed by each coloring action, both the weight and UNCOLOR set need to be updated. When a vertex v_i is assigned the current color, the weight w_i corresponding to it will be decreased by 1 by doing $w_i = w_i - 1$. Those vertices with weight equals to 0 will be removed from UNCOLOR (i.e., UNCOLOR = UNCOLOR - v_i). If the vertex violates any constraints or its weight is larger than 0, then this vertex will remain in UNCOLOR for next iteration. The process of ColorVertexI stops when either the UNCOLOR set is empty or no feasible colors can be assigned to any vertices in UNCOLOR set.

Although ColorVertexI limits the number of defective edges to the minimum extent, there is a high probability that not all vertices get colored due the rigorous coloring constraints of the algorithm. To further color those remaining vertices, we propose ColorVertexII. As a supplement to ColorVertexI, ColorVertexII releases some of the hard requirements by allowing certain adjacent vertices to share the same color. However, with the overall goal of increasing the survivability of a networked system, such release should still follow certain principles. To be specific, instead of targeting at controlling the number of defective edges (keep it as 0), ColorVertexII shifts its focus to minimizing the size of the maximal CVG. For better understanding, we use an example to illustrate our point. Given two graphs in Fig. 3. The left graph has 3 defective edges ($\{v_1, v_7\}$, $\{v_3, v_7\}$, $\{v_6, v_7\}$) but none of them share a common vertex; the graph on the right contains 3 defective edges ($\{v_1, v_4\}$, $\{v_2, v_4\}$, $\{v_4, v_8\}$) but all share a common vertex v_4. Accordingly, the maximal infectable number in the left graph is 2 (assuming the attack starts from one node), whereas for the graph on the right, this number is 4. Hence, if an attack takes place on both graphs, the potential damage in the left graph is smaller than that in the other graph even though the left graph has a larger number of defective edges.

After ColorVertexI, if UNCOLOR set is empty, it returns a perfect coloring solution where no adjacent nodes share same colors. Otherwise, ColorVertexII is called after ColorVertexI finishes. It tries every color one by one in the UNCOLOR set and choose one with the least penalties. Since penalty occurs when defective edges appear, least penalties means that with the color assigned to the

---

Algorithm 1. Color Assignment Algorithm

Input: (1) Graph $G = (V, E, W)$; (2) Available colors are ordered and represented by integers
    $1, 2, \cdots, k$; (3) Ordering ω of vertices in V; (4) Constraint sets C_h and C_s;
Output: A color assignment of k colors, 1 through k, to vertices of G represented by an array.
1: initialize array X
2: **for** $l \leftarrow 1$ to $n - 1$ **do**
3:     pick unlabelled $v \in V$ at random
4:     $label(v) \leftarrow l$
5: **end for**
6: UNCOLOR $\leftarrow V$
7: UNCOLOR $\leftarrow$ ApplyConstraint(G, C_h)
8: **for** i from the smallest to largest integer (color) **do**
9:     **for** each vertex e in UNCOLOR **do**
10:         ColorVertexI(G, C_s, i, e)
11:     **end for**
12: **end for**
13: **if** (UNCOLOR $== \emptyset$) **then** exit
14:     **for** each vertex e in UNCOLOR **do**
15:         ColorVertexII(G, C_s, e)
16:     **end for**
17: **end if**
18:
19: **procedure** APPLYCONSTRAINT(G, C_h)
20:     **for** for each vertex j related by constraint $c_h(j) \in C_h$ **do**
21:         $color(X[j]) \leftarrow c_h(j).\varepsilon$
22:         update w_j and UNCOLOR
23:     **end for**
24:     return(UNCOLOR)
25: **end procedure**
26:
27: **procedure** COLORVERTEXI(G, C_s, i, e)
28:     **for** each vertex r that directly connects to e **do**
29:         check $L(r)$ and C_s to see if i is a valid color for e
30:         If so, $color(X[e]) \leftarrow i$
31:         update w_e and UNCOLOR
32:     **end for**
33: **end procedure**
34:
35: **procedure** COLORVERTEXII(G, C_h, e)
36:     size $= \infty$
37:     Select color $icolor$ that results in the smallest CVG
38:     $color(X[e]) \leftarrow icolor$
39:     update w_e and UNCOLOR
40: **end procedure**

---

particular vertex, it forms up a smaller CVG compared to all other colors. This process repeats until UNCOLOR set is empty.

4.3 Algorithm Complexity Analysis

Initially, n nodes in graph G are available for coloring. In ColorVertexI, as all available colors (k) have to be tentatively assigned to every node, so there are $n * k$ checks in this step. Suppose there are n remaining uncolored nodes in the worst case, each node with w_i colors needs to be assigned, in ColorVertexII we need $n * w_i * k$ rounds to pick the optimal color for each of them. To satisfy the algorithm constraints, after each color allocation, ColorVertexII also needs to check the size of the CVGs containing the current node in order to find the optimal color assignment with the minimal value. This makes the time complexity of ColorVertexII $O(n * k + n * w_{avg} * n_i * k)$, where w_{avg} is the average number of weights for all of the nodes in the network, and $O(n^2 * k)$ in the worst case

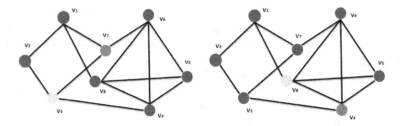

Fig. 3. Two random graphs with different software assignments

(the expanded vertex set size for each color in ColorVertexII is as large as the entire graph when n_i becomes n).

It is easy to show that if colors are fully available at each vertex during the coloring phase of our algorithm, i.e., $|L(v_i)| = k$, and the maximum degree in the graph $\Delta = max_{0 \neq i \neq N} d(v_i)$, an optimal software assignment can eliminate the existence of defective edges if the number of available colors for the to-be-colored node $k \geq \Delta + 1$. This matches the well-known conclusion in graph coloring that, the chromatic number of a graph is at most $\Delta + 1$ [20]. It is also practically useful to derive a theoretical lower bound of $m = |C|$ on an arbitrary graph for a software assignment solution. However, it is difficult to analyze its lower bound when the system requirements and constraints vary across the network without restricting the constraints. For the case where there is no constraints, the lower bound of chromatic number had been discussed and proved [21]. Another extreme case is when all vertices of graph have been completely colored by pre-defined constrains. In this case, the chromatic number is exactly the number of colors of the graph.

5   Evaluations

In this section, we present simulation results for evaluating the performance of our method with respect to the above-mentioned requirements.

5.1   Simulation Setup

Recall that our model is built on top of undirected graph G as the abstraction of networked systems (Section 2.1). To fully investigate the performance of our algorithm in arbitrary systems, we use three representative topologies to characterize the behaviors of different systems. Specifically, we consider three types of graphs with different degree distributions: random graph, regular graph and power-law graph. A regular graph does not have high connectivity in many cases and thus long and circuitous routes are required to reach other nodes. Typical examples of regular graphs includes lattice and ring lattice graph, which can be used to characterize the behavior of each vertex that depends upon the behavior of its nearest neighbors. In a random graph, each pair of vertices are connected with the same probability and the degrees of each vertex are distributed according to a binomial distribution. In a power-law graph, the degree distribution satisfies a power law. It contains highly connected nodes (hubs) and is a good model for the highly connected systems. Scale-free networks follow power-law and many well-known networks such as WWW and social networks are believed to be scale-free [22]. We believe these three types of graphs provide a reasonable coverage range of realistic networked systems.

In this simulation, we generate graphs using *igraph* package in R with approximately the same average degree of 8. Given approximately the same degree settings across tested graphs, we observe if network connectivity affects the defense capability of our method. The default size for graphs in our experiment is 1000. Since our proposed mechanism only targets on networked systems with central authority (so that assigning software could be possible), the size of network chosen for experiment is reasonable and adequate to illustrate the results of our study. All simulation results here are presented as the average of 50 trials.

To evaluate our approach under various settings, we run the simulations with different combinations of the number of colors and weights, which is denoted as *#color* and *#weight*, respectively. The total *#color* in the "color pool", represents the unique number of software choices available for hosts to choose from, and *#weight* represents the average number of distinct software finally installed on each host. We further define $r = \#weight/\#color$. In our simulation we set *#color* to 30 by default. We believe 30 is a reasonable number to illustrate the properties of our algorithm (Section 6 will discuss how to reduce the number of colors for a real system). In order to see how the number of average weight impacts the performance metrics, *#weight* is set to be an integer value ranging from 1 to 20. Intuitively, the larger r, the less heterogeneity of the system. We avoid choosing values larger than 20 because when it exceeds 20, the whole system becomes almost homogeneous.

5.2   Simulation Metrics

We adopt two metrics while evaluating the performance of our approach, including 1) the maximal number of nodes that can be possibly compromised; 2) the average size of isolated CVGs. For the first metric, we define S as the number of nodes contained in the largest CVG, denoting the number of machines compromised under the worst-case attacks. Nodes within the maximal CVGs are always attackers' first choice to penetrate into the network. In addition to that, we also consider the average size of CVGs, which indicates the overall robustness of the system. Although solely depending on the average size of CVGs may not directly indicate the survivability of the system, when taking it into considerations together with S, it can somehow be used to present separate infections caused by an attack. We use a symbol $\bar{s}$ to denote the average size of CVGs in the system.

5.3 Simulation Results

Impact of r. First, we use the power-law graph as an example to show how $r = \#weight/\#color$ impacts the heterogeneity of a system. Fig. 4 shows the variation of the largest CVG size S in responding to the changes of $\#weight$ and $\#color$ in a power-law graph.

We observe that given the same $\#color$, when $\#weight$ increases, the CVG size S becomes greater. In addition to the general distribution, we also notice that all three lines with different $\#color$ generate relatively flat trends at the beginning and are followed by a sharp increase when r reaches 0.4. Before this critical point, S remains relatively small (i.e., when $r < 0.4$, S is less than 50). However, after r exceeds 0.4, S begins to increase rapidly.

The simulation results indicate that the degree of heterogeneity our algorithm can create actually depends on the value of r. In general greater r tends to generate larger CVG, which in turn indicates a more homogeneous system. For instance, when $\#weight$ equals to $\#color$ ($r = 1$), there is only one component in the graph (the worst case). The results also suggest very limited decrease of the CVG size when r is less than 0.4. Hence, for systems already with a r value less than 0.4, there is little need to reduce the $\#weight$ (e.g., by decreasing the number of software packages to be installed in each host) to prevent automated attacks.

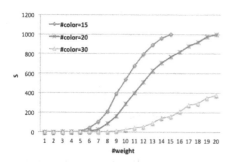

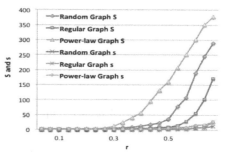

Fig. 4. S as a function of $\#weight$ and $\#color$

Fig. 5. Performance on three representative graphs

Impact of Network Topology. Next we conduct simulation to see how different network topologies might affect the CVG size (S) and the average size of isolated CVGs ($\bar{s}$). As can be seen from Fig. 5, although the same "flat to sloping" trends are also observed in all three different topologies, we find that the CVG size of a power-law graph actually starts to increase at a relatively low r value (0.4) as compared to the cases of a random graph (when $r = 0.5$) and a regular graph (when $r = 0.6$). The difference in "turning point" is due to the distinct connectivity of each kind of topology. Given the existence of high connectivity nodes in a power-law network, large CVGs tend to be more easily formed than in the other two types of graphs. In contrast, as characterized by low connectivity and relatively high cliquishness [23], a regular graph only generates large CVGs with larger r.

Besides the measurement on the CVG size, we also monitor the average size of all CVGs $\bar{s}$. Unlike our prior observations, we find that the distribution $\bar{s}$ with r increases gently this time. Although there also appear to be some turning points in all three distributions, even if r exceeds the threshold, $\bar{s}$ remains relatively small values (when r reaches 0.6, $\bar{s}$ of three graphs is still smaller than 50) as compared to the CVG sizes. The explanation of this phenomenon is that, when a CVG is formed (after r exceeds the threshold), the sizes of CVGs become polarized. That is, except the maximal ones which are very large, the other CVGs are relatively small (sizes between 1 to 50).

The above results are useful as they suggest that organizations with limited budget or software availability can still enhance their system heterogeneity by changing the underlying topology if possible.

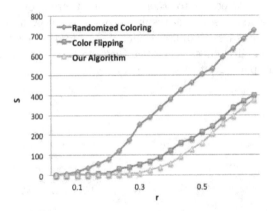

Fig. 6. Comparison with other algorithms

Comparison with Other Algorithms. We next compare our algorithm with two related algorithms, randomized coloring and color flipping, as proposed in a previous study [5]. In randomized coloring, each node picks a tentative color uniformly at random from the color pool, whereas color flipping extends the random coloring by allowing each node performs a local search amongst its immediate neighbors to switch colors to decrease the number of locally defective edges. Besides, we also compare our algorithm with the optimal solution based on brute-force search. We compare these algorithms in terms of the CVG size (S) as a function of r. Results are plotted in Fig. 6. As we can see from the figure, our algorithm outperforms both randomized coloring and color flipping methods by creating smaller CVGs given the same r.

Scalability and Computational Overhead. Finally, we repeat the experiment on graphs of larger size and measure the computational overhead introduced by our algorithm. Even though Fig. 7 shows the average time required by this assignment algorithm grows exponentially with size of the network, it still suggests our algorithm can be applied to large systems with thousands of nodes with acceptable time overhead. As showed in Fig. 7, in a commodity PC, it takes about 10 minutes to assign colors to 10 thousand nodes. The simulation result confirms the practicability of our algorithm.

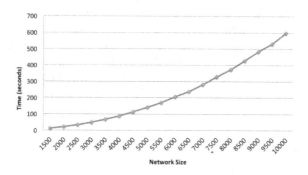

Fig. 7. Time overhead (in seconds)

6   Discussion and Future Work

Source of Diverse Software. In our problem setting, software diversity could be caused by a number of factors. First, installing different types of software on adjacent machines is itself a type of software diversity. One might doubt that if enterprises are willing to invest amounts of resources (e.g., purchasing licenses, training employees) to realize the mechanism. However, there is always a trade-off between security and costs. We believe the insights from the simulation results could help to ease the issue of finding the balance. Second, software of the same type might be implemented independently. For example, a number of web browsers are freely available, e.g., Firefox, IE, Chrome, so we may assume their vulnerabilities are different [6], and consider them as different colors. Third, with new compiler technique [24], each download of a piece of software could be a variant version of the client software which may not share the same vulnerability.

Vulnerabilities in Software. Another thing needs to be clarified in the context is that we do not actually need full knowledge of vulnerabilities (e.g., types and the exact number) in the software to be assigned. Given a software assignment solution, no matter how many vulnerabilities residing in a software product, even if it has an unknown vulnerability, CVGs of the graph remain the same. For the same reason, we can further shrink the size of "color pool" by considering multiple software packages as one single software product that can be represented by using a single color. For instance, all the standard software packages (including network services) come with Windows 7 in a batch, so the entire package of the standard Windows 7 distribution will only considered as one color. The edge between two adjacent hosts is defective as long as they both install Windows 7. For each (third-party) application installed later on, it may be considered as one color if it provides some network services.

Severity Level of Vulnerability. In reality, vulnerabilities often have different levels of severity. The risks of some vulnerabilities are minor while some may be quite significant. For two CVGs of the same size, a more severe vulnerability (e.g., gain complete control of a system) could result in a far more serious damage compared to a mild vulnerability (e.g., allow an attacker to collect some types of user information). As such, we may use different values to represent different levels of damage that could be resulted from an attack, and our objective of optimization will then become to minimize the overall damage by the attack. In our future work we will devise a new algorithm by taking into account this dimension.

7   Conclusions

In this work, we proposed a method for effectively containing automated attacks via software diversity. By building up a heterogeneous networked system, our defense mechanism increases the complexity of the networked system by utilizing off-the-shelf diverse software. Given the practical problems of software assignment, we presented a software assignment algorithm based on graph multi-coloring with real world constraints and system prerequisites. We analyzed the effectiveness of our methodology through extensive simulation study.

Acknowledgement. The work of Sencun Zhu was supported in part by NSF grant CCF-1320605 and a Google gift. We also thank the reviewers for helpful comments.

References

1. Lala, J.H., Schneider, F.B.: It monoculture security risks and defenses. IEEE Security & Privacy 7(1), 12–13 (2009)
2. Stamp, M.: Risks of monoculture. Communications of the ACM 47(3), 120 (2004)
3. Zhang, Y., Vin, H., Alvisi, L., Lee, W., Dao, S.K.: Heterogeneous networking: a new survivability paradigm. In: Proceedings of the 2001 Workshop on New Security Paradigms, pp. 33–39. ACM (2001)
4. Yang, Y., Zhu, S., Cao, G.: Improving sensor network immunity under worm attacks: a software diversity approach. In: Proceedings of the 9th ACM International Symposium on Mobile Ad Hoc Networking and Computing, pp. 149–158. ACM (2008)
5. O'Donnell, A.J., Sethu, H.: On achieving software diversity for improved network security using distributed coloring algorithms. In: Proceedings of the 11th ACM Conference on Computer and Communications Security, pp. 121–131. ACM (2004)
6. Han, J., Gao, D., Deng, R.H.: On the effectiveness of software diversity: A systematic study on real-world vulnerabilities. In: Flegel, U., Bruschi, D. (eds.) DIMVA 2009. LNCS, vol. 5587, pp. 127–146. Springer, Heidelberg (2009)

7. Snow, K.Z., Monrose, F., Davi, L., Dmitrienko, A., Liebchen, C., Sadeghi, A.R.: Just-in-time code reuse: On the effectiveness of fine-grained address space layout randomization. In: 2013 IEEE Symposium on Security and Privacy (SP), pp. 574–588. IEEE (2013)

8. Giuffrida, C., Kuijsten, A., Tanenbaum, A.S.: Enhanced operating system security through efficient and fine-grained address space randomization. In: USENIX Security Symposium (2012)

9. Davi, L.V., Dmitrienko, A., Nürnberger, S., Sadeghi, A.R.: Gadge me if you can: secure and efficient ad-hoc instruction-level randomization for x86 and arm. In: Proceedings of the 8th ACM SIGSAC Symposium on Information, Computer and Communications Security, pp. 299–310. ACM (2013)

10. Philippaerts, P., Younan, Y., Muylle, S., Piessens, F., Lachmund, S., Walter, T.: Code pointer masking: Hardening applications against code injection attacks. In: Holz, T., Bos, H. (eds.) DIMVA 2011. LNCS, vol. 6739, pp. 194–213. Springer, Heidelberg (2011)

11. Jafarian, J.H., Al-Shaer, E., Duan, Q.: Openflow random host mutation: transparent moving target defense using software defined networking. In: Proceedings of the First Workshop on Hot Topics in Software Defined Networks, pp. 127–132. ACM (2012)

12. Salamat, B., Jackson, T., Gal, A., Franz, M.: Orchestra: intrusion detection using parallel execution and monitoring of program variants in user-space. In: Proceedings of the 4th ACM European Conference on Computer Systems, pp. 33–46. ACM (2009)

13. Jensen, T.R., Toft, B.: Graph coloring problems, vol. 39. John Wiley & Sons (2011)

14. Chang, R.Y., Tao, Z., Zhang, J., Kuo, C.C.: A graph approach to dynamic fractional frequency reuse (ffr) in multi-cell ofdma networks. In: IEEE International Conference on Communications, ICC 2009, pp. 1–6. IEEE (2009)

15. Voigt, M.: List colourings of planar graphs. Discrete Mathematics 120(1), 215–219 (1993)

16. Hujter, M., Tuza, Z.: Precoloring extension. ii. Graph classes related to bipartite graphs. Acta Mathematica Universitatis Comenianae 62(1), 1–11 (1993)

17. Bulatov, A.A.: H-coloring dichotomy revisited. Theoretical Computer Science 349(1), 31–39 (2005)

18. Tuza, Z.: Graph colorings with local constraints-a survey. Discussiones Mathematicae Graph Theory 17(2), 161–228 (1997)

19. Borodin, A., Ivan, I., Ye, Y., Zimny, B.: On sum coloring and sum multi-coloring for restricted families of graphs. Theoretical Computer Science 418, 1–13 (2012)

20. Welsh, D.J., Powell, M.B.: An upper bound for the chromatic number of a graph and its application to timetabling problems. The Computer Journal 10(1), 85–86 (1967)

21. Bollobás, B.: The chromatic number of random graphs. Combinatorica 8(1), 49–55 (1988)

22. Scale-free networks, https://en.wikipedia.org/wiki/Scale-free_network

23. Premo, L.: Local extinctions, connectedness, and cultural evolution in structured populations. Advances in Complex Systems 15(01n02) (2012)

24. Jackson, T., Salamat, B., Homescu, A., Manivannan, K., Wagner, G., Gal, A., Brunthaler, S., Wimmer, C., Franz, M.: Compiler-generated software diversity. In: Moving Target Defense, pp. 77–98. Springer (2011)

FSquaDRA: Fast Detection
of Repackaged Applications

Yury Zhauniarovich[1], Olga Gadyatskaya[1,2], Bruno Crispo[1],
Francesco La Spina[1], and Ermanno Moser[1]

[1] Department of Information Engineering and Computer Science,
University of Trento, Trento, Italy
{zhauniarovich,gadyatskaya,crispo,laspina,moser}@disi.unitn.it
[2] Interdisciplinary Center for Security, Reliability and Trust,
University of Luxembourg, Luxembourg City, Luxembourg

Abstract. The ease of Android applications repackaging and prolifer-
ation of application clones in Google Play and other markets call for
new effective techniques to detect repackaged code and combat distribution of cloned applications. Today all existing techniques for repackaging
detection are based on code similarity or feature (e.g., permission set)
similarity evaluation. We propose a new approach to detect repackaging based on the resource files available in application packages. Our
tool called FSquaDRA performs a quick pairwise application comparison (full pairwise comparison for 55,000 applications in just 80 hours on
a laptop), as it measures how many identical resources are present inside
both packages under analysis. The intuition behind our approach is that
malicious repackaged applications still need to maintain the "look and
feel" of the originals by including the same images and other resource
files, even though they might have additional code included or some of
the original code removed.

To evaluate the reliability of our approach we perform a comparison
of the FSquaDRA similarity scores with the code-based similarity scores
of AndroGuard for a dataset of randomly selected application pairs, and
our results demonstrate strong positive correlation of the FSquaDRA
resource-based score with the code-based similarity score.

Keywords: Smartphones, Repackaging, Mobile applications.

1 Introduction

Mobile ecosystems today represent a huge and fast growing market. Success
stories of such companies as Rovio (with the Angry Birds game) attract to the
mobile business vast amounts of developers. Yet, the developers can suffer from
monetary and reputation losses when their applications are stolen and appear
on the markets *repackaged*.

The problem of application (app for short) stealing on Android stems from
the fact that at present it is not very difficult to repackage an Android app.

V. Atluri and G. Pernul (Eds.): DBSec 2014, LNCS 8566, pp. 130–145, 2014.

Applications are usually signed with a self-signed certificate. Thus, an adversary can easily change the code and sign the app with his own certificate. At present, neither the official Google Play market nor alternative markets do not detect if an application has been repackaged. At the same time, there is a strong aspiration from adversaries to steal applications. They can earn monetary profits either by changing the revenue destination of advertisement libraries, or by embedding malware, which can transform phones into controllable "zombies". Thus, to maintain the healthiness of the ecosystem there is a strong need to detect the repackaged applications and prevent their distribution.

Currently the problem of Android app repackaging is widely explored and several solutions to identify plagiarized applications were proposed, e.g., [9,7,6,10,16,12]. All these solutions are based on features extracted from the app code. However, it is clear that the code itself is often impacted by the repackaging process: the added malicious functionality (new advertisement libraries and/or malware code) modifies the code of the app. Additionally, the usage of obfuscation libraries during repackaging can further modify the code [11]. Moreover, adversaries can simply replicate some initial behaviour of an app (so called app spoofing [14]). Obviously, the detection rates of repackaging for a code similarity-based techniques decrease under the influence of these factors. Notice that the availability of various tools like smali/backsmali [4] or apktool [3] greatly alleviates the task of code changing and application repackaging.

Yet, it is not only the code that defines an app. Nowadays, smartphones have powerful processors, advanced video and audio systems that are able to support screens with very high resolutions and to produce sounds of high quality. These factors lead to the constant demand of attractive apps. Therefore, to become popular an app should not only include the code with interesting functionality, but should also contain attractive layouts, images and other supplementary resources, which become an integral part of the user experience. These resource files (resources, for short) are delivered on the device packaged together with the code, and are now an inseparable part of modern mobile apps.

This paper proposes an approach to detect repackaged apps based on comparison of the content of the resource files forming Android app packages. Our approach relies on the observation that usually Android packages (apk files) include a significant number of resources, and that malicious repackagers aim to change the applications in a way they resemble the originals as much as possible. Therefore, the code parts may change but the resource files (including icons, images, music and video files, etc.) often remain the same.

To be practical, the approach of detecting repackaged applications based on resource files comparison needs to be fast enough, considering the vast number of Android apps (currently there are more then 700,000 apps only in the official market). Thus, a simple pairwise comparison of all files inside two compared apps is not quite scalable because the complexity is proportional to the product of the number of files inside two packages multiplied by the average size of a file. Luckily, during the process of app signing a hash of each file inside the apk is computed and stored in the package. We leverage this information to compute the similarity of applications. Thus, our approach is fast enough to be used even for comparing applications pairwise.

To our knowledge, we are the first who propose to detect Android repackaged applications based on similarities in resource files, and not on the ones in the code. This paper contains the following contributions:

- We propose a novel technique to detect repackaged Android applications based on files included in the packages.
- Using the peculiarities of Android app signing process we develop a very fast algorithm that can be used for pairwise comparison of apps. FSquaDRA managed to compare on average 6700 app pairs per second on our dataset using a commodity hardware. This number shows that our approach clearly outperforms all available solutions based on pair-wise code comparison.
- Understanding the importance of Android app repackaging problem we release our tool as open-source[1] to drive the research in this direction.
- We evaluate the practicality of our approach by comparing the resource-based similarity score produced by FSquaDRA with the code-based similarity score computed by the open-source AndroGuard tool [8,2]. Our experiments show that the FSquaDRA similarity score is strongly correlated with the Andro-Guard code similarity score.
- We evaluate the effectiveness of the FSquaDRA on a dataset with more than 55000 applications crawled on Google Play and 7 alternative markets, and report repackaging rates for this dataset.

2   Our Approach

Android applications are spread across the devices in the form of Android packages (`apk` files) that contain code, manifest, libraries and resource files compressed in a `zip` archive. Thus, each app includes not only the code, but also a large set of supplementary files being an integral part of the Android package. This is confirmed by our dataset that consists of 55000 apps. For this dataset on average there are 315.56 files inside an Android package with maximum value of 11099 files and minimum of 4 (we present the details of our dataset later on).

Previously, to detect repackaged applications researchers considered predominantly the code (`classes.dex`) and the manifest `AndroidManifest.xml` files. We propose to use the full set of files inside apks to detect repackaging.

Our intuitions are as follows. An adversary, who clones an application, seeks to resemble the original one as much as possible, thus, increasing the probability of the clone installation. In Android apps code is loosely coupled with resources giving the adversary a possibility to easily change the code. For example, the legitimate Opera Mini application and its repackaged version containing malware [13] coincide in 230 out of 234 files inside those packages.

For the scope of this paper we consider two cases of repackaging: (malicious) *plagiarism*, when two application packages include the same files but are signed

---

[1] https://github.com/zyrikby/FSquaDRA

by different developers (with different certificates), and (benign) *rebranding*, when two application packages include the same files and are signed by the same certificate.

Using binary comparison of files, which constitute two Android applications, it is possible to understand to what extent these two apps are similar. Unfortunately, binary comparison is not a cheap operation. Moreover, a file in the first app should be compared against each file in the second package. These overheads may be considerably reduced using comparison of the file digests (hashes). Our tool uses this technique to calculate the similarity between two applications. At the same time, digest computation against the content of a file requires considerable resources consumption and, thus, directly cannot be used in a tool that has to process significant amount of apks. To overcome this limitation we use the hashes calculated during the application signing process. Thus, the overhead for hash computations does not affect our tool. To facilitate the understanding of our algorithm we first describe the code signing process used in Android.

Android application signing background. An unsigned `apk` file contains a compiled code and a set of resources. In Android, all Java code is compiled into one file called `classes.dex`. Moreover, some of the xml files can also be compiled into a binary format. Besides compiled files, an Android package usually contains non-compiled resource such as icons, drawables, text files, different binary files, etc. This archive is then signed with the standard Java signing tool called *jarsigner*. This tool creates a special directory inside the archive called `META-INF`, where it stores the information related to the code signing process.

We are only interested in the first step of the signing process, which produces the main manifest file (`MANIFEST.MF`). During this step the *jarsigner* tool calculates a digest of each file inside the unsigned `apk` and writes it into the `MANIFEST.MF` file. On Android, the *SHA1* algorithm is used to compute the digest of file content.

The manifest file consists of the main attributes section and and a set of per-entry attributes, one entry for each file contained in the unsigned apk file. These per-entry attributes store information about the file name (relative path) and the digest encoded using the `base64` format. Therefore, after the first step of application signing process a SHA1 digest of the content of each file is available in the manifest file. These hash values are later used in our tool.

The algorithm and implementation details. Protocol 1 describes the algorithm implemented in FSquaDRA for pairwise comparison of apps. In Line 2 of Protocol 1 we select all apk files located under the directory, the path to which is specified by the variable *path* provided as an argument. After that, in Lines 6-10 FSquaDRA extracts the required information from the apk files. At first, our tool gets the name of the file. Then it extracts the attributes of the apk using the `getApkAttributesToMemory` method. In particular, it iterates over the entries in the `MANIFEST.MF` file and writes the results into a map, which key corresponds to the relative path of a file inside the package and value is equal to the SHA1 hash of the file. Additionally, during this step FSquaDRA extracts

Protocol 1. The algorithm of application comparison

```
1:  ApkAttr_list ← [  ]
2:  Apk_list ← getApkFileList(path)
3:  \\ Get application attributes
4:  for all A_i ∈ Apk_list do
5:      ApkName_i ← getApkName(A_i)
6:      Attr_i ← getApkAttributesToMemory(A_i)
7:      Add (fileName_i, Attr_i) to ApkAttr_list
8:  end forall
9:  size ← length(ApkAttr_list)
10: \\ Pairwise comparison of applications
11: for (k = 0; k < size; k + +) do
12:     hashes_k ← getFileHashesSet(Attr_k)
13:     certs_k ← getCertHashes(Attr_k)
14:     for (l = k + 1; l < size; l + +) do
15:         hashes_l ← getFileHashesSet(Attr_l)
16:         certs_l ← getCertHashes(Attr_l)
17:         jSim ← getJaccardIndex(hashes_k, hashes_l)
18:         sameCert ← certsTheSame(certs_k, certs_l)
19:         OUT: ApkName_k, ApkName_l, sameCert, jSim
20:     end for
21: end for
```

the developer certificates, which have been used for the application signing, and stores into *Attr* object the digests computed over these certificates. This allows us to reduce the memory consumption of FSquaDRA and speed up the certificate comparison process. The name of the app file along with the object *Attr_i* containing all required application attributes are stored into the *ApkAttr_list* list.

Lines 15-25 show how the comparison of applications is performed. The similarity score (the FSquaDRA similarity, or the *fss* score for short) corresponds to the Jaccard similarity coefficient (expressed by Formula 1) computed over the sets of file hashes extracted in Line 8.

$$jSim(H_k, H_l) = \frac{|H_k \cap H_l|}{|H_k \cup H_l|} \tag{1}$$

We implemented our algorithm in Java. We did not parallelize it intentionally (i.e., our tool runs in a single-thread program). This allows us to calculate the net time required to run our comparisons and predict the execution time and memory consumption. An increase of a dataset results in the linear growth of the execution time for attributes extraction, while the pairwise comparison operation cumulative time rises quadratically (in the number of apks under consideration). In the current implementation the memory consumption grows linearly with the number of applications. The code is availabe under the Apache-2.0 license[2].

3   Evaluation

Our dataset consists of 55,779 Android applications. The dataset collection was performed during June-July of 2013. During this period we explored 8 different markets: the official *Google Play*[3] market (13,223 apps; including 500 top

---

[2] https://github.com/zyrikby/FSquaDRA
[3] https://play.google.com/store/apps

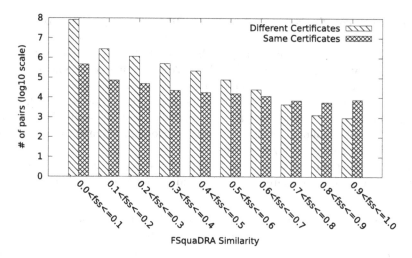

Fig. 1. Histogram of app repackaging rates detected with FSquaDRA (logarithmic scale)

free apps for each category) and 7 third-party stores: *androidbest*[4] (1662 apps), *androiddrawer*[5] (2857 apps), *androidlife*[6] (1678 apps), *anruan*[7] (4232 apps), *appsapk*[8] (2679 apps), *pandaapp*[9] (14,143 apps), and *SlideME*[10] (15,305). Our dataset occupies 317.4 GB of disk space.

We have run FSquaDRA on the collected app dataset on a Mac Book Pro laptop with 2.9 GHz Intel Core i7 Processor with 2 cores, and 8GB 1600 Mhz DDR3 memory. FSquaDRA required 15.10 hours to load all apk attributes in memory for our complete dataset, and 64.41 hours to compute the similarity scores for all apk pairs ($>10^9$) in our dataset consuming less than 6GB of RAM. On the dataset FSquaDRA performs on average 6700 app pair comparisons per second. We consider these results quite encouraging, as pairwise app comparison for code-based similarity metrics cannot be executed in comparable time.

Figure 1 presents a histogram of positive fss scores distribution for our dataset of 55779 applications (in logarithmic scale). Notice that the app pairs with $fss>0$ constitute approximately 5.41% of the total app pairs number for our dataset. To simplify presentation we break down the fss values into 10 bins in the range $(0, 1]$. In Fig. 1 we can see that the vast majority of the application pairs with detected resource similarity have the fss score in the range $(0, 0.1]$, and that for the fss score in the range $(0.7, 1]$ there are more app pairs

---

[4] http://androidbest.ru/

[5] http://www.androiddrawer.com/

[6] http://androidlife.ru/

[7] http://www.anruan.com/

[8] http://www.appsapk.com/

[9] http://android.pandaapp.com/

[10] http://slideme.org/

with the same certificate detected by FSquaDRA than app pairs with different certificates. We provide more insight why this is the case in the sequel.

To evaluate the quality of our approach we would like to compare our results with some state-of-art code similarity-based repackaging detection technique, e.g., [16,15,7,10]. Unfortunately, these tools were not released publicly, and we were not able to obtain them. Similar problem was also reported in [11], where the authors used AndroGuard as a freely available tool for comparison of code similarity in apks. Following this approach, we use AndroGuard to provide us a metrics of code similarity for app pairs.

The main question we would like to investigate is whether the FSquaDRA similarity metrics is correlated with the AndroGuard code similarity metrics. This can be interpreted twofold:

- *Problem of false positives.* For apps that FSquaDRA classifies as similar, are they similar also according to the AndroGuard classification (and vice-versa)? If our tool classifies an app pair as similar, but there is no actual code similarity, this pair can be interpreted as false positive. It is obvious that it is impossible to completely avoid false positives for FSquaDRA because common resources, such as, e.g., open source sound and image files, can increase the FSquaDRA metrics, while the code would be different. So here we are interested in strong correlation of the similarity metrics values.
- *Problem of false negatives.* For apps that FSquaDRA classifies as completely different, are there many app pairs sharing code similarities according to AndroGuard? Again, it is not possible to completely avoid false negatives due to the different nature of code similarity and resource similarity, but we would like to assert that the false negatives rate is not too high.

Notice that in this section we interpret the AndroGuard code similarity score as the ground truth. We have performed manual inspection of some application pairs to confirm the findings of FSquaDRA (reported further), but it is impossible to inspect manually a substantial subset of our dataset. Therefore we have to rely on the code similarity metrics as the ground for evaluating FSquaDRA reliability.

The AndroGuard algorithm which computes the similarity score (*ags* for short) of two apps is presented in [8]. The similarity score is based on the analysis of Dalvik code of an app pair and detection of identical, similar and different (new or deleted) methods in the apps. To perform this, the algorithm a) generates a signature for each method of each application, b) identifies all methods that are identical in both apps, c) discovers all methods that are similar. A signature is generated based on the method control flow information, used API calls and exceptions inside the method. If two signature hashes are identical then the methods are considered identical. To compute the similarity between methods Normalized Compression Distance (NCD) [5] is used.

AndroGuard however was found to be not very reliable, as its similarity metrics was discovered to be not commutative. That is, for two apks A and B, it could be that $ags^*(A, B) \neq ags^*(B, A)$, where ags^* is the value computed by the AndroGuard tool directly. We have decided to still use the existing Andro-

Guard implementation, but to adjust the AndroGuard score. We have experimented with a series of app pairs, and have established that the metrics $ags = (ags^*(A,B) + ags^*(B,A))/2$ is more faithful than the original ags^* similarity score, and we have used this metrics for comparison with FSquaDRA results.

To compute a similarity value for two applications AndroGuard takes significantly more time than FSquaDRA, and it was not possible to compute the similarity metrics for the whole app corpus we have crawled. E.g., it takes approximately 65 seconds on average to compare one pair of apps using AndroGuard (the actual time of comparison depends a lot on the similarity of apps in the pair; it takes significantly less time to compare very similar apps than completely different ones). We cannot also rely on a straightforward random selection of app pairs, because it is clear from Fig. 1 that, e.g., the share of app pairs with fss similarity in the range (0, 0.2] is a lot larger than the share of app pairs in (0.8, 1.0], which is as interesting. Therefore, we have performed a random selection of 100 app pairs with same certificate and 100 app pairs with different certificates from each bin with non-null fss metrics, and we have computed the AndroGuard similarity metrics for these pairs (2000 pairs total). This selection enables the best selection of an app pairs corpus with different fss metrics, and without strong predominance of some fss value range. To evaluate the false negative rates we have randomly selected 100 apk pairs with same certificate and 100 apk pairs with different certificates from the dataset with $fss=0$.

Table 1 presents summary statistics computed for the randomly selected app pairs. Notice that for non-null fss values we compare separately app pairs with same certificate and with the different ones, as these two groups are different by nature. This observation is indeed reinforced by the data we have. Fig. 2(a) presents a scatterplot of the fss and ags similarity metrics values for the selected app pairs with different certificates (potentially plagiarised). We can see the strong correlation of the values from the figure. This is confirmed by the data: the standard Pearson's product-moment correlation computed for data in this figure is 0.791. Notice that any value ≥ 0.5 is commonly considered as strong correlation. Testing for the null-hypothesis (that true correlation is non existent) for this dataset gives that the 95% confidence interval is [0.767, 0.813]; and the p-value$\approx 10^{-16}$, so we can safely reject the null-hypothesis. The sample mean of the difference (fss-ags) for each selected app pair with different certificates is approximately equal to -0.047, with standard t-test rejecting the null-hypothesis (the p-value$\approx 10^{-12}$), and the 95% confidence interval for true mean [-0.052, -0.029]. The standard deviation for the difference (fss-ags) is 0.186. We also present a boxplot for this difference in Fig. 3(a).

These data confirm that FSquaDRA can be an effective tool to detect repackaged applications, as the fss similarity values for app pairs with different certificates are highly correlated with code-based similarity metrics of AndroGuard; and the average difference in the similarity metrics produced by FSquaDRA and by AndroGuard is not significant.

Fig. 2(b) presents a scatterplot of the fss and ags similarity metrics for the randomly selected apk pairs signed with the same certificate (potentially rebranded). The standard Pearson's product-moment correlation for this dataset is approximately 0.58 (the null-hypothesis on correlation is rejected, with 95% confidence interval for correlation [0.538, 0.62] , and p-value $\approx 10^{-16}$). This can be still interpreted as a strong correlation, but it is less strong than for the apk pairs with different certificate. The sample mean for the difference (fss-ags) in this dataset is approximately equal to -0.27 (standard t-test reports 95% confidence interval for true mean [-0.292, -0.259], and the null-hypothesis for sample difference mean being zero is rejected with p-value$\approx 10^{-16}$). This means that on average for apks signed with the same certificate FSquaDRA tends to estimate their similarity score noticeably lower than the code-based similarity score computed by AndroGuard. These findings can be intuitively explained by the fact that developers tend to reuse the code patterns across their products. For app pairs signed with the same certificate it is clear that they can contain similar code snippets with high probability. Therefore higher code similarity score is expectable.

We can also see from Fig. 2(b) that there is a lot of app pairs with very high AndroGuard similarity score, but varying FSquaDRA similarity score, which are most probably the pairs impacting the correlation coefficient for this dataset. We have manually inspected some of these pairs and have managed to find several patterns, when such situations occur. One of the most common observed case is when the same code is used for displaying different content. For instance, in our dataset we found several applications, which were developed to display books. For every book a single application has been developed. All these applications use the same code but the resources (the book chapters) are different. Thus, our tool shows low similarity score (because still some files, e.g., `classes.dex`, are the same), while according to the code similarity score the applications in the pair are the same. Similar behaviour we also witnessed with other categories of applications, which display the same type of content, e.g., for wallpaper apps and widgets. Another interesting example, which falls into this category, is when the apps in the pair provide a UI customization functionality for the third application. In this case, AndroGuard produces high similarity score for such pairs of apps, while because of the difference of the UI components FSquaDRA reports low similarity.

The lower correlation of the metrics can be also attributed to the usage of the same ad libraries. This happens when the fraction of the code produced by a developer significantly smaller than the ones brought by ad libraries. In this case AndroGuard falsely detects applications as repackaged, while FSquaDRA produces more credible results (because the applications are different).

Fig. 3(b) presents a boxplot for the sample difference (fss-ags). In comparison with Fig. 3(a), we can notice that for apk pairs with the same signature the range of the similarity scores difference is larger. Our data suggests that FSquaDRA may not be as efficient for detecting repackaging in apps signed with the same certificate (rebranded), as it is for the apps signed with different certificates (plagiarized). Nevertheless, correlation of the FSquaDRA score with the code-based similarity score of AndroGuard is still strong (>0.5).

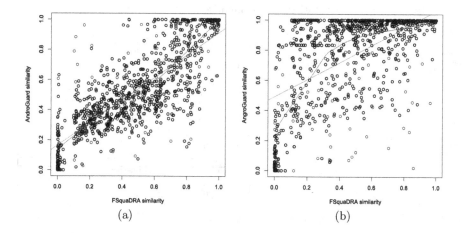

Fig. 2. Scatterplots of FSquaDRA similarity vs. AndroGuard similarity for the pairs: a) signed with different certificates; b) signed with the same certificate. The red line is the line of best fit, the blue curve is the LOWESS (locally weighted scatterplot smoothing line).

Finally, let us consider the difference (fss-ags) for the randomly selected app pairs with fss=0. The sample mean of (fss-ags), or, simply, of the ags similarity score taken with the negative sign, for these app pairs is approximately -0.041, with the 95% confidence interval for the true mean [-0.051, -0.0309], and the standard deviation for this dataset is approximately equal to 0.0737. Thus, FSquaDRA does not error a lot on average. From these statistics we can see that for apk pairs not marked as similar by FSquaDRA AndroGuard does not see significant code similarity either, even for applications signed with the same certificate. Therefore we can conclude that if developers do not include any similar resouces in apps, they also mostly do not reuse code (this is often the case of apps produced by companies). We do not report the correlation coefficient for this type of dataset, as the fss score equals to 0.

4   Cross-Market Repackaging

After asserting that FSquaDRA produces similarity metrics that is valuable for detecting repackaged applications, being strongly correlated with the code similarity metrics, we look into repackaging rates corresponding to the markets under consideration, and investigate clusters of repackaged applications. Notice that clearly any FSquaDRA score greater than 0 for a pair of apks can be an indication that these apks are clones. However, to increase the certainty of detecting clones we have chosen the fss value of 0.7 to be a reliable threshold for repackaging. Based on our observations, we consider it a good starting point for resource similarity score sufficient to reliably detect clones, and we leave the task of identifying the threshold precisely for future work.

Table 1. Summary statistics for comparison of the fss and ags metrics

Sample	Statistics	Value	Details
App pairs with non-null fss with different certificates in comparison with ags; 1000 app pairs	Mean of difference fss - ags	-0.04122781	Standard one sample t-test 95% confidence interval: [-0.05278174, -0.02967388] p-value = 4.62e-12
	Standard deviation for difference fss - ags	0.1861895	
	Median	-0.04799	
	Correlation coefficient of fss and ags values	0.7919082	Pearson's product-moment correlation 95% confidence interval [0.7675988, 0.8139426] p-value $\leq$ 2.2e-16
App pairs with non-null fss with same certificates in comparison with ags; 1000 app pairs	Mean of difference fss - ags	-0.276119	Standard one sample t-test 95% confidence interval: [-0.2928976, -0.2593405] p-value = 2.2e-16
	Standard deviation for difference fss - ags	0.2703832	
	Median	-0.25180	
	Correlation coefficient of fss and ags values	0.580733	Pearson's product-moment correlation 95% confidence interval [0.5381128, 0.6203911] p-value $\leq$ 2.2e-16
App pairs with null fss with mixed certificates in comparison with ags; 200 app pairs	Mean of difference fss - ags	-0.04124	Standard one sample t-test 95% confidence interval: [-0.05152188, -0.03095351] p-value = 1.777e-13
	Standard deviation for difference fss - ags	0.07375432	
	Median	-0.01304	
2200 app pairs, fss including app pairs with the same ags; and different certificates, and with fss=0 and fss>0	Mean of difference fss - ags	-0.14800	Standard one sample t-test 95% confidence interval: [-0.1585031, -0.1374917] p-value = 2.2e-16
	Standard deviation for difference fss - ags	0.2512748	
	Median	-0.09894	
	1st quartile	-0.27380	
	3rd quartile	0.00000	
	Correlation coefficient of fss and ags values	**0.7149053**	Pearson's product-moment correlation 99% confidence interval [0.6869681, 0.7407324] p-value ¡ 2.2e-16

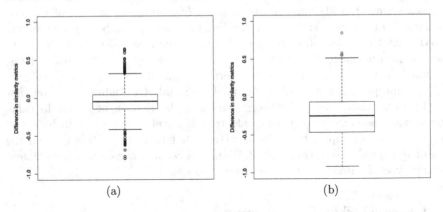

(a)   (b)

Fig. 3. Boxplot of the difference of FSquaDRA similarity with AndroGuard similarity for app pairs with fss>0: a) signed with different certificates; b) sighed with the same certificate

Cross-market comparison. Table 2 presents the repackaging rates of Google Play applications cloned in other markets. Under the assumption that the Google Play market is the source of original applications, this table reports how many cloned pairs were detected with the fss score greater than 0.7, and the total number of apk pairs with fss>0 for all markets of our study compared with Google Play (the corresponding subset of our dataset). In this experiment we have compared each crawled apk in Google Play with each apk crawled in the considered third party markets. We also provide the processing time required for each market comparison with Google Play. Notice that for all markets the number of app pairs with the fss score greater than 0.7 is not very significant. To understand better how the big is the subset of potentially repackaged applications we also provide the total number of app pairs with $fss>0$ detected, and the number of pairs with $fss>0$ and signed with different certificates.

From Table 2 we can observe that the markets with the highest repackaging rates are androiddrawer (16.16% of app pairs have similarity of resources $fss>0$) and Google Play (10.31% of app pairs have $fss>0$). We suspect that this is the case because these markets are more popular sources of apps, in comparison with others; and malicious repackagers that seek acquiring significant ad revenues or big user base for their botnets may target more popular markets. Yet, this intuition needs to be confirmed with more data, and there can be other plausible explanations.

Table 2. Results of experiments, each market in comparison with Google Play

Market	Repackaging Rates				Time	
	Same signature # pairs ($fss>0.7$)	Different signature # pairs ($fss>0.7$)	Total $fss>0$ (% of total pair #)	Total $fss>0$ with diff. cert. (% of total pair #)	Loading apk attributes in memory	Processing
androidbest	27	10	714258 (3.25%)	713194 (3.24%)	14.16 min	12.274 min
androiddrawer	528	14	6108547 (16.16%)	6097437 (16.14%)	15.46 min	56.02 min
androidlife	41	44	1145396 (5.16%)	1143400 (5.15%)	14.24 min	15.67 min
anruan	106	97	3349271(5.985%)	3347895 (5.982%)	15.26 min	36.11 min
appsapk	422	86	2105334 (5.94%)	2094716 (5.91%)	15.66 min	22.52 min
Google Play	1897	1301	9019858 (10.31%)	8985401 (10.27%)	13.28 min	59.97 min
pandaapp	755	381	10741872 (5.74%)	10726743 (5.73%)	28.52 min	136.65 min
SlideME	475	579	9496874 (4.69%)	9481029 (4.68%)	25.96 min	97.07 min

Application clusters. Repackaged applications can form clusters (a set of repackaged apps stemming from some original application). We tried to elicit and analyze strongly connected clusters containing applications with very similar resources. The results produced by FSquaDRA can be interpreted as an undirected labelled graph, where nodes correspond to the applications in our dataset and edges represent similarity relationship between two applications, labelled with the fss similarity score. Thus, to find the clusters of applications we used the following algorithm. At first, we selected all pairs, which had shown the FSquaDRAsimilarity value more than 0.7. After that in the resulting graph we searched for connected components (i.e., set of connected nodes), which corresponded to application clusters. We looked for clusters that have 3 and more nodes. Using this approach we discovered 71 cluster, the largest of which included 9 applications.

We have investigated manually some of the clusters, and we report on the largest two of them (smaller clusters are not reported for the lack of space). The largest cluster with 9 nodes contains applications from 3 different markets (4 from Google Play, 4 from SlideME and 1 from appsapk), all signed with different certificates. The nodes are connected with 8 edges; similarity scores for app pairs not connected by an edge vary in the range [0.61, 0.7). The cluster with 8 applications contains packages distributed on 5 different markets (2 come from Google Play, 3 from SlideME, 1 from anruan, and 2 from pandapp). These 8 applications are connected by 7 nodes, and the fss scores for the app pairs not connected by an edge vary in [0.4, 0.6). In this cluster 3 applications (from anruan and pandapp) were signed by the same certificate, and others were signed with different certificates.

After we manually inspected all applications in these clusters, we discovered that these apps were legitimate applications and not maliciously repackaged. These "false positives" appeared because all apps in the cluster used the same popular library ActionBarSherlock [1], which is supplied with lots of files. Additionally, the applications contained a very limited number of their own unique files, and thus FSquaDRA falsely detected them as repackaged applications. We performed also an analysis using AndroGuard and found out that the code files were also very poisoned with this library. AndroGuard similarity scores for these clusters were in the range [0.46, 0.96]. Therefore, in the shadow of the methodology selected for our analysis this is still a good result for our tool. However, this example clearly shows that it is desirable to implement techniques for automatic library resources detection and exclusion, similarly as it is done for code in [7,15]. We leave this problem for the future work.

5   Related Work

Existing works in repackaging detection on Android mostly focus on code similarity and do not consider the resource similarity, in contrast to FSquaDRA. Unfortunately, it is impossible to compare our tool with others because existing research tools, excluding AndroGuard, are not publicly available.

In [16] the authors search repackaged applications in third-party markets using Google Play as a baseline. A tool called DroidMOSS uses fuzzy hashing of code to calculate a fingerprint of the app and then computes the edit distance between two fingerprints to compute the similarity score. The analysis performed in [16] shows that 5-13% applications hosted in alternative markets are repackeged. These conclusions agree with our finddings reported in Sec. 4.

In the paper [15] the authors further investigate the problem of repackaged apps and concentrate on detection of piggybacked applications (repackaged apps that carry a malicious payload). To find these apps the authors perform code decoupling into primary and non-primary modules, and compute a fingerprint for each primary module, which contains the main functionality. After that while iterating over the fingerprints the linearithmic algorithm detects apps with similar primary modules, which are considered as piggybacked candidates. Finally, piggybacked apps are detected comparing the sets of non-primary modules of these similar apps. The experiments show the presence of 1.3% piggybacked apps in the dataset.

Paper [6] presents the DNADroid tool detecting cloned (plagiarized) applications. Using the semantic similarity of apps the tool detects potential clone candidates. At the second step, the tool extracts Program Flow Graph of each method in compared applications, and, based on the subgraph isomorphism problem as a final criteria of method similarity, computes similarity score of the apps. DNADroid managed to detect 191 cloned pairs (0% false positives was reported). The authors also compared their tool with AndroGuard [2]. On 191 pairs AndroGuard failed for 24 pairs and produced very low similarity score for 10 pairs meaning that it missed 18% of the pairs found by DNADroid. Continuing the work on DNADroid [6] Crussell et al. developed a new tool AnDarwin [7], which extracts features from app code and compares them, instead of pairwise comparisons of code, allowing to perform large-scale analysis of Android applications. On a dataset of 265,359 third-party apps collected from 17 markets DNADroid detected 4,295 cloned and 36,106 rebranded applications (cloned apps with the same signature).

The authors in the work [12] concentrate on investigation which applications are likely to suffer from being plagiarised, and how to detect plagiarised applications uploaded to a market. The authors analysed the meta-information of 158,000 applications. They detected that 29.4% of applciations are more likely to be plagiarised, based on the assumption that it was more likely that a malicious developer would use for plagiarising the applications, which alredy contained the permissions needed to perform malicios actions.

The paper [10] presents another approach to detect code reuse among Android apps. To discover the similarities between the code they use k-grams of Dalvik opcode sequences as features. To obtain app representation they apply hashing to the extracted features. The Juxtapp tool can detect (a) buggy and vulnerable code reuse (b) known malware instances and (c) pirated applications. To assess the Juxtapp efficiency the authors ran the experiment of pairwise comparison on a set of 95.000 Android apps (an Amazon EC2 cluster with 25 slave nodes was used) that lasted about 200 minutes. As for effectiveness, among the apps from Android Market the authors identified 174 samples containing vulnerable patterns in the in-app billing code and 239 apps containing those in the code using Licence Verification Library. Moreover, they identified 34 new instances of known malware in the alternative Anzhi market.

Recently, a framework for evaluating Android application repackaging detection algorithms has been proposed [11]. In the paper the authors classify currently available approaches for detection of repackaged applications and present a framework that can be used to assess the effectiveness of this kind of algorithms. The framework translates Dalvik bytecode into Java code, applies obfuscation techniques and packs back the code into the Dalvik representation. To assess the effectiveness of a tool is run over real and modified by the framework app. The authors proposed to assess repackaging detection algorithms by broadness (i.e., how an algorithm can stand to obfuscation techniques applied separately) and by depth (i.e., if an algorithm is resilient to techniques applied sequentially). As the case study, the authors applied the framework to AndroGuard [2] – the only publicly available tool for repackaging detection. The results show that Andro-Guard can successfully combat with different obfuscation techniques and, thus, can be widely used to detect repackaged applications. Notice that FSquaDRA will successfully pass the tests of [11], because it does not rely on code similarity.

6   Conclusions

In this paper we present an approach to detect Android application repackaging based on the apk resource files, and an implementation of this approach in the FSquaDRA tool. Leveraging hash files of resources already present in apks, FSquaDRA is capable of fast pairwise apk comparison. It computes the Jaccard similarity score for compared apks and classifies them as similar if substantial number of resource files are the same in both packages.

We have evaluated practicality of FSquaDRA in two aspects: whether it gives results similar to the code-based app repackaging detection techniques, and whether it is fast enough to handle significant number of apks. Our results are encouraging. The FSquaDRA resource similarity score is strongly correlated with the AndroGuard code similarity score, especially for the apks signed with different certificates, and thus, potentially, plagiarized. FSquaDRA is also has good performance, as it was able to process a dataset of more than 55000 apks on a laptop in less than 80 hours. Notice that our implementation was not optimized for better performance, as it is single-threaded. Yet, the approach can be easily parallelized using different parallelization algorithms for pairwise comparison.

The obvious limitation of the current tool is that an adversary who is familiar with the approach can easily change all resource files in the package to make his plagiarized application virtually undetectable by FSquaDRA. Resource similarity metrics can be hardened against this by looking into files themselves rather than just comparing the digests, but it will lead to performance losses (which can become comparable with those of the code-based repackaging detection techniques if implemented reasonably). The most promising, to our point of view, is a hybrid approach, when repackaged applications are detected using both approaches, code and resource comparison. We believe this is a very interesting research direction.

Another interesting future work direction is to look into the data produced by FSquaDRA looking for patterns and interesting findings, such as the fact that on average applications signed with the same certificate have higher code similarity score than resource similarity score, while this difference is not so evident in the apps signed with different certificates.

FSquaDRA opens an avenue of enhancement for app plagiarism detection algorithms, and not only for Android. For other ecosystems, such as iOS or Windows Phone, that request the developers to submit the full source code and resources before publishing apps on the market our technique can be used to improve the on-market plagiarism detection algorithms by complementing the code similarity-based approaches.

Acknowledgements. This work has been partially supported by the FP7-ICT SecCord Project 316622 funded by the EU, and the TENACE PRIN Project (grant no. 20103P34XC) funded by the Italian MIUR.

References

1. ActionBarSherlock, http://actionbarsherlock.com/
2. AndroGuard: Reverse engineering, Malware and goodware analysis of Android applications, https://code.google.com/p/androguard/
3. Android-apktool: A tool for reverse engineering Android apk files, https://code.google.com/p/android-apktool/
4. Smali: An assembler/disassembler for Android's dex format, https://code.google.com/p/smali/
5. Cilibrasi, R., Vitányi, P.M.B.: Clustering by compression. IEEE Transactions on Information Theory 51, 1523–1545 (2005)
6. Crussell, J., Gibler, C., Chen, H.: Attack of the clones: Detecting cloned applications on android markets. In: Foresti, S., Yung, M., Martinelli, F. (eds.) ESORICS 2012. LNCS, vol. 7459, pp. 37–54. Springer, Heidelberg (2012)
7. Crussell, J., Gibler, C., Chen, H.: Scalable semantics-based detection of similar android applications. In: Proc. of Esorics 2013 (2013)
8. Desnos, A.: Android: Static analysis using similarity distance. In: Proc. of HICSS 2012, pp. 5394–5403 (2012)
9. Gibler, C., Stevens, R., Crussell, J., Chen, H., Zang, H., Choi, H.: Adrob: examining the landscape and impact of android application plagiarism. In: Proc. of MobiSys 2013, pp. 431–444 (2013)
10. Hanna, S., Huang, L., Wu, E., Li, S., Chen, C., Song, D.: Juxtapp: A scalable system for detecting code reuse among android applications. In: Flegel, U., Markatos, E., Robertson, W. (eds.) DIMVA 2012. LNCS, vol. 7591, pp. 62–81. Springer, Heidelberg (2013)
11. Huang, H., Zhu, S., Liu, P., Wu, D.: A framework for evaluating mobile app repackaging detection algorithms. In: Huth, M., Asokan, N., Čapkun, S., Flechais, I., Coles-Kemp, L. (eds.) TRUST 2013. LNCS, vol. 7904, pp. 169–186. Springer, Heidelberg (2013)
12. Potharaju, R., Newell, A., Nita-Rotaru, C., Zhang, X.: Plagiarizing smartphone applications: attack strategies and defense techniques. In: Barthe, G., Livshits, B., Scandariato, R. (eds.) ESSoS 2012. LNCS, vol. 7159, pp. 106–120. Springer, Heidelberg (2012)
13. Protalinski, E.: Warning: New Android malware tricks users with real Opera Mini (July 2012), http://www.zdnet.com/warning-new-android-malware-tricks-users-with-real-opera-mini-7000001586/
14. Vidas, T., Christin, N.: Sweetening android lemon markets: measuring and combating malware in application marketplaces. In: Proc. of CODASPY 2013, pp. 197–208 (2013)
15. Zhou, W., Zhou, Y., Grace, M., Jiang, X., Zou, S.: Fast, scalable detection of "piggybacked" mobile applications. In: Proc. of CODASPY 2013, pp. 185–196 (2013)
16. Zhou, W., Zhou, Y., Jiang, X., Ning, P.: Detecting repackaged smartphone applications in third-party android marketplaces. In: Proc. of CODASPY 2012, pp. 317–326 (2012)

'Who, When, and Where?'
Location Proof Assertion for Mobile Devices

Rasib Khan, Shams Zawoad, Md Munirul Haque, and Ragib Hasan

Department of Computer and Information Sciences
University of Alabama at Birmingham
{rasib,zawoad,mhaque,ragib}@cis.uab.edu

Abstract. In recent years, location of mobile devices has become an important factor. Mobile device users can easily access various customized applications from the service providers based on the current physical location information. Nonetheless, it is a significant challenge in distributed architectures for users to prove their presence at a particular location in a privacy-protected and secured manner. So far, researchers have proposed multiple schemes to implement a secure location proof collection mechanism. However, such location proof schemes are subject to tampering and not resistant to collusion attacks. Additionally, the location authority providing a location proof is assumed to be honest at all times. In this paper, we present the fundamental requirements of any location proof generation scheme, and illustrate the potential attacks possible in such non-federated environments. Based on our observations, we introduce a concept of witness oriented endorsements, and describe a collusion-resistant protocol for asserted location proofs. We provide an exhaustive security analysis of the proposed architecture, based on all possible collusion models among the user, location authority, and witness. We also present a prototype implementation and extensive experimental results to adjust different threshold values and illustrate the feasibility of deploying the protocol in regular devices for practical use.

Keywords: Location Assertion, Location Proof, Proof Protocol, Security, Witness Endorsement.

1 Introduction

Location-based services for mobile devices have achieved great popularity in recent times. Authentication, authorization, access control, accounting, and similar critical actions can be associated with the geographical locations of the devices. The location information is then used by service providers to provide diverse location-based services to the users [1]. However, unsecured location reporting mechanisms may have effects on trivial cases, such as, in social-games like FourSquare [2], and may even be of national security, as that of spoofing Drones with false location data [3].

A location proof for a user is verified with respect to the identity of the user, the location in question, and the time of visit. However, self-reported information regarding location presence can be easily spoofed. Global Positioning System (GPS) coordinates, cell triangulation in mobile phones, and IP address tracking are all susceptible to manipulation for making false location claims [4]. Conversely, automated location reporting violates users' privacy and introduces centralization bottleneck in the architecture [5].

V. Atluri and G. Pernul (Eds.): DBSec 2014, LNCS 8566, pp. 146–162, 2014.

There have been numerous proposals for user initiated location proof generation [1, 6–9]. The localization authority covering the area utilizes some secure distance-bounding mechanism to ensure the user's presence [10–12]. However, existing mechanisms overlook collusion attacks in their models. In a collusion attack, participating entities go into a mutual agreement and agrees to create counterfeit location proofs. Hence, the fake proofs resemble an actual proof and can be utilized by the user as a false evidence of presence at that location. The related works thus far have not considered any third-party endorsement for location proofs, which makes the schemes vulnerable to collusion attacks [1, 4–15].

This paper presents a distributed witness-oriented architecture for generating secure location proofs which is resistant to collusion attacks. The following scenario illustrates the practicality of a secure location proof mechanism.

A pharmaceutical agent travels around different places hoping to get a sale for the pharmaceutical company. Upon returning to office, he makes an expense claim for the money paid at the hotel where he was staying during the traveling period. However, in addition to the bill of receipt from the hotel, the company requires a proof of presence that the sales agent was actually residing at that specific hotel. Thus, the agent provides his secured proof of presence, which was collected from the hotel. The proof was also securely asserted by the hotel manager, or any other witness available at the hotel. The finance department of the company then validates the endorsed proof and pays the incurred cost to the sales agent.

Contributions. The contributions of this paper are as follows:

1. We have introduced a novel solution for obtaining distributed secure location proofs for mobile devices. The architecture allows generating witness-oriented asserted location proofs in a distributed environment which incorporates an additional endorsement by a third entity to ensure a collusion-resistant location proof.
2. We have presented an exhaustive security analysis of the proposed architecture against a detailed combinatorial study for collusion models and different attacks in the working protocol.
3. We have illustrated the feasibility of the proposed architecture for practical use using a proof-of-concept implementation. The prototype is used in an extensive experimental process to identify attacks and adjust the threshold values for the protocol.

The rest of the paper is organized as follows. We discuss related work in Section 2. Section 3 introduces the key terminologies and concepts in location proof systems. Section 4, discusses the potential attacks and challenges in a location proof generation scheme. We present our secure assertion oriented scheme in Section 5, and provide a security analysis in Section 6. The prototype implementation and simulation results have been presented in Section 7. Section 8 describes our experimental process to set the threshold values, and finally conclude in Section 9

2   Related Work

Location reporting mechanisms require a reliable and tamper proof architecture to preserve the integrity of the data. Traditional GPS systems are effective in general purpose location reporting [16]. However, it is not a suitable option in terms of security and indoor tracking. Recent papers have proposed a combination of GPS signals with cellular tower triangulation and identifying the access network channel. Gabber *et al.* [17] utilized multi-channel information to verify the location. Unfortunately, malicious entities can bypass such combinatorial schemes [1, 8]. Additionally, GPS signatures [18] are not useful since they are open to spoofing attacks [8].

Hardware oriented localization techniques [19–21] measure signal attenuation and asynchronous measurement of round trip times to verify the presence of a certain user device in the vicinity [10, 22–25]. However, location reporting using signal attenuation can easily be manipulated by an attacker in close proximity of the devices. Furthermore, all of these mechanisms suffer from channel noise, limitations with line-of-sight, and complexity of deployment. In our design, we have considered a three-party interactive solution. We have used timing thresholds between each pair of communicating parties to ensure three-way proximity.

Collection of secure location proofs from a manager was discussed by Waters *et al.* [9]. Another approach for creating secure location proofs has been described by Saroiu *et al.* [1]. However, these schemes require highly coupled entities with a monolithically centralized architecture. Trusted platform module and virtual machine based attestation for trusted sensor readings have been proposed by Saroiu *et al.* [26] and Gilbert *et al.* [7] respectively. Luo *et al.* presented a method for obtaining privacy-preserved location proofs using a random nonce between the user and the provider [8]. Khan *et al.* presented a model for chaining location proofs in a chronological order for secure provenance [27].

Limitations of Current Research: In a free-to-act environment, participating entities may go into a mutual agreement and collude to produce a fake proof of presence. Furthermore, the person operating a mobile device may override certain operations on the device and manipulate the proofs. Such collusions between the parties can provide each other illegitimate benefits. Additionally, we consider the location authority to be possibly malicious as well. Given the location authority manipulates the proofs, most protocols that we have discussed so far will collapse. Furthermore, the flexibility and distributed mode of operation supported by such an architecture should be able to sustain the entropy, randomness, and falsified data generated by misbehaving entities in the environment.

3   Modelling a Secure Location Assertion

In this section, we present the notions of witnesses and assertions, the terminologies, and the models for creating and verifying secure location assertions.

3.1   Witnesses and Assertions

In everyday life, two parties considering each other as untrustworthy necessitates the involvement of a witness. In addition to the two parties involved in the information exchange, a witness provides a notarization of the statement. The notarized statement is then redistributed among the two parties, which bears the endorsement by the witness as an additional enforcement of the truth value of the content.

We utilize the same concept to create location proofs and have the proof asserted by a co-located witness. In this context, a witness is a spatio-temporally co-located entity with the user and the location authority. A witness will assert proofs only when willing to do so, and will not assert otherwise. Devices willing to assert location proofs sends a registration request to the available location authority. In a commercially deployed scenario, the incentive of the witness can be based on awarded 'points' depending on valid assertions. The 'points' would add to the trust value of a witness and may be redeemed for membership benefits from the service provider. The assertions may also be used by the witness to prove co-location with the user. The witness can withdraw from the witness-list at any time by sending a withdrawal request to the location authority.

3.2 Terminologies

We have introduced certain terminologies in the description of our models, and also in designing the scheme for secure location proof assertion. A **User** U is a mobile entity that visits a location. The user is identified with a mobile device, which is used to determine his location and store the location proofs. A **Site** S is a physical region within a finite area under the coverage of one location authority. A **Location Authority** L is a stationery entity, which is responsible for providing location proofs for a particular site, and owns a unique identifier. A **Witness** W is a mobile user who can assert a location proof for the presence of another mobile device at a particular location. The presence of the witness does not imply an eye-witness, but rather a spacio-temporal co-location with the user at the site S. A **Witness List** WL provides the listing of all registered witnesses under the coverage of the location authority at a given time. Witnesses are registered against their cypto-ID. The witness list is preserved at the location authority and is used to provide the proof of witness's presence at the site. A **Crypto-Id** CID is a cryptographic identity for the user and witnesses, used in all phases of the protocol, ensuring privacy of the entities participating in the process. The users and witnesses will have the cypto-ID tagged with their certificates. A **Location Proof** LP is a token of evidence received by a user when visiting a specific site, and an **Asserted Proof** AP is a location proof LP asserted by a valid witness using his crypto-ID. Finally, an **Auditor** is an authority who is presented with an asserted location proof and confirms the legitimacy of the user's claim of presence at the particular site.

3.3 Threat Model

The two main targets considered in our threat model are the place and time of location proofs corresponding to a user. An adversary should not be able to create a proof for a location that the user has not visited, or a proof for a different time than the actual time of visit. An additional target is the identity and location privacy of users and witnesses. An attacker may create a dossier of users visiting a given location, and learn the location history and identities of other users it has encountered in the past. Unlike previous works [1, 8, 9], we assume the users, location authorities, or witness devices may be malicious and can collude with one another. It is assumed that the user has full access to the storage and computation of the device, can run an application on the device, and can delete, modify, tamper, or insert any content in the data stored on the device. The location authority or the user can create a puppet witness to produce false asserted proofs. We assume that no entities share their private keys at any point, and a three-way collusion scenario does not exist. We assume mobile devices are non-shareable private properties and the physical security of the phone depends on the user himself. Additionally, typical attacks such as MAC address fingerprinting are prevented via known techniques such as MAC address cloning [28]. According to the protocol, we assume the presence of at least one witness at the given site who is willing to provide an assertion.

3.4   System Model

We assume the mobile devices carried by users are WiFi enabled. The devices have local storage for storing the proofs. A device visiting a site can find the location authority over the wireless network. It is assumed that the user, location authority, and witness can access each others' public key for a given Crypto-Id. The location authority periodically updates the available witness list. Witnesses are chosen at random for asserting a location proof. Upon completion of a schematic communication between the entities, the user is presented with a location proof and is stored on the user's device. At a later time, the user presents the location proof to an auditor.

4   Security and Challenges in Location Proofs

This section includes the fundamental security challenges which exist in any location proof protocol. We present the previous studies and illustrate the possible attacks in such distributed architectures for generating location proofs.

4.1   Challenges and Attacks

In our opinion, possibility of tampering with data in distributed flexible environments has a higher probability compared to any centralized architectures. Hence, we aim at making location assertions tamper-evident, assuming that all information are susceptible to tampering, as opposed to being tamper-proof. Therefore, we focus on ensuring detection of different types of attacks while generating a proof of presence. We list the potential attacks as follows.

False presence: A malicious user can create a fake location proof on his own, without being physically present at the location. The fake proof is supposed to resemble an actual proof, which the user could have actually collected from a valid location authority.

False timestamping *(backdating, future dating)*: In a backdating attack, the user and the location authority colludes to create a proof for a past time. Conversely, in future dating, the location authority and a user colludes to generate a proof with a future timestamp.

Implication: A location authority and/or a witnesses can falsely accuse a user of his presence at a certain location. In this case, the malicious location authority and witness colludes to generate a false proof of presence for the user.

False assertion: A user can collude with a witness, and generate a falsely asserted location proof. The truth value in such a fake proof is reinstated with the assertion received from the other user.

Denial of presence: A user can visit a location and at a later time, deny his presence at that location. In such a case, the user actually denies the validity of a certain location proof that has been been generated upon his presence at that particular location.

Proof switching: The user is expected to have full access to all storage facilities on his mobile device. Hence, the user utilizes the legitimate proof and manipulates the information to create a false proof for a different location.

Relay attack: A user can use a proxy to relay the requests and collect a location proof. Alternatively, a location authority can maliciously relay assertion requests with the witness not being present at the site.

Sybil attack: A Sybil attack occurs when a single user generates multiple presence and identities [29]. A user can launch a Sybil attack by generating multiple identities representing a user and a witness and provide false endorsements for location proofs.

Denial of witness's presence: At the time of proof verification, the user can claim the absence of witnesses at the site or falsely claim an assertion to be counterfeit. The user and the location authority may also collude and claim the non-availability of witnesses.

Privacy violation: An attacker may capture an asserted location proof generated for a user, and discover the identity of the user and/or the witness.

5   A Secure Location Proof Assertion Scheme

In this section, we present the design, schematic definitions, architecture and the protocol for a secure location proof assertion scheme.

5.1   Schematic Description of Secure Location Proof Assertion

In this section, we define the schematic description of each message in all steps of the protocol, in sequence of their occurrences. Initially, the user U, sends a proof request, $PReq$, to the location authority, L.

$$pReq = < CID_U, t_U > \qquad (1)$$

Here, in expression 1, CID_U is the cryptographic identity of the user U, and t_U, is the timestamp from the user U's mobile device. To state that, user U has visited a site with location authority identifier L, at time t_L – the current time at the location authority L, the location authority prepares a location statement LS as follows:

$$LS = < CID_U, L, t_L > \qquad (2)$$

Hence, the location authority creates a location proof LP, to be sent to the user U, using the location statement LS, formed in expression 2. Additionally, the location authority L also forms the assertion request $AReq$ for LP to be sent to witness W.

$$LP = AReq = < LS, S_L(LS) > \qquad (3)$$

Here, in expression 3, $S_L(LS)$ represents the digital signature computed on location statement LS, from expression 2, using the location authority's private key. Thus, the location proof LP is sent to user U, and an assertion request $AReq$ is sent to the witness W. Next. the asserted statement AS is created by a witness W to assert the $AReq$. The assertion statement is prepared as follows:

$$AS = < CID_W, CID_U, L, h(LP), t_W > \qquad (4)$$

In expression 4, CID_W and CID_U are the cryptographic identifiers for the witness W, and the user U respectively. Additionally, t_W is the signed asserted timestamp from the witness' mobile device. The witness includes $h(LP)$, a cryptographic hash of the LP. Subsequently, the witness W prepares an assertion A, as shown below.

$$A =< AS, S_W(AS) >$$ (5)

The assertion in expression 5 includes an asserted statement AS from expression 4, and $S_W(AS)$ is a signature computed by the asserting witness W on AS. Thus, an asserted proof of presence at site S, created by the witness W, is a pair of values: the location proof LP, and the assertion A. The asserted location proof, ALP is defined as thus:

$$ALP =< LP, A >$$ (6)

The user U receives ALP as shown in expression 6, and issues a verification request $VReq$ to be sent to the witness W as follows:

$$VReq =< ALP, LP, h(ALP, LP), t_u >$$ (7)

In expression 7, the user U had already received the location proof LP (expression 3) and the asserted location proof ALP (expression 6). The user includes a signed timestamp t_u for the current time on the user's device, and $h(ALP,LP)$, a cryptographic hash function on both the location proof LP and the asserted proof ALP. The verification response V, sent by the witness W is defined as:

$$V =< R, t_{WV} >$$ (8)

Here, $R \in \{YES, NO\}$, and t_{WV} is the response timestamp for the witness verification from the witness' mobile device. The verification statement VS is thus defined as follows:

$$VS =< V, S_W(V) >$$ (9)

In expression 9, V is the verification response from expression 8, and $S_W(V)$ is a signature computed by the witness W on V. Finally, the acknowledgement $ALPAck$ is created by user U and sent to the location authority L as follows:

$$ALPAck =< S_U(LP, AS), h(LP, AS), t_t >$$ (10)

The acknowledgement $ALPAck$ shown in expression 10 includes $S_U(LP,AS)$, a cryptographic signature from user U, on the location proof LP and the assertion statement AS. This is then sent to the location authority L, to be stored, as a receipt for the asserted location proof received by the user U.

5.2 Location Assertion Protocol Architecture

In our proposed architecture, we assume that each entity is registered with a service provider. Users, witnesses, and location authorities register with the centralized system, with a unique identification criteria, such as the Social Security Number, passport number, driving license, and trade license. The entities will get a crypto-ID tagged with a certificate containing the public/private keypair. This is the only component which requires a centralized mode of operation. However, we claim that this is a one-time procedure, and does not constitute any obstruction as a bottleneck in rest of the protocol. Secondly, there exists a mechanism to distribute the public certificates for all the entities. The user U, witness W, and

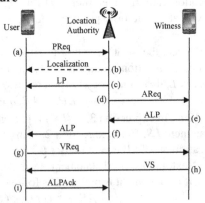

Fig. 1. Sequence Diagram for the Location Assertion Protocol

the location authority L, should be able to collect each other's public-key certificates. Finally, it is given that all communications between the user U, the location authority L, and the witness W, take place over secure socket layer (SSL) connections and public key encryption. The sequence of interaction for creating an asserted location proof is illustrated in figure 1 and is described as below.

(a) **Location authority discovery and proof request:** Each location is identified by a unique global identifier and are publicly available (via a lookup), or that the location authorities periodically broadcast their information on the local network. The user obtains the identity of the location authority and sends a location proof request $PReq$ to the location authority L, as shown in expression 1.

(b) **Secure localization:** Upon receiving the $PReq$ message, the location authority runs a secure localization step to determine whether the device is actually present there.

(c) **Location proof generation:** The location authority L generates the location proof LP, as shown in expression 3, and sends it to the requesting user.

(d) **Proof assertion request:** The location authority L has a witness list WL consisting of the available witnesses willing to serve for asserting location proofs. The location authority L sends an assertion request $AReq$, as shown in expression 3, to a randomly selected witness W from the witness list WL.

(e) **Asserted message creation:** The witness W receives the assertion request $AReq$ and verifies the location statement LS included within $AReq$. Upon a successful verification of all information, the asserted location proof ALP, as shown in expression 6, is sent to the location authority L.

(f) **Assertion verification and relay:** The location authority L receives and verifies the asserted location proof ALP. The location authority L verifies the time lapse between sending an assertion request $AReq$ and receiving the asserted location proof ALP, i.e., difference between t_L available from ALP and the current time at the location authority L. A maximum threshold for the time difference is enforced to detect any proxy forwarding delay by the witness. Upon successful verification, the location authority L relays the asserted location proof ALP to the user U.

(g) **Verification request:** Once the user U has received both the location proof LP and the asserted location proof ALP, he sends the verification request $VReq$ directly to the witness, as shown in expression 7.

(h) **Verification response:** The witness W receives the verification request $VReq$ and validates the assertion provided earlier. The witness calculates the difference between the time t_W, available in the assertion statement AS (expression 4), with the current time on the witness device. An acceptable threshold for the time difference ensures that the user is not a proxy relay attack. If successful, the witness W creates a verification statement VS, as shown in expression 9, and sends it to the user U.

(i) **Location proof receipt:** Finally, user U receives the verification statement VS from the witness W. The user U verifies the difference between the time in the verification request t_u, and the current time on the user's device when it receives the verification response. A maximum threshold for the delay ensures that the witness is not proxying the assertion and the verification requests. Once verified, the user creates an acknowledgement $ALPAck$, as shown in expression 10, and sends it to the location authority L. The user U then stores the asserted location proof ALP on his device for the specific site S, and hence, completes the protocol.

Subsequently, the location authority L stores the receipt for the location proof and maintains a publicly visible list of these tickets. At every epoch, it publishes the current state of this list along with a signature. The published list is used to prevent back-dating and future-dating attacks.

6   Security Analysis

In this section, we present an analysis of the security properties of our schemes. We start by enumerating the different types of attackers and combination of collusions among the existing entities. Furthermore, we analyse how our scheme can protect against attacks, which are possible in such colluded environments.

6.1   Collusion Patterns

We define the following symbols: honest user U, malicious user $\bar{U}$, honest location authority L, malicious location authority $\bar{L}$, honest witness W, and a malicious witness $\bar{W}$. The eight possible combinations for collusion patterns and the corresponding attacks are shown in table 1. The protocol ensures mutual communication among all entities. Thus, any collusions leading to a fake proof generation can be easily identified by the valid entity at specific stages of the protocol. A thorough analysis on each collusion pattern is presented in the following sub-section.

Table 1. Collusion Models and Corresponding Threats

Notation	Attack
U L W	No collusion.
$\bar{U}$ L W	False proofs, reordering, denial of presence, proof switching, relay attack.
U $\bar{L}$ W	Denial of service, implication.
U L $\bar{W}$	False endorsement, privacy.
U $\bar{L}\bar{W}$	Implication, relay attack, replay attack.
$\bar{U}$ L $\bar{W}$	False endorsement, relay attack, Sybil attack.
$\bar{U}\bar{L}$ W	False proofs, relay attack, replay attack.
$\bar{U}\bar{L}\bar{W}$	False proofs.

6.2   Threat Analysis

We have made a thorough security analysis of all the possible combinations of the user, location authority, and the witness. Table 1 summarizes the different attack scenarios and the corresponding threats.

[ULW] All honest entities do not imply a threat of generating false location proofs.

[$\bar{U}$LW] A malicious user $\bar{U}$ can request false location proofs. However, if the location authority L and witness W are honest, this attack does not succeed. An honest location authority L will not sign a false location proof. Additionally, an honest witness W will not endorse a location statement which is not accompanied by a proof from the location authority L. In case of a relay attack, the proxy forwarding delay can be detected in step (h) of the protocol, and thus can be rejected.

[U$\bar{L}$W] The dishonest location authority $\bar{L}$ will never have the final receipt from the user U and thus cannot create a false proof. The honest witness W will also not assert a location proof, unless it can detect user U's presence. The malicious location authority $\bar{L}$ may provide a false timestamp. However, an honest witness will not endorse a proof if the timestamp differs a lot from its own timestamp. Additionally, any illegitimate information by the malicious location authority will force the user U, or the witness W to forfeit the asserted location proof protocol.

[UL$\bar{W}$] A malicious witness $\bar{W}$ cannot do any harm, other than denial of service and privacy violation of the user U. However, the cryptographic identity of the user CID_U does not allow the malicious witness $\bar{W}$ to reveal the user's actual identity. Furthermore, a falsely asserted location proof will be discarded by the location authority L, before the location authority L relays the asserted location proof to the user U.

[U$\bar{L}\bar{W}$] A malicious location authority $\bar{L}$ can collude with a dishonest witness $\bar{W}$ and create false location proofs for a user. However, if the user never participated in a proof protocol with the location authority, such an attack will not work. The malicious location authority $\bar{L}$ can give a user a backdated or a future dated timestamp. Subsequently, a colluding malicious witness $\bar{W}$ can endorse such a false timestamped proof. However, the user U finally verifies the location proof and the asserted location proof, and has the option of discarding the protocol by not sending the final receipt for the asserted location proof. A relay attack can also be identified by the user U between step (h) and step (i). The malicious location authority $\bar{L}$ also has the option for storing a previous proof, endorsed by a valid witness W, and use it later to launch a replay attack. However, the user U directly communicates with the witness during endorsement verification. Thus, in case of any discrepancy with the timing threshold, the user U can discard the proof completely.

[$\bar{U}$L$\bar{W}$] A malicious user $\bar{U}$ and a colluding witness $\bar{W}$ cannot create falsely asserted location proofs. The location authority L denies to cooperate with the dishonest user $\bar{U}$ and the witness $\bar{W}$, based on the comparison of the timestamps t_U and t_W, or any invalid information included in the process of asserting the location proof. A Sybil attack is also possible in this case. However, the centralized registration system, a requirement of the architecture, prevents a user $\bar{U}$ to create a witness profile $\bar{W}$ on the same device. Additionally, the location authority warrants for witness devices which are already registered at the location authority L. A relay attack with a proxy user $\bar{U}$ and a proxy witness $\bar{W}$ is also detected by the location authority L in steps (b) and (f) respectively.

[$\bar{U}\bar{L}$W] A malicious user $\bar{U}$ and a dishonest location authority $\bar{L}$ can collude to create a false proof with backdated or future-dated timestamp. The falsely created asserted location proof can be utilized to launch a relay and a replay attack. However, an honest witness W will not endorse a false proof with an incorrect timestamp. In step (h), from the time difference between t_W and the current time on the device, the witness can successfully identify a relay or a replay attack and will refrain from sending a positive response to the user $\bar{U}$ in the verification phase.

[$\bar{U}\bar{L}\bar{W}$] A three way collusion is not considered in our scheme. However, a backdated attack can be detected by the auditor if checks the published accumulator by the location authority for the epoch corresponding to the proof timestamp. The only attack that is possible here is a post-dating attack, when the user $\bar{U}$, location authority $\bar{L}$, and witness $\bar{W}$, collude to create a location proof with a future timestamp, and $\bar{L}$ does not publish it in the epoch report. However, we claim that any distributed security protocol without centralized monitoring requires at least one entity which is valid. Hence, the successful completion of any security protocol is protected against the legitimate entity, who plays the role of the situational verifier. Nonetheless, an auditor may impose a stricter proof model involving asserted location proof statements from multiple closely located location authorities to verify the actual presence.

7 System Evaluation

In this section we present the performance of the designed architecture illustrated utilizing a prototype implementation. Additionally, we present a comparative analysis of our protocol against a similar protocol proposed by Luo *et al.* [8].

7.1 Protocol Implementation

To evaluate the feasibility and performance of the protocol, we developed the prototype applications for location authority, user and witness. Applications for user and witness were built on the Android platform. In our experiment, for simluating a user, we used a *HTC Evo 4G* smart phone with *Android 2.3.3* operating system. The witness was simulated on a *Motorola XT875* smart phone, with *Android 4.0.3* operating system. The location authority was implemented as a desktop application, using *JDK 1.6*, and ran it on *OSX 10.8.2*, equipped with *Intel Core i5 1.7 GHz* processor and *4GB 1600 MHz DDR3* RAM. For the testbed network, we used WiFi for communication among the different entities in the protocol, and generated the asserted location proofs. We used the RSA (2048 bit) for generating signatures and encryption of the packets. Additionally, we used SHA-256 for generating the hash values. We assume that all the three entities have access to each other's public keys. Hence, the processing delay does not include the time to access the key over the network.

7.2 Performance Analysis

We evaluated the performance of three important steps of the protocol from the user application. We recorded the timestamps at different phases of the protocol for 100 complete execution cycles. Initially, we recorded the time lapsed after sending a proof request *PReq* to the location authority *L*, and eventually receiving a location proof *LP*. We denote this as *LProof Received* time. Subsequently, we recorded the time lapsed between sending the verification request *VReq* and receiving the verification statement *VS* from the witness *W*, which is denoted here as *VS Received* time. Finally, we measured the time required to complete the whole protocol. Figure 2a represents the time required for each step in every iteration, and figure 3 illustrates the average time required for the individual steps.

In our proposed scheme, the mean time for *LProof Received* and *VS Received* were 228 milliseconds and 362 milliseconds respectively. Although the computation needed for generating the location proof *LP* and the verification statement *VS* is similar (generating the packet then signing it), the *VS Received* time is higher than the *LProof Received* time. This behavior is natural, as the witness's device has less computation power than the location authority's device.

In the protocol, the location authority *L* forwards the asserted location proof *ALP* to the user *U*. In the end, the location authority *L* receives the acknowledgement *ALPAck* receipt from the user *U*. We measured the time required between these two steps.

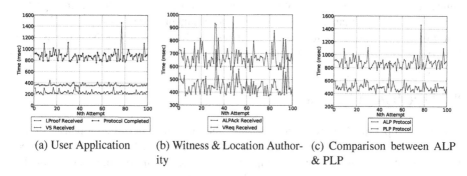

(a) User Application   (b) Witness & Location Author-   (c) Comparison between ALP
                             ity   & PLP

Fig. 2. Protocol Performance Evaluation

The time measurement is noted as *ALPAck Received* on figure 2b, which depicts this processing delay for each iteration. Additionally, the average time required for *ALPAck Received* is shown in figure 3.

The witness W, sends the asserted location proof *ALP* to the location authority L. The witness then W waits for the verification request *VReq* from the user. The time required between sending the asserted location proof *ALP* and receiving the verification request *VReq* is important from the witness's point of view. We measured the processing delays between these two steps, which is denoted as *VReq Received*. Figure 2b illustrates the time for each iteration on the witness's device, with the average time shown in figure 3.

7.3 Performance Comparison

To perform a comparative analysis of our proposed protocol (Asserted Location Proof or *ALP* protocol), we selected another secure location proof protocol, namely 'Proactive Location Proof' or *PLP* protocol, proposed by Luo *et al.* in [8]. Both the protocols were compared based on their time of completion for receiving the location proof. Figure 2c illustrates the time required to complete each protocol. The average processing time for the *ALP* protocol is 877 milliseconds, whereas that of the *PLP* protocol is

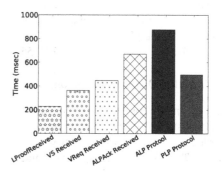

Fig. 3. Average Time Required for Different Steps of the Protocol

496 milliseconds. Given the fact that we have more phases in our protocol including numerous encryption and decryption operations, the *ALP* should be taking a longer processing time. However, the comparison demonstrates that the processing time for ALP is still comparable to rather simplistic models like PLP. Additionally, none of the other protocols so far have neither considered collusion attacks nor the presence of malicious location authority.

The results above show some overhead processing in our proposed protocol. However, it provides an extra level of security by getting the assertion from the witness, hence adding to the trust value of such location proofs. The completion time for the protocol is still less than 1 second, which is a reasonable latency for practical usage. Addition of the witness increases the attack surface for the protocol. Nonetheless, we have proved in section 6 that our proposed protocol is resilient to all combinations of collusion attacks.

8   Threshold Adjustment

We applied a practical approach to determine the thresholds in different phases of the asserted location proof protocol. Resistance against relay attacks have been illustrated using the following experimental setup, where we adjust the optimal values for the threshold according to the requirements of the system.

8.1   Threshold Initialization

We need three threshold values to identify relay attacks in the protocol. At first, in step *(f)* of our protocol, the location authority L verifies the time lapse between sending *AReq* and receiving *ALP*, $\Delta(LA_{AReq-ALP})$, using the threshold T_{LW} to identify a proxy witness. In step *(h)*, the witness measures the required time between sending *ALP* and receiving *VReq*, $\Delta(W_{ALP-VReq})$, and compares this time with the threshold T_{WU} to detect the presence of a proxy user. Finally, in step *(i)*, the user measures the elapsed time between sending *VReq* and receiving *VS*, $\Delta(U_{VReq-VS})$, and compares it with the threshold T_{UW} to identify the presence of a proxy witness. The initial threshold value is set as the mean time of completion for the given phases of the scheme, which was calculated from 100 experimental executions of the protocol. Subsequently, the threshold was set at that value to detect the presence of proxy users or witnesses. The mean values for $\Delta(LA_{AReq-ALP})$, $\Delta(W_{ALP-VReq})$, and $\Delta(U_{VReq-VS})$ are thus set to values for T_{LW}, T_{WU}, T_{UW} at 240.754, 552.464, and 346.004 milliseconds respectively.

8.2   Variable-Distance Threshold Measurements

The next phase of the work included a variable-distance setup for the protocol. The recorded times were used to justify the values for T_{LW}, T_{UW}, and T_{WU}. We placed the user U, witness W, and the location authority LA at varying distances and recorded the time measurements for each of $\Delta(U_{VReq-VS})$, $\Delta(LA_{AReq-ALP})$, and $\Delta(W_{ALP-VReq})$. The recorded times for each of the values for varying distances are shown in table 2.

The recorded times show that the time intervals tend to increase as the distance between the entities are increased. Additionally, we observed that the previously set val-

Table 2. Variable-Distance Measurements

Case	Dist. (ft)	Time (ms)
U - W	33	381.093
$\Delta(U_{VReq-VS})$	62	383.232
	80	383.232
	100	453.131
W - LA	3	235.178
$\Delta(LA_{AReq-ALP})$	30	251.032
	50	230.801
	70	349.787
U - LA	36	487.437
$\Delta(W_{ALP-VReq})$	93	512.459
	110	2120.656
	132	1949.892

ues for the thresholds do not suffice the purpose of determining the proxy attacks in each

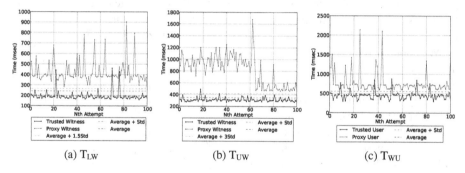

(a) T_{LW} (b) T_{UW} (c) T_{WU}

Fig. 4. Threshold Identification

of the cases. Therefore, the next phase for adjusting the threshold included performing a relay attack using a proxy witness and user. Subsequently, we utilized the measurements from the relay attack to adjust our threshold values using a sliding threshold model.

8.3 Relay Attacks using Proxy

The value of the thresholds have been determined using relay attacks. We executed a relay attack using a proxy to forward messages between two networks. In the first case, we utilized a proxy to relay packets to a remote network to a witness which is not not spatially co-located with user and location authority. We calculated the time lapse between sending *VReq* and receiving *VS* for this attack scenario. The recorded T_{LW}'s and T_{UW}'s for both trusted and proxy witnesses are shown in figure 4a and figure 4b respectively. Next, we performed a similar experiment using a user proxy. The proxy was present to relay the packets to the user on the remote network. The recorded T_{WU}'s for both the trusted and proxy users are shown in figure 4c.

8.4 Sliding Threshold Model

We utilized a sliding threshold model to determine optimal values for T_{LW}, T_{UW}, and T_{WU}. Initially, we started with a minimum value to specify the optimal threshold, and observed the percentage of attacks successfully identified. Additionally, we also calculated the percentage of false alarms when the threshold is set at the given value.

For determining an optimal T_{UW}, we set the initial threshold at [Mean (μ) + Standard Deviation (σ)]. The threshold for T_{UW} was thus at 552.46 milliseconds, and the corresponding attack identification and false alarm was found to be at 100% and 6% respectively.

The threshold was set at different incremental values to reduce the false alarm rate in the protocol. The next experimental threshold was set at [$\mu + 1.3\sigma$], where the attack identification was still at 100%, while the false alarm had dropped to 14%. With a gradual increase of the threshold, we saw no decrease in the percentage of attacks identified, but the false alarm rate reduced to 5% by the time we reached [$\mu + 2\sigma$]. With T_{UW} set at [$\mu + 3\sigma$], the attack identification was still 100% but the false alarms has reduced to only 1%. As we increased the threshold beyond [$\mu + 3\sigma$], we observed the false alarm rate reduced to the point where it was still 1%, and the percentage of attack identification had started to drop. At this point, the sliding threshold was thus fixed at $[\mu + 3\sigma]$ for T_{UW}. The values from our simulation has been summarized in table 3.

We applied the same sliding threshold model to determine the threshold values for T_{LW} and T_{WU} respectively. Upon similar experimental evaluations as above, the optimal threshold for T_{LW} has thus been set at $[\mu + 1.5\sigma]$, with a value of 264.7 milliseconds. The corresponding attack identification and false alarm rates are 100% and 3% respectively.

Similarly, the optimal threshold for T_{WU} has been found to be at $[\mu + \sigma]$ with a value of 552.46 milliseconds. The corresponding attack identification and false alarm rates are 100% and 6% respectively. The results from the sliding threshold model for T_{LW} and T_{WU} in presented in table 3.

Table 3. Justification of Threshold Values

Threshold	Step	Value	(%)Attack Detection	(%)False Alarm
T_{WU}	$\mu + \sigma$	**552.46**	100	6
	$\mu + 1.3\sigma$	583.50	99	6
	$\mu + 1.5\sigma$	604.20	93	6
	$\mu + 1.7\sigma$	624.89	73	5
T_{LW}	$\mu + \sigma$	240.8	100	6
	$\mu + 1.3\sigma$	255.14	100	4
	$\mu + 1.5\sigma$	**264.7**	100	3
	$\mu + 1.8\sigma$	279.04	100	3
	$\mu + 2\sigma$	286.5	98	3
T_{UW}	$\mu + \sigma$	346	100	15
	$\mu + 1.5\sigma$	363.5	100	10
	$\mu + 1.8\sigma$	374	100	8
	$\mu + 2\sigma$	381	100	5
	$\mu + 2.3\sigma$	391.5	100	3
	$\mu + 2.5\sigma$	398.5	100	2
	$\mu + 3\sigma$	**416.01**	100	1
	$\mu + 3.5\sigma$	433.51	100	1
	$\mu + 4.3\sigma$	461.51	98	1

9   Conclusion

Collection and verification of location proofs have significant real-life applications in location-based services. In this paper, we introduced a novel architecture for obtaining secure asserted location proofs from a location authority and a spatio-temporally co-located witness. Our design is set up on a tamper-evident platform, in contrast to a tamper-proof concept. We illustrate how our proposed scheme provides defense against all possible forms of attacks and collusion models within the entities. Currently, we are developing an algorithm for multi-metric selection of witnesses from the list of currently registered witnesses based on their trust values in the protocol. For further research, we will extend the protocol and implement a granular concept of information visibility to preserve user privacy. We are also working on secure location provenance chains to allow auditors to validate the user's order of presence at different locations.

Acknowledgement. This research was supported by a Google Faculty Research Award and the Department of Homeland Security Grant #FA8750-12-2-0254.

References

1. Saroiu, S., Wolman, A.: Enabling new mobile applications with location proofs. In: Proc. of HotMobile, pp. 1–6 (2009)
2. VanGrove, J.: Foursquare cracks down on cheaters (April 2010),
   http://mashable.com/2010/04/07/foursquare-cheaters/

3. Maduako, I.: Wanna hack a drone? possible with geo-location spoofing! (July 26, 2012), http://geoawesomeness.com/?p=893

4. Tippenhauer, N.O., Rasmussen, K.B., Popper, C., Capkun, S.: iPhone and iPod location spoofing: Attacks on public WLAN-based positioning systems. SysSec Technical Report, ETH Zurich (April 2008)

5. Blumberg, A.J., Eckersley, P.: On locational privacy, and how to avoid losing it forever (August 2009), https://www.eff.org/wp/locational-privacy

6. Davis, B., Chen, H., Franklin, M.: Privacy-preserving alibi systems. In: Proc. of ASIACCS, pp. 34–35. ACM (2012), http://doi.acm.org/10.1145/2414456.2414475

7. Gilbert, P., Cox, L.P., Jung, J., Wetherall, D.: Toward trustworthy mobile sensing. In: Proc. of HotMobile, pp. 31–36. ACM (2010)

8. Luo, W., Hengartner, U.: Proving your location without giving up your privacy. In: Proc. of HotMobile, pp. 7–12 (2010)

9. Waters, B.R., Felten, E.W.: Secure, private proofs of location. Technical report TR-667-03, Princeton University (January 2003)

10. Brands, S., Chaum, D.: Distance bounding protocols. In: Helleseth, T. (ed.) EUROCRYPT 1993. LNCS, vol. 765, pp. 344–359. Springer, Heidelberg (1994)

11. Chiang, J.T., Haas, J.J., Hu, Y.-C.: Secure and precise location verification using distance bounding and simultaneous multilateration. In: Proc. of WiSec, pp. 181–192. ACM (2009)

12. Rasmussen, K.B., Čapkun, S.: Realization of RF distance bounding. In: Proceedings of the USENIX Security Symposium (2010)

13. Narayanan, A., Thiagarajan, N., Lakhani, M., Hamburg, M., Boneh, D.: Location privacy via private proximity testing. In: Proc. of NDSS (2011)

14. Traynor, P., Schiffman, J., La Porta, T., McDaniel, P., Ghosh, A.: Constructing secure localization systems with adjustable granularity using commodity hardware. In: Proc. of GLOBECOM 2010, pp. 1–6 (2010)

15. Brassil, J., Netravali, R., Haber, S., Manadhata, P., Rao, P.: Authenticating a mobile device's location using voice signatures. In: Proc. of WiMob, pp. 458–465. IEEE (October 2012)

16. Enge, P., Misra, P.: Special issue on global positioning system. Proceedings of the IEEE 87(1), 3–15 (1999)

17. Gabber, E., Wool, A.: How to prove where you are: tracking the location of customer equipment. In: Proc. of ACM CCS, pp. 142–149. ACM (1998)

18. Denning, D.E., MacDoran, P.F.: Location-based authentication: Grounding cyberspace for better security. Computer Fraud & Security 1996(2), 12–16 (1996)

19. Capkun, S., Hubaux, J.: Secure positioning of wireless devices with application to sensor networks. In: Proc. of INFOCOM, vol. 3, pp. 1917–1928. IEEE (2005)

20. Sastry, N., Shankar, U., Wagner, D.: Secure verification of location claims. In: Proceedings of the 2nd ACM Workshop on Wireless Security (WiSe), pp. 1–10. ACM (2003)

21. Čapkun, S., Čagalj, M.: Integrity regions: authentication through presence in wireless networks. In: Proc. of ACM WiSe, pp. 1–10. ACM (2006)

22. Aruba Networks, Inc., Dedicated air monitors? you decide (2006), http://www.arubanetworks.com/technology/tech-briefs/dedicated-air-monitors/

23. Pandey, S., Anjum, F., Kim, B., Agrawal, P.: A low-cost robust localization scheme for wlan. In: Proc. of WICON, p. 17. ACM (2006)

24. Tao, P., Rudys, A., Ladd, A.M., Wallach, D.S.: Wireless lan location-sensing for security applications. Computing Reviews 45(8), 489–490 (2004)

25. Youssef, M., Youssef, A., Rieger, C., Shankar, U., Agrawala, A.: Pinpoint: An asynchronous time-based location determination system. In: Proceedings of the 4th International Conference on Mobile Systems, Applications and Services, pp. 165–176. ACM (2006)
26. Saroiu, S., Wolman, A.: I am a sensor, and i approve this message. In: Proc. of HotMobile, pp. 37–42 (2010)
27. Khan, R., Zawoad, S., Haque, M., Hasan, R.: OTIT: Towards secure provenance modeling for location proofs. In: Proc. of ASIACCS. ACM (2014)
28. Martinovic, I., Zdarsky, F., Bachorek, A., Jung, C., Schmitt, J.: Phishing in the wireless: Implementation and analysis. In: Proceedings of IFIP SEC, pp. 145–156 (2007)
29. Douceur, J.R.: The sybil attack. In: Druschel, P., Kaashoek, M.F., Rowstron, A. (eds.) IPTPS 2002. LNCS, vol. 2429, pp. 251–260. Springer, Heidelberg (2002)

Design Patterns for Multiple Stakeholders in Social Computing

Pooya Mehregan and Philip W. L. Fong

Department of Computer Science
University of Calgary
Calgary, AB, Canada
{pmehrega,pwlfong}@ucalgary.ca

Abstract. In social computing, multiple users may have privacy stakes in a content (e.g., a tagged photo). They may all want to have a say on the choice of access control policy for protecting that content. The study of protection schemes for multiple stakeholders in social computing has captured the imagination of researchers, and general-purpose schemes for reconciling the differences of privacy stakeholders have been proposed.

A challenge of existing multiple-stakeholder schemes is that they can be very complex. In this work, we consider the possibility of simplification in special cases. If we focus on specific instances of multiple stakeholders, are there simpler design of access control schemes? We identify two design patterns for handling a significant family of multiple-stakeholder scenarios. We discuss efficient implementation techniques that solely rely on standard SQL technology. We also identify scenarios in which general-purpose multiple-stakeholder schemes are necessary. We believe that future work on multiple stakeholders should focus on these scenarios.

Keywords: Social Computing, Privacy, Multiple Stakeholders, Discretionary Access Control, Owner, Controller, Design Pattern.

1 Introduction

The advent of social computing has brought about fundamental changes in our understanding of Discretionary Access Control (DAC). In traditional DAC, such as the Graham-Denning model [6, 12], every object is associated with a distinguished user known as the *owner* of that object. Ownership in DAC is not about property rights. Rather, the owner is the user who has full administrative privileges over that object: i.e., that user is granted the privileges to administrate the access control policies of the resource. Every object has exactly one owner, though ownership is transferrable. The owner may selectively delegate some administrative privileges to other users known as the *controllers* of the object. This classical picture requires revision in the face of the new privacy needs of social computing.

In social computing, users often annotate contents that are originally contributed by others (e.g., commenting, liking). At other times, contents come to

V. Atluri and G. Pernul (Eds.): DBSec 2014, LNCS 8566, pp. 163–178, 2014.
© IFIP International Federation for Information Processing 2014

be associated with users other than the original contributors (e.g., photo tagging). There are also scenarios in which multiple users co-contribute a piece of information (e.g., friendship articulation). In all these scenarios, multiple users have a privacy stake in a given content: they all have an interest in determining the access control policy for the content. The classical picture of one owner delegating administrative duties to trusted controllers is no longer valid. Different stakeholders of the same content now have diverse privacy preferences, and they do not necessarily agree with one another. Yet, existing social computing systems still insist that the visibility of a content is controlled by a unique "owner". The privacy shortcomings of such a practice have been well-documented [19].

Squiccinarini *et al.* [15, 16] were the first to identify the need to take into account the often diverse privacy preferences of all stakeholders when the access control policy of a resource is to be selected. Subsequent works (e.g., [19, 21]), especially the seminal contributions of Squiccinarini *et al.* [15–17] and Hu *et al.* [7–9], have firmly established the necessity and feasibility of access control schemes that reconcile the diverse protection needs of multiple stakeholders. Such schemes have come to be called by different names, such as co-ownership [15–17], collaborative privacy management/control [8, 15, 17], and multiparty access control [7, 9]. For the sake of neutrality, we choose to call this phenomenon *multiple stakeholders*. Many of the proposed schemes for multiple stakeholders are very general, equipped with conflict resolution mechanisms that are not easy to understand by a regular user.

In this paper, we raise the question of *simplification*: Are there cases in which general-purpose multiple-stakeholder schemes are *overkill*? If we focus on specific instances of multiple stakeholders (e.g., liking, photo tagging, etc), can we honor the diverse privacy preferences of the stakeholders through *simple* designs of access control schemes? Our answers to these questions are univocally affirmative. Our goal is not to question the value of general-purpose schemes for multiple stakeholders. (There are instances in which general-purpose schemes are absolutely irreplaceable, as we shall see in §8.) Rather, our goal is to sharpen future discussions of multiple stakeholders, and to put forward access control schemes that can be used today, by social computing vendors such as Facebook and Google+. Specifically, our contributions are the following:

1. We propose two design patterns [5] for addressing a large number of multiple-stakeholder instances (§3, §4). Out of the five examples of multiple stakeholders that are quoted in the literature, our design patterns can address the privacy needs of three of them.
2. We identify previously unpublished privacy breaches in some of the above instances of multiple stakeholders, and propose ways to prevent them (§5).
3. We propose an implementation strategy for the design patterns that rely solely on standard SQL technology (§6), and demonstrate that the resulting performance meets the responsiveness requirements of web applications (§7).
4. We carefully identify scenarios in which general-purpose schemes of multiple stakeholders are needed (§8).

2   Related Work

The first work that identifies and addresses the problem of multiple stakeholders is that of Squicciarini et al. [15, 16]). In their proposal, whenever the privacy policy of a co-administrated object is to be decided, stakeholders are asked to take part in an auction. Stakeholders earn credits by creating objects and sharing their ownerships with other users. Using their credits, the stakeholders give their highest bid for the privacy policy they want to be selected for the co-administrated object. Then, the highest bid wins the auction and the privacy policy associated with the winning bid is adopted. The stakeholders then get taxed from their credits, with amounts depending on how dominant their roles were in determining the outcome of auction (winning privacy policy). The auction is based on a mechanism called Clarke-Tax, which in turn is a special case of Vickrey-Clarke-Groves (VCG). Inference techniques based on Folksonomies have also been proposed to prevent repetition of auctions for similar objects which are co-administrated by the same stakeholders. The biggest drawback for this work is its low usability. Users will have difficulty figuring out how the auction works and how to translate their privacy to a bid amount. The need for usability is later addressed in a subsequent work of Squicciarini et al. [17], in which majority-voting is used in place of complex auctions.

The work in [19] not only points out the problem of multiple stakeholders (that some stakeholders do not have control over the objects for which they have a privacy stake), but also demonstrates concretely its consequences. Specifically, the authors demonstrated how inference attacks may result from not addressing the privacy preferences of stakeholders. They also considered a simple solution in which the conjunction of the stakeholders' privacy preferences are taken as the access control policy for the co-administrated object.

In [21], stakeholders collaborate in authoring a policy for a co-administrated object. The policy can be edited by each of the stakeholders, with the following restrictions. Every policy is divided into two parts: (a) the **weak conditions** and (b) the **strong conditions**. Weak conditions are *negotiable* conditions of access. Each stakeholder can freely modify the weak conditions, even if they are contributed by other stakeholders. The strong conditions are *non-negotiable* conditions of access. When a stakeholder contributes a strong condition, the authorship is recorded. Only the author of a strong condition can revise it. Conflict resolution is performed manually. For example, when the strong conditions become overly restrictive for a stakeholder, there is the option for revising the object itself (e.g., blurring parts of a picture) in order to inspire other stakeholders to relax their strong conditions.

In the seminal work of Hu and Ahn [7, 9], a comprehensive requirement analysis for the problem of multiple stakeholders is given. Different types of controllers (i.e., stakeholders) are distinguished: the **owner** is the user whose profile is hosting the co-administrated object; the **contributor** is the user who contributes the co-owned object to the owner's profile; **stakeholders** are users who have been "tagged" in the co-administrated object; **distributers** are users who have re-shared the co-administrated object on their profiles. Each stakeholder specifies for the co-administrated object her preferred privacy policies as well as a sensitivity level. The latter is a normalized quantity representing the perceived privacy sensitivity of the object. Obviously, the privacy policies specified by the various controllers may not agree with one another. This is the first work that draws connection between conflict resolution and policy composition. Voting schemes have been proposed for resolving conflicts among the policies specified by the controllers.

In [8], another scheme for conflict resolution has been proposed. The fundamental assumption is that there is a trade-off between the need for privacy and the desire to share. The two are operationalized into two corresponding quantities: privacy risk and sharing loss. A quantitative scheme is devised to trade off the two quantities.

In the works above, the various instances of the multiple-stakeholder problem are treated in a uniform manner, hence a generic solution is proposed for all the problem instances. This approach does not take into account the idiosyncrasies of different instances of multiple stakeholders, which occasionally admit straightforward and efficient solutions. This is the topic to which we now turn.

3   Design Pattern: Simple Annotations

A *design pattern* is a reusable software design for a recurring software design problem [5]. In this and the next section, we discuss respectively two design patterns for two well-defined families of multiple-stakeholder scenarios. This section presents a design pattern known as *Simple Annotations*.

3.1   Setting

Social computing systems support not only the sharing of contents, but also further social interactions that are prompted by the initial sharing of contents. Examples of such social interactions include commenting, liking, tagging and resharing. We use the term *annotations* to refer to these secondary contents that are associated with a shared content. Annotations that are not further annotated are said to be *simple*. The more complex subject of *higher order annotations* (i.e., annotations of annotations) is discussed in the next section.

The author of an annotation can be different from the author of the annotated content. When an annotated content is displayed, the annotations are displayed along with it. In mainstream social computing systems, the author of the annotated content is taken to be the DAC owner of the *content-annotations aggregate*: i.e., the author of the annotated content is the one who can specify the privacy setting of both the original content and its annotations.

3.2   Privacy Challenges

The problem of the mainstream design is that *the authors of annotations also have privacy stakes in the visibility of the content-annotations aggregate, and yet they have absolutely no say in the visibility of the annotations that they authored.* In fact, we accept the following as a general design principle in the context of multiple stakeholders.

Design Principle 1. *Every stakeholder of a content shall have a say on the access control policy that protects the content.*

The users of Facebook came to notice this issue when the Ticker [10, 18, 20] (a real-time news feed which appears at side of the Facebook page) started showing the friends of users their activities such as what they have liked, commented and shared. Facebook claims that, Ticker is not breaching users' privacy since no privacy setting has been changed and the information showed in Ticker is already there and visible by those who can view it in the Ticker. That is, the privacy settings of the annotated (i.e., liked, commented, or shared) contents already allow access to the the content-annotations aggregate. Below is Facebook's announcement regarding the privacy of News Feed and Ticker [4]:

> *"People included in the audience of the post can see your comment or like in News Feed or ticker as well as other places around Facebook. You can check who something is shared with by going to the post and hovering over the audience icon."*

What Facebook fails to appreciate is that the privacy preferences of annotation authors are not honoured. When a user likes a content, she has absolutely no control over who may or may not be able to see that she likes the content. In the following, we explain in concrete terms how the privacy of annotation authors are breached in the cases of liking, tagging and (re)sharing.

Liking. In Facebook, users can *"like"* (also *"+1"* in Google+) a content to show their support for, affirmation of, or interest in that content. When the content is displayed, a total number of "likes" is also displayed, and the viewer of the content may also follow a link to display the full list of users who have liked the content. When the list is displayed, the following information of each liker is displayed: (a) display name, (b) thumbnail picture, and (c) link to profile.

A user who expresses her affirmation of a content may want the "like" to be displayed with discretion. For example, liking a political commentary may lead to troubles in certain countries, and yet, expressing such affirmations is an important democratic expression. Currently, there is no mechanism in Facebook that would allow the liker to control the visibility of his or her likes.

Tagging. Users can *tag* one another in today's social network systems. Facebook, Google+ and Instagram all have this feature. Specifically, users can tag one another in contents such as pictures, videos and textual information like statuses, comments and captions, usually by means of a mention tag '@' followed by the display name of a user.

The tagging of photos has been a classical example for multiple stakeholders in the literature [7–9, 15, 17, 19]. When a user uploads a photo in which other users appear, the former is disclosing potentially sensitive information about the latter. This by itself is a privacy issue, but this is not an instance of the multiple-stakeholder problem. It becomes a multiple-stakeholder scenario when the latter users are tagged by the former user — when the identities of these users are explicitly associated with the photo. These tags will be displayed together with the photo. It was not long ago that Facebook introduced a privacy setting that requires users to ask for other users' consent before they can get them tagged in a content.

Sharing. Facebook users can reshare a content that is originally posted by another user. There are two types of reshares in Facebook: (a) **link reshares** and (b) **content reshares**.

In link reshares, a user u posts a URL l along with a caption. A viewer v of the posting can reshare l (without the caption). There are two ways in which user privacy can be breached. First, the original posting of l by u shows both the total number of reshares, as well as a link that lists all the resharers. When this link is followed, the identity of v will be disclosed. The situation is analogous to that of liking. Second, the resharing of l by v is displayed with the phrase "via u", which discloses the identity of u. The situation is analogous to tagging.

In content reshares, a user u uploads some content c (e.g., photo) to Facebook. A viewer v of c can reshare c. Again, there are two privacy concerns in play here. First, the identity of v appears in a list associated with the posting of c by u. As noted above, this is analogous to liking. Second, u is clearly a stakeholder for the resharing of c by v. User u specifies a policy $p_{u,c}$ for controlling access to c, and v specifies a policy $p_{v,c}$ for controlling access to the reshared c. A user w can access the reshared c when $p_{u,c} \wedge p_{v,c}$ is satisfied.

3.3   Solution: Separation of Protection

Previous works in multiple stakeholders take the content-annotations aggregate as an indivisible entity, and thus attempt to address the multiple-stakeholder problem at that level. Our use of the term "aggregate" to refer to a content and its annotations is intended to make explicit the fact that we are not dealing with an atomic entity, but rather a composite one. Recognizing this, we articulate the following design principle.

Design Principle 2. *If every component of an aggregate entity can have a different set of stakeholders, then each component should be protected separately by a different access control policy.*

The applicability of the above principle depends on the allocation of stakeholders.

Notice that a stakeholder of an annotated content also has a privacy stake in its annotations, for the latter convey information about the former.

Design Principle 3. *Every stakeholder of an annotated content is a stakeholder of its annotations.*

In short, an annotation **inherits** all the stakeholders of the content to which it annotates. These stakeholders are called **inherited stakeholders**. Stakeholders of a content that are not inherited are called **principal stakeholders**.

Consider, for instance, a hypothetical social computing system in which every content has exactly one principal stakeholder, namely, the author of that content. Applying Design Principle 3, a simply annotated content has exactly one stakeholder (i.e., the content's author), while a simple annotation has two stakeholders (i.e., the annotated content's author and the annotation's author). Since every component of a content-annotations aggregate has a different set of stakeholders, Design Principle 2 mandates that each must be protected by a separate policy.

How then are we to assign an access control policy to each component? Our goal is to simplify the design of protection schemes for multiple stakeholders. Consequently, we make two design choices that are aimed at producing simple and yet effective protection. The first decision is to minimize the effort of policy specification that needs to be performed by a user.

Design Decision 4. *Every stakeholder u of content c has a **preferred policy** $p_{u,c}$ that expresses the privacy preference of u for c. If u is a principal stakeholder of c, then u will explicitly specify $p_{u,c}$. Otherwise, u is an inherited stakeholder of c, c is an annotation of some content c', and u is also a stakeholder of c': then $p_{u,c} = p_{u,c'}$.*

In short, preferred policies are **inherited** by annotations. A second design choice is to realize Design Principle 1 by simple conjunction of preferred policies.

Design Decision 5. *Suppose $S_c = \{u_1, \ldots, u_k\}$ is the set of stakeholders for content c, and their preferred policies for c are $p_{u_1,c}, \ldots, p_{u_k,c}$. Then the access control policy p_c for content r is $\bigwedge_{u \in S_c} p_{u,c}$.*

We use the following examples to illustrate how the design works out in practice.

Liking. The author of a content c that can be liked will specify a preferred policy p_1 for c. Because the content author is the sole and principal stakeholder of the content, the visibility of c is controlled solely by p_1. When another user "likes" c, she will be given the opportunity to specify a preferred policy p_2 for this like entry. The access control policy for this like entry is $p_1 \wedge p_2$.

When c is displayed, the total number of likes will be displayed, together with a link for displaying the "likers". When that link is followed, *not all likers are displayed.* The system will check the access control policy of each like entry, and display only those that are accessible by the viewer.

Tagging. In the same vein, every tag is protected separately from the content to which the tag belong. The content itself is protected solely by the preferred policy of its author, who is the principal stakeholder of the content. The principal stakeholder of a tag is the user identified by the tag. This user will specify a preferred policy for the tag. The author of the original content is an inherited stakeholder of the tag. Consequently, each tag is protected by the conjunction of two preferred policies: (a) the preferred policy of the content, and (b) the preferred policy of the user who is being tagged. When the content is displayed, only a subset of its tags are displayed. Tags for which the access control policy is not satisfied are not displayed. To simplify policy specification, a user may have a default policy for controlling the visibility of tags that identify her.

Sharing. Recall the three kinds of privacy concerns surrounding link and content resharing. First, the listing of resharers along with the original posting is analogous to liking, and thus can be handled by a scheme like the one we proposed above for liking. Second, the "via" clause in a reshared link behaves like a tag, and thus it can be handled by a scheme like the one we proposed above for tagging. Third, a reshared content is protected in Facebook using exactly the same design as outlined in Design Decisions 4 and 5, which speak to the robustness of these two design decisions.

4   Design Pattern: Higher Order Annotations

The design pattern we present in this section handles *higher order annotations*. That is, an annotation can be further annotated. The classical example of such higher order annotations is commenting. A posting in a forum can be annotated by comments, which in turn can be further commented on.

4.1   Replying Comments

In most of today's social network systems and online communities, users are able to leave comments on the contents created by themselves or other users. One type of comments mimic the structure of emails. In this type of comments, a user explicitly selects the content that her comment replies to (just like replying to an email). This is a common practice in forums and online communities. Therefore, comments of this type constitute a tree-like structure with the original content as the root of the tree and different threads of comments become branches of the tree. We call this type of comments *replying comments* because of their resemblance to replying emails. Facebook has added replying comments in the posts that have several hundreds of comments. However, the depth of the tree of comments cannot grow more than two in this case.

Design Principles 1, 2 and 3, and Design Decisions 4 and 5 all apply to this setting. Suppose $c_0, c_1, \ldots, c_k$ is a thread of contents, such that c_0 is a non-annotation content (root), and c_i is annotated by c_{i+1}. Let u_i be the author (and thus principal stakeholder) of c_i. Then the stakeholders of c_k are $u_0, u_1, \ldots, u_k$. Each u_i must explicitly specify a preferred policy p_i for c_i. Preferred policies are inherited, and thus the access control policy for c_k is the conjunction $\bigwedge_{i=0}^{k} p_i$.

4.2   Appending Comments

Replying comments do not cover all types of commenting mechanisms in social computing. A notable exception is the mechanism that we call *appending comments*, which is widely deployed in many social network systems. A comment that a user creates gets appended to the end of all the existing comments for the original contents (hence appending comments). Unlike replying comments, this type of comments has less structure than replying comments, and thus it makes the allocation of stakeholders more ambiguous. In the worst case, a newly introduced appending comment may be (implicitly) responding to all the existing comments (and thus annotating all preceding comments as well as the original content). Consequently, rather than a tree structure, the original content and its appending comments form a sequence $c_0, c_1, \ldots, c_k$, where c_0 is the original content, and $c_1, \ldots, c_k$ are the appending comments.

Applying Design Principles 1, 2 and 3, and Design Decisions 4 and 5 to this situation yields the following. Suppose u_i is the author (and thus principal stakeholder) of c_i, and p_i is the preferred policy explicitly specified by u_i for c_i. The stakeholders of c_i are $u_0, u_1, \ldots, u_i$. Therefore, the access control policy for c_k will be the conjunction $\bigwedge_{i=0}^{k} p_i$. Note the difference between this conjunction and the one for replying comments. In the case of replying comments, the access control policy of a comment is the conjunction of the preferred policies of the *ancestors* of that comment. In the case of appending comments, the access control policy of a comment is the conjunction of the preferred policies of all the *preceding* comments.

4.3   Hybrid Solution for Comments

The scheme proposed above for appending comments has a drawback analogous to a well-known problem in Low Watermark Model of Biba [2]. The accessibility of comments becomes increasingly restrictive as users create more and more comments: if a user is able to view a highly restrictive comment (restrictive in terms of access control policy), then this user will not be able to leave a comment with a less restrictive access control policy.

To overcome this drawback, we propose a hybrid solution, in which a user may annotate a content by either appending comment or replying comment. Comments are by default appending comments. The author of an appending comment implicitly consents to adopting the most liberal preferred policy (i.e., everyone). Consequently, the access control policy of an appending comment will be the same as the access control policy of the content to which the appending comment is annotating. If a user wants to explicitly specify a preferred policy, then the user may introduce a replying comment (she will need to point to a specific comment to which she is replying). This preferred policy will not affect the accessibility of the appending comments at a higher level. This prevents the low-watermark effect of pure appending comments, but also provides flexibility of protection offered by replying comments. It is easy to add this feature to an existing social computing system that features appending comments.

5   Relationship Disclosure via Annotations

Annotations create a channel by which user relationships can be inferred. Facebook (also Google+) discloses the "audience" of a content to its viewers.

The "audience" is essentially the access control policy of the content. Suppose users u and v prefer to hide their friendship from other users. To that end, they set the accessibility of their friend lists to *"only me"*. Suppose further that u shares a content c with *friends*, and subsequently v likes c, but v sets the preferred policy of the like to "everyone". Suppose now an observer w comes along. User w is a friend of u, and thus w can view c. When w examines the audience of c, w becomes aware that only friends of u can view c. User w then notices that v likes c. Now w can infer that v is a friend of u. What u and v are not aware is that simply by making c and its annotations visible could lead to the disclosure of their relationships.

The above inference is possible because w can identify the audience of c. We believe that Facebook (also Google+) discloses the audience of a content in order to warn annotators of the visibility of the content. Our solution of protecting an annotated content and its annotations separately (§3 and §4) removes the need for disclosing the "audience" of a content. Without knowing the exact access control policy, the attacker cannot infer relationships with certainty.

Suppose we are paranoid, and we worry that the observer w may be able to guess that the access control policy of the above content is *"friends"* (maybe by observing that other contents of u are usually protected by the *"friends"* policy). Then relationship disclosure will still be possible. We propose here another solution which tackles this paranoia. Suppose p_c is the access control policy of a content c that is created by user u. Suppose $p_{v,a}$ is the preferred policy of an annotation a of c, where a is contributed by v. Suppose p_f is the access control policy of the friend list of u. Then we set the access control policy p_a of annotation a to be $p_c \wedge p_{v,a} \wedge p_f$. In general, relationship inference can be prevented if the access control policy that protects an annotation (p_a) is at least as restrictive as the one protecting the relationship (p_f).

6   Implementation Strategy

The two design patterns presented in §3 and §4 refrain from displaying all annotations (as is done in existing social computing systems). Instead, each annotation is guarded by a separate access control policy, and only the accessible annotations are displayed. This last feature calls for special implementation techniques.

Open Accessibility Queries. A typical Policy Decision Point (PDP) must perform what we call **definite accessibility checks** in order to test whether a given requestor may access a *given* resource. To list the annotations that are accessible by a requestor, a naive implementation will make a database query to collect all annotations, and then procedurally iterate through the annotations, filtering away the ones that fail the accessibility check. Such an implementation is likely unacceptable in performance.

A more efficient implementation will push the work of accessibility filtering to the database management system, which is equipped with highly efficient indexing and query optimization technologies. In essence, we need to be able to

Table	Columns	Indexes
Friends	ID (int)	Clustered: ID (Primary Key)
	UserID1 (int)	Non-Clustered: UserID1 and UserID2
	UserID2 (int)	Non-Clustered: UserID1 Include UserID2
		Non-Clustered: UserID2 Include UserID1
Resources	ResourceID (int)	Clustered: ResourceID (Primary Key)
	PolicyID (int)	Non-Clustered: ParentID and RootID Include ResourceID
	OwnerID (int)	Non-Clustered: OwnerID and ParentID
	ParentID (int)	Non-Clustered: ParentID
	RootID (int)	Non-Clustered: PolicyID and ParentID Include ReaourceID and OwnerID
		Non-Clustered: RootID Include ResourceID
Users	UserID (int)	Clustered: UserID (Primary Key)

Fig. 1. Database tables and their columns and indexes

evaluate **open accessibility queries**: *Given a requestor, find all the accessible resources of a certain kind (e.g., annotations of a given content).*

There are two variations to this query: one involving only simple annotations, and the other involving higher order annotations. We present in the following the high-level idea of how open accessibility queries can be answered in each case, using solely standard SQL technologies.

Modelling a Social Network System. Figure 1 shows the relational database tables that we use as basis for articulating our implementation strategy. Real implementations will probably contain more details, but we believe our tables capture the essence of a social network system. The *Users* table tracks user identifiers. The *Friends* table captures friendship among users. The *Resources* table captures resources, their preferred policies (enumerated type: only me, friends, friends of friends, everyone), author, and, in the case of annotations, the content to which this resource is annotating as well as the root of the annotation tree.

Open Accessibility Queries via Views. To support open accessibility queries, a view (V_Access) can be created to relate users to resources that the former can access (Fig. 2). Such a view allows us to query the set of resources that a given user may access. The view is the union of four different views, one for each of the four modes of access (i.e., only me, friends, friends of friends, everyone). Each of the four views relates users to resources with policies granting the corresponding mode of access.

Fig. 3 shows stored procedures for retrieving those annotations of a given resource that are accessible to a given user: one procedure for simple annotations, and another for higher order annotations. The reason for using stored procedures instead of inline queries is to optimize the execution time.

7 Performance Evaluation

This section demonstrates that the performance of the implementation strategy as proposed in the last section has reasonable performance.

```
CREATE VIEW View_Friends AS
SELECT f1.UserID1, f1.UserID2 FROM Friends AS f1
UNION ALL
SELECT f2.UserID2, f2.UserID1 FROM Friends AS f2

CREATE VIEW V_Owner_Acc AS
SELECT RootID, ParentID, ResourceID, OwnerID AS UserID
FROM Resources

CREATE VIEW V_Friends_Acc AS
SELECT r.RootID, r.ParentID, r.ResourceID, v.UserID2 AS UserID
FROM Resources AS r
  JOIN View_Friends AS v ON r.OwnerID = v.UserID1
WHERE (r.PolicyID = 1) OR (r.PolicyID = 2)

CREATE VIEW V_FOF_Acc AS
SELECT r.RootID, r.ParentID, r.ResourceID, F2.UserID2 AS UserID
FROM Resources AS r
  JOIN View_Friends AS F1 ON r.OwnerID = F1.UserID1
    JOIN View_Friends AS F2 ON F1.UserID2 = F2.UserID1
WHERE (r.PolicyID = 2)

CREATE VIEW V_Everyone_Acc AS
SELECT r.RootID, r.ParentID, r.ResourceID, u.UserID
FROM Resources AS r
  CROSS JOIN Users AS u
WHERE (r.PolicyID = 3)

CREATE VIEW V_Access AS
SELECT * FROM V_Owner_Acc UNION SELECT * FROM V_Friends_Acc
  UNION SELECT * FROM V_FOF_Acc UNION SELECT * FROM V_Everyone_Acc
```

Fig. 2. View definitions for reverse accessibility check

7.1   Dataset

Social Network Data. We used an anonymized social network dataset (4,847,571 nodes and 68,993,773 edges) created from LiveJournal [1, 11] and hosted by Stanford Large Network Dataset Collection. LiveJournal is a social network with estimated 10 to 100 millions of users. Users can have blogs and add one another as friends. Friendship in LiveJournal is directed. We therefore created a database view to represent the symmetric closure of the friendship relation, thereby making friendship symmetric as in Facebook.

Resources Data. We generate the resources that are being protected by access control. Each resource has a privacy policy chosen uniformly at random from $\{0, 1, 2, 3\}$, where 0, 1, 2 and 3 correspond to *Only Me, Friends, Friends of Friends* and *Everyone* respectively. These are the default privacy policies available in Facebook. Each resource's owner is selected uniformly at random from the set of all users in the dataset. Each resource can be either a content or an annotation. Denote by R the set of all resources, C the set of (non-annotation) contents, and A the set of annotations. We have: $R = C \uplus A$. We design two separate configurations of experiments, one for simple annotations and another for higher order annotations. As a result, the way we relate annotations to

```
CREATE PROCEDURE SP_Can_Access @UserID INT, @ResourceID INT AS
BEGIN
SELECT r.ResourceID FROM
( SELECT va.ResourceID FROM View_Access AS va
   WHERE (va.UserID = @UserID) AND (va.ResourceID = @ResourceID) )t
    JOIN Resources AS r ON r.ParentID = t.ResourceID
      JOIN View_Access AS va ON va.ResourceID = r.ResourceID
WHERE va.UserID = @UserID
END


CREATE PROCEDURE SP_Recursive_Can_Access @UserID INT, @ResourceID INT AS
BEGIN
WITH Recursive_Can_Access (ResourceID, Level) AS
 (SELECT ResourceID, 0 AS LEVEL
   FROM View_Access
   WHERE ResourceID = @ResourceID AND UserID = @UserID
   UNION ALL
   SELECT va.ResourceID, LEVEL + 1
   FROM View_Access AS va
     JOIN Recursive_Can_Access AS r ON va.ParentID = r.ResourceID
   WHERE va.UserID = @UserID AND va.RootID = @ResourceID)
SELECT ResourceID, LEVEL
FROM Recursive_Can_Access
END
```

Fig. 3. Procedures for retrieving simple and higher order annotations

contents differ for each configuration. Below we show how we relate annotations to contents in each configuration.

The Simple Annotations Configuration. We randomly generate a function $f : A \to C$ to assign annotations to contents. The generation of f is controlled by a parameter ratio $= \left\lfloor \frac{|A|}{|C|} \right\rfloor$, which is the average number of annotations that each content has. Function f maps each element in domain A to an element in codomain C uniformly at random with probability $\frac{1}{|C|}$.

The Higher Order Annotations Configuration. We randomly generate a function $f : A \to R$ to map annotations to resources. We generation of f is again controlled by the parameter ratio $= \left\lfloor \frac{|A|}{|C|} \right\rfloor$. The constraint which function f must satisfy is that annotation assignment must result in a *forest* (disjoint union of trees) over R (no circles).

7.2 Setup

The experiments are conducted both on a consumer-scale machine (aka local) and the Microsoft cloud called Windows Azure (aka Azure). The results from both environments are reported. We repeat the experiments in two characteristically different computing environments to give an idea of the range of performance that one can expect in reality. The consumer-scale machine is but a notebook computer, and thus it represents the pessimistic lower bound of performance. The Azure environment is likely more representative of the kind of server-side capability that a social computing vendor possesses.

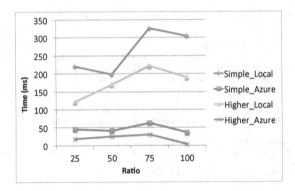

Fig. 4. Performance figures for the two experimental configurations, each repeated in both the local and Azure environment

The local machine is equipped with Microsoft SQL Server (2005 and 2012) and 64-bit Windows 7 Professional (Service Pack 1), and has the following hardware configuration: 2.4 GHz Intel Core 2 Duo Processor, 4 GB 1067 MHz DDR3 Memory, SATA disk. The database is later migrated to Windows Azure, and experiments are conducted on the SQL server provided in Windows Azure. The database is hosted on a Windows Azure server located in north central USA. Most of the experiments on Azure are run around midnight when we conjecture there is less load on the server.

7.3   Measurements

For each of the two configurations (simple annotations and higher order annotations), we measure the execution time of submitting the corresponding query in Fig. 3 to the SQL Server. The measurement is repeated for 1000 times, each with randomly chosen arguments (repetitive arguments are avoided), and the average execution time is computed. Each query receives two arguments: (a) a user of the social network and (b) a content. The users are chosen in such a way that they have access to the content itself according to that content's access control policy. The result set for these queries are the annotations of that content for which the user is allowed to access.

7.4   Results and Interpretation

Fig. 4 shows the response time for retrieving accessible annotations. Note that, when a consumer-scale machine (local) is used, the retrieval time is between 100--350 milliseconds. When a server-scale machine (Azure) is used, the retrieval time is no higher than 70 milliseconds.

According to [14, Chapter 5] and [13], the following response time limits must be considered in interactive applications. (1) 0.1 second is the limit for the users to feel that system works instantaneously and that they are directly performing the manipulation (typing in a text box and viewing the text typed simultaneously). (2) 1.0 second is the limit for the users to keep their flow of thoughts and they feel they are freely navigating (although they feel the delay, they also feel the computer is working). (3) 10 seconds is the limit to keep users attention. Taking into consideration network latency (30 − 300 milliseconds for web sites such as Facebook [3]), and using server-scale machines like Windows Azure, response time remains in the acceptable range of 0.1 to 1.0 second.

8   Discussions and Future Work

Of the five classical examples of multiple stakeholders (i.e., tagging, commenting, sharing, foreign contents, and friendship articulation), the design patterns proposed in this work can address three of them with very simple designs of access control. The core observation that we depend on is Design Principle 2, which asserts that components of composite objects should be protected by separate access control policies when the stakeholders of the components are different.

The above implies that there are two classes of multiple-stakeholder scenarios that cannot be addressed in the manners suggested in this work.

1. *Joint Assertions*. Some contents are atomic: they are not made up of separately identifiable components. An example is the assertion of a relationship between two parties. Such contents are created under the consent of multiple parties (e.g., befriending requires the consent of the two friends), and thus multiple stakeholders are involved.

2. *Collaborative Authoring*. Some contents, such as wiki pages, are composite, but each must be taken as a whole. These contents are results of collaboration among multiple authors, and yet authorship is attributed to the entire product and cannot be attributed to the parts. Thus the finished product affects the privacy of multiple stakeholders.

In these 2 cases, general-purpose schemes for multiple stakeholders [7–9, 15–17, 21] are absolutely irreplaceable. Future work in the study of protection schemes for multiple stakeholders should focus on the above two classes of scenarios.

Acknowledgments. This work is supported in part by an NSERC Discovery Grant and a Canada Research Chair.

References

1. Backstrom, L., Huttenlocher, D., Kleinberg, J., Lan, X.: Group formation in large social networks: Membership, growth, and evolution. In: Proceedings of KDD 2006, Philadelphia, PA, USA, pp. 44–54. ACM (2006)
2. Biba, K.J.: Integrity considerations for secure computer systems. Technical Report ESD-TR-76-372, Electronic Systems Division, Air Force Systems Command, United States Air Force (April 1977)

3. CityCloud. Some interesting bits about latency (August 2012), `https://www.citycloud.com/city-cloud/some-interesting-bits-about-latency/`
4. Facebook Help Center (August 2013), `https://www.facebook.com/help/www/255898821192992`
5. Gamma, E., Helm, R., Johnson, R., Vlissides, J.: Design Patterns. Addison Wesley (1994)
6. Graham, G.S., Denning, P.J.: Protection: Principles and practice. In: Proceedings of the 1972 AFIPS Spring Joint Computer Conference, Atlantic City, New Jersey, USA, vol. 40, pp. 417–429 (May 1972)
7. Hu, H., Ahn, G.-J.: Multiparty authorization framework for data sharing in online social networks. In: Li, Y. (ed.) DBSec 2011. LNCS, vol. 6818, pp. 29–43. Springer, Heidelberg (2011)
8. Hu, H., Ahn, G.-J., Jorgensen, J.: Detecting and resolving privacy conflicts for collaborative data sharing in online social networks. In: Proceedings of ACSAC 2011, Orlando, Florida, USA, pp. 103–112 (2011)
9. Hu, H., Ahn, G.-J., Jorgensen, J.: Multiparty access control for online social networks: Model and mechanisms. IEEE Transactions on Knowledge and Data Engineering (2013)
10. Kumar, M.: How Facebook Ticker Exposing Your Information and Behavior Without Your Knowledge (October 2011), `http://thehackernews.com/2011/10/how-facebook-ticker-exposing-your.html`
11. Leskovec, J., Lang, K.J., Dasgupta, A., Mahoney, M.W.: Community structure in large networks: Natural cluster sizes and the absence of large well-defined clusters. Internet Mathematics 6(1), 29–123 (2009)
12. Li, N., Tripunitara, M.V.: On safety in discretionary access control. In: Proceedings of IEEE S&P 2005, Oakland, CA, USA, pp. 96–109 (May 2005)
13. Miller, R.B.: Response time in man-computer conversational transactions. In: Proceedings of the 1968 AFIPS Fall Joint Computer Conference, Part I, San Francisco, CA, USA, vol. 33, pp. 267–277 (December 1968)
14. Nielsen, J.: Usability Engineering. Morgan Kaufmann (1993)
15. Squicciarini, A.C., Shehab, M., Paci, F.: Collective privacy management in social networks. In: Proceedings of WWW 2009, Madrid, Spain, pp. 521–530 (2009)
16. Squicciarini, A.C., Shehab, M., Wede, J.: Privacy policies for shared content in social network sites. The VLDB Journal 19(6), 777–796 (2010)
17. Squicciarini, A.C., Xu, H., Zhang, X.L.: CoPE: Enabling collaborative privacy management in online social networks. Journal of the American Society for Information Science 62(3), 521–534 (2011)
18. The Social CMO. New Facebook Ticker Is Invasion of Privacy (September 2011), `http://www.thesocialcmo.com/blog/2011/09/new-facebook-ticker-is-invasion-of-privacy/`
19. Thomas, K., Grier, C., Nicol, D.M.: Unfriendly: Multi-party privacy risks in social networks. In: Atallah, M.J., Hopper, N.J. (eds.) PETS 2010. LNCS, vol. 6205, pp. 236–252. Springer, Heidelberg (2010)
20. Washbrook, C.: Facebook's Ticker Privacy Scare, and What You Should Do About It (September 2011), `http://nakedsecurity.sophos.com/2011/09/26/facebook-ticker-privacy-scare/`
21. Wishart, R., Corapi, D., Marinovic, S., Sloman, M.: Collaborative privacy policy authoring in a social networking context. In: Proceedings of IEEE POLICY 2010, Fairfax, VA, USA, pp. 1–8 (2010)

Collaboratively Solving the Traveling Salesman Problem with Limited Disclosure

Yuan Hong[1], Jaideep Vaidya[2], Haibing Lu[3], and Lingyu Wang[4]

[1] SUNY-Albany
hong@albany.edu
[2] Rutgers University
jsvaidya@business.rutgers.edu
[3] Santa Clara University
hlu@scu.edu
[4] Concordia University
wang@concordia.ca

Abstract. With increasing resource constraints, optimization is necessary to make the best use of scarce resources. Given the ubiquitous connectivity and availability of information, collaborative optimization problems can be formulated by different parties to jointly optimize their operations. However, this cannot usually be done without restraint since privacy/security concerns often inhibit the complete sharing of proprietary information. The field of privacy-preserving optimization studies how collaborative optimization can be performed with limited disclosure. In this paper, we develop privacy-preserving solutions for collaboratively solving the traveling salesman problem (TSP), a fundamental combinatorial optimization problem with applications in diverse fields such as planning, logistics and production. We propose a secure and efficient protocol for multiple participants to formulate and solve such a problem without sharing any private information. We formally prove the protocol security under the rigorous definition of secure multiparty computation (SMC), and demonstrate its effectiveness with experimental results using real data.

Keywords: Privacy, Secure Multiparty Computation, Optimization.

1 Introduction

Collaboration amongst different parties occurs frequently in the modern business world. Given the increasing resource constraints, it makes sense for different companies to jointly optimize their operations in delivering, production planning, scheduling, inventory control, etc. Indeed, joint optimization has led to significant savings when successfully carried out. However, such collaboration is normally the exception, rather than the rule. The reason for this is the high degree of trust required, wherein proprietary data has to be shared with an external party which can then carry out the optimization. To deal with this, privacy-preserving solutions have been developed to enable collaborative optimization for several specific problems [1–5]. In this paper, we focus on the traveling salesman problem (TSP). TSP is a fundamental optimization problem, and can be used

V. Atluri and G. Pernul (Eds.): DBSec 2014, LNCS 8566, pp. 179–194, 2014.

in many applications such as logistics, planning, and production. We first show how a simple two-party collaborative TSP can be formulated [1]:

Example 1. There are two shipping companies, denoted *Alice* and *Bob*, which offer delivery services among seven cities, City $1, \ldots, 7$. Figure 1 shows the city connectivity and corresponding delivery cost for both companies.

A client E_C wants to decide which shipping company to employ in order to ship their goods to a list of cities (e.g., $1, 2, 3, 5$, and 6) with the lowest overall cost. However, E_C is reluctant to let either *Alice* or *Bob* know its list of cities before signing the contract, and *Alice* and *Bob* also do not want to share all their delivery cost information with E_c or other parties. How can E_C make this decision under such privacy concerns?

The prior solution [1] is to let E_C securely solve "Two" two-party TSPs with *Alice* and *Bob* "respectively", and then choose the lower cost obtained from *Alice* and *Bob*.

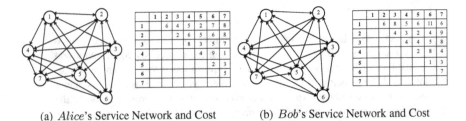

	1	2	3	4	5	6	7
1		6	4	5	2	7	8
2			2	6	5	6	8
3				8	3	5	7
4					4	9	1
5						2	3
6							5
7							

	1	2	3	4	5	6	7
1		6	8	5	6	11	6
2			4	3	2	4	9
3				4	4	5	8
4					2	8	4
5						1	3
6							7
7							

(a) *Alice*'s Service Network and Cost   (b) *Bob*'s Service Network and Cost

Fig. 1. Two-party Collaboration in [1]

While this enables E_C to choose the lowest cost provider, it does not enable the lowest cost overall, since it forces one company to be used to do all of the shipments. In this paper, we tackle the privacy concerns in a multiparty TSP (rather than two-party TSP [1]) in which the global minimum cost can be further reduced from all the participants, detailed as below.

Cost Reduction. Assume that the optimal solutions derived for E_C from Alice and Bob in Figure 1 are 1) "*Alice* : $1 \rightarrow 5 \rightarrow 6 \rightarrow 2 \rightarrow 3 \rightarrow 1$" with total cost 2+2+6+2+4=16, and 2) "*Bob* : $1 \rightarrow 5 \rightarrow 6 \rightarrow 2 \rightarrow 3 \rightarrow 1$" with total cost 6+1+4+4+8=23. Per the work in [1], E_C then employs *Alice* to deliver their goods to the destinations due to $16 < 23$. However, Bob indeed offers cheaper shipping rates among some cities, e.g., $5 \rightarrow 6 \rightarrow 2$. If E_C can employ both shipping companies to deliver goods, even though on the same route "$1 \rightarrow 5 \rightarrow 6 \rightarrow 2 \rightarrow 3 \rightarrow 1$", the global cost could be $2 + 1 + 4 + 2 + 4 = 13 < 16 < 23$. As more shipping companies participate in the collaboration, significant cost saving can be realized.

Practicability and Availability. In reality, many companies need to make decisions for the delivery of considerable number of cities. From the economic perspective, they normally do not always contract with only one shipping company for all of their destinations. Then, the two-party TSP in [1] clearly cannot meet the practical cost-minimizing demand of E_C. Besides this, such TSP has many other drawbacks. Specifically, if neither *Alice* nor *Bob* is able to complete the delivery for E_C by their own: e.g., *Alice*

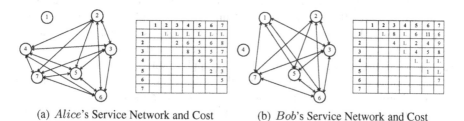

(a) *Alice*'s Service Network and Cost   (b) *Bob*'s Service Network and Cost

Fig. 2. Limited Shipping Service Network ("L" means unavailable service)

cannot deliver any shipping to City 1 while *Bob* cannot deliver shipping between City 1 and 2 (Figure 2), then the model in [1] cannot provide a solution.

To address the above limitations, we formulate and securely solve a novel cost-reducible collaborative TSP, which enables the client to find the global minimum cost from one or more shipping companies, and enables the shipping companies not to lose their clients for their service limitation. Indeed, securely solving a fundamental optimization problem like TSP gives great insights to all its the applications with limited information disclosure. With similar settings, our problem formulation and solver can be equally applicable to the proprietary information protection in many other real-world applications such as arranging school bus routes for one or more outsourced companies to pickup the children, scheduling service calls at cable firms, and manufacturing circuit board by drilling holes with machines from different entities [6]. Therefore, the main contributions of this paper are summarized as below:

- We propose a new efficient secure communication protocol to solve the novel cost-reducible collaborative TSP under semi-honest adversarial model – all parties follow the protocol but they are curious to derive private information from each other.
- We give end-to-end security proof for our secure communication protocol under the rigorous definition of Secure Multiparty Computation (SMC) [7, 8], whereas only the security of some building blocks was proven in the two-party TSP [1].
- We demonstrate the effectiveness of our approach with experiments on real data.

The remainder of this paper is organized as follows. We first briefly review the related literature in Section 2. Then we define the problem in Section 3, and present the secure communication protocol in Section 4. We give security and cost analysis in Section 5. Section 6 demonstrates the experimental results. Finally, we conclude this paper and discuss the future work in Section 7.

2 Related Work

We briefly review some of the relevant work on privacy-preserving collaborative (viz. distributed) optimization. Li and Atallah [9] addressed the collaborative linear programming problem between two parties where the objective function and constraints can be arbitrarily partitioned, and proposed a secure simplex method for such problem based on homomorphic encryption and scrambled circuit evaluation. Vaidya [10] proposed a secure revised simplex approach with homomorphic encryption and secure comparison, which is more efficient than Li and Atallah's approach [9]. Catrina and Hoogh [11] presented a solution to solve distributed linear programs based on secret sharing. The protocols utilized a variant of the simplex algorithm and secure computation with fixed-point rational numbers, optimized for such application.

Apart from a direct cryptographic protocol, another typical approach is to transform the original problem into a different space, solve it in that transformed space, and then reconstruct the solution. Du [12] and Vaidya [13] transformed the linear programming problem by multiplying a monomial matrix to both the constraint matrix and the objective function, assuming that one party holds the objective function while the other party holds the constraints. Bednarz et al. [14, 15] pointed out a potential attack to the above transformation approach, which has been resolved in [3, 16]. In addition, Mangasarian presented two transformation approaches for horizontally partitioned linear programs [17] and vertically partitioned linear programs [18] respectively. Li et al. [19] extended the transformation approach [17] for horizontally partitioned linear programs with equality constraints to inequality constraints. Hong and Vaidya identified a potential inference attack to Mangasarian and Li's transformation based approach, and revised the transformation with significantly enhanced security guarantee in [20].

There has also been work on creating privacy-preserving solutions for collaborative combinatorial optimization problems (especially those that are NP-hard). Hong et al. [4] presented a privacy-preserving approach for the well known graph coloring problem. The solution is based on tabu search. The work most relevant to our problem is that of Sakuma et al [1] who proposed a genetic algorithm for securely solving two-party distributed traveling salesman problem (TSP). They consider the case that one party holds the cost vector/matrix while the other party holds the tour vector/matrix. The TSP that is completely partitioned among multiple parties has been discussed but not solved in [1]. In this paper, we consider a cost-reducible collaborative TSP amongst multiple (more than two) parties, and securely solve it with simulated annealing based protocol, which facilitates us to formally prove the security for the approach. Our approach falls under the framework of secure multiparty computation [7, 8, 21, 22], wherein any function can be securely computed without revealing anything to each party except its input, output, and anything that can be derived from them.

3   Problem Formulation

3.1   TSP and Simulated Annealing

TSP is a NP-hard optimization problem that is defined as follows[23]: given a set of cities and the distances between every pair of cities, finding the shortest route that visits all the cities exactly once and returns to the original city (minimizing overall distance). Note that in a more general sense, distance between cities can be replaced with cost.

Simulated annealing is a generic probabilistic meta-heuristic that is widely used to solve this NP-hard problem when the input is large [23]. Simulated annealing was inspired from thermodynamics, based on the behavior of metals cooling and annealing [24]. The basic idea behind simulated annealing is to move from one state (solution) to another state (a neighboring solution), until a good enough solution is found, or the given computation budget has been exhausted. Note that the move is probabilistic in that we may move to a worse solution or choose to stay in the same state even if a better solution has been found some of the times. In TSP, given the traveling route, denoted as x, the objective function of simulated annealing is to minimize $f(x)$ and the algorithm iteratively moves from solutions to their neighboring solution. At each stage, the probability of making a transition from a solution to the neighboring solution is based on an acceptance probability function for two solutions and a sensitivity parameter "Temperature" T. The algorithm is briefly summarized as below:

1. initialize a solution x by randomly selecting a traveling route.
2. randomly pick a neighboring solution x' of x by 2-Opt neighborhood [25], swapping the visited order of two cities. For example, if $x =$ "1$\rightarrow$ 3 $\rightarrow$ 2 $\rightarrow$ 4", then $x =$ "1 $\rightarrow$ 3 $\rightarrow$ 4 $\rightarrow$ 2" is its neighboring solution.
3. decide whether to move to the new solution with the probability computed from $f(x)$, $f(x')$ and the sensitivity parameter T. If yes, update the current solution.
4. repeat step 2,3 until achieving the iteration threshold or a satisfactory solution.

3.2 Cost-Reducible Collaborative TSP

In a TSP, $G = (V, E)$ is a complete undirected graph where V and E represent the set of cities and (cost) weighted edges respectively. Cost-reducible collaborative TSP involving k shipping companies and one client, where all involved shipping companies successively "Relay" the goods for client E_C on the overall route for further cutting the cost. Then, we define it as k-Relaying Traveling Salesman Problem (k-RTSP).

Definition 1 (k-RTSP). *Assume n cities, and k shipping companies $P_1, \ldots, P_k$ that hold k different cost matrices/vectors $y_1, \ldots, y_k$, and a client E_C who needs to visit a subset of cities once (finally returning to the original city, as in a Hamiltonian Cycle). Then, k-RTSP is defined as: find the optimal traveling route and minimum total cost for E_C's cities, where every segment of the traveling route is served by the shipping company quoting the cheapest rate among all k shipping companies.*

k-RTSP's optimal traveling route is jointly computed by k shipping companies and the client. If $k = 1$, k-RTSP turns into a two-party TSP [1] since no relay is required.

Vectors in k-RTSP. Intuitively k shipping companies' cost vectors can be written as:

Table 1. k Shipping Companies' Cost Vectors

$$y_1 = (y^1_{(1,2)}, \ldots, y^1_{(1,n)}, y^1_{(2,3)}, \ldots, y^1_{(2,n)}, \ldots, y^1_{(n-1,n)})$$
$$\vdots$$
$$y_k = (y^k_{(1,2)}, \ldots, y^k_{(1,n)}, y^k_{(2,3)}, \ldots, y^k_{(2,n)}, \ldots, y^k_{(n-1,n)})$$

As shown in Figure 2, if one shipping company does not serve delivery between two cities, e.g., P_1 does not deliver between City 1 and 2, we let $y^1_{(1,2)}$ be a sufficiently large number L. Similarly, client's traveling route vector can be expressed as a boolean vector $x = (x_{(1,2)}, \ldots, x_{(1,n)}, x_{(2,3)}, \ldots, x_{(2,n)}, \ldots, x_{(n-1,n)})$ where $x_{(i,j)} = 1$ means e_{ij} is included in E_C's traveling route;otherwise 0.

Note that the length of vectors x and $y_1, \ldots, y_k$ is the total number of city pairs $d = n(n-1)/2$. For simplicity of notations, we use $j = 1, \ldots, d$ to indicate the index of $n(n-1)/2$ elements in each of the $k+1$ vectors.

Cost Function and Solution. In k-RTSP, every $x_{(i,j)} = 1$ in x (e_{ij} is included in the route) is assigned to a shipping company with cheapest cost (we denote this process as "Route Assignment"). Then x can be drilled down to k boolean vectors for k different shipping companies, for example as below:

Table 2. Route Assignment for Traveling Route Vector

	$x = (0, 1, 0, 1, 0, 0, 1, 0, 0, 1, 0, 0, 0, 0, 0, 0, 0, 1, 0, 0)$
Alice	$x_1 = (0, 0, 0, 0, 0, 0, 1, 0, 0, 0, 0, 0, 0, 0, 0, 0, 0, 0, 0, 0)$
Bob	$x_2 = (0, 0, 0, 0, 0, 0, 0, 0, 0, 1, 0, 0, 0, 0, 0, 0, 0, 1, 0, 0)$
Carol	$x_3 = (0, 1, 0, 1, 0, 0, 0, 0, 0, 0, 0, 0, 0, 0, 0, 0, 0, 0, 0, 0)$

Denoting $x_{ij} \in \{0,1\}$ ($i = 1, \ldots, k$ and $j = 1, \ldots, d$) as whether shipping company P_i delivers goods for the jth corresponding pair of cities or not, the length-d vector x is then drilled down to k length-d vectors $x_1, \ldots, x_k$ in route assignment. Thus, $\{x_1, \ldots, x_k\}$ is the solution of k-RTSP, which is finer-grained than x. Moreover, the cost function of k-RTSP can be derived as $f(x_1, \ldots, x_k) = \sum_{i=1}^{k} x_i \cdot y_i = \sum_{i=1}^{k} (\sum_{j=1}^{d} x_{ij} y_{ij})$.

4 Privacy-Preserving Algorithm

Simulated annealing is an efficient meta-heuristic for conventional TSP, thus we build the secure solver for k-RTSP by securing the simulated annealing algorithm. First, we consider the extension of the algorithm to solve k-RTSP (no security), all the parties repeat the following procedures until they find a near-optimal solution:

Client E_C proposes a solution $x = \{x_1, \ldots, x_k\}$ and its neighboring solution $x' = \{x'_1, \ldots, x'_k\}$ to all the shipping companies $P_1, \ldots, P_k$, then $P_1, \ldots, P_k$ jointly compute the energy of two solutions $f(x_1, \ldots, x_k)$ and $f(x'_1, \ldots, x'_k)$, and finally compute the probability of moving from x to x':

$$Prob = \min\{1, exp(-\frac{f(x'_1, \ldots, x'_k) - f(x_1, \ldots, x_k)}{T})\} \qquad (1)$$

If x' outperforms x, solution will move from x to x' with $Prob = 1$; if x' is worse than x, there still exists a probability to move from x to x' (to avoid local optimum).

More importantly, all parties should jointly compute the result without revealing any private information in every iteration. To achieve this, we present a secure communication protocol to solve k-RTSP without private information disclosure.

4.1   Building Blocks

Simulated annealing iteratively computes the energy of various pairs of neighboring solutions and decides whether to move or not. Thus, the secure communication protocol based on it also repeatedly calls some secure functions, which are considered as *Building Blocks* of the protocol. We briefly describe them below:

Secure Scalar Product. The cost function of k-RTSP is given as $f(x_1, \ldots, x_k) = \sum_{i=1}^{k} x_i \cdot y_i$ where client E_C holds the traveling route vectors $x_1, \ldots, x_k$ and shipping companies $P_1, \ldots, P_k$ hold $y_1, \ldots, y_k$ respectively. Thus, we implement a secure scalar product protocol based on Paillier's Homomorphic Cryptosystem [26] to securely compute the function (Algorithm 1). *Notice that every party only holds a random number – the sum of the random numbers is the scalar product which is also unknown to everyone besides the private inputs.*

Algorithm 1. Secure Scalar Product

Input: Traveling route vector $x = \{x_1, \ldots, x_k\}$, cost vectors $y_1, \ldots, y_k$
Output: $f(x_1, \ldots, x_k) = \sum_{i=1}^{k} x_i \cdot y_i$ co-held by all $k + 1$ parties

1. Client E_C creates a public/private key pair (pk, sk), and encrypts $x_1, \ldots, x_k$ to $Enc_{pk}(x_1), \ldots, Enc_{pk}(x_k)$ with its pk
2. E_C sends $Enc_{pk}(x_1), \ldots, Enc_{pk}(x_k)$ and pk to all k shipping companies $P_1, \ldots, P_k$
3. **for** each party $P_i, i = 1, \ldots, k$ **do**
4. P_i generates a random integer r_i, encrypts it with the public key pk, computes the encrypted scalar product as: $Enc_{pk}(x_i)^{y_i} * Enc_{pk}(r_i) = Enc_{pk}(x_i \cdot y_i + r_i)$, and sends it back to E_C
5. E_C decrypts $Enc_{pk}(x_i \cdot y_i + r_i)$ with its private key sk and obtains a random share $s_i = x_i \cdot y_i + r_i$
   {Finally, E_C privately holds random numbers $\forall i \in [1, k], s_i = x_i \cdot y_i + r_i$, and $\forall i \in [1, k], P_i$ privately holds random numbers $-r_i$. The sum of all the shares $f(x_1, \ldots, x_k) = \sum_{i=1}^{k} x_i \cdot y_i$ is unknown to all parties.}

Secure Comparison. In simulated annealing, given temperature T, Equation 1 is used to determine if solution $x = \{x_1, \ldots, x_k\}$ should be moved to $x' = \{x'_1, \ldots, x'_k\}$ or not. In every iteration, $\min\{1, exp(-\frac{f(x'_1, \ldots, x'_k) - f(x_1, \ldots, x_k)}{T})\}$ should be compared with a random number $\eta \in [0, 1)$ [27]: if $\min\{1, exp(-\frac{f(x'_1, \ldots, x'_k) - f(x_1, \ldots, x_k)}{T})\} > \eta$, then move $x = \{x_1, \ldots, x_k\}$ to $x' = \{x'_1, \ldots, x'_k\}$; otherwise, not.

We employ FairplayMP [28] to securely compare the outputs of two functions, thus we need to compare: $f(x_1, \ldots, x_k) - f(x'_1, \ldots, x'_k)$ and $T \log \eta$, where the inputs for $f(x_1, \ldots, x_k)$ and $f(x'_1, \ldots, x'_k)$ are the random shares held by all $k + 1$ parties (generated from Algorithm 1).

Note that, if $f(x_1, \ldots, x_k) - f(x'_1, \ldots, x'_k) > T \log \eta$, client E_C moves $x = \{x_1, \ldots, x_k\}$ to $x' = \{x'_1, \ldots, x'_k\}$ regardless of whether x' is better than x or not; else, the move does not occur. Note that if the temperature T is lowered, simulated annealing algorithm only accepts moving from x to a worse solution x' with closer energy $f(x'_1, \ldots, x'_k)$ and $f(x_1, \ldots, x_k)$. This guarantees the accuracy of the meta-heuristic.

In secure comparison, similarly, each party cannot learn any input from each other, and only client E_C knows the comparison result ">" or "$\leq$".

4.2 Two-Level Secure Simulated Annealing (TSSA)

Different from the traditional TSP, k-RTSP has two categories of neighboring solutions since up to k possible costs are available for every pair of cities in G. First, like the well-known TSP, we can find the 2-Opt [25] neighboring solution x' by permuting the visited order of two cities, e.g., $x = 1 \rightarrow 2 \rightarrow 3$ and $x' = 1 \rightarrow 3 \rightarrow 2$. Second, for every solution, e.g., $x = 1 \rightarrow 2 \rightarrow 3$, each route segment ($1 \rightarrow 2$ and $2 \rightarrow 3$) can be potentially assigned to Alice, Bob or Carol in "Route Assignment". Then, $x = 1 \rightarrow 2 \rightarrow 3$ (with a particular route assignment) should have $3^2 - 1 = 8$ neighboring solutions by choosing different combinations of shipping companies, reflected in $\{x_1, \ldots, x_k\}$. Ideally, if $y_1, \ldots, y_k$ are known to client E_C, E_C can simply select the shipping company with the lowest cost on each segment of the route. However, in secure k-RTSP model, such information is masked and absolutely unknown to E_C. Therefore, we have to run meta-heuristics again to find the optimal route assignment for every solution (traveling route) generated in neighboring route search.

In summary, while securely running the protocol, a top-level simulated annealing is called to search traveling route vector x. For every new solution x, bottom-level simulated annealing will be executed to search the neighborhoods in "Route Assignment". As soon as a near-optimal solution of "Route Assignment" for x is found, x *and its optimal route assignment* will be updated as the current solution. After that, top-level simulated annealing continues to repeatedly traverse x's neighboring traveling route vectors. Therefore, we denote this two level meta-heuristic based protocol as *Two-level Secure Simulated Annealing (TSSA)*.

4.3 Secure Communication Protocol

Our secure communication protocol (TSSA shown in Algorithm 2) ensures that any party cannot learn any private information from each other. More specifically, at Line 1, the protocol is initialized; the loop for top-level simulated annealing is executed between Line 2-22; at Line 3-5, E_C drills down current solution (x, derived from top-level simulated annealing) and initializes the bottom-level simulated annealing, whose loop executes between Line 6-13; in the bottom-level loop, current solution (bottom level) is updated at Line 10-11, and the bottom-level cooling is implemented at Line 13; At Line 19-20 in the top-level loop, current solution for TSSA is updated, and the top-level cooling is implemented at Line 22. TSSA algorithm searches the optimal traveling route vector where the embedded bottom-level simulated annealing is called to search the optimal route assignment for every solution. For any traveling route x and its neighboring solution x' obtained in the top-level simulated annealing, their corresponding optimal route assignments are found by separate bottom-level simulated annealing respectively. Thus, the current best route (with its optimal route assignment) moves toward the optimal traveling route (with the optimal route assignment) of k-RTSP. Here, it is worth noting that:

Algorithm 2. Two-level Secure Simulated Annealing

Input: Client E_C's initial traveling route x; Shipping companies cost vectors $y_1, \ldots, y_k$; Initial
temperature T_1, T_2; Cooling coefficient ρ_1, ρ_2; $\eta \in [0, 1)$

Output: Near-optimal route $best\{x\}$ and the route assignment $best\{x_1, \ldots, x_k\}$

1. $iter_1 \leftarrow 0$; $best\{x\} \leftarrow x$; $best\{x_1, \ldots, x_k\} \leftarrow \{x_1, \ldots, x_k\}$
   {Top-level simulated annealing searches the optimal route with optimal route assignment}
2. **while** $iter_1 < max\_iter_1$ **do**
3. $iter_2 \leftarrow 0$
       {Bottom-level simulated annealing for the optimal route assignment of $best\{x\}$}
4. E_C drills down $best\{x\}$ with a random route assignment: $\{x_1, \ldots, x_k\}$
5. $best_1\{x_1, \ldots, x_k\} \leftarrow \{x_1, \ldots, x_k\}$
6.   **while** $iter_2 < max\_iter_2$ and $route\_assigned(best\{x\}) = 0$ **do**
7. E_C gets $best_1\{x_1, \ldots, x_k\}$'s random neighboring route assignment: $\{x'_1, \ldots, x'_k\}$
8.   Call Algorithm 1 twice to securely compute $f(x_1, \ldots, x_k) = \sum_{i=1}^{k} x_i \cdot y_i$ and
   $f(x'_1, \ldots, x'_k) = \sum_{i=1}^{k} x'_i \cdot y_i$ among all $k + 1$ parties
9.   Call secure comparison (FairplayMP [28]) to compare $f(x_1, \ldots, x_k) - f(x'_1, \ldots, x'_k)$
   and $T_2 \log \eta$ among all $k + 1$ parties
10.   **if** $f(x_1, \ldots, x_k) - f(x'_1, \ldots, x'_k) > T_2 \log \eta$ **then**
11. $best_1\{x_1, \ldots, x_k\} \leftarrow \{x'_1, \ldots, x'_k\}$
12. $iter_2 + +$
13. $T_2 \leftarrow \rho_2 T_2$ (cooling down after several iterations)
14. $route\_assigned(best\{x\}) = 1$
15. E_C gets a random neighboring route of $best\{x\}$: x'
       {Bottom-level simulated annealing for the optimal route assignment of x'}
16.   All $k + 1$ parties repeat Step 3-15 to obtain the near-optimal route assignment for x':
   $best_2\{x_1, \ldots, x_k\}$ and $route\_assigned(x') = 1$
17.   Call Algorithm 1 twice to securely compute $f(best_1\{x_1, \ldots, x_k\})$ and
   $f(best_2\{x_1, \ldots, x_k\})$ among all $k + 1$ parties
18.   Call secure comparison (FairplayMP [28]) to compare $f(best_1\{x_1, \ldots, x_k\})$ -
   $f(best_2\{x_1, \ldots, x_k\})$ and $T_1 \log \eta$ among all $k + 1$ parties
19.   **if** $f(best_1\{x_1, \ldots, x_k\}) - f(best_2\{x_1, \ldots, x_k\}) > T_1 \log \eta$ **then**
20. E_C updates: $best\{x\} \leftarrow x'$; $route\_assigned(best\{x\}) = 1$; $best\{x_1, \ldots, x_k\} \leftarrow$
   $best_2\{x_1, \ldots, x_k\}$
21. $iter_1 + +$
22. $T_1 \leftarrow \rho_1 T_1$ (cooling down after several iterations)
23. Return $best\{x\}$ and $best\{x_1, \ldots, x_k\}$

- To compute the energy of any solution, all parties securely compute the scalar product using Algorithm 1, and each party holds a share of the result. To determine whether move or not, all parties implement FairplayMP [28] to securely compare the functions with their input shares. Finally, only client E_C knows the comparison result and whether move or not.

- For top and bottom-level simulated annealing, we use different sensitivity parameters: initial temperature T_1 and T_2, cooling coefficient ρ_1, ρ_2 (note that the temperature will be lowered after several iterations). We also setup different maximum number of iterations for top and bottom-level simulated annealing respectively max_iter_1 and max_iter_2.

- In order to improve efficiency, we define an indicator $route\_assigned(x) \in \{0, 1\}$ to avoid running the route assignment for every route x twice in the protocol – as a neighboring solution and the current solution respectively. If the optimal route assignment for x has been found in previous iterations, we let $route\_assigned(x) = 1$; Otherwise, 0. At Line 6, we examine the status of $route\_assigned(x)$ before going to the bottom-level simulated annealing.

- At Line 23, E_C learns only the near-optimal route $best\{x\}$ and its near-optimal route assignment $best\{x_1, \ldots, x_k\}$ (as the output of the protocol). We do not allow E_C to learn the total optimal cost during executing the protocol (before all parties contracting) because of some potential malicious inference attack slightly going beyond the semi-honest model: if the minimum cost is revealed to E_C, then E_C can use any two cities as the input to get the minimum cost (viz. the cost between two known cities, which is the corresponding shipping company's proprietary information). More severely, the minimum cost of every pair of cities and the corresponding shipping company might be inferred by E_C by repeating such malicious attack for multiple times. Although the SMC/protocol security is not violated in the above attacking scenario under semi-honest adversarial model, we still unreveal the total optimal cost for mitigating such risk.

5   Security and Cost Analysis

A formal security proof can be provided under the framework of Secure Multiparty Computation (SMC). Under the framework of SMC, a secure protocol reveals nothing in semi-honest model if all the messages received by every party can be simulated in polynomial time by knowing only the input and output of the SMC protocol [7, 8].

Theorem 1. *TSSA protocol reveals only the near-optimal traveling route $best\{x\}$ and the route assignment $best\{x_1, \ldots, x_k\}$ to client E_C in semi-honest model.*

Proof. We first look at the steps that do not need communication between different parties in the protocol. Notice that all the candidate solutions are proposed by E_C in TSSA, then most of the steps are locally implemented by E_C, e.g., finding the neighboring solution (either the traveling route or the route assignment), updating the current solution based on the comparison, and reducing the temperature in simulated annealing. These steps can be simulated by simply executing those steps.

In addition, we must simulate each party's view (all the received messages in the protocol) that requires communication in polynomial time. More specifically, client E_C and k shipping companies $P_1, \ldots, P_k$ iteratively communicate with each other in Secure Scalar Product (Algorithm 1) and Secure Comparison. We now examine the messages received by each party.

Client E_C's view: First, while calling the secure scalar product computation every time, E_C receives k encrypted random shares. k random shares are the actual messages received by E_C in those steps. W.l.o.g., E_C gets $s_i = x_i \cdot y_i + r_i$ from shipping company P_i. All the random shares generated in all iterations can be simulated by generating a random from the *uniform probability distribution over $\mathcal{F}$*, assuming that s_i is scaled to fixed precision over a closed field, enabling such a selection. Thus, $Prob[s_i = t] = Prob[r_i = t - s_i] = \frac{1}{\mathcal{F}}$, and all the shares can be simulated in polynomial time.

Second, E_C receives a series of comparison results from FairplayMP [28]. To simulate the sequence of comparison results (">" or "$\leq$"), the inverse step of the simulated annealing can be utilized. Specifically, E_C starts from the near-optimal traveling route, and then finds the given neighboring solutions in sequence by running TSSA inversely (note that temperature increase can be imposed to tune the sensitivity of the moving probability in the inverse optimization). While comparing $f(x'_1, \ldots, x'_k)$ − $f(x_1, \ldots, x_k)$ and $T_2 \log \eta$ in the bottom-level simulated annealing, if the result is ">", the simulator outputs an "1", otherwise "0". Now we discuss how to simulate them in polynomial time.

Recall that all the searched solutions are known to E_C in sequence, but the energy of any state (which is the sum of the local random shares) is unknown to E_C since E_C does not know the cost vectors from every shipping company. Fortunately, since E_C knows its final traveling route $best\{x\}$, we can use the same simulator in [10] to simulate a cost function in polynomial time. Then, the energy of two compared states (solutions) can be polynomially simulated as well simply because both solutions are regarded as the input for E_C (E_C proposes the candidate solutions). Consequently, we can simulate "1" or "0" for two reasons: 1) the probability of generating each of them is deterministic with Equation 1, and 2) another parameter η is uniformly distributed in $[0, 1)$. Therefore, a sequence of such comparison results in E_C's view can be simulated in polynomial time. Similarly, the sequence of comparison results for top-level simulated annealing can be simulated with the same polynomial machine.

In summary, applying the Composition Theorem [8], client E_C learns only the near-optimal traveling route $best\{x\}$ and the route assignment $best\{x_1, \ldots, x_k\}$.

Shipping Company $\forall i \in [1, k]$, P_i's View: In the protocol, every shipping company only receives the random shares in secure scalar product computation and E_C's public key pk. As analyzed above, the random shares can be simulated in polynomial time using the same machine as E_C's random share. Therefore, applying the Composition Theorem [8], every shipping company only learns the public key pk in the protocol. This completes the proof.

Besides the protocol security guaranteed by the SMC theory, it would be useful if we can simultaneously resolve the inferences from the messages received before and after the move. Coincidentally, simulated annealing provides excellent mechanism to naturally mitigate such inference attack. Specifically, unlike many other meta-heuristics, simulated annealing runs probabilistically and allows moving from the current solution to a *worse neighboring solution*. Due to the above uncertainty and the unrevealed overall cost in any solution, it is difficult for E_C to infer any private information, e.g., which solution outperforms its neighboring solution. Thus, the inference attack (which actually does not compromise the SMC protocol security) could be mitigated.

Cost Analysis: Given a k-RTSP with n cities, the maximum number of iterations of the top and bottom level simulated annealing is given as max_iter_1 and max_iter_2 respectively. For simplicity of notation, we denote them as $O(m)$. We now discuss the communication and computation cost required in the TSSA protocol.

Communication Cost. In TSSA protocol, only secure scalar product computation and secure comparison request multiparty communication. First, while calling the secure scalar product computation, it needs one round communication between E_C and each shipping company. Then, the communication cost of total secure scalar product computation is $O(2m^2 * k * n(n-1)/2) = O(m^2n^2k)$ messages of bit communication. Second, the number of communication messages in every secure comparison is equal to the number of computing parties [29]. Then, the communication cost of total secure comparison is $O(m(2m+1)k) = O(m^2k)$ messages of bit communication. Moreover, public key pk is delivered from E_C to all k shipping companies (every party can use the same public key in all iterations, thus pk can be considered as offline cost). Therefore, the communication complexity of the protocol is $O(m^2n^2k)$.

Computation Cost. First, E_C locally finds the neighboring solution, moves the solution and updates the temperature in both top and bottom-level simulated annealing. The computation cost of the above process is ignorable compared to cryptographic work. Second, if we estimate the runtime for a single secure scalar product computation and a single secure comparison as t_s and t_c respectively, the total computation cost based on cryptography can be written as $(2m^2 * k) * t_s + m(2m+1) * k * t_c \approx 2m^2k(t_s + t_c)$.

6   Experimental Validation

We first present the experimental setting and then discuss the results.

Datasets. We conduct experiments on four real datasets collected from National Imagery and Mapping Agency [6]. Each dataset is derived from a country (Canada, Japan, Italy and China), where the cost of travel between cities is the Euclidean distance computed from the coordinates. We randomly select six sets of cities from each of the four datasets with the size (number of cities n) $200, 400, 600, 800, 1000$ and 1200. This matches the experimental setup in [1], which makes it comparable for the two-party case. Note that we repeat every experiment 10 times by changing the initial city in every test, and average all the results returned from all 10 experiments running on each of the 4 different datasets.

Problem Setup. To formulate k-RTSP, we need to set the costs for the k parties. To do this, we generate $k-1$ noise values by sampling from the gaussian distribution with mean 0 and an appropriate variance (1/3 of the cost). Then, we obtain k different costs for every pair of cities (the original plus the $k-1$ noise added values) and randomly assign them to the k different parties, where k is selected as $2, 4, 6, 8, 10$ and 12.

Meta-heuristics Setup. We initialize the temperature for two-level simulated annealing and the cooling parameters as $T_1 = 1000$, $\rho_1 = 50\%$ and $T_2 = 1000$, $\rho_2 = 20\%$. If no better solution can be found in 50 iterations, we apply cooling. If no better solution can be found in 20 times cooling, we terminate the meta-heuristics (note that the termination criteria can be alternatively established as a maximum threshold for the total number of iterations).

Cost Estimation of Large Scale Input. For small and medium scale input, we can directly capture the computation cost. Since our protocol iteratively utilizes the cryptographic building blocks, we can estimate the computation cost for large scale input.

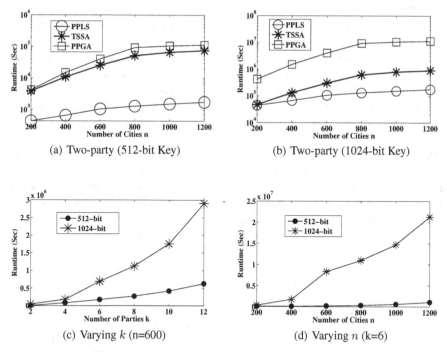

Fig. 3. Computation Cost Evaluation

The runtime can be obtained through multiplying the cost of running a unit building block by the overall required count. We do this for the tests with runtime more than 10^4 seconds (approx. 3 hours).

6.1   Computation Cost Comparison (Two-party)

Under the same experimental setup for the two party TSP, we compare the computation cost of our two-level secure simulated annealing (TSSA) with Sakuma and Kobayashi's two algorithms – Privacy-preserving local search (PPLS) and Privacy-preserving genetic algorithm (PPGA) [1]. Since only two parties are involved, the bottom-level simulated annealing would not be triggered in TSSA.

We set the key length in Paillier's Homomorphic cryptosystem [26] as 512 bits and 1024 bits, and the size of the circuit (number of gates) in FairplayMP [28] as 512 (a benchmark setup). Figure 3(a) and 3(b) show the runtime of TSSA, PPLS and PPGA for the key length of 512 bits and 1024 bits respectively. As expected, the computation cost of TSSA lie between that of PPLS and PPGA. This is consistent with the fact that 2-Opt local search performs efficiently yet produce the worst result [28, 30]. More specifically, when the number of cities n increases from 200 to 1200, with 512-bit key, TSSA consumes approximately 1.5 hour – 20 hours; with 1024-bit key, TSSA spends approximately 20 hours – 5 days. The computation cost increases polynomially in both scenarios.

6.2 Results of k-RTSP

In the multiparty case, we evaluate the performance of solving k-RTSP with TSSA in two facts: the efficiency of the solver and the quality of k-RTSP's optimal solution. Efficiency can be reflected as the computation cost (viz. runtime) of the algorithm. Figure 3(c) and 3(d) demonstrate the scalability of our TSSA algorithm. The runtime grows polynomially as the number of shipping companies k or the number of cities n increases. Since TSSA is provably secure for all $k + 1$ parties, the most expensive runtime shown in the figure (1200 cities, key length of 1024-bit, $k = 6$) is still tolerable (around 10 days).

On the other hand, we define two measures to evaluate the quality of k-RTSP's optimal solutions: "Cost Reduction Ratio" $= 1 - \frac{c}{c_{max}}$ and "Heuristic Error" $= \frac{c}{c_{min}} - 1$. Given a specific traveling route to visit all cities, c_{max} denotes the maximum possible cost (the highest cost is chosen between every pair of consecutively visited cities on the route), c is the optimal solution derived from TSSA algorithm and c_{min} denotes the minimum possible cost (the lowest cost is chosen between every pair of consecutively visited cities on the route).

Table 3. Quality of Near-optimal Solutions

(a) Cost Reduction Ratio

Inputs	$k = 2$	$k = 4$	$k = 6$	$k = 8$	$k = 10$
$n = 200$	0.272	0.256	0.245	0.23	0.211
$n = 400$	0.301	0.292	0.285	0.269	0.241
$n = 600$	0.324	0.318	0.312	0.303	0.293
$n = 800$	0.339	0.335	0.328	0.32	0.317
$n = 1000$	0.352	0.344	0.339	0.336	0.332
$n = 1200$	0.361	0.353	0.348	0.344	0.339

(b) Heuristic Error

Inputs	$k = 2$	$k = 4$	$k = 6$	$k = 8$	$k = 10$
$n = 200$	0.025	0.032	0.041	0.063	0.075
$n = 400$	0.038	0.047	0.054	0.073	0.084
$n = 600$	0.052	0.066	0.085	0.094	0.111
$n = 800$	0.081	0.085	0.116	0.128	0.137
$n = 1000$	0.127	0.142	0.154	0.164	0.183
$n = 1200$	0.161	0.171	0.18	0.192	0.199

TSSA protocol gives good results for k-RTSP if $CostReRatio$ is high and $Error$ is low. To validate this on large-scale inputs, we simplify TSSA by running it without cryptographic work, which does not distort the returned near-optimal solutions. Table 3 present the "Cost Reduction Ratio" and "Heuristic Error", where $k = 2, \ldots, 10$ and $n = 200, \ldots, 1200$. First, the cost reduction ratio increases with the increase of the problem size. This fact is true because, when the client needs to visit more cities, the maximum possible cost becomes extremely high, then great saving can be realized. With the growth of k, maximum possible cost would be slightly higher for the same k-RTSP, however the heuristic cannot always find the route assignment for every pair of cities. Then, cost reduction ratio decreases as k goes large. Second, the heuristic error represents the difference between the near-optimal solution obtained by TSSA and the minimum possible cost. The data in Table 3(b) implies that the error grows while enlarging either k or n. This is the nature of heuristics.

Finally, cost reduction ratio between 0.211 and 0.361 shows a considerable saving in delivery, and the heuristic error (which primarily reflects the error produced in bottom-level simulated annealing) between 0.25 and 0.199 shows the effectiveness of our TSSA meta-heuristic algorithm.

7 Conclusion and Future Work

In this paper, we formulate and study the privacy issues in the cost-reducible collaborative TSP where the global cost can be further reduced by allowing multiple companies to collaboratively provide a shared solution. We then proposed an effective privacy-preserving approach (TSSA protocol) to securely derive the near-optimal solution within a reasonable time. We formally proved the security of the TSSA protocol and validated the efficiency as well as the quality of the optimal solution with real data. In the future, we will further mitigate the inference attack in addition to the SMC protocol security by proposing schemes that require multiple parties to jointly propose neighboring solutions (like [4]), and also improve the efficiency of the communication protocol by either developing secure solvers based on the recent cryptographic tools (e.g., Sharemind [31], PICCO [32]) or incorporating problem transformation into the algorithm without compromising security. We also intend to generalize the simulated annealing based communication protocol to solve more NP-hard problems with limited information disclosure.

References

1. Sakuma, J., Kobayashi, S.: A genetic algorithm for privacy preserving combinatorial optimization. In: GECCO, pp. 1372–1379 (2007)
2. Clifton, C., Iyer, A., Cho, R., Jiang, W., Kantarcioglu, M., Vaidya, J.: An approach to identifying beneficial collaboration securely in decentralized logistics systems. Management & Service Operations Management 10(1) (2008)
3. Hong, Y., Vaidya, J., Lu, H.: Secure and efficient distributed linear programming. Journal of Computer Security 20(5), 583–634 (2012)
4. Hong, Y., Vaidya, J., Lu, H., Shafiq, B.: Privacy-preserving tabu search for distributed graph coloring. In: SocialCom/PASSAT, pp. 951–958 (2011)
5. Hong, Y., Vaidya, J., Wang, S.: A survey of privacy-aware supply chain collaboration: From theory to applications. Journal of Information Systems (to appear, 2014)
6. http://www.math.uwaterloo.ca/tsp/
7. Yao, A.C.: How to generate and exchange secrets. In: Proceedings of the 27th IEEE Symposium on Foundations of Computer Science, pp. 162–167. IEEE Computer Society, Los Alamitos (1986)
8. Goldreich, O.: Encryption Schemes. In: The Foundations of Cryptography, vol. 2. Cambridge University Press (2004)
9. Li, J., Atallah, M.J.: Secure and private collaborative linear programming. In: Proceedings of the 2nd International Conference on Collaborative Computing: Networking, Applications and Worksharing, November 17-20, pp. 1–8 (2006)
10. Vaidya, J.: A secure revised simplex algorithm for privacy-preserving linear programming. In: AINA 2009: Proceedings of the 23rd IEEE International Conference on Advanced Information Networking and Applications (2009)
11. Catrina, O., de Hoogh, S.: Secure multiparty linear programming using fixed-point arithmetic. In: Gritzalis, D., Preneel, B., Theoharidou, M. (eds.) ESORICS 2010. LNCS, vol. 6345, pp. 134–150. Springer, Heidelberg (2010)
12. Du, W.: A Study of Several Specific Secure Two-party Computation Problems. PhD thesis, Purdue University, West Lafayette, Indiana (2001)
13. Vaidya, J.: Privacy-preserving linear programming. In: SAC, pp. 2002–2007 (2009)

14. Bednarz, A., Bean, N., Roughan, M.: Hiccups on the road to privacy-preserving linear programming. In: Proceedings of the 8th ACM Workshop on Privacy in the Electronic Society, WPES 2009, pp. 117–120. ACM, New York (2009)
15. Bednarz, A.: Methods for Two-party Privacy-preserving Linear Programming. PhD thesis, The University of Adelaide, Adelaide, Australia (2012)
16. Hong, Y., Vaidya, J., Lu, H.: Efficient distributed linear programming with limited disclosure. In: Li, Y. (ed.) DBSec 2011. LNCS, vol. 6818, pp. 170–185. Springer, Heidelberg (2011)
17. Mangasarian, O.L.: Privacy-preserving horizontally partitioned linear programs. Optimization Letters 6(3), 431–436 (2012)
18. Mangasarian, O.L.: Privacy-preserving linear programming. Optimization Letters 5(1), 165–172 (2011)
19. Li, W., Li, H., Deng, C.: Privacy-preserving horizontally partitioned linear programs with inequality constraints. Optimization Letters 7(1), 137–144 (2013)
20. Hong, Y., Vaidya, J.: An inference-proof approach to privacy-preserving horizontally partitioned linear programs. Optimization Letters 8(1), 267–277 (2014)
21. Goldreich, O., Micali, S., Wigderson, A.: How to play any mental game - a completeness theorem for protocols with honest majority. In: Proceedings of the 19th ACM Symposium on the Theory of Computing, pp. 218–229. ACM, New York (1987)
22. Ben-Or, M., Goldwasser, S., Wigderson, A.: Completeness theorems for non-cryptographic fault-tolerant distributed computation. In: Proceedings of the 20th Annual ACM Symposium on Theory of Computing, pp. 1–10 (1998)
23. Papadimitriou, C.H., Steiglitz, K.: Combinatorial optimization: algorithms and complexity. Prentice-Hall, Inc., Upper Saddle River (1982)
24. Kirkpatrick, S., Gelatt Jr., C.D., Vecchi, M.P.: Optimization by simulated annealing. Science 220(4598), 671–680 (1983)
25. Croes, G.A.: A method for solving traveling salesman problems. Operations Research 6(6), 791–812 (1958)
26. Paillier, P.: Public-key cryptosystems based on composite degree residuosity classes. In: Stern, J. (ed.) EUROCRYPT 1999. LNCS, vol. 1592, pp. 223–238. Springer, Heidelberg (1999)
27. Metropolis, N., Rosenbluth, A.W., Rosenbluth, M.N., Teller, A.H., Teller, E.: Equation of state calculations by fast computing machines. The Journal of Chemical Physics 21, 1087 (1953)
28. Ben-David, A., Nisan, N., Pinkas, B.: Fairplaymp: a system for secure multi-party computation. In: Proceedings of the 15th ACM Conference on Computer and Communications Security, CCS 2008, pp. 257–266. ACM, New York (2008)
29. Ioannidis, I., Grama, A.: An efficient protocol for yao's millionaires' problem. In: Hawaii International Conference on System Sciences (HICSS-36), Waikoloa Village, Hawaii, January 6-9, pp. 205–210 (2003)
30. Kim, B.-I., Shim, J.-I., Zhang, M.: Comparison of tsp algorithms. In: Project for Models in Facilities Planning and Materials Handling (1998)
31. Bogdanov, D., Laur, S., Willemson, J.: Sharemind: A framework for fast privacy-preserving computations. In: Jajodia, S., Lopez, J. (eds.) ESORICS 2008. LNCS, vol. 5283, pp. 192–206. Springer, Heidelberg (2008)
32. Zhang, Y., Steele, A., Blanton, M.: Picco: a general-purpose compiler for private distributed computation. In: ACM Conference on Computer and Communications Security, pp. 813–826 (2013)

ELITE: zEro Links Identity managemenT systEm*

Tarik Moataz[1,2], Nora Cuppens-Boulahia[2], Frédéric Cuppens[2], Indrajit Ray[1], and Indrakshi Ray[1]

[1] Dept. of Computer Science, Colorado State University, Fort Collins, CO 80523
{tmoataz,indrajit,iray}@cs.colostate.edu
[2] Institut Mines-Télécom, Télécom Bretagne, Cesson Sévigné, France
{nora.cuppens,frederic.cuppens}@telecom-bretagne.eu

Abstract. Modern day biometric systems, such as those used by governments to issue biometric-based identity cards, maintain a deterministic link between the identity of the user and her biometric information. However, such a link brings in serious privacy concerns for the individual. Sensitive information about the individual can be retrieved from the database by using her biometric information. Individuals, for reasons of privacy therefore, may not want such a link to be maintained. Deleting the link, on the other hand, is not feasible because the information is used for purposes of identification or issuing of identity cards. In this work, we address this dilemma by hiding the biometrics information, and keeping the association between biometric information and identity probabilistic. We extend traditional Bloom filters to store the actual information and propose the SOBER data structure for this purpose. Simultaneously, we address the challenge of verifying an individual under the multitude of traits assumption, so as to guarantee that impersonation is always detected. We discuss real-world impersonation use cases, analyze the privacy limits, and compare our scheme to existing solutions.

1 Introduction

Many nations are increasingly using biometric based systems for national identity cards for their citizens. Examples of these are the proposed project of Carte Nationale d'Identité Biométrique of the French government (see http://www.service-public.fr/actualites/002101.html) and the AADHAAR project undertaken by the Unique Identification Authority of India (see http://uidai.gov.in). These governments are building large biometric database systems to issue social security cards, health insurance cards etc. The main objective is to efficiently provide citizen services via accurate identity verification. For this purpose, these systems maintain a database of sensitive personal information, called the *identity database*, a *biometric database* containing individual's biometric information, and a *deterministic link* between the identity

---

* This work was partially supported by the U.S. National Science Foundation under Grant No. 0905232.

V. Atluri and G. Pernul (Eds.): DBSec 2014, LNCS 8566, pp. 195–210, 2014.

of the individual in the identity database and her biometric information in the biometric database. This link, which is a primary-key/foreign-key relationship between the two databases, allows querying the identity database using the biometric information from the biometric database. The link helps to ensure that any improper access to the identity database via impersonation is detected and potentially prevented.

Impersonation can happen at many stages of the biometric system operation. We are interested in two specific situations, the so called "First application for biometric card" scenario where the user is applying for the issue of a biometric based identity card, and the "Renewal without a document or ID card loss" scenario, where a user is applying for a replacement card.

First application for biometric card: During the first application, the applicant goes through an eligibility determination step. If the user is eligible and her biometric information does not exist in the biometric database, then the application is accepted. If the individual provides an identity that already exists in the identity database then it is a case of *impersonation*.

Renewal without a document: During the renewal phase, the applicant has to go through the verification step in order to determine if he already exists in the system. Renewal can take place if and only if the relevant biometric information already exists in the biometric database. If the individual gives a different identity that is not associated with his biometric information it is a case of impersonation.

The deterministic link between biometric information and identity help detect such impersonations. In almost all existing biometric information management systems that we have studied however, this link is public and not protected. Consequently, it brings forth serious privacy concerns for the individuals. Biometric information is, surprisingly, easily available without consent. For example, fingerprints can be easily picked up from different surfaces. An attacker who is targeting a specific individual and has acquired by subterfuge that individual's biometric information and also has access to the identity database can then easily cause a privacy breach for the targeted individual. (Note that, by simply accessing the identify database, the attacker cannot launch such a targeted attack.) Consequently, individuals who are concerned about their privacy, may want these deterministic links between the identity database and the biometric database removed. Unfortunately, since removing the link is not an option, we investigate in this work if a *probabilistic link* between biometric information and identity can maintain user privacy and at the same time preserve all the functionalities of the system.

One possible solution to this problem is to keep the information in the biometric database encrypted, so that the identity is linked to encrypted biometric data. If the attacker cannot correlate the illegally obtained biometric information with the encrypted information stored in the database, the attacker will not be able to breach privacy of the individual. Several works aim to provide biometric privacy employing variants of this theme [11,14,17], although they do not address the same problem as ours. In fact, these techniques cannot be used as native constructions to solve our problem. Under these setups, proper identification would work only if an individual could be associated with one and only one stored biometric information. Unfortunately, owing to the vagaries of biometric capture devices, a physical biometric pattern can have several captured versions – the so called *multitude of traits* issue. These versions are not totally different and have considerable similarities. However, they are rarely exactly the same. An identification based on two similar pieces of biometric information is always possible with different levels of accuracy and efficiency. However, these similarities quickly vanish when the biometric information is encrypted. This is one of the reasons why biometric information is traditionally stored as plaintext, although the work of Bringer et al. [5] proposes an error-tolerant searchable encryption scheme that can be used to solve this problem [1] albeit at the expense of very high computational overhead making it impractical for large scale deployment.

The Setbase approach proposed by Adi Shamir [18] was the first scheme to address the problem of converting a deterministic association between biometric information and identity into a probabilistic one. This scheme stores the biometric information as plaintext. The relation *one to one* is replaced by a relation n to n where n is the size of a subset of identities set. The idea centers around fixing a number m of subsets without fixing their size. This results in m subsets of identities, and their associated subsets of biometrics. Consequently, each identity is associated to many (the size of the subset) biometrics and, vice versa, each biometric information is associated with many identities. This concept makes the biometric-identity association private. The approach allows one to detect impersonation with a certain probability but not as accurately as a deterministic *one to one* mapping. There have quite a few works that explored the underlying principles of the Setbase approach and quantify various parameters [12,13]. However, the Setbase approach has several issues that prevent it from being adopted in practice. First of all, the association between a given subset of identities and the corresponding subset of biometric information represents a valuable information and should be kept secret. If there is an attacker (including insiders) who knows that a given person is in a subset S_i, it will enable the attacker to usurp this identity if the attacker and the individual share the same subset. For this reason, the association is encrypted using a probabilistic asymmetric semantically secure scheme that hides the association. Moreover, keys should be kept secret in order to protect the system while biometric information is stored as plaintext without any transformation, encryption or obfuscation. Finally, any deletion is impossible in the Setbase approach which makes the scheme not deployable.

In this paper, we present a novel scheme called ELITE (acronym for zEro Links Identity managemenT systEm) that allows a probabilistic link between biometric information and identity. We describe an initial construction called ELITE-1 that introduces the fundamental principles of the scheme. We then refine this to propose ELITE-2 – the second and main construction. ELITE-1 assumes that the biometric information stored in the database and the biometric information retrieved from the biometric capture device during the verification are the same. We propose a novel probabilistic data structure called "Stored Object Bloom Filter" (SOBER, for short) for storing identities, which is based on the traditional Bloom Filters. We then adapt the Greedy algorithm proposed by Azar et al. [2] in the context of the *balls in bins* problem, to insert identities in the SOBER structure. We show how to determine if an individual is in the system during one of the two phases discussed earlier. For the second construction, we take into account the issue of *multitude of traits*. In ELITE-2, the storage and the creation of biometric templates is based on the scheme of R. Capelli et al. [7]. ELITE-2 ensures that even if the captured biometric information is considered different, we are able to store them in a secret way and at the same time preserve the ELITE-1 functionalities. Our proposed scheme has many advantages over the Setbase approach [18] namely, (i) creating a probabilistic link between the biometrics and the identities while maintaining a high impersonation detection rate, (ii) better control over the privacy and impersonation detection dilemma, (iii) biometric information not stored in a plaintext, yet the multitude of traits issue addressed, (iv) more efficient scheme with a constant search complexity and reduced storage space while deletion can still be performed.

2   ELITE: zEro Links Identity managemenT systEm

In real world biometric system, there is always a phase during which the system enrolls new individuals and issues their biometric ID cards or passports. During this phase, a deterministic link between the identity and the biometric information needs to be maintained. We assume that the enrollment phase is not compromised and that this link is deleted directly after the issuance. The ELITE scheme deals with issues related to storing the biometric information in the database after the biometric ID card has been issued – the *storage phase* – and verifying whether an individual is in the system or not – the *search phase*.

We extend the classical Bloom filter data structure [3] to develop the ELITE solution. We call this data structure "Stored Object Bloom filtER (SOBER)". It enables the separation of the identity from the biometric information by making the link between biometric information and identity probabilistic. The scheme also hides the biometric information so that it is impossible to recover stored information. ELITE-1 employs a multiple choice identity allocation algorithm, **Greedy** [2] that has been proposed in the context of the *balls in bins* problem. It allows the insertion of a number of identities in the SOBER data structure. In the following, we first introduce the Stored Object Bloom Filter data structure, present the Greedy algorithm, and then discuss the construction of the ELITE-1 scheme. We present an example to discuss how our system works and then analyze the privacy features of the scheme.

2.1   Preliminaries

Stored Object Bloom Filter - SOBER Bloom filters [3] are probabilistic data structures that permit testing membership of an element in a group. Bloom filter as a structure does not allow the storage of the element, but only the membership verification of an element. The most important feature of a Bloom filter is that the time complexity for membership verification is constant i.e. $O(1)$. SOBER is a $\langle key - value \rangle$ data structure that has similar construction as a normal Bloom filter with the additional feature that the cells can contain extra information. In the following, we first discuss the construction steps of SOBER, then describe how to search for an element using this probabilistic data structure.

SOBER construction. Briefly, a classical Bloom Filter works as follows. Let us consider a set of n elements $S = \{a_1, ..., a_n\}$ and r independent hash functions $h_{k_j} : \{0,1\}^* \to [0, m]$ where m is the size of an array $\mathcal{A}$. We initialize all cells of $\mathcal{A}$ to zero. For each a_i in S and $j \in [1, r]$, we compute the value $h_{k_j}(a_i)$. The output of each hash function represents the index to a cell in array $\mathcal{A}$ whose value will be set to 1. This is shown on the left side in Figure 1. To test whether an element a' is a member of the set S, we have to only calculate $h_{k_1}(a'), ..., h_{k_r}(a')$. If for each $j \in [1, r], \mathcal{A}(h_{k_j}(a')) = 1$ then we can conclude that $a' \in S$ (with a high probability), otherwise $a' \notin S$. Note that, in some membership verification cases, we can have a false positive for elements whose identities were not stored in the Bloom filter. However, the false positive rate can be arbitrarily reduced.

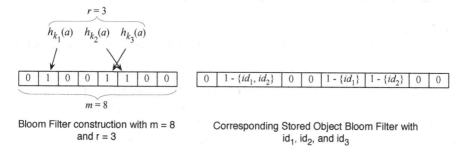

Bloom Filter construction with m = 8 and r = 3

Corresponding Stored Object Bloom Filter with id_1, id_2, and id_3

Fig. 1. Relation between traditional Bloom Filter and SOBER

The proposed Stored Object Bloom Filter data structure can be seen as a combination of the Bloom filter with Storage (BFS) [4] and the classical Bloom filter. In BFS data structure, each cell contains a set of values depending on the output of the hash functions while in the basic bloom filter a zero or one value is stored (for fast membership detection). Each cell in the SOBER data structure can be considered as a $\langle key, value \rangle$ cell, where $key \in \{0,1\}$ and the value is a set of elements. This is illustrated on the right side in Figure 1.

Greedy algorithm for inserting identities into SOBER. The insertion of identities in the SOBER data structures can be mapped to the classical *balls in bins* problem. In literature, there are many techniques that enable this kind of insertion, such as, the uniform insertion with a single choice insertion and multiple choice insertion. These schemes were constructed for different purposes but their main objective is to decrease the maximum load for every bin, that is the number of balls in any given bin. We are particularly interested in this article to the second type of insertion, namely, the multiple choice insertion. Moreover, we are interested in the special setting where the number of balls is larger than the number of bins but with a constant ratio. The selection of a multiple choice rather than the single choice scheme is mainly based on certain privacy issues that we are going to explain later on. We use the "Greedy" algorithm proposed in [2] for our purpose. Let l denote the number of balls and m the number of bins. $\mathbf{Greedy}(\mathcal{U}, d)$ is the balls in bins insertion algorithm that places the next ball into the less loaded bin among d bins sampled uniformly at random from $\mathcal{U}$.

2.2 ELITE-1 Scheme Construction

Storage phase Let us consider the set of n biometric information $\mathbf{b} = \{b_1, \ldots, b_n\}$ and the corresponding identity set $\mathbf{id} = \{id_1, \ldots, id_n\}$.

1. Create an empty SOBER data structure (all cells initialized with value 0) with size equal to m and r independent hash functions $h_i : \{0, 1\}^* \to [\![0, m]\!]$.
2. For $1 \leq i \leq n$, hash the biometric information b_i in the set by applying the r hash functions and store a 1 in each location of SOBER corresponding to the output of the hash function. If the cell location is already a 1, leave it as 1.
3. Insert one identity value id_i corresponding to b_i uniformly at random in one of the r cell locations identified by outputs of the hash functions when applied to b_i.
4. For $1 \leq i \leq n$, insert l times the same identity id_i associated with b_i in l positions in SOBER following the $\mathbf{Greedy}(\mathcal{U}, d)$, regardless of whether the cell position is 0 or 1. If id_i is already in a cell of SOBER by virtue of step 3, do not duplicate id_i in that cell but consider it one of the l insertions.
5. Create a look-up table $\mathcal{L}$ of n rows. Each row contains the identity id_i and the indexes of corresponding cells in SOBER where id_i has been inserted and the application of the hash functions on the corresponding biometric information b_i resulted in a 1 in the cell. (Note that at the end of the previous step there can be some cells with a 0 but still containing id_i. Those cells will not be included in a row of $\mathcal{L}$.)

The search phase begins by taking a biometric information b_j of some individual and hashing it r number of times. If each of those r cells in SOBER indexed by the outputs of the hash functions contains a 1, then there is a match and we proceed with the verification of the identity.

Search phase Given the biometric information b_j and the identity id_j:

1. Create an empty set I.
2. Apply the r hash functions $h_i(b_j)$ for $1 \leq i \leq r$, if $h_i(b_j) = 1$ insert the associated identities in I.
3. If $id_j \in I$, then the individual is in the system.

2.3   Discussion

Let us consider a set of biometrics $\{b_1, b_2, b_3, b_4, b_5\}$ with corresponding identities $\{id_1, id_2, id_3, id_4, id_5\}$, a SOBER with size equal to 12, and 3 independent hash functions. Assume that l is equal to 2. A possible construction is shown in Tables 1(a) and 1(b). We take the case of the identity id_5 and the corresponding biometric b_5 to discuss the construction of the lookup-table and SOBER. Let the cells in SOBER identified by the application of the hash functions on b_5 (step 2 of storage phase) be 6, 7 and 12. Thus those positions contain a 1. Step 3 of the algorithm then inserts id_5 in position 12 (say). Let us now assume that step 4 identifies positions 6 and 12 to be the ones where id_5 should be inserted. (It is just a coincidence that the hash functions on b_5 also identified 6 and 12 as among the positions that should contain 1.) We insert id_5 in position 6. Since id_5 is already in position 12 by virtue of step 3, we do not duplicate but count it as the second insertion. Note, that in this step we could have had an insertion of id_5 in a cell which contains a 0. The lookup table now contains the values 6, 12 as addresses in SOBER for id_5.

Table 1. Possible construction of ELITE-1 system

(a) Look-up table of identities

Identity	Address in SOBER
id_1	9
id_2	2
id_3	2
id_4	12
id_5	6,12

(b) SOBER with $r = 3$ and $m = 12$. The cells are numbered 1 through 12 left to right from top to bottom.

$0\text{-}\{id_3\}$	$1 - \{id_3, id_2\}$	$0\text{-}\{id_3\}$	$1\text{-}\{id_1\}$
0	$1\text{-}\{id_5, id_2\}$	$1 - \{id_4\}$	$0\text{-}\{id_2\}$
$1 - \{id_1\}$	$0\text{-}\{id_4\}$	$0\text{-}\{id_1\}$	$1 - \{id_5, id_4\}$

Observations: In our approach, the system does not store the plain text of the biometric information of registered users. The information stored in SOBER will be used to verify the existence of the user's biometric information. Further, the *look-up table of identities* acts as a proof of whether the user is registered in the system without leaking any information about his biometric information. This look-up table also allows easy deletion of an identity from the information base. Since ELITE-1 knows the positions of the cells in SOBER that contain the identity, we can delete it without altering the other identities or any information in the data structure. Finally, even if the system has knowledge of the type of hash functions, it is very difficult to restore the real biometric information. This is because even using brute force many biometrics can give the same result (the result of a hash function is equal to 1 in the same identity position). We will see in the privacy and computational analysis that the search is constant in time owing to the Bloom feature of SOBER, and storage complexity is far below the Setbase approach. This makes real world deployment practical.

Fraud determination: Based on the example, we now discuss the fraud use cases presented earlier in Section 1. We address the first application use case first. Suppose that there is an applicant who comes to an agency for the first application. The first phase to perform is the verification of his biometric information. This verification consists of a search step on the SOBER biometric base. Referring to the SOBER base given in Tables 1a and 1b, let b be the new biometric information of this applicant id. We calculate the output of the three hash functions $h_i(b)$. We can have the following results:

- If $\exists i \in [1, r]$ such that $h_i(b) = 0$ and $id \notin \mathcal{L}$ then neither the biometric information nor the identity exist in the system. In this case, the individual is truly a new user.
- If $h_1(b) = 4, h_2(b) = 2, h_3(b) = 6$ then the biometric information exists in SOBER. If $id \in I = \{id_1, id_2, id_3, id_5\}$ such that the given identity of the applicant was on the identity base, the system then assumes that the applicant has made an error to be addressed for a first application service.
- The biometric information exists in SOBER but the identity does not exist in the look-up table $\mathcal{L}$. This is an attempt of identity theft or impersonation.

For the second use case (renewal without document), the applicant wants to renew his ID card when the biometric information already exists in the system. Suppose that $h_1(b) = 4, h_2(b) = 2, h_3(b) = 6$, $id \notin I = \{id_1, id_2, id_3, id_5\}$ and $id \in \mathcal{L}$. In this case, the applicant is not the person that he claims to be. So this is an impersonation case. In fact, the system proves this by showing that the biometric information provided by the individual exists in the SOBER, and the identity is not in the set I. Note that for this specific example, it is easy for the attacker to usurp the system since we deal with a small set of identities. However this task is going to be more difficult in real world deployment since this set will be much larger. The size of the identity set I has to be parametrized by the administrator so that the privacy and the fraud detection can follow the administrator's expectation of the system.

2.4   Privacy Analysis

The construction phase reveals that the size of the identity set I is crucial for privacy and for reliable impersonation detection. In the following section, we present an analysis that aims to determine the appropriate values that will allow us to create a reliable system. The analysis is dependent on four variables: m the size of the SOBER structure (the number of cells, that is), k the number of hash functions, n the number of identities and l the number of random insertions into SOBER for each identity. We first define the degree of privacy and the probability of fraud detection.

Definition 1. *Let I be the set of retrieved identities during the search phase. The degree of privacy p_P for any individual is a ratio equal to: $p_P = \frac{1}{|I|}$, where $|I|$ denotes the size of the set I.*

Definition 2. *Let I be the set of retrieved identities during the search phase. The probability of fraud p_F for the two use cases defined in Section 1 are as follows:*

$$p_F = \begin{cases} \frac{1}{|I|} & \text{use case -- first application for biometric card} \\ \\ \frac{|I|}{n} & \text{use case -- renewal without a document} \end{cases}$$

The above definitions capture the fact that the size of identity set I controls the rate of fraud and at the same time the degree of privacy of individuals. In fact, the probability to detect fraud in our first use case is equal to $\frac{1}{|I|}$, where I is the number of unique identities in the identity set I. On the other hand, for our second use case, the probability p_F that a attacker gives a different identity in the same identity set I is equal to $\frac{|I|}{n}$. Moreover, if the size of the identity set increases the privacy level of users also increases. Thus, a small privacy degree p_P reflects a high privacy level.

It is clear that there is a trade off between the privacy level that the system offers, the reliability of fraud detection and the difficulty to mislead the system. Indeed, if the set of unique identities gets larger, the attacker gets a higher chance of cheating the system; on the other hand, if the set of unique identities gets larger, users get better privacy. The degree of privacy is based on how evenly we distribute the identities over all positions of the SOBER data structure. The best scenario will be a case where every position stores exactly $\frac{l \cdot n}{m}$ identities. However, a random insertion of identities cannot guarantee this result. Thus, we have used the Greedy algorithm to decrease the maximum load of every position in order to be as close to the ideal situation as we can. Moreover, decreasing the maximum load will increase the minimum load (i.e. the minimum number of identities in any cell). One may be led to believe that a deterministic identity insertion will be better in our scenario. However, it is not the case from a security perspective. This is because having a deterministic insertion algorithm will leak information about the strategy of identity insertion. Consequently, for any internal adversary the task of identity deletion will be straightforward.

Essentially, we want to have a SOBER data structure where empty positions are very rare, almost non-existent. Empty positions refer to those positions in the SOBER data structure that do not contain any identity. We employ a classical problem known as the *the occupancy problem* [8], that gives us the exact probability of finding an empty position. We will show that, using the Greedy algorithm, we can control the minimum and maximum load of every cell in SOBER data structure and consequently disperse the identities in a uniform manner throughout the entire data structure.

Decreasing the false positive rate in SOBER: SOBER is a probabilistic data structure that involves some false positives. Let p_f denote the probability of a false positive. We first determine the appropriate values to minimize the false positive rate. Let us consider a SOBER with a size equal to m associated with k hash functions. We have n entries. Each insertion in the SOBER will imply insertion of $l + 1$ same identity values uniformly at random. We consider hash functions as random functions. We can show that for $k = \frac{m}{n} \ln(2)$, the probability of false positives is the minimum and is equal to $p_f = 2^{-k}$.

Probability of an empty cell in the SOBER data structure: Let us assume that insertion of identities are made uniformly at random with a single choice, i.e. every identity has one random choice to get into a given cell. We have $l \cdot n$ identities and m cells. We denote by $X_{n.l,m}$ the number of empty cells after all insertions. We can show that the probability that all cells contain at least one identity is equal to: $\Pr(X_{n.l,m} = 0) = \sum_{i=0}^{n}(-1)^i \binom{m}{i}(1 - \frac{i}{m})^{n.l}$. This formula can be approximated [9] to: $\Pr(X_{n.l,m} = 0) \simeq e^{-\lambda}$, where $\lambda = m.e^{-\frac{n.l}{m}}$.

Minimum/Maximum load of any cell: The Greedy algorithm ensures with a high probability [20] a maximum load equal to $\frac{n \cdot l}{m} + \sqrt{\frac{n \cdot l \cdot \ln(m)}{m}}$ in the case where $n \cdot l > m \cdot ln(m)$. While the maximum load defines the upper bound of the number of identities by cell, the minimum load is very important as well, since it controls the minimum size of the set I in the worst case. The following theorem gives the behavior of the minimum load of the *Greedy($\mathcal{U}$, 2)* algorithm. We omit the proof for lack of space.

Theorem 1. *Let $n \cdot l$ be the number of identities, m the size of the SOBER data structure and $d = 2$ the parameter of the Greedy algorithm. Let p be a positive real number. Then, we have with a probability at least equal to $1 - \frac{n \cdot k}{ln(2)} \cdot e^{-\frac{l \cdot ln(2) \cdot p^2}{2k}}$ the minimum load of any bin to be larger or equal to: $\frac{(1-p) \cdot l \cdot ln(2)}{k}$*

A direct consequence of Theorem 1 is that the number of identities in the worst case with a probability equal to $1 - p(l, k, n, p)$ is equal:

$$|I| = (1 - p) \cdot l \cdot ln(2)$$

where $p(l, k, n, p) = \frac{n \cdot k}{ln(2)} \cdot e^{-\frac{l \cdot ln(2) \cdot p^2}{2k}}$. We can control the minimum load by choosing a proper value of l for a fixed number of hash functions as well as a fixed population. This implies that the administrator can control the privacy of fraud p_F as well as the degree of privacy p_P. We should emphasize that the bigger the set I the more private the individual's biometric is but with lesser fraud detection ratio. This latter ratio should be carefully selected by authorities for a fair use of the system.

3   ELITE-2 Solution for Multitude of Traits Issue

The ELITE-1 scheme assumes that the user is associated with only one biometric information that has an exact match during the verification phase. This, however, is not true in real life [10]. In fact, we should differentiate between the biometric information as a physical characteristic of the individual, and the numerical biometric information after being captured by an image sensor. Note that, a physical biometric information can also have several versions. However, these versions are not totally different and have some similarities. So an identification of two similar biometrics can always be possible; only the accuracy and the efficiency are the main issues. This identification is mainly based on how the biometric information is digitized, and how robustly a biometric information can be represented such that similar biometrics will match even if they are distorted.

In literature, there are several biometric indexing techniques that can be variously classified depending on the features used [18]. Examples are global features such as the average of ridge-line frequency over the whole biometric information, local ridge-line orientations, minutiae and other features obtained from the biometric pattern. In the following, we are interested in the minutiae indexing technique presented in [6,7]. This technique introduces a biometric information indexing based on Minutiae Cylinder-Code, MCC. We provide in the following the details of the MCC approach.

3.1 Minutiae Cylinder-Code Overview

The MCC representation is a fixed-radius approach relying on minutiae features of the biometric information. MCC involves three dimensional representations of minutiae into cylinders. Each physical biometric information β can be seen as a set of minutiae that represents a template $\mathcal{T}$ of β such that $\mathcal{T} = \{m_1, \cdots, m_n\}$. Each minutia m_i is defined by its location (x_{m_i}, y_{m_i}) and its orientation in the space θ_{m_i}. The MCC transformation associates each minutia with a local space (cylinder) that encodes spacial and directional relationship with the neighboring minutiae. Each cylinder is divided into multiple cells and each cell contains a value depending on the neighboring minutiae. We will not go into the details of MCC. We describe next the verification steps done using the locality-sensitive hash functions [15].

We represent each biometric information as a set of binary vectors B. Each binary vector b_m corresponds to a MCC transformation of a given minutia m in the template of the biometric information $\mathcal{T}$ such that, $B = \{\mathbf{b_m} \mid m \in \mathcal{T} \text{ and } MCC(m) = \mathbf{b_m}\}$.

For two biometrics β_1 and β_2 having respectively the templates $\mathcal{T}_1$ and $\mathcal{T}_2$, we generate the binary vector sets for both templates B_1 and B_2. A similarity measure between these two biometric information can be done using Hamming distance [19] such that, $hds(\mathcal{T}_1, \mathcal{T}_2) = \frac{\sum_{\mathbf{b} \in \mathbf{B_2}} max_{\mathbf{b_j} \in B_1}(1 - (\frac{d_H(\mathbf{b}, \mathbf{b_j})}{n})^p)}{|B_1|}$ where n represents the size of each binary vector, p a parameter controlling the shape of the similarity and d_H the Hamming distance, with $hds(\cdot)$ near to 0 means no similarity, and a $hds(\cdot)$ near to one means a maximum of similarity. We have to point out that this similarity measure may not be the best choice for MCC comparison, and there are many other more suited measures discussed in detail in [6]. For the sake of simplicity we have chosen the Hamming distance similarity measure.

At this point, we cannot directly integrate the MCC transformation in our ELITE solution, since we cannot apply a Hamming computation over hashed values of biometrics templates if we store them in our SOBER. In fact, using MCC representation, we can avoid computing Hamming distance and replace it by locality-sensitive hash function (LSH) [7]. LSH can be viewed as projecting a n size vector into h size vector where $h < n$. The idea behind the use of LSH is that similar n size vectors still remain similar by projecting them into h size vectors.

The LSH approach consists of selecting k hash functions f_{H_1} defined by randomly choosing k arrival position subsets H_1, H_2,...,H_k. In order to compute the projection of a vector, we apply the k-hash functions; the output of each hash function is a binary vector with a size equal to h. Thus, using LSH, the Hamming distance similarity can be estimated [16] such that :

$$hds(\mathcal{T}_1, \mathcal{T}_2) \cong \frac{\sum_{\mathbf{b} \in \mathbf{B_2}} max_{\mathbf{b_j} \in B_1}(C(\mathbf{b}, \mathbf{b_j}))^{\frac{p}{h}})}{|B_1|.k^{\frac{p}{h}}} \tag{1}$$

where $C(\mathbf{b}, \mathbf{b_j}) = \sum_{i=1}^{l} \delta[f_{H_i}(\mathbf{b}) - f_{H_i}(\mathbf{b_j})]$ and δ is a Dirac symbol equal to 1 in case of equality and zero in the other case. We refer the reader to [7] to the experimental results on multiple well known biometrics databases.

Summing up, since we do not require computing Hamming distance for an identification, the MCC representation and the multiple LSH solution can be integrated to the ELITE scheme in order to handle identification under the multitude of traits issue, while at the same time providing a probabilistic link between individuals and their biometric information. In the following we describe the solution ELITE-2.

3.2   ELITE-2 Construction

Let us consider a set of n biometrics considered as n templates, where each template is a set of minutiae, and the associated set of n identities $\mathbf{id} = \{id_1, \cdots, id_n\}$. After applying the MCC transformation, the result will be a set of n binary vectors such that $\mathbf{B} = \{B_1, \cdots, B_n\}$. Let us consider s locality-sensitive hash functions (LSH) defined by a random sampling of arrival spaces such that $H_1, \cdots, H_s$, the size of each arrival space being equal to h. We should underline the fact that the size h will determine later the size of the SOBER filters. In the following, we describe the storage phase as well as the search (i.e. verification) phase.

Storage phase. First, we create s SOBERs with the same set of r independent hash functions $h_1, \cdots, h_r$, where each SOBER has a size equal to 2^h. Each cell in each SOBER will be divided into two lists. The first list will contain the identifier couples of each minutia transformation – for example $(1, 2)$ denotes the second minutia of the first biometry (instead of containing one or zero value) – and the second list contains the identities. Let us consider the MCC transformation of the ith biometric information $B_i = \{b_{i,1}, \cdots, b_{i,t}\}$ and the associated identity id_i. For each $b_{i,j} \in B_i$, the algorithm proceeds in these steps:

1. For each $1 \leq k \leq s$, apply the r independent hash functions $h_1, \cdots, h_r$ such that $\{SOBER_k[h_1(f_{H_k}(b_{i,j}))] = (i,j), \cdots, SOBER_k[h_r(f_{H_k}(b_{i,j}))] = (i,j)\}$,

2. For each $1 \leq k \leq s$, insert the identity id_i in l cell of each SOBER$_k$ following the Greedy algorithm,

3. Insert only one value of id_i in only one SOBER uniformly at random in the positions where the r hash functions outputted has an outputted result.

4. Create a row in the look-up table $\mathcal{L}$ which contains the identity id_i and the corresponding positions in the random selected SOBER where id_i belongs to cells where hash functions outputted a 1's result for the biometric information B_i.

We reiterate these steps for all binary vectors B_i. At the end we will output s filled out SOBERS which represents the new biometric database.

Search phase. The input of this phase is a scanned physical biometric information and an identity id. We want to verify whether the biometric information exists or not in the biometric database. The first step is to transform the scanned biometric information using the MCC representation. The output of the MCC representation is a binary vector set B. In order to perform the verification we follow these steps:

1. Create t empty collusion sets $C_1, \cdots, C_t$ and t empty identity sets $(I_1, \cdots, I_t)$,

2. For $1 \leq k \leq s$, for $1 \leq i \leq t$, compute the value $h_1(f_{H_k}(b_i)), \cdots, h_r(f_{H_k}(b_i))$ and retrieve from
   $\{SOBER_k[h_1(f_{H_k}(b_{i,j}))], \cdots, SOBER_k[h_r(f_{H_k}(b_{i,j}))]\}$ the couple (or couples) existing in all the corresponding positions as well as all the corresponding identities. Store them respectively in C_i and I_i.

3. For $1 \leq i \leq t$, rearrange the list C_i such that for each couple we give a score that represents the number of images of the corresponding couple in C_i, that is, the number of hash functions that collide between the new entry and existing biometric information(s).

4. Based on $C_1, \cdots, C_t$, select the maximum number of occurrences that belongs to the same template, then calculate the similarity based on the equation 1. If the similarity is bigger than a minimum that the administrator defines, the biometric information exists.

5. If $id \in I = \{I_1, \cdots, I_t\}$, conclude that the identity belongs to the system.

We should point out that the size of I is very important since it represents the parameter of privacy that we have explained in previous section (see Definition 1). In addition, the size of the SOBER is 2^h, which is equal to all the possibilities of hash function space H_i. On the other hand, the number of entries for each SOBER is equal to $n \times t$ where n is the number of biometrics and t the number of minutiae in each biometric information. (In practice $t \cong 70$ [7]). In order to have the minimum false positives and decrease the collision in the same SOBER for different binary vectors b, we should verify the following equation: $r = \frac{2^h}{n.t} ln(2)$.

In addition, tuples stored in the SOBER cells do not disclose any information about the identity. A number of these couples exist in the construction so as to maintain a link between minutiae and not to individuals' identity. This link allows one to determine the number of collusions for each stored minutiae in relation to others in the same template, as shown in the search phase.

From privacy perspective, the analysis can be done following the same steps as ELITE-1. The only main difference is the number of SOBERs (the number of minutiae associated with each biometric information is considered as a single entry).

3.3   Complexity Analysis

The storage complexity of ELITE-1 is dependent on the number of instances of identities, which is equal to l for each identity. If n represents the number of identities, the storage complexity is equal to $\mathcal{O}(n \cdot l)$. ELITE-2 represents a solution that can accommodate the multitude of traits issue, which ELITE-1 cannot, while maintaining the advantage of the basic ELITE-1 scheme. ELITE-2 derives its power from the constant search time of SOBER. However since the ELITE-2 construction requires the use of s bloom filters, the search time is equal to $\mathcal{O}(s)$. On the other hand, the use of s Bloom filters increases the storage complexity to $\mathcal{O}(s \cdot n \cdot l)$. (Here we do not take into account the constant factor of number of minutiae, which is in the order of ~ 70 minutiae per biometric information). ELITE-2 takes into consideration the multitude of traits for deletion of biometrics while keeping identities unlinked to their hidden biometrics. Table 2 presents a functional and computational comparison between the Setbase approach and the two ELITE solutions.

Table 2. Comparison between ELITE-(1,2) and Setbase approach

Scheme	Search complexity	Storage complexity	Multitude of traits	Hidden biometric information	Delete operation
ELITE-1	$\mathcal{O}(1)$	$\mathcal{O}(n.l)$	no	yes	yes
ELITE-2	$\mathcal{O}(s)$	$\mathcal{O}(s.n.l)$	yes	yes	yes
Setbase approach	$\mathcal{O}(n)$	$\mathcal{O}(n\lvert B\rvert)$	yes	no	no

ELITE-2 has many privacy advantages compared to the Setbase approach, specially with regards to the flexibility it offers for the choice of the rate of impersonation detection. In the Setbase approach, the rate is equal to m/n, where m is the size of each subset and n the size of whole population. Since the number of subsets are fixed, the m factor increases, which decreases linearly the detection rate. In ELITE-2, the randomization factor can be dynamically changed depending on the authorities' expectations. In ELITE-2, fixing the size of the

SOBER is mandatory before inserting elements. This can be a shortcoming to overcome if the distribution of population growth is not pre-determined (which is typically the case). However, even if we made the assumption of an unknown population growth, a good way to proceed is to divide each SOBER into chunks (each chunk is a different SOBER with its own hash functions) that we fill up depending on the population growth.

4   Conclusion

One of the biggest concerns of biometric based systems such as the ones used for issuing biometric based identity cards is that the systems include a deterministic link between the biometric information of an individual and her identity. Since the system also contains sensitive private information, such deterministic links can cause identity thefts for an individual when an attacker misuses a externally obtained biometric information to impersonate a registered user. In this work, we presented two constructions, ELITE-1 and ELITE-2, that render the association between the biometric information and the identity probabilistic. ELITE-2 improves upon ELITE-1 to address the challenges posed by the multitude of traits issue. We provide a theoretical analysis of the privacy guarantees of the ELITE scheme. We discuss how real-world impersonations can be detected. Finally, we provide analytical results of the storage and search complexities of the two schemes.

Future work involves a thorough new stateful algorithm that takes dynamically into consideration the distribution of identities during the storage phase in order to have more precise control over the probabilistic parameters. In addition, we plan to investigate how our scheme ELITE-1 can be applied to other applications, such as, keeping the relationship between an individual and his genetic information secret.

References

1. Adjedj, M., Bringer, J., Chabanne, H., Kindarji, B.: Biometric Identification over Encrypted Data Made Feasible. In: Prakash, A., Sen Gupta, I. (eds.) ICISS 2009. LNCS, vol. 5905, pp. 86–100. Springer, Heidelberg (2009)
2. Azar, Y., Broder, A.Z., Karlin, A.R., Upfal, E.: Balanced Allocations. In: Proceedings of the 26th Annual ACM Symposium on Theory of Computing, pp. 593–602. ACM, Chicago (1994)
3. Bloom, B.H.: Space/Time Trade-offs in Hash Coding with Allowable Errors. Communications of the ACM 13(7), 422–426 (1970)
4. Boneh, D., Kushilevitz, E., Ostrovsky, R., Skeith III, W.E.: Public Key Encryption That Allows PIR Queries. In: Menezes, A. (ed.) CRYPTO 2007. LNCS, vol. 4622, pp. 50–67. Springer, Heidelberg (2007)
5. Bringer, J., Chabanne, H., Kindarji, B.: Error-Tolerant Searchable Encryption. In: Proceedings of IEEE International Conference on Communications, Dresden, Germany, pp. 1–6 (June 2009)

6. Cappelli, R., Ferrara, M., Maltoni, D.: Minutia Cylinder-Code: A New Representation and Matching Technique for Fingerprint Recognition. IEEE Transaction on Pattern Analysis and Machine Intelligence 32(12), 2128–2141 (2010)
7. Cappelli, R., Ferrara, M., Maltoni, D.: Fingerprint Indexing Based on Minutia Cylinder-Code. IEEE Transaction on Pattern Analysis and Machine Intelligence 33(5), 1051–1057 (2011)
8. Feller, W.: An Introduction to Probability Theory and Its Applications: Volume One. John Wiley & Sons (1968)
9. Host, L.: Some Asymptotic Results For Occupancy Problems. The Annals of Probability 5(6), 1028–1035 (1977)
10. Jain, A.K., Bolle, R.M., Pankanti, S.: Biometrics: Personal Identification in Networked Society. Springer (1999)
11. Jain, A.K., Nandakumar, K., Nagar, A.: Biometric Template Security. EURASIP Journal on Advances in Signal Processing 2008 (2008)
12. Justus, B., Cuppens, F., Cuppens-Boulahia, N., Bringer, J., Chabanne, H., Cipiere, O.: Define Privacy-preserving Setbase Drawer Size Standard: A ϵ-closeness Perspective. In: Proceedings of the 11th Annual International Conference on Privacy, Security and Trust, Tarragona, Catalonia, Spain, pp. 362–365 (July 2013)
13. Justus, B., Cuppens, F., Cuppens-Boulahia, N., Bringer, J., Chabanne, H., Cipiere, O.: Enhance Biometric Database Privacy: Defining Privacy-Preserving Drawer Size Standard for the Setbase. In: Wang, L., Shafiq, B. (eds.) DBSec 2013. LNCS, vol. 7964, pp. 274–281. Springer, Heidelberg (2013)
14. Kevenaar, T.A.M., Korte, U., Merkle, J., Niesing, M., Ihmor, H., Busch, C., Zhou, X.: A Reference Framework for the Privacy Assessment of Keyless Biometric Template Protection Systems. In: Proceedings of the Special Interest Group on Biometrics and Electronic Signatures, Darmstadt, Germany, pp. 45–56 (September 2010)
15. Kushilevitz, E., Ostrovsky, R., Rabani, Y.: Efficient Search for Approximate Nearest Neighbor in High Dimensional Spaces. In: Proceedings of the 30th Annual ACM Symposium on the Theory of Computing, Dallas, Texas, USA, pp. 614–623 (May 1998)
16. Mimaroglu, S., Simovici, D.A.: Approximate Computation of Object Distances by Locality-Sensitive Hashing. In: Proceedings of the 4th International Conference on Data Mining, Las Vegas, Nevada, USA, pp. 714–718 (July 2008)
17. Schmidt, G.J., Soutar, C., Tomko, G.J.: Fingerprint Controlled Public Key Cryptographic System. Patent #US5541994 A. Mytec Technologies Inc. (July 1996)
18. Shamir, A.: Adding Privacy to Biometric Databases: The Setbase Approach. Presentation at the 31st International Conference of Data Protection and Privacy (2009), http://www.privacyconference2009.org/program/Presentaciones/common/pdfs/adhi_shamir_madrid.pdf (last accessed September 23, 2013)
19. Steane, A.M.: Error Correcting Codes in Quantum Theory. Physical Review Letters 77(5), 793 (1996)
20. Talwar, K., Wieder, U.: Balanced Allocations: The Weighted Case. In: Proceedings of the Thirty-ninth Annual ACM Symposium on Theory of Computing, STOC 2007, pp. 256–265. ACM, New York (2007)

Dynamic Workflow Adjustment
with Security Constraints

Haibing Lu[1], Yuan Hong[2], Yanjiang Yang[3], Yi Fang[1], and Lian Duan[4]

[1] Santa Clara University
{hlu,yfang}@scu.edu
[2] University at Albany
hong@albany.edu
[3] I2R Singapore
yyang@i2r.a-star.edu.sg
[4] New Jersey Institute of Technology
lian.duan@njit.edu

Abstract. Dynamic workflow adjustment studies how to minimally adjust existing user-task assignments, when a sudden change occurs, e.g. absence of users, so that all tasks are being attended and no constraint is violated. In particular, we study two key questions: (i) Will the workflow still be satisfiable given a change? (ii) If the answer is yes, how to find a satisfying assignment with the minimum perturbation to the old system? We consider various types of changes, including absence of a user, addition of a separation-of-duty constraint, addition of a binding-of-duty constraint, and revocation of a user-to-task authorization, study their theoretical properties and formulate them into the well-studied Boolean satisfiability problem, which enables a system engineer without much technical background to solve problems by using standard satisfiability solvers. A step further, towards more efficient solutions for our specific problems, we propose customized algorithms by adapting and tailoring the state-of-art algorithms inside standard solvers. Our work would have implications for business process management, staffing, and cost planning.

Keywords: workflow, security, dynamic, satisfiability.

1   Introduction

A workflow can be defined as a set of tasks and dependencies that control the coordination requirements among these tasks [2]. A workflow example is an information system for an online pharmacy store, which involves a set of tasks, e.g. order entry, medication assessment, billing, and shipping, a set of employees with different roles, e.g. pharmacist and non-technical staff, and a set of constraints, e.g. non-technical staff cannot perform medication assessment, and a person who does credit check cannot perform billing due to the fraud concern.

The problem of allocating users to tasks to comply with a given authorization policy and also fulfil the workflow requirement, is important in access control and has received considerable attention in the literature. However, there still lack studies from the dynamic perspective, despite a few papers looking into this problem, e.g. [17,5].

V. Atluri and G. Pernul (Eds.): DBSec 2014, LNCS 8566, pp. 211–226, 2014.

Indeed, many factors of a workflow are dynamically changing, e.g. a user is absent due to sickness, the right of a user to access a certain task is temporarily revoked due to frequent mistakes, and a user has to step way from a task due to an emerging conflict of interest. A poorly designed workflow, although might be working at the current moment, is vulnerable to future changes and may cause huge troubles both financially and operationally to an organization. So it is crucial to study the resilience and flexibility of a workflow system with respect to various types of changes. It is also important to investigate how much disruption to an existing system is necessary to make a satisfying workflow assignment when a sudden change occurs.

In this paper, we formulate and study dynamic workflow adjustment with various changes, which is to make a workflow assignment with the minimum perturbations to the current workflow system, while complying with the authorization policy and all associated constraints. Specific types of dynamic changes considered include absence of a user, addition of a separation-of-duty constraint, addition of a binding-of-duty constraint, and revocation of a user-to-task authorization. To tackle dynamic workflow adjustment with various changes, we provide Boolean satisfiability model formulations, which enable a workflow engineer without much technical background to solve the problems with standard solvers.

Due to the hardness nature of dynamic workflow adjustment, it is of practical importance to have efficient and customized algorithms, rather than resorting to standard solvers, which rarely take account of the characteristics of individual problems. A significant difference of dynamic workflow adjustment from the conventional workflow assignment problem is that a satisfying assignment for the system before the change is already available, which should be taken advantage of, rather than designing a new assignment from scratch like a standard solver does. More importantly, finding the satisfying workflow assignment, closest to the old assignment, is our ultimate goal, as a satisfying workflow assignment with much disruption to the old system is of no value in practice. We are thus motivated to customize the state-of-art algorithms for the Boolean satisfiability problem to our unique problems.

Our work would have practical implications on workflow planning, staffing, and cost budgeting. By studying the resilience of a workflow system against different types of changes, a system manager can plan ahead to minimize the expected loss. By studying the minimum required perturbation to the old assignment to make a satisfying assignment, the manager can have a better understanding of the strategic importance of a specific position or an employee and thus make a better and more flexible workflow system.

2   Problem Definitions

Many types of workflow assignment constraints have been studied in the literature, e.g. [5,17,9,4]. Following their research, we consider skill constraints, separation-of-duty constraints, binding-of-duty constraints, and performing constraints.

Skill constraints, also called static constraints, refer to that a task has to be performed by persons with necessary skills or credentials. Skill constraints are typically enforced by role-based access control (RBAC) [13] due to its various advantages, e.g.

low administrative cost and support of permission inheritance through role hierarchy. The basic idea of RBAC is to associate roles with tasks and then assign roles to users, so that a user is authorized to all tasks that are associated with the roles assigned to him/her. For instance, a pharmacist role is associated with tasks of ordering entry, credit check, fulfilling order, mediation assessment, shipping, and billing. So any employee with the pharmacist role can perform all associated tasks. The literature of RBAC, e.g. [10,11,16], typically denotes user-task assignments by UPA, user-role assignments by UA, and role-task assignment by PA, in which UA and PA can deduce UPA. Since this paper assumes roles are stable, to ease the modeling, we consider and denote user-task assignments by A, which is a binary matrix, i.e. $x_{ij} = 1$ means user i is permitted to perform task j; otherwise not. Note that in our paper, authorization is different from actual assignment. Authorization of $x_{ij} = 1$ only means user i has necessary credentials (or skills) to perform task j. For instance, a pharmacist is permitted to perform the billing task, but may not be assigned to the billing task.

A separation-of-duty (SoD) constraint is to distribute responsibilities to prevent from fraud and error. For instance, many companies require that a person can not perform both purchasing and billing tasks to avoid embezzlement. The conventional perception of a separation-of-duty constraint is a pair of conflicting tasks that no one can perform simultaneously. This paper considers a separation-of-duty constraint from a more general perspective by including conflict-of-interest constraints, as they both advocate decentralization of tasks. An example of conflict-of-interest constraint is that in order to provide an objective review a funding proposal reviewer is not allowed to review the proposal of the person whom he/she had worked with or supervised. So in our paper, a separation-of-duty constraint is defined and denoted by s_{ijkl}, which states that if user i performs task j, then user k is not allowed to perform task l. As such, the conventional definition of a pair of conflicting tasks j and l can be described as $\bigcup_{\forall i} s_{ijil}$.

A binding-of-duty (BoD) constraint specifies the binding relation of tasks. For instance, a person who changes a password must be the person who creates the password. In our paper, it is defined and denoted by b_{ijkl}, stating that if user i performs task j, then user k has to perform task l. Note that our definition is different from and more general than the conventional definition of a BoD constraint, which refers to that bound tasks have to be performed by the same subject. In some cases, a binding relation can be associated with multiple subjects. For instance, a company may specify that the manager who approves a project proposal must come from the same department as the proposal submitter due to the same knowledge background. By our BoD definition, a conventional BoD constraint on binding task j and l can be described as $\bigcup_{\forall i} b_{ijil}$.

A performing constraint specifies that every task needs to be performed by at least one user; in other words, no unattended task. The constraint can be represented by $\sum_i x_{ij} \geq 1, \forall j$.

In this paper, we consider and study four types of changes that may interrupt a running workflow system. They are: (1) absence of a user, (2) addition of a SoD constraint, (3) addition of a BoD constraint, and (4) revocation of an authorization.

A common obstruction to a workflow system is the change of users. Addition of a user does not cause constraint conflicts, although the system engineer needs to assign appropriate tasks to the new user, the study of which is out of the scope of this paper.

When user i is absent, a performing constraint may be violated, e.g. task j becomes unattended if user i was the only one performing the task. If another user is to replace the absent user, other types of constraint conflicts, e.g. SoD and BoD, may occur. So to prevent potential loss, a workflow designer has to plan ahead by investigating the workflow resilience to such a type of changes. Two questions are faced. First, will a workflow still be satisfiable after a change occurs? Second, which might be more important, what is the satisfying workflow assignment with the minimum disruption to the old system? By satisfying, we mean the workflow assignment does not cause any constraint conflict. The second question is more important because a satisfying workflow assignment with much disruption to the old system is of no practical value. To answer the two questions, we define the following problem.

Problem 1. Given users U, tasks T, user-task authorizations A, BoD constraints B, SoD constraints S, existing satisfying user-task assignment $\tilde{X}$, and a number δ, if user i' is absent, does there exist a satisfying workflow assignment X such that $\sum_{ij} |x_{ij} - \tilde{x}_{ij}| \leq \delta$?

δ is the threshold for the amount of disruption. When δ is greater than $\sum_{ij} |\tilde{x}_{ij}|$, problem 1 is the formulation of the first question. Indeed, problem 1 is the representation of the decision version of the second question. So by solving problem 1 multiple times with different values of δ, one can find the answer for the second question.

A BoD constraint may be added or deleted, when a user's responsibilities changed, user relations evolved, task characteristics are updated, etc. Addition of a BoD constraint may cause the existing workflow assignment to be unsatisfying, while deletion of a BoD constraint does not impact the satisfiability. Addition of a BoD constraint gives rise to the same two questions. First, will the addition of a SoD constraint make the workflow unsatisfiable? Second, how to find a satisfying workflow assignment without the minimum disruption to the old system? The two questions are formulated as problem 2.

Problem 2. Given users U, tasks T, user-task authorizations A, BoD constraints B, SoD constraints S, and existing satisfying user-task assignments $\tilde{X}$ and a number δ, if a BoD constraint $b_{i'j'k'l'}$ is added, does there exist a satisfying workflow assignment X such that $\sum_{ij} |x_{ij} - \tilde{x}_{ij}| \leq \delta$?

Addition of a SoD constraint $s_{i'j'k'l'}$ may also cause constraint conflicts if $\tilde{x}_{i'j'} = 1$ and $\tilde{x}_{k'l'} = 1$ both hold in the old workflow system. Will the change cause the system to a standstill? How much effort is required to make another satisfying workflow system? The two questions can be answered by solving the following problem.

Problem 3. Given users U, tasks T, user-task authorizations A, BoD constraints B, SoD constraints S, and existing satisfying user-task assignments X and a number δ, if a SoD constraint $s_{i'j'k'l'}$ is added, does there exist a satisfying workflow assignment X such that $\sum_{ij} |x_{ij} - \tilde{x}_{ij}| \leq \delta$?

Authorization might be added or revoked in the middle of a process. As addition of an authorization, e.g. a staff may be upgraded to the pharmacist role after getting the licence, does not cause any type of constraint conflicts studied in this paper, so in terms of change of authorization we only consider the revocation case. Revocation of authorization may occur when a user becomes disqualified for certain tasks. For instance, a pharmacist is permitted to process shipment. But if he frequently makes mistakes, then his permission to that task may be suspended or revoked. The problem is that when his assignment to the shipment task is canceled, we have to find another person to replace that person, if that person is the only one assigned to that job in the old workflow system. There might be multiple persons with the authorization to the shipment task. But an assignment decision may cause other types of conflicts, e.g. SoD and BoD. In that case, we may have to make more changes to resolve cascaded conflicts. To investigate the satisfiability and resilience of the workflow to such a type of change, we define the following problem.

Problem 4. Given users U, tasks T, user-task authorizations A, BoD constraints B, SoD constraints S, existing satisfying user-task assignment $\tilde{X}$, and a number δ, if authorization $a_{i'j'}$ is revoked, does there exist a satisfying workflow assignment X such that $\sum_{ij} |x_{ij} - \tilde{x}_{ij}| \leq \delta$?

3   Theoretical Study

Finding a satisfying workflow assignment without any constraint conflict from scratch has been proven to be NP-hard [5]. The difference in our dynamic workflow adjustment problems is that there was a satisfying workflow assignment available. Intuitively, it should not be difficult to examine the workflow satisfiability under a change by tweaking the previous workflow assignment. But it turns out a dynamic workflow adjustment problem can be as difficult as the workflow design problem.

In this section, we will prove the dynamic workflow adjustment problem in the case of one user being absent is NP-complete based on some known results.

Statement 1. *The problem of determining when a planar map, i.e. it can be drawn on the plane in such a way that its edges intersect only at their endpoints, is three-colorable is NP-complete [15].*

Statement 2. *Every planar map is 4-colorable [1].*

Theorem 1. *Problem 1 is NP-complete.*

A decision problem is NP-complete if it belongs to NP and also can be reduced to a NP-complete problem.

Given a new workflow assignment, one can examine its difference from the old assignment and its satisfiability in polynomial time. So problem 1 belongs to NP.

Consider a special case of problem 1 with δ being a large number, so the decision problem asks whether a workflow is satisfiable when a user is absent. The satisfiability problem can be reduced to planar 3-colorability. Statements 1 and 2 show that any planar graph has a 4-coloring solution, but hard to find a 3-coloring solution. An instance of problem 1 can be represented by $\{U, T, A, C, B, X, U_i\}$, which denote users, tasks, authorizations, conflict-of-interest constraints, binding-of-duty constraints, previous assignments and the user who is absent. A planar map can be represented by regions $\{r_i\}$. We denote $col : r_i \rightarrow \{1, 2, 3, 4\}$ to be a 4-coloring solution, such that $col(r_i) \neq col(r_j)$ if r_i and r_j are adjacent. For each planar map instance, we can construct an equivalent instance of problem 1 as the follows:

- For U, let it be $\{u_1, u_2, u_3, u_4\}$;
- For T, create a task t_i to correspond to each region R_i of the map;
- For A, users are allowed to execute all tasks;
- For C, include $\{s_{1i1j}, s_{2i2j}, s_{3i3j}, s_{4i4j}\}$, i.e. separation-of-duty constraint on t_i and t_j, if r_i and r_j are adjacent;
- For B, let it be empty;
- For X, let x_{ij} be 1 if $col(r_j) = i$ so that X are feasible assignments to the above constraints C;
- For u_i, let it be any user.

When a user is absent, the constructed instance of problem 1 becomes equivalent to finding a 3-coloring solution to a planar map. So problem 1 is NP-complete.   □

4 Model Formulation

To tackle the dynamic workflow adjustment problems, one straightforward approach is to formulate them with well-studied models and then take advantage of existing solvers, which can save much effort for a system engineer. We find that the dynamic workflow adjustment problems can be modeled as Boolean satisfiability problems, which are well studied and have many good algorithms as well as available public/commercial software packages. Boolean satisfiability problem, commonly abbreviated as SAT, is probably one of the most studied problems in computer science, and has a range of applications in electronic design automation and artificial intelligence. SAT is historically notable as the first problem proven to be NP-complete. However, SAT is widely used because conflict-driven clause learning (CDCL) SAT solvers [14] are so effective in practice.

The dynamic workflow adjustment problems can be formulated as Boolean satisfiability problems, which enable one to adopt exiting SAT solvers. Before we provide their SAT formulations, we firstly examine the constraints.

A BoD constraint b_{ijkl} requires user k to perform task l when user i performs task j. In other words, if x_{ij} is TRUE, x_{kl} has to be TRUE, which can be expressed by:

$$(\neg x_{ij} \bigvee x_{kl}).$$

When x_{ij} is TRUE, $\neg x_{ij}$ is FALSE. Then in order to make the clause to be TRUE, x_{kl} has to be TRUE.

A SoD constraint s_{ijkl} forbids user k from performing task l when user i performs task j. In other words, one of x_{ij} and x_{kl} has to be FALSE, which can be expressed by the clause:

$$(\neg x_{ij} \bigvee \neg x_{kl}),$$

because in order to make the clause to be TRUE, the negation of one of x_{ij} and x_{kl} has to be TRUE.

A performing constraint requires that each task t_j needs to be performed by at least one person. In other words, one of x_{ij} has to be TRUE, which can be expressed by the clause:

$$(\bigvee_{i \in A_j} x_{ij}),$$

where A_j denotes the set of users with the authorization to task t_j.

Before any change happens, the workflow is satisfied by the current user-task assignments $\{\tilde{X}_{ij}\}$, which means the following CNF expression is TRUE:

$$(\bigwedge_{\forall s_{ijkl}} (\neg \tilde{X}_{ij} \bigvee \neg \tilde{X}_{kl})) \bigwedge (\bigwedge_{\forall b_{ijkl}} (\neg \tilde{X}_{ij} \bigvee \tilde{X}_{kl})) \bigwedge (\bigwedge_{\forall j} (\bigvee_{i \in A_j} \tilde{X}_{ij})).$$

Consider problem 1, which essentially tries to answer two questions: whether the workflow is satisfiable when user i' is absent? what is the satisfying assignment with the minimum perturbation to the old assignment?

The first question can be formulated as the SAT problem of finding an assignment of TRUE and FALSE values to variables $\{x_{ij}\}$ to satisfy the CNF expression:

$$E_1 = (\bigwedge_{\forall s_{ijkl}|i \neq i'} (\neg x_{ij} \bigvee \neg x_{kl})) \bigwedge (\bigwedge_{\forall b_{ijkl}|i \neq i'} (\neg x_{ij} \bigvee x_{kl})) \bigwedge (\bigwedge_{\forall j} \bigvee_{i \in A_j|i \neq i'} x_{ij})),$$

which contains the clause representation of all workflow assignment constraints.

The second question can be described as the weighted MAX-SAT problem with the CNF expression:

$$E_2 = E_1 \bigwedge (\bigwedge_{\forall i|i \neq i'} ((x_{ij} \bigvee \neg x_{ij}) \bigwedge (\tilde{x}_{ij} \bigvee \neg x_{ij}) \bigwedge (x_{ij} \bigvee \neg \tilde{x}_{ij}) \bigwedge (\tilde{x}_{ij} \bigvee \neg \tilde{x}_{ij}))).$$

Clauses $(x_{ij} \bigvee \neg x_{ij}) \bigwedge (\tilde{x}_{ij} \bigvee \neg x_{ij}) \bigwedge (x_{ij} \bigvee \neg \tilde{x}_{ij}) \bigwedge (\tilde{x}_{ij} \bigvee \neg \tilde{x}_{ij})$ are used to evaluate the equality of x_{ij} and $\tilde{x}_{ij}$, as the clauses are TRUE if and only if the value of x_{ij} is the same as $\tilde{x}_{ij}$. We let the weights on all clauses in E_1 be a sufficiently large number and the weights on the other clauses be 1. So to maximize such a weighted MAX-SAT problem, clauses in E_1 must be satisfied, as they carry significantly large weights. As such, we guarantee that the optimal solution to the weighted MAX-SAT problem corresponds to a satisfying workflow assignment. Therefore, the constructed weighted MAX-SAT problem is equivalent to the original minimal perturbation problem.

Consider problem 2, addition of a BoD constraint $s_{i'j'k'l'}$. Whether the workflow is satisfiable after the change can be formulated as a SAT problem with the expression:

$$E_3 = E_1 \bigwedge (\neg x_{ij} \bigvee x_{kl}).$$

The problem of finding a satisfying assignment with the minimum perturbation after the BoD constraint change can be formulated as a MAX-SAT problem of the CNF expression:

$$E_4 = E_3 \bigwedge (\bigwedge_{\forall i|i \neq i'} ((X_i \bigvee \neg X_i) \bigwedge (\tilde{X}_i \bigvee \neg X_i) \bigwedge (X_i \bigvee \neg \tilde{X}_i) \bigwedge (\tilde{X}_i \bigvee \neg \tilde{X}_i)))$$

with the weights on clauses of E_3 being a significantly large number and the weights on the other clauses being 1.

Consider problem 3, addition of a SoD constraint $s_{i'j'k'l'}$. Whether the workflow is satisfiable after the change can be formulated as a SAT problem with the expression:

$$E_5 = E_1 \bigwedge (\neg x_{i'j'} \bigvee \neg x_{k'l'}).$$

The problem of finding a satisfying assignment with the minimum perturbation after the SoD constraint change can be formulated as a MAX-SAT problem of the CNF expression:

$$E_6 = E_5 \bigwedge (\neg x_{i'j'} \bigvee \neg x_{k'l'}) \bigwedge (\bigwedge_{\forall i | i \neq i'} ((X_i \bigvee \neg X_i)$$

$$\bigwedge (\tilde{X}_i \bigvee \neg X_i) \bigwedge (X_i \bigvee \neg \tilde{X}_i) \bigwedge (\tilde{X}_i \bigvee \neg \tilde{X}_i)))$$

with the weights on clauses of E_5 being a significantly large number and the weights on the other clauses being 1.

Consider problem 4, revocation of authorization $a_{i'j'}$. Whether the workflow is satisfiable after the change can be formulated as a SAT problem with the CNF expression:

$$E_7 = (\bigwedge_{\forall s_{ijkl}} (\neg \tilde{X}_{ij} \bigvee \neg \tilde{X}_{kl})) \bigwedge (\bigwedge_{\forall b_{ijkl}} (\neg \tilde{X}_{ij} \bigvee \tilde{X}_{kl})) \bigwedge (\bigwedge_{\forall j} (\bigvee_{i \in A'_j} \tilde{X}_{ij})).$$

The problem of finding a satisfying assignment with the minimum perturbation after the SoD constraint change can be formulated as a MAX-SAT problem of the CNF expression:

$$E_8 = E_7 \bigwedge (\bigwedge_{\forall i | i \neq i'} ((x_i \bigvee \neg x_i) \bigwedge (\tilde{X}_i \bigvee \neg x_i) \bigwedge (x_i \bigvee \neg \tilde{x}_i) \bigwedge (\tilde{x}_i \bigvee \neg \tilde{x}_i)))$$

with the weights on clauses of E_7 and $(\neg x_{i'j'} \bigvee \neg x_{k'l'})$ being a significantly large number and the weights on the other clauses being 1.

5 Customized Algorithms

Resorting to existing optimization and SAT solvers is a common approach for the access control community to tackle encountered problems, e.g. [10,5,17]. However, a disadvantage of solvers is that they are designed as a universal platform for all feeded problems and thus disregard the properties of individual problems that could be used to design more efficient algorithms.

Unlike designing a workflow assignment from scratch, the dynamic workflow adjustment problems have an important piece of information available, the previous satisfying assignment. To make a satisfying workflow assignment, an intuitive way is to tweak the previous conflicting assignment instead of trying to make up the whole assignment from empty as a solver would do. In this section, we will present customized algorithms for the dynamic workflow adjustment problems. As they are based on the start-of-art algorithms for the SAT problem, so we firstly give a brief introduction on them.

5.1 State-of-Art SAT Algorithms

The state-of-art SAT algorithms are DPLL [7] and CDCL (a modern variant of DPLL) [14,12]. Both CDCL and DPLL algorithms are complete, backtracking-based, tree search algorithms for deciding the satisfiability of a CNF expression. At each step, the algorithms choose a variable, assign a value to it, simplify the formula and then check if the simplified formula is satisfiable. If it is true, the original formula is satisfiable. Otherwise, assume the opposite value to the variable. If it is not satisfiable either, the algorithm backtracks to a higher level. The difference between CDCL and DPLL is that the DPLL algorithm backtracks to the next higher level, which is referred to as chronical backtracking, while the CDCL algorithm may go up more levels by using clause learning, which is referred to as non-chronical backtracking.

Both algorithms speed up the backtracking by the eager use of the unit propagation rule at each step.

Unit propagation. If a clause is a *unit clause*, i.e. it contains only a single unassigned literal, this clause can only be satisfied by assigning the necessary value to make this literal true. Thus, no choice is necessary. In practice, it would lead to deterministic cascades of units and could avoid a large part of the naive search space. For example, consider the expression of $(x_1 \bigvee x_2) \bigwedge (\neg x_2 \bigvee x_3)$. If the literal x_1 has assumed FALSE, then $(x_1 \bigvee x_2)$ becomes a unit clause and x_2 has to assume TRUE to make the clause TRUE. As a cascade effect, $(\neg x_2 \bigvee x_3)$ becomes a unit clause and x_3 has to assume TRUE to make the clause TRUE.

5.2 Basic Algorithm

Instead of designing an algorithm for each presented problem, we introduce and study a basic problem, sharing the commonality with all dynamic workflow adjustment problems, and its algorithm can be applied to all problems with simple problem-specific configurations. The basic problem is defined as follows.

Problem 5. Given a list of perturbations $PList$ to a previously satisfying workflow assignment $\tilde{X}$, which leads to performing constraint conflicts only and no other types of constraint conflicts, does there exist a satisfying workflow assignment X with $\sum_{ij} |x_{ij} - \tilde{x}_{ij}| \leq \delta$ and without changing any given perturbation in $PList$?

Note that problem 5 limits existing conflicts to performing constraint conflicts only. So to resolve such a problem, at the beginning we only need to focus on how to find users to cover the unattended tasks. For each unattended task, there might be multiple users with rights to access. If we randomly pick and assign a user to an unattended task, other types of constraint conflicts, e.g. SoD and BoD, might be triggered. If one tries to fix a cascaded constraint conflict, more constraint conflicts could be generated. In the worse cases, we may end up in an infinite loop. So to effectively solve the problem, we need a strategy on how to make perturbations at each step.

Inspired by the DBLL and CDCL algorithms, we present a complete, backtracking-based, tree search algorithm, stated in Algorithm 1. The basic idea is that at each step we pick an unattend task and then select an authorized user to cover it. If the selected perturbation causes SoD and BoD constraint conflicts, we make further perturbations to resolve those conflicts, as the unit propagation does in the CDCL and DPLL algorithms. In particular, if user i is assigned to the unattended task j and a SoD constraint s_{ijil} is violated because user i was assigned to task l, we perturb both x_{il} and x_{kl} from 1 to 0. If a BoD constraint b_{ijil} is violated because user i was not assigned to task l, then we perturb both x_{il} and x_{kl} from 0 to 1 as well. The algorithm is written in a

---

Algorithm 1. BasicPerturb(X, A, B, S, PList, δ, DLevel)

1: **if** DLevel==0 **then**
2:     **return** UNSATISFIABLE
3: **end if**
4: NewPerturbations←PickPerturbation(X, A, B, C, PList);
5: **if** NewPerturbation==$\emptyset$ **then**   ▷ No satisfying assignment
6:     DLevel←DLeve-1;
7:     Backtrack();   ▷ Chronological Backtracking
8: **else**
9:     NewPerturbations←Propagate(X, A, B, C, PList, NewPerturbations);
10:    **if** IsConflict()==TRUE **then**
11:        NeighborSearch();   ▷ Search neighboring nodes
12:    **else if** IsSatisfied()==TRUE **then**
13:        **return** SATISFIABLE
14:    **else**
15:        DLevel←DLevel+1;
16:        PList←PList∪NewPerturbations;
17:        Perturb(X, A, B, C, PList, DLevel);
18:    **end if**
19: **end if**

---

recursive form as the *BasicPerturb()* function and stated in Algorithm 1. The arguments of the *BasicPerturb()* function are X, the original user-task assignments, A, the user-task authorizations, B, BoD constraints, S, SoD constraints, $PList$, the given list of perturbations, δ, the maximal amount of allowed perturbations, and $DLevel$, the level of searching. The algorithm description is as follows.

- Lines 1-3 state that if $DLevel$ becomes 0, the problem is determined unsatisfiable. The value of $DLevel$ indicates the searching level and is set to 1 when the algorithm starts. So if $DLevel$ becomes 0, it means the whole searching space has been traversed and no satisfying solution has been found.
- At line 4, the *PickPerturbation()* function is to select an unattend task first and then assign an authorized user to it. Note that if the selected user causes unsolvable conflicts, we will keep trying to find another authorized user to the unattend task without considering other unattended tasks. If no feasible user exists, then the whole search at the current level fails and has to move back to the next parent node. The selection of a task and a user is called branching. There are many branching heuristics. Our general rule is to select the task with more restrictions (e.g., more associated constraints, less authorized users) and the user with more freedom (e.g, less assignments, more authorizations). Branching rules indeed play an important role in a search tree algorithm. We will have a more detailed discussion later.
- Lines 5-8 state that the algorithm backtracks, if no satisfying assignment can be found. Again, note that at each level only one task is selected. If we failed in finding a user for it, we do not consider other unattend task at this level, because the search at the current level is doomed to fail. In such a case, the search moves back to the next parent node. Note that this papers only uses the chronological backtracking strategy, which is also used in the DBLL algorithm. A non-chronological

backtracking strategy, which allows to jump to a higher level by learning the traversed route and has been used in the modern SAT solvers, might be used to reduce the searching time. Non-chronological backtracking may be beneficial to our problems. But we leave the study in the future work.

- At line 9, the *Propagate()* function propagates the picked perturbation. As *PickPerturbation()* is to fix a performing constraint conflict, i.e. assigning an authorized user to an unperformed task, such a perturbation decision may cause BoD and SoD constraint conflicts. In such cases, the algorithm makes more perturbations to fix the cascaded BoD and SoD constraint conflicts. If a BoD (or SoD) constraint b_{ijkl} (or s_{ijkl})is violated, the assignments of $x_{ij} = 1$ and $x_{kl} = 1$ are canceled. Note that the *Propagate()* function does not resolve further cascaded performing constraint conflicts. The *Propagate* function is similar to the unit propagation procedure used in the SAT solvers.
- At lines 10-12, the *IsConflict()* function checks whether the new perturbations cause a conflict. In particular, we check two types of conflicts. One is the number of the total perturbations made so far. If it exceeds the maximum accepted number δ, then the search along this route has failed. The other one is that whether any new perturbation changes a previous perturbation decision. If so, then the search has failed also, because a loop has occurred. When either case happens, *NeighborSearch()* is called to find another authorized user to the picked unattended task.
- At lines 13-14, the *IsSatisfied()* function checks whether the new perturbations make a satisfying workflow management system.
- Lines 16-18 are executed when the evaluation of the *IsSatisfied()* function is FALSE. *PList* is updated by including new perturbations and then the search continues.

5.3   Problem-Specific Configurations

All studied dynamic workflow adjustment problems can adopt algorithm 1 with some problem-specific configurations. To demonstrate how it works, we will run it on a toy online pharmacy example. There are 7 task, T1 - T7: order entry, credit check, fulfil order, medication assessment, shipping, billing, and update legers respectively. There are four roles: P (pharmacist), T (technical staff), N (non-technical staff), and A (accountant). The task-role relation and personnel assignments are written in Table 1. There are 4 employees: David, Sam, John, and Eva. There are a SoD constraint on T2 and T6, a SoD constraint on T3 and T6, and a BoD constraint on T6 and T7. All these are depicted in Figure 1.

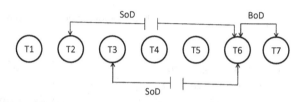

Fig. 1. An Order Fulfillment Process Diagram for an Online Pharmacy

Absence of User. For problem 1, we can directly apply algorithm 1 by setting the starting perturbation list $PList$ as $\{\forall j, X_{ij} : 1 \rightarrow 0\}$, where i is the absent user. $PList$ is a set of assignment deletion and does not cause any other types of constraint conflicts, except performing constraint conflicts. So $PList$ satisfies the algorithmic requirement. For illustration, suppose Eva is absent and the maximum accepted number of perturbations is 3. An algorithm execution example is shown in Figure 2. At level 1, the assignment of T6 and T7 are empty, because Eva is absent and she is the only user who was performing them. At level 2, we pick the unattended task T7 first and then assign John it. As a result, T6 has to be assigned to John due to the BoD constraint on T6 and T7. As it propagates, the assignment of John to T3 is deleted, because of the SoD constraint on T6 and T3. At this point, other than performing constraint conflicts, there is no other type of constraint conflict. So it proceeds to level 3. By selecting T3 and assigning Sam to it, we find a satisfying workflow assignment, as all tasks are attended by at least one authorized employee, no constraint conflict exists, and the number of total perturbations is 3.

Table 1. Task-Role Relation and Personnel Assignment

	T1	T2	T3	T4	T5	T6	T7
Associated	P	P	P	P	P	P	P
Roles	T	T	T		T	T	T
	N		A		N	N	A
	A				A	A	
Assignment	David	Sam	John	John	David	Eva	Eva
	(N)	(T)	(P)	(P)	(N)	(A)	(A)

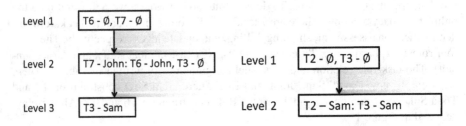

Level 1	T6 - ∅, T7 - ∅
Level 2	T7 - John: T6 - John, T3 - ∅
Level 3	T3 - Sam

| Level 1 | T2 - ∅, T3 - ∅ |
| Level 2 | T2 – Sam: T3 - Sam |

Fig. 2. Absence of Eva   **Fig. 3.** Addition of a BoD Constraint (T2, T3)

Addition of BoD Constraint. Algorithm 1 can also be applied to the case when a BoD constraint is added. A BoD constraint b_{ijkl} requires $x_{kl} = 1$ if $x_{ij} = 1$. b_{ijkl} causes a conflict when $x_{ij} = 1$ and $X_{kl} = 0$ in the old system. To resolve a BoD constraint conflict, a simple way is to delete both assignments. It may lead to performing constraint conflicts. If so, we can simply call algorithm 1 by making $PList$ as $\{x_{ij} : 1 \rightarrow 0, x_{kl} : 1 \rightarrow 0\}$, which only causes performing constraint conflicts.

Suppose a BoD constraint on T2 and T3 is added to Figure 1. An algorithm execution example is shown in Figure 3. At level 1, the assignments of T2 and T3 are set as empty. At level 2, select T2 and assign Sam to T2, as Sam has authorization to T2. Due to the BoD constraint on T2 and T3, Sam is assigned to T3 as well, which constitutes a satisfying workflow system. Note that a branching rule indeed is very important for the algorithm efficiency. As if we assign other authorized user to T2, it may cause conflicts and then have to return to make another selection. We will discuss branching rules and how to use them to improve algorithm efficiency later.

Addition of SoD Constraint. Algorithm 1 can also apply to the case when a SoD constraint is added with some simple configurations. A SoD constraint s_{ijkl} requires $x_{ij} = 1$ and $x_{kl} = 1$ cannot both hold. So addition of s_{ijkl} may cause a SoD constraint conflict if $X_{ij} = 1$ and $X_{kl} = 1$ both hold in the old system. To resolve the conflict, we simply delete assignments of $x_{ij} = 1$ and $x_{kl} = 1$, and then directly adopt algorithm 1 by making $PList$ as $\{x_{ij} : 1 \to 0, X_{kl} : 1 \to 0\}$.

To illustrate it, suppose a SoD constraint on T3 and T4 is added to Figure 1 and the maximum accepted number of perturbations is 3. An algorithm execution example is shown in Figure 4. At level 1, the assignments of T3 and T4 are set as empty. At level 2, John is assigned to the unattended task T4. At level 3, Eva is assigned to T3 first. As a result, the assignment of Eva to T6 is deleted because of the SoD constraint on T3 and T6, and then the assignment of Eva to T7 is deleted because of the BoD constraint. Since the number of the currently total perturbations exceeds 3, the assignment of Eva to T3 fails and the searching goes back. Alternatively, Sam is assigned to T3, which constitutes a satisfying workflow system.

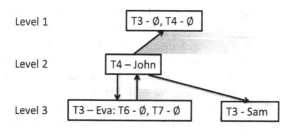

Fig. 4. Addition of a SoD Constraint (T3, T4)

Revocation of Authorization. Problem 4 can directly adopt algorithm 1 by making $PList$ as $x_{ij} : 1 \to 0$, when the authorization of $a_{ij} = 1$ is revoked, which only causes performing constraint conflicts.

To illustrate it, suppose John is forbidden from accessing T3, due to his frequent mistakes on fulling orders, despite his role allows him to access T3. Again, we assume the maximum accepted number of perturbations is 3. An algorithm execution example is shown in Figure 5. At level 1, the assignment of T3 is set as empty due to the authorization revocation. At level 2, Eva is picked and assigned to T3. As a result, the assignment

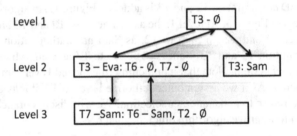

Fig. 5. Revocation of John - T3

of Eva to T6 becomes illegal and is deleted due to the SoD constraint on T3 and T6. Furthermore, the assignment of Eva to T7 has to be deleted due to the BoD constraint on T6 and T7. Then the execution proceeds to level 3. As T6 and T7 are unattended, Sam is selected and assigned to T7. As a result, Sam is assigned to T6 due to the BoD constraint on T6 and T7, and then the assignment of Sam to T2 has to be deleted due to the SoD constraint on T2 and T7. At this point, the number of total perturbation has exceeds 3. So the assignment of Sam to T2 fails. Since the assignment of Eva to T7 was changed at the upper level and is tabued at the current level, so there is no feasible assignment for T7. Then the search moves back. Then, Sam is selected and assigned to T3, which constitutes a satisfying workflow system.

5.4 Branching Heuristics

Branching plays an important role in a search tree algorithm. Indeed, CDCL and DPDL usually refer to a set of algorithms with different branching heuristics. A good branching rule may find a satisfying solution quickly. For instance, consider the example of Figure 5. If we assign Sam to T3 in the first place, then we obtain a satisfying workflow assignment immediately without wasting time on searching other branches. By playing with some synthetic data sets, we find that that in order to find a satisfying solution quickly, a good branching strategy should prioritize an unattended task with more restrictions and a user with more freedom. In particular, we sum up the following experiences.

- *Pick a task with less authorized users.* The motivation is to narrow search space. If there are a few authorized users, then we only need to consider those few options. For instance, considering Figure 2, when Eva is absent and leaves T6 and T7 unattend, we pick T7 over T6. As there are fewer assignment options available for T7, it will be quick for us to reach a conclusion whether the current branch is satisfiable.
- *Pick a task with more associated constraints.* The motivation is also to narrow search space. If we pick a task with more associated constraints, when a user is assigned to the picked task, those associated constraints may be triggered and thus many other personnel assignments are determined through propagation. So we can quickly conclude whether this rout is satisfying.

- *Pick a user with less assignments.* The motivation is to increase the chance of constituting a satisfying solution. By picking a user with less assignments, it would be less likely that the assignment causes conflicts later.
- *Pick a user with less associated constraints.* The motivation is the same as above. By picking a user with less associated constraints, we can assign that person more freely and expect less conflicts later.

Note that algorithm 1 can also be applied to the complex cases that many types of changes occur the same time. As Algorithm 1 requires the beginning perturbation list $PList$ causes performing constraint conflicts only, so we only need to resolve other types of constraint conflicts firstly, e.g. for addition of s_{ijkl} (or b_{ijkl}) delete assignments of $x_{ij} = 1$ and $x_{kl} = 1$.

6 Related Work

The work most related to ours is Basin et al. [5], which studies the optimal workflow adjustment problem. One main difference is that we study the optimal workflow adjustment problem with respect to each specific type of changes, e.g. SoD and BoD, and consider the minimum perturbation to the old workflow system as the objective. Another difference is in the approach to solve the problem. We not only provide SAT model formulations for the studied problems, but also present customized algorithms by modifying the state-of-art SAT algorithms, which should have more practical importance than model formulations, in particular given that the workflow adjustment problems are NP-hard in nature. Another work that is related to ours is the workflow resiliency problem introduced by Wang and Li [17]. They study whether a workflow can be executed successfully if a given number of users is unavailable. Their problem can be viewed as a special case of our dynamic adjustment problem, as they consider only one specific type of changes and have no constraint on the amount of perturbations. In [6], Crampton was the first to study the decision problem whether an allocation of users to tasks exists for a given workflow such that an authorization policy is satisfied . In [17], Wang and Li call it the workflow satisfiability problem and prove it is NP-complete for their authorization model. Some papers, e.g. [3], consider the different delegation models for workflows, which allow the assignment of access rights available to a user to another user. Some papers study the characteristics of SoD and BoD and their impacts the design of an access control system, e.g. [8].

7 Conclusion

In this paper, we formulated and studied the optimal dynamic workflow adjustment problems with respect to various type of changes, including absence of a user, addition of a SoD constraint, addition of a BoD constraint, and revocation of an authorization. We provide SAT model formulations to the studied problems. In addition, we provide customized algorithms inspired by the state-of-art SAT algorithms.

References

1. Appel, K., Haken, W.: Every planar map is four colorable. Illinois Journal of Mathematics 21(3), 429–567 (1977)
2. Atluri, V., Chun, S.A., Mazzoleni, P.: A chinese wall security model for decentralized workflow systems. In: Proceedings of the 8th ACM Conference on Computer and Communications Security, CCS 2001, pp. 48–57. ACM, New York (2001)
3. Atluri, V., Warner, J.: Supporting conditional delegation in secure workflow management systems. In: Proceedings of the Tenth ACM Symposium on Access Control Models and Technologies, SACMAT 2005, pp. 49–58. ACM, New York (2005)
4. Bai, X., Gopal, R., Nunez, M., Zhdanov, D.: On the prevention of fraud and privacy exposure in process information flow. INFORMS J. on Computing 24(3), 416–432 (2012)
5. Basin, D., Burri, S.J., Karjoth, G.: Optimal workflow-aware authorizations. In: Proceedings of the 17th ACM Symposium on Access Control Models and Technologies, SACMAT 2012, pp. 93–102. ACM, New York (2012)
6. Crampton, J.: A reference monitor for workflow systems with constrained task execution. In: Proceedings of the Tenth ACM Symposium on Access Control Models and Technologies, SACMAT 2005, pp. 38–47. ACM, New York (2005)
7. Davis, M., Logemann, G., Loveland, D.: A machine program for theorem-proving. Commun. ACM 5(7), 394–397 (1962)
8. Li, N., Tripunitara, M.V., Bizri, Z.: On mutually exclusive roles and separation-of-duty. ACM Trans. Inf. Syst. Secur. 10(2) (May 2007)
9. Li, N., Tripunitara, M.V., Wang, Q.: Resiliency policies in access control. In: Proceedings of the 13th ACM Conference on Computer and Communications Security, CCS 2006, pp. 113–123. ACM, New York (2006)
10. Lu, H., Vaidya, J., Atluri, V.: Optimal boolean matrix decomposition: Application to role engineering. In: IEEE 24th International Conference on Data Engineering, pp. 297–306 (2008)
11. Lu, H., Vaidya, J., Atluri, V., Hong, Y.: Constraint-aware role mining via extended boolean matrix decomposition. IEEE Transactions on Dependable and Secure Computing 9(5), 655–669 (2012)
12. Moskewicz, M.W., Madigan, C.F., Zhao, Y., Zhang, L., Malik, S.: Chaff: engineering an efficient sat solver. In: Proceedings of the 38th Annual Design Automation Conference, DAC 2001, pp. 530–535. ACM (2001)
13. Sandhu, R.S., Coyne, E.J., Feinstein, H.L., Youman, C.E.: Role-based access control models. Computer 29(2), 38–47 (1996)
14. Silva, J.A.P.M., Sakallah, K.A.: Grasp: a new search algorithm for satisfiability. In: Proceedings of the 1996 IEEE/ACM International Conference on Computer-Aided Design, ICCAD 1996, pp. 220–227. IEEE Computer Society (1996)
15. Stockmeyer, L.: Planar 3-colorability is polynomial complete. SIGACT News 5(3), 19–25 (1973)
16. Vaidya, J., Atluri, V., Guo, Q., Lu, H.: Edge-rmp: Minimizing administrative assignments for role-based access control. Journal of Computer Security 17(2), 211–235 (2009)
17. Wang, Q., Li, N.: Satisfiability and resiliency in workflow authorization systems. ACM Trans. Inf. Syst. Secur. 13(4), 40:1–40:35 (2010)

Consistent Query Plan Generation
in Secure Cooperative Data Access

Meixing Le[1], Krishna Kant[2], and Sushil Jajodia[3]

[1] Cisco Corp.
meile@cisco.com
[2] Temple Univ.
kkant@temple.edu
[3] Geoerge Mason Univ.
jajodia@gmu.edu

Abstract. In this paper, we consider restricted data sharing between a set of parties that wish to provide some set of online services requiring such data sharing. We assume that each party stores its data in private relational databases, and is given a set of mutually agreed set of authorization rules that may involve joins over relations owned by one or more parties. Although the query planning problem in such an environment is similar to the one for distributed databases, the access restrictions introduce significant additional complexity that we address in this paper. We examine the problem of efficiently enforcing rules and generating query execution plans in this environment. Because of the exponential complexity of optimal query planning, our query planning algorithm is heuristics based but produces excellent, if not optimal, results in most of the practical cases.

Keywords: Rule enforcement, Consistent query planning, Cooperative data access.

1 Introduction

Providing rich services to clients with minimal manual intervention or paper documents requires the enterprises involved in the service path to collaborate and share data in an orderly manner. For instance, to enable automated shipping of merchandise and status checking, the e-commerce vendor and shipping company should be able to exchange relevant information, perhaps by enabling queries to retrieve data from each other's databases. Similarly, in order to provide integrated payment and payment status services to the client, the e-commerce vendor needs to share data with the credit card companies or other vendors that specialize in payment processing. There may even be a need for some data sharing between the payment processing and shipping companies so that the issue of payment for shipping can be smoothly handled.

Traditionally, such cross enterprise data access has been implemented in ad hoc ways. In particular, incoming queries may not be allowed to directly access

V. Atluri and G. Pernul (Eds.): DBSec 2014, LNCS 8566, pp. 227–242, 2014.

the databases maintained by a company, and instead handled via some intermediate module. This has the advantage of isolation but could be quite inefficient. More significantly, cross-enterprise data access is typically driven by bilateral agreements between the two parties that no other party knows anything about. While attractive from isolation perspective, such bilateral agreements introduce a high degree of cost, complexity, and inefficiency into the processes. In particular, bilateral agreements may require more data to be exposed to other parties so that it is possible to answer complex queries that require composition of data from multiple parties. Bilateral agreements also rule out possibilities of sharing computation results between parties. For instance, if the e-commerce company needs to get information involving join of data over three parties (e.g., the e-commerce company itself, a warehouse, and a shipping company), under bilateral agreements, we have to bring the relevant data from the other two parties to the e-commerce company first and then do joins. With multiparty interactions enabled, such data may already be available. The purpose of this paper is to explore the general *multi-party collaboration* model and to develop algorithms for safely implementing the authorization rules so that only desired data can be accessed by authorized parties.

We assume that the multi-party data sharing is driven by twin consideration of business need and privacy; therefore, the rules are expected to grant sufficient privileges for answering the agreed upon set of queries but no more. We assume that the collaborating parties generally trust one another and play by the rules. Typically, this would be enforced through legal and financial provisions in the agreements, but there may still be a need to take the "trust-but-verify" approach. The verification issue is beyond the scope of this paper and will be addressed in future work. The purpose of this paper is to focus on efficient mechanisms for executing queries in what amounts to a distributed database with access restrictions. To the best of our knowledge this is the first work of its kind, even though query planning in distributed databases has been considered extensively.

Although the enterprise data may appear in a variety of forms, this paper focuses on the relational model, with *authorization rules* specifying access to certain attributes over individual relations and their meaningful joins (e.g., join over key attributes). For simplicity and schema level treatment, we do not consider tuple selections as part of the rules in this paper. The problem then is to find ways of enforcing the rules and constructing efficient query plans.

Since each party is likely to frame rules from its own perspective, the rules taken together may suffer from inconsistency, unenforceability, and other issues. The consistency problem refers to the fact that if a party is provided access to two relations, say R and S, it is very difficult to prevent it from joining these relations, but the rule may deny access to $R \bowtie S$. Our previous research has addressed this issue [12] and here we simply assume that the rules are *upwards closed*, i.e., access to R and S will automatically enable access to $R \bowtie S$. The enforceability problem can be illustrated as follows: If a party P is given access to $R \bowtie S$ but it and no other party has access to both R and S, it is not possible to actually compute $R \bowtie S$. We have examined this problem in [13]. In some cases, enforceability requires introducing a trusted third party [14] that is given sufficient access rights to perform the operation in question (e.g., $R \bowtie S$ in our example). Third parties bring in their own security risks, and we do not consider them in this paper. We instead focus on generating efficient query plans in an environment without any trusted third parties, and do so in two steps:

1) We examine each authorization rule and check whether the rule can be totally enforced (or implemented) among the collaborating parties. Since this issue has been addressed in [13], we do not focus on this step here.

2) We build a safe and efficient query plan based on the available rule enforcement steps. We discuss the complexity of finding optimal answer in our scenario, and how it differs from classical query processing. We then propose an efficient algorithm that derives query plans based on a greedy heuristic. We prove that our algorithms are both correct and complete, and experimentally show the quality of the results.

The rest of the paper is organized as follows. Following the related work in Section 2, the problem is defined formally in Section 3. Section 4 analyzes the complexity of query planning. Section 5 then describes the algorithm for generating query plans.

2 Related Work

The problem of collaborative data access has been considered in the past, and this has inspired our multi-party collaboration approach. In particular, De-Capitani, et.al. [7] consider such a model and discuss an algorithm to check if a query with a given query plan tree can be safely executed. However, this work does not address the problem of how the given rules are implemented and how the query plan trees are generated. The same authors have also proposed a possible architecture for the collaborative data access in [8] but this work does not address query planning. As we shall show shortly, *regular query optimizers cannot be used here since they do not comprehend access restrictions and may fail to generate some possible query plans.*

There are also existing works on distributed query processing under protection requirements [4,15] which consider a limited access pattern called binding pattern. It is assumed that the accessible data is based on some input data. For instance, a party can provide names and ID's of some individuals, it may be allowed to access their medical records. This is a completely different model from ours. There are also many classical works on query processing in centralized and distributed systems [3,11,5], but they do not deal with constraints from the data owners, which differs from our work.

Answering queries that takes advantage of materialized views is another well investigated research direction. Some of these works focus on query optimization [9] which use materialized views to further optimize existing query plans. In our case, we need to generate a query plan from scratch. Some works use views for maintaining physical data independence and for data integration [16]. They assume the scenario where data is organized in different formats and comes from different sources, and accessing data via views may not provide the complete information to answer the queries. Using authorization views for fine-grained access control is discussed in [17], and [19] analyzed the query containment problem under such access control model. Similarly, conjunctive queries are used to evaluate the query equivalence and information containment, and the work [10] presented several theoretical results. Compared to these works, our data model is homogeneous across the parties, and our authorization model not only puts constraints based on relational views but also the interactions among collaborating parties. Consequently, generating a query plan in our scenario is even more complicated. Some results from these works can be complementary to our work and can be used to further optimize the query plans generated by our approach. However, this is out of the scope of this paper.

In addition, there are services such as Sovereign joins [2] to provide third party join services; we can think this as one possible third party model in our scenario. There is also some research [1,6,18] about how to secure the data for out-sourced database services. These methods are also useful for enforcing the authorization rules, but we consider the scenario without any involvement of third parties.

3   Problem and Definitions

We consider a group of collaborating parties each with its own relational database but with collectively known key attributes and authorizations that allow for useful joins among the tables. We assume that the join schema is also collectively known, and we only consider select-project-join (SPJ) queries. To enable working at the schema level, selections are treated like projections (i.e., attributes mentioned in selection predicates are assumed to be accessible). We also allow an incoming query to be answered by any party that has the required authorizations. The basic query planning problem is as follows: Given a set of authorization rules $\mathcal{R}$ on n cooperating parties, and a query q authorized by $\mathcal{R}$, find an efficient query execution plan for q that is consistent with the rules $\mathcal{R}$.

3.1   A Running Example

In the following, we use a running e-commerce scenario with four parties: (a) *E-commerce*, denoted as E, is a company that sells products online, (b) *Customer_Service*, denoted C, that provides customer service functions (potentially for more than one Company), (c) *Shipping*, denoted S, provides shipping services (again, potentially to multiple companies), and finally (d) *Warehouse*, denoted W, is the party that provides storage services. To keep the example simple, we assume that each party owns but one table described as follows. In reality, each party may have several tables that are available for collaborative access, in addition to those that are entirely private and thus not relevant for collaborative query processing.

1. E-commerce (<u>order_id</u>, product_id, total) as E
2. Customer_Service (<u>order_id</u>, issue, agent) as C
3. Shipping (<u>order_id</u>, addr, delivery_type) as S
4. Warehouse (<u>product_id</u>, location) as W

The relations are self-explanatory, with underlined attributes indicating the key attributes. In the following, we use *oid* to denote *order_id* for short, *pid* for *product_id*, and *delivery* for *delivery_type*. The possible join schema is given in figure 1. Relations E, C, S can join over their common attribute *oid*; relation E can join with W over the attribute *pid*. The relations are in BCNF, and the only FD (Functional Dependency) in each relation is the underlined key attribute determining the non-key attributes. To keep our discussion simple, we do not consider foreign keys in this paper. Foreign keys are unlikely to be used for linking data across organizational boundaries; nevertheless, our model can be easily extended to consider foreign key constraints.

3.2 Definitions and Authorization Model

An authorization rule r_t is a triple $[A_t, J_t, P_t]$, where J_t is called the join path of the rule, A_t is the authorized attribute set, and P_t is the party authorized to access the data.

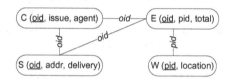

Fig. 1. The given join schema for the example

Definition 1. *A* **join path** J_t *is the result of a series of joins over the relations* $JR_t = \{R_1, R_2...R_n\}$ *with specified equi-join predicates* $(A_{l1}, A_{r1}), (A_{l2}, A_{r2})...$ (A_{ln}, A_{rn}) *among them, where* (A_{li}, A_{ri}) *are the lists of join attributes from two relations. The* **length** *of a join path is the cardinality of* JR_t.

The authorized attributes is given by A_t part of the rule r_t, which we assume to include all key attributes as well. Table 1 shows all the rules in our example system. (The last column specifies the party to which the authorization is given.) Since our analysis does not deal with selections directly, all attributes appearing in selection predicates are treated as projection attributes. Thus, a query q can be represented by a pair $[A_q, J_q]$, where A_q is the set of attributes appearing in the Selection and Projection predicates. For instance, the SQL query "**q**: Select $oid, total, addr$ From E Join S On $E.oid = S.oid$ Where $delivery = $ 'ground'" can be represented as the pair $[A_q, J_q]$, where A_q is the set $\{oid, total, addr, delivery\}$; J_q is the join path $E \bowtie_{oid} S$. We say $J_i \cong J_j$ (join path equivalence) if any tuple in J_i appears in J_j and vice versa. Then, a query q is **authorized** if there exists a rule r_t such that $J_t \cong J_q$ and $A_q \subseteq A_t$. In other words, the rule and the authorized query must have the equivalent join paths.

To answer a query that is authorized by the rules, we still need a **query execution plan** (or "query plan" for short) where each of the steps corresponds to an authorized and realizable operation. In our model, the query execution plan pl can also be represented with a triple $[A_{pl}, J_{pl}, P_{pl}]$ just like a rule. Here, the join path not only for local joins but also counts the data transmitted between the parties as we will discuss later. For this plan to be valid, it is necessary that $J_{pl} \cong J_q$ and $A_q \subseteq A_{pl}$. We introduce the notion of consistent query

Table 1. Auth. rules for running Example

#	Authorized attribute set	Auth. Join Path	To
1	{pid, location}	W	P_W
2	{oid, pid}	E	P_W
3	{oid, pid, location}	$E \bowtie_{pid} W$	P_W
4	{oid, pid, total}	E	P_E
5	{oid, pid, total, issue}	$E \bowtie_{oid} C$	P_E
6	{oid, pid, total, issue, addr}	$S \bowtie_{oid} E \bowtie_{oid} C$	P_E
7	{oid, pid, location, total, addr}	$S \bowtie_{oid} E \bowtie_{pid} W$	P_E
8	{oid, pid, issue, agent, total, addr, delivery}	$S \bowtie_{oid} E \bowtie_{oid} C \bowtie_{pid} W$	P_E
9	{oid, addr, delivery}	S	P_S
10	{oid, pid, total}	E	P_S
11	{oid, pid, total, addr, delivery}	$E \bowtie_{oid} S$	P_S
12	{oid, pid, total, location}	$E \bowtie_{pid} W$	P_S
13	{oid, location, pid, total, addr, delivery}	$S \bowtie_{oid} E \bowtie_{pid} W$	P_S
14	{oid, pid}	E	P_C
15	{oid, issue, agent}	C	P_C
16	{oid, pid, issue, agent}	$E \bowtie_{oid} C$	P_C
17	{oid, pid, issue, agent, total, addr, location}	$S \bowtie_{oid} C \bowtie_{oid} P_C$ $E \bowtie_{pid} W$	P_C

plan next, and only consistent plans are considered safe to answer the queries.

The desired query plan can be represented hierarchically where at each level, a number of sub-plans are combined to get the next higher level plan. The access plans for basic relations owned by the parties form the bottom level in this structure. For instance, there is a query plan to retrieve all the information of rule r_3 in Table 1, and such a plan contains a join over two subplans based on rules r_1 and r_2 respectively. The subplan for r_1 is to access table W on P_W. The subplan for r_2 is an access plan reading table S at P_S, and another operation transmitting the data from P_S to P_W. The example plan authorized by r_3 has the $J_{pl} = E \bowtie_{pid} W$, and $A_{pl} = \{oid, pid, location\}$. We say a rule r_t **authorizes** ($\succeq$) a plan pl, if $J_{pl} \cong J_t$, $P_{pl} = P_t$, and $A_{pl} \subseteq A_t$.

Definition 2. *An operation in a query plan is* **consistent** *with the given rules* $\mathcal{R}$, *if for the operation, there exist rules that authorize access to the input tuples of the operation and to the resulting output tuples.*

For the three types of operations in our scenario, we give the corresponding conditions for consistent operation.

1. For a projection (π) to be consistent with the rule set $\mathcal{R}$, there must be a rule r_p that authorizes ($\succeq$) the input information.
2. Join ($\bowtie$) is a binary operation where two input subplans pl_{i1} and pl_{i2} produce the resulting plan $pl_o = pl_{i1} \bowtie pl_{i2}$. For a join operation to be consistent with $\mathcal{R}$, all the three plans need to be authorized by rules. Since join is performed at a single party, and rules are upwards closed, if the input plans are authorized by rules, the join operation is consistent.
3. Data transmission ($\rightarrow$) involves an input plan pl_i on a party P_i and an output plan pl_o for a party $P_o \neq P_i$. If there are rules $r_i, r_o \in R$ with equivalent

join paths (i.e., $J_i \cong J_o$), and $r_i \succeq pl_i, r_o \succeq pl_o$, then the data transmission operation is consistent with $\mathcal{R}$.[1]

For our example, rule r_8 authorizes P_E to get information on the join path $(S \bowtie E \bowtie C \bowtie W)$. Also note that although the attribute set of rule r_{11} is contained in that of rule r_8, there is no rule for P_E to get these attributes on the join path of $(E \bowtie S)$. Therefore, party S, the owner of rule r_{11} cannot send these attributed to P_E.

Definition 3. *A query execution plan pl is* **consistent** *with the rules* $\mathcal{R}$, *if for each step of the operation in the plan is consistent with the given rule set* $\mathcal{R}$.

3.3   Inadequacy of Classical Query Planning

Generating a consistent plan that answers an authorized query in our scenario is much more complex than the well studied problem of query planning for distributed databases (without any access restrictions). We illustrate this by an example. Suppose that there are two collaborating parties P_R and P_S with database schemas $R(\underline{A}, B, C)$, and $S(\underline{A}, D, E)$ respectively (A is the key attribute for both relations). The party P_R has an authorization rule $r_R = \{A, B, C, D\}, R \bowtie S$ (in addition to access to its own data). The party P_S has two authorization rules: $r_{S1} = \{A, B\}, R$ and $r_{S2} = \{A, B, C, D, E\}, R \bowtie S$. Let us now consider how to generate a consistent plan to answer a query for $\{A, B, C, D, E\}$ over the join path of $R \bowtie S$.

In classical query planning, we will generate a query plan tree and try to assign the appropriate operations to different parties. There is no constraint of data access in classical case. Therefore, either party P_R or P_S can retrieve the other relation and do the join to answer the query. From performance considerations, semi-joins [11] are usually used in the distributed query processing. However, in our case, even a semi-join is not enough to generate the consistent query plan for the query. It is clear that neither P_R and P_S can obtain the desired result with just one join. If we use the semi-join method, the only possibility is that P_R sends $\{A\}$ to P_S; P_S does the join and ships $\{A, D\}, R \bowtie S$ back to P_R, which then computes $\{A, B, C, D\}, R \bowtie S$ by doing another join. This, in turn is passed back to party P_S, which then obtains the desired result. In contrast, if we use regular join, then party P_S can have at best the attributes $\{A, B, D, E\}, R \bowtie S$ through one join operation.

To generate the consistent plan for answering the query, it is required that we do the semi-join first, and party P_R again sends the $\{A, B, C\}, R \bowtie S$ to party P_S. Another join operation at party P_S could then give the required query results. Figure 2 illustrates the situation. Each box is a rule, and the authorization rule that authorizes the query is in dashed box. The numbers on the arrows indicate the ordered steps for the consistent query plan. It is clear that generating

---

[1] If P_i is sending information with attributes not in A_o, P_i should do a projection operation $\pi_{A_o}(pl_i)$ first.

a consistent query plan under the data access constraints can be lot more complicated than for distributed query planning. In the following section, we show the complication of query processing in cooperative data access environment.

4   Complexity of Query Planning

From performance perspective, we always want consistent and optimal query plans with minimal costs. Unfortunately, finding the optimal query plan is *NP-hard* in such a cooperative data access scenario.

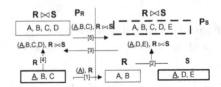

Fig. 2. Illustration of Query Planning

Theorem 1. *Finding the optimal query plan to answer an authorized query is NP-hard.*

Proof. The optimization of set covering problem is known to be NP-hard. In the set covering problem, there is a set of elements $U = \{A_1, A_2, ..., A_n\}$, and there is also a set of subsets $S = \{S_1, S_2, ...S_m\}$ where S_i is a set of elements from U and is assigned a cost. The task is to find a subset of S, say C, that has minimal total cost and covers all the attributes in set U. We can convert this set covering problem into the cooperative query planning problem and thereby prove that the optimal query planning problem is also NP-hard.

Consider 2 basic relations R and S which can join together over a key attribute A_0, distinct from the element set U that we will also use as attributes in our construction. We assign all the attributes in U to relation R, which will have the schema $\{A_0, A_1, A_2, ..., A_n\}$. For each S_i in S, we make an authorization rule $\{A_0, S_i\}$ on relation S. Thus, for $m + 1$ parties, $P_0, P_1 ... P_n$ have the following authorization rules:

1. Party P_0 owns R and has a rule r_0 that authorizes the desired query for retrieving the entire set U over the join path $J = R \bowtie (\bowtie_{i=1}^n S_i)$. Note that P_0 cannot unilaterally obtain the join path J.
2. Each of the other parties P_i, $i = 1 ... n$, has a rule r_i on the relation S with attributes $S_i \bigcup \{A_0\}$.

Note that P_0 cannot locally do the join $R \bowtie S$, but other parties can enforce their rules r_i locally, and their costs are known. Therefore, for P_0 to answer the query, it needs a plan bringing attributes from other parties and merging them at P_0 (multi-way join on attribute A_0) to answer the query. The optimal plan needs to choose the rules with minimal costs, and the union of their attribute sets must cover the query attribute set. If the optimal query plan can be found in polynomial time, the set covering problem also has a polynomial solution, which proves the assertion.   □

4.1 Query Plan Cost Model

It is reasonable to assume that the number of tuples in the relations are known. Assuming we have the historical statistic information of the tables, so we can estimate the join results accurately. The notion of *join selectivity* [11], a number between 0 and 1.0 provides an estimate for the size of the joined relation. We assumed that the join selectivity between the relations are known so that the number of tuples in a join path can be estimated.

The cost of a query plan mainly includes two parts: 1) cost of the join operations, and 2) cost of data transmission among the parties. We assume joins are done by nested loop and indices on join attributes are available. Let $Size()$ denote the number of tuples in the relation, and $Pages()$ is the number of pages in the relation. Consider two relations R and S, of which R is the smaller one, i.e., $Size(R) < Size(S)$. Let α denote the output cost of generating each tuple in the results, and let $P_{(X,Y)}$ denote the known join selectivity. Let β denote the per I/O cost. Assuming the cost of finding matching tuples in S is 1. Then the cost of a join operation between R and S can be estimated as:

$$\alpha(Size(R) * Size(S) * P_{(R,S)}) + \beta(Pages(R) + Size(R) * 1)$$

The costs of data transmission is only decided by the size of the data being shipped. Let γ denote the per tuple cost for data transmission. Then the cost of moving $R \bowtie S$ from a party to another is given by: $\gamma(Size(R) * Size(S) * P_{(R,S)})$

It is worth noticing that our algorithm does not tie to any specified cost model, this is one easy cost model that we can adopt.

4.2 Enumerating All Query Plans

Unlike classical query planning, we face a number of hurdles, as illustrated next. To generate a consistent plan for a query, we first need a plan that enforces the query join path. This can be further joined with other plans to get all the requested attributes. Obviously, in order to consider a join path of length n, one needs to consider all top level join subpaths of with lengths k and $n - k$ for suitable values of k. Unfortunately, this is insufficient. Since a longer join path will generally produce relations with fewer tuples, it is often desirable to consider joins of overlapping relations in cooperative data access environment. For instance, generating a join path of $R \bowtie S \bowtie T$ may be better done as $(R \bowtie S) \bowtie (S \bowtie T)$ instead of, say, $(R \bowtie S) \bowtie (T)$. It all depends on the authorization rules setting in the environment as well as the sizes of relations and costs of operations.

An added difficulty is that we can't just pick the subpaths based on the join cost – we also need to pay attention to the attributes we are able to access by doing the join. For instance, if the goal is to answer $\{A, B, C, D\}$ on join path $R \bowtie S \bowtie T$, we may have two ways of getting it: (a) A subplan pl_1 that yields that attribute set $\{A, B\}$, and (b) A higher cost subplan pl_2 that yields the attribute set $\{A, C, D\}$. Since we need more work to get missing attributes, at this stage we can't even pick one of these, and instead must keep both. Thus, in general, we need to maintain many "partial" plans. For each such partial plan, we then need to consider the problem of retrieving the missing attributes. This, in turn, requires checking all possible combinations of relevant rules, followed by a recursive procedure to find enforcement plan for the chosen relevant rules. It is clear that the exhaustive enumerate to find the globally optimal answer can be extremely expensive.

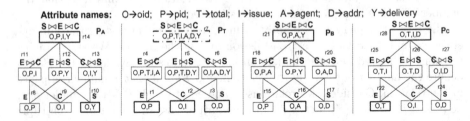

Fig. 3. A simple worst case example

We illustrate the complexity of exhaustive enumeration via the case of join path length of 3 for our running example. In figure 3, there are four parties P_A, P_T, P_B, P_C and they all have rules on equivalent join paths. The attribute names are simplified to save space. In the example, an incoming query asks for all the attributes $\{O, P, T, I, A, D, Y\}$ on $(S \bowtie E \bowtie C)$ and only r_7 (dashed box) can authorize the query.

Although there are many ways to enforce the query join path $S \bowtie E \bowtie C$, none of them can totally enforce all the query attributes. The possible ways to enforce the join path locally on P_t is $3*(1+2) = 9$ (each join path of length 2 can join with other two rules of length 2 and one rule of length 1). Considering other 3 parties, we have $(3 * 4 * (1 + 2 * 4)) * 4 = 432$ (considering join across parties) different ways of enforcing the join path, and these plans result in 10 different missing attribute sets (although there are many enforcement plans, many of their enforced attribute sets are overlapped). For each of them, we need to check the ways to get missing attributes. For example, if the missing attribute set is $\{total, agent, delivery\}$. Then, there are 12 relevant rules having the missing attributes, and the possible combinations to consider are $2^{12}-1$.

5   Consistent Query Planning

Due to the difficulties in enumerating all possible ways of answering a query, we consider using a greedy algorithm.

5.1   Greedy Query Planning Algorithm

To find an efficient consistent query plan, we always choose the optimal query plan to enforce the join path first, and then apply greedy set covering mechanism on the missing attributes (the attributes cannot be enforced with the join path enforcement plan) to find required relevant rules (rules authorize subplans for the complete query plan). The optimal enforcement plan for a join path on a specified party can be pre-determined by extending the rule enforcement checking algorithm in a dynamic programming way [13]. As discussed, the selected plan usually results in a missing attribute set. To get these attributes, we explore the graph structure to decompose the target rule r_t (the rule authorizes the incoming query q) into a set of relevant rules that can provide these attributes. We record the required operations among these rules, and then recursively find ways to enforce these rules to generate a query plan.

As the join path enforcement plan enforces J_t, it can be extended to get missing attributes that appear in the relevant rules of basic relations on all J_t-**cooperative parties** (cooperative parities which have authorization rules on join path J_t). This can be done through semi-join operations. In such cases, the party P_t can send only the join attributes to its J_t-cooperative party, and the receiving party does a local join to get these attributes and send it back. P_t then performs another join to add these attributes to the query plan. The remaining missing attributes can always be found in the relevant rules on J_t-cooperative parties. However, these relevant rules are defined on join paths instead of basic relations. Similar to the above case, the missing attributes carried by these relevant rules can be brought to the final plan by performing semi-join operations.

The next step is to determine these **relevant rules** (rules can provide missing attributes and the join paths include a subset of relations of J_t). Here, we always pick the relevant rule that covers the most attributes in the missing attribute set until all the missing attributes are covered by the picked rules. This is a greedy approach, and is similar in spirit to the approximate algorithms used for the set covering problem. The relevant rules effectively allow us to decompose the rule (i.e., express in terms of) rules with smaller join paths. The missing attributes are also reduced in the process by considering the rules involving basic relations. During the decomposition, the algorithm associates the set of attributes with the decomposed rule that are the missing attributes expected to be delivered by this rule. We record the operations between the existing plan and these decomposed ones. If they are on the same party, a join operation between them is recorded. Otherwise, a semi-join operation is recorded. Since each decomposed rule can be further decomposed, the algorithm uses a queue to process the rules until all the rules are on basic relations. This decomposition process gives the hierarchal relationships among rules that indicate how required attributes can be added to the final plan. After this step, the query plan is going to use all the attributes that available locally (all the picked relevant rules on the same party P_t), and it removes these duplicate attributes (non-key attributes) from remote parties (via projections).

The decomposition process gives a set of rules, but we also need the subplans to enforce the join paths of these rules so as to generate a complete plan. To achieve that, we inspect the join paths of these decomposed rules from bottom-up. We use another priority queue to keep all the join paths from the decomposed relevant rules, and the shortest join path is always processed first. This allows the use of results from the enforcement plans of sub join paths as much as possible. The algorithm uses the best enforcement plan for each join path as discussed. When an enforcement plan of a join path is retrieved, the algorithm combines previously recorded operations to generate the subplan for the decomposed rule on such join path. Finally, the algorithm finds the plans for each join paths in the queue, and generates the final query plan with a series of ordered operations starting from the basic relations. The entire process is summarized in Algorithm 4.

5.2 Properties of the Algorithm

In this section we show that the query planning algorithm is correct.

Theorem 2. *A query plan generated by Query Planning Algorithm is consistent with the set of rules* $\mathcal{R}$.

The proof is omitted as it's straightforward according to our definition of query plan consistency.

5.3 Preliminary Performance Evaluation of the Algorithm

Require: The structure of rule set $\mathcal{R}$, Incoming query q
Ensure: Generate a plan answering q.
1.   **if** There is a rule r_t, $J_t \cong J_q$ and $A_q \subseteq A_t$ **then**
2.   Missing attribute set $A_m \leftarrow A_q$
3.   Initialize queue Q, and priority queue P
4.   Enqueue r_t to Q with A_m
5.   **while** Queue Q is not empty **do**
6.   Dequeue rule r_t and the associated A_m
7.   **for** Each J_t-cooperative party **do**
8.   Finds the attribute set A_b from basic relations
9. $A_m \leftarrow A_m \setminus A_b$
10.   Record connections between r_b and r_t
11.   **while** $A_m \neq \emptyset$ **do**
12.   **for** Each relevant rule r_s on P_{co} **do**
13.   Find the rule with max $A_m \cap A_s$
14.   Enqueue the rule r_s with $\pi(A_m)$
15.   Enqueue the join path J_s to priority queue P
16.   Record connections between r_s and r_t
17. $A_m = A_m \setminus A_s$
18.   **while** The priority queue P is not empty **do**
19.   Dequeue the rule r_s with join path J_s
20.   Add the path to enforce J_s to plan
21.   **for** Each J_s-cooperative party **do**
22.   **if** The party has recorded A_b on J_s **then**
23.   Add ($\bowtie$ / $\rightarrow$) operations between r_b and r_s
24.   **for** Each decomposed rule r_d from r_s **do**
25.   Add ($\bowtie$ / $\rightarrow$) operations between r_d and r_s
26. **else**
27.   The query q cannot be answered

Fig. 4. Query Planning Algorithm

Finding a globally optimal query plan is not only NP-hard for the situation we are considering, it is also extremely difficult to systematically and efficiently enumerate all possible cases with large number of parties and rules. In view of this and the space limitations of the paper, we only illustrate comparative performance for the following three situations, all relating to our running e-commerce example.

Here we assume that the selected join path enforcement plan carries the maximal attributes along with it. Since we do not have any assumptions on the sizes of the relations and join selectivities between them, we cannot calculate the exact costs of the plans to compare the them. For simplicity, we use the number of joins as the metric to evaluate the efficiency of the plans. This would be a good representation of actual cost if all the relations have roughly the same size.

Example 1. Consider the situation in figure 3 and given the same query discussed before which only rule r_7 can authorize, the *optimal* plan should be as follows: join the three rules on basic relations which are r_1, r_2, r_3 at P_t to enforce the join path of $S \bowtie E \bowtie C$ with attribute set $\{oid, pid, issue, addr\}$. Then P_t sends the *oid* on the join path of $S \bowtie E \bowtie C$ to other three parties P_A, P_B, P_C, and does semi-joins with each of the party to obtain the missing attributes $\{total, agent, delivery\}$ one from each party. Finally, P_t does a local join with this information got from remote parties and such a plan answering the query. The related rules for the consistent query plan are marked using bold boxes in the figure. In this case study, our greedy algorithm generates the same optimal plan. The optimal way to enforce join path $S \bowtie E \bowtie C$ is the local enforcement at P_t, and our plan also gets the missing attributes via semi-join operations. Note that manually finding the optimal plan is easy only under the assumption that all the relations are of the same size.

Example 2. Consider a query with the join path $S \bowtie C \bowtie E \bowtie W$, and an attribute set that includes every attribute of rule r_8 except *delivery*. Figure 5 illustrates the rules corresponding to our running example. Unrelated rules are removed, and rules on

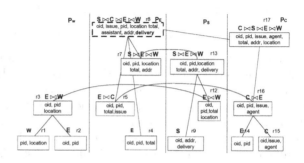

Fig. 5. Simplified relevance graph

the graph are applied in the generated query plan. For such a query, our algorithm first finds the optimal way to enforce the join path, which can be represented as

$$[((r_1 \bowtie r_2 \to P_S) \bowtie r_9) \to P_E] \bowtie [r_{14} \bowtie r_{15} \to P_E] \tag{1}$$

This plan results in a missing attribute set $\{total, agent\}$. Next, the algorithm adds a local join with rule r_4 to retrieve *total*, and a semi-join with rule r_{16} to obtain the attribute *agent* because P_E and P_C are J_8-cooperative parties (J_8 is equivalent to J_{17}). Here, r_{16} is enforced during the join path enforcement. In figure 5, the solid lined between rules indicates the steps for enforcing the query join path, and the dashed lines are the operations for retrieving missing attributes. The dashed box shows the rule r_8 which authorizes the query. In fact, there are only two ways to enforce the query join path in this example. The other way is to perform $r_9 \bowtie r_{10}$ first and then join with r_{12} at party P_S. By doing that, the plan can carry the attribute *total* and only has *agent* as missing attribute. However, if we compare the two plans, the difference is that our plan gets the attribute *total* via a join among relation E and join path $S \bowtie C \bowtie E \bowtie W$, and the latter plan performs the join among E and S at party P_S. Since the longer join path usually has fewer tuples, the former plan is better. As for the missing attribute *agent*, it can only be retrieved from party P_S, and getting it from r_{16} is better than r_{15}. Therefore, the query plan generated by our algorithm is again the optimal plan.

Example 3. Here we consider a situation where the algorithm does not produce an optimal plan. Consider a query which is the same as rule r_4. As shown in figure 6, the bold boxes are used in enforcing the query join path $S \bowtie E \bowtie C$ by our algorithm, which is

$$[(r_8 \bowtie r_9 \to P_T) \bowtie r_1] \qquad (2)$$

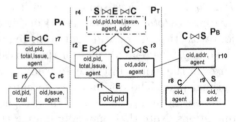

Fig. 6. A simple non-optimal example

The other way to enforce it is to enforce rule r_7 at party P_A first, and send the results to party P_T to enforce R_2 and join with R_3. That is

$$[(r_8 \bowtie r_9 \to P_T) \bowtie (r_5 \bowtie r_6 \to P_T)] \qquad (3)$$

As the latter plan requires one more join and data transmission operation, our plan to enforce the query join path appears better. However, the latter plan has no missing attribute, and our plan needs to enforce rule r_7 again to retrieve attributes $\{total, issue\}$ which includes more operations. Therefore, our plan is not optimal in this case. However, compared to the optimal plan, our generated plan only has one extra step involving r_1 joining with r_3, which means that the cost difference between the two plans is likely not significant.

Due to the space limitations, we have listed only 3 detailed case studies here. In addition, we have evaluated other example queries based on our running example given in Table 1. Table 2 lists seven other examples. The second column shows the queries in "attribute set, join path" format, and the third column shows the consistent query plans generated by our algorithm. The symbols π, $\bowtie$ and $\to$ correspond to the projection, join and data transmission operations. The last column shows whether the generated query plan is optimal, and it turns out that the plan is indeed optimal in all seven cases. This is typical of the behavior we have seen so far, although because of the complexities generating optimal query plans we have so far been unable to generate and test cases in large numbers. We, however, believe that the algorithm does produce optimal or near optimal solution in nearly all practical situations.

Complexity of the Algorithm. Assuming N_q rules are locally relevant to the query q, the number of relevant rules on J_t-cooperative parties is N_r, and C is a constant to record operations. The overall worst case complexity of our greedy algorithm is $O(N_q * N_r^2 * C)$, which is $O(N^3)$ (N is the total number of rules).

Table 2. Illustration of quality of some generated query plans

#	Example Query	Gerenated Query Plan	Optimal?
1	{oid, pid, location}, $E \bowtie W$	$r_1 \bowtie r_2$ on P_W	Yes
2	{oid, pid, total, issue}, $E \bowtie C$	$(\pi(oid)r_{14} \bowtie \pi(oid, issue)r_{15} \to P_E) \bowtie r_4$	Yes
3	{oid, pid, total, addr}, $E \bowtie S$	$\pi(oid, addr)r_9 \bowtie \pi(oid, pid, total)r_{10}$	Yes
4	{oid, pid, total, delivery}, $S \bowtie E \bowtie W$	$(\pi(pid)r_1 \bowtie r_2 \to P_S) \bowtie \pi(oid, delivery)r_9 \bowtie \pi(oid, total)r_{10}$	Yes
5	{oid, pid, total, addr}, $S \bowtie E \bowtie W$	$((\pi(pid)r_1 \bowtie r_2 \to P_S) \bowtie \pi(oid, addr)r_9 \to P_E) \bowtie \pi(oid, total)r_4$	Yes
6	{oid, pid, total, addr}, $S \bowtie C \bowtie E \bowtie W$	$((\pi(pid)r_1 \bowtie r_2 \to P_S) \bowtie \pi(oid, addr)r_9 \to P_E) \bowtie (\pi(oid)r_{14} \bowtie \pi(oid, issue)r_{15} \to P_E)\pi(oid, total)r_4$	Yes
7	{oid, pid, agent}, $S \bowtie C \bowtie E \bowtie W$	$((\pi(pid)r_1 \bowtie r_2 \to P_S) \bowtie \pi(oid)r_9 \to P_E) \bowtie (\pi(oid)r_{14} \bowtie \pi(oid, agent)r_{15} \to P_E) \to P_C$	Yes

6 Conclusions and Future Work

In previous research work, a flexible data authorization model has been proposed to meet the security requirements for collaborative computing among different data owners in a collaborative environment. A regular query optimizer cannot give consistent query plans under the constraints of these rules. In this paper, we propose an algorithm to generate corresponding efficient consistent query plans for answerable queries.

For the future work, we will study the problem of making the unenforceable rules to be enforceable. We can consider using a trusted third party to enforce the rules, and we may also augment the given set of rules. Trusted third parties can be also used to improve the consistent query planning. To evaluate of our approaches comprehensively, we will study the cooperative relationships among enterprises in various real world scenarios, and test our mechanism under these cases. In addition, we will investigate the problem where data are horizontally fragmented and distributed among different parties, which adds selection to the picture. In fact, extension of the model to include limited forms of selection is one area that we wish to pursue in the future. We also plan to extend our model to more general applications that involve non-numeric data (e.g., textual or image data) where the regular join operation may be not be the most interesting operation. Finally, we wish to examine the issue of verifying whether the collaborative parties are really following the rules as advertised or may be behaving in undesirable ways.

References

1. Aggarwal, G., Bawa, M., Ganesan, P., Garcia-Molina, H., Kenthapadi, K., Motwani, R., Srivastava, U., Thomas, D., Xu, Y.: Two can keep A secret: A distributed architecture for secure database services. In: CIDR, pp. 186–199 (2005)
2. Agrawal, R., Asonov, D., Kantarcioglu, M., Li, Y.: Sovereign joins. In: Proceedings of the 22nd International Conference on Data Engineering, ICDE 2006, Atlanta, GA, USA, April 3-8, p. 26. IEEE Computer Society (2006)

3. Bernstein, P.A., Goodman, N., Wong, E., Reeve, C.L., Rothnie Jr., J.B.: Query processing in a system for distributed databases (SDD-1). ACM Transactions on Database Systems 6(4), 602–625 (1981)

4. Calì, A., Martinenghi, D.: Querying data under access limitations. In: Proceedings of the 24th International Conference on Data Engineering, ICDE 2008, Cancún, México, April 7-12, pp. 50–59. IEEE (2008)

5. Chaudhuri, S.: An overview of query optimization in relational systems. In: Proceedings of the 7th ACM SIGACT-SIGMOD-SIGART Symposium on Principles of Database Systems, pp. 34–43 (1998)

6. Ciriani, V., De Capitani di Vimercati, S., Foresti, S., Jajodia, S., Paraboschi, S., Samarati, P.: Keep a few: Outsourcing data while maintaining confidentiality. In: Backes, M., Ning, P. (eds.) ESORICS 2009. LNCS, vol. 5789, pp. 440–455. Springer, Heidelberg (2009)

7. De Capitani di Vimercati, S., Foresti, S., Jajodia, S., Paraboschi, S., Samarati, P.: Controlled information sharing in collaborative distributed query processing. In: ICDCS 2008, Beijing, China (June 2008)

8. De Capitani di Vimercati, S., Foresti, S., Jajodia, S., Paraboschi, S., Samarati, P.: Authorization enforcement in distributed query evaluation. Journal of Computer Security 19(4), 751–794 (2011)

9. Goldstein, J., Larson, P.: Optimizing queries using materialized views: a practical, scalable solution. In: Proceedings of the 2001 ACM SIGMOD International Conference on Management of Data, pp. 331–342 (2001)

10. Halevy, A.Y.: Answering queries using views: A survey. VLDB Journal 10(4), 270–294 (2001)

11. Kossmann, D.: The state of the art in distributed query processing. ACM Computer Survey 32(4), 422–469 (2000)

12. Le, M., Kant, K., Jajodia, S.: Access rule consistency in cooperative data access environment. In: 8th International Conference on Collaborative Computing: Networking, Applications and Worksharing (CollaborateCom2012), pp. 11–20 (October 2012)

13. Le, M., Kant, K., Jajodia, S.: Consistency and enforcement of access rules in cooperative data sharing environment. In: Computers and Security (November 2013)

14. Le, M., Kant, K., Jajodia, S.: Rule enforcement with third parties in secure cooperative data access. In: Wang, L., Shafiq, B. (eds.) DBSec 2013. LNCS, vol. 7964, pp. 282–288. Springer, Heidelberg (2013)

15. Li, C.: Computing complete answers to queries in the presence of limited access patterns. VLDB Journal 12(3), 211–227 (2003)

16. Pottinger, R., Halevy, A.Y.: Minicon: A scalable algorithm for answering queries using views. VLDB J. 10(2-3), 182–198 (2001)

17. Rizvi, S., Mendelzon, A., Sudarshan, S., Roy, P.: Extending query rewriting techniques for fine-grained access control. In: Proceedings of the 2004 ACM SIGMOD International Conference on Management of Data, SIGMOD 2004 (2004)

18. Sion, R.: Query execution assurance for outsourced databases. In: VLDB, pp. 601–612. ACM (2005)

19. Zhang, Z., Mendelzon, A.O.: Authorization Views and Conditional Query Containment. In: Eiter, T., Libkin, L. (eds.) ICDT 2005. LNCS, vol. 3363, pp. 259–273. Springer, Heidelberg (2005)

Hunting the Unknown
White-Box Database Leakage Detection

Elisa Costante[1], Jerry den Hartog[1], Milan Petković[1,2], Sandro Etalle[1,3],
and Mykola Pechenizkiy[1]

[1] Eindhoven University of Technology, The Netherlands
{e.costante,j.d.hartog,m.petkovic,s.etalle,m.pechenizkiy}@tue.nl
[2] Philips Research Europe, High Tech Campus, The Netherlands
[3] University of Twente, The Netherlands

Abstract. Data leakage causes significant losses and privacy breaches worldwide. In this paper we present a *white-box* data leakage detection system to spot anomalies in database transactions. We argue that our approach represents a major leap forward w.r.t. previous work because: i) it significantly decreases the False Positive Rate (FPR) while keeping the Detection Rate (DR) high; on our experimental dataset, consisting of millions of real enterprise transactions, we measure a FPR that is orders of magnitude lower than in state-of-the-art comparable approaches; and ii) the white-box approach allows the creation of self-explanatory and easy to update profiles able to explain *why* a given query is anomalous, which further boosts the practical applicability of the system.

Keywords: Leakage Detection, Privacy, Data Security, Anomaly Detection.

1 Introduction

Data is valuable; databases, storing customer and confidential business data, represent a core asset for any organization. This makes data leakage, i.e. the unauthorized/unwanted transmission of data and information [1], a major threat. The harm caused by a data leakage includes economic loss, damage to the reputation and decrease of the customers' trust. In case the leakage involves personal or sensitive information, legal liability for not complying with data protection laws also comes into play. To reduce these enormous costs and comply with legislation, timely detection of data leakage is essential.

Insiders threats, e.g. malevolent or simply careless employees, are amongst the top sources of data leakage: because of their right to access internal resources, such as databases, insiders can cause significant damages [2]. According to [3], data leaked from database accounts for most of the records disclosed in 2012.

Access Control (AC) mechanisms [4] aim to guarantee that only users that have the rights can access certain data and as such form a first line of defense against data leakage. However, AC has some limitations. For example, AC rules

V. Atluri and G. Pernul (Eds.): DBSec 2014, LNCS 8566, pp. 243–259, 2014.
© IFIP International Federation for Information Processing 2014

might be not expressive enough and, especially in dynamic context, might require frequent and costly updates. In addition, AC might reduce data availability which is critical in emergency situations (e.g. in healthcare domains) or productivity (e.g. time loss to ask for permission to access certain documents). As a result, organisations often apply relaxed AC policies by giving users access to more information than they actually need [5], which obviously also reduces the AC effectiveness against data leakage. Beside AC, tools and methodologies exist for data leakage detection and prevention [6], which mainly differ in the location where they operate (e.g. network, workstation or database). In this paper we act at a database level: in this way we can detect leakages at a very early stage, i.e. when sensitive data is leaving its primary source.

Academic solutions to database leakage detection typically work by monitoring database traffic in terms of SQL queries. Existing solutions can be divided into *signature-based* and *behavioural-based* systems [7]. Generally, in signature-based systems a blacklist defines the set of dangerous or denied access patterns. On the other hand, behavioural-based systems automatically learn permitted access patterns by observing 'normal' activities and mark every anomaly as potential threat. The main problem of signature-based approaches is that they can only detect well-known attacks, whereas behavioural-based approaches have the great potential of detecting unknown database attacks. In addition, by automatically generating fine-grained profiles, behavioural-based solutions require less human-effort thus offering the best possible detection at the lowest cost. These advantages make behavioural-based approaches widely adopted in literature [8–15]. However, these approaches have also drawbacks. The first problem is the high False Positive Rate (FPR) they usually generate. Since each false alert has to be analyzed by the security officer to establish whether it indicates a real threat or not, false positives have a high operational cost. In network anomaly detection [16, 17] (a different yet similar field), a system starts to be "usable in practice" when it shows a FPR in the order of 0,01%, a rate by far not attained by present database anomaly detection systems. The second drawback is that current solutions provide little or no support for alert handling. Usually, when an alert is raised, it prompts an investigation process carried out by the security officer. It is important to support the security officer in making a correct and efficient decision by providing as much useful information as possible on the nature of the alert. In this respect, signature-based systems have an 'unfair' advantage: when they raise an alert, they can say exactly which signature is violated and why this violation may constitute a problem. On the other hand, behaviour-based solutions usually accompany a raised alert with a *deviation degree* or an *anomaly score* which is virtually useless to the officer as it does not clearly state "what is going on". Explaining the reason of an alert is generally more difficult for anomaly detection systems because of their *black-box* nature, i.e. the underlying engine (be it a neural network or a machine learning classifier) is difficult to understand and update, properties which are particularly important to reduce the number of false positives and to understand the meaning of an alert.

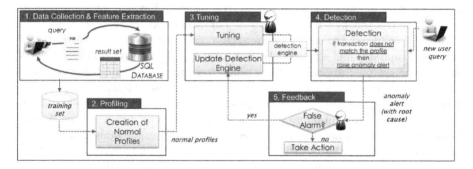

Fig. 1. Framework Overview

To enable practical detection of unknown database leakage threats we introduce what, to the best of our knowledge, is the first *white-box* behavioural-based
database leakage detection system. As opposed to existing black-box solutions,
which only flag a transaction as anomalous or not, the white-box approach enables the extrapolation of the root cause of an alarm. Our system creates self-
explanatory and easy to update histogram-based profiles of database usage by
observing SQL queries and raises an alarm when a query does not match the
profiles. Finally, the system provides a feedback mechanism enabling the officer
to mark an alarm as false positive, so that the system can be updated accordingly to avoid the repetition of the same mistake. Thanks to this new approach,
our system strongly mitigates the aforementioned problems, namely:

- the white-box approach makes profiles and detection rules self-explanatory,
  so that users can easily modify them to improve the system accuracy;
- when an alarm is raised, the system explicitly indicates the alarm's root
  cause, facilitating the user in handling the alarms;
- the feedback mechanism permits to progressively reduce the FPR.

To validate the proposed solution, we carried out two sets of experiments, the
first one using a database consisting of more than two million real transactions
taken from a company database and the second one taken from a simulated
scenario. In these experiments we benchmarked the systems against the ones
presented in [9] and [10]. According to these tests, our system achieves a very
high Detection Rate (DR) with a FPR which is one or two orders of magnitude
lower (i.e. better) than the approaches used for comparison.

2   The Framework

The solution we present in this paper targets two core objectives, namely i) max-
imizing the DR of known and unknown threats; and ii) minimizing the FPR,
i.e. the number of normal transactions erroneously marked as anomalous. To
meet these objectives it is necessary to have a rich feature space, i.e. a set of
features describing database transactions able to capture database usage at a

fine-grain, so that even small deviations from usual behaviour can be detected. Figure 1 shows the five main phases of our framework. The first phase, the *Data Collection and Feature Extraction*, captures users (SQL) transactions (select/insert/update) and extracts the feature space. The output of this phase is the *training set*, used during *Profiling* phase to construct normal behaviour profiles. Once profiles are ready the security officer can use the *Tuning* to inspect them and verify whether they are complete, and optionally decide to extend the profiling period. The tuning generates a *detection engine* which is used during *Detection* to flag each new incoming query as normal or anomalous. In case of an anomalous query, an alert which clearly states why the detector considers it as an anomaly is raised. Finally, when an alarm is raised, the *Feedback* mechanism allows the security officer to flag it as false positive, which cause an immediate update of profiles and detection engine so that the same mistake is not repeated.

2.1 Data Collection and Feature Extraction

Definition 1 (Feature Space). *The* feature space $F = \langle f_1, f_2, ..., f_n \rangle$ *is the list of query characteristics, including its syntax, result and context (features), used to represent a query.*

The feature space determines the level of details of the profiles we build, and the kind of attacks that can be detected. Table 1 describes our feature space; features can be divided into three groups: *syntax-centric*, *context-centric*, and *result-centric*. Each type of feature helps in detecting specific threats. For example, syntax-centric features, by profiling the kind of queries users usually make, enable the detection of leakages caused by e.g. privileges misuses. By using context-centric features it is possible to detect misuses related to database usage at unusual location or time. Finally, result-centric features represent the only way to spot leakages caused by the access to illegitimate data values (see Table 1). To construct the feature space it is necessary to monitor user's activities in terms of SQL queries. Several ways to capture users' queries are discussed in [18]. To learn representative profiles it is important that during data collection all queries normally submitted to the database are captured to form a training set w.r.t. our definitions.

Definition 2 (Query). *A query Q is a list of n-query values, with one query value $Q(f_i)$ for each feature f_i.*

Definition 3 (Feature Values). *Each feature f_i has a type and an associated finite set of values $V_i = \{v_{i,1}, \ldots, v_{i,m_i}\}$ that the feature can take.*

Definition 4 (Training Set). *The set of queries collected during the monitoring period, comprises our training set $T = \{Q_1^t, Q_2^t, ..., Q_k^t\}$, containing the k queries which will be used to build normal profiles.*

2.2 Profiling

Profiles should be able to completely describe normal database usage, i.e. which queries are submitted, when, at which location, what results are retrieved and

Table 1. Feature classification and feature utility in detecting specific threats

	Feature	Detected Threats
Syntax Centric	Query (command, tables, columns)	These features help in detecting leakages due to users accessing information out of their working scope (e.g. due to *excessive privileges granted* or *misuse of privileges*).
	Where Clause (length, special chars, columns and tables)	*SQL Injection* and *XSS attacks* usually act on the syntax of a query to inject malicious (SQL) statements which can be used to extract sensitive information from the database. Dangerous injected statements usually contain specific keywords that can be monitored to help the detection.
Context Centric	Response Code	Specific codes are given for specific database events, e.g. failing login attempts. Multiple failures might indicate a *password guess* attack, which might start a data leakage.
	Client/DBMS USERID/ROLE	Identifying which end-user and with which role or which client application is responsible of anomalous activities is helpful for *accountability reasons*.
	Timestamp, IP Address	Access from unusual location or at unusual time might indicate the credentials have been stolen e.g. someone is carrying on a *masquerade attack*.
Result Centric	N. of Records and Bytes	Retrieving a large quantity of data (e.g. copying customer list) might indicate a data leakage/misuse is taking place.
	Result Set	The results returned by a query helps in detecting misuses where the query syntax is legitimate (e.g. a doctor can access the table *disease* and *patient*) but the data retrieved are not (e.g. the doctor access records of patients she does not treat).

so on. Normal usage may be related to different entities, e.g., the *user* or the *role* submitting the query. Thus different profiles may be needed for different 'entities'. The first step in the profiling process is choosing the entity for which profiles are built.

Definition 5 (Profiling Feature). *The* profiling feature $\bar{f} \in F$ *represents the entity we want to profile. We use $\bar{x}$ for the value of x for the profiling feature, e.g. $\bar{i}$ is the index of the profiling feature, $\bar{f} = f_{\bar{i}}$, $\bar{V} = V_{\bar{i}}$ is the set of profiling values, $\bar{m} = m_{\bar{i}}$ is the size of this set, etc.*

Definition 6 (Histogram). *A threshold t is a number $\in [0,1]$ or a label in $\{anomalous, normal\}$. We define anomalous < 0 and $1 <$ normal. A bin is a frequency freq $\in N$ together with a threshold t. A histogram h_i for feature f_i has a size $|h_i|$ representing the number of queries it contains, and assigns a bin $bin(v, h_i)$ to each value $v \in V_i$ that f_i can take. Given a value $v \in V_i$ and a histogram h_i we write:*
- *$freq(v, h_i)$ for the frequency in $bin(v, h_i)$;*
- *$t(v, h_i)$ for the threshold in $bin(v, h_i)$;*
- *$prob(v, h_i)$ for $\frac{freq(v, h_i)}{|h_i|}$, the probability of v in h_i.*

To build the histograms the training set T is first divided into $\bar{m}$ subsets $S_1, S_2, ..., S_{\bar{m}}$. In each subset S_j, the queries have the same value on the profiling feature (namely $v_{\bar{i},j}$). For example, if we choose the *userid* as profiling feature $\bar{f}$ and in the training set $\bar{f}$ only takes 2 different values e.g., $\bar{v}_1 = rob$ and $\bar{v}_2 = sally$, then the training set will be divided into $\bar{m} = 2$ subsets, containing respectively the queries executed by *rob* and *sally*. At this point the creation of the profiles can start. Note that when building the profiles (and during detection), we make a restriction in assuming that features are *independent* of each other (the implications of this assumption are discussed in Section 4).

Definition 7 (Profile). *A profile H is a list of histograms for each feature except $\bar{f}$. The profile set P gives a profile for each profiling value $\bar{v} \in \bar{V}$. We write $H^{\bar{v}}$ to refer to the profile for the profiling value $\bar{v}$ (e.g. H^{rob} or H^{sally}). We write $h_i^{\bar{v}}$ to refer to the histogram for feature f_i in the profile $H^{\bar{v}}$.*

Note that different features are of different data types (*nominal, numeric, time* and *set*) and could have wide ranges. To create meaningful profiles we need to create group (or bins) of query values, e.g. 'Timestamp' can be grouped according to the work shift. A key challenge in the creation of the histograms is the definition of an optimal size of its bins –*bin width*– which depends on the feature data type. For *nominal* features, we can simply take a bin for each different value encountered. This approach does not work for *numeric* features as it would lead to an explosion in number of bins. Instead ranges of values are used. The size of the ranges has to be a right balance between narrow (many bins with low frequency, risk of increasing false positives) and wide (few bins with high frequency, risk of missing anomalous queries). For *time* features, bins can be defined as e.g. hours, days or work shift according to the domain. With a *set* feature, e.g. the tables used in a query, one could consider two different approaches to define the bins; i) create a different bin for each set; or ii) create a different bin for each element of the set. In the first approach we care about the exact combination of values. In the second only about which values occur. In addition, in the second approach a single query could count towards multiple bins. In this paper we apply the second approach (we omit a deeper discussion of the differences between the two approaches for reason of space).

To finalize the profiling we normalize the histograms into a probability distribution. The transformation is done by dividing the frequency of each bin by the size of the histogram which (right after training) is equal to the size of the related subset S_j, thus giving $prob(v_{i,j}, h_i) = \frac{freq(v_{i,j})}{|S_j|}$. Normalization is useful to deal with different size of different subsets, e.g. a user more active than another.

Once the histograms have been built, they will represent the normal behaviour: during detection if all the values of a query fall in bins with high frequency, the query will be considered normal, while it will be considered anomalous if at least one value falls in a bin with low or zero frequency.

This way of profiling allows great flexibility. First of all, by setting the profiling feature it is possible to create different profiles, e.g. a profile per *userid* and a profile per *role* to check whether users' activities match with their correspondent role. Furthermore, the usage of histograms allows 'online learning': the profile is built one instance at a time which means it is not necessary to retrain the complete model (as it happens e.g. with clustering) in case a new transaction has to be added to the system.

2.3   Tuning

In existing solutions the training set is usually assumed to be *attack-free* and *exhaustive*, i.e. it is representative w.r.t. normal behaviour. Drawbacks of these assumptions are: i) if an attacker is already active during the data collection, the *attack-free* assumption can lead to failing to detect some leakages and misuses; and ii) the *exhaustive* assumption can contribute to the explosion of false positives in case normal behaviour is not fully represented. To detach from these assumptions, we provide a tuning mechanism to allow a security expert to inspect and adapt normal profiles.

During the tuning, the expert can set a *global threshold*, representing the minimum probability each bin of the training set must satisfy to be considered normal. The global threshold is used to globally label all bins of all histograms of all profiles: if the bin probability is lower than the threshold, the bin is marked as *anomalous*, it is marked as *normal* otherwise. The global threshold can be seen as a measure of the level of tolerance towards rare values: a threshold of zero means that every query in the training set is considered legitimate (attack-free assumption), while a threshold higher than zero means that *rare* values (i.e. value which probability is below threshold) are considered anomalous, hence they will cause an alarm. A zero threshold also means that all the alarms generated during detection are caused by *new values*, thus a high number of false positives in this setting implies the training does not exhaustively represent normal behaviour.

To allow profile manipulation, after setting the global threshold, it is possible to manually flag each bin as *normal* or *anomalous*. For example, if the *delete* command is always anomalous then it can be flagged as such. In this way the expert can have a general rule of thumb (the global threshold) for initially uniformly labeling all the bins, and the fine-grain mechanism to add exceptions to the general rule. The set of profiles with labeled bins forms the *detection engine*.

2.4   Detection and Feedback Loop

After training, the detection engine analyzes incoming queries w.r.t. normal behaviour profiles to determine whether they are anomalous or not.

Definition 8 (Anomalous Query). *Consider a query Q by entity $\bar{v} = Q(\bar{f})$. Writing $v_i = Q(f_i)$ for the value Q assumes for feature f_i and $h_i^{\bar{v}}$ for the histogram for f_i in profile $H^{\bar{v}}$ we define: i) $R(Q) = \{f_i : prob(v_i, h_i^{\bar{v}}) <= t(v_i, h_i^{\bar{v}})\}$, the root cause set containing the features which values are anomalous; ii) Anomalous(Q) = true $\iff$ $R(Q) \neq \emptyset$, which says whether a query is anomalous or not; iii)AnomalyScore(Q) = $\prod\limits_{f_i \in R(Q)} \frac{1}{prob(v_i, h_i^{\bar{v}})}$, a score which quantifies how likely anomalous Q is (but not how harmful it is).*

In case Q is anomalous an alarm is raised, as shown in Figure 2. Alarms are listed together with the related profile (*sally* in the example), the anomaly score, the root cause set and the anomalous query text. The *anomaly score* is bigger than zero for anomalous queries (rarer values contribute more to the score).

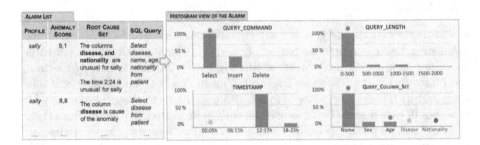

Fig. 2. Detection Results: how alarms can be presented to the security officer

The *root cause set* contains the features which values have no correspondent bin, or fall in one labeled as anomalous, thus causing the alarm. Knowing the root causes of an anomaly helps the security officer in handling the alarm. For a query to be anomalous, it is sufficient that a single feature has a value falling in an anomalous/not existent bin. Of course, several features can cause the anomaly, in which case the anomaly score will be higher and the root cause list wider. When a value has no correspondent bin, i.e. a previously unseen value, we use a minimum probability (rather than zero) to avoid division by zero.

When an alarm is raised the security officer has to handle it. Consider the first alarm shown on the left side of Figure 2, caused by *sally* using the columns *disease* and *nationality*, and submitting the query at *2:24 am*. When the officer selects the alarm, the values of the query (circles) are represented w.r.t. the related profile (histograms) as shown on the right side of the figure. A circle over a bin (bar) means that the query value for that feature falls in that bin. The officer can provide feedback about every alarm, i.e. she can mark each root cause as *true positive* or *false positive*. A true positive means that a specific value represent an actual anomaly and that the officer wants to be warned every time it occurs. A false positive instead means that one of the causes of an alarm is benign and it should not cause an alarm any longer. Circles can be green (for normal values), yellow (for values which have still to be evaluated by the officer), and red (for values which have been previously marked as *true positive*, e.g. *nationality*). For example, assuming that *sally* is entitled to use the column *disease*, the officer will mark such value as a false positive, which will cause a refinement of our profiles: the profile *sally* will be updated by adding a new bin with the value *disease* to the corresponding histogram; the bin frequency will be incremented of a unit, and the threshold will be set to *normal*. This implies that if *sally* uses the column *disease* again, no alarm will be raised. In addition, the other alarms related to *sally* will be updated accordingly, meaning that if an alarm is caused by the use of *disease*, e.g. the second alarm in Figure 2, it will be deleted from the list. In this way a single officer's feedback can result in the deletion of multiple alarms, hence reducing the officer's working load.

3   Evaluation

In this section, we validate our system by addressing the following questions:
- How effective is our framework. To this end, we made an experimental evaluation of its Detection Rate (DR) and its False Positive Rate (FPR).
- How does it compare with existing solutions, in particular with Kamra et al. [9] and Wu et al. [10]. To help the comparison we use Receiver Operating Characteristics (ROC) curves [19] and Area Under the Curve (AUC) values.
- What is the added value of the feedback mechanism? We test this by measuring the impact a feedback operation has in reducing the FPR.

3.1   Methodology

We implemented our framework as a RapidMiner (http://rapidminer.com/) extension, and made experiments with two different datasets, one with 2 Gb of real enterprise transactions, the other one with simulated queries. Both datasets were divided into a Training Set ($\sim$ 70% of the dataset) used to learn the profiles, and a Testing Set (the remaining $\sim$ 30%) used as input for the detection engine. To measure the *FPR* we assume both datasets are attack-free (the global threshold is set to zero), which is a common practice in this domain. In this way every alarm raised on the Testing Set can be considered a false positive. Beside the training and the testing set we also have distinct Attack Sets containing malicious query specifically crafted for each dataset. In these settings, we measure *FPR* and DR as:
- *FPR=(#alarms raised on the testing set)/(cardinality of the testing set)*
- *DR = (#alarms raised on the attack set)/(cardinality of the attack set)*

  The Enterprise Dataset (ED) is taken from the log of an operational database of a large IT company, with about 100 users, owning 4 different roles. We collected a total of 2,349,198 transactions (1,644,437 in the Training Set and 704,761 in the Testing Set), and extracted the features listed in Table 2. Note that the Result Set (RS) and the client application *role* are not available for this dataset. In addition, we have an Attack Set composed of 107 malicious queries devised and executed by the security administrator of the database, logged in as one of the profiled users. These queries represent real threats to the enterprise since they access sensitive information normal employees do not normally access (e.g. other employees' *password* or *user ids*).

  The Simulated Dataset (SD) was constructed using the healthcare management system GnuHealth (http://health.gnu.org). We simulated *normal behaviour* (validated by domain experts) consisting of an *admin* and different users of a hospital, where *doctors* and *nurses* take care of *patients* suffering from different *diseases*. The Simulated Dataset contains a total of 30,492 queries (21,344 in the Training Set and 9,148 in the Testing Set); in addition, we simulated two attacks:
- *Attack 1*: the admin looks at parts of the database (e.g. the table *patient*) which she should have no interest in (277 malicious queries);

Table 2. Features extracted during the experiments

	Feature	Type	White-Box without RS	White-Box with RS	Kamra et al. (c-quiplet)	Kamra et al. (m-quiplet)	Kamra et al. (f-quiplet)	Wu et al.
	QUERY_COMMAND	nominal	v	v	v	v	v	v
	QUERY_LENGTH	numeric	v	v				
	QUERY_COL_SET	set	v	v			v	
	QUERY_COL_NUM	numeric	v	v	v	v		v
	QUERY_TABLE_SET	set	v	v		v	v	v*
Syntax	QUERY_TABLE_NUM	numeric	v	v	v			
Centric	QUERY_SELECT_ALL	nominal	v	v				
	WHERE_TABLE_SET	set	v	v		v	v	v*
	WHERE_TABLE_NUM	numeric	v	v	v			
	WHERE_COL_SET	set	v	v			v	
	WHERE_COL_NUM	numeric	v	v	v	v		
	WHERE_LENGTH	numeric	v	v				
	WHERE_SPEC_CHAR	numeric	v	v				
	OS_USERNAME	nominal	v	v				
	CLIENT_APP_UID	nominal	v	v	v**	v**	v**	v**
Context	CLIENT_APP_ROLE	nominal	v	v	v**	v**	v**	v**
Centric	RESPONSE_CODE	nominal	v	v				
	TIMESTAMP	time	v	v				v
	IP_ADDRESS	nominal	v	v				v
	BYTES_NUM	numeric		v				
Result	ROWS_NUM	numeric		v				
Centric	DISEASE	nominal		v				
	PATIENT_ID	nominal		v				

v - feature used by the approach
v* - the *tables* in the *from* and in the *where* clause are grouped in a single feature
v** - *role* and *userid* are mutually exclusively used as labels

– *Attack 2*: a general practitioner, who only treats patients with generic disease (e.g. *flu, cough*) accesses data of patients with *HIV* (26 malicious queries). Note that queries in *Attack 2* have been specifically crafted to be detected based on RS features only.

To compare our framework to competing proposals from literature, we reproduced the systems of [9, 10] and we measured their FPR and DR on both datasets. Both approaches apply Naïve Bayes to learn the *userid* (or *user role*) class: an alarm is raised if the class predicted by the classifier differs from the actual one. The main difference between the two solutions is given by the features used to learn the classifier: Kamra et al. adopt a pure syntax-centric approach while Wu et al. add context-centric features. The Kamra et al. solution has three variants – c-quiplet, m-quiplet and f-quiplet – which differs in how fine grained their feature space is. When comparing the results, it is important to note that our approach differs from [9, 10] not only in the algorithm, but also in the following aspects. First, we consider more features: Table 2 shows the feature space used in our solution and those used by the other two approaches. Secondly, we can take into account the RS; this is however only present in the Simulated Dataset, and for this dataset we made two separate measurements: one with the the RS and the other without. Finally, our system is devised from scratch to include a feedback loop. However, to guarantee fairness, the feedback has not been used when comparing our results with those of [9, 10].

Generally, a detector performs well if it shows both a low FPR (costs) and a high DR (benefits). FPR and DR depend on the *true* and *false* alarms raised by a detector. Recall that an alarm is raised if *anomaly score* > 0 in our solution, and if *prediction* ! = *actual class* for the solutions in [9, 10]. To plot ROC curves we measure FPR and DR for varying values of a decision threshold t. The threshold t is used to vary the output of the detectors as follows: for our solution an alarm will be raised if *anomaly score* > t, while for [9, 10] an alarm will be generated if *prediction* ! = *actual class* and the *prediction probability* > t. To compare different detectors we plot their ROC curves in a single graph: the best detector is the one which ROC curve passes closer to the upper left point (0,1) (zero costs, maximum benefits). In case ROCs intersect, it might be difficult to visually spot which method performs better, thus we reduce ROC curves into a single scalar value: the AUC. Note that outside the ROC context we assume the use of the default value for t which is 0 for all the considered approaches and which leads to the best FPR-DR tradeoff.

3.2   Results

Table 3 presents the performance of different solutions over the Enterprise Dataset, with *userid* as profiling feature. The results show that, while the DR is high (100%) for every solution, the White-Box approach has the lowest FPR (1.65%), which is 7 times better than the best results amongst the comparing approaches (Kamra et al., m-quiplet, FPR of 12.24%). Our solution is also the one with the best FPR-DR tradeoff, as shown by the ROC curves in Figure 3 and by the highest AUC value (0.987). This means we can provide the best benefit at the lowest cost, hence we consistently reduce the officer's work load.

On the Simulated Dataset, we could test the performance of our solution also in presence of RS. Results over this dataset, with *userid* as profiling feature, are shown in Table 4 and confirm the outstanding FPR of the White-Box solution which is orders of magnitude lower than the one of compared approaches (1.09% without RS and 1.41% with RS, versus 44.00% of Wu et al., the next in order with the lowest FPR). Interestingly, the addition of the RS features results in a slight increase of FPR, but it does allow us to detect *Attack 2*, which was devised explicitly to be detectable only in presence of RS information (therefore *Attack 2* should not be detected by syntax-based approaches). With these settings, it is not surprising that the White-Box solution without RS has DR2 = 0.0%: it misses the potential of detecting *Attack 2*. What is surprising is that DR2 is different from zero for the competing approaches: in principle, neither of them – being syntax-based – should be able to detect this (note that a random guess detector also has a DR different from zero). On the other hand, when we add RS features we obtain the highest DR (80.77%). Note that although we fail to detect all malicious queries in *Attack 2*, we actually manage to detect the attack and to warn the security officer that a specific user is acting strangely. Finally, the White-Box solution with RS is the one offering the best FPR-DR tradeoff as shown by the ROC in Figure 4 (DR1 and DR2 are combined to plot the ROC).

Table 5 shows the results of our test when the *user role* is chosen as profiling feature. The results refer to the Simulated Dataset only as role information is not available in the Enterprise Dataset. The table shows that FPR is generally

Table 3. Results for Enterprise Dataset (*userid* profiles)

	FPR	DR	AUC
White-Box (without RS)	**1.65%**	100%	**0.987**
White-Box (with RS)	*na*	*na*	*na*
Kamra et al. (c-quiplet)	15.00%	100%	0.927
Kamra et al. (m-quiplet)	12.24%	100%	0.951
Kamra et al. (f-quiplet)	12.67%	100%	0.981
Wu et al. (standard)	13.03%	100%	0.957

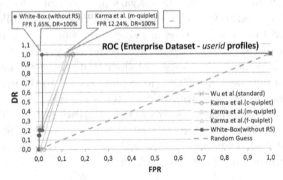

Fig. 3. ROC curves comparison - Enterprise Dataset (*userid* profiles)

Table 4. Results for Simulated Dataset (*userid* profiles)

	FPR	DR1	DR2	AUC
White-Box (without RS)	**1.09%**	100%	0.00%	0.948
White-Box (with RS)	1.41%	100%	**80.77%**	**0.980**
Kamra et al. (c-quiplet)	72.18%	98.92%	53.85%	0.584
Kamra et al. (m-quiplet)	71.03%	100%	76.92%	0.406
Kamra et al. (f-quiplet)	69.58%	100%	73.08%	0.422
Wu et al. (standard)	44.00%	100%	42.31%	0.824

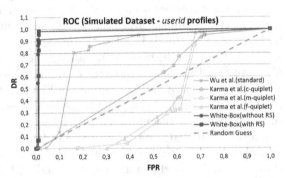

Fig. 4. ROC curves comparison - Simulated Dataset (*userid* profiles)

Table 5. Results for Simulated Dataset (*role* profiles)

	FPR	DR1	DR2	AUC
White-Box (without RS)	**0.38%**	100%	0.00%	0.954
White-Box (with RS)	0.91%	100%	**80.77%**	**0.984**
Kamra et al. (c-quiplet)	40.04%	100%	3.85%	0.687
Kamra et al. (m-quiplet)	50.73%	100%	0.00%	0.517
Kamra et al. (f-quiplet)	50.87%	100%	0.00%	0.518
Wu et al. (standard)	29.34%	100%	0.00%	0.823
Wu et al. (hierarchical)	27.68%	100%	0.00%	0.839

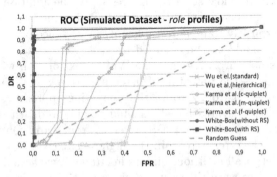

Fig. 5. ROC curves comparison - Simulated Dataset (*role* profiles)

Table 6. Feedback Impact on FPR (*userid* profiles)

	Feedback Operation	Enterprise DS		Simulated DS	
		FPR (%)	FP (#)	FPR (%)	FP (#)
White-Box (without RS)	0	1.65%	11596	1.09%	100
	1	1.17%	8234	1.08%	99
	4	0.05%	327	1.04%	95
	7	0.05%	318	1.01%	92
White-Box (with RS)	0	na	na	1.41%	129
	1	na	na	1.40%	128
	4	na	na	1.13%	104
	7	na	na	1.09%	98

lower, while DR is either less than or equal to the results obtained when *userid* is chosen as profiling feature (see Table 4). This is because, especially in large enterprises, *userid* profiles are more specific than *user role* profiles. The better FPR is due to the fact that the engine is less sensitive to small variations; the "lower" DR to the fact that profiles are less specific. As shown in the table, the White-Box solution (with and without RS) has the same DR for both *userid* and *role* profiles. In the case of *Attack 1* this is due to the fact that we have only one user with role *admin*, which makes role and user profiles identical. In the case of *Attack 2* the same DR means that none of the other doctors ever looked at disease HIV, thus if any doctor looks at it, an alarm will be raised. Note that if we add a doctor who treats patients with HIV to the normal behaviour scenarios, DR2 would likely decrease. In overall, as shown by the ROC curves in Figure 5, the White-Box solution with RS performs better than the others (AUC=0.984), with a small cost in terms of FPR (0.91%).

Impact of the Feedback Loop. A novel component of our framework is a feedback loop mechanism that allows to iteratively decreasing the FPR. All the results shown in the previous section did not take advantage of this feedback mechanisms to ensure a more fair comparison with the other systems in the literature [9, 10]. Table 6 shows how the feedback loop mechanism actually improves the FPR. The table refers to *userid* profiles, and shows that in the enterprise dataset, only 7 feedback operations are enough to drop the FPR from 1.65% to 0.05% (from 11596 to 318 alarms). On the simulated dataset, 7 feedback operations reduce the FPR from 1.09% to 1.01% and from 1.41% to 1.09% respectively in the solution without and with RS. Note that – as expected – the impact of a single feedback operation is higher when multiple false alarms are caused by the same feature value, e.g. in the enterprise dataset a single feedback operation eliminated 3362 false alarms. It is worth mentioning that a single feedback operation consists of only few mouse clicks: those necessary to mark an alarm as false positive. Finally, note that none of the existing solutions offer a built-in feedback mechanism, mainly because it would require a complete re-training of the detection engine, which is not necessary in our framework.

4   Discussion, Limitations and Future Work

As our experimental validation has shown, our framework boosts the practical applicability of anomaly-based database leakage detection by presenting the highest DR with a FPR which is orders of magnitude lower when compared to existing solutions. In addition, the FPR can be further reduced by applying the *feedback loop* to eliminate false positives. Finally, the white-box nature of our solution clearly states the causes of an anomaly, hence helping the officer in handling the alerts. We believe the good results achieved mainly depend on our fine-grained profiles, which allow creating a more faithful model of usage behaviour. On the other hand, we think there are several reasons why the other approaches (we compared to) present a high FPR. First of all, the other solutions use Naïve Bayes which inherently depends on the user's ids (or role) distribution of activities: their performance are usually better with training sets in which actions are evenly distributed amongst users. However, relying on this assumption is a strong limitation in database leakage detection where query data flows are generally not uniformly distributed. Secondly, these solutions have a limited feature space which does not allow to creating fine-grained profiles. However, since Naïve Bayes is not designed to take advantage of each feature in a specific way as we do, we expect that a larger feature space would not significantly improve performance of the other approaches (initial tests seem to confirm this).

Although the general good results, our solution still has some limitations we need to address. The major limitation is due to the feature independency assumption used to build profiles. This assumption implies that anomalous queries for which each individual feature by itself is normal cannot be detected. For example, it might be normal that *sally delete* on column *age* and *select* on column *disease*, however the fact that she *delete* on column *disease* might represent a misuse that is currently undetected. To address this problem, we aim at applying data mining techniques (rule-mining in particular) to find combination of features that discriminate anomalies from normal behaviour. The second limitation is related to the detection per single query. In the current implementation, each query is individually analyzed and labeled by the detection engine. In this way, attacks that are split over multiple queries (or multiple sessions) might not be detected. Extending our solution to detect anomalies which involve groups of queries is another interesting path we intend to follow. Finally, several improvements can be made to the feedback mechanism e.g., by adding a signature-based approach to let the officer define fine-grained exception rules.

5   Related Work

Database Leakage Detection Solutions. Available database leakages detection solutions mainly differ for the type of features (*syntax-centric, context-centric,* or *result-centric*) used for representing normal behaviour.

The works presented in [8–10] are syntax-centric. In [8] the authors build normal behaviour profiles based on the assumption that SQL commands and their order in each database transaction are relevant. During detection, if an attacker executes valid queries but in an incorrect order, an alert is raised. In [9] normal profiles are built using a Naïve Bayes classifier. The system learns to predict the *userid* or the *role* based on the SQL command and on the tables and columns in the query. When a new query arrives, in case the userid (or the role) predicted by the classifier mismatch the actual value, an alarm is raised. In [10] the approach is very similar to the one in [9], with an extended feature space.

Pure syntax-centric approaches have to deal with some structural limitations. For example, they fail to detect situations where the type of query submitted is normal but the data retrieved is anomalous. These considerations are at the basis of the solution proposed in [12], that suggests to profile normal behaviour based on the data users retrieve. A mixed approach combining result-centric and context-centric is used in [13] where a mining algorithm is used to define association rules between context and result set. In this way the same request may be legitimate if performed within one context but abnormal within another. Finally, in [14] syntax-centric and result-centric approaches are combined. Normal profiles are represented in terms of statistical distribution: if a new query does not match the original probability distribution, it will be considered anomalous.

Anomaly Detection Techniques. Behaviour-based solutions detect potential database leakages by identifying deviations from normal behaviour, a problem generally known as *anomaly detection*. Anomaly detection techniques can be divided into supervised, semi-supervised, and unsupervised [20]. In *supervised* approaches, it is assumed that the training set contains queries labeled either as *normal* or as *anomalous*. In the *semisupervised* approach the assumption is that the training set contains only labels for normal transactions. Finally, in the *unsupervised* approach no labels are needed: the dataset is sought for intrinsic similarities that can be modeled so that outliers can easily pop out.

In the context of database leakage detection a labeled dataset is very hard to obtain, thus unsupervised techniques are those used the most in this field. Examples of unsupervised techniques include clustering, association rules, and statistical methods. Clustering techniques group similar instances of the training set according to a distance or similarity function. Any sample that does not belong to any cluster is considered an anomaly. A major drawback of clustering techniques is that the number of clusters has to be defined a-priori. In addition, a complete re-training is necessary if a new sample has to be added to the model. Association rules have the main advantage of being self-explanatory, thus creating a white-box system. However, they have a high computational cost and high memory consumption [21]. Finally, statistical methods are based on the probabilistic model generated from the training set: if the probability of the new data instance to be generated by such probabilistic model is very low, then the instance is considered an outlier. Statistical methods includes Hidden Markov Models (HMM) and histogram analysis. HMMs are very good to model temporal relationships, however, the high computational and memory cost, together with the high number of parameters that need to be set can discourage their usage [7, 21]. Histogram-based are the simplest nonparametric statistical techniques. The profiles of normal data are based on the construction of a histogram of frequencies for each feature of the feature space. This technique is computationally inexpensive, and generates a self-explanatory model. Its simplicity and intrinsic white-box structure, together with the support to the *online learning* – no need of retraining when a model update is required– make this solution the best candidate when a model easy to understand and to update is required.

6 Conclusions

In this paper, we presented a white-box behaviour-based database leakage detection system. Our experimental validation shows that our approach provides high DR for different kinds of attacks, both syntax and result set related, by keeping a low FPR. Especially, the FPR is orders of magnitude lower than that of comparable solutions (1.65% over the Enterprise Dataset), thus boosting the practical applicability of our solution. The number of false positives can be further reduced thanks to the feedback loop. Furthermore, the white-box nature of the solution creates self-explanatory profiles and allows the extraction of the root causes of an alarm. As future work we aim at enhancing our system to cope with current limitations and to extend the validation process to other (real) datasets.

Acknowledgment. This work has been partially funded by the Dutch program COMMIT under the THeCS project.

References

1. Gordon, P.: Data Leakage - Threats and Mitigation. Technical report, SANS Institute (2007)
2. Software Engineering Institute: 2011 CyberSecurity Watch Survey. Technical report, Software Engineering Institute, Carnegie Mellon University (2011)
3. Verizon: The 2013 Data Breach Investigations Report. Technical report (2013)
4. Samarati, P., de Vimercati, S.: Access control: Policies, models, and mechanisms. Foundations of Security Analysis and Design (2001)
5. Caputo, D., Maloof, M., Stephens, G.: Detecting insider theft of trade secrets. In: S&P. IEEE (2009)
6. Shabtai, A., Elovici, Y., Rokach, L.: A survey of data leakage detection and prevention solutions. Springer (2012)
7. Patcha, A., Park, J.: An overview of anomaly detection techniques: Existing solutions and latest technological trends. Computer Networks (2007)
8. Fonseca, J., Vieira, M., Madeira, H.: Integrated intrusion detection in databases. In: Bondavalli, A., Brasileiro, F., Rajsbaum, S. (eds.) LADC 2007. LNCS, vol. 4746, pp. 198–211. Springer, Heidelberg (2007)
9. Kamra, A., Terzi, E., Bertino, E.: Detecting anomalous access patterns in relational databases. The VLDB Journal (2007)
10. Wu, G.Z., Osborn, S.L., Jin, X.: Database intrusion detection using role profiling with role hierarchy. In: Jonker, W., Petković, M. (eds.) SDM 2009. LNCS, vol. 5776, pp. 33–48. Springer, Heidelberg (2009)

11. Bockermann, C., Apel, M., Meier, M.: Learning SQL for database intrusion detection using context-sensitive modelling (Extended abstract). In: Flegel, U., Bruschi, D. (eds.) DIMVA 2009. LNCS, vol. 5587, pp. 196–205. Springer, Heidelberg (2009)
12. Mathew, S., Petropoulos, M., Ngo, H.Q., Upadhyaya, S.: A data-centric approach to insider attack detection in database systems. In: Jha, S., Sommer, R., Kreibich, C. (eds.) RAID 2010. LNCS, vol. 6307, pp. 382–401. Springer, Heidelberg (2010)
13. Gafny, M., Shabtai, A., Rokach, L., Elovici, Y.: Applying unsupervised context-based analysis for detecting unauthorized data disclosure. In: CCS. ACM (2011)
14. Santos, R.J., Bernardino, J., Vieira, M., Rasteiro, D.M.L.: Securing Data Warehouses from Web-Based Intrusions. In: Wang, X.S., Cruz, I., Delis, A., Huang, G. (eds.) WISE 2012. LNCS, vol. 7651, pp. 681–688. Springer, Heidelberg (2012)
15. Chung, C.Y., Gertz, M., Levitt, K.: Demids: A misuse detection system for database systems. In: Integrity and Internal Control Information Systems (2000)
16. Bolzoni, D., Etalle, S., Hartel, P.H.: Panacea: Automating attack classification for anomaly-based network intrusion detection systems. In: Kirda, E., Jha, S., Balzarotti, D. (eds.) RAID 2009. LNCS, vol. 5758, pp. 1–20. Springer, Heidelberg (2009)
17. Hadžiosmanović, D., Simionato, L., Bolzoni, D., Zambon, E., Etalle, S.: N-Gram against the Machine: On the Feasibility of the N-Gram Network Analysis for Binary Protocols. In: Balzarotti, D., Stolfo, S.J., Cova, M. (eds.) RAID 2012. LNCS, vol. 7462, pp. 354–373. Springer, Heidelberg (2012)
18. Jin, X., Osborn, S.L.: Architecture for data collection in database intrusion detection systems. In: Jonker, W., Petković, M. (eds.) SDM 2007. LNCS, vol. 4721, pp. 96–107. Springer, Heidelberg (2007)
19. Fawcett, T.: An introduction to ROC analysis. Pattern Recognition Letters (2006)
20. Chandola, V., Banerjee, A., Kumar, V.: Anomaly detection. ACM Computing Surveys (2009)
21. Mazhelis, O.: One-class classifiers: a review and analysis of suitability in the context of mobile-masquerader detection. South African Computer Journal (2006)

Incremental Analysis of Evolving Administrative Role Based Access Control Policies

Silvio Ranise[1] and Anh Truong[1,2]

[1] Security and Trust Unit, FBK-Irst, Trento, Italia
[2] DISI, Università degli Studi di Trento, Italia

Abstract. We consider the safety problem for Administrative Role-Based Access Control (ARBAC) policies, i.e. detecting whether sequences of administrative actions can result in policies by which a user can acquire permissions that may compromise some security goals. In particular, we are interested in sequences of safety problems generated by modifications (namely, adding/deleting an element to/from the set of possible actions) to an ARBAC policy accommodating the evolving needs of an organization. or resulting from fixing some safety issues. Since problems in such sequences share almost all administrative actions, we propose an incremental technique that avoids the re-computation of the solution to the current problem by re-using much of the work done on the previous problem in a sequence. An experimental evaluation shows the better performances of an implementation of our technique with respect to the only available approach to solve safety problems for evolving ARBAC policies proposed by Gofman, Luo, and Yang.

1 Introduction

Today, the administration of access control policies is key to the security of many IT systems that need to evolve in rapidly changing environments and dynamically finding the best trade-off among a variety of needs. Permissions to perform administrative actions must be restricted since security officers can only be partially trusted. In fact, some of them may collude to—inadvertently or maliciously—modify the policies so that untrusted users can get security-sensitive permissions. A way to restrict administrative permissions is to specify a set of administrative actions, each one identifying conditions about which administrators can modify certain policies. Despite this restriction, taking into consideration the effect of all possible sequences of administrative actions turns out to be a difficult task because of the huge number of ways in which actions can be interleaved and the resulting explosion in the generated policies. Thus, push-button analysis techniques are needed to identify *safety* issues, i.e. administrative actions generating policies by which a user can acquire permissions that may compromise some security goals. This is known as the *safety problem*, which amounts to establish whether there exists a (finite) sequence of administrative actions, selected from a set of available ones, that applied to a given initial policy, yields a policy in which a user gets certain permissions.

V. Atluri and G. Pernul (Eds.): DBSec 2014, LNCS 8566, pp. 260–275, 2014.
© IFIP International Federation for Information Processing 2014

To further complicate the problem, administrative actions tend to evolve over time in order to correct potential security issues revealed after solving safety problems or to accommodate the changing needs of an organization. After each change, administrators may wish to solve safety problems to check if a security issue has been fixed or if the change introduced a new security issue. Since typical changes have the form of sequences of simple operations that add/delete an action to/from the available set of administrative actions, the available technique for safety analysis is invoked on "similar" problems—i.e. safety problems that share almost all administrative actions. It would be thus good to compute the result for the new problem instance by re-using as much as possible the computations performed for the previous problem instance and possibly performing only those computations needed to take into account the change in the set of administrative actions. This is an example of *incremental* computation [15].

In this paper, we propose an incremental technique capable of solving sequences of safety problems for Role-Based Access Control (RBAC) policies [20]; the administrative actions we consider are those of the Administrative RBAC model (ARBAC) [19]. We derive an incremental version of our procedure for analyzing single instances of the ARBAC safety; see, e.g., [18]. This amounts to computing a symbolic representation of the set of RBAC policies from which the goal is reachable, called the set of *backward* reachable states. We do this by re-using the set of backward reachable states computed to solve a "similar" instance of the ARBAC safety problem. In some situations, this is easy: consider adding a new administrative action when the answer to the previous instance of the problem was "reachable." The answer to the new instance of the problem is obviously again "reachable" since the administrative actions used in the previous instance to show reachability can still be used to solve the new instance, that simply contains one more action. In other situations, finding an answer to a similar safety problem is more complex: consider adding a new administrative action when the answer to the previous instance of the problem was "unreachable." The answer to the new instance of the problem requires additional computations in order to understand if the set of backward reachable states has been enlarged and the new action may turn the answer from "unreachable" to "reachable" or not. As we will see, our procedure tries to recognize situations in which it is easy to infer an answer from previous computations while deferring additional computations when this cannot be avoided.

As observed in [15], the theoretical criteria commonly used to evaluate the performances of non-incremental procedures can be unsatisfactory when considering incremental changes. (Recall that solving single instances of ARBAC safety problems is PSPACE-complete; see, e.g., [21].) Additionally, "from a practical standpoint incremental algorithms that do not have "good" theoretical performance [...] can give satisfactory performance in practice" [15]. For these reasons, we have performed an experimental evaluation of an implementation of our incremental procedure on randomly generated safety problems. We have compared our procedure with those in [8,9]: the results clearly show the advantages of our approach.

Related work. Deriving incremental versions of batch algorithms is a much studied topic in several fields of Computer Science; we point the reader to [15] for a general overview on incremental computation.

There is a long line of works on the safety analysis of access control policies started with the seminal work in [11]. The idea underlying such works is to reduce safety analysis to graph manipulation [13,3,22] or fix-point computation performed either by Logic Programming—as in [14]—or model checking—as in [14,23,4,2,5,12,6,18]!. All these works do not consider incremental analysis.

The first work to propose the analysis of evolving ARBAC policies is [8,9]. Besides arguing the importance of incremental analysis, [8,9] propose incremental versions of the algorithms for analyzing ARBAC policies of [23]. This work is our main source of inspiration: we share the same motivations and take a similar approach by proposing an incremental version of our technique for the automated analysis of ARBAC policies [18]. The main difference is in the underlying model checking procedure: we use an implicit (symbolic) representation of the set of RBAC policies obtained by applying administrative actions whereas [8,9] use the explicit-state model checking technique of [23]. More recently, [10] presents a symbolic analysis procedure—based on a sophisticated Logic Programming technique, called abduction—for rule-based administrative policies, which are also capable of expressing changes to the policy rules. A comparison with our approach or that of [8,9] is complex because of the differences in expressive power. On the one hand, the rule-based administrative policies of [10] can express only a sub-set of the ARBAC policies since they do not support, e.g., negations in the conditions to apply an action. On the other hand, they can express modifications of RBAC policies that cannot be expressed by ARBAC policies (the interested reader is pointed to [10] for details). For this reason, we compare our technique with those of [8,9] only (see Section 5 below).

Plan of the paper. Section 2 introduces the background on the safety of ARBAC policies. Section 3 summarizes our symbolic procedure to solve safety problems, that is made incremental in Section 4. Our implementation and its experimental evaluation are discussed in Section 5. The paper concludes in Section 6.

2   RBAC and ARBAC

In *Role-Based Access Control (RBAC)* [20], access decisions are based on the roles that individual users have as part of an organization. Permissions are grouped by role name and correspond to various uses of a resource. Roles can have overlapping responsibilities and privileges, i.e. users belonging to different roles may have common permissions. For the purpose of safety analysis, without loss of generality (see, e.g., [21]), we ignore role hierarchies (a remark on this assumption is at the end of this section). Let U be a set of users, R a set of roles, and P a set of permissions. Users are associated to roles by a binary relation $UA \subseteq U \times R$ and roles are associated to permissions by another binary relation $PA \subseteq R \times P$. A user u is a *member* of role r when $(u, r) \in UA$. A user u *has permission* p if there exists a role $r \in R$ such that $(r, p) \in PA$ and u is a member of r. A *RBAC policy* is a tuple (U, R, P, UA, PA).

Administrative RBAC (ARBAC) [19] controls how RBAC policies may evolve through administrative actions that assign or revoke user memberships into roles. Usually (see, e.g., [23]), administrators may only update the relation UA while PA is fixed. Thus, a RBAC policy is a tuple (U, R, UA) or simply UA when U and R are clear from the context. This simplification is assumed in several works in the literature and we also adopt it in this paper (a remark on the significance of this assumption is at the end of this section).

The set of possible administrative actions is defined by rules specifying the which roles an administrator should or should not have—this is also called the *administrative domain* of the rule—and which roles a user should have to get a role assigned or revoked. An administrative domain is specified by a *pre-condition*, i.e. a finite set of expressions of the forms r or $\bar{r}$ (for $r \in R$). A user $u \in U$ *satisfies* a pre-condition C if, for each $\ell \in C$, u is a member of r when ℓ is r or u is not a member of r when ℓ is $\bar{r}$ for $r \in R$. Permission to assign users to roles is specified by a ternary relation *can_assign* containing tuples of the form (C_a, C, r) where C_a and C are pre-conditions, and r a role. Permission to revoke users from roles is specified by a binary relation *can_revoke* containing tuples of the form (C_a, r) where C_a is a pre-condition and r a role. In both cases, we say that C_a is the *administrative pre-condition*, C is a *(simple) pre-condition*, r is the *target role*, and a user u_a satisfying C_a is the *administrator*. When there exist users satisfying the administrative and the simple (if the case) pre-conditions of an administrative action, the action is *enabled*. The relation *can_revoke* is only binary because simple pre-conditions are useless when revoking roles [23].

The semantics of the administrative actions in the set ψ of rules obtained by the disjoint union of rules in *can_assign* and *can_revoke* is given by the binary relation $\rightarrow_\psi$ defined as follows: $UA \rightarrow_\psi UA'$ iff there exist users u_a and u in U such that either (*i*) there exists $(C_a, C, r) \in$ *can_assign*, u_a satisfies C_a, u satisfies C (i.e. (C_a, C, r) is enabled), and $UA' = UA \cup \{(u, r)\}$ or (*ii*) there exists $(C_a, r) \in$ *can_revoke*, u_a satisfies C_a (i.e. (C_a, r) is enabled), and $UA' = UA \setminus \{(u, r)\}$. A *run* of the administrative actions in $\psi := ($*can_assign, can_revoke*$)$ is a sequence $UA_0, UA_1, ..., UA_n, ...$ such that $UA_i \rightarrow_\psi UA_{i+1}$ for $i \geq 0$.

The safety problem for ARBAC policies. A pair (u_g, R_g) is called a *(RBAC) goal* for $u_g \in U$ and R_g a finite set of roles. The cardinality $|R_g|$ of R_g is the *size* of the goal. Given an initial RBAC policy UA_0, a goal (u_g, R_g), and administrative actions $\psi = ($*can_assign, can_revoke*$)$; (an instance of) the *user-role reachability problem*, identified by the tuple $\langle UA, \psi, (u_g, R_g) \rangle$, consists of checking if there exists a finite sequence $UA_0, UA_1, ..., UA_n$ (for $n \geq 0$) where (i) $UA_i \rightarrow_\psi UA_{i+1}$ for each $i = 0, ..., n-1$ and (ii) u_g is a member of each role of R_g in UA_n.

Sometimes, to simplify the solution of user-role reachability problems, *separate administration* has been assumed (see, e.g., [23]), which amounts to requiring that administrative and regular roles are disjoint. This permits to consider just one user, omit administrative users and roles so that the tuples in *can_assign* are pairs composed of a simple pre-condition and a target role and the pairs in *can_revoke* reduce to target roles only. Although our approach does not need such an assumption, we make use of it in the examples to simplify the technical development and in the experiments of Section 5 to streamline the comparison with the approach in [8,9].

Remark. In [19], modifications to role hierarchies are allowed. Since they closely reflect the structure of the organizations in which the policies are used, we believe that their modifications should be rare as they imply substantial changes to the organizations themselves. Thus, we decided to disregard administrative actions modifying the role hierarchy of RBAC policies.

In [19], it is also possible to modify the permission-role assignment relation PA by administrative actions similar to those in ψ for UA (obtained by simply replacing users with permissions). There exists a reduction [21] for the problem of checking if a user can be assigned a given set of permissions—called the *user-permission reachability problem*—into a (finite) set of independent user-role and permission-role reachability problems. A *permission-role reachability problem* consists of answering questions of the form: can a set of permissions be assigned to a given set of roles by applying a finite sequence of actions modifying the relation PA? Given the similarities between the actions modifying PA and UA, analysis techniques for the user-role reachability problem can be easily adapted to the permission-role reachability problem [21]. As a consequence, the incremental analysis techniques described in the following can be extended to take care of administrative actions modifying also PA.

3 Solving User-Role Reachability Problems

Our approach [4,2,5,18] to solve single instances of user-role reachability problems is based on a symbolically representing user-role reachability problems and then invoking a symbolic model checking procedure. More precisely, we represent RBAC policies, administrative actions, and goals by formulae of first-order logic. Then, we use simple logical manipulations and theorem proving techniques to iteratively compute the symbolic representation of sets of backward reachable states. Technically, we use the definitions and results in [17].

We assume a class $\mathcal{L}$ of first-order formulae and define an $\mathcal{L}$-based *symbolic transition system* S ($\mathcal{L}$-STS, for short) to be a triple $\langle V, In, Tr \rangle$ where V is the (finite) set of system variables of S, In is an assertion of $\mathcal{L}$ describing all the initial states of S and Tr is a (finite) set of assertions of $\mathcal{L}$. The assertion In contains some or all the system variables V; we also write $In(V)$ to emphasize this. Each member tr of Tr is an assertion of $\mathcal{L}$ containing some or all the system variables in V and the primed system variables in $V' = \{v'|v \in V\}$ where v' indicates the values of v after the execution of the transition; we also write $tr(V, V')$ to emphasize this.

We take $\mathcal{L}$ to be the *Bernays-Shönfinkel-Ramsey* (*BSR*) [16] fragment of first-order logic; sometimes called Effectively-Propositional Logic (EPR), see, e.g., [17]. An assertion of BSR has the form $\exists X.\forall Y.\varphi(X, Y)$ where X and Y are (disjoint) sets of variables and φ is a quantifier-free formula—called the *matrix*—containing equality, predicates, and constants but no functions. The translation procedure 1 shows how to obtain a symbolic representation of a user-role reachability problem. The idea is to consider the roles in R as unary predicates,

Procedure 1. The translation procedure TR

Require: $P = \langle\langle U, R, UA\rangle, \psi, (u_g, R_g)\rangle$ is a user-role reachability problem

Ensure: $S = \langle V, In, Tr\rangle$ is a $\mathcal{L}$-based STS and G is an assertion of $\mathcal{L}_G$

1. $V \leftarrow R$ { Roles are considered as unary predicates }
2. $In \leftarrow \forall x. \bigwedge_{r \in R}(r(x) \Leftrightarrow \bigvee_{(u,r)\in UA} x = u)$
3. $Tr \leftarrow \{[\alpha] | \alpha \in \psi\}$
4. $G \leftarrow \exists x. x = u_g \wedge \bigwedge_{r_g \in R_g} r_g(x)$

$$
[\alpha] := \begin{cases} \exists a, x. \forall y. \begin{pmatrix} \bigwedge_{r \in C_a} r(a) \wedge \bigwedge_{\overline{r} \in C_a} \neg r(a) \wedge \\ \bigwedge_{r \in C} r(x) \wedge \bigwedge_{\overline{r} \in C} \neg r(x) \wedge \\ r_t{}'(y) \Leftrightarrow (y = x \vee r_t(y)) \wedge Id(R \setminus \{r_t\}) \end{pmatrix} & \text{if } \alpha = (C_a, C, r_t) \\[2em] \exists a, x. \forall y. \begin{pmatrix} \bigwedge_{r \in C_a} r(a) \wedge \bigwedge_{\overline{r} \in C_a} \neg r(a) \wedge \\ r_t(x) \wedge \\ r_t{}'(y) \Leftrightarrow (y \neq x \wedge r_t(y)) \wedge Id(R \setminus \{r_t\}) \end{pmatrix} & \text{if } \alpha = (C_a, r_t) \end{cases}
$$

so that $r(u)$ can be interpreted as $(u, r) \in UA$. The auxiliary translation function $[\cdot]$ maps rules in *can_assign* or *can_revoke* to BSR formulae, where $Id(R^*)$ abbreviates $\bigwedge_{r \in R^*} r'(y) \Leftrightarrow r(y)$. Intuitively, $Id(R^*)$ means that all the roles in $R^* = R \setminus \{r_t\}$ are left unchanged by the administrative action with target role r_t. The BSR formula In does not contain existential quantifiers and it is called a *universal BSR formula*. Dually, the BSR formula G, representing the goal of the user-role reachability problem, does not contain universal quantifiers and it is called an *existential BSR formula*.

Example 1. We illustrate how TR works by means of an example taken from [23]. For simplicity, we assume separate administration (recall the definition at the end of Section 2). Let $U = \{u_1\}$, $R = \{r_1, ..., r_8\}$, initially $UA := \{(u_1, r_1), (u_1, r_4), (u_1, r_7)\}$, rules $(\{r_1\}, r_2)$, $(\{r_2\}, r_3)$, $(\{r_3, \overline{r_4}\}, r_5)$, $(\{r_5\}, r_6)$, $(\{\overline{r_2}\}, r_7)$, and $(\{r_7\}, r_8)$ are in *can_assign*, rules (r_1), (r_2), (r_3), (r_5), (r_6), and (r_7) are in *can_revoke*, and the goal be $(u_1, \{r_6\})$.

TR works by first introducing the unary predicates $r_1, ..., r_8$ in V. Then, it forms the following universal formula In from UA:

$$
\forall x. \begin{pmatrix} (r_1(x) \Leftrightarrow x = u_1) \wedge (r_4(x) \Leftrightarrow x = u_1) \wedge (r_7(x) \Leftrightarrow x = u_1) \wedge \\ \neg r_2(x) \wedge \neg r_3(x) \wedge \neg r_5(x) \wedge \neg r_6(x) \wedge \neg r_8(x) \end{pmatrix} .
$$

The translation of $(\{r_5\}, r_6)$ in *can_assign* is $\exists x. \forall y. (r_5(x) \wedge (r_6{}'(y) \Leftrightarrow (y = x \vee r_6(y))) \wedge Id(R \setminus \{r_6\}))$, that of (r_1) in *can_revoke* is $\exists x. \forall y. (r_1(x) \wedge (r_1{}'(y) \Leftrightarrow (y \neq x \wedge r_1(y))) \wedge Id(R \setminus \{r_1\}))$, and that of the goal is $G := \exists x. (r_6(x) \wedge x = u_1)$. □

Given the translation procedure 1, we can now explain how solving the reachability problem for BSR-based STS is equivalent to solving user-role reachability problems. First, define a *state* of a BSR-based STS $S = \langle V, In, Tr\rangle$ to be a mapping from the set V to a user-role assignment relation such that $(u, r) \in UA$ when $r(u)$ holds. Then, define a run of S as a (possibly infinite) sequence $s_0, s_1, ...$ of states such that s_0 satisfies (in the sense of first-order logic) In and for every

---

Procedure 2. The backward reachability procedure BR

Input: $S = \langle V, In, Tr \rangle$ is a $\mathcal{L}$-based STS and G is an assertion of $\mathcal{L}$
Output: answer to the reachability problem for S and G
1. $P \leftarrow G;\ B \leftarrow \mathit{false};$
2. **while** $(P \wedge \neg B$ is satisfiable$)$ **do**
3.   **if** $(In \wedge P$ is satisfiable$)$ **then**
4.   **return reachable**
5.   **end if**
6. $B \leftarrow P \vee B;$
7. $P \leftarrow Pre(Tr, P);$
8. **end while**
9. **return unreachable**

$i = 0, 1, ...$, we have that s_i, s_{i+1} satisfy tr for some tr in Tr. Let $s_0, ..., s_n, ...$ be a run of S, we say that s_n is *reachable* from s_0 for $n \geq 1$. The *reachability problem* for a STS S and a *goal* assertion G of BSR amounts to establish if there exists a run $s_0, ..., s_n, ...$ of S such that s_n satisfies (in the sense of first-order logic) G. By definition of states of a BSR-STS, it is easy to transform sequences of states to sequences of RBAC policies. Thus, the answer to a user-role reachability problem P is the same to that of the reachability problem for a BSR-STS S and goal G when $(S, G) = \mathrm{TR}(P)$.

We are now left with the problem of solving reachability problems for BSR-STSs. We use the approach in [17], summarized in Procedure 2. BR tries to compute an assertion of $\mathcal{L}$, stored in B, characterizing all states from which those satisfying G are reachable by executing finitely many transitions in Tr. If the loop terminates at iteration n, then B stores such an assertion since it contains the disjunction of the n pre-images of G (stored in P). The pre-image of an assertion K of $\mathcal{L}$ containing the system variables in V relative to a transition tr in Tr is defined as follows:

$$Pre(tr, K) := \exists V'.(tr(V, V') \wedge K(V'))$$

and characterizes the set of states from which those satisfying assertion K are reachable. By abuse of notation, we write $Pre(Tr, K)$ instead of $Pre(\bigvee_{tr \in Tr} tr, K)$. Simple logical manipulations show that Pre is *monotonic in its first argument*, i.e. if $Tr_1 \subseteq Tr_2$ then $Pre(Tr_1, K) \Rightarrow Pre(Tr_2, K)$ is valid.

Let us consider the n-iteration of the loop in BR, P stores $Pre^n(Tr, G)$ and B stores $\bigvee_{i=0}^{n} Pre^i(Tr, G)$, where $Pre^0(Tr, G) := G$ and $Pre^{k+1}(Tr, G) := Pre(Tr, Pre^k(Tr, G))$ for $k = 0, ..., n-1$. Upon termination of BR, the assertion in B is the set of *backward reachable states (from G)*. The formulae checked for satisfiability at lines 2 and 3 are

$$Pre^n(Tr, G) \wedge \neg \bigvee_{i=0}^{n-1} Pre^i(Tr, G) \tag{1}$$

$$In \wedge Pre^n(Tr, G), \tag{2}$$

respectively. Checking the satisfiability of (1) is the *fix-point test* since it is equivalent (by refutation) to verifying the validity of $Pre^n(Tr, G) \Rightarrow \bigvee_{i=0}^{n-1} Pre^i(Tr, G)$ while the converse, i.e. the validity of $\bigvee_{i=0}^{n-1} Pre^i(Tr, G) \Rightarrow Pre^n(Tr, G)$ holds by definition of pre-image. The un-satisfiability of (2) at every iteration $i \leq n$ implies the un-satisfiability of $In \wedge \bigvee_{i=0}^{n} Pre^i(Tr, G)$. This means that checking that none of the states characterized by the assertion in B are allowed as initial states of S is equivalent to verify that there is no state satisfying G that is also reachable from an initial state and G is unreachable (cf. line 9 of Procedure 2).

Theorem 1 ([17]). BR *is a decision procedure for the reachability problem of BSR-STSs.*

The main argument underlying the proof of this result is two-fold. First, the satisfiability checks at line 2 and 3 of Procedure 2 are decidable. To see this, observe that formulae (1) and (2) can be rewritten to logically equivalent BSR formulae, whose satisfiability is well-known to be decidable (see, e.g., [16]). Efficient theorem proving techniques (see, e.g., [17])—available in Satisfiability Modulo Theories (SMT) solvers—can be used in practice to tackle such satisfiability checks. Second, the procedure always terminates by using a standard technique for proving termination (see [17] for details).

Let $\texttt{Solve}(P) = \texttt{BR}(\texttt{TR}(P))$ for a user-role reachability problem P.

Corollary 1. Solve *decides the user-role reachability problem.*

This follows from Theorem 1 and the fact that $r(u)$ is interpreted as $(u, r) \in UA$.

Example 2. Let us consider again the user-role reachability problem in Example 1. The BSR formula representing the (fix-point) set of backward reachable states obtained by invoking BR is

$$\exists x. \begin{pmatrix} (r_6(x) \wedge x = u_1) \vee (r_5(x) \wedge x = u_1) \vee (r_3(x) \wedge \neg r_4(x) \wedge x = u_1) \vee \\ (r_2(x) \wedge \neg r_4(x) \wedge x = u_1) \vee (r_1(x) \wedge \neg r_4(x) \wedge x = u_1) \end{pmatrix} \quad (3)$$

It is not difficult to verify that the initial RBAC policy UA (see again Example 1) is not in the set of states represented by (3), by checking that the conjunction of In—representing UA and (3) is unsatisfiable (recall that this check can be done automatically because of the decidability of BSR formulae). We are thus entitled to conclude that the goal $(u_1, \{r_6\})$ is unreachable.   □

Remark. By properties stated and proved in [17] (from which Corollary 1 derives), we observe that Solve is capable of solving user-role reachability problem for a *finite but unknown number of users*. This means that our technique for safety analysis is capable of coping with dynamic situations in which users may join or leave the organization in which the RBAC policies are administered. This dramatically enlarges the scope of applicability of the analysis and thus the usefulness of its results. For lack of space, we cannot discuss the reasons of this; the interested reader is pointed to [17]. The incremental version of Solve developed below inherits this feature.

4   Incremental Analysis of Evolving ARBAC Policies

An *evolving ARBAC policy* is a pair $(\psi; \omega)$ where ψ is the "original" set of rules and ω is a finite sequence of operations of the form add(α) or delete(α). Applying add(α) (delete(α), respectively) to ψ generates a new set of rules $\psi \cup \{\alpha\}$ ($\psi \setminus \{\alpha\}$, respectively). The sequence $P_0, ..., P_n$ of user-role reachability problems induced by an evolving ARBAC policy $(\psi; op_1, ..., op_n)$ and an initial user-role reachability problem $P = \langle UA, \psi, (u_g, R_g) \rangle$ is such that $P_0 = P$ and $P_i = \langle UA, \psi_i, (u_g, R_g) \rangle$ where ψ_i is obtained from ψ_{i-1} by applying the operation op_i for $i = 1, ..., n$. We now derive an incremental version of the procedure Solve capable of re-using the set of backward reachable states computed to solve P_{i-1} to infer an answer for P_i.

The following two observations are the basis of our approach. First, under certain conditions, it is possible to derive the answer to P_i from that of P_{i-1} without invoking the symbolic reachability procedure BR (Procedure 2). Second, it is possible to design an "incremental" version of BR, denoted iBR, capable of re-using a symbolic representation of the set of backward reachable states computed in a previous invocation. While such a procedure—called, iBR—will be described in Section 4.1, for the time being, it is sufficient to know that it takes as input a BSR-STS $S = \langle V, In, Tr \rangle$ and a goal formula G together with the reference B to a formula representing the set of backward reachable states computed in a previous invocation of iBR. It then returns either (unreachable, ϵ), with ϵ being the empty sequence, iff G is unreachable from In by applying a finite sequence of transitions in Tr or (reachable, σ) with σ being a non-empty sequence of transitions in Tr leading from In to G. The pre-condition of iBR is that

$$\text{there exist } n \geq 0 \text{ and } \widehat{Tr} \subseteq Tr \text{ such that } B \text{ refers to } \bigvee_{i=0}^{n} Pre^i(\widehat{Tr}, G). \quad (4)$$

We emphasize that, when invoking iBR(S, G, B), the parameters S and G are passed by value whereas B by reference so that, upon returning, B refers to the newly computed set of backward reachable states. We assume that after an invocation to iBR, (4) holds again, i.e. (4) is an invariant of iBR. If $n = 0$, then the formula above reduces to *false* and iBR($S, G, false$) is equivalent to BR(S, G), except for the capability of returning the sequence of transitions leading from an initial state to one satisfying the goal G together with reachable.

We are now ready to describe the incremental version SolveEvolving of Solve, shown in Procedure 3. The original user-role reachability problem $\langle UA, \psi, (u_g, R_g) \rangle$ is translated (by invoking TR, c.f. Procedure 1), solved from scratch (the third parameter of iBR refers to *false* meaning that there is no previous knowledge about the set of backward reachable states), and the user is notified of the result via notify (line 1). Such a procedure simply prints out a message reporting if the user-role reachability problem under consideration (identified with original or the operation op that has been applied) is reachable or unreachable and, in the first case, also shows the sequence σ of administrative actions leading from the initial RBAC policy to one satisfying the goal. Afterwards (lines 2-25), the processing of the sequence ω of operations for adding or deleting administrative actions is started until none is left. At each iteration, an operation op in ω is

Procedure 3. SolveEvolving

Input: Original user-role reachability problem $\langle UA, \psi, (u_g, R_g) \rangle$ and
sequence ω of operations

1. $(S, G) \leftarrow \text{TR}(\langle UA, \psi, (u_g, R_g) \rangle)$; $(res, \sigma) \leftarrow \text{iBR}(S, G, false)$; notify(original, res, σ);

2. **while** ($\omega \neq \epsilon$) **do**
3. $op \leftarrow \text{first}(\omega)$; $\omega \leftarrow \text{rest}(\omega)$;
4.   **if** ($res = \text{reachable}$) **then**
5.   **if** ($op = \text{add}(\alpha)$) **then**
6. $S \leftarrow S \oplus [\alpha]$;
7.   **else if** ($op = \text{delete}(\alpha)$) **then**
8. $S \leftarrow S \ominus [\alpha]$; $B \leftarrow \text{Filter}(B, \alpha)$;
9.   **if** ($\alpha \in \sigma$) **then**
10. $(res, \sigma) \leftarrow \text{iBR}(S, G, B)$;
11.   **end if**
12.   **end if**
13.   **else if** ($res = \text{unreachable}$) **then**
14.   **if** ($op = \text{add}(\alpha)$) **then**
15. $S \leftarrow S \oplus [\alpha]$;
16.   Let r_t be the target role of α and $F \leftarrow \begin{cases} \exists x. r_t(x) & \text{if } \alpha \in can\_assign \\ \exists x. \neg r_t(x) & \text{if } \alpha \in can\_revoke \end{cases}$
17.   **if** ($F \Rightarrow B$ is valid) **and** ($Pre([\alpha], B) \Rightarrow B$ is invalid) **then**
18. $(res, \sigma) \leftarrow \text{iBR}(S, G, B)$;
19.   **end if**
20.   **else if** ($op = \text{delete}(\alpha)$) **then**
21. $S \leftarrow S \ominus [\alpha]$; $B \leftarrow \text{Filter}(B, \alpha)$;
22.   **end if**
23.   **end if**
24.   notify(op, res, σ);
25. **end while**

considered (line 3) and one among the following four cases (lines 5-6, 7-12, 14-19, or 20-22) is executed depending on the answer res to the previous problem and the type of the operation op. In each, the translation of a rule α is added (line 6 or 15) to or deleted (line 8 or 21) from S, where $S \oplus [\alpha] = \langle V, In, Tr \cup \{[\alpha]\} \rangle$ and $S \ominus [\alpha] = \langle V, In, Tr \setminus \{[\alpha]\} \rangle$ when $S = \langle V, In, Tr \rangle$. Let $P_0, ..., P_n$ be the sequence of user-role reachability problems induced by the evolving ARBAC policy $(\psi; \omega)$, it is easy to see that $(S, G) = \text{TR}(P_i)$ at iteration $i = 0, ..., n$ of the loop when executing SolveEvolving(P, ω). We now describe each case in detail.

Let $\overline{P} = \langle UA, \overline{\psi}, (u_g, R_g) \rangle$ and $\overline{S} = \text{TR}(\overline{P}) = \langle V, In, \overline{Tr} \rangle$ be the user-role reachability problem and the content of the variable S at the previous iteration of the loop, respectively, together with $\overline{res}$ and $\overline{\sigma}$ be the values stored in the variables res and σ, respectively, at the previous iteration of the loop.

(lines 5-6) $\overline{res}$ is reachable and op is add(α): indeed, the goal (u_g, R_g) is still reachable since all the actions in $\overline{\sigma}$ are in $\overline{\psi} \cup \{[\alpha]\}$, i.e. are still available in the new user-role reachability problem. So, there is no need to invoke iBR and

SolveEvolving can notify the user that the answer is again $(\overline{res}, \overline{\sigma})$ (line 24). It is easy to see that the invariant (4) of iBR still holds at the end of the current iteration of the loop.

(lines 7-11) $\overline{res}$ is reachable and op is delete(α): after removing α from S, we invoke the function Filter so that B now contains the formula

$$\bigvee_{j=0}^{m} Pre^{j}(\overline{Tr} \setminus \{[\alpha]\}, G) \tag{5}$$

describing the sub-set of backward reachable states of those computed by the last invocation of iBR not taking into account the action α being deleted (for some $m \geq 0$). I.e. (5) is the post-condition of the function Filter, whose efficient implementation will be described in Section 4.1. Since (5) holds after the invocation of Filter, it is easy to see that also the invariant (4) of iBR holds at the end of the current iteration of the loop. Then, we consider two cases. If the deleted action α is not in the sequence $\overline{\sigma}$ of administrative actions leading from the initial policy to one satisfying the goal, then SolveEvolving can immediately notify the user that the answer is again $(\overline{res}, \overline{\sigma})$ (line 24). Otherwise (i.e. α is in $\overline{\sigma}$), we invoke iBR on the new reachability problem $\overline{S} \ominus [\alpha]$ and the user is notified of the newly computed values of res and σ (line 24).

(lines 14-19) $\overline{res}$ is unreachable and op is add(α): we consider depending on the fact that the set $\overline{B}$ of backward reachable states is affected or not by the addition of the administrative action α. To verify this, we first build the formula F (line 16) which is satisfied by any set of states in which the target role r_t of α is assigned (if $\alpha \in can\_assign$) or not (if $\alpha \in can\_revoke$) to some user. Then, it is checked whether F is contained in $\overline{B}$ ($F \Rightarrow B$ is valid or, by refutation, $F \wedge \neg B$ is unsatisfiable) but the set of states described by the pre-image of $\overline{B}$ with respect to $[\alpha]$ is not included in $\overline{B}$ ($Pre([\alpha], \overline{B}) \Rightarrow \overline{B}$ is invalid or, by refutation, $Pre([\alpha], \overline{B}) \wedge \neg \overline{B}$ is satisfiable). Notice that both checks are decidable because of the decidability of the satisfiability of BSR formulae. If $\alpha \in can\_assign$ and the check fails, then $\overline{B}$ is unaffected by the addition of α since either the target role r_t is assigned to no user in $\overline{B}$ or the pre-image of $\overline{B}$ with respect to $[\alpha]$ is already in the fix-point; similarly, when $\alpha \in can\_revoke$. If the check succeeds, iBR is invoked on the updated set $\overline{S} \oplus [\alpha]$ of transition formulae and the goal G while considering the previously computed set $\overline{B}$ of backward reachable states. In both cases, it is not difficult to see that that the invariant (4) of iBR is maintained at the end of the current iteration.

Example 3. Let $\overline{P}$ be the user-role reachability problem in Example 1. Recall that the set of backward reachable states is represented by (3) in Example 2. Now, consider the following three problems all derived from $\overline{P}$ by adding action

- $(\{r_3\}, r_7)$: $F = \exists x. r_7(x)$, $F \Rightarrow$ (3) is invalid, SolveEvolving can notify that the answer is **unreachable**;
- $(\{r_1\}, r_3)$: $F = \exists x. r_3(x)$, $F \Rightarrow$ (3) is valid, $Pre([(\{r_1\}, r_3)], (3))$ is $\exists x. (r_1(x) \wedge \neg r_4(x) \wedge x = u_1)$, which is the last disjunct in (3) and thus $Pre([(\{r_1\}, r_3)], (3)) \Rightarrow$ (3) is trivially valid, SolveEvolving can notify that the answer is **unreachable**;

– $(\{r_1\}, r_5)$: $F = \exists x.r_5(x)$, $F \Rightarrow (3)$ is valid, $Pre([(\{r_1\}, r_5)], (3))$ is $\exists x.(r_1(x) \wedge x = u_1)$ that is not in (3), and thus $Pre([(\{r_1\}, r_5)], (3)) \Rightarrow (3)$ is invalid, and we need to invoke iBR on the new reachability problem.   □

(lines 20-22) $\overline{res}$ is unreachable and op is delete(α): indeed, the goal (u_g, R_g) is still unreachable since, at the previous iteration of the loop, we had that $In \wedge \bigvee_{i=0}^{n} Pre^i(\overline{Tr}, G)$ was unsatisfiable as $\overline{res}$ is unreachable. Now, observe that $\bigvee_{j=0}^{m} Pre^j(\overline{Tr} \setminus \{[\alpha]\}, G) \Rightarrow \bigvee_{i=0}^{n} Pre^i(\overline{Tr}, G)$ is valid since Pre is monotonic with respect to its first argument (as stated in Section 3). From these, by simple Boolean reasoning, we can conclude that $In \wedge \bigvee_{j=1}^{m} Pre^j(\overline{Tr} \setminus \{[\alpha]\}, G)$ is also unsatisfiable. Because of the post-condition (5) of Filter, it is easy to see that the invariant (4) of iBR is maintained.

Example 4. Let $\overline{P}$ be again the user-role reachability problem in Example 1. Consider removing action $(\{r_2\}, r_3)$ from $\overline{P}$. It is easy to see that the goal is still unreachable. By invoking the function Filter, variable B refers to the formula

$$\exists x. \left((r_6(x) \wedge x = u_1) \vee (r_5(x) \wedge x = u_1) \vee (r_3(x) \wedge \neg r_4(x) \wedge x = u_1) \right), \quad (6)$$

which is obtained by deleting the pre-image of the goal w.r.t. $(\{r_2\}, r_3)$, namely $\exists x.(r_2(x) \wedge \neg r_4(x) \wedge x = u_1)$ and $\exists x.(r_1(x) \wedge \neg r_4(x) \wedge x = u_1)$. SolveEvolving can consider new operations with the new set of backward reachable states.   □

4.1   iBR and Filter

Procedures iBR and Filter use a decorated version of formulae. Let ϵ denote the empty sequence and σ be a (finite, possibly empty) sequence of administrative actions, i.e. either $\sigma = \epsilon$ or there exists $l \geq 1$ such that $\sigma = \alpha_1; \ldots; \alpha_l$ for α_i an administrative action with $i = 1, ..., l$. If K is a BSR formula, then K^σ is a *decorated BSR formula* for σ a sequence of administrative actions. The logical reading of the decorated BSR formulae K^σ is simply the BSR formula K; for instance, $K_1^{\sigma_1} \Rightarrow K_2^{\sigma_2}$ is equivalent to $K_1 \Rightarrow K_2$. We will also use Boolean combinations of standard and decorated BSR formulae, its logical meaning is simply obtained by forgetting the decorations; for example, the meaning of $K_1 \wedge K_2^\sigma$ is simply $K_1 \wedge K_2$ with σ a sequence of administrative actions.

We derive the incremental version iBR of BR by performing the following two modifications on the code of Procedure 1. First, we replace line 1 with

if $(B = false)$ then $P \leftarrow G^\epsilon$; else $P \leftarrow B$; end if

i.e. variable P contains the goal G decorated by the empty sequence ϵ when there is no information about previous reachability problems; otherwise, P contains the set of states computed in a previous invocation of iBR (recall that B is a parameter passed by reference). The second modification concerns the computation of pre-images: $Pre([\alpha], K^\sigma)$ is the BSR formula $Pre([\alpha], K)$ decorated by the sequence $\alpha; \sigma$ of administrative actions. It is thus not difficult to see that variables P and B contain decorated BSR formulae of the form

$$\bigvee_{i=0}^{m} K_i^{\sigma_i} \quad (7)$$

for some $m \geq 0$, K_i is a decorated BSR formula for $i = 0, ..., m$ (as before, the formula reduces to *false* when $m = 0$). The last modification to the code of Procedure 1 refers to the conditional at lines 3-5. Recalling (7), we can assume that the decorated version of (2) has the form $In \wedge (7)$. Such a formula is satisfiable iff there exists $i^* \in \{0, ..., m\}$ such that $In \wedge K_i^{\sigma_i}$ is so. Thus, we replace lines 3-5 with the following

> **for** $i = 0$ **to** m **do**
>   **if** $(In \wedge K_i^{\sigma_i}$ is satisfiable) **then** (reachable, σ_i) **end if**
> **end for**

which allows iBR to return the sequence of administrative actions making a goal reachable, by simply reading the decoration σ_i of a disjunct $K_i^{\sigma_i}$ of the decorated BSR formula stored in P. The fact that (4) is an invariant of iBR can be shown by a case-analysis on the result returned by the previous invocation of iBR.

Filter also exploits decorated BSR formulae. Let (7) be the formula in B and α an administrative action, Filter(B, α) returns the decorated BSR formula $\bigvee_{j \in J} K_j^{\sigma_j}$ for $J = \{j \in \{0, ..., m\} | \alpha \notin \sigma_j\}$. It is easy to verify that the post-condition (5) holds.

5   Implementation and Experiments

We have used Python to implement SolveEvolving in a system called IASASP. The tool is an evolution of ASASP [1,18], which can be seen as an implementation of Solve (introduced immediately before Corollary 1, towards the end of Section 3). The implementation of iBR is done by invoking the model checker MCMT [7] to re-use its capability of saving the symbolic representation of the set of backward reachable states to a file and consider it for later invocations. Below, we describe an experimental evaluation comparing IASASP with an implementation of the approach in [8,9] on a set of randomly generated benchmark problems. We consider four versions of the technique in [8,9]: *IncFwd1*, *IncFwd2*, and *LazyInc* are based on the forward reachability algorithm of [23] and assume separate administration whereas *IncFwdWSA* is an incremental forward algorithm for user-role reachability problems not assuming separate administration. The reader interested in the description of these algorithms is pointed to [8,9]; for this paper, it is sufficient to know that these algorithms incorporate ideas (of increasing degree of sophistication) to permit the re-use of previously computed sets of reachable states.

We consider six sets of benchmarks whose characteristics are shown in tables T1, T2, and T3 of Figure 1. The user-role reachability problems in $B_1, ..., B_4$ assume separate administration whereas those in B_5 and B_6 do not (first column of T1). The initial user-role reachability problems in $B_1, ..., B_4$ share the same (empty) initial RBAC policy and the same set ψ_1 of administrative actions (second column of T1 under 'Initial problem'). The problems in B_5 and B_6 have two distinct (non-empty) initial RBAC policies (UA_1 and UA_2, respectively) and share the same set ψ_2 of administrative actions. The answer to the initial user-role reachability problem is shown in column 'Answer' of T1 and the time t_1 taken by our tool and that t_2 taken by the tool of [8,9] are in column 'Time' with

T1	Separate Administration	Initial Problem			$|\omega|$	Number of instances
			Answer	Time		
B_1	Yes	$\langle \emptyset, \psi_1, g_1 \rangle$	Reach.	43.28/78.16	1	32
B_2	Yes	$\langle \emptyset, \psi_1, g_2 \rangle$	Unreach.	41.15/80.22	1	32
B_3	Yes	$\langle \emptyset, \psi_1, g_1 \rangle$	Reach.	43.28/78.16	3, 5, 7, 10, 15, 20	15
B_4	Yes	$\langle \emptyset, \psi_1, g_2 \rangle$	Unreach.	41.15/80.22	3, 5, 7, 10, 15, 20	15
B_5	No	$\langle UA_1, \psi_2, g_3 \rangle$	Reach.	45.19/83.65	1	32
B_6	No	$\langle UA_2, \psi_2, g_4 \rangle$	Unreach.	61.42/116.73	1	32

T2	$|can\_assign|$	$|can\_revoke|$	Total
ψ_1	313	64	377
ψ_2	296	55	351

T3	g_1	g_2	g_3	g_4
Size	5	2	3	1

Fig. 1. Characteristics of the 6 benchmark sets

the format t_1/t_2 (both in seconds). The actions in ψ_1 are randomly generated following the approach in [23] while the actions in ψ_2 are those of the university ARBAC policy in [23]. The number of elements in can_assign and can_revoke (with their sum) are show in T2. The problems in B_1 and B_3 (B_2 and B_4, respectively) share the same goal g_1 (g_2, respectively). The size of the goals (i.e. the number of roles) in the problems are in T3. As shown in column '$|\omega|$' of T1, the length of the sequences ω of "add" and "delete" actions in B_1, B_2, B_5, and B_6 is 1; this means that the tools need to solve just one user-role reachability problem besides the initial one for instances in these benchmark sets. The length of the sequences ω of "add" and "delete" actions in B_3 and B_4 is $\ell = 3, 5, 7, 10, 15, 20$; this means that the tools need to solve ℓ user-role reachability problems besides the initial one. For problems in B_1, B_2, B_5, and B_6, we consider 32 distinct instances of sequences of actions of length 1 while for those in B_3 and B_4, we consider 15 distinct instances of sequences of actions of increasing length $\ell = 3, 5, 7, 10, 15, 20$ (see column 'Number of instances' of T1).

All the experiments were performed on an Intel QuadCore (3.6 GHz) CPU with 16 GB Ram running Ubuntu 11.10. The timings of the tools on the problems in the six benchmarks are reported in Figure 2; they are in seconds, are obtained by averaging the times taken over the number of instances indicated in the last column of T1 (cf. Figure 1), and measure the performance of processing the sequence ω of operations being considered, not including the time used to solve the initial user-role reachability problem since we want to compare the performances of the two approaches in handling changes to the set of administrative operations, not in solving single instance problems. However, notice how IASASP is better than the tool of [8,9] on the initial (single instance) problems in the benchmarks $B_1, ..., B_6$ by considering the column 'Time' in Table T1 of Figure 1. Any operation can affect the reachability of the goal in the benchmarks that we consider. The table on the upper-left corner and the two plots refer to benchmark sets B_1, B_2, B_3, and B_4 under separation administration whereas the table on the upper-right corner to B_5 and B_6 that do not assume separate administration. In almost cases, IASASP performs and scales better than the

Operation in ω	Time					Operation in ω	Time	
	IncFwd1	IncFwd2	LazyInc	IASASP			IncFwdWSA	IASASP
B_1 add can_assign	0	10.31	0	0.01		add can_assign	10.07	0.03
delete can_assign	69.72	11.14	11.14	1.75		delete can_assign	8.62	4.84
add can_revoke	0	1.07	0	0.01	B_5 add can_revoke	5.14	0.03
delete can_revoke	12.15	1.72	1.72	0.47		delete can_revoke	2.35	1.31
add can_assign	132.93	68.79	68.79	5.23		add can_assign	32.27	5.35
delete can_assign	0	12.09	0	0.01		delete can_assign	6.76	0.03
B_2 add can_revoke	19.67	1.25	1.25	0.69	B_6 add can_revoke	11.2	1.05
delete can_revoke	0	6.44	0	0.01		delete can_revoke	0.46	0.03

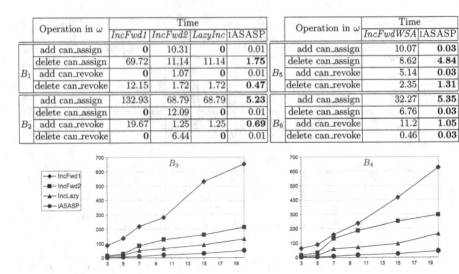

Fig. 2. Comparison of our approach with that of [8,9] on the six benchmark sets

techniques of [8,9] as shown by the two plots in Figure 2. IASASP performs better than the best version (*IncLazy*) of the techniques in [8,9] and clearly outperforms the worse version (*IncFwd1*). For instance in B_4, IASASP processes sequences of length 20 of operations in around 50 seconds whereas *IncLazy* takes more than 150 seconds, *IncFwd2* around 300 seconds, and *IncFwd1* takes more than 600 seconds. The better performances of our approach are due to the sophisticated techniques put in place in SolveEvolving to detect when the addition or deletion of an administrative action does not change the answer to the new instance of the reachability problem.

6   Conclusion

The paper discusses an algorithm for the automated analysis of evolving AR-BAC policies. The idea is to re-use the previously computed sets of backward reachable states in order to infer the answer to "similar" user-role reachability problems. An experimental evaluation shows that our incremental procedure performs better than the state-of-the-art techniques in [8,9]. As future work, we plan to extend our experiments on problems under non-separate administration and to compare IASASP also with the backward reachability algorithm in [9].

Acknowledgments. We thank the authors of [8,9] for making the code of their tool available to us and the help in using it. We also thank the anonymous reviewers for their constructive criticisms.

References

1. Alberti, F., Armando, A., Ranise, S.: ASASP: Automated Symbolic Analysis of Security Policies. In: Björner, N., Sofronie-Stokkermans, V. (eds.) CADE 2011. LNCS, vol. 6803, pp. 26–33. Springer, Heidelberg (2011)

2. Alberti, F., Armando, A., Ranise, S.: Efficient Symbolic Automated Analysis of Administrative Role Based Access Control Policies. In: ASIACCS. ACM Pr. (2011)
3. Ammann, P., Lipton, R., Sandhu, R.: The expressive power of multi-parent creation in monotonic access control models. JCS 4(2&3), 149–196 (1996)
4. Armando, A., Ranise, S.: Automated Symbolic Analysis of ARBAC-Policies. In: Cuellar, J., Lopez, J., Barthe, G., Pretschner, A. (eds.) STM 2010. LNCS, vol. 6710, pp. 17–34. Springer, Heidelberg (2011)
5. Armando, A., Ranise, S.: Scalable Automated Symbolic Analysis of ARBAC Policies by SMT Solving. JCS 20(4), 309–352 (2012)
6. Ferrara, A.L., Madhusudan, P., Parlato, G.: Policy Analysis for Self-administrated Role-Based Access Control. In: Piterman, N., Smolka, S.A. (eds.) TACAS 2013 (ETAPS 2013). LNCS, vol. 7795, pp. 432–447. Springer, Heidelberg (2013)
7. Ghilardi, S., Ranise, S.: MCMT: A Model Checker Modulo Theories. In: Giesl, J., Hähnle, R. (eds.) IJCAR 2010. LNCS, vol. 6173, pp. 22–29. Springer, Heidelberg (2010)
8. Gofman, M., Yang, P.: Efficient Policy Analysis for Evolving Administrative Role Based Access Control. Int. J. of Software and Informatics (to appear, 2014)
9. Gofman, M.I., Luo, R., Yang, P.: User-role reachability analysis of evolving administrative role based access control. In: Gritzalis, D., Preneel, B., Theoharidou, M. (eds.) ESORICS 2010. LNCS, vol. 6345, pp. 455–471. Springer, Heidelberg (2010)
10. Gupta, P., Stoller, S.D., Xu, Z.: Abductive analysis of administrative policies in rule-based access control. In: Jajodia, S., Mazumdar, C. (eds.) ICISS 2011. LNCS, vol. 7093, pp. 116–130. Springer, Heidelberg (2011)
11. Harrison, M.A., Ruzzo, W.L., Ullman, J.D.: Protection in Operating Systems. Communications of ACM 19(8), 461–471 (1976)
12. Jayaraman, K., Ganesh, V., Tripunitara, M., Rinard, M., Chapin, S.: Automatic Error Finding for Access-Control Policies. In: CCS. ACM (2011)
13. Koch, M., Mancini, L.V., Parisi-Presicce, F.: Decidability of Safety in Graph-Based Models for Access Control. In: Gollmann, D., Karjoth, G., Waidner, M. (eds.) ESORICS 2002. LNCS, vol. 2502, pp. 229–244. Springer, Heidelberg (2002)
14. Li, N., Tripunitara, M.V.: Security analysis in role-based access control. ACM TISSEC 9(4), 391–420 (2006)
15. Ramalingam, G., Reps, T.: A Categorized Bibliography on Incremental Computation. In: Proc. of POPL, pp. 502–510. ACM (1993)
16. Ramsey, F.P.: On a Problem of Formal Logic. Proceedings of the London Mathematical Society s2-30(1), 264–286 (1930)
17. Ranise, S.: Symbolic Backward Reachability with Effectively Propositional Logic— Applications to Security Policy Analysis. FMSD 42(1), 24–45 (2013)
18. Ranise, S., Truong, A., Armando, A.: Boosting Model Checking to Analyse Large ARBAC Policies. In: Jøsang, A., Samarati, P., Petrocchi, M. (eds.) STM 2012. LNCS, vol. 7783, pp. 273–288. Springer, Heidelberg (2013)
19. Sandhu, R., Bhamidipati, V., Munawer, Q.: The ARBAC97 model for role-based control administration of roles. ACM TISSEC 1(2), 105–135 (1999)
20. Sandhu, R., Coyne, E., Feinstein, H., Youmann, C.: Role-Based Access Control Models. IEEE Computer 2(29), 38–47 (1996)
21. Sasturkar, A., Yang, P., Stoller, S.D., Ramakrishnan, C.R.: Policy Analysis for Administrative Role Based Access Control. TCS 412(44), 6208–6234 (2011)
22. Soshi, M., Maekawa, M., Okamoto, E.: The Dynamic-Typed Access Matrix Model and Decidability of the Safety Problem. IEICE-TF (1), 1–14 (2004)
23. Stoller, S.D., Yang, P., Ramakrishnan, C.R., Gofman, M.I.: Efficient policy analysis for administrative role based access control. In: CCS. ACM Press (2007)

Mining Attribute-Based
Access Control Policies from Logs*

Zhongyuan Xu and Scott D. Stoller

Department of Computer Science, Stony Brook University, USA

Abstract. Attribute-based access control (ABAC) provides a high level of flexibility that promotes security and information sharing. ABAC policy mining algorithms have potential to significantly reduce the cost of migration to ABAC, by partially automating the development of an ABAC policy from information about the existing access-control policy and attribute data. This paper presents an algorithm for mining ABAC policies from operation logs and attribute data. To the best of our knowledge, it is the first algorithm for this problem.

1 Introduction

ABAC is becoming increasingly important as security policies become more dynamic and more complex. In industry, more and more products support ABAC, using a standardized ABAC language such as XACML or a vendor-specific ABAC language. In government, the Federal Chief Information Officer Council called out ABAC as a recommended access control model [1, 4]. ABAC allows "an unprecedented amount of flexibility and security while promoting information sharing between diverse and often disparate organizations" [4]. ABAC overcomes some of the problems associated with RBAC, notably role explosion [4].

ABAC promises long-term cost savings through reduced management effort, but manual development of an initial policy can be difficult and expensive [4]. *Policy mining* algorithms promise to drastically reduce the cost of migrating to ABAC, by partially automating the process.

Role mining, i.e., mining of RBAC policies, is an active research area and a currently relatively small (about $70 million) but rapidly growing commercial market segment [3]. In contrast, there is, so far, relatively little work on ABAC policy mining. We recently developed an algorithm to mine an ABAC policy from an ACL policy or RBAC policy [10].

However, an ACL policy or RBAC policy might not be available, e.g., if the current access control policy is encoded in a program or is not enforced by a computerized access control mechanism. An alternative source of information about the current access control policy is operation logs, or "logs" for short. Many software systems produce logs, e.g., for auditing, accounting, and accountability

---

* This material is based upon work supported in part by NSF under Grant CNS-0831298.

V. Atluri and G. Pernul (Eds.): DBSec 2014, LNCS 8566, pp. 276–291, 2014.

purposes. Molloy, Park, and Chari proposed the idea of mining policies from logs and developed algorithms for mining RBAC policies from logs [6].

The main challenge is that logs generally provide incomplete information about entitlements (i.e., granted permissions). Specifically, logs provide only a lower bound on the entitlements. Therefore, the generated policy should be allowed to include *over-assignments*, i.e., entitlements not reflected in the logs.

This paper presents an algorithm for mining ABAC policies from logs and attribute data. To the best of our knowledge, it is the first algorithm for this problem. It is based on our algorithm for mining ABAC policies from ACLs [10]. At a high level, the algorithm works as follows. It iterates over tuples in the user-permission relation extracted from the log, uses selected tuples as seeds for constructing candidate rules, and attempts to generalize each candidate rule to cover additional tuples in the user-permission relation by replacing conjuncts in attribute expressions with constraints. After constructing candidate rules that together cover the entire user-permission relation, it attempts to improve the policy by merging and simplifying candidate rules. Finally, it selects the highest-quality candidate rules for inclusion in the generated policy.

Several changes are needed to our algorithm for mining ABAC policies from ACLs to adapt it to mining from logs. When the algorithm generalizes, merges, or simplifies rules, it discards candidate rules that are invalid, i.e., that produce over-assignments. We modify those parts of the algorithm to consider those candidate rules, because, as discussed above, over-assignments must be permitted. To evaluate those candidate rules, we introduce generalized notions of rule quality and policy quality that quantify a trade-off between the number of over-assignments and other aspects of quality. We consider a metric that includes the normalized number of over-assignments in a weighted sum, a frequency-sensitive variant that assigns higher quality to rules that cover more frequently used entitlements, along the lines of [6], and a metric based on a theory quality metric in inductive logic programming [7, 8].

ABAC policy mining is similar to inductive logic programming (ILP), which learns logic-programming rules from facts. Mining ABAC policies from logs and attribute data is similar to ILP algorithms for learning from positive examples, because those algorithms allow the learned rules to imply more than the given facts (i.e., in our terminology, to have over-assignments). We implemented a translation from ABAC policy mining to Progol [8], a well-known ILP system.

We evaluated our algorithm and the ILP-based approach on some relatively small but non-trivial handwritten case studies and on synthetic ABAC policies. The results demonstrate our algorithm's effectiveness even when the log reflects only a fraction of the entitlements. Although the original (desired) ABAC policy is not reconstructed perfectly from the log, the mined policy is sufficiently similar to it that the mined policy would be very useful as a starting point for policy administrators tasked with developing that ABAC policy.

2 ABAC Policy Language

This section presents the ABAC policy language used in our work. It is adopted from [10]. We consider a specific ABAC policy language, but our approach is general and can be adapted to other ABAC policy languages. Our ABAC policy language contains the common ABAC policy language constructs, except arithmetic inequalities and negation, which are left for future work.

Given a set U of users and a set A_u of user attributes, user attribute data is represented by a function d_u such that $d_u(u, a)$ is the value of attribute a for user u. There is a distinguished user attribute uid that has a unique value for each user. Similarly, given a set R of resources and a set A_r of resource attributes, resource attribute data is represented by a function d_r such that $d_r(r, a)$ is the value of attribute a for resource r. There is a distinguished resource attribute rid that has a unique value for each resource. We assume the set A_u of user attributes can be partitioned into a set $A_{u,1}$ of *single-valued user attributes* which have atomic values, and a set $A_{u,m}$ of *multi-valued user attributes* whose values are sets of atomic values. Similarly, we assume the set A_r of resource attributes can be partitioned into a set $A_{r,1}$ of *single-valued resource attributes* and a set of $A_{r,m}$ of *multi-valued resource attributes*. We assume there is a distinguished atomic value $\perp$ used to indicate that an attribute's value is unknown.

A *user-attribute expression* (UAE) is a function e such that, for each user attribute a, $e(a)$ is either the special value $\top$, indicating that e imposes no constraint on the value of a, or a set (interpreted as a disjunction) of possible values of a excluding $\perp$. We refer to $e(a)$ as the *conjunct* for a. A UAE e *uses* attribute a if $e(a) \neq \top$. Let attr(e) denote the set of attributes used by e.

A user u *satisfies* a UAE e, denoted $u \models e$, iff $(\forall a \in A_{u,1}. e(a) = \top \vee \exists v \in e(a). d_u(u, a) = v)$ and $(\forall a \in A_{u,m}. e(a) = \top \vee \exists v \in e(a). d_u(u, a) \supseteq v)$. For multi-valued attributes, we use the condition $d_u(u, a) \supseteq v$ instead of $d_u(u, a) = v$ because elements of a multi-valued user attribute typically represent some type of capabilities of a user, so using $\supseteq$ expresses that the user has the specified capabilities and possibly more. For example, suppose $A_{u,1} = \{\text{dept}, \text{position}\}$ and $A_{u,m} = \{\text{courses}\}$. The function e_1 with $e_1(\text{dept}) = \{\text{CS}\}$ and $e_1(\text{position}) = \{\text{grad}, \text{ugrad}\}$ and $e_1(\text{courses}) = \{\{\text{CS101}, \text{CS102}\}\}$ is a user-attribute expression satisfied by users in the CS department who are either graduate or undergraduate students and whose courses include CS101 and CS102.

In examples, we may write attribute expressions with a logic-based syntax, for readability. For example, the above expression e_1 may be written as dept $=$ CS $\wedge$ position $\in \{\text{ugrad}, \text{grad}\} \wedge$ courses $\supseteq \{\text{CS101}, \text{CS102}\}$. For an example that uses $\supseteq\in$, the expression e_2 that is the same as e_1 except with $e_2(\text{courses}) = \{\{\text{CS101}\}, \{\text{CS102}\}\}$ may be written as dept $=$ CS $\wedge$ position $\in \{\text{ugrad}, \text{grad}\} \wedge$ courses $\supseteq\in \{\{\text{CS101}\}, \{\text{CS102}\}\}$, and is satisfied by graduate or undergraduate students in the CS department whose courses include either CS101 or CS102.

The *meaning* of a user-attribute expression e, denoted $[\![e]\!]_U$, is the set of users in U that satisfy it. User attribute data is an implicit argument to $[\![e]\!]_U$. We say that e *characterizes* the set $[\![e]\!]_U$.

A *resource-attribute expression* (RAE) is defined similarly, except using the set A_r of resource attributes instead of the set A_u of user attributes. The semantics of RAEs is defined similarly to the semantics of UAEs, except simply using equality, not $\supseteq$, in the condition for multi-valued attributes in the definition of "satisfies", because we do not interpret elements of multi-valued resource attributes specially (e.g., as capabilities).

Constraints express relationships between users and resources. An *atomic constraint* is a formula f of the form $a_{u,m} \supseteq a_{r,m}$, $a_{u,m} \ni a_{r,1}$, or $a_{u,1} = a_{r,1}$, where $a_{u,1} \in A_{u,1}$, $a_{u,m} \in A_{u,m}$, $a_{r,1} \in A_{r,1}$, and $a_{r,m} \in A_{r,m}$. The first two forms express that user attributes contain specified values. This is a common type of constraint, because user attributes typically represent some type of capabilities of a user. Let $\mathrm{uAttr}(f)$ and $\mathrm{rAttr}(f)$ refer to the user attribute and resource attribute, respectively, used in f. User u and resource r *satisfy* an atomic constraint f, denoted $\langle u, r \rangle \models f$, if $d_u(u, \mathrm{uAttr}(f)) \neq \bot$ and $d_r(u, \mathrm{rAttr}(f)) \neq \bot$ and formula f holds when the values $d_u(u, \mathrm{uAttr}(f))$ and $d_r(u, \mathrm{rAttr}(f))$ are substituted in it.

A *constraint* is a set (interpreted as a conjunction) of atomic constraints. User u and resource r *satisfy* a constraint c, denoted $\langle u, r \rangle \models c$, if they satisfy every atomic constraint in c. In examples, we write constraints as conjunctions instead of sets. For example, the constraint "specialties $\supseteq$ topics $\wedge$ teams $\ni$ treatingTeam" is satisfied by user u and resource r if the user's specialties include all of the topics associated with the resource, and the set of teams associated with the user contains the treatingTeam associated with the resource.

A *user-permission tuple* is a tuple $\langle u, r, o \rangle$ containing a user, a resource, and an operation. This tuple means that user u has permission to perform operation o on resource r. A *user-permission relation* is a set of such tuples.

A *rule* is a tuple $\langle e_u, e_r, O, c \rangle$, where e_u is a user-attribute expression, e_r is a resource-attribute expression, O is a set of operations, and c is a constraint. For a rule $\rho = \langle e_u, e_r, O, c \rangle$, let $\mathrm{uae}(\rho) = e_u$, $\mathrm{rae}(\rho) = e_r$, $\mathrm{ops}(\rho) = O$, and $\mathrm{con}(\rho) = c$. For example, the rule $\langle \text{true, type=task} \wedge \text{proprietary=false}, \{\text{read, request}\}, \text{projects} \ni \text{project} \wedge \text{expertise} \supseteq \text{expertise}\rangle$ used in our project management case study can be interpreted as "A user working on a project can read and request to work on a non-proprietary task whose required areas of expertise are among his/her areas of expertise." User u, resource r, and operation o *satisfy* a rule ρ, denoted $\langle u, r, o \rangle \models \rho$, if $u \models \mathrm{uae}(\rho) \wedge r \models \mathrm{rae}(\rho) \wedge o \in \mathrm{ops}(\rho) \wedge \langle u, r \rangle \models \mathrm{con}(\rho)$.

An *ABAC policy* is a tuple $\langle U, R, Op, A_u, A_r, d_u, d_r, Rules \rangle$, where U, R, A_u, A_r, d_u, and d_r are as described above, Op is a set of operations, and $Rules$ is a set of rules.

The user-permission relation induced by a rule ρ is $[\![\rho]\!] = \{\langle u, r, o \rangle \in U \times R \times Op \mid \langle u, r, o \rangle \models \rho\}$. Note that U, R, d_u, and d_r are implicit arguments to $[\![\rho]\!]$.

The user-permission relation induced by a policy π with the above form is $[\![\pi]\!] = \bigcup_{\rho \in Rules} [\![\rho]\!]$.

3   Problem Definition

An *operation log entry* e is a tuple $\langle u, r, o, t \rangle$ where $u \in U$ is a user, $r \in R$ is a resource, $o \in Op$ is an operation, and t is a timestamp. An *operation log* is a sequence of operation log entries. The user-permission relation induced by an operation log L is $UP(L) = \{\langle u, r, o \rangle \mid \exists t.\ \langle u, r, o, t \rangle \in L\}$.

The input to the *ABAC-from-logs policy mining problem* is a tuple $I = \langle U, R, Op, A_u, A_r, d_u, d_r, L \rangle$, where U is a set of users, R is a set of resources, Op is a set of operations, A_u is a set of user attributes, A_r is a set of resource attributes, d_u is user attribute data, d_r is resource attribute data, and L is an operation log, such that the users, resources, and operations that appear in L are subsets of U, R, and Op, respectively. The goal of the problem is to find a set of rules *Rules* such that the ABAC policy $\pi = \langle U, R, Op, A_u, A_r, d_u, d_r, Rules \rangle$ maximizes a suitable policy quality metric.

The policy quality metric should reflect the size and meaning of the policy. Size is measured by *weighted structural complexity* (WSC) [5], and smaller policies are considered to have higher quality. This is consistent with usability studies of access control rules, which conclude that more concise policies are more manageable. Informally, the WSC of an ABAC policy is a weighted sum of the number of elements in the policy. Specifically, the WSC of an attribute expression is the number of atomic values that appear in it, the WSC of an operation set is the number of operations in it, the WSC of a constraint is the number of atomic constraints in it, and the WSC of a rule is a weighted sum of the WSCs of its components, namely, $\mathrm{WSC}(\langle e_u, e_r, O, c \rangle) = w_1 \mathrm{WSC}(e_u) + w_2 \mathrm{WSC}(e_r) + w_3 \mathrm{WSC}(O) + w_4 \mathrm{WSC}(c)$, where the w_i are user-specified weights. The WSC of a set of rules is the sum of the WSCs of its members.

The meaning $[\![\pi]\!]$ of the ABAC policy is taken into account by considering the differences from $UP(L)$, which consist of over-assignments and under-assignments. The over-assignments are $[\![\pi]\!] \setminus UP(L)$. The under-assignments are $UP(L) \setminus [\![\pi]\!]$. Since logs provide only a lower-bound on the actual user-permission relation (a.k.a entitlements), it is necessary to allow some over-assignments, but not too many. Allowing under-assignments is beneficial if the logs might contain noise, in the form of log entries representing uses of permissions that should not be granted, because it reduces the amount of such noise that gets propagated into the policy; consideration of noise is left for future work. We define a policy quality metric that is a weighted sum of these aspects:

$$Q_{\mathrm{pol}}(\pi, L) = \mathrm{WSC}(\pi) + w_o \,|\, [\![\pi]\!] \setminus UP(L) \,|\, /\, |U| \tag{1}$$

where the *policy over-assignment weight* w_o is a user-specified weight for over-assignments, and for a set S of user-permission tuples, the frequency-weighted size of S with respect to log L is $|S|_L = \sum_{\langle u, r, o \rangle \in S} \mathrm{freq}(\langle u, r, o \rangle, L)$, where the relative frequency of a user-permission tuple in a log is given by the *frequency function* $\mathrm{freq}(\langle u, r, o \rangle, L) = |\{e \in L \mid \mathrm{userPerm}(e) = \langle u, r, o \rangle\}| / |L|$, where the user-permission part of a log entry is given by $\mathrm{userPerm}(\langle u, r, o, t \rangle) = \langle u, r, o \rangle$.

For simplicity, our presentation of the problem and algorithm assume that attribute data does not change during the time covered by the log. Accommodating changes to attribute data is not difficult. It mainly requires re-defining the notions of policy quality and rule quality (introduced in Section 4) to be based on the set of log entries covered by a rule, denoted $\llbracket \rho \rrbracket_{LE}$, rather than $\llbracket \rho \rrbracket$. The definition of $\llbracket \rho \rrbracket_{LE}$ is similar to the definition of $\llbracket \rho \rrbracket$, except that, when determining whether a log entry is in $\llbracket \rho \rrbracket_{LE}$, the attribute data in effect at the time of the log entry is used.

4   Algorithm

Our algorithm is based on the algorithm for mining ABAC policies from ACLs and attribute data in [10]. Our algorithm does not take the order of log entries into account, so the log can be summarized by the user-permission relation UP_0 induced by the log and the frequency function freq, described in the penultimate paragraph of Section 3.

Top-level pseudocode appears in Figure 1. We refer to tuples selected in the first statement of the first while loop as *seeds*. The top-level pseudocode is explained by embedded comments. It calls several functions, described next. Function names hyperlink to pseudocode for the function, if it is included in the paper, otherwise to the description of the function.

The function addCandRule($s_u, s_r, s_o, cc, uncovUP, Rules$) in Figure 2 first calls computeUAE to compute a user-attribute expression e_u that characterizes s_u, and computeRAE to compute a resource-attribute expression e_r that characterizes s_r. It then calls generalizeRule($\rho, cc, uncovUP, Rules$) to generalize rule $\rho = \langle e_u, e_r, s_o, \emptyset \rangle$ to ρ' and adds ρ' to candidate rule set $Rules$. The details of the functions called by addCandRule are described next.

The function computeUAE(s, U) computes a user-attribute expression e_u that characterizes the set s of users. Preference is given to attribute expressions that do not use uid, since attribute-based policies are generally preferable to identity-based policies, even when they have higher WSC, because attribute-based generalize better. Similarly, computeRAE(s, R) computes a resource-attribute expression that characterizes the set s of resources. Pseudocode for computeUAE and computeRAE are omitted. The function candidateConstraint(r, u) returns a set containing all of the atomic constraints that hold between resource r and user u. Pseudocode for candidateConstraint is straightforward and omitted.

The function generalizeRule($\rho, cc, uncovUP, Rules$) in Figure 3 attempts to generalize rule ρ by adding some of the atomic constraints in cc to ρ and eliminating the conjuncts of the user attribute expression and/or the resource attribute expression corresponding to the attributes used in those constraints, i.e., mapping those attributes to $\top$. We call a rule obtained in this way a *generalization* of ρ. Such a rule is more general than ρ in the sense that it refers to relationships instead of specific values. Also, the user-permission relation induced by a generalization of ρ is a superset of the user-permission relation induced by ρ. generalizeRule($\rho, cc, uncovUP, Rules$) returns the generalization ρ' of ρ with the best quality according to a given rule quality metric. Note that ρ' may cover tuples that are already covered (i.e., are in UP); in other words, our algorithm can generate policies containing rules whose meanings overlap.

A *rule quality metric* is a function $Q_{\mathrm{rul}}(\rho, UP)$ that maps a rule ρ to a totally-ordered set, with the ordering chosen so that larger values indicate high quality. The second argument UP is a set of user-permission tuples. Our rule quality metric assigns higher quality to rules that cover more currently uncovered user-permission tuples and have smaller size, with an additional term that imposes a penalty for over-assignments, measured as a fraction of the number of user-permission tuples covered by the rule, and with a weight specified by a parameter w_o', called the *rule over-assignment weight*.

$$Q_{\mathrm{rul}}(\rho, UP) = \frac{|[\![\rho]\!] \cap UP|}{|\rho|} \times (1 - \frac{w_o' \times |\mathrm{overAssign}(\rho)|}{|[\![\rho]\!]|}).$$

In generalizeRule, *uncovUP* is the second argument to Q_{rul}, so $[\![\rho]\!] \cap UP$ is the set of user-permission tuples in UP_0 that are covered by ρ and not covered by rules already in the policy. The loop over i near the end of the pseudocode for generalizeRule considers all possibilities for the first atomic constraint in cc that gets added to the constraint of ρ. The function calls itself recursively to determine the subsequent atomic constraints in c that get added to the constraint.

We also developed a frequency-sensitive variant of this rule quality metric. Let $Q_{\mathrm{rul}}^{\mathrm{freq}}$ denote the frequency-weighted variant of Q_{rul}, obtained by weighting each user-permission tuple by its relative frequency (i.e., fraction of occurrences) in the log, similar to the definition of λ-distance in [6]. Specifically, the definition of $Q_{\mathrm{rul}}^{\mathrm{freq}}$ is obtained from the definition of Q_{rul} by replacing $|[\![\rho]\!] \cap UP|$ with $|[\![\rho]\!] \cap UP|_L$ (recall that $|\cdot|_L$ is defined in Section 3).

We also developed a rule quality metric $Q_{\mathrm{rul}}^{\mathrm{ILP}}$ based closely on the theory quality metric for inductive logic programming described in [7]. Details of the definition are omitted to save space.

The function mergeRules(*Rules*) in Figure 3 attempts to improve the quality of *Rules* by removing redundant rules and merging pairs of rules. A rule ρ in *Rules* is *redundant* if *Rules* contains another rule ρ' such that every user-permission tuple in UP_0 that is in $[\![\rho]\!]$ is also in $[\![\rho']\!]$. Informally, rules ρ_1 and ρ_2 are merged by taking, for each attribute, the union of the conjuncts in ρ_1 and ρ_2 for that attribute. If adding the resulting rule ρ_{mrg} to the policy and removing rules (including ρ_1 and ρ_2) that become redundant improves policy quality and does not introduce over-assignments where none existed before, then ρ_{mrg} is added to *Rules*, and the redundant rules are removed from *Rules*. As optimizations (in the implementation, not reflected in the pseudocode), meanings of rules are cached, and policy quality is computed incrementally. mergeRules(*Rules*) updates its argument *Rules* in place, and it returns a Boolean indicating whether any rules were merged.

The function simplifyRules(*Rules*) attempts to simplify all of the rules in *Rules*. It updates its argument *Rules* in place, replacing rules in *Rules* with simplified versions when simplification succeeds. It returns a Boolean indicating whether any rules were simplified. It attempts to simplify each rule in several ways, including elimination of subsumed sets in conjuncts for multi-valued attributes, elimination of conjuncts, elimination of constraints, elimination of elements of sets in conjuncts for multi-valued user attributes, and elimination of

// *Rules is the set of candidate rules*
Rules = ∅
// *uncovUP contains user-permission tuples*
// *in UP$_0$ that are not covered by Rules*
uncovUP = *UP$_0$*.copy()
while ¬*uncovUP*.isEmpty()
  // *Select an uncovered tuple as a "seed".*
  ⟨*u, r, o*⟩ = some tuple in *uncovUP*
  cc = candidateConstraint(*r, u*)
  // *s$_u$ contains users with permission* ⟨*r, o*⟩
  // *and that have the same candidate*
  // *constraint for r as u*
  s$_u$ = {*u'* ∈ *U* | ⟨*u', r, o*⟩ ∈ *UP$_0$*
    ∧ candidateConstraint(*r, u'*) = *cc*}
  addCandRule(*s$_u$*, {*r*}, {*o*}, *cc*, *uncovUP*, *Rules*)
  // *s$_o$ is set of operations that u can apply to r*
  s$_o$ = {*o'* ∈ *Op* | ⟨*u, r, o'*⟩ ∈ *UP$_0$*}
  addCandRule({*u*}, {*r*}, *s$_o$*, *cc*, *uncovUP*, *Rules*)
end while

// *Repeatedly merge and simplify*
// *rules, until this has no effect*
mergeRules(*Rules*)
while simplifyRules(*Rules*)
  && mergeRules(*Rules*)
  skip
end while
// *Select high quality rules into Rules'.*
Rules' = ∅
Repeatedly move highest-quality rule
from *Rules* to *Rules'* until
$\sum_{\rho \in Rules'} [\![\rho]\!] \supseteq UP_0$, using
UP$_0$ \ [[*Rules'*]] as second argument to
Q$_{rul}$, and discarding a rule if it does
not cover any tuples in *UP$_0$* currently
uncovered by *Rules'*.
return *Rules'*

Fig. 1. Policy mining algorithm. The pseudocode starts in column 1 and continues in column 2.

function addCandRule(*s$_u$*, *s$_r$*, *s$_o$*, *cc*, *uncovUP*, *Rules*)
// *Construct a rule ρ that covers user-perm. tuples* {⟨*u, r, o*⟩ | *u* ∈ *s$_u$* ∧ *r* ∈ *s$_r$* ∧ *o* ∈ *s$_o$*}.
e$_u$ = computeUAE(*s$_u$*, *U*); *e$_r$* = computeRAE(*s$_r$*, *R*); *ρ* = ⟨*e$_u$*, *e$_r$*, *s$_o$*, ∅⟩
ρ' = generalizeRule(*ρ, cc, uncovUP, Rules*); *Rules*.add(*ρ'*); *uncovUP*.removeAll([[*ρ'*]])

Fig. 2. Compute a candidate rule *ρ'* and add *ρ'* to candidate rule set *Rules*

overlap between rules. The detailed definition is similar to the one in [10] and is omitted to save space.

4.1   Example

We illustrate the algorithm on a small fragment of our university case study (*cf.* Section 5.1). The fragment contains a single rule *ρ$_0$* = ⟨true, *type* ∈ {gradebook}, {addScore, readScore}, crsTaught ∋ crs⟩ and all of the attribute data from the full case study, except attribute data for gradebooks for courses other than cs601. We consider an operation log *L* containing three entries: {⟨csFac2, cs601gradebook, addScore, t$_1$⟩, ⟨csFac2, cs601gradebook, readScore, t$_2$⟩, ⟨csStu3, cs601gradebook, addScore, t$_3$⟩}. User csFac2 is a faculty in the computer science department who is teaching cs601; attributes are position = faculty, dept = cs, and crsTaught = {cs601}. csStu3 is a CS student who is a TA of cs601; attributes are position = student, dept = cs, and crsTaught = {cs601}. cs601gradebook is a resource with attributes type = gradebook, dept = cs, and crs = cs601.

Our algorithm selects user-permission tuple ⟨csFac2, cs601gradebook, addScore⟩ as the first seed, and calls function candidateConstraint to compute the set of atomic constraints that hold between csFac2 and cs601gradebook; the result is

function generalizeRule(ρ, cc, $uncovUP$, $Rules$)
// ρ_{best} is best generalization of ρ
$\rho_{\text{best}} = \rho$
// $gen[i][j]$ is a generalization of ρ using
// $cc'[i]$
$gen = $ new Rule[cc.length][3]
for $i = 1$ **to** cc.length
$\quad f = cc[i]$
$\quad$ // generalize by adding f and eliminating
$\quad$ // conjuncts for both attributes used in f.
$\quad gen[i][1] = \langle \text{uae}(\rho)[\text{uAttr}(f) \mapsto \top],$
$\quad\quad\quad \text{rae}(\rho)[\text{rAttr}(f) \mapsto \top],$
$\quad\quad\quad \text{ops}(\rho), \text{con}(\rho) \cup \{f\}\rangle$
$\quad$ // generalize by adding f and eliminating
$\quad$ // conjunct for user attribute used in f
$\quad gen[i][2] = \langle \text{uae}(\rho)[\text{uAttr}(f) \mapsto \top], \text{rae}(\rho),$
$\quad\quad\quad \text{ops}(\rho), \text{con}(\rho) \cup \{f\}\rangle$
$\quad$ // generalize by adding f and eliminating
$\quad$ // conjunct for resource attrib. used in f.
$\quad gen[i][3] = \langle \text{uae}(\rho), \text{rae}(\rho)[\text{rAttr}(f) \mapsto \top],$
$\quad\quad\quad \text{ops}(\rho), \text{con}(\rho) \cup \{f\}\rangle$
end for
for $i = 1$ **to** cc.length **and** $j = 1$ **to** 3
$\quad$ // try to further generalize $gen[i]$
$\quad \rho'' = \text{generalizeRule}(gen[i][j], cc[i+1..],$
$\quad\quad\quad\quad uncovUP, Rules)$
$\quad$ **if** $Q_{\text{rul}}(\rho'', uncovUP) > Q_{\text{rul}}(\rho_{\text{best}},$
$\quad\quad\quad\quad uncovUP)$
$\quad\quad \rho_{\text{best}} = \rho''$
$\quad$ **end if**
end for
return ρ_{best}

function mergeRules($Rules$)
// Remove redundant rules
$redun = \{\rho \in Rules \mid \exists \rho' \in Rules \setminus \{\rho\}.$
$\quad\quad [\![\rho]\!] \cap UP_0 \subseteq [\![\rho']\!] \cap UP_0\}$
$Rules$.removeAll($redun$)
// Merge rules
$workSet = \{(\rho_1, \rho_2) \mid \rho_1 \in Rules \wedge \rho_2 \in Rules$
$\quad\quad \wedge \rho_1 \neq \rho_2 \wedge \text{con}(\rho_1) = \text{con}(\rho_2)\}$
while not($workSet$.empty())
$\quad (\rho_1, \rho_2) = workSet$.remove()
$\quad \rho_{\text{mrg}} = \langle \text{uae}(\rho_1) \cup \text{uae}(\rho_2),$
$\quad\quad\quad \text{rae}(\rho_1) \cup \text{rae}(\rho_2),$
$\quad\quad\quad \text{ops}(\rho_1) \cup \text{ops}(\rho_2), \text{con}(\rho_1)\rangle$
$\quad$ // Find rules that become redundant
$\quad$ // if merged rule ρ_{mrg} is added
$\quad redun = \{\rho \in Rules \mid [\![\rho]\!] \subseteq [\![\rho_{\text{mrg}}]\!]\}$
$\quad$ // Add the merged rule and remove redun-
$\quad$ // dant rules if this improves policy quality
$\quad$ // and does not introduce over-assignments.
$\quad$ // where none existed before.
$\quad$ **if** $Q_{\text{pol}}(Rules \cup \{\rho_{\text{mrg}}\} \setminus redun) < Q_{\text{pol}}(Rules)$
$\quad\quad \wedge (\text{noOA}(\rho_1) \wedge \text{noOA}(\rho_2) \Rightarrow \text{noOA}(\rho_{\text{mrg}}))$
$\quad\quad Rules$.removeAll($redun$)
$\quad\quad workSet$.removeAll($\{(\rho_1, \rho_2) \in workSet \mid$
$\quad\quad\quad \rho_1 \in redun \vee \rho_2 \in redun\}$)
$\quad\quad workSet$.addAll($\{(\rho_{\text{mrg}}, \rho) \mid \rho \in Rules$
$\quad\quad\quad \wedge \text{con}(\rho) = \text{con}(\rho_{\text{mrg}})\}$)
$\quad\quad Rules$.add(ρ_{mrg})
$\quad$ **end if**
end while
return true if any rules were merged

Fig. 3. Left: Generalize rule ρ by adding some formulas from cc to its constraint and eliminating conjuncts for attributes used in those formulas. $f[x \mapsto y]$ denotes a copy of function f modified so that $f(x) = y$. $a[i..]$ denotes the suffix of array a starting at index i. Right: Merge pairs of rules in $Rules$, when possible, to reduce the WSC of $Rules$. (a, b) denotes an unordered pair with components a and b. The union $e = e_1 \cup e_2$ of attribute expressions e_1 and e_2 over the same set A of attributes is defined by: for all attributes a in A, if $e_1(a) = \top$ or $e_2(a) = \top$ then $e(a) = \top$ otherwise $e(a) = e_1(a) \cup e_2(a)$. noOA($\rho$) holds if ρ has no over-assignments, i.e., $[\![\rho]\!] \subseteq UP_0$.

$cc = \{\text{dept} = \text{dept}, \text{crsTaught} \ni \text{crs}\}$. addCandRule is called twice to compute candidate rules. The first call to addCandRule calls computeUAE to compute a UAE e_u that characterizes the set s_u containing users with permission $\langle \text{addScore}, \text{cs601gradebook}\rangle$ and with the same candidate constraint as csFac2 for cs601gradebook; the result is $e_u = (\text{position} \in \{\text{faculty}, \text{student}\} \wedge \text{dept} \in \{\text{cs}\} \wedge \text{crsTaught} \supseteq \{\{\text{cs601}\}\})$. addCandRule also calls computeRAE to compute a resource-attribute expression that characterizes $\{\text{cs601gradebook}\}$; the result is $e_r = (\text{crs} \in \{\text{cs601}\} \wedge \text{dept} \in \{\text{cs}\} \wedge \text{type} \in \{\text{gradebook}\})$. The set of operations considered in this call to addCandRule is simply $s_o = \{\text{addScore}\}$. addCandRule then calls generalizeRule, which generates a candidate rule ρ_1 which initially has e_u, e_r and s_o in the first three components, and then atomic constraints in cc are added to ρ_1, and conjuncts in e_u and e_r for attributes used in cc are eliminated; the result is $\rho_1 = \langle \text{position} \in \{\text{faculty}, \text{student}\}, \text{type} \in \{\text{gradebook}\},$ $\{\text{addScore}\}, \text{dept} = \text{dept} \wedge \text{crsTaught} \ni \text{crs}\rangle$, which also covers the third log entry. Similarly, the second call to addCandRule generates a candidate rule $\rho_2 = \langle \text{position} \in \{\text{faculty}\}, \text{type} \in \{\text{gradebook}\}, \{\text{addScore}, \text{readScore}\}, \text{dept} = \text{dept} \wedge \text{crsTaught} \ni \text{crs}\rangle$, which also covers the second log entry.

All of $UP(L)$ is covered, so our algorithm calls mergeRules, which attempts to merge ρ_1 and ρ_2 into rule $\rho_3 = \langle \text{position} \in \{\text{faculty}, \text{student}\}, \text{type} \in \{\text{gradebook}\},$ $\{\text{addScore}, \text{readScore}\}, \text{dept} = \text{dept} \wedge \text{crsTaught} \ni \text{crs}\rangle$. ρ_3 is discarded because it introduces an over-assignment while ρ_1 and ρ_2 do not. Next, simplifyRules is called, which first simplifies ρ_1 and ρ_2 to ρ_1' and ρ_2', respectively, and then eliminates ρ_1' because it covers a subset of the tuples covered by ρ_2'. The final result is ρ_2', which is identical to the rule ρ_0 in the original policy.

5   Evaluation Methodology

We evaluate our policy mining algorithms on synthetic operation logs generated from ABAC policies (some handwritten and some synthetic) and probability distributions characterizing the frequency of actions. This allows us to evaluate the effectiveness of our algorithm by comparing the mined policies with the original ABAC policies. We are eager to also evaluate our algorithm on actual operation logs and actual attribute data, when we are able to obtain them.

5.1   ABAC Policies

Case Studies. We developed four case studies for use in evaluation of our algorithm, described briefly here. Details of the case studies, including all policy rules, various size metrics (number of users, number of resources, etc.), and some illustrative attribute data, appear in [10].

Our *university case study* is a policy that controls access by students, instructors, teaching assistants, registrar officers, department chairs, and admissions officers to applications (for admission), gradebooks, transcripts, and course schedules. Our *health care case study* is a policy that controls access by nurses, doctors, patients, and agents (e.g., a patient's spouse) to electronic health records (HRs) and HR items (i.e., entries in health records). Our *project management case study* is a policy that controls access by department managers, project leaders, employees, contractors, auditors, accountants, and planners to budgets, schedules, and tasks associated with projects. Our *online video case study* is a policy that controls access to videos by users of an online video service.

The number of rules in the case studies is relatively small (10 ± 1 for the first three case studies, and 6 for online video), but they express non-trivial policies and exercise all the features of our policy language, including use of set membership and superset relations in attribute expressions and constraints. The manually written attribute dataset for each case study contains a small number of instances of each type of user and resource.

For the first three case studies, we generated a series of synthetic attribute datasets, parameterized by a number N, which is the number of departments for the university and project management case studies, and the number of wards for the health care case study. The generated attribute data for users and resources associated with each department or ward are similar to but more numerous than the attribute data in the manually written datasets. We did not bother creating synthetic data for the online video case study, because the rules are simpler.

Synthetic Policies. We generated synthetic policies using the algorithm proposed by Xu and Stoller [10]. Briefly, the policy synthesis algorithm first generates the rules and then uses the rules to guide generation of the attribute data; this allows control of the number of granted permissions. The algorithm takes N_{rule}, the desired number of rules, as an input. The numbers of users and resources are proportional to the number of rules. Generation of rules and attribute data is based on several probability distributions, which are based loosely on the case studies or assumed to have a simple functional form (e.g., uniform distribution).

5.2   Log Generation

The inputs to the algorithm are an ABAC policy π, the desired completeness of the log, and several probability distributions. The *completeness* of a log, relative to an ABAC policy, is the fraction of user-permission tuples in the meaning of the policy that appear in at least one entry in the log. A straightforward log generation algorithm would generate each log entry by first selecting an ABAC rule, according to a probability distribution on rules, and then selecting a user-permission tuple that satisfies the rule, according to probability distributions on users, resources, and operations. This process would be repeated until the specified completeness is reached. This algorithm is inefficient when high completeness is desired. Therefore, we adopt a different approach that takes advantage of the fact that our policy mining algorithm is insensitive to the order of log entries and depends only on the frequency of each user-permission tuple in the log. In particular, instead of generating logs (which would contain many entries for popular user-permission tuples), our algorithm directly generates a *log summary*, which is a set of user-permission tuples with associated frequencies (equivalently, a set of user-permission tuples and a frequency function).

Probability Distributions. An important characteristic of the probability distributions used in synthetic log and log summary generation is the ratio between the most frequent (i.e., most likely) and least frequent items of each type (rule, user, etc.). For case studies with manually written attribute data, we manually created probability distributions in which this ratio ranges from about 3 to 6. For case studies with synthetic data and synthetic policies, we generated probability distributions in which this ratio is 25 for rules, 25 for resources, 3 for users, and

3 for operations (the ratio for operations has little impact, because it is relevant only when multiple operations appear in the same rule, which is uncommon).

5.3 Metrics

For each case study and each associated attribute dataset (manually written or synthetic), we generate a synthetic operation log using the algorithm in Section 5.2 and then run our ABAC policy mining algorithms. We evaluate the effectiveness of each algorithm by comparing the generated ABAC policy to the original ABAC policy, using the metrics described below.

Syntactic Similarity. Jaccard similarity of sets is $J(S_1, S_2) = |S_1 \cap S_2| / |S_1 \cup S_2|$. Syntactic similarity of UAEs is defined by $S_{\text{syn}}^{\text{u}}(e, e') = |A_u|^{-1} \sum_{a \in A_u} J(e(a), e'(a))$. Syntactic similarity of RAEs is defined by $S_{\text{syn}}^{\text{r}}(e, e') = |A_r|^{-1} \sum_{a \in A_r} J(e(a), e'(a))$. The syntactic similarity of rules $\langle e_u, e_r, O, c \rangle$ and $\langle e_u', e_r', O', c' \rangle$ is the average of the similarities of their components, specifically, the average of $S_{\text{syn}}^{\text{u}}(e_u, e_u')$, $S_{\text{syn}}^{\text{r}}(e_r, e_r')$, $J(O, O')$, and $J(c, c')$. The *syntactic similarity* of rule sets *Rules* and *Rules'* is the average, over rules ρ in *Rules*, of the syntactic similarity between ρ and the most similar rule in *Rules'*. The *syntactic similarity* of policies π and π' is the maximum of the syntactic similarities of the sets of rules in the policies, considered in both orders (this makes the relation symmetric). Syntactic similarity ranges from 0 (completely different) to 1 (identical).

Semantic Similarity. Semantic similarity measures the similarity of the entitlements granted by two policies. The *semantic similarity* of policies π and π' is defined by $J(\llbracket \pi \rrbracket, \llbracket \pi' \rrbracket)$. Semantic similarity ranges from 0 (completely different) to 1 (identical).

Fractions of Under-Assignments and Over-Assignments. To characterize the semantic differences between an original ABAC policy π_0 and a mined policy π in a way that distinguishes under-assignments and over-assignments, we compute the fraction of over-assignments and the fraction of under-assignments, defined by $|\llbracket \pi \rrbracket \setminus \llbracket \pi_0 \rrbracket| / |\llbracket \pi \rrbracket|$ and $|\llbracket \pi_0 \rrbracket \setminus \llbracket \pi \rrbracket| / |\llbracket \pi \rrbracket|$, respectively.

6   Experimental Results

This section presents experimental results using an implementation of our algorithm in Java. The implementation, case studies, and synthetic policies used in the experiments are available at http://www.cs.stonybrook.edu/~stoller/.

Over-Assignment Weight. The optimal choice for the over-assignment weights w_o and w_o' in the policy quality and rule quality metrics, respectively, depends on the log completeness. When log completeness is higher, fewer over-assignments are desired, and larger over-assignments weights give better results. In experiments, we take $w_o = 50c - 15$ and $w_o' = w_o/10$, where c is log completeness. In a production setting, the exact log completeness would be unknown, but a rough estimate suffices, because our algorithm's results are robust to error in this estimate. For example, for case studies with manually written attribute data, when the actual log completeness is 80%, and the estimated completeness used to compute w_o varies from 70% to 90%, the semantic similarity of the original and mined policies varies by 0.04, 0.02, and 0 for university, healthcare, and project management, respectively.

Experimental Results. Figure 4 shows results from our algorithm. In each graph, curves are shown for the university, healthcare, and project management case studies with synthetic attribute data with N equal to 6, 10, and 10, respectively (average over results for 10 synthetic datasets, with 1 synthetic log per synthetic dataset), the online video case study with manually written attribute data (average over results for 10 synthetic logs), and synthetic policies with $N_{rule} = 20$ (average over results for 10 synthetic policies, with 1 synthetic log per policy). Error bars show standard deviation. Running time is at most 12 sec for each problem instance in our experiments.

For log completeness 100%, all four case study policies are reconstructed exactly, and the semantics of synthetic policies is reconstructed almost exactly: the semantic similarity is 0.98. This is a non-trivial result, especially for the case studies: an algorithm could easily generate a policy with over-assignments or generate more complex rules. As expected, the results get worse as log completeness decreases. When evaluating the results, it is important to consider what levels of log completeness are likely to be encountered in practice. One datapoint comes from Molloy *et al.*'s work on role mining from real logs [6]. For the experiments in [6, Tables 4 and 6], the actual policy is not known, but their algorithm produces policies with 0.52% or fewer over-assignments relative to $UP(L)$, and they interpret this as a good result, suggesting that they consider the log completeness to be near 99%. Based on this, we consider our experiments with log completeness below 90% to be severe stress tests, and results for log completeness 90% and higher to be more representative of typical results in practice.

Syntactic similarity for all four case studies is above 0.87 for log completeness 60% or higher, and is above 0.93 for log completeness 80% or higher. Syntactic similarity is lower for synthetic policies, but this is actually a good result. The synthetic policies tend to be unnecessarily complicated, and the mined policies are better in the sense that they have lower WSC. For example, for 100% log completeness, the mined policies have 0.98 semantic similarity to the synthetic policies (i.e., the meaning is almost the same), but the mined policies are simpler, with WSC 17% less than the original synthetic policies.

Semantic similarity is above 0.7 for log completeness 60% or higher, and above 0.89 for log completeness 80% or higher, for synthetic policies and for case studies other than healthcare. The semantic similarity is lower for healthcare, because the over-assignment weight given by the above formula is not optimal for this policy. In fact, if the optimal value of w_o is used for each log completeness, the semantic similarity for healthcare is always above 0.99. Better automated tuning of w_o is a direction for future work.

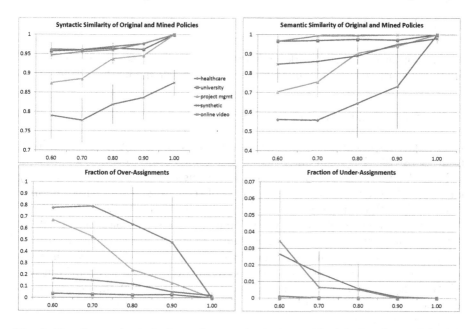

Fig. 4. Top: Syntactic similarity and semantic similarity of original and mined ABAC policies, as a function of log completeness. Bottom: Fractions of over-assignments and under-assignments in mined ABAC policy, as a function of log completeness. The legend (omitted from some graphs to save space) is the same for all four graphs.

The fractions of over-assignments and under-assignments are below 0.24 and 0.05, respectively, when log completeness is 80% or higher, for synthetic policies and for case studies other than healthcare. The fractions are higher for health-care, because w_o is not well chosen, as discussed above.

Comparison of Rule Quality Metrics. The above experiments use the first rule quality metric, Q_{rul}, in Section 4. We also performed experiments using $Q_{\mathrm{rul}}^{\mathrm{freq}}$ and $Q_{\mathrm{rul}}^{\mathrm{ILP}}$ on case studies with manually written attribute data and synthetic policies. We found that there is no clear winner between Q_{rul} and $Q_{\mathrm{rul}}^{\mathrm{freq}}$ (sometimes one is better, sometimes the other is better), and $Q_{\mathrm{rul}}^{\mathrm{ILP}}$ gives worse results overall.

Comparison with Inductive Logic Programming. To translate ABAC policy mining from logs to Progol [8], we used the translation of ABAC policy mining from ACLs to Progol in [10, Sections 5.5, 16], except negative examples corresponding to absent user-permission tuples are omitted from the generated program, and the statement set(posonly)? is included, telling Progol to use its algorithm for learning from positive examples. For the four case studies with manually written attribute data (in contrast, Figure 4 uses synthetic attribute for three of the case studies), for log completeness 100%, semantic similarity of the original and Progol-mined policies ranges from 0.37 for project management and healthcare to 0.93 for online video, while our algorithm exactly reconstructs all four policies.

7   Related Work

We are not aware of prior work on ABAC mining from logs. The closest topics of related work are ABAC mining from ACLs and role mining from logs.

7.1   ABAC Policy Mining from ACLs

Our policy mining algorithm is based on our algorithm for ABAC policy mining from ACLs [10]. The main differences are described in Section 1.

Ni *et al.* investigated the use of machine learning algorithms for security policy mining [9]. In the most closely related part of their work, a supervised machine learning algorithm is used to learn classifiers (analogous to attribute expressions) that associate users with roles, given as input the users, the roles, user attribute data, and the user-role assignment. Perhaps the largest difference between their work and ABAC policy mining is that their approach needs to be given the roles and the role-permission or user-role assignment as training data; in contrast, ABAC policy mining algorithms do not require any part of the desired high-level policy to be given as input. Also, their work does not consider anything analogous to constraints.

Association rule mining is another possible basis for ABAC policy mining. However, association rule mining algorithms are not well suited to ABAC policy mining, because they are designed to find rules that are probabilistic in nature and are supported by statistically strong evidence. They are not designed to produce a set of rules that completely cover the input data and are minimum-sized among such sets of rules. Consequently, unlike our algorithm, they do not give preference to smaller rules or rules with less overlap.

7.2   Role Mining from Logs

Gal-Oz *et al.* [2] assume that logs record sets of permissions exercised together in one high-level operation. Their role mining algorithm introduces roles whose sets of assigned permissions are the sets of permissions in the log. Their algorithm introduces over-assignments by removing roles with few users or whose permission set occurs few times in the log and re-assigning their members to roles with more permissions. Their algorithm does not use attribute data.

Molloy *et al.* apply a machine learning algorithm that uses a statistical approach, based upon a generative model, to find the policy that is most likely to generate the behavior (usage of permissions) observed in the logs [6]. They give an algorithm, based on Rosen-Zvi et al.'s algorithm for learning Author-Topic Models (ATMs), to mine meaningful roles from logs and attribute data, i.e., roles such that the user-role assignment is statistically correlated with user attributes. Their approach can be adapted to ABAC policy mining from logs, but its scalability in this context is questionable, because the adapted algorithm would enumerate and then rank all tuples containing a UAE, RAE and constraint (i.e., all tuples with the components of a candidate rule other than the operation set), and the number of such tuples is very large. In contrast, our algorithm never enumerates such candidates.

Zhang *et al.* use machine learning algorithms to improve the quality of a given role hierarchy based on users' access patterns as reflected in operation logs [12, 11]. These papers do not consider improvement or mining of ABAC policies.

References

1. Federal Chief Information Officer Council: Federal Identity Credential and Access Management (FICAM) Roadmap and Implementation Guidance, ver. 2.0 (2011)
2. Gal-Oz, N., Gonen, Y., Yahalom, R., Gudes, E., Rozenberg, B., Shmueli, E.: Mining roles from web application usage patterns. In: Furnell, S., Lambrinoudakis, C., Pernul, G. (eds.) TrustBus 2011. LNCS, vol. 6863, pp. 125–137. Springer, Heidelberg (2011)
3. Hachana, S., Cuppens-Boulahia, N., Cuppens, F.: Role mining to assist authorization governance: How far have we gone? International Journal of Secure Software Engineering 3(4), 45–64 (2012)
4. Hu, V.C., Ferraiolo, D., Kuhn, R., Friedman, A.R., Lang, A.J., Cogdell, M.M., Schnitzer, A., Sandlin, K., Miller, R., Scarfone, K.: Guide to Attribute Based Access Control (ABAC) Definition and Considerations (Final Draft). NIST Special Publication 800-162, National Institute of Standards and Technology (September 2013)
5. Molloy, I., Chen, H., Li, T., Wang, Q., Li, N., Bertino, E., Calo, S.B., Lobo, J.: Mining roles with multiple objectives. ACM Trans. Inf. Syst. Secur. 13(4) (2010)
6. Molloy, I., Park, Y., Chari, S.: Generative models for access control policies: applications to role mining over logs with attribution. In: Proc. 17th ACM Symposium on Access Control Models and Technologies (SACMAT). ACM (2012)
7. Muggleton, S.H.: Inverse entailment and progol. New Generation Computing 13, 245–286 (1995)
8. Muggleton, S.H., Firth, J.: CProgol4.4: a tutorial introduction. In: Dzeroski, S., Lavrac, N. (eds.) Relational Data Mining, pp. 160–188. Springer (2001)
9. Ni, Q., Lobo, J., Calo, S., Rohatgi, P., Bertino, E.: Automating role-based provisioning by learning from examples. In: Proc. 14th ACM Symposium on Access Control Models and Technologies (SACMAT), pp. 75–84. ACM (2009)
10. Xu, Z., Stoller, S.D.: Mining attribute-based access control policies. Computing Research Repository (CoRR) abs/1306.2401 (June 2013), http://arxiv.org/abs/1306.2401 (revised January 2014)
11. Zhang, W., Chen, Y., Gunter, C.A., Liebovitz, D., Malin, B.: Evolving role definitions through permission invocation patterns. In: Proc. 18th ACM Symposium on Access Control Models and Technologies (SACMAT), pp. 37–48. ACM (2013)
12. Zhang, W., Gunter, C.A., Liebovitz, D., Tian, J., Malin, B.: Role prediction using electronic medical record system audits. In: AMIA Annual Symposium Proceedings, pp. 858–867. American Medical Informatics Association (2011)

Attribute-Aware Relationship-Based Access Control for Online Social Networks*

Yuan Cheng, Jaehong Park, and Ravi Sandhu

Institute for Cyber Security
University of Texas at San Antonio
yuan@ycheng.org, {jae.park,ravi.sandhu}@utsa.edu

Abstract. Relationship-based access control (ReBAC) has been adopted as the most prominent approach for access control in online social networks (OSNs), where authorization policies are typically specified in terms of relationships of certain types and/or depth between the access requester and the target. However, using relationships alone is often not sufficient to enforce various security and privacy requirements that meet the expectation from today's OSN users. In this work, we integrate attribute-based policies into relationship-based access control. The proposed attribute-aware Re-BAC enhances access control capability and allows finer-grained controls that are not available in ReBAC. The policy specification language for the user-to-user relationship-based access control (UURAC) model proposed in [6] is extended to enable such attribute-aware access control. We also present an enhanced path-checking algorithm to determine the existence of the required attributes and relationships in order to grant access.

Keywords: Access Control, Attribute, Social Networks.

1 Introduction

Authorization decisions in traditional access control models (e.g., discretionary access control, mandatory access control, role-based access control, etc.) are primarily based on identities, group or role memberships, and security labels, etc. However, they fail to cope with the scalability and dynamicity of online social networks (OSNs). In OSNs, it is not practical for users to specify all the users who can access their information in a traditional way. Instead, Relationship-based Access Control (ReBAC) [7,9] has emerged as the most prevalent access control mechanism for OSNs. With ReBAC, resource owners can specify access control of their information based on their relationships with others, without knowing the user name space of the entire network or all their possible direct or indirect contacts. Accordingly, relationship-based access control has been recognized as a key requirement for security and privacy in OSNs [10], and has been commonly adopted in real world OSN systems since it keeps the balance between ease-of-use and flexibility.

---

* This work is partially supported by grant CNS-1111925 from the US National Science Foundation.

V. Atluri and G. Pernul (Eds.): DBSec 2014, LNCS 8566, pp. 292–306, 2014.

Despite its popularity in both theory and practice, current ReBAC is still far from perfect. Most ReBAC systems merely focus on type, depth or strength of the relationships, lacking support for some topology-based and history-based access control policies that are of rich social significance. For example, they cannot express policies such as "at least five common friends" or "friendship request pending" that require global or contextual information of the social graph. In addition to relationships, attributes of users (such as age, location, identity) also need to be taken into account when determining access. Without introducing attributes, policies like "a common friend named Tom" cannot be described in current ReBAC languages. We suggest that combining these attributes of users and relationships with ReBAC would provide users more versatile and flexible access control on their data.

In this work, we discuss the benefits of incorporating attribute-based access control (ABAC) into an existing ReBAC model. We formalize a new policy specification based on the previous UURAC policy language [6], addressing the access requirements in terms of the attributes of users, relationships and social graphs. Several examples are provided to show the usage of the proposed attribute-aware ReBAC policy language. The path-checking algorithm for finding a qualified path in [6] is also extended to simultaneously check whether the attribute-based requirements are satisfied. We briefly compare the complexity of the algorithm with the original UURAC algorithm, and discuss the changes.

2   Background and Motivation

In this section, we review existing ReBAC literature followed by discussion on potential benefits of adding attribute-based policies to ReBAC.

2.1   ReBAC

Access control based on interpersonal relationships has become the de facto standard solution for OSNs in practice. This is called relationship-based access control (ReBAC) [10]. A number of ReBAC solutions have been proposed in the literature. From these solutions, we can identify at least three decision factors of relationship type, relationship depth, and relationship strength (e.g., trust) that are used in ReBAC.

Some solutions proposed to associate trust with ReBAC, allowing people to specify the strength of their connections by assigning trust values to relationships. Carminati et al. proposed a series of ReBAC models for OSNs, where trust level, type and depth of the user-to-user relationships are identified as decision factors for authorization [3,4]. In their work, trust values of multiple relationships of the same type on a path can be calculated to form an indirect trust between users that are not directly connected. In [2], Carminati et al. introduced a semantic web based ReBAC solution, which defines authorization, administration and filtering policies to control the access. Another semantic web-based approach proposed by Masoumzadeh et al. allows both users and the system to express policies based on access control ontologies [15].

Fong et al. presented a Facebook-like access control model, featuring four types of policies that cover four different aspects of access in OSNs [8]. The four policies can regulate user search, traversal of the social graph, communication between users, and normal access to objects owned by users. The model mimics the privacy setting used in Facebook at the time of the paper was written. As such it lacks support for multiple types and depth of relationships. Fong et al. also built a formal ReBAC model for social computing applications on top of a modal logic language specification [7]. This model enables support for multiple types and direction of relationships. The model has been subsequently extended for improved flexibility and efficiency [1, 9].

Cheng et al. proposed a user-to-user relationship-based access control (UU-RAC) model with a regular expression-based policy specification language [6]. User-to-resource and resource-to-resource relationships are added to the model in their subsequent work on the URRAC model [5]. Both models are founded on the characteristics identified in Activity Control (ACON) [16, 17].

2.2   Beyond Relationships

ReBAC takes advantage of the structure of OSN systems and offers users a simple and effective way for configuring their access control policies. However, ReBAC suffers from two shortcomings. First, most of the ReBAC models rely on the type, depth, or strength of relationships, but cannot exploit more complicated topological information contained in the social graph. For example, many ReBAC proposals can determine whether there exists a qualified relationship path on the graph, but their policy languages cannot express requirements on multiple occurrences of such paths. Second, ReBAC generally lacks support for various contextual information of users and relationships available in OSNs. Such contextual information also called attributes can be utilized for finer-grained access control. In addition to the normal relationship information, some of the attribute examples are user's name, age, role, location, trust in other users, duration of relationships, and so on. Let us consider two examples of attribute-based policies that are applied on ReBAC.

Common Friends. The very nature of OSNs encourages new connections. To help users expand their connections, OSNs normally suggest some new connection candidates to a user based on number of common friends they share, for example. This is typically used as a tool for social promotion, but it can be applied to access control as well. Alice can allow a user who is not currently her friend but shares a certain number of common friends with her to access some of her contents. She can also specify that Bob must be a common friend of her and an access requester in order for the requester to get access. In regular ReBAC system, these policies cannot be expressed as they only check the existence of certain relationships but do not count the number of such relationships. Also, due to lack of support for node attributes, ReBAC policies are not able to distinguish particular users on the relationship paths.

Transitive Trust. Consider a scenario where relationships are associated with an attribute of trust value, which denotes the strength of connection between two users. Since each user only knows a few direct friends, it is expected that more users are likely to be connected indirectly through their existing connections. Trust values between direct connections are used to compute the transitive trust, indicating the strength of such indirect relationships. A line of research has been addressing the area of trust in OSNs [11, 12, 14], where trust is combined with relationship type and depth as parameters to determine access. However, many limitations can be found in these works. Some only consider a single relationship type, others consider the case of multiple types but lack support for trust comparison and calculation between different types or paths. If we treat trust as an attribute of relationships, it can be mixed with other attributes of users and thus enable finer-grained access control policies, despite the multiple relationship types or paths.

3 Preliminaries

The UURAC model introduced by Cheng et al. [6] captures user-to-user relationships in OSNs for authorization purpose, and defines a regular expression-based policy specification language. We briefly summarize UURAC model as our proposed model is based on it.

3.1 Basic Notations

In UURAC, $\Sigma = \{\sigma_1, \sigma_2, \ldots, \sigma_n, \sigma_1^{-1}, \sigma_2^{-1}, \ldots, \sigma_n^{-1}\}$ denotes the set of relationship types. Given a relationship type $\sigma_i \in \Sigma$, the inverse of the relationship is $\sigma_i^{-1} \in \Sigma$. An action has an active form and a passive form, denoted $action$ and $action^{-1}$, respectively. If Alice pokes Bob, the action is $poke$ from Alice's viewpoint, whereas it is $poke^{-1}$ from Bob's viewpoint.

3.2 UURAC Model Components

The UURAC model components are illustrated in Figure 1. **Accessing user** (u_a) represents an acting user who requests an access to a target and carries **accessing user policies** (AUP) which controls the accessing user's access to targets. Each **action** represents an operation initiated by an accessing user against a target. An action is denoted as $action$ for the accessing user but $action^{-1}$ for the target. The targets can be either **target user** (u_t) (e.g., a user pokes another user) or **target resource** (r_t). There is also a **controlling user** (u_c) who controls an access to a resource that has user-to-resource (U2R) relationship with her such as the owner of the resource. An access to a target user is controlled based on the **target user policies** (TUP) that are configured using user-to-user (U2U) relationships between the target user and the access requesters, while an access to a target resource is controlled based on **target resource policies**

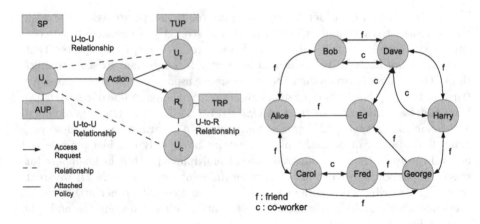

Fig. 1. Model components   **Fig. 2.** A sample social graph

(TRP) that are configured using U2U relationships between the controlling user and the access requester.

An access request $\langle u_a, act, target \rangle$ denotes the initiation of an access, where $act \in Act$ specifies the type of access requested by the accessing user on the target. If u_a requests to interact with another user, $target$ is $u_t \in U$. If u_a tries to access a resource owned by another user u_c, $target$ is resource $r_t \in R$ where R is a finite set of resources in OSN.

A policy defines the rules that determine how authorization is regulated. Policies can be either system-specified or user-specified. **System-specified policies** (SP) are system-wide rules enforced by the OSN system while user-specified policies are applied to specific users or resources. User-specified policies include AUP, TUP, and TRP.

3.3 Social Graph

As shown in Figure 2, OSN is abstracted as a directed labeled simple graph, where each node indicates a user and each edge corresponds to a U2U relationship. The social graph of an OSN is modeled as a triple $G = \langle U, E, \Sigma \rangle$ where

- U is a finite set of registered users in the system, represented as nodes on the graph,
- $\Sigma = \{\sigma_1, \sigma_2, \ldots, \sigma_n, \sigma_1^{-1}, \sigma_2^{-1}, \ldots, \sigma_n^{-1}\}$ denotes a finite set of relationship types, where each type specifier σ denotes a relationship type supported in the system, and
- $E \subseteq U \times U \times \Sigma$, denoting social graph edges, is a set of existing user relationships.

For every $\sigma_i \in \Sigma$, there is $\sigma_i^{-1} \in \Sigma$ representing the inverse of relationship type σ_i. We require that the original relationship and its inverse twin always exist on the social graph simultaneously. Given a user $u \in U$, a user $v \in U$ and a relationship type $\sigma \in \Sigma$, a relationship (u, v, σ) expresses that there exists a relationship of type σ starting from user u and terminating at v. It always has an equivalent form (v, u, σ^{-1}).

4 $UURAC_A$ Model

In this section, we extend the UURAC model to facilitate attribute-aware Re-BAC policy specification and enforcement.[1]

4.1 Attributes in OSNs

OSNs maintain a massive amount of data about attributes of users and resources. Users keep profile information as required by the OSNs, such as name, age, gender, etc. When a piece of resource is uploaded to the OSN, the resource provider is also able to attach some metadata about the resource. We can define policies based on this attribute information associated with users and resources. However, the majority of ReBAC systems have focussed on some particular aspects of relationships, such as type, depth, and strength. This makes ReBAC relatively simple and efficient, but also limits the use of ReBAC in terms of control capability. In recent years, studies on attribute-based access control (ABAC) have shown that various contextual information of user, resource, and computing environment could be utilized for highly flexible and finer-grained controls [13,18,19]. However, current ABAC solutions are not likely to be readily usable on top of a ReBAC in OSNs. While typical ABAC models only consider the attributes of accessing user, target resource and sometimes computing environment, attribute-aware ReBAC needs to specify which attributes and whose attributes (i.e., user attributes, relationship attributes) on the relationship path between accessing users and target/controlling users should be examined.

For attribute-aware ReBAC, we identify three types of attributes: node (user/resource) attribute, edge (relationship) attribute and count attribute, as follows.

Node Attributes. Users and resources are represented as nodes on the social graph. Users carry attributes that define their identities and characteristics, such as name, age, gender, etc. Resource attributes may include title, owner, date, etc.

Edge Attributes. Each edge is associated with attributes that describe the characteristics of the edge. Such attributes may include relationship weights, types, and so on.

Both edge attributes and node attributes can apply to a single object or multiple objects. An example of attributes for multiple edges is the transitive trust between two nodes that are not directly connected. For instance, trust values of two or more edges need to be considered to calculate overall trust between

---

[1] We reiterate that in UURAC only user-to-user relationships are considered so resources can only occur as the target of a relationship path. The relationship path itself can only include users.

accessing user and target/controlling user. Attributes describing multiple nodes are more commonly seen in OSNs, such as average age, common location, or common alma mater between people. Relevant node and edge attributes can be also assembled to enable policy combinations. For instance, Alice may specify a policy saying that "only users who have more than 0.5 trust with Bob can access."

Count Attribute. Count attribute neither describes nor is associated with any node or edge. It depicts the occurrence requirement for the attribute-based path specification, specifying the lower bound of the occurrences of such path.

4.2   Attribute-Based Policy Formulation

Attribute-based policy specifies access control requirements that are related to the attributes of users and their relationships. Here, we formally define the basic attribute-based policy language.

- N and E are nodes and edges, respectively;
- $NA_k(1 \leq k \leq K)$ and $EA_l(1 \leq l \leq L)$ are the pre-defined attributes for nodes and edges, respectively, where K is the number of node attributes and L is the number of edge attributes;
- $ATTR(n)$ and $ATTR(e)$ are attribute assignments for node n and edge e, respectively, where $ATTR(n) \in NA_1 \times NA_2 \times \cdots \times NA_K$, and $ATTR(e) \in EA_1 \times EA_2 \times \cdots \times EA_L$. Each attribute has only single value for its domain.

On the relationship path between two users in OSNs, there may exist many other users connected with different relationships. Each user or relationship carries attributes, which can be utilized for specifying access control rules. In some cases, the attributes of all users or relationships on the path need to be considered. Sometimes, attributes of only certain users or relationships are used. As shown in Table 1, we use the universal quantifier $\forall$ and the existential quantifier $\exists$ to denote "all" and "at least one" user(s) or relationship(s), respectively. The notation [ ] is used to represent ranges on the relationship path while { } denotes a set of users/relationships located at a specific distance on the path between accessing user and target/controlling user. In order to express a range or exact

Table 1. Attribute quantifiers

$\forall$ [+m, -n]	All entities from the mth to the nth last, $m + n \leq h$ where m and n are non-negative integers and h is a hopcount limit
$\forall$ [+m, +n]	All entities from the mth to the nth, $m \leq n \leq h$
$\forall$ [-m, -n]	All entities from the mth last to the nth last, $h \geq m \geq n$
$\exists$ [+m, -n]	One entity from the mth to the nth last, $m + n \leq h$
$\exists$ [+m, +n]	One entity from the mth to the nth, $m \leq n \leq h$
$\exists$ [-m, -n]	One entity from the mth last to the nth last, $h \geq m \geq n$
$\forall$ $\{2^{\{\pm N\}}\}$	All entities in this set
$\exists$ $\{2^{\{\pm N\}}\}$	One entity in this set

position on the path, we use plus and minus signs to indicate the forward (from the start) and backward directions (from the end), followed by a number that denotes the position from the front or the back. Note that indicator for users starts from 0 while indicator for relationships begins from 1. For example, for users, +0 means the starting user and -1 represents the second last user on the path; while for relationships, +1 indicates the first relationship on the path and -2 means the second last. The plus-minus sign in the last two rows denotes the forward or backward direction rather than its normal mathematical meaning.

An attribute-base policy rule is composed of a *quantifier* specifying the quantity of certain node/edge attributes, a boolean function of these node/edge attributes $f(ATTR(N), ATTR(E))$, and a count attribute predicate $count \geq i$, as follows.

$$\langle quantifier, f(ATTR(N), ATTR(E)), count \geq i \rangle$$

Note that the quantifier is applied to a node/edge function, but not to the count attribute predicate. For instance, R1 specifies a rule saying that "there must be at least five common connections between the requester and the owner, whose occupation is student". In R2 and R3, the count attribute predicate is not used and this is shown as '_', which indicates $count \geq 1$ in default. Here, the policy contains a rule indicating that "a user who is connected through adults whose addresses are 'Texas' can access". R3 requires that on a path between the accessing user and target/controlling user, users in three specific distances must be adults.

- $R1 : \langle \exists [+1, -1], occupation(u) = \text{``student''}, count \geq 5 \rangle$
- $R2 : \langle \forall [+1, -1], (age(u) \geq 18) \wedge (address(u) = \text{``Texas''}), \_ \rangle$
- $R3 : \langle \forall \{+1, +2, -1\}, (age(u) \geq 18), \_ \rangle$

4.3 Policy Specifications

Attribute-based policies are applied on certain relationship paths between accessing user and target/controlling user. For this, we extend the regular expression-based policy specification language proposed in [6]. Table 2 defines a list of notations used in the policy specification language.

Attribute-aware UURAC policies include two parts: a requested action, and a graph rule that conditions the access based on the social graph. As shown in Table 3, we identify several different types of policies. Actions are denoted in the passive form act^{-1} in target user policy and target resource policy, since target user/resource is always the recipient of the action. Target resource policy has an extra parameter u_c, indicating the controlling user of the resource. The differentiation of active and passive form of an action does not apply to system-specified policies, as these policies are not associated with any particular entity in action. However, when specifying a system policy for a resource, we can optionally refine the resource in terms of resource type ($r.typename, r.typevalue$).

Table 4 defines the syntax for the graph rules using Backus-Naur Form (BNF). Each graph rule specifies a *startingnode* and a *pathrule*. Starting node denotes the user where the policy evaluation starts. A path rule represents a collection of path specs. Each path specification consists of a pair $(path, hopcount)$ that specifies the relationship path pattern between two users and the maximum number of edges on the path, which need to be satisfied in order to get access. Multiple path specifications can be connected with conjunctive "∧" and disjunctive "∨" connectives. "¬" over path specifications denotes absence of the specified pair of relationship pattern and hopcount limit. The pattern of relationship path $path$ represents a sequence of type specifiers from the starting node to the evaluating node.

Unlike in UURAC, we add a new term $AttPolicy$ to the grammar to facilitate attribute-based policies. It can be found either after the whole path specification $(path, hopcount)$ or a segment of the path pattern $path$. The one that applies to $(path, hopcount)$ is called global attribute-based policy. When it follows a segment of $path$, it is a local attribute-based policy that only applicable for this segment. For simplicity, the examples hereafter only use global attribute-based policies.

We now show how attribute-based rules can be applied to some examples within UURAC$_A$.

Example 1: Node attribute and count attribute policy. Alice wants to reveal her profile to users who share at least five common student friends. She can specify the following policy for her friends of friends:

– P1: $\langle profile\_access, (u_a, ((ff, 2): \exists[+1, -1], occupation(u) = \text{"student"}, count \geq 5))\rangle$

If she wants to allow someone who shares a common friend Bob with her to see her profile, the policy can be represented as follows:

– P2: $\langle profile\_access, (u_a, ((ff, 2): \exists[+1, -1], name(u) = \text{"Bob"}, \_)))\rangle$

For P1, the system needs to find paths that match $(ff, 2)$ and check the occupation attribute of users on the paths. If there exist at least five such paths, u_a is allowed to see the profile information of the target. For P2, once a $(ff, 2)$ path

Table 2. Policy specification notations

Concatenation (·)	Joins multiple characters $\sigma \in \Sigma$ or Σ itself end-to-end, denoting a series of occurrences of relationship types.
Asterisk (*)	Represents the union of the concatenation of σ with itself zero or more times.
Plus (+)	Denotes concatenating σ one or more times.
Question Mark (?)	Represents occurrences of σ zero or one time.
Disjunctive Connective (∨)	Indicates the disjunction of multiple path specs.
Conjunctive Connective (∧)	Denotes the conjunction of multiple path specs.
Negation (¬)	Implies the absence of the specified pair of relationship type sequence and hopcount.
Colon(:)	Separates relationship pattern and attribute-based policies

Table 3. Access control policy representations

Accessing User Policy	$\langle act, graphrule \rangle$
Target User Policy	$\langle act^{-1}, graphrule \rangle$
Target Resource Policy	$\langle act^{-1}, u_c, graphrule \rangle$
System Policy for User	$\langle act, graphrule \rangle$
System Policy for Resource	$\langle act, (r.typename, r.typevalue), graphrule \rangle$

Table 4. Grammar for graph rules

$GraphRule \rightarrow$ "(" $StartingNode$ "," $PathRule$ ")"
$PathRule \rightarrow AttPathSpecExp \,|\, AttPathSpecExp \; Connective \; PathRule$
$AttPathSpecExp \rightarrow PathSpecExp \,|\, PathSpecExp$ " : " $AttPolicy$
$Connective \rightarrow \vee \,|\wedge$
$PathSpecExp \rightarrow PathSpec \,|$ "¬" $PathSpec$
$PathSpec \rightarrow$ "(" $AttPath$ "," $HopCount$ ")" $\,|$ "(" $EmptySet$ "," $HopCount$ ")"
$HopCount \rightarrow Number$
$AttPath \rightarrow Path \,|\, Path$ " : " $AttPolicy$
$Path \rightarrow TypeSeq \,|\, TypeSeq \; Path$
$EmptySet \rightarrow \emptyset$
$TypeSeq \rightarrow AttTypeExp \,|\, AttTypeExp$ "." $TypeSeq$
$AttTypeExp \rightarrow TypeExp \,|\, TypeExp$ " : " $AttPolicy$
$TypeExp \rightarrow TypeSpecifier \,|\, TypeSpecifier \; Wildcard$
$AttPolicy \rightarrow$ use dedicated parser to process
$StartingNode \rightarrow u_a |u_t| u_c$
$TypeSpecifier \rightarrow \sigma_1 |\sigma_2| \ldots |\sigma_n| \sigma_1^{-1} |\sigma_2^{-1}| \ldots |\sigma_n^{-1}| \Sigma$
$Wildcard \rightarrow$ " * " $|$ "?" $|$ " + "
$Number \rightarrow [0-9]+$

is found and the name of the user on the path equals to Bob, the system would grant access.

Example 2: Edge attribute policy. Alice grants users to access *Photo1* if the user is within 3 hops away and can reach her on a path with a minimum 0.5 trust value of friend relationships on each hop. Such policy is specified as follows:

– P3: $\langle read, Photo1, (u_a, ((f*, 3) : \forall [+1, -1], trust(r) \geq 0.5, \_)) \rangle$

The system will check each edge on the path to ensure its trust value meets the requirement, before granting access.

Example 3: Capturing a UURAC policy. The following policy only contains relationship-based requirements $(f*, 3)$, where node/edge attributes and count attribute are both empty:

– P4: $\langle poke, (u_a, (f*, 3) : \exists [+0, -0], \_, \_)) \rangle$

The UURAC$_A$ model is seamlessly compatible with the UURAC model. The example 3 shows how UURAC policy can be captured in UURAC$_A$.

Algorithm 1. $AccessEvaluation(u_a, act, target)$

---

1. (Policy Collecting Phase)
2. **if** $target = u_t$ **then**
3. $AUP \leftarrow u_a$'s policy for act, $TUP \leftarrow u_t$'s policy for act^{-1}, $SP \leftarrow$ system's policy for act
4. **else**
5. $u_c \leftarrow owner(r_t)$, $AUP \leftarrow u_a$'s policy for act, $TRP \leftarrow u_c$'s policy for act^{-1} on r_t, $SP \leftarrow$ system's policy for $act, r.type$
6. (Policy Evaluation Phase)
7. **for all** policy in AUP, TUP/TRP and SP **do**
8.   Extract graph rules ($start, path\ rule$) from policy
9.   **for all** graph rule extracted **do**
10.   Determine the starting node, specified by $start$, where the path evaluation starts
11.   Determine the evaluating node which is the other user involved in access
12.   Extract path rules $path\ rule$ from graph rule
13.   Extract each path spec $path, hopcount$ and/or attribute rule $attpolicy$ from path rules
14.   Simultaneously path-check each path spec and evaluate the corresponding attribute rule using Algorithm 2
15.   Evaluate a combined result based on conjunctive or disjunctive connectives between path specs
16. Compose the final result from the result of each policy

---

5   Algorithm

This section addresses the access evaluation of UURAC$_A$. UURAC [6] provides a path-checking algorithm to find a qualified path between the access requester and the target (or the resource owner) that meets the ReBAC requirements. To enforce attribute-based policies, the access evaluation should incorporate attribute-based policies during path-checking. One may run attribute checking on the result paths found by the UURAC algorithm. However, this is likely to be inefficient. In this paper, we present a modified path-checking algorithm to incorporate an attribute-based policy evaluation on the fly during path finding process.

Access Evaluation Procedure. Access requests can be evaluated as described in Algorithm 1. For an access request $(u_a, act, target)$, the system fetches u_a's policy about act, $target$'s act^{-1} policy and the system-specified policy for act. The decision module extracts path specification $(path, hopcount)$ and attribute-based rules $attpolicy$ from these policies. It runs the path-checking algorithm to determine the result for each policy. During path-checking, the decision module also needs to keep track of all of the involved attributes and make sure they satisfy the attribute-based policies. Finally, the results of all chosen policies in evaluation are composed into a single result. The existence of multi-user policies may raise policy conflicts. To resolve this, we can adopt the conflict resolution policy proposed in [5], which is based on a disjunctive, conjunctive, or prioritized strategy.

Algorithm 2. $DFSPathChecker(G, path, hopcount, s, t, globalattpol)$

1. $DFA \leftarrow REtoDFA(path)$; $currentPath \leftarrow NIL$; $d \leftarrow 0$
2. $stateHistory \leftarrow$ DFA starts at the initial state
3. Extract the quantifier symbol and interval/set information from $globalattpol$
4. Get the required rules for attributes of edges and nodes $f(ATTR(E), ATTR(N))$
5. Fetch the requirements of count attribute "$count \geq i$". If it is omitted, "$count \geq 1$".
6. Assign temporary space for attributes according to the size of the interval/set and the hopcount limit
7. Initialize counter $count \leftarrow 0$
8. **if** $hopcount \neq 0$ **then**
9.   **return** DFST(s)

Algorithm 3. $DFST(u)$

1. **if** $d + 1 > hopcount$ **then**
2.   **return** FALSE
3. **else**
4.   **for all** (v, σ) where (u, v, σ) *in* G **do**
5.   **switch**
6.   **case 1** $v \in currentPath$
7.   **break**
8.   **case 2** $v \notin currentPath$ and $v = t$ and DFA with transition σ is at accepting state
9.   **if** v and (u, v, σ) is within the range specified by quantifier **then**
10. $attrList \leftarrow attrList.(ATTR(v), ATTR(u, v, \sigma))$
11.   **if** $f(ATTR(v), ATTR(u, v, \sigma)) = TRUE$ **then**
12. $count \leftarrow count + 1$
13.   **if** $count \geq i$ **then**
14. $d \leftarrow d + 1$; $currentPath \leftarrow currentPath.(u, v, \sigma)$
15. $currentState \leftarrow$ DFA takes transition σ
16. $stateHistory \leftarrow stateHistory.(currentState)$
17.   **return** TRUE
18.   **else**
19. $attrList \leftarrow attrList \backslash (ATTR(v), ATTR(u, v, \sigma))$
20.   **else**
21. $d \leftarrow d + 1$; $currentPath \leftarrow currentPath.(u, v, \sigma)$
22. $currentState \leftarrow$ DFA takes transition σ
23. $stateHistory \leftarrow stateHistory.(currentState)$
24.   **return** TRUE
25.   **break**
26.   **case 3** $v \notin currentPath$ and $v = t$ and transition σ is valid for DFA but DFA with transition σ is not at accepting state
27.   **break**
28.   **case 4** $v \notin currentPath$ and $v = t$ and transition σ is invalid for DFA
29.   **break**
30.   **case 5** $v \notin currentPath$ and $v \neq t$ and transition σ is invalid for DFA
31.   **break**
32.   **case 6** $v \notin currentPath$ and $v \neq t$ and transition σ is valid for DFA
33. $d \leftarrow d + 1$; $currentPath \leftarrow currentPath.(u, v, \sigma)$
34. $currentState \leftarrow$ DFA takes transition σ
35. $stateHistory \leftarrow stateHistory.(currentState)$
36.   **if** (DFST(v)) **then**
37.   **return** TRUE
38.   **else**
39. $d \leftarrow d - 1$; $currentPath \leftarrow currentPath \backslash (u, v, \sigma)$
40. $attrList \leftarrow attrList \backslash (ATTR(v), ATTR(u, v, \sigma)$
41. $previousState \leftarrow$ last element in $stateHistory$
42.   DFA backs off the last taken transition σ to $previousState$
43. $stateHistory \leftarrow stateHistory \backslash (previousState)$
44.   **return** FALSE

Attribute-Aware Path Checking Algorithm. The path-checking algorithm, as shown in Algorithm 2, uses a depth-first search (DFS) strategy to traverse the social graph G from a starting node s. The mission is to find relationship paths between the starting node s and the evaluating node t, that satisfy the policy. The pair of path pattern $path$ and hopcount limit $hopcount$ specifies the relationship-based requirements, whereas $globalattpol$ indicates the attribute-based rules.

Let us consider the example policy P1 in Section 4.3: $\langle profile\_access,$ $(u_a, ((ff, 2): \exists[+1, -1], occupation(u) = \text{“}student\text{”}, count \geq 5))\rangle$. The grammar extracts the starting node u_a and splits the relationship-based rules $(ff, 2)$ and the attribute-based rules "$\exists[+1, -1]$, $occupation(u) = \text{“}student\text{”}, count \geq 5$". Algorithm 2 then constructs a DFA (deterministic finite automata) from the regular expression ff. This is done by the function $REtoDFA()$. Variables $currentPath$ and $stateHistory$ are initialized to NIL and the initial DFA state, respectively. The attribute-based rule is divided into three parts: "$\exists[+1, -1]$", "$occupation(u) = \text{‘}student\text{’}$" and "$count \geq 5$". "$\exists[+1, -1]$" quantifies the whole path between the access requester and the target (or the resource owner) to which the following node attribute function applies. "$occupation(u) = \text{‘}student\text{’}$" is a function of node attributes that checks the occupation of the users on the path. The count attribute predicate "$count \geq 5$" specifies the required number of qualified relationship paths. To store the attribute values of nodes and edges during traversal in this example, we need space for attributes of 1 node and 2 edges. In general, if the interval is $[+a, -b]$ and the hopcount limit is c, we need to assign space for attributes of (c - a - b + 1) nodes and (c - a - b) edges.

After setting the hopcount indicator d to 0, Algorithm 2 launches the DFS traversal function $DFST()$, shown in Algorithm 3, from the starting node. Given the node u, the algorithm first makes sure taking one step forward does not violate the hopcount limit. Otherwise, it has to exit and return to the previous node. If further traversal is allowed, the algorithm starts to pick an edge (u, v, σ) from the collection of all incident edges leaving u one by one. According to the path pattern ff in the example, at the first step, the algorithm specifically looks for an unvisited edge of type f terminating at a node other than the evaluating node (case 6). If such edge is found, let's say (u_a, u_1, f), the algorithm increments d by 1, adds the edge to $currentPath$, moves the DFA from the initial state by taking transition f and updates the DFA state history accordingly. It also adds the corresponding attributes of edge (u_a, u_1, f) and node u_1 to the attribute list $attrList$ for later evaluation, since u_1 is 1 hop away from u_a and thus is within the range $[+1, -1]$. The algorithm then continues to run $DFST()$ on the new node u_1. From node u_1, it repeats the previous process again by checking the hopcount limit and picking new incident edges. Since the hopcount limit is 2, the algorithm has to find an unvisited edge of type f that terminates at t (case 2). Once the edge (u_1, t, f) is discovered, the algorithm goes on to find the corresponding attributes for evaluation. $[+1, -1]$ indicates that we also need to check the attributes of the second last node on the path, which is u_1. Since we already added u_1's attributes to the list, the algorithm simply runs attribute function $f(ATTR(u_1))$ to see if it satisfies the requirements. If yes, we then check the count attribute, which is *count* in this case. The policy says it requires five qualified paths, thus the algorithm has to increment the counter and return to the previous node to search for another 4 paths. If $(u_a, u_1, f)(u_1, t, f)$ is the fifth path we found, $DFST(u_1)$ should return true and all its previous $DFST()$ calls as well. Eventually, it makes Algorithm 2 to return true, indicating we found the necessary amount of paths that satisfy the policy. If the node/edge attributes do not match the requirements, the algorithm removes the attributes from the list (line 18-19) and try the next edge. After finishing edge searching at this level and returning to the previous $DFST()$ call (line 38-43), it has to drop the edge and reset all variables to the previous values. Algorithm 2 returns false after all incident edges leaving u_a have been unsuccessfully searched.

The proof of correctness of this algorithm is fundamentally the same as the algorithm for UURAC [6]. The new algorithm neither brings in more edges to be considered nor increases the depth of recursive traversal to be taken. Hence, its complexity is still bounded between $O(dmin^{Hopcount})$ and $O(dmax^{Hopcount})$, where $dmin$ and $dmax$ stand for the minimum and maximum out-degree of node, and $Hopcount$ denotes the hopcount limit. Attribute-base check introduces additional overhead when the algorithm finds a possible qualified path. The overhead costs are proportional to the amount of attributes as well as the type of attribute functions considered in the policy, which is not related to the structure of the social graph.

6 Conclusion

This paper presents an extended UURAC model for OSNs that utilizes both relationship-based and attribute-based policies for determining access. Attribute information of users and their relationships are as important as the social graph in OSNs with respect to access control. We formalized the attribute-based policies and extended the grammar for policy specifications. The policy language supports expressing requirements on attributes of some or all of the users and relationships on the path. While it could be possible to further extend the proposed model for even finer-grained attribute-based controls, the proposed model provides a solid foundational mechanism for ReBAC that also allows attribute-based access control.

References

1. Bruns, G., Fong, P.W., Siahaan, I., Huth, M.: Relationship-based access control: its expression and enforcement through hybrid logic. In: Proceedings of the Second CODASPY, pp. 117–124. ACM (2012)
2. Carminati, B., Ferrari, E., Heatherly, R., Kantarcioglu, M., Thuraisingham, B.: A semantic web based framework for social network access control. In: Proceedings of the 14th SACMAT, pp. 177–186. ACM (2009)

3. Carminati, B., Ferrari, E., Perego, A.: Rule-based access control for social networks. In: Meersman, R., Tari, Z., Herrero, P. (eds.) OTM 2006 Workshops. LNCS, vol. 4278, pp. 1734–1744. Springer, Heidelberg (2006)
4. Carminati, B., Ferrari, E., Perego, A.: Enforcing access control in web-based social networks. ACM TISSEC 13(1), 6 (2009)
5. Cheng, Y., Park, J., Sandhu, R.: Relationship-based access control for online social networks: beyond user-to-user relationships. In: PASSAT 2012, pp. 646–655. IEEE (2012)
6. Cheng, Y., Park, J., Sandhu, R.: A user-to-user relationship-based access control model for online social networks. In: Cuppens-Boulahia, N., Cuppens, F., Garcia-Alfaro, J. (eds.) DBSec 2012. LNCS, vol. 7371, pp. 8–24. Springer, Heidelberg (2012)
7. Fong, P.W.: Relationship-based access control: protection model and policy language. In: Proceedings of the First CODASPY, pp. 191–202. ACM (2011)
8. Fong, P.W.L., Anwar, M., Zhao, Z.: A privacy preservation model for facebook-style social network systems. In: Backes, M., Ning, P. (eds.) ESORICS 2009. LNCS, vol. 5789, pp. 303–320. Springer, Heidelberg (2009)
9. Fong, P.W., Siahaan, I.: Relationship-based access control policies and their policy languages. In: Proceedings of the 16th SACMAT, pp. 51–60. ACM (2011)
10. Gates, C.: Access control requirements for Web 2.0 security and privacy. IEEE Web 2.0 (2007)
11. Golbeck, J., Hendler, J.: Inferring binary trust relationships in web-based social networks. ACM Transactions on Internet Technology (TOIT) 6(4), 497–529 (2006)
12. Golbeck, J.A.: Computing and Applying Trust in Web-based Social Networks. PhD thesis, University of Maryland at College Park, College Park, MD, USA (2005)
13. Jin, X., Krishnan, R., Sandhu, R.: A unified attribute-based access control model covering DAC, MAC and RBAC. In: Cuppens-Boulahia, N., Cuppens, F., Garcia-Alfaro, J. (eds.) DBSec 2012. LNCS, vol. 7371, pp. 41–55. Springer, Heidelberg (2012)
14. Kruk, S.R., Grzonkowski, S., Gzella, A., Woroniecki, T., Choi, H.-C.: D-FOAF: Distributed identity management with access rights delegation. In: Mizoguchi, R., Shi, Z.-Z., Giunchiglia, F. (eds.) ASWC 2006. LNCS, vol. 4185, pp. 140–154. Springer, Heidelberg (2006)
15. Masoumzadeh, A., Joshi, J.: OSNAC: an ontology-based access control model for social networking systems. In: SocialCom 2010, pp. 751–759. IEEE (2010)
16. Park, J., Sandhu, R., Cheng, Y.: ACON: activity-centric access control for social computing. In: 2011 Sixth International Conference on Availability, Reliability and Security (ARES), pp. 242–247. IEEE (2011)
17. Park, J., Sandhu, R., Cheng, Y.: A user-activity-centric framework for access control in online social networks. IEEE Internet Computing 15(5), 62–65 (2011)
18. Shen, H., Hong, F.: An attribute-based access control model for web services. In: PDCAT 2006, pp. 74–79. IEEE (2006)
19. Yuan, E., Tong, J.: Attributed based access control (ABAC) for web services. In: Proceedings of the IEEE ICWS, pp. 561–569. IEEE (2005)

Randomly Partitioned Encryption for Cloud Databases

Tahmineh Sanamrad[1], Lucas Braun[1], Donald Kossmann[1],
and Ramarathnam Venkatesan[2]

[1] Systems Group, Computer Science Departement, ETH Zurich, Switzerland
`{sanamrat,braunl,donaldk}@inf.ethz.ch`
[2] Microsoft Research, Redmond CA, USA
`venkie@microsoft.com`

Abstract. With the current advances in Cloud Computing, outsourcing data has
never been so tempting. Along with outsourcing a database comes the privacy
versus performance discussion. Order-Preserving Encryption (OPE) is one of
the most attractive techniques for database encryption since it allows to execute
range and rank queries efficiently without decrypting the data. On the other hand,
people are reluctant to use OPE-based techniques in practice because of their
vulnerability against adversaries with knowledge of the domain, its frequency
distribution and query logs. This paper formally defines three real world driven
attacks, called *Domain Attack*, *Frequency Attack* and *Query Log Attack*, typically launched by an honest-but-curious database or systems administrator. We
also introduce measures to capture the probability distribution of the adversary's
advantage under each attacker model. Most importantly, we present a novel technique called *Randomly Partitioned Encryption* (RPE) to minimize the adversary's
advantage. Finally, we show that RPE not only withstands real world database
adversaries, but also shows good performance that is close to state-of-art OPE
schemes for both, read- and write-intensive workloads.

Keywords: Database Encryption, Efficient Query Processing, Domain Attack,
Frequency Attack, Query Log Attack, Randomly Partitioned Encryption.

1 Introduction

Believing the trade press, cloud computing is the next big thing. Cloud computing
promises reduced cost, flexibility, improved time to market, higher availability, and
more focus on the core business of an organization. Virtually all players of the IT industry are jumping on the cloud computing band wagon. The only issue that seems to be
able to stop cloud computing are security concerns [8]. The events that motivated this
work were privacy violations in a *private* cloud by *honest-but-curious* adversaries.[1]

Encryption is a possible way to protect data against such attackers. The spectrum of
available encryption schemes ranges from strong semantically secure (but typically inefficient) encryption schemes to weak (but efficient) encryption schemes. The problem
that *Randomly Partitioned Encryption* tries to solve is to combine the advantages of low-
security/high-performance schemes like OPE [1] with high-security/low-performance

---

[1] Adversaries that do not actively manipulate data, but try to infer information as defined in [19].

V. Atluri and G. Pernul (Eds.): DBSec 2014, LNCS 8566, pp. 307–323, 2014.

schemes like Probabilistic AES (AES in CBC mode [19]), in order to achieve *good security* and *reasonable performance*. Performance refers to the average query response times of the TPC-H benchmark, while security, in this paper, is the ability to resist the following attacks (thoroughly defined in section 3):

- **Domain Attack:** The Adversary has knowledge of the plaintext domain.
- **Frequency Attack:** The Adversary has knowledge of the plaintext domain and its frequency distribution.
- **Query Log Attack:** The Adversary has knowledge of the plaintext domain and has access to the database query logs.

1.1 Background and State of the Art

The main idea of *RPE* is to randomly partition the domain and apply an order preserving encryption scheme to each partition. This makes *RPE* a partially order-preserving encryption as each partition is ordered, but the total order is hidden. In the following, we try to summarize the state of the art in the context of existing OPE schemes and argue why they cannot withstand *Domain, Frequency* and *Query Log Attack*. A more detailed overview of related work can be found in section 9.

Order-Preserving Encryption (OPE). An order-preserving symmetric encryption (OPE) scheme is a deterministic symmetric encryption scheme whose encryption algorithm produces ciphertexts that preserve numerical ordering of the plaintexts. This property makes OPE very attractive for database applications, since it allows efficient range and rank query processing on encrypted data. However, the order relationship between plaintext and ciphertext remains intact after encryption, making it an easy target for a *Domain Attack*. Moreover, being deterministic, makes OPE particularly vulnerable against *Frequency Attacks*. OPE was first proposed in the database community by Agrawal et al. [1], and treated cryptographically for the first time by Boldyreva et al. in [7], followed by [6], [20], [23], [33] in search for an "ideal object". However, the problem of dealing with *Domain* and *Frequency Attacks* remains.

Probabilistic Order-Preserving Encryption (Prob-OPE). A probabilistic order-preserving encryption scheme is a probabilistic symmetric encryption scheme whose algorithm not only produces ciphertexts that preserve numerical ordering of the plaintexts, but also generates different ciphertexts for the same plaintext. This property flattens out the original frequency distribution of the plaintext values, therefore resisting any statistical analysis. Examples are [11], [18], [31], [35]. However, probabilistic schemes still leak total order and are exposed to *Domain Attacks*.

Partially Order Preserving Encryption (POP). A partially order-preserving encryption scheme is a symmetric encryption scheme whose algorithm partitions the domain. Within each partition the order is preserved but across the partitions the order is distorted. There are several ways how to partition the domain: [17], [26] partition the domain into several bins. These solutions are secure against *Domain Attacks*, but vulnerable against *Frequency and Query Log Attacks* because the queries leak the bin boundaries. *RPE* on the other hand, partitions the data in a fine-grained manner and proposes a security-tunable method to rewrite queries.

1.2   Contributions and Main Results

To the best of our knowledge, this paper is the first that formally defines *Domain Attack*, *Frequency Attack* and *Query Log Attack*. Moreover, we introduce three novel encryption methods and analyze their security under these attacks. We start with a scheme that protects against the *Domain Attack* which we call *Deterministic Randomly Partitioned Encryption* (Det-RPE). We then make this scheme probabilistic (Prob-RPE) in order to address the *Frequency Attack* and finally introduce a new query-rewrite mechanism called *Fixed-Range Query Rewrite* (FR) to additionally protect RPE from *Query Log Attacks*. FR can be applied to both, Det-RPE and Prob-RPE, yielding two additional encryption schemes called Det-RPE-FR, resp. Prob-RPE-FR.

What is more, we assess the security and performance of these three encryption methods and compare them to relevant related work. Table 1 shows a summary of this assessment. The first three columns depict security and have a tick if a method is secure against a certain attack (a tick in brackets means that the security depends on a tuning parameter). The last column shows a very rough performance measure that states whether or not range queries can be answered within 30 minutes in the 10-GB TPC-H dataset. As we can see, the three *RPE* variants are Pareto-optimal as they have unique privacy/performance characteristics that differentiate them from existing solutions.

Table 1. Qualitative Security & Performance Analysis of selected Database Encryption Schemes

Adversary Model	Domain Attack	Frequency Attack	Query Log Attack	Performance
OPE [1], [6], [7], [20], [23], [33], [34]	✗	✗	✗	✓
Modular OPE [6]	✓	✗	✗	✓
Probabilistic OPE [11], [18], [35]	✗	✓	✗	✓
Partially OPE [17], [26]	[✓]	✗	✗	✗
AES-CBC [19]	✓	✓	✓	✗
Det-RPE	✓	✗	✗	✓
Prob-RPE	✓	✓	✗	✓
Det-RPE-FR	✓	✗	[✓]	✓
Prob-RPE-FR	✓	✓	[✓]	✓

One important feature of our methods is their composability. RPE schemes can be composed with any order-preserving encryption scheme approved by the security community, thereby inheriting their latest breakthroughs. Additionally, by adding a layer of randomness on top of a chosen underlying OPE scheme, RPE schemes amend the weaknesses of OPE schemes.

1.3   Overview

The remainder of this paper is organized as follows: Section 2 presents our assumed client-server architecture. Section 3 formally defines the newly introduced adversary models. Section 4 starts with describing the basic idea of *Randomly Partitioned Encryption*, then formally defines Det-RPE and analyses the security of Det-RPE and other OPE schemes under *Domain Attack*. Section 5 formally defines *Probabilistic RPE* and analyses its security under *Frequency Attack*. In Section 6, the *Fixed Range Query Rewrite* mechanism is explained and its security is analyzed under *Query Log Attack*. Section 7 and 8 describe implementation details and how they influence performance of the TPCH benchmark. Section 9 discusses related work in detail and section 10 briefly concludes.

2 Client-Server Architecture

Figure 1a shows the traditional client-server architecture of running applications on top of a database system. The application or end user issues SQL statements to the database server. The database server executes these SQL statements and returns the results.

Figure 1b shows the extended architecture assumed in this paper. This architecture has also been assumed by all related work on client-side database security; e.g. in [3], [9], [24], [27]. In this architecture, the application remains unchanged and issues the same (unencrypted) SQL statements as in the traditional system of Figure 1a. The confidentiality is implemented as part of an *Encryption Layer*. The *Encryption Layer* has two significant methods: First,

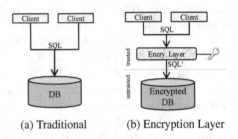

(a) Traditional   (b) Encryption Layer

Fig. 1. Client-Server Database Architecture

rewriting the queries and updates that are to be submitted to the encrypted database. Second, *decrypting and post-processing* the query results returned from the encrypted database. Thus, the *Encryption Layer* encapsulates encryption/decryption and makes security issues transparent to the application developer and end user.

The *Encryption Layer* is assumed to be *thin* and *trusted*. Thin means that not much computational power is needed to implement the *Encryption Layer*; the heavy weight-lifting of executing joins, aggregates, etc. is expected to be carried out in the database. It should be possible to deploy the *Encryption Layer* on a smart phone or laptop. The goal is to omit any administration requirements for the *Encryption Layer*.

3 Adversary Models

A couple of concrete usecases from the financial industry have given birth to new adversary models for cloud databases. These models have not been cryptographically treated so far. In this section we formally introduce the new adversary models and security metrics.

Notation. Let $\mathcal{X}$ be the set of plaintext values in a domain, and $\mathcal{Y}$ be the set of ciphertext values. The size of $\mathcal{X}$ is denoted as $X = |\mathcal{X}|$; the same applies for the size of $\mathcal{Y}$, $Y = |\mathcal{Y}|$. Plaintext elements are denoted as x and ciphertext elements as y. Additionally, we define the Key space to be $\mathcal{K}eys$ and K is denoted as an element from the key space. $\mathcal{K}$ is a function that randomly selects an element from $\mathcal{K}eys$, denoted as $K \xleftarrow{\$} \mathcal{K}eys$. The $\$$ sign on top of the $\leftarrow$ shows that the selection was random. Let $\mathcal{E}nc$ be the encryption function having a key, K, and a plaintext value, x, as its input parameters; thus, we have: $y = \mathcal{E}nc(K, x)$. Symmetrically, $\mathcal{D}ec$ will be the decryption function, taking y and K as input, yielding: $x = \mathcal{D}ec(K, y)$. Let $Rank_x$ be the rank of x in $\mathcal{X}$. Symmetrically, we have $Rank_y$ which denotes the rank of y in $\mathcal{Y}$. Let $rank$ be the function that returns the rank of an element in its corresponding space. The frequency distribution of $\mathcal{X}$ and $\mathcal{Y}$ is denoted as $\mathcal{F}_\mathcal{X}$ and $\mathcal{F}_\mathcal{Y}$ respectively. Let $freq$ be the function that returns the frequency of an element in its corresponding space.

3.1 Domain Attack

Domain Attack is launched by an adversary, $\mathcal{A}^D$ that has a-priori knowledge of the plaintext domain. In our motivating usecase from the financial industry, the database administrator had a list of all customers and needed to retrieve other relevant account information for selected customers.

Rank One-Wayness. In order to measure the success probability of $\mathcal{A}^D$, in breaking an encryption scheme, $\mathcal{ES}$, we introduce a new notion called Rank One-Wayness (ROW). The ROW advantage is defined to be the probability of Experiment 1 returning *1*.

$$Adv_{ES}^{ROW}(\mathcal{A}^D) = Pr[Exp_{ES}^{ROW}(\mathcal{A}^D) = 1)] \tag{1}$$

Experiment 1 . $\text{Exp}_{ES}^{ROW}(\mathcal{A}^D)$

1: $K \xleftarrow{\$} \mathcal{K}eys; x \xleftarrow{\$} \mathcal{X}$
2: $y \leftarrow \mathcal{E}nc(K, x)$
3: $Rank_y \leftarrow rank(y)$
4: $x' \xleftarrow{\$} A^D(\mathcal{X}, Rank_y)$
5: **if** $x = x'$ **then return** 1
6: **else return** 0

To further clarify Experiment 1, let us consider the following example. Let $\mathcal{X} = \{'Beatles', 'Metallica', 'U2'\}$ and $\mathcal{ES} = OPE$. Assume the ciphertext space to be $\mathcal{Y} = \{143, 465, 706\}$. We start the experiment by choosing a random element from $\mathcal{X}$, for instance $'Metallica'$ and encrypt it. We provide $\mathcal{A}^D$ with $\mathcal{X}$ and $Rank_{465} = 2$. $\mathcal{A}^D$ has to return an element from $\mathcal{X}$ which he thinks corresponds to the second element of $\mathcal{Y}$. The probability that $\mathcal{A}^D$ guesses $'Metallica'$ correctly is called the *ROW advantage*.

3.2 Frequency Attack

A *Frequency Attack* is an attack that is launched by an adversary, $\mathcal{A}^{DF}$ that has a-priori knowledge of the plaintext values as well as their frequency distribution.

Frequency One-Wayness. In order to measure the success probability of $\mathcal{A}^{DF}$ in breaking an encryption scheme, $\mathcal{ES}$, we introduce a new notion called Frequency One-Wayness (FOW). The FOW advantage is defined to be the probability of Experiment 2 returning *1*.

$$Adv_{ES}^{FOW}(\mathcal{A}^{DF}) = Pr[Exp_{ES}^{FOW}(\mathcal{A}^{DF}) = 1] \tag{2}$$

Again we illustrate this with an example. Let $\mathcal{X} = \{'Beatles', 'Beatles', 'U2'\}$ and $\mathcal{ES} = OPE$. The ciphertext space will be $\mathcal{Y} = \{143, 143, 706\}$. We start the experiment by choosing a random element from $\mathcal{X}$, for instance $'Beatles'$ and encrypt it. We give $\mathcal{A}^{DF}$, $\mathcal{X}$, $\mathcal{F}_{\mathcal{X}} = \{2, 1\}$ and $freq_{143} = 2$. $\mathcal{A}^{DF}$ has to return an element from $\mathcal{X}$ which he thinks corresponds to the element of $\mathcal{Y}$ that appears twice. The probability that $\mathcal{A}^{DF}$ guesses correctly is called the *FOW advantage*.

Experiment 2 . $\mathrm{Exp}_{ES}^{FOW}(\mathcal{A}^{DF})$

1: $K \xleftarrow{\$} Keys; x \xleftarrow{\$} \mathcal{X}$
2: $y \leftarrow \mathcal{E}nc(K, x)$
3: $Freq_y \leftarrow freq(y)$
4: $x' \xleftarrow{\$} A^{DF}(\mathcal{X}, \mathcal{F}_x, Freq_y)$
5: **if** $x = x'$ **then return** 1
6: **else return** 0

3.3 Query Log Attack

A *Query Log Attack* is launched by an adversary, $\mathcal{A}^Q$, that in addition to domain knowledge, has access to the database query logs, Q_{DB}. In our concrete usecase, since the adversary is the database administrator, access to query logs is granted to him. Depending on the encryption scheme, the query logs may reveal more information about the underlying data than what the encryption scheme was initially intended to leak. Thus, it is crucial to add query log analysis to the list of possible cryptanalysis on database encryption schemes. In general, the query logs leak (1) content, (2) origin (e.g. an IP address of the client submitting the query), (3) frequencies, and (4) time stamp of the query. In this paper we will focus on the *Query Content*. How to perform query analysis and what an adversary can obtain from it, depends on the underlying encryption scheme.

We define the success probability of $\mathcal{A}^Q$ as his advantage to break the Rank One-Wayness of the underlying encryption scheme, $\mathcal{ES}$. Similar to Experiment 1, the adversary, $\mathcal{A}^Q$, is given the plaintext domain, $\mathcal{X}$, a ciphertext rank, $Rank_y$, and additionally the database query logs, Q_{DB}. In the end, $\mathcal{A}^Q$ is asked to return the underlying plaintext, x. The ROW advantage of $\mathcal{A}^Q$ is formulated as:

$$Adv_{ES}^{ROW}(\mathcal{A}^Q) = Pr[Exp_{ES}^{QLA}(\mathcal{A}^Q) = 1] \tag{3}$$

Experiment 3 . $\mathrm{Exp}_{ES}^{ROW}(\mathcal{A}^Q)$

1: $K \xleftarrow{\$} Keys; x \xleftarrow{\$} \mathcal{X}$
2: $y \leftarrow \mathcal{E}nc(K, x)$
3: $Rank_y \leftarrow rank(y)$
4: $x' \xleftarrow{\$} A^Q(\mathcal{X}, Rank_y, Q_{DB})$ ▷ note the additional argument Q_{DB}
5: **if** $x = x'$ **then return** 1
6: **else return** 0

4 Deterministic RPE

This section presents the deterministic *Randomly Partitioned Encryption* scheme (Det-RPE). The key idea of RPE is to take an existing weak encryption method such as OPE as in [1], [6], [7], [20], [34] as a building block and to enhance its security by applying it separately on different random partitions of the data called *Runs*. In contrast to other partially order preserving encryption schemes, such as [26], [17] where they bin the plaintext domain in random-length (or fixed ranged) partitions, RPE creates partially ordered partitions called *Runs* by randomly assigning each domain value to a *Run*; thereby creating more uncertainty.

Figure 2a shows the workings of a traditional OPE encryption function. It receives a plaintext, x, and produces a ciphertext, y, and τ is the set of input parameters that $\mathcal{E}nc$ takes (e.g. a secret key). Figure 2b shows how RPE composes this traditional scheme to become more secure and have a number of additional operational advantages (e.g., support for updates). Instead of a single $\mathcal{E}nc$ function per domain, RPE makes use of

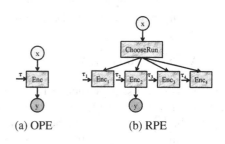

(a) OPE   (b) RPE

Fig. 2. RPE Principle

U encryption functions per domain, $\mathcal{E}nc_1, \mathcal{E}nc_2, \ldots, \mathcal{E}nc_U$, where U is the number of *Runs*. These U functions possibly all have the same structure (e.g. order-preserving using MOPE [6]) and just differ in the secret key they use. Given a plaintext, x, *ChooseRun* generates a number between 1 and U and encrypts x using the corresponding $\mathcal{E}nc$ function, i.e. $y = \mathcal{E}nc_{ChooseRun(x)}(x)$.

Depending on the *ChooseRun* function and the structure of the $\mathcal{E}nc$ function, the composed encryption scheme of Figure 2b can have different properties. The performance overhead of RPE (as compared to no encryption) depends on the number of runs, U; In the extreme case of $U = 1$, RPE is the same as $\mathcal{E}nc$ which is typically a weak, yet high performance encryption scheme. In the other extreme, $U = \infty$, RPE is the same as *random* which corresponds to a strong yet low performance encryption scheme.

Deterministic RPE (abbreviated as Det-RPE) is a deterministic encryption scheme because a deterministic *ChooseRun* and a deterministic $\mathcal{E}nc$ function are used. Determinism of the *ChooseRun* function can be achieved by making its output depend on the plaintext, x, i.e. by using a *pseudo-random* function. Our Det-RPE construction has to generate two sets of keys, one set for the runs and the other for the *ChooseRun* function.

Table 2. Det-RPE Example: $U = 2$

Clear Text	Run 1	Run 2	Code ($\langle$ run, y $\rangle$)
Beatles		1	$\langle 2, 1 \rangle$
Beatles		1	$\langle 2, 1 \rangle$
Beatles		1	$\langle 2, 1 \rangle$
Elton John	1		$\langle 1, 1 \rangle$
Madonna		2	$\langle 2, 2 \rangle$
Madonna		2	$\langle 2, 2 \rangle$
Metallica		3	$\langle 2, 3 \rangle$
Nelly Furtado	2		$\langle 1, 2 \rangle$
Tina Turner	3		$\langle 1, 3 \rangle$

The encryption function of Det-RPE then composes the *ChooseRun* function with the encryption function of a typical OPE scheme. Det-RPE can be composed with any OPE scheme from [1, 6, 7, 20, 33, 34].

Construction 1. *Let $\mathcal{OPE} = (\mathcal{K}, \mathcal{E}nc, \mathcal{D}ec)$ be a deterministic order-preserving encryption scheme. We define a deterministic RPE scheme, $\mathcal{D}et\text{-}\mathcal{RPE}(\mathcal{K}_{dRPE}, \mathcal{E}nc_{dRPE}, \mathcal{D}ec_{dRPE})$, as follows:*

- $\mathcal{K}_{dRPE}$ *runs $\mathcal{K}$ independently for each run and returns U keys, namely $(K_1, ..., K_U)$. Also, it runs $\mathcal{K}$ independently to generate K_{map} for the ChooseRun function.*

- $\mathcal{E}nc_{dRPE}$ takes K_u and x, as input where $u = ChooseRun(K_{map}, x)$. Then it returns u and $y = \mathcal{E}nc(K_u, x)$, i.e. (u, y).
- $\mathcal{D}ec_{dRPE}$ takes (u, y) as input and returns $x = \mathcal{D}ec(K_u, y)$.

Table 2 gives an example of a set of customer names encrypted with *Det-RPE* with $U = 2$ using an OPE scheme where $\mathcal{U}$ denotes the set of runs and $|\mathcal{U}| = U$.

4.1   Analysis of Domain Attack

An ordinary OPE scheme such as in [1], [6], [7], [20], [23], [33], [34] allows the domain adversary, $\mathcal{A}^D$, to efficiently break the encryption by solely using sorting. In other words: $Adv_{OPE}^{ROW}(\mathcal{A}^D) = 1$. On the other hand, a Modular OPE scheme, as proposed in [6], is resilient against a Domain Attack as shown in Lemma 1.

Lemma 1. *ROW-advantage of $\mathcal{A}^D$ on Modular OPE is:*

$$Adv_{MOPE}^{ROW}(\mathcal{A}^D) = Pr[Exp_{MOPE}^{ROW}(A) = 1] = \frac{1}{X} \tag{4}$$

Proof. In order to win Experiment 1 on MOPE, the adversary needs to know the modular offset. Since offset is chosen randomly from $\mathcal{X}$, the adversary will win the game with a probability of $\frac{1}{X}$.

Nevertheless, MOPE is vulnerable to the Known Plaintext Attacks, where the adversary additionally has one or more plaintext-ciphertext pairs. In that case, MOPE collapses into OPE.

The Probabilistic OPE schemes such as in [11], [18], [35] have the following ROW advantage against a Domain Attack:

Lemma 2. *(proof in [25]) ROW-advantage of $\mathcal{A}^D$ on Prob-OPE is:*

$$Adv_{Prob\text{-}OPE}^{ROW}(\mathcal{A}^D) = Pr[Exp_{Prob\text{-}OPE}^{ROW}(\mathcal{A}^D) = 1] = \frac{\binom{Rank_y - 1}{Rank_x - 1}\binom{Y - Rank_y}{X - Rank_x}}{\binom{Y-1}{X-1}} \tag{5}$$

RPE amends all variants of OPE schemes to a great extent by randomly partitioning the domain into *Runs*, thereby breaking the total order into U partial orders. According to [5, 13], the problem of finding the right total order out of U partial orders is classified as inapproximable.

Lemma 3. *(proof in [25]) ROW-advantage of $\mathcal{A}^D$ on Det-RPE is defined as:*

$$Adv_{Det\text{-}RPE}^{ROW}(\mathcal{A}^D) = Pr[Exp_{Det\text{-}RPE}^{ROW}(\mathcal{A}^D) = 1] = \frac{\binom{Rank_x - 1}{Rank_{(y,r)} - 1}\binom{X - Rank_x}{\frac{X}{U} - Rank_{(y,r)}}}{\binom{X}{\frac{X}{U}}} \tag{6}$$

The probability distribution conforms to a negative hypergeometric probability distribution which applies to sampling without replacement from a finite population, in our case the domain, $\mathcal{X}$. As random selections are made from the population, each subsequent draw decreases the population causing the probability of success to change with each draw. The detailed proofs of Lemma 2 and 3 are quite involved and can be found in our technical report [25].

An important observation to make from Equations 5 and 6 is that the ROW advantage not only depends on the domain size but also on the rank of the plaintext in the domain. Consequently, extreme values of the domain (e.g. "AAA" or "ZZZ") are breaking the uniformity of the probability distribution. In order to fix this problem, Det-RPE can be composed with Modular OPE [6] to form a ring structure to hide these extreme values.

In Figure 3 the ROW advantage is plotted for each encryption scheme. As a baseline we plot the advantage of an adversary that outputs a random x regardless of the domain. This is considered to be "ideal" and is exactly what Modular OPE [6] achieves. We see that Det-RPE helps an OPE scheme (in that case ROPE from [7]) with high ROW advantage to get close to the "ideal" threshold by increasing the number of runs.

The equations presented in this section can be tuned to meet the *user's negligibility requirement*. For example, in Equation 6, depending on the domain size, the number of runs can be tuned to meet the security/performance requirements of the system. The higher the number of runs, the closer one gets to the "ideal" threshold, but also the bigger is the performance overhead.

Table 3. Prob-RPE with $U = 2$

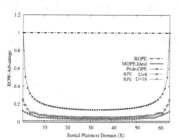

Fig. 3. ROW advantage under Domain Attack

Customer Name	Run 1	Run 2	Prob-Code ($\langle$ run, y $\rangle$)
Beatles		1	$\langle 2, 1 \rangle$
Beatles		2	$\langle 2, 2 \rangle$
Beatles	1		$\langle 1, 1 \rangle$
Elton John		3	$\langle 2, 3 \rangle$
Madonna	2		$\langle 1, 2 \rangle$
Madonna		4	$\langle 2, 4 \rangle$
Metallica	3		$\langle 1, 3 \rangle$
Nelly Furtado	4		$\langle 1, 4 \rangle$
Tina Turner		5	$\langle 2, 5 \rangle$

5   Probabilistic RPE

In this section we present the probabilistic variant of Randomly Partitioned Encryption (Prob-RPE). RPE is made probabilistic in two ways: (a) by using a probabilistic order preserving encryption scheme within each run, such as proposed in [35] and (b) by assigning the same plaintext value to different runs to guarantee database dynamism and improve security.

In *Probabilistic RPE*, *ChooseRun* is defined as a *random function*. For each plaintext element, x, *ChooseRun* randomly selects a run, u. Afterwards, x is to be encrypted in u. Table 3 gives an example of such a Prob-RPE encryption scheme where the same value can even have multiple codes within a single run. For instance, Beatles has two codes in *Run 2* and one code in *Run 1*, in other words $Beatles = \{\langle 2, 1 \rangle, \langle 2, 2 \rangle, \langle 1, 1 \rangle\}$.

We formally construct Prob-RPE as follows:

Construction 2. *Let $Prob\text{-}\mathcal{OPE}(\mathcal{K}_p, \mathcal{E}nc_p, \mathcal{D}ec_p)$ be a probabilistic order-preserving encryption scheme from [35]. We define a probabilistic RPE scheme, $Prob\text{-}\mathcal{RPE}(\mathcal{K}_{pRPE}, \mathcal{E}nc_{pRPE}, \mathcal{D}ec_{pRPE})$, as follows:*

- *$\mathcal{K}_{pRPE}$ runs $\mathcal{K}_p$ independently for each run and returns U keys, namely $(K_1, ..., K_U)$.*
- *$\mathcal{E}nc_{pRPE}$ takes K_u and x, as input where $u = ChooseRun()$. Then it returns u and $y = \mathcal{E}nc_p(K_u, x)$, i.e. (u, y).*
- *$\mathcal{D}ec_{pRPE}$ takes (u, y) as input and returns $x = \mathcal{D}ec_p(K_u, y)$.*

The query rewrite mechanisms for RPE have been thoroughly explained in [25]. To give an intuition on how queries are rewritten using RPE, consider a query that asks for all customers with name LIKE ''M%'' in the example of Table 3 for Prob-RPE. This query must be rewritten to:

```
SELECT * FROM Customer
  WHERE (run = 1 AND ( 1 < y < 4))
    OR (run = 2 AND ( 3 < y < 5))
```

5.1 Analysis of Frequency Attack

A known weakness of a deterministic encryption scheme is its inability to hide the original frequency distribution of the plaintext domain, specially if the plaintext domain has a skewed frequency distribution. Since OPE, Modular OPE and Det-RPE are all deterministic encryption schemes, the FOW-advantage introduced in Section 3.2 of $\mathcal{A}^{DF}$ depends on the plaintext frequency distribution, namely $F_\mathcal{X}$. In other words, if the original frequency distribution is uniform then the adversary's advantage is also uniform, i.e. best security. Nevertheless, if the original frequency distribution is skewed, then the adversary's advantage is different and depends on the number of elements having the same frequency.

Corollary 1. *Let $y = \mathcal{E}nc(K, x)$ and $G = \{w | w \in \mathcal{X} \wedge freq_\mathcal{X}(w) = freq_\mathcal{Y}(y)\}$ be the set of distinct plaintext values having the same frequency as y. Then, the FOW-advantage of the $\mathcal{A}^{DF}$ adversary on a deterministic encryption scheme is defined as his winning probability in Experiment 2:*

$$Adv_{DET}^{FOW}(\mathcal{A}^{DF}) = Pr[Exp_{DET}^{FOW}(A) = 1] = \frac{1}{|G|} \tag{7}$$

Remark 1. *A deterministic encryption scheme is optimally safe against a Frequency Attack if and only if $F_\mathcal{X}$ is uniform. A uniform $F_\mathcal{X}$ implies a maximum $|G|$ where $|G| = X$, i.e. $|G|$ equals the domain size.*

Remark 2. *Probabilistic OPE and Prob-RPE as described in this section, take care of a skewed probability distribution by each time creating a new ciphertext for a plaintext value. This way the skewed frequency distribution of the plaintext domain is mapped to a uniform frequency distribution in the ciphertext space i.e. the FOW advantage under frequency attack is optimal which is $\frac{1}{X}$.*

6 Fixed Range Query Rewrite

In Section 3.3, we have introduced an attack that is based on the information that an attacker can extract from the query logs. The query logs are said to be dangerous, when they carry more information about the underlying encryption scheme than the encrypted data in the database.

To see what type of queries can be dangerous for each of the encryption schemes presented in this paper, we introduce the concept of a *Query Simulator*. A *Query Simulator* generates queries by looking at the encrypted data. Thus, if we are dealing with a query which can be simulated just by looking at the encrypted data, that query is called *simulatable*. Otherwise, the query is dangerous and can be exploited to break the guarantees of the underlying encryption scheme. Typically, in both, probabilistic and partially order preserving schemes, such as in [17], [26], [35] to support efficient query processing, the queries reveal essential information about the certain initial values. Therefore, RPE conceals the total order which can be reconstructed by query log analysis. Table 4 presents a summary of the simulatable SQL operators in combination with the encryption schemes presented in this paper.

Table 4. SQL Operator Simulatability for different Encryption Schemes

SQL-Operator	OPE	MOPE [6]	Prob-OPE [18], [35]	POP [17], [26]	Det-RPE	Prob-RPE	*-RPE-FR
WHERE (=, !=)/IN	✓	✓	✗	✗	✓	✗	✓
WHERE (<, >)/LIKE(Prefix%)	✓	✓	✗	✗	✗	✗	✓
Equi-Join	✓	✓	✗	✗	✓	✓	✓
TOP N	✓	✗	✗	✗	✓	✗	✓
ORDER BY (sort)	✓	✓	✓	✗	✓	✓	✓
MIN/MAX	✓	✗	✗	✗	✓	✗	✓

Table 4 shows that all SQL Operators are simulatable for OPE. Nevertheless, OPE is not safe against *Query Log Attack* because the adversary has domain knowledge and can therefore launch a *Domain Attack*. Probabilistic OPE and Partially OPE schemes seem at first sight to be more secure, but on the other hand queries are not simulatable in those schemes, i.e. query log attack breaks them.

Our approach, RPE, is most of the time simulatable except for range queries. Thus, there are two solutions to this problem: (1) Suppress the range queries, (2) Using *Fixed Range Query Rewrite* mechanisms. In this section we will elaborate the second option.

The idea of *Fixed Range Query Rewrite* is to divide the ciphertext space, $\mathcal{Y}$ into k disjoint fixed-sized sub-ranges of size r, fr_i where $i = 1, ..., k$ and $|fr_i| = r$. Whenever a range query is asked, the smallest units that are returned are those *fixed ranges* that contain the user's results.

Table 5. Two fixed ranges of size 3, $r = 3$

Fixed Range	Customer Names	Run 1	Run 2	Code ($\langle$ run, y $\rangle$)
fr_1	Beatles		3	$\langle 2, 3 \rangle$
	Elton John	1		$\langle 1, 1 \rangle$
	Madonna		5	$\langle 2, 5 \rangle$
fr_2	Metallica		9	$\langle 2, 9 \rangle$
	Nelly Furtado	6		$\langle 1, 6 \rangle$
	Tina Turner	7		$\langle 1, 7 \rangle$

As an example, consider Table 5 where deterministic RPE has been used for encryption. The client submits the query: SELECT name FROM customer WHERE name > 'Lady Gaga'. Using Det-RPE the query should be rewritten to: SELECT name FROM customer WHERE (run = 1 AND 3 < code < 10) OR (run = 2 AND 3 < code < 10).

However, since this query is revealing some information about the partition rela-tionships, we will use fixed range query rewrite mechanisms. Thus, the original query will be rewritten as follows to cover both fixed ranges, fr_1 and fr_2 that contain the result: SELECT name FROM customer WHERE (run = 1 AND 0 < code < 10) OR (run = 2 AND 0 < code < 10).

This is the whole table in this example. The result includes two additional false positives, namely, "Beatles" and "Elton John" that will be filtered out during the post-processing. Obviously, using *Fixed Ranged Query Rewrite* returns a super-set of the result that needs to be post-filtered and leads to performance loss. On the other hand, the security guarantees and analysis will deviate from what we have discussed earlier in Section 4.

6.1 Analysis of Query Log Attack

According to Table 4, OPE schemes are safe against query analysis, however Modular OPE cannot safely handle min/max and rank queries. Probabilistic OPE cannot handle range queries without revealing the borders, so using *Fixed Ranged Query Rewrite* pro-tects the encryption scheme from query log analysis. In case of RPE, range queries are problematic because they help to reconstruct the total order, which is exactly what RPE is trying to hide. Hence, *Fixed Ranged Query Rewrite* helps again to limit the ROW ad-vantage under query log attack. Assuming we have a uniform code distribution within a range in all runs, Equation 6 changes into:

$$Adv_{\text{Det-RPE-FR}}^{\text{ROW}}(\mathcal{A}^Q) = Pr[Exp_{\text{Det-RPE-FR}}^{\text{ROW}}(\mathcal{A}^Q) = 1] \quad = \frac{\binom{Rank_x^{fr}-1}{Rank_{(y,r)}^{fr}-1}\binom{r-Rank_x^{fr}}{\frac{r}{u}-Rank_{(y,r)}^{fr}}}{\binom{r}{\frac{r}{U}}}$$

$$(8)$$

Informally speaking, the randomness is no more distributed throughout the domain, but is only available within the fixed range. From Equation 8 we reach the following conclusions:

- If $U = r$ then we have a uniform probability distribution. This means although no range query is possible within a fixed range (like having AES in each range). Among different fixed ranges, range queries are possible.
- Getting better security is achievable by both increasing the range size and the num-ber of runs. However they both come at the cost of performance.
- Range size is the main parameter whereas the domain size does not play a role anymore.

7 Database Functionality

After the security assessment of RPE, we also want to compare its supported function-ality to the state-of-the-art. Table 6 summarizes which SQL operators can be efficiently implemented for which encryption technique. We can see that the RPE variants sup-port most of the desired SQL operators, which allows them to be used in practice while semantically secure encryption schemes (like e.g. AES in CBC mode or fully homomorphic encryption schemes[12] become inefficient as soon as we want to ask range, in, order-by or group-by queries. RPE also allows indexes to be build on top of it as usual. For a full description on *query rewrite* and *referential integrity*, we refer the curious reader to our Technical Report [15].

Table 6. Supported SQL Operators: State of the Art vs. RPE

SQL-Operator	OPE	MOPE[6]	POP[17, 26]	Det-RPE	Prob-RPE	FHE [12]	AES-CBC [19]
DISTINCT	✓	✓	✗	✓	✗	✗	✗
WHERE (=, !=)	✓	✓	✓	✓	✓	✗	✗
WHERE ($<, >$)	✓	✓	✓	✓	✓	✗	✗
LIKE(Prefix%)	✓	✓	✓	✓	✓	✗	✗
LIKE(%Suffix)	✗	✗	✗	✗	✗	✗	✗
IN	✓	✓	✓	✓	✓	✗	✗
Equi-Join	✓	✓	✓	✓	✓	✗	✗
Non Equi-Join	✓	✓	✓	✓	✓	✗	✗
TOP N	✓	✗	✗	✓	✗	✗	✗
ORDER BY	✓	✓	✗	✓	✓	✗	✗
SUM	✗	✗	✗	✓	✓	✓	✗
MIN/MAX	✓	✗	✗	✗	✗	✗	✗
GROUP BY	✓	✓	✗	✓	✗	✗	✗

8 Performance Analysis and Experimental Results

In order to measure to what extent missing SQL operator influence query performance, we implemented the TPC-H benchmark on the architecture shown in figure 1. We have executed a number of experiments with different varying parameters, e.g. the number of runs or the number of codes per value in a single run for Prob-RPE. We measured total response time, post-processing time, network cost and query compilation time. For space reasons we only present the most important results and reference to our technical report [25] for the complete numbers and explanations.

All experiments were conducted on two separate machines for client and server. The client was written in Java, ran on a machine with 24 GB of memory and communicated to the database server using JDBC. The server machine had 132 GB of memory available and hosted a MySQL 5.6 database. Both machines had 8 cores and ran a Debian-based Linux distribution. We measured end-to-end response time for all queries in separation, thereby using a scaling factor of 10 (which means that the size of the plaintext data set is 10 GB). Metrics used in aggregate functions (e.g., volume of orders) and surrogates (e.g., order numbers) were left unencrypted while all other (sensitive) attributes, such as names, dates, etc. were encrypted. Whenever SQL operators on encrypted data were not supported, the entire data was shipped and then aggregated and filtered during the post-processing step at the encryption layer. Wherever the TPC-H benchmark defines an index on an attribute a, we created the same index on the encrypted value of a as well as a composite index on (a_run, a).

Figure 4 shows the response time for different encryption functions compared to *Plain*, which is the response time for query processing on unencrypted data. *Det-OPE* is a deterministic OPE scheme as proposed by [7] and was used as a gold standard to compare against two different RPE variants that both used fixed-range query rewrite. The deterministic RPE version is denoted by *Det-RPE-FR*, while *Prob-RPE-FR* stands

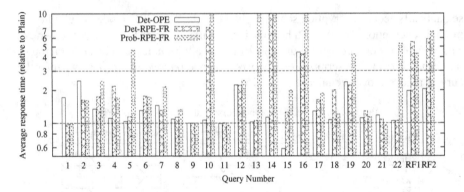

Fig. 4. TPC-H response times of different encryption functions relative to Plain, scaling factor 10

for the probabilistic version. We can see that for a majority of queries and RPE variants, response time is at most three times higher than *Plain* and twice as high as *Det-OPE*. Sometimes, it is even smaller than the baselines because the partitioning (together with the composite indexes) allows for parallelized query processing, which was employed in the presence of Top-N queries. As expected, *Prob-RPE-FR* can add significant overhead. However, we believe this overhead to be reasonable as the security gain is substantial as shown in the previous sections. We also measured the performance of deterministic AES-ECB [19], but did not include the results in the graph because most queries did not finish withing 30 minutes and therefore had an overhead ranging from about 20x to 200x. AES-CBC [19], a representative of semantically secure encryption schemes, would perform even worse.

The number of runs, U, is an important parameter of all RPE schemes. Figure 5 shows how the running time of Det-RPE-FR increases with the number of runs for the first six TPCH queries and relative to *Plain*. We chose these queries because they cover a wide spectrum of different operators (range predicates, aggregates, Top N, sub-selects, etc.). Overall, it can be seen that the curves are fairly flat. Only for Q6, there is a significant (but still linear) increase in the re-

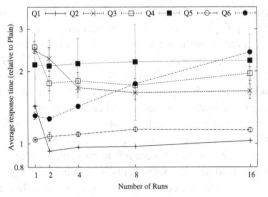

Fig. 5. Response Time of TPC-H Queries 1 to 6 for Det-RPE-FR, vary U from 1 to 16

sponse time with a growing number of runs. Q2 and Q3 are Top N queries and are therefore executed with a degree of parallelism equal to U, which result in a decreasing response time. Q1, Q4 and Q5 have a similar behavior like most TPCH-queries: their curves stay fairly flat. This shows that partitioning does generally not hurt RPE.

9   Related Work

To fill the gap between no security/high performance and high security/low performance, there have been a number of proposals for encryption techniques that support query processing without decrypting the data. Examples are [2], [9], [14]. However, these approaches return a superset of the desired result and lose a lot of time into decrypting and filtering out the false positives.

On the other hand, the goal of fully homomorphic encryption (FHE) [30], [10], [12], [22], [28] is to strongly encrypt the data and process it directly without decryption. [32] shows, at a conceptual level, how FHE can be used in databases. However, when taken to practice, databases explode in size because of the huge keys required by FHE. Therefore, the practicality of FHE in databases is an open question and no performance evaluation has been published so far.

Another important class of encryption techniques for databases are variants of order-preserving encryption (OPE), first introduced by Agrawal et al. [1]. Examples include *Random (Modular) OPE* [6], [7], *Mutable OPE* [23], *Indistinguishability-based OPE* [20], *Generalized OPE* [33], [34], *Structure Preserving Database Encryption* [11], *Probabilistic OPE* [35], *OPE with Splitting and Scaling* [31], *Multivalued OPE* [18], *Multivalued partial OPE* [17], and *Chaotic OPE* [26]. RPE is based on Random OPE and Modular Random OPE from [6], [7], but very different from all the other OPE derivatives in the sense that it either solves a different problem (i.e. addresses different attacks) or uses different techniques. Systems that exploit OPE are *CryptDB* [24] and *Monomi* [29]. RPE can be integrated into these systems to make them more secure.

Secure hardware has recently been exploited in the *TrustedDB* [4] and *Cipherbase* [3] projects. They are an interesting approach, but how to reach good performance, especially for analytical workloads, is still open. Again, RPE can be plugged-in into these systems in order to allow for faster, but still secure query processing.

Most commercial database products support strong encryption using AES [19], e.g. Oracle [21] and Microsoft SQL Server [16]. Unfortunately, they only support encryption for *data at rest* at the disk level, which means that these approaches do not address attacks issued by a curious database administrator or any other party that can access to the data in memory.

10   Conclusion

This paper presented different variants of *Randomly Partitioned Encryption*, a set of novel methods for encrypting cloud databases, thereby addressing real world attacker scenarios like *Domain, Frequency* and *Query Log* attacks. To the best of our knowledge, this is the first time that these attacks were formally defined and their success probability with respect to both, existing order-preserving encryption schemes, and the proposed RPE variants, analyzed. Moreover, the paper showed that the additional performance cost introduced by these new encryption schemes is reasonably small and gave a detailed overview of similar and related work in the literature.

References

[1] Agrawal, R., et al.: Order preserving encryption for numeric data. In: Proceedings of the 2004 ACM SIGMOD International Conference on Management of Data, pp. 563–574. ACM (2004)

[2] Agrawal, R., et al.: Privacy-preserving data mining. ACM Sigmod Record 29(2), 439–450 (2000)

[3] Arasu, A., et al.: Orthogonal Security with Cipherbase. In: CIDR. Citeseer (2013)

[4] Bajaj, S., et al.: TrustedDB: a trusted hardware based database with privacy and data confidentiality. In: Proceedings of the 2011 ACM SIGMOD International Conference on Management of Data, pp. 205–216. ACM (2011)

[5] Berger, B., et al.: Approximation alogorithms for the maximum acyclic subgraph problem. In: Proceedings of the First Annual ACM-SIAM Symposium on Discrete Algorithms, pp. 236–243. Society for Industrial and Applied Mathematics (1990)

[6] Boldyreva, A., Chenette, N., O'Neill, A.: Order-preserving encryption revisited: Improved security analysis and alternative solutions. In: Rogaway, P. (ed.) CRYPTO 2011. LNCS, vol. 6841, pp. 578–595. Springer, Heidelberg (2011)

[7] Boldyreva, A., Chenette, N., Lee, Y., O'Neill, A.: Order-preserving symmetric encryption. In: Joux, A. (ed.) EUROCRYPT 2009. LNCS, vol. 5479, pp. 224–241. Springer, Heidelberg (2009)

[8] Chow, R., et al.: Controlling data in the cloud: outsourcing computation without outsourcing control. In: Proceedings of the 2009 ACM Workshop on Cloud Computing Security, pp. 85–90. ACM (2009)

[9] Damiani, E., et al.: Balancing confidentiality and efficiency in untrusted relational DBMSs. In: Proceedings of the 10th ACM Conference on Computer and Communications Security, pp. 93–102. ACM (2003)

[10] ElGamal, T.: A public key cryptosystem and a signature scheme based on discrete logarithms. In: Blakely, G.R., Chaum, D. (eds.) CRYPTO 1984. LNCS, vol. 196, pp. 10–18. Springer, Heidelberg (1985)

[11] Elovici, Y., Waisenberg, R., Shmueli, E., Gudes, E.: A structure preserving database encryption scheme. In: Jonker, W., Petković, M. (eds.) SDM 2004. LNCS, vol. 3178, pp. 28–40. Springer, Heidelberg (2004)

[12] Gentry, C.: A fully homomorphic encryption scheme. PhD thesis. Stanford University (2009)

[13] Guruswami, V., et al.: Beating the random ordering is hard: Inapproximability of maximum acyclic subgraph. In: IEEE 49th Annual IEEE Symposium on Foundations of Computer Science, pp. 573–582. IEEE (2008)

[14] Hacigümüş, H., et al.: Executing SQL over encrypted data in the database-service-provider model. In: Proceedings of the 2002 ACM SIGMOD International Conference on Management of Data, pp. 216–227. ACM (2002)

[15] Hildenbrand, S., et al.: Query processing on encrypted data in the cloud. Tech. rep. 735. Department of Computer Science, ETH Zurich (2011)

[16] Hsueh, S.: Database encryption in SQL server 2008 enterprise edition. Microsoft, SQL Server Technical Article (2008)

[17] Kadhem, H., et al.: A Secure and Efficient Order Preserving Encryption Scheme for Relational Databases. In: KMIS, pp. 25–35 (2010)

[18] Kadhem, H., et al.: MV-OPES: Multivalued-order preserving encryption scheme: A novel scheme for encrypting integer value to many different values. IEICE Transactions on Information and Systems 93(9), 2520–2533 (2010)

[19] Katz, J., et al.: Introduction to modern cryptography: principles and protocols. CRC Press (2007)

[20] Malkin, T., et al.: Order-Preserving Encryption Secure Beyond One-Wayness. Tech. rep. Citeseer (2013)

[21] Nanda, A.: Transparent Data Encryption. Oracle Magazine (2005)

[22] Paillier, P.: Public-key cryptosystems based on composite degree residuosity classes. In: Stern, J. (ed.) EUROCRYPT 1999. LNCS, vol. 1592, pp. 223–238. Springer, Heidelberg (1999)

[23] Popa, R.A., et al.: An ideal-security protocol for order-preserving encoding. In: 2013 IEEE Symposium on Security and Privacy (SP), pp. 463–477. IEEE (2013)

[24] Popa, R.A., et al.: Cryptdb: protecting confidentiality with encrypted query processing. In: Proceedings of the Twenty-Third ACM Symposium on Operating Systems Principles, pp. 85–100. ACM (2011)

[25] Sanamrad, T., et al.: POP: a new encryption scheme for dynamic databases. Tech. rep. 782. Department of Computer Science, ETH Zurich (2013)

[26] Seungmin, L., et al.: Chaotic order preserving encryption for efficient and secure queries on databases. IEICE Transactions on Information and Systems 92(11), 2207–2217 (2009)

[27] Sion, R.: Secure data outsourcing. In: Proceedings of the 33rd International Conference on Very Large Data Bases, pp. 1431–1432. VLDB Endowment (2007)

[28] Smart, N.P., Vercauteren, F.: Fully homomorphic encryption with relatively small key and ciphertext sizes. In: Nguyen, P.Q., Pointcheval, D. (eds.) PKC 2010. LNCS, vol. 6056, pp. 420–443. Springer, Heidelberg (2010)

[29] Tu, S., et al.: Processing analytical queries over encrypted data. In: Proceedings of the 39th International Conference on Very Large Data Bases, pp. 289–300. VLDB Endowment (2013)

[30] van Dijk, M., Gentry, C., Halevi, S., Vaikuntanathan, V.: Fully homomorphic encryption over the integers. In: Gilbert, H. (ed.) EUROCRYPT 2010. LNCS, vol. 6110, pp. 24–43. Springer, Heidelberg (2010)

[31] Wang, H., et al.: Efficient secure query evaluation over encrypted XML databases. In: Proceedings of the 32nd International Conference on Very Large Data Bases, pp. 127–138. VLDB Endowment (2006)

[32] Wang, S., et al.: Is Homomorphic Encryption the Holy Grail for Database Queries on Encrypted Data? Technical report, Department of Computer Science, UCSB (2012)

[33] Wozniak, S., et al.: Beyond the ideal object: towards disclosure-resilient order-preserving encryption schemes. In: Proceedings of the 2013 ACM Workshop on Cloud Computing Security Workshop, pp. 89–100. ACM (2013)

[34] Xiao, L., et al.: A Note for the Ideal Order-Preserving Encryption Object and Generalized Order-Preserving Encryption. In: IACR Cryptology ePrint Archive 2012, p. 350 (2012)

[35] Yang, Z., Zhong, S., Wright, R.N.: Privacy-preserving queries on encrypted data. In: Gollmann, D., Meier, J., Sabelfeld, A. (eds.) ESORICS 2006. LNCS, vol. 4189, pp. 479–495. Springer, Heidelberg (2006)

Towards Secure Cloud Database
with Fine-Grained Access Control

Michael G. Solomon, Vaidy Sunderam*, and Li Xiong**

Department of Mathematics & Computer Science
Emory University
Atlanta, Georgia 30322, USA
{msolo01,vss,lxiong}@emory.edu

Abstract. Outsourcing data to cloud environments can offer ease of access, provisioning, and cost benefits, but makes the data more vulnerable to disclosure. Loss of complete control over the data can be offset through encryption, but this approach requires an omniscient third party key authority to handle key management, increasing overhead complexity. We present the ZeroVis framework that provides confidentiality for data stored in a cloud environment without requiring a third party key manager. It combines fine-grained access control with the ability to search over encrypted data to allow existing applications to migrate to cloud environments with very minimal software changes, while maintaining data provider control over who can consume that data.

Keywords: Confidentiality, Searchable Encryption, Ciphertext Policy, Fine-grained Access Control, Cloud.

1   Introduction

An agreement with a Cloud Service Provider (CSP) [13] to store data in a public, community, or hybrid cloud environment can provide the benefits of outsourced maintenance and capability to alter capacity based on demand [3]. However, the cost of outsourcing data storage is diminished control over data security [25, 16]. CSP environments are untrusted [10] in which local levels of control cannot be attained [17, 16]. Traditional access control methods are often insufficient for CSP [17, 19] hosted databases. Lacking sufficient confidentiality controls not only exposes the data to additional vulnerabilities, but is also possibly a violation of laws, regulations, or contract terms [22].

The primary challenge is to extend confidentiality assurances into untrusted domains [19]. Since different data consumers have different privileges, data access must be individualized and restricted to authorized consumers. And to be functionally effective, the protected data must be searchable without incurring

* Research supported in part by NSF grant OCI-1124418 and AFOSR DDDAS grant FA9550-12-1-0240.
** Research supported in part by NSF grant CNS-1117763 and AFOSR DDDAS grant FA9550-12-1-0240.

V. Atluri and G. Pernul (Eds.): DBSec 2014, LNCS 8566, pp. 324–338, 2014.

excessive overhead or exposing any of the protected data to any entities in the untrusted environment [5].

A common method to protect data in any untrusted environment is to encrypt data before sending it outside the trusted domain [9]. In multi-user database scenarios, solutions using most traditional encryption implementations are suboptimal, requiring an additional key-management layer thereby degrading performance and scalability [32, 20, 8].

Traditional data encryption techniques require a single key, or a pair of keys, to encrypt and decrypt each data item. The most fine-grained approach to using encryption for data stored in a database requires a separate key for each cell (each column within a row), and a trusted key authority to store keys and manage access to them based on pre-determined access criteria. The opposite extreme approach would be to use a single key or key pair to encrypt and decrypt all protected cells in the database, an approach similar to various transparent data encryption schemes [11, 7]. This approach makes it easier to manage keys but introduces a single point of compromise. A balance between the two extremes is to define partitions of encrypted data (the set of encrypted cells in a database that share the same encryption/decryption key), and are often implemented as roles [30]. While this approach is a good compromise between minimum and maximum granularity, the common use of key access managers does still grant access control authority to the key access manager, instead of giving the authority to the data provider.

Table 1. Data Access Example: Research teams and contexts of interest

Team	Treatment	Research Context	Description
A	Z51.11	Cancer	Effectiveness of different treatment
B	E66.09	Nutritional health	Impact of obesity on heart disease
C	Z51.11	Tobacco use AND Heart disease	Impact of lifestyle and heart disease on cancer treatment effectiveness
D	Modified Diet	Nutrition	Measurable benefits of various diets

Running Example. Difficulties with balancing data protection and ease of access are common in medical data collection. Consider the following scenario. Four research teams, A, B, C, and D, need patient data. Table 1 shows four research teams, along with the specific treatments they are studying and the general context of their work. The primary challenge to be addressed is to obtain current data that is pertinent to their research, while complying with HIPAA rules and patient constraints. Patient constraints allow a patient to control who can access her data, such as researchers, medical service providers, and next of kin to access her data. A patient can submit her data with constraints, such as "allow authorized cancer researchers to access my data".

Contributions. We propose a framework that addresses the need of confidentiality in an untrusted environment along with maintaining *data provider control*

over *data consumer access* without an omniscient key manager. Our framework, termed ZeroVis[1], combines the ability to search across encrypted data [24] with fine-grained access control [1] to provide confidentiality protection, searchability for efficient access, and data owner initiated access control, all in an untrusted storage environment. Our framework will provide a one-to-many (one data provider to many data consumers) data confidentiality layer that can be accessed by existing legacy applications to allow current host-bound applications to migrate to a cloud storage environment and maintain confidentiality.

Our framework does not require a trusted third party to manage encryption keys for data providers and consumers. Nor does it require specific permission for each new data consumer (e.g. research team). In essence, each data provider (patient) specifies an access policy (based on attributes rather than identities) for her data that determines who can access protected portions of her data. Traditional key management schemes require a key manager to associate authorized data providers and authorized data consumers with keys (a many-to-many relationship). Our framework assumes the existence of an attribute manager that maintains valid attributes for authorized data consumers (instead of many keys), regardless how many partitions they can access.

Given our running example, assume that a patient received treatment at an oncologist's office. The patient specified that the data to describe and record the visit is saved with the following access policy:
"treatment='Z51.11' AND (context=cancer OR context=tobacco use)" (i.e. only data consumers that possess the treatment attribute with a value of Z51.11[2] and the context attribute with either the values of cancer or tobacco can access her data.)

Our framework proposes the use of CP-ABE (Ciphertext Policy Attribute Based Encryption) [1] to control access to data based on the data consumer's attributes. Only consumers who possess attributes that satisfy the ciphertext's access policy can decrypt. In the running example, all research teams can retrieve any encrypted database row. However, only A and C can decrypt the data since their attributes (treatment and context) satisfy the CP-ABE access policy. Our framework also utilizes layered encryption in combination with CP-ABE to support efficient query processing on encrypted data. In this paper we present an implementation of our framework and a performance study with different database sizes the demonstrate the feasibility of our proposed approach.

2 Related Work

The ZeroVis framework most closely relates to searchable encryption and distributed/federated encryption key management. Broadcast encryption [12] was first proposed as a solution to the problem of sending secure transmissions from

---

[1] Like flying an instrument approach with limited or no visibility - only pilots with proper equipment, clearance, and the current local frequencies can land.
[2] Z51.11 is the ICD10 code for "Encounter for antineoplastic chemotherapy", which also corresponds to the ICD9 code V58.11.

one site to an arbitrary number of recipients. This scheme is similar to ours, but differs in its reliance on a known hierarchical distribution pattern and set of privileged users. Later work based on [12] increases scalability [23] [18] and even integrate Attribute Based Encryption techniques for greater utility [31].

Attribute Based Encryption (ABE) [14] addressed the problem of encrypting data for an arbitrary number of recipients. Unlike broadcast encryption, ABE keys are derived instead of simply shared. Goyal proposed an extension to Identity Based Encryption (IBE) [2] that uses attributes and access policies, not distinct identities, to encrypt and decrypt data. The two primary forms of ABE are Ciphertext Policy ABE (CP-ABE) and Key Policy ABE (KP-ABE). KP-ABE embeds the access policy in the user's private key [14], while CP-ABE embeds the access policy in the ciphertext [1]. KP-ABE gives control over who can decrypt data to the key generator, while CP-ABE ensures that the encryptor (data owner) retains control over who can decrypt her data [1]. ABE solves the problem of providing access to private data for specified recipient without traditional key management issues, and is proposed in several outsourcing secure data schemes [27, 15, 28], but the technique alone does not map well to encrypting data for storage in a database due to its lack of a mechanism to efficiently search encrypted data. Li et. al. [21] uses both CP-ABE and KP-ABE schemes to store personal health record (PHR) data in a semi-trusted environment. Their proposed framework extends the basic ABE notion to include Multi-Authority ABE (MA-ABE) [4] to allow different attribute authorities with different data needs to collectively generate users' secret keys based on distinct sets of user attributes. This approach of securing PHR data focuses primarily on storing documents and does not address the problem of efficiently searching across many PHR data items.

CryptDB [24] is research software that addresses the performance limitations of accessing encrypted data stored in a database. Multiple copies of each encrypted column are stored, using different encryption algorithms, to support many requirements of common application queries. Although CryptDB does solve the access performance issue, it relies on distinct keys that are bound to user identities. Further, CryptDB focuses primarily on transaction related queries. The Monomi [26] project uses many of CryptDB's techniques to address analytical queries, extending the CryptDB concept by splitting query processing between the server and the client. While more scalable than CryptDB for analytical queries, it still does not provide a scalable method for one-to-many encryption.

Verifiable Attribute-based Keyword Search over Outsourced Encrypted Data (VABKS) [29] uses ABE to provide access control and solves the problem of searching across encrypted data in the cloud by adding encrypted keyword indexes to the ABE payload. While VABKS does provide searchability for ABE encrypted data, the technique is document-centric, requiring a defined list of searchable keywords for each ABE item, limiting its usefulness for searching across many database items.

Our approach builds on selected concepts from each of the above, and adds data provider controlled access control to better address efficient encrypted data access and overcome difficulties associated with distributed access control.

3   Problem Definition and Building Blocks

Consider a database D, with tables T_1 .. T_i. Each Table contains rows R_1 .. R_j, each with columns C_1 .. C_k. Clients access the database contents as data providers (DP), data consumers (DC), or as both roles. Data providers store data in the database (INSERT, UPDATE), and data consumers retrieve data from the database (SELECT). In a database that uses client-based encryption to protect stored data, clients access data in one or more columns (C_1, C_2, ..., C_k) from one or more rows (R_1, R_2, ..., R_j) from one or more tables (T_1, T_2, ..., T_i). Data providers encrypt data before storing it in the database and data consumers must decrypt data after retrieving it from the database. In this model, the database only stores encrypted versions of protected cells and never sees the plaintext version of the data. The primary problem with this approach is in the difficulty of generating and managing the keys to encrypt and decrypt data. Data providers and data consumers must share keys to access data, and the number of keys grows with a higher level of desired fine-grained access (i.e. a need for more encryption partitions.)

We built the ZeroVis framework on two primary building blocks, Ciphertex Policy Attribute Based Encryption (CP-ABE), and CryptDB. Each component brings desirable features to ZeroVis, but neither one solves our problem alone.

Ciphertex Policy Attribute Based Encryption. A CP-ABE scheme provides fine-grained access control over data [1]. CP-ABE associates a user with a set of descriptive attributes to generate the user's secret key, SK. Data are encrypted under an access policy such that only users whose attributes match the access policy can decrypt the data. To encrypt a message M using CP-ABE, the encryptor provides an access policy which is expressed as a boolean expression containing selected attributes and values for M. Figure 1 shows the access policy presented earlier in a tree structure. The message is then encrypted based on the access structure, T. Decryptors generate SK based on their attributes. A decryptor is only able to decrypt ciphertext, CT, when her SK satisfies the access policy used to encrypt the message. Unauthorized users cannot decrypt CT even if they collude and combine their disjoint attributes.

CP-ABE defines the following four essential functions:

1. Setup(): Input security parameter, output public parameter (PK), for encryption, and master key (MK), to generate user secret keys.
2. Encrypt: Input message M, access structure T, public parameter PK, output ciphertext CT.
3. KenGen: Input set of user's attributes SX and MK, output secret key SK for SX.

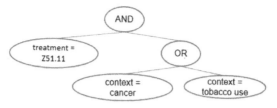

treatment=Z51.11 AND ((context=cancer) OR context=tobacco use))

Fig. 1. CP-ABE Access Tree)

4. Decrypt: Input CT, SK. If SK satisfies access structure in CT, return M, else return NULL.

CP-ABE works well for encrypting individual shared data where the file's name or identifier is known, but there is no provision for searching ciphertext, thereby making CP-ABE alone insufficient for database queries.

CryptDB. CryptDB is a DBMS that provides confidentiality for data stored on an untrusted database server [24]. The system provides near-transparent confidentiality by intercepting database queries and rewriting them in such a way as to execute over encrypted data. Decryption for consumption never occurs on the server, only at the trusted proxy. CryptDB also incorporates an encryption strategy that can adjust the encryption level of each column based on user queries. At runtime, the CryptDB proxy analyzes each query and determines the encryption needs based on the query components. The proxy will either then map each query component to an encrypted data item or request an encryption layer adjustment. All data is initially stored by CryptDB encrypted into several layers, with each layer encrypted with one of six encryption methods. The resulting value is called "encryption onion". CryptDB will only "peel" an onion layer (decrypt the outer layer) if a query requires an inner layer to successfully complete. This dynamic ability to alter encryption layers gives CryptDB the flexibility to maintain confidentiality while still responding to query requirements. The database server peels onion layers with user defined functions, and will never remove the innermost layer that would expose the original plaintext. Although CryptDB does provide the ability to select and search encrypted data on an untrusted sever, it still requires user-based encryption keys. CryptDB must rely on an external authority to enforce key management, including authorizing multiple consumers to decrypt a provider's data.

4   ZeroVis Framework

4.1   Framework Overview

To overcome the problems described in the previous section, our approach integrates CP-ABE with the ability to search across encrypted data, e.g. as provided

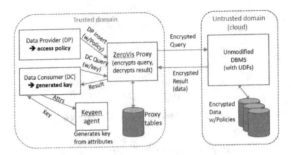

Fig. 2. ZeroVisibility Cloud Framework

in CryptDB, to synthesize a solution that supports single data provider encryption accessible by multiple data consumers for data stored in an untrusted environment, along with the ability to efficiently retrieve the data without decrypting in the cloud.

Figure 2 shows the ZeroVis framework. The core of our framework is the ZeroVis proxy which is responsible for encrypting data and queries and decrypting query results. The data provider submits data along with access policies through ZeroVis Proxy which encrypts the data via CP-ABE and searchable encryption and stores the encrypted data through an unmodified DBMS. A data consumer submits a query along with a pre-generated secret key, SK, (generated from the data consumer's attributes) through the ZeroVis proxy which encrypts the query. The DBMS returns encrypted results of the query to the ZeroVis proxy, which decrypts the results and returns the plaintext to the data consumer.

One additional requirement of a complete framework in a production environment is an Attribute Authority (AA). The AA is responsible for authorizing users, and managing attributes associated with those users. The framework depends on the AA to supply authenticated attributes for each authenticated user, and to prevent unauthorized users from submitting queries through the framework. Users can submit queries directly to the untrusted DBMS, but without the necessary master key from the AA, decryption attempts are unsuccessful.

4.2 Data Insertion and Encryption

To encrypt data, the DP provides the trusted proxy with the plaintext data and an access policy. Figure 3 shows the data flow with an example INSERT query. The trusted proxy encrypts the plaintext data, translates the query components into their encrypted counterparts (for query elements that are stored encrypted in the DBMS), and submits the encrypted payload, along with the embedded access policy, to the DBMS. Notice in Figure 3 there are 2 ciphertext values. The first represents existing CryptDB encryption and the second depicts the new CP-ABE CT added by ZeroVis.

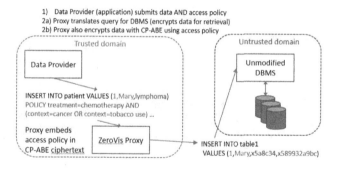

Fig. 3. Submitting Data (INSERT)

4.3 Data Retrieval and Decryption

To decrypt data, a DC must first generate a secret key, SK, based on her attributes. In most implementations, a trusted AA will generate a key for each identity upon new user registration. The DC provides a set of descriptive attributes, SX, such as treatment and context interest areas (for our running example). Attributes can describe an entity's state, status, or authorized interest areas. The AA generates SK based on the supplied SX and returns SK to the DC on demand. For example, a research team member may possess attributes "treatment=Z51.11, context=cancer".

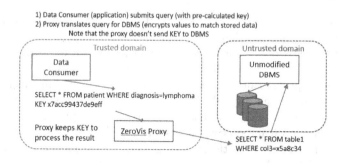

Fig. 4. Retrieving Data (SELECT request)

The DC then presents SK (generated by the AA) to the trusted proxy when attempting to access encrypted data. The trusted proxy translates the supplied query elements into their encrypted counterparts (for query elements that are stored encrypted in the DBMS), and submits the query, depicted in figure 3. The proxy then translates the returned data from the encrypted state, CT, as stored in the DBMS, depicted in figure 4, into plaintext state, M, for the application. The CP-ABE decryption algorithm will only return plaintext message, M, when the supplied SK satisfies the data's embedded access policy that was provided

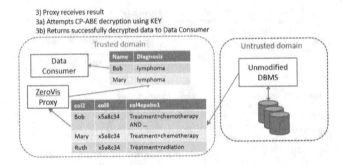

Fig. 5. Retrieving Data (SELECT response)

by the DP. If the supplied key does not satisfy the access policy the proxy simply returns a null value.

The process of modifying data (UPDATE) is essentially a combination of a data retrieval operation followed by a data submission operation. While the process of updating data is straightforward, the implementation of the framework would need to ensure updates are well-behaved and do not allow unauthorized data or policy modifications. Users updating data must possess SK to retrieve data and an access policy to encrypt changes. Traditional access controls would be necessary to limit data and policy updates to authorized users.

4.4   Implementation

Our test implementation of ZeroVis was built on the architecture described above. The data consumer issues queries to the ZeroVis proxy. The ZeroVis proxy re-writes each query and submits it to the mySQL database server. We built the ZeroVis proxy by modifying the CryptDB proxy, which was built by modifying mysql-proxy. Both CryptDB and ZeroVis can be implemented using other proxy software and any DBMS the chosen proxy supports. Both the ZeroVis proxy and the MySQL database server run on computers running Linux. ZeroVis supports both interactive clients through a shell prompt and existing applications through a connection to the proxy. Both client types require that users register with an AA.

We implemented the ZeroVis framework by integrating CP-ABE into CryptDB proxy. CryptDB provides query re-writing and capability to search across encrypted data. The addition of CP-ABE as a new encryption method within CryptDB gives the framework one-to-many encryption capability. The first change to CryptDB was to create a new column for each protected column. CryptDB normally creates 2 or 3 columns to store encrypted data using different methods to support different types of queries. The new column for each plaintext column stores the CP-ABE CT. We added a new encryption layer, ABE, to each onion definition, added a new ABE security level, and added a new class to handle CP-ABE encryption and decryption operations. The new class uses cpabe-toolkit functions to encrypt and decrypt data. We modified the CryptDB proxy query re-writing code to replace requested columns with CP-ABE columns. We retain the CryptDB obfuscated column names in the queries to allow the database to select data using searchable data. The database then returns only CP-ABE encrypted data. The proxy attempts to decrypt each column and returns successfully decrypted data to the client.

With the new functionality in place to handle CP-ABE, we extended the proxy to fetch the user's CP-ABE SK, based on the MySQL database user id. The private key will be provided by the AA in more robust implementations. Additional modifications to the proxy also fetch and store the current user's default access policy for CP-ABE encryption operations. The ZeroVis system currently creates CP-ABE CT for every encrypted column. The CP-ABE encryption uses the current user's access policy. Decryption uses the current user's SK, previously generated using the CP-ABE keygen() function. Future work will extend the supported SQL syntax to allow users to optionally provide access policies with every query.

5   Performance Results

Experiment Setup. Our performance assessment is based on a straightforward CP-ABE addition to CryptDB as described above. Our goal was to determine the additional overhead CP-ABE added to the existing CryptDB implementation. We created multiple copies of test databases, all based on subsets of the TPC-C[6] benchmark database. Test databases of different sizes were built by altering the number of rows in the item, warehouse, and district tables, all based on cardinality relationships defined in the TPC-C specification. The resulting 5 test databases DB-a, DB-b, DB-c, DB-d, DB-e have row cardinality of 1912, 2975, 7156, 18622, 35756 respectively, which are approximately increasing in a logarithmic scale. We created sets of queries, both single row and multiple row returned sets, to assess the general performance of the ZeroVis framework. The queries were simple, single table INSERT statements to load varying size subsets of the TPC-C database, and single table SELECT statements to retrieve 1 row (150 SELECTs) and sets (150 SELECTs) from the item, stock, and customer tables. The SELECT queries to retrieve sets of rows were randomly generated to select a range from the domain of each table. The test sever had an Intel Core 2 2.0 GHz(x2) processor with 3GB RAM running Ubuntu 13.10. The client/proxy computer had an Intel Core i7 2.4 GHz(x8) processor with 16GB RAM running Ubuntu 13.10. The two computers were connected via a 100Mbit/s Ethernet connection.

Results. Adding CP-ABE results in an additional encryption operation for each protected column, adding substantial observed space and computation time overhead. CryptDB, without CP-ABE, is approximately 26% slower (throughput loss) than native MySQL [24] when running the TPC-C benchmark. Encryption and decryption times are linearly related to the number of leaf nodes in the CP-ABE access policy. According to Bethenourt et al, [1], their implementation of CP-ABE took approximately 0.5 seconds to encrypt a payload with 20 policy leaf nodes, while only taking 0.04 seconds to decrypt. One reason why the encryption operation is so much slower is that it includes parsing and processing the provided policy. The decrypt operation does not directly interact with attributes. Generating the key, based on supplied attributes, is a separate function that must be completed prior to any decryption attempt.

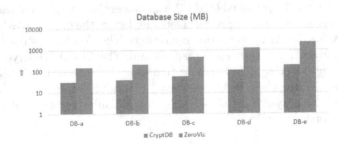

Fig. 6. Resulting DB Sizes for test DBs (of logarithmically increasing row cardinality)

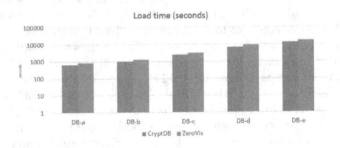

Fig. 7. Database load time

Figure 6 shows the resulting database size (in MB) of the 5 test databases with varying row cardinality (approximately increasing in a logarithmic scale) for CryptDB (without CP-ABE) and ZeroVis (with CP-ABE) respectively. As the figure illustrates, the overhead incurred by ZeroVis increases linearly with the row cardinality. The current implementation stores a complete CP-ABE ciphertext payload for every protected database column, which includes the access policy and the encrypted data. Our future work will explore reducing redundancy through consolidating CP-ABE access policies which we expect will significantly decrease the overhead.

Figure 7 shows the load time for each database instance. The ZeroVis computational overhead is a result of the additional CP-ABE calculations. As mentioned above, the current test ZeroVis implementation constructs the access policy tree for each column, even if all columns share the same policy. It is expected that reducing CP-ABE access policy redundancy will also reduce computational overhead for future ZeroVis framework versions and result in ZeroVis performing more closely to CryptDB.

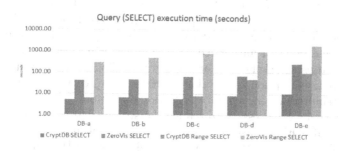

Fig. 8. Database Query time

Figure 8 shows times for queries that return single rows, and sets of rows (range queries). We submitted 300 SELECT queries for each database instance, 150 distinct queries and 150 range queries. The queries were scaled to consider the range of data stored in each database (randomly generated to exercise the full range of data in each table). Queries use both indexed and non-indexed criteria. The disparity between CryptDB and ZeroVis performance for range queries is due to ZeroVis' current larger data storage requirements. Additional tests with the proxy and sever running on a single machine showed that network costs were not responsible for the higher overhead of ZeroVis. The queries in our test returned most of the columns from each table, requiring CP-ABE decryption operations for each column. While decrypting multiple columns is normal expected behavior, the redundancy of storing and transporting multiple copies of the access policy for each column increases the workload.We believe reducing redundant CP-ABE operations and normalizing the access policy storage technique will reduce ZeroVis' computational overhead and additional costs of the framework, resulting in performance closer to CryptDB than the current ZeroVis implementation.

6   Conclusions and Future Work

In this paper we showed how combining CP-ABE with encrypted data searching solves the problem of storing and retrieving confidential data from an untrusted environment, while giving the data provider control over who accesses her data. While other frameworks provide some of these capabilities, ours is the only one to our knowledge that accomplishes this without relying on traditional key management techniques. Our framework is the first to specifically address the need for one-to-many encryption in a database environment, which requires support for efficient queries across encrypted data.

This paper describes the initial ZeroVis framework implementation. Future framework changes are necessary to create a more production viable framework.A specific requirement for a trusted AA needs to be included. Although we only generally described the need for the AA,the AA will be an integral component of a completed framework. It will be responsible for authorizing users, securely storing their attributes, and providing the ZeroVis proxy with sufficient authentication information and attributes to properly handle encryption and decryption operations for authorized users. The AA will act as the layer of protection that stops attackers from arbitrarily providing unauthorized attributes to the CP-ABE encryption/decryption functions. The AA will also manage the master key required for encryption/decryption operations.

Additional work is necessary to reduce the storage and computational overhead of CP-ABE. Others have already studied this problem, including Constant-size CP-ABE (CP-ABE) [31] and techniques discussed in [18] and [1]. We will also explore normalizing the CP-ABE ciphertext,which is currently a concatenation of the access policy and the encrypted payload. The access policy comprises over 90% of the ciphertext size. Denormalizing the CP-ABE ciphertext will reduce the storage (and network transmission) requirements for multiple columns that share the same access policy.

References

[1] Bethencourt, J., Sahai, A., Waters, B.: Ciphertext-policy attribute-based encryption. In: IEEE Symposium on Security and Privacy, pp. 321–334. IEEE Computer Society (2007)

[2] Boneh, D., Franklin, M.: Identity-based encryption from the weil pairing. In: Kilian, J. (ed.) CRYPTO 2001. LNCS, vol. 2139, pp. 213–229. Springer, Heidelberg (2001)

[3] Carroll, M., van der Merwe, A., Kotze, P.: Secure cloud computing: Benefits, risks and controls. In: Information Security South Africa (ISSA), pp. 1–9 (August 2011)

[4] Chase, M., Chow, S.S.M.: Improving privacy and security in multi-authority attribute-based encryption. In: Proceedings of the 16th ACM Conference on Computer and Communications Security, CCS 2009, pp. 121–130. ACM, New York (2009)

[5] Chow, R., Golle, P., Jakobsson, M., Shi, E., Staddon, J., Masuoka, R., Molina, J.: Controlling data in the cloud: Outsourcing computation without outsourcing control. In: Proceedings of the 2009 ACM Workshop on Cloud Computing Security, CCSW 2009, pp. 85–90. ACM, New York (2009)

[6] Transaction Processing Performance Council. Tpc benchmark c, standard specification version 5 (2001)

[7] Deshmukh, Pasha A., Qureshi, et al.: Transparent data encryption–solution for security of database contents. arXiv preprint arXiv:1303.0418 (2013)

[8] De Capitani di Vimercati, S., Foresti, S., Jajodia, S., Paraboschi, S., Samarati, P.: Over-encryption: Management of access control evolution on outsourced data. In: Proceedings of the 33rd International Conference on Very Large Data Bases, VLDB 2007, pp. 123–134. VLDB Endowment (2007)

[9] Elmasri, R.A., Navathe, S.B.: Fundamentals of Database Systems [With Access Code]. Addison Wesley Publishing Company Incorporated (2011)

[10] Farcasescu, M.R.: Trust model engines in cloud computing. In: 2012 14th International Symposium on Symbolic and Numeric Algorithms for Scientific Computing (SYNASC), pp. 465–470 (September 2012)

[11] Ferretti, L., Colajanni, M., Marchetti, M., Scaruffi, A.E.: Transparent access on encrypted data distributed over multiple cloud infrastructures. In: The Fourth International Conference on Cloud Computing, GRIDs, and Virtualization, CLOUD COMPUTING 2013, pp. 201–207 (2013)

[12] Fiat, A., Naor, M.: Broadcast encryption. In: Stinson, D.R. (ed.) CRYPTO 1993. LNCS, vol. 773, pp. 480–491. Springer, Heidelberg (1994)

[13] Gowrigolla, B., Sivaji, S., Masillamani, M.R.: Design and auditing of cloud computing security. In: 2010 5th International Conference on Information and Automation for Sustainability (ICIAFs), pp. 292–297 (December 2010)

[14] Goyal, V., Pandey, O., Sahai, A., Waters, B.: Attribute-based encryption for fine-grained access control of encrypted data. In: Proceedings of the 13th ACM Conference on Computer and Communications Security, CCS 2006, pp. 89–98. ACM, New York (2006)

[15] Ibraimi, L., Petkovic, M., Nikova, S., Hartel, P., Jonker, W.: Ciphertext-policy attribute-based threshold decryption with flexible delegation and revocation of user attributes. Univeristy of Twente, Tech. Rep. (2009)

[16] Jansen, W., Grance, T., et al.: Guidelines on security and privacy in public cloud computing. NIST Special Publication 800:144 (2011)

[17] Khan, K.M., Malluhi, Q.: Establishing trust in cloud computing. IT Professional 12(5), 20–27 (2010)

[18] Kim, J., Susilo, W., Au, M.H., Seberry, J.: Efficient semi-static secure broadcast encryption scheme. In: Cao, Z., Zhang, F. (eds.) Pairing 2013. LNCS, vol. 8365, pp. 62–76. Springer, Heidelberg (2014)

[19] Kulkarni, G., Chavan, N., Chandorkar, R., Waghmare, R., Palwe, R.: Cloud security challenges. In: 2012 7th International Conference on Telecommunication Systems, Services, and Applications (TSSA), pp. 88–91 (October 2012)

[20] Lee, W.-B., Lee, C.-D.: A cryptographic key management solution for hipaa privacy/security regulations. IEEE Transactions on Information Technology in Biomedicine 12(1), 34–41 (2008)

[21] Li, M., Yu, S., Zheng, Y., Ren, K., Lou, W.: Scalable and secure sharing of personal health records in cloud computing using attribute-based encryption. IEEE Transactions on Parallel and Distributed Systems 24(1), 131–143 (2013)

[22] Mather, T., Kumaraswamy, S., Latif, S.: Cloud Security and Privacy: An Enterprise Perspective on Risks and Compliance. Theory in practice. O'Reilly Media (2009)

[23] Phan, D.-H., Pointcheval, D., Shahandashti, S.F., Strefler, M.: Adaptive cca broadcast encryption with constant-size secret keys and ciphertexts. International Journal of Information Security 12(4), 251–265 (2013)

[24] Popa, R.A., Redfield, C.M.S., Zeldovich, N., Balakrishnan, H.: Cryptdb: Protecting confidentiality with encrypted query processing. In: Proceedings of the Twenty-Third ACM Symposium on Operating Systems Principles, SOSP 2011, pp. 85–100. ACM, New York (2011)

[25] Shen, Z., Tong, Q.: The security of cloud computing system enabled by trusted computing technology. In: 2010 2nd International Conference on Signal Processing Systems (ICSPS), vol. 2, pp. V2–11–V2–15 (July 2010)

[26] Tu, S., Frans Kaashoek, M., Madden, S., Zeldovich, N.: Processing analytical queries over encrypted data. Proc. VLDB Endow. 6(5), 289–300 (2013)

[27] Yu, S., Wang, C., Ren, K., Lou, W.: Achieving secure, scalable, and fine-grained data access control in cloud computing. In: 2010 Proceedings IEEE INFOCOM, pp. 1–9 (March 2010)

[28] Yu, S., Wang, C., Ren, K., Lou, W.: Attribute based data sharing with attribute revocation. In: Proceedings of the 5th ACM Symposium on Information, Computer and Communications Security, ASIACCS 2010, pp. 261–270. ACM, New York (2010)

[29] Zheng, Q., Xu, S., Ateniese, G.: Vabks: Verifiable attribute-based keyword search over outsourced encrypted data. Cryptology ePrint Archive, Report 2013/462 (2013), http://eprint.iacr.org/

[30] Zhou, L., Varadharajan, V., Hitchens, M.: Enforcing role-based access control for secure data storage in the cloud. The Computer Journal 54(10), 1675–1687 (2011)

[31] Zhou, Z., Huang, D.: On efficient ciphertext-policy attribute based encryption and broadcast encryption: Extended abstract. In: Proceedings of the 17th ACM Conference on Computer and Communications Security, CCS 2010, pp. 753–755. ACM, New York (2010)

[32] Zou, X., Dai, Y.-S., Bertino, E.: A practical and flexible key management mechanism for trusted collaborative computing. In: The 27th Conference on Computer Communications, INFOCOM 2008., pp. 538–546. IEEE (April 2008)

Practical Private Information Retrieval from a Time-Varying, Multi-attribute, and Multiple-Occurrence Database

Giovanni Di Crescenzo, Debra Cook, Allen McIntosh, and Euthimios Panagos

Applied Communication Sciences, NJ, USA
{gdicrescenzo,dcook,amcintosh,epanagos}@appcomsci.com

Abstract. We study the problem of privately performing database queries (i.e., keyword searches and conjunctions over them), where a server provides its own database for client query-based access. We propose a cryptographic model for the study of such protocols, by expanding previous well-studied models of keyword search and private information retrieval to incorporate a more practical data model: a time-varying, multi-attribute and multiple-occurrence database table.

Our first result is a 2-party private database retrieval protocol. Like all previous work in private information retrieval and keyword search, this protocol still satisfies server time complexity linear in the database size.

Our main result is a private database retrieval protocol in a 3-party model where encrypted data is outsourced to a third party (i.e., a cloud server), satisfying highly desirable privacy and efficiency properties; most notably: (1) *no unintended information* is leaked to clients or servers, and only minimal 'access pattern' information is leaked to the third party; (2) for each query, all parties run in time *only logarithmic* in the number of database records; (3) the protocol's runtime is practical for real-life applications, as shown in our implementation where we achieve response time that is *only a small constant* slower than commercial non-private protocols like MySQL.

1 Introduction

As reinforced by current technology trends (e.g., 'Big Data', 'Cloud-based Data Retrieval'), in today's computer system there is critical need to efficiently store, access and manage massive amounts of data. While data management and storage systems evolve to take these new trends into account, privacy considerations, already of great interest, become even more important. To partially address privacy needs, database-management systems can use private database retrieval protocols, where clients submit queries and receive matching records in a way so that clients do not learn anything new about the database records (other than the content of the matching records), and database servers do not learn which queries are submitted. The research literature has attempted to address these issues, by studying private database retrieval protocols in limited database models and with limited efficiency properties. In this paper we address some of these limitations, by using a practical database model, and proposing a participant and privacy model in which data is outsourced to a third party (in encrypted form) and practical private database retrieval protocols are possible.

V. Atluri and G. Pernul (Eds.): DBSec 2014, LNCS 8566, pp. 339–355, 2014.
© IFIP International Federation for Information Processing 2014

Our Contribution. Continuing the well-studied areas of private information retrieval (PIR) [4,17] and keyword search (KS) [3,2,9], we propose a more practical database model, capturing record payloads, multiple attributes, possibly equal attribute values across different database records, and multiple answers to a given query and insertion/deletion of database records. In this model, we define suitable correctness, privacy and efficiency requirements, by showing previously not discussed technical reasons as to why we cannot use the exact same requirements from the PIR and KS areas.

We then design a first database retrieval protocol that satisfies the desired privacy properties (i.e., the server learns no information about the query value other than the number of matching records, and the client learns no information about the database other than matching database records) in our novel and practical database model (i.e., a time-varying, multi-attribute and multiple-occurrence table). This protocol is based on oblivious pseudo-random function evaluation protocols and PIR protocols and still has server time complexity linear in the database size (a source of great inefficiency in previous PIR and KS protocols), a drawback dealt with in our next result.

After expanding the participant model with a third party (i.e., a cloud server, as in the database-as-a-service model [13]), we design a second protocol, *only based on pseudo-random functions (implemented as block ciphers)*, where both server and third party run queries in logarithmic time and the following privacy properties hold: the server learns nothing about the query value, the client learns nothing about the database in addition to the payloads associated with the matching records, and the third party learns nothing about the query value or the database content, other than the repeating of queries from the client and repeated access to the encrypted data structures received by the server at initialization. Thus, we solve the long-standing problem of achieving efficient server runtime at the (arguably small) cost of a 'third-party'-server and some 'access-pattern' type leakage to this third party. We stress that this protocol has efficient running time not only in an asymptotic sense, but in a sense that makes it ready for real-life applications (where such form of leakage to the third party is tolerable), answering another long-standing question in the PIR area. In our implementation, we reached our main design goal of achieving response time to be *only a small constant* slower than commercial non-private protocols like MySQL. Solving a number of technical challenges posed by the new data model (including a reduction step via a novel multiplicity database) using simple and practical techniques was critical to achieve this goal. The privacy loss traded for such a practicality property is rather minimal, as neither the client nor the server learn anything new, and the third party does not learn anything about the plain database content or the plain queries made, but just an 'unlabeled histogram' describing the relative occurrences of (encrypted) matching records and (encrypted) query values within the protocol. (Techniques from [14] can be used to mitigate privacy loss from such leakage as well.) In all our protocols, we only consider privacy against a semi-honest adversary, as there are known techniques, based on the general paradigm of [11], to compile such protocols and achieve privacy against malicious adversaries. Almost all formal definitions and proofs are omitted due to space restriction.

Related Work. Our work revisits and extends work in the PIR and KS areas, which have received a large amount of attention in the cryptography literature. (See, e.g., [18].) Both areas consider rather theoretical data models, as we now discuss. In PIR, a database is modeled as a string of n bits, and the query value is an index $i \in \{1, \ldots, n\}$. In KS, the data models differ depending on the specific paper we consider; the closest data model to ours is the one from [9], where a database is a set of records with per-record payloads, but has a single attribute, admits a single matching record per query and no record insertions/deletions. The inefficiency of the server runtime in PIR and KS protocols has been well documented (see, e.g., [20]). Some results attempted to use a third party and make the PIR query subprotocol more efficient but require a practically inefficient preprocessing phase [7].

In both PIR and KS, the database owner is the server that hosts the plain data. In some related research areas, such as oblivious RAM (starting with [12]), and searchable symmetric encryption (starting with [19]), the database owner is the client that uses the server to host a carefully prepared and encrypted version of the data. In public-key encryption with keyword search (starting with [2]) the data is provided in encrypted form by multiple independent servers to a third party that helps satisfying a client's query. Because of these critical differences, results in the cited areas do not solve the problem addressed by PIR and KS and use substantially different techniques, which are not directly comparable to ours.

In the project supporting this paper, other performing teams like ours came up with different and interesting solutions to similar problems. The closest published work from any of these teams that we are aware of consists of [15]. Among the many differences, the cited paper uses random oracles and public-key cryptography operations, which we do not use since random oracles have been proved to likely not exist and public-key cryptography operations are known to be less efficient than symmetric-key ones. Finally, our database retrieval protocols well combine with database policy compliance protocols from [6] that allow a server to authorize (or not) queries by a client according to a specific policy, while maintaining privacy of queries and policy.

2   Models and Requirements

Data and Query Models. We model a *database* as an n-row, m-column matrix $D = (A_1, \ldots, A_m)$, where each column is associated with an *attribute*, denoted as A_j, for $j = 1, \ldots, m$. The first $m - 1$ columns are *keyword attributes*, and the last column $P = A_m$, is a *payload* attribute. A *database entry* is denoted as keyword $A_j(i)$ or, in the case $j = m$, as payload $p(i) = A_m(i)$. The database *schema* is the collection of parameters n, m and of the description of each *domain* associated with each of the m attributes, and to which database entries belong. The database schema is assumed to be publicly known to all parties. A database row is also called *record*, and is assumed to have the same length ℓ_r (if data is not already in this form, techniques from [8] are used to efficiently achieve this property), where ℓ_r is constant with respect to n. We consider a *database update* as an addition, deletion, or change of a single record, and refer to the *current database* (resp., *current database schema*), as the database (resp., database schema) obtained after any previously occurred updates. A *query* q is modeled to refer to one or more database attributes and to contain one or more *query values* from the relative attribute domains. We will mainly consider KS queries, such as: "SELECT $*$ FROM $main$ WHERE attribute_name $= v$," where v is the query value.

A *valid response* to such a query consists of all payloads $p(i)$, for $i \in \{1, \ldots, n\}$, such that $A_j(i) = v$, if attribute_name $= A_j$, for some $j \in \{1, \ldots, m-1\}$. We say that the records in a valid response *match* the query. We will also discuss extensions of our techniques to other query types, such as conjunctions (via logical AND gates) of KS queries. The number of records containing the same query value v at attribute A_j is also called the j-*multiplicity* of v in the database, and is briefly denoted as $m_j(v)$. KS queries are always made to a specific attribute A_j, for some $j \in \{1, \ldots, m-1\}$, and therefore in their discussion the index j is omitted to simplify notation and discussion.

Participant Models. We consider the following *efficient* (i.e., running in probabilistic polynomial-time in a common security parameter 1^σ) participants. The *client* is the party, denoted as C, that is interested in retrieving data from the database. The *server* is the party, denoted as S, holding the database (in the clear), and is interested in allowing clients to retrieve data. The *third party*, denoted as TP, helps the client to carry out the database retrieval functionality and the server to satisfy efficiency requirements during the associated protocol. By 2-*party model* we denote the participant model that includes C, S and no third party. By 3-*party model* we denote the participant model that includes C, S, and TP. (See Figure 1,2 for a comparison of the two participant models.)

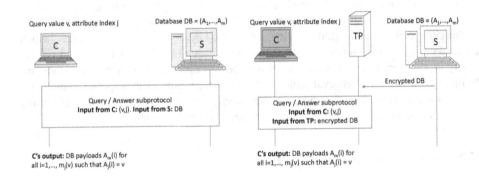

Fig. 1. Structure of our 2-party DR protocol   **Fig. 2.** Structure of our 3-party DR protocol

Database Retrieval Protocols. In the above data, query, and participant models, we consider a *database retrieval* (briefly, DR) protocol as an evolution of the KS protocol, as defined in [9] (in turn, an evolution of the PIR protocol, as defined in [17]), with the following three main model and functionality extensions, which are consistent with the functioning of typically deployed databases: (1) databases contain multiple attributes (or columns with keywords); (2) each database attribute can have multiple occurrences of the same keyword; and (3) database entries may change as a result of record addition and deletion. Specifically, we define a DR protocol as a triple (Init, Query, Update) of subprotocols, as follows. The initialization subprotocol Init is used to set up data structures and cryptographic keys before C's queries are executed. The query subprotocol Query allows C to make a single query to retrieve (possibly multiple) matching database records. The record update subprotocol Update allows S to periodically update the data structures and cryptographic keys set during the Init subprotocol, as a result of a record addition or deletion. As a first attempt, we target DR protocols that satisfy the following (informal) list of *requirements*:

1. *Correctness*: the DR protocol allows a client to obtain all payloads from the current database associated with records that match its issued query;
2. *Privacy*: the DR protocol preserves privacy of database content and query values, ideally only revealing what is leaked by system parameters known to all parties and by the intended functionality output (i.e., all payloads in matching records to C);
3. *Efficiency*: the protocol should have low time, communication and round complexity; ideally, a constant number of messages per query, and time and communication sublinear in the number n of database records.

It turns out that, as written, these requirement cannot be exactly satisfied, and the missing properties are different depending on whether we consider the 2-party or the 3-party model. Thus, we continue with formal definitions common to both models, and then defer different formal definitions of privacy and efficiency to later sections.

Preliminary Requirement Notations: Let σ be a security parameter. A function is *negligible* if for all sufficiently large natural numbers $\sigma \in \mathcal{N}$, it is $< 1/p(\sigma)$, for any polynomial p. A *DR protocol execution* is a sequence of executions of subprotocols $(\mathsf{Init}, \mathsf{qu}_1, \ldots, \mathsf{qu}_q)$, where $qu_i \in \{\mathsf{Query}, \mathsf{Update}\}$, for $i = 1, \ldots, q$, for some q polynomial in σ, and all subprotocols are run on inputs provided by the involved parties (i.e., a database from S, query values from C, and database updates from S). We only consider *stateless* Query subprotocols, in that they can depend on the outputs of Init and Update subprotocols but not on the output of previous Query subprotocols.

Correctness: for any DR protocol execution, and any inputs provided by the participants, in any execution of a Query subprotocol, the probability that C obtains all records in the current database that match C's query value input to this subprotocol, is 1.

Background Primitives. A *random function R* is a function that is chosen with distribution uniform across all possible functions with some pre-defined input and output domains. A *keyed function $F(k, \cdot)$* is a *pseudo-random function* (PRF, first defined in [10]) if, after key k is randomly chosen, no efficient algorithm allowed to query an oracle function O can distinguish whether O is $F(k, \cdot)$ or O is a random function R (over the same input and output domain), with probability greater than $1/2$ plus a negligible quantity. An *oblivious pseudo-random function evaluation protocol* (oPRFeval, first defined in [9]) is a protocol between two parties A, having as input a string k, and B, having as input a key x for a PRF F. The protocol's outcome is a private function evaluation of the value $F(k, x)$, returned to B (thus, without revealing any information about x to B, or any information about k to A). oPRFeval protocols were constructed in [9,16] using number-theoretic hardness assumptions.

A *single-database private information retrieval protocol* (PIR, first defined in [17]) is a protocol between two parties A, having as input a value $i \in \{1, \ldots, n\}$, and B, having as input a database represented as a sequence of equal-length values $x = (x[1], \ldots, x[n])$ The protocol consists in a private retrieval of the value $x[i]$, returned to A (thus, without revealing any information about i to B or about $x[1], \ldots, x[i-1], x[i+1], \ldots, x[n]$ to A). A *semi-private* PIR protocol is a protocol where privacy only consists of preventing to reveal any information about i to B. Several PIR and semi-private

PIR protocols have been presented in the cryptographic literature, starting with [17], using number-theoretic hardness assumptions.

3   Two-Party Database Retrieval

We define privacy and efficiency requirements in the 2-party model in Section 3.1 and describe our first DR protocol (for KS queries in the 2-party model) in Section 3.2.

3.1   Privacy and Efficiency in the 2-Party Model

Informally, our privacy and efficiency requirements are modified with respect to our first attempt in Section 2, so that a 2-party DR protocol can leak the number of matching records to S, has communication complexity sublinear in n if the number of matching records is also sublinear in n, and allows S to run in time linear in the number n of database records. A formal treatment follows.

Privacy: Informally speaking, we require the subprotocols in a DR protocol execution do not leak information beyond the following:

1. Init: the database schema, as part of overall system parameters, will be known to all participants;
2. Query, based on query value v, attribute index j, and the current database: the pair $(j, m_j(v))$ will be known by S and all payloads $\{p(i) : i = i(1), \ldots, i(m_j(v))\}$ such that $A_j(i(1)) = \cdots = A_j(i((m_j(v)))) = v$ will be obtained by C, as a consequence of the correctness requirement;
3. Update: on input a record addition or deletion to the current database, the current database (after the update) will be known by S, as a consequence of the correctness requirement, and the current database schema (after the update), as part of overall system parameters, will be known by all participants.

Given this characterization of the intended leakage, a formal privacy definition can be derived using known definition techniques from simulation-based security and composable security frameworks often used in the cryptography literature.

Consistently with the literature on secure function evaluation, PIR and KS protocols, it might have seemed reasonable to just require that no new information about the query value is revealed to S, as we hoped to achieve in our first attempt in Section 2. It turns out that this level of privacy cannot be obtained, as we now explain. Let us consider a specific execution of subprotocol Query within a DR protocol execution. Since more than one record may match C's query value v, by the correctness property, at the end of this execution of subprotocol Query, C must be able to compute all payloads $p(i(1)), \ldots, p(i(m_j(v)))$ corresponding to records matching v, where $m_j(v)$ denotes the multiplicity of v in the j-th database attribute A_j. Moreover, since the executions of the Init, Update protocols only leak the database schema to C, and since subprotocol Query is stateless, all previous subprotocol executions in the DR protocol execution, do not help in computing all matching records to this specific execution of subprotocol Query. In other words, C must be able to compute all matching records from the communication received during this specific execution of subprotocol Query. By a standard application of Shannon's source coding theorem (see, e.g., [5]), this implies that the communication exchanged in this execution is an upper bound to the entropy H of payloads $p(i(1)), \ldots, p(i(m_j(v)))$ (over the probability distribution of the source that generates the database payloads). Thus, we obtain the following

Proposition 1. For any v, let $cc(v)$ denote the number of bits exchanged in an execution of subprotocol Query on input query value v and attribute index j. It holds that $cc(v) \geq H(p(i(1)), \ldots, p(i(m_j(v))))$.

In Proposition 1, the entropy term is maximized when database payloads are randomly and independently distributed, in which case the communication exchanged in each execution of subprotocol Query leaks an upper bound on the value $m_j(v)$, i.e., the number of matching records, to *both* C and S. Accordingly, we target the design of protocols that may leak $m_j(v)$ also to S during each execution of subprotocol Query on input query value v and attribute index j (as formulated in the above privacy requirement).

Efficiency: A DR protocol's *round complexity* (resp., *communication complexity*) is the max number of messages (resp., the max length of all messages), as a function of the system parameters n, m, σ, required by any of the Init, Query, Update subprotocols, for any inputs to them. A DR protocol's *S-time complexity* for subprotocol π is the max running time (as a function of the system parameters n, m, σ) required by S in subprotocol $\pi \in \{$Init, Query, Update$\}$, over all possible inputs to it. Asymptotic requirements consistent with the literature on PIR and KS protocols include the following: (1) the communication complexity of each execution of protocol Query is sublinear in n; (2) the S-time complexity in each execution of protocol Query is sublinear in n. Requirement (1) is achieved by PIR and KS protocols in the literature when up to a single record is sent as a reply to each query. However, in our DR protocols, a query could be matched by a possibly linear number of records; accordingly, we only require the communication complexity to be sublinear *whenever so is the number of matching records*. Requirement (2), when coupled with the privacy requirement that an execution of the Init protocol only leaks minimal information to C, is known to be unachievable in the 2-party model (or otherwise privacy of the query value v would not hold against the server), as discussed in many papers including [17,9].

3.2 Our Protocol

Our 2-party DR protocol for KS queries follows the general structure outlined in Figure 1 and satisfies the following

Theorem 1. Under the existence of oPRFeval protocols [9] and (single-database) PIR protocols [17], there exists (constructively) a DR protocol $\pi_1 = ($Init$_1$, Query$_1$, Update$_1)$ for KS queries in the 2-party model, satisfying:
1. correctness
2. privacy against C (i.e., it only leaks the matching records to C);
3. privacy against S (i.e., it only leaks the queried attribute and the number of matching records to S);
4. communication complexity of Query$_1$ is $o(n)$ if so is the number of matching records;

5. round complexity of Query_1 is $O(\log n)$;
6. the S-time complexity in Query_1 (resp. Init_1) (resp., Update_1) is $O(n)$ (resp., is $O(n)$) (resp., is $O(\log n)$).

The protocol π_1 claimed in Theorem 1 is presented in two steps: first, we describe a DR protocol $\pi_0 = (\mathsf{Init}_0, \mathsf{Query}_0)$ in the restricted data model where all keywords in each database attribute are distinct, and no record additions or deletions happen, and then we describe the DR protocol π_1 that builds on π_0 to remove these restrictions.

The DR Protocol π_0. Informally speaking, this protocol is a combination of a KS protocol, denoted as Protocol 2 in [9] (in turn building on a semi-private KS protocol from [3]), and an oPRFeval protocol for computing a pseudo-random function f, as follows.

Init_0. On input database $D = (A_1, \ldots, A_m)$, S returns a pseudo-random version of the database, denoted as $prD = (prA_1, \ldots, prA_{m-1}, A_m)$, and computed by replacing keyword entries $A_j(i)$ with pseudo-random values $prA_j(i) = f_k(A_j(i))$ for all $j = 1, \ldots, m-1$ and $i = 1, \ldots, n$, where k is a random key. (That is, keyword entries are replaced by pseudo-random versions of them, but payloads in A_m remain unchanged).

Query_0. On input query value v and attribute index j from C, and key k and database prD from S, the following steps are run:
1. C and S run an oPRFeval protocol to return $f_k(v)$ to C;
2. C sends j to S
3. C and S run the semi-private KS protocol from [3], where C uses $f_k(v)$ as query value and S provides (prA_j, A_m) as a 2-column database. At the end of the protocol, C can compute the record $A_m(i)$ such that $prA_j(i) = f_k(v)$, if any.

Here, the semi-private KS protocol from [3] consists of using a PIR protocol, such as the one from [17], to probe a conventional search data structure built by S on top of the pseudo-database keywords in a way that is oblivious to S.

Protocol π_0 can be shown to be a DR protocol in the following restricted data model: (1) no database records are added or deleted; (2) for each $j = 1, \ldots, m-1$ the database entries $A_j(1), \ldots, A_j(n)$ relative to the j-th attribute are all distinct. We remove these two restrictions by combining the following ideas: S can transform the original database into one where each column A_j has distinct keywords (or payload), by computing a *padded database*, where keywords are padded with a multiplicity counter; S can compute a preliminary *multiplicity database* to let C obtain the multiplicity of its query value from S using protocol π_0; given the multiplicity of the query value, C can request the matching records by making one query for each matching record to the padded database, using again protocol π_0; updating the padded and multiplicity databases and associated data structures can be done efficiently by careful choices of padding and data structures. We stress that revealing the multiplicity value to C does not provide any more information than sending the matching records (which C is entitled to receive). A more formal description follows.

The DR Protocol π_1. Based on the above DR protocol $\pi_0 = (\mathsf{Init}_0, \mathsf{Query}_0)$, we define protocol $\pi_1 = (\mathsf{Init}_1, \mathsf{Query}_1, \mathsf{Update}_1)$ as follows.

Init_1. On input database $D = (A_1, \ldots, A_m)$, S builds an associated padded database $pD = (pA_1, \ldots, pA_m)$, as follows. The payload pA_m is equal to A_m. Then, for each $j = 1, \ldots, m-1$, and each $i = 1, \ldots, n$, the keyword $pA_j(i)$ is defined as

$(A_j(i), mc(i, j))$ where $mc(i, j)$ is the multiplicity counter from $\{1, \ldots, n\}$ such that $A_j(i)$ is the $mc(i, j)$-th occurrence of value $A_j(i)$ within array $(A_j(1), \ldots, A_j(n))$; Then S builds an associated multiplicity database $mD = (mA_1, \ldots, mA_m)$, as follows. For each $j = 1, \ldots, m - 1$, and each $i = 1, \ldots, n$, the keyword $mA_j(i)$ is defined exactly as $pA_j(i)$. The payload $mA_m(i)$ is denoted as $m'_j(v)$, where $m'_j(v)$ is defined as $m_j(v)$ when $mc(i, j) = 1$ and a null string $\bot$ of the same length otherwise. Finally, S runs Init_0 to compute pseudo-random versions $prpD$ and $prmD$ of databases pD and mD, respectively, and to send the schema for databases mD and pD to C.

Query$_1$. On input query value v and attribute index j for C, and key k and databases $prpD, prmD$ for S, the following steps are run:

1. C and S run subprotocol Query$_0$ on input database $prmD$ from S, and query value $(v, 1)$ and attribute index j from C. Let $p(i)$ be the payload obtained by C at the end of this protocol, for some $i \in \{1, \ldots, n\}$. If $p(i) = \bot$ then the protocol stops. Otherwise C sets the value $m_j(v) = p(i)$.

2. For $t = 1, \ldots, m_j(v)$, C and S run subprotocol Query$_0$ on input database $prpD$ from S, and query value (v, t) and attribute index j from C.

Update$_1$. In subprotocol Update$_1$, we consider record addition and record deletion operations, and on each of them, we need to efficiently update any values changing as a result of these operations; specifically:

1. the data structures required in π_0;
2. the multiplicity value $m'_j(v)$ used in mD;
3. the multiplicity counters $mc(i, j)$ in the padding structures used in pD and mD;
4. the database schema for both pD and mD; and
5. the pseudo-random databases $prpD$ and $prmD$.

First, with respect to (1), we observe that the data structures used in π_0 are those from [3] and are conventional data structures with the only requirement of performing search in logarithmic time. Our added requirement of having efficient insertion and deletion does not require a modification of the data structures, since many of the data structures used in [3] (e.g., binary search trees) can be used to perform logarithmic-time search, insertion and deletion. Then, the values in (2), (4), and (5) can be updated in time constant with respect to n, as follows. As for (2), updating the multiplicity value $m'_j(v)$ only requires to change one payload entry $mA_m(i)$ in the multiplicity database mD, regardless of the multiplicity of v, and can be done in $O(\log n)$. As for (4), S can just update the database schema for both pD and mD and send those to C. As for (5), S can again use key k to recompute new $f_k(pD_j(i))$ and $f_k(mD_j(i))$ values.

With respect to values in (3), we now describe how to update the multiplicity counters $mc(i, j)$ after a record update. In the addition case, a record would also be added in the databases pD and mD, and the multiplicity counter $mc(i, j)$ in the added record is set to $m_j(v) + 1$. In the deletion case, a record would also be deleted in the databases pD and mD, and we cannot stop there as this would likely create a discontinuity in the sequence of multiplicity counters $mc(i, j)$ (e.g., when $m_j(v) \geq 3$, deleting the record with multiplicity counter 2 would leave only records with counters 1 and 3). Instead, S resets the multiplicity counter of i-th record such that $mc(i, j) = m_j(v)$ as equal to the multiplicity counter of the just deleted record, thus keeping no discontinuity in the sequence of multiplicity counters.

4   Three-Party Database Retrieval

We define privacy and efficiency requirements in the 3-party model in Section 4.1 and describe our second DR protocol (for KS queries in the 3-party model) in Section 4.2.

4.1   Privacy and Efficiency in the 3-Party Model

Informally, our privacy and efficiency requirements are modified with respect to our first attempt in Section 2, so that a 3-party DR protocol can leak the number of matching records as well as 'access-pattern' leakage, to TP, and has communication complexity sublinear in n if the number of matching records is also sublinear in n. (In particular, we keep the requirement that S and TP have to run in time sublinear in the number n of database records.) A formal treatment follows.

Privacy: The privacy leakage we allow in the 3-party model has two differences with respect to the 2-party model: the number of matching records is now leaked to TP instead of S; moreover, the following additional leakage to TP is allowed: repeated (or not) occurrences of the same query made by C, and repeated (or not) accesses to the same initialization information sent by S to TP at the end of the initialization protocol. Informally speaking, we require the subprotocols in a DR protocol execution in the 3-party model to not leak any information beyond the following:

1. Init: the database schema, as part of overall system parameters, will be known to all participants and an additional string eds (for encrypted data structures) will be known to TP; here, eds is encrypted under one or more keys unknown to TP and its length is known from quantities in the database schema;

2. Query, based on query value v, attribute index j, and the current database: all payloads $\{p(i) : i = i(1), .., i(m_j(v))\}$ such that $A_j(i(1)) = \cdots = A_j(i((m_j(v)))) = v$ will be obtained by C, as a consequence of the correctness requirement; the pair $(j, m_j(v)))$, all bits in eds read by TP according to the instructions in the Query protocol, and which previous executions of Query used the same query value v, will be known to TP;

3. Update: on input a record addition or deletion to the current database, the current database (after the update) will be known to S, as a consequence of the correctness requirement, and the current database schema (after the update), as part of overall system parameters, will be known by all participants; all bits in eds read and/or modified by TP according to the instructions in the Update protocol will be known to TP, who will also determine up to one record previously or currently present in the database containing the same query value as the one in the added/deleted record.

Given this characterization of the intended leakage, a formal privacy definition can be derived using known definition techniques from simulation-based security and composable security frameworks often used in the cryptography literature.

Using a direct extension of Proposition 1 to the 3-party model, we can prove an analogue result with respect to leaking $m_j(v)$ to the coalition of S and TP. Thus, different

3-party DR protocols could leak $m_j(v)$ only to S, or only to TP, or somehow split this leakage between S and TP. Having to choose between one of these options, we made the practical consideration that privacy against S (i.e., the data owner) is typically of greater interest than privacy against TP (i.e., the cloud server helping C retrieve data from S) in many applications, and therefore we focused in this paper on seeking protocols that leak $m_j(v)$ to TP and nothing at all to S. The other definitional choice of leaking repetition patterns (even though not actual data) to TP is not due to a theoretical limitation, but seems a rather small privacy price to pay towards achieving the very efficient S and TP time-complexity requirements discussed below.

Efficiency: The definition of a 3-party DR protocol's *round complexity, communication complexity* and *S-time-complexity* are naturally extended from those of 2-party DR protocols. We also define the *TP-time-complexity* by naturally adapting the server time-complexity definition. As for 2-party protocols, we require that 3-party DR protocols have communication complexity to be sublinear whenever so is the number of matching records. Contrarily to 2-party protocols, we do require that the S-time complexity and the TP-time complexity in each execution of protocol Query is sublinear in n, whenever is the number of matching records is sublinear in n (and achieving this property is one of the major goals in the constructions in this paper). We also target a practical *response time* efficiency requirement: the response time within a Query execution is only a small constant c worse than the response time within the same subprotocol for a non-private protocol such as MySQL.

4.2   Our Protocol

Our 3-party DR protocol for KS queries follows the general structure outlined in Figure 2 and satisfies the following

Theorem 2. Under the existence of a PRF, there exists (constructively) a DR protocol $\pi_2 = (\mathsf{Init}_2, \mathsf{Query}_2, \mathsf{Update}_2)$ for KS queries in the 3-party model, satisfying:
1. correctness
2. privacy against C (i.e., it only leaks the matching records to C);
3. privacy against S (i.e., it does not leak anything to S);
4. privacy against TP (i.e., it only leaks number of matching records, the repetition of query values and the repeated access to initialization encrypted data structures);
5. communication complexity of Query_2 (resp. Init_2) (resp., Update_2) is $o(n)$ if so is the number of matching records (resp., is $O(n)$) (resp., is $O(\log n)$);
6. S-time complexity in Query_2 (resp. Init_2) (resp., Update_2) is $O(1)$ (resp., is $O(n)$) (resp., is $O(\log n)$);
7. TP-time complexity in Query_2 (resp. Init_2) (resp., Update_2) is $o(n)$ if the number of matching records is $o(n/logn)$ (resp., is $O(n)$) (resp., is $O(\log n)$);
8. round complexity of Query_2 is $O(1)$.

Informally, our protocol π_2 is obtained by performing several improvements in the 3-party model to protocol π_1 (which was designed in the 2-party model). As done for π_1, we first construct a DR protocol $\pi_0' = (\mathsf{Init}_0', \mathsf{Query}_0')$ in a restricted data model, and then a DR protocol π_2 that uses π_0' and the ideas of multiplicity database and padded database to obtain a DR protocol in our more general data model.

The DR Protocol π_0'. Informally speaking, this protocol is a simplified construction of π_0, taking advantage of the 3-party model.

Init_0'. On input database $D = (A_1, \ldots, A_m)$, where $A_1, \ldots, A_{m-1}$ contain keywords and A_m contains a payload, S first computes a shuffled version sD of database D; that is, $sD = (sA_1, \ldots, sA_m)$, where $sA_j(\rho(i)) = A_j(i)$ for $j = 1, \ldots, m$ and $i = 1, \ldots, n$, where ρ is a random permutation over $\{1, \ldots, n\}$. Then, similarly as in Init_0, S computes a pseudo-random version of the database sD, denoted as $prsD = (prsA_1, \ldots, prsA_m)$, and computed by replacing keyword entries $sA_j(i)$ with pseudo-random entries $prsA_j(i) = f_k(sA_j(i))$ for all $j = 1, \ldots, m$ and $i = 1, \ldots, n$, where k is a random key and f is a pseudo-random permutation (here, using a permutation instead of a function will later facilitate C's decryption of any received payloads). Moreover, S generates a search data structure (i.e., a binary search tree $iTree_j$) over the keywords $prsA_j(1), \ldots, prsA_j(n)$ in $prsD$, for $j = 1, \ldots, m - 1$. Then, S sends $(iTree_1, \ldots, iTree_{m-1}), prsD$ to TP and the key k to C, in addition to sending the database schema to both parties.

Query_0'. In this protocol, C takes as input key k, a query value v and attribute index j, S takes as input key k and database D, and TP takes as input $(iTree_1, \ldots, iTree_{m-1})$, $prsD$. On these inputs, the protocol goes as follows:

1. C computes $f_k(v)$ and sends $(f_k(v), j)$ to TP
2. TP searches for $f_k(v)$ in the search data structure $iTree_j$
3. If TP finds i such that $f_k(v) = prsA_j(i)$, then
   $\quad TP$ sends the associated (encrypted) payload $prsA_m(i)$ to C
   $\quad C$ computes the (plain) payload as $f_k^{-1}(prsA_m(i))$

We note that Query_0' significantly simplifies Query_0 in that C can directly compute $f_k(v)$, without need to run an oPRFeval protocol, and TP can directly search for $f_k(v)$ in the data structure $iTree_j$, without need to run a semi-private PIR protocol.

Protocol π_0' can be shown to be a DR protocol in the 3-party model and in the following restricted data model: (1) the database entries do not change; (2) for each $j \in \{1, \ldots, m\}$ the database entries $A_j(1), \ldots, A_j(n)$ relative to the j-th attribute are all distinct. We remove these two restrictions exactly as done in Section 3: we generate π_2 from π_0' using a padded database, a multiplicity database, and composing $m_j(v) + 1$ times protocol π_0'. A more formal description is included for completeness.

The DR Protocol π_2. Based on $\pi_0' = (\mathsf{Init}_0', \mathsf{Query}_0', \mathsf{Update}_0')$, we define protocol $\pi_2 = (\mathsf{Init}_2, \mathsf{Query}_2, \mathsf{Update}_2)$ as follows.

Init_2. On input database $D = (A_1, \ldots, A_m)$, S first runs Init_0', thus sending $prsD$ and $(iTree_1, \ldots, iTree_{m-1})$ to TP and k to C, and D's schema to both C and TP. Then S builds an associated padded database $pD = (pA_1, \ldots, pA_m)$, and an associated multiplicity database $mD = (mA_1, \ldots, mA_m)$, exactly as done in Init_1. Finally, S runs Init_0' to compute pseudo-random and shuffled versions $prspD$ and $prsmD$ of databases pD and mD, respectively, and to send the schema for databases mD and pD to C.

Query_2. On input query value v and attribute index j for C, and key k and databases $prspD, prsmD$ for S, the following steps are run:

1. C and TP run subprotocol Query$_0'$ on input database $prsmD$ from TP, and query value $(v, 1)$ and attribute index j from C. Let $p(i)$ be the payload obtained by C at the end of this protocol, for some $i \in \{1, \ldots, n\}$. If $p(i) = \perp$ then the protocol stops. Otherwise C sets the value $m_j(v) = p(i)$.

2. For $t = 1, \ldots, m_j(v)$, C and TP run subprotocol Query$_0'$ on input database $prspD$ from TP, and query value (v, t) and attribute index j from C, who thus obtains payloads $p(i(1)), \ldots, p(i(m_j(v)))$, $i(1), \ldots, i(m_j(v)) \in \{1, \ldots, n\}$, from $prspD$;

3. For $t = 1, \ldots, m_j(v)$, C computes the t-th original payload from D as $f_k^{-1}(p(i(t)))$, where k is the key obtained during the execution of Init_0'.

Update$_2$. We consider record addition and record deletion operations, and on each of them, we need to efficiently update any changed values; specifically:

1. the data structures required in π_0';
2. the multiplicity value $m_j'(v)$ used in mD;
3. the multiplicity counters $mc(i, j)$ in the padding structures used in pD and mD;
4. the database schema for pD and mD;
5. the data structures $(iTree_1, \ldots, iTree_{m-1})$; and
6. the pseudo-random and shuffled databases $prsmD$ and $prspD$.

The updates for values in (1)-(4) are done as in Update$_1$. The updates to the data structure $iTree$ are conventional data structure updates in the presence of one insertion or one deletion. As for (6), S can again use key k to recompute new $f_k(pD_j(i))$ and $f_k(mD_j(i))$ values. Several approaches would work to update the permutation ρ; here is an example: upon a record insertion, the newly inserted record is considered the $(n + 1)$-th record in D and $\rho(n + 1)$ is defined as $= n + 1$; upon a deletion of the i-th record, the value $\rho(n)$ is defined as $= i$.

5   Extension: Conjunction Formulae

We extend the KS protocols from Sections 3, 4 to the conjunction formulae over KS queries; that is, the AND of c KS queries, for some $c \geq 1$.

A first approach would be to process, in parallel, an individual KS query for each term in the conjunction, and then having TP compute the intersection across the matching sets. This approach is clearly undesirable both for privacy and efficiency reasons. With respect to privacy, such a protocol would reveal to C the multiplicity of the query value in each conjunct, which is not necessarily computable from the number of records matching all conjuncts. With respect to efficiency, it is not hard to find examples of conjunctive queries for which at least one conjunct is matched by a linear number of records, but the number of records matching all conjuncts is sublinear in n. On such queries, the communication complexity would be linear even though the information to which C is entitled by the DR protocol functionality is sublinear.

To avoid both problems, we designed the following 'combined-index' approach. In the initialization subprotocol, a specific combined index on the tuple of attribute values can be created by concatenating the attribute names and query values, thus allowing the conjunction to be treated as a single keyword query. For example, a conjunctive query of $A_1 = a_1$ and $A_2 = a_2$ becomes a single KS query $A_1 A_2 = a_1 a_2$. The combined index for $A_1 A_2$ is treated exactly as indices for single attributes. The initialization, insertion and deletion subprotocols are the same as those for KS queries, working on the cartesian product of the domain. C runs the KS query algorithm using the combined attribute values. Good properties of the method include: support of conjunctive queries with an arbitrary number of conjuncts; it is only necessary to create a single combined index for each set of attribute values as opposed to each permutation of the attribute values (i.e. only an index for $A_1 A_2$ is necessary, not one for $A_1 A_2$ and one for $A_2 A_1$); and querying on the single index is faster than querying on multiple indices and determining the intersection of the results. The unattractive property is that it requires one index for each supported conjunctions, resulting in an exponential (in c) number of indices if all possible conjunctions have to be supported. Still, many practical formulae can be addressed, as the scenario where the number of attributes is constant with respect to n is the most typical, and storage is an inexpensive resource nowadays.

6   Performance Evaluation

We present performance results for KS queries and boolean formulae over KS queries for a small number of queries executed using our 3-party protocol π_2 (implemented with an additional SSL/TLS layer). MySQL was used for obtaining baseline results in a non-private setting using the same schema and records as for π_2.

Setup. We used 5 different database sizes: 10K, 100K, 1M, 10M, and 100M records. All records were stored in a single database table containing the following columns:

Column	Type	Format	Population Approach
FirstName	VARCHAR	16 Bytes	Randomly chosen, average 1K multiplicity
LastName	VARCHAR	16 Bytes	Randomly chosen, average 1K multiplicity
Gender	ENUM	Male or Female	Randomly chosen
Number	INTEGER	8 Bytes	Randomly chosen and distinct
DoB	DATE	YYYY-MM-DD	Randomly chosen in [1940-01-01, 1990-12-31]
Notes1	TEXT	64 Bytes	Random sentences from ebooks in [1]
Notes2	TEXT	256 Bytes	Random sentences from ebooks in [1]

The S and TP processes and an instance of MySQL server version 5.5.28 were running on a Dell PowerEdge R710 server with two Intel Xeon X5650 2.66Ghz processors, 48GB of memory, 64-bit Ubuntu 12.04.1 operating system, and connected to a Dell PowerVault MD1200 disk array with 12 2TB 7.2K RPM SAS drives in RAID6 configuration. Database clients were running on a Dell PowerEdge R810 server with two Intel Xeon E7-4870 2.40GHz processors, 64 GB of memory, 64-bit Red Hat Enterprise Linux Server release 6.3 operating system, and connected to the Dell PowerEdge R710 server via switched Gigabit Ethernet. Regular TCP/IP connections were used for MySQL. We built MySQL indices on *FirstName, LastName, Gender*, and *Number*. We built keyword indices for our protocol π_2 on *FirstName, LastName, Number*, and a combined index on *FirstName, Gender*. The following query templates were used for executing database queries. Each query was executed five times using different values, and the average query response was used.

Q1: SELECT * FROM main WHERE Number = value
Q2: SELECT * FROM main WHERE FirstName = value AND Gender = value

Q3: SELECT * FROM main WHERE FirstName = value AND LastName = value
Q4: SELECT * FROM main WHERE FirstName = value OR LastName = value

We implemented a B^+-tree as the search data structure (used as attribute index) due to its sub-linear search performance for disk-resident data. We note that for query Q3, we did not build a combined index, but, for sake of performance comparisons, we implemented an alternative conjunction protocol (a work in progress, omitted here) with yet unclear privacy properties. Also, for Q4, we implemented a disjunction protocol where the parties simply run the query protocol for both queries at the disjuncts (also a work in progress, since disjunction protocols with improved privacy may be desirable).

Results. Figures 3, 4 show the performance results for our protocol π_2 and mySQL, respectively. For all database sizes, Q1-Q4 matched 1, 500, 1000 and 2000 records, respectively. We observe that the database size has minimal impact on query response time. This was expected since the same number of records were matched by each query.

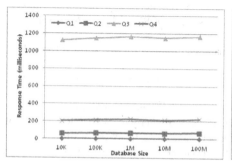

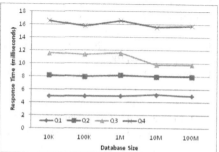

Fig. 3. Our 3-party query performance   **Fig. 4.** MySQL query performance

Our protocol π_2's performance (~2ms) is better than MySQL (~5ms) for Q1 despite the additional overhead of SSL/TLS communications, because of the minimalistic approach used by our implementation, in terms of simpler query execution and data structures, compared to traditional database management systems. When the number of matched records increases, MySQL outperforms our protocol by a factor of around 8.6, 119.1, and 14.4 for Q2, Q3, and Q4, respectively. Unlike MySQL, where once the first match is found in the B^+-tree data structure used for the queried column then a simple forward scan of the tree leaf pages is needed for locating all matches, our protocol performs a separate scan of the search data structure (a B^+-tree) for each matched value. Because these scans are for ciphertext values, it is highly unlikely that any two scans will traverse the same path from the root of the B^+-tree down to the same leaf page. Thus, the number of I/O operations required for fetching B^+-tree leaf pages into the in-memory cache for locating matched records is proportional to the number of matched records. Our protocol's response times in Q3 are more than 17 times slower than response times in Q2 despite the fact that they have the same structure and, in addition, Q3 matched twice as many records as Q2. Furthermore, Q3 is 5 times slower than Q4 although Q4 resulted in twice as many matched records. The main reasons for this are the inefficiency of the protocol used for Q3 as well as the fact that Q2 was answered using a combined index, while Q3 and Q4 required scanning of two B^+-tree indices.

Acknowledgements. This work was supported by the Intelligence Advanced Research Projects Activity (IARPA) via Department of Interior National Business Center (DoI/NBC) contract number D13PC00003. The U.S. Government is authorized to reproduce and distribute reprints for Governmental purposes notwithstanding any copyright annotation hereon. Disclaimer: The views and conclusions contained herein are those of the authors and should not be interpreted as necessarily representing the official policies or endorsements, either expressed or implied, of IARPA, DoI/NBC, or the U.S. Government.

References

1. Project gutenberg, http://www.gutenberg.org
2. Boneh, D., Di Crescenzo, G., Ostrovsky, R., Persiano, G.: Public key encryption with keyword search. In: Cachin, C., Camenisch, J.L. (eds.) EUROCRYPT 2004. LNCS, vol. 3027, pp. 506–522. Springer, Heidelberg (2004)
3. Chor, B., Gilboa, N., Naor, M.: Private information retrieval by keywords. IACR Cryptology ePrint Archive (1998)
4. Chor, B., Kushilevitz, E., Goldreich, O., Sudan, M.: Private information retrieval. J. ACM 45(6), 965–981 (1998)
5. Cover, T.M., Thomas, J.A.: Elements of information theory, 2nd edn. Wiley (2006)
6. Di Crescenzo, G., Feigenbaum, J., Gupta, D., Panagos, E., Perry, J., Wright, R.N.: Practical and privacy-preserving policy compliance for outsourced data. In: WAHC (2014)
7. Di Crescenzo, G., Ishai, Y., Ostrovsky, R.: Universal service-providers for private information retrieval. J. Cryptology 14(1), 37–74 (2001)
8. Di Crescenzo, G., Shallcross, D.: On minimizing the size of encrypted databases. In: Atluri, V., Pernul, G. (eds.) DBSec 2014. LNCS, vol. 8566, pp. 361–368. Springer, Heidelberg (2014)
9. Freedman, M.J., Ishai, Y., Pinkas, B., Reingold, O.: Keyword search and oblivious pseudorandom functions. In: Kilian, J. (ed.) TCC 2005. LNCS, vol. 3378, pp. 303–324. Springer, Heidelberg (2005)
10. Goldreich, O., Goldwasser, S., Micali, S.: How to construct random functions. J. ACM 33(4), 792–807 (1986)
11. Goldreich, O., Micali, S., Wigderson, A.: How to play any mental game or a completeness theorem for protocols with honest majority. In: STOC, pp. 218–229 (1987)
12. Goldreich, O., Ostrovsky, R.: Software protection and simulation on oblivious RAMs. J. ACM 43(3), 431–473 (1996)
13. Hacigümüs, H., Iyer, B.R., Li, C., Mehrotra, S.: Executing SQL over encrypted data in the database-service-provider model. In: SIGMOD Conference, pp. 216–227 (2002)
14. Islam, M.S., Kuzu, M., Kantarcioglu, M.: Access pattern disclosure on searchable encryption: Ramification, attack and mitigation. In: NDSS (2012)
15. Jarecki, S., Jutla, C.S., Krawczyk, H., Rosu, M.-C., Steiner, M.: Outsourced symmetric private information retrieval. In: ACM Conference on Computer and Communications Security, pp. 875–888 (2013)
16. Jarecki, S., Liu, X.: Efficient oblivious pseudorandom function with applications to adaptive OT and secure computation of set intersection. In: Reingold, O. (ed.) TCC 2009. LNCS, vol. 5444, pp. 577–594. Springer, Heidelberg (2009)

17. Kushilevitz, E., Ostrovsky, R.: Replication is not needed: Single database, computationally-private information retrieval. In: FOCS, pp. 364–373 (1997)
18. Ostrovsky, R., Skeith III, W.E.: A survey of single-database private information retrieval: Techniques and applications. In: Okamoto, T., Wang, X. (eds.) PKC 2007. LNCS, vol. 4450, pp. 393–411. Springer, Heidelberg (2007)
19. Song, D.X., Wagner, D., Perrig, A.: Practical techniques for searches on encrypted data. In: IEEE Symposium on Security and Privacy, pp. 44–55 (2000)
20. Wang, S., Ding, X., Deng, R.H., Bao, F.: Private information retrieval using trusted hardware. In: Gollmann, D., Meier, J., Sabelfeld, A. (eds.) ESORICS 2006. LNCS, vol. 4189, pp. 49–64. Springer, Heidelberg (2006)

LPM: Layered Policy Management
for Software-Defined Networks [*]

Wonkyu Han[1], Hongxin Hu[2] and Gail-Joon Ahn[1]

[1] Arizona State University, Tempe, AZ 85287, USA
{whan7,gahn}@asu.edu
[2] Clemson University, Clemson, SC 29634, USA
hhu@desu.edu

Abstract. Software-Defined Networking (SDN) as an emerging paradigm in networking divides the network architecture into three distinct layers such as application, control, and data layers. The multi-layered network architecture in SDN tremendously helps manage and control network traffic flows but each layer heavily relies on complex network policies. Managing and enforcing these network policies require dedicated cautions since combining multiple network modules in an SDN application not only becomes a non-trivial job, but also requires considerable efforts to identify dependencies within a module and between modules. In addition, multi-tenant SDN applications make network management tasks more difficult since there may exist unexpected interferences between traffic flows. In order to accommodate such complex network dynamics in SDN, we propose a novel policy management framework for SDN, called layered policy management (LPM). We also articulate challenges for each layer in terms of policy management and describe appropriate resolution strategies. In addition, we present a proof-of-concept implementation and demonstrate the feasibility of our approach with an SDN-based simulated network.

Keywords: Policy Management, Software-Defined Networking, Security.

1 Introduction

Traditional network environments are ill-suited to meet the requirements of today's enterprises, carriers, and end users. Software-Defined Networking (SDN) was recently introduced as a new network paradigm which is able to provide unprecedented programmability, automation, and network control by decoupling the control and data layers, and logically centralizing network intelligence and state [6]. A typical architecture of SDN consists of three distinct layers such as application, control, and data layers. Network applications in the application layer can communicate with an SDN controller via an open interface and define network-wide policies based on a global view of the network provided by the controller. The SDN controller, which resides in the control layer, manages network services, and provides an abstract view of the network to the application layer. At the same time, the controller translates policies defined by applications into actual rules for processing packets, which are identifiable by the data layer.

---

[*] This work was partially supported by the grant from Department of Energy (DE-SC0004308).

V. Atluri and G. Pernul (Eds.): DBSec 2014, LNCS 8566, pp. 356–363, 2014.

The multi-layered SDN architecture significantly helps manage and process network traffic flows. However, each layer of SDN architecture heavily relies on complicated network policies and managing those policies in SDN requires not only dedicated cautions but also considerable efforts. Our study reveals that such a multi-layered architecture brings great challenges in policy management for SDN as follows:

- **Policy management in SDN application layer:** An SDN application could employ multiple modules, such as Firewall (FW), Load-Balance (LB), Route, and Monitor, to process the same flow by composing rules produced by those modules [9]. However, such a task is not trivial since rules may overlap each other within a module (intra-module dependency) or between modules (inter-module dependency).
- **Policy management in SDN control layer:** In SDN control layer, there may exist multiple SDN applications running on top of a controller and they might jointly process the same traffic flow. In such a situation, flow rules from different applications that process the same flow may also overlap each other (inter-application dependency) and even lead to policy conflicts [10].
- **Policy management in SDN data layer:** In SDN data layer, different flows may go through the same switches and rules defining different flows in the same flow table may also overlap each other (intra-table dependency). In such a case, an unintended modification of a flow path could happen.

To address the above-mentioned challenges, we propose a novel framework for managing policies with respect to three layers in SDN architecture. In SDN application layer, we adopt a policy segmentation mechanism to compute and eliminate intra-module and inter-module dependencies, and enable a secure and efficient policy composition. In SDN control layer, our framework identifies inter-application dependencies and provides two kinds of resolution strategies. In addition, we propose a flow isolation mechanism to resolve intra-table dependencies in SDN data layer. We also provide a prototype implementation of our framework in an open SDN controller and evaluate our approach using a real-world network configuration and an emulated OpenFlow network.

This paper is organized as follows. Section 2 overviews our framework and presents policy management challenges and corresponding resolution strategies based on three layers of SDN architecture. In Section 3, we describe our implementation details and evaluation results followed by the related work discussed in Section 4. Section 5 concludes this paper.

2 Layered Policy Management (LPM) Framework

2.1 Overview

Our LPM framework enables a layered policy management with respect to three layers of SDN architecture as illustrated in Figure 1.

In SDN application layer, a main challenge comes from policy composition in an SDN application, where intra-module and inter-module dependencies should be addressed. Partially or entirely overlapped rules in a module make nontrivial intra-module

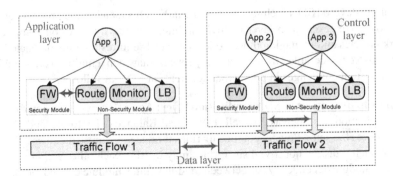

Fig. 1. Multi-layered SDN policy management: (i) application layer; (ii) control layer; and (iii) data layer

dependencies and make the process of policy composition more difficult. In addition, inter-module dependencies between security and non-security modules may cause security challenges due to inappropriate composition sequence and dynamic packet modification. Our framework addresses insecure and inefficient policy composition issues in an SDN application and adopts a policy segmentation mechanism to address those issues.

In SDN control layer, multiple applications in an SDN controller processing the same flow may cause inter-application dependencies. As shown in Figure 1, `App 2` and `App 3` intend to process the same flow `Flow 2`, thereby the policies produced by two applications may conflict with each other. Our framework also leverages the policy segmentation mechanism to eliminate the conflicts and applies two resolution strategies by allowing them to jointly process the same flow or assigning dependent applications with different priorities to break inter-application dependencies.

In SDN data layer, each physical switch stores a number of flow rules with corresponding priorities into its flow table. A rule defining one flow, such as `Flow 1` in Figure 1, with a lower priority might be affected by another rule for another flow, such as `Flow 2` in Figure 1, with a higher priority, causing intra-table dependency. Since intra-table dependency might change the behaviors of associated flows, our framework provides a flow isolation mechanism to address such an issue.

2.2   Policy Management in SDN Application Layer

Considerations and Challenges. While an SDN application with multiple modules processes a network traffic flow, a fundamental consideration is to address intra-module and inter-module dependencies in policy composition. To illustrate these issues, we adopt two kinds of policy composition operators introduced in [9]. "*Parallel*" operator (|) means the *union* of two modules and generates a set of packet processing rules which should be applied to the same flow simultaneously. "*Sequential*" operator ($\gg$) stands for the serialization of modules so that the matching rules would be performed one by one on the same flow. We next investigate several policy management challenges in SDN application layer.

Firewall Policy
r_1: src = 10.0.x.x, dst = 1.2.3.x → deny
r_2: dst = 1.2.3.4 → allow
r_3: src = 10.0.0.x, dst = 1.2.3.x → deny

Route Policy
r_5: src = 10.0.0.x, dst = 1.2.3.4 → fwd(1)
r_6: src = 10.2.2.2, dst = 1.2.x.x → fwd(2)
r_7: src = 10.2.2.2, dst = 1.2.3.x → fwd(3)

Load-balance Policy
r_4: src = 10.0.1.1, dst = 1.2.x.x → src = 10.2.2.2

Monitor Policy
r_8: src = 10.0.1.1, dst = 1.2.10.11 → count
r_9: src = 10.1.x.x, dst = 1.2.3.4 → count

Fig. 2. Sample policies defined by four different network modules

(1) *Intra-module and inter-module dependency*: Assume that there exist four different modules in an SDN application, such as Firewall (FW), Load-Balance (LB), Route, and Monitor, and all rules in each module have been sorted by their priorities as depicted in Figure 2. In FW policy, r_1, r_2, and r_3 are mutually dependent, and r_2 and r_3 are partially overlapped by r_1, representing intra-module dependencies. In addition, the rule r_1 in FW policy is dependent with both r_4 in LB policy and r_5 in Route policy, representing inter-module dependencies. Furthermore, since r_2 in FW policy is dependent with r_9 in Monitor policy, FW module is dependent with all other modules which implies that determining inter-module dependencies requires considerable efforts.

(2) *Insecure and inefficient policy composition*: Suppose that two modules in an SDN application are sequentially composed, represented as $LB \gg FW$. In this case, r_4 in LB policy modifies packets' source IP address to 10.2.2.2 and could enable malicious packets to bypass the firewall since r_1 in FW policy cannot block these packets. Hence, we could notice that an inaccurate sequence during the composition may cause security breaches in SDN applications. In addition, a programmer may want to compose two modules in parallel, such as $FW \mid Route$. We could observe that all rules in FW policy are dependent with r_5 in Route policy. Since r_1 has the highest priority, r_1 and r_5 can be jointly combined and the following rule can be obtained: $src = 10.0.0.x, dst = 1.2.3.4 \longrightarrow deny, fwd(1)$. Indeed, r_5 is not necessary to be composed with FW rules, since the FW rule r_1 ultimately blocks packets matching the rule pattern. Therefore, we could also observe that it is obviously inefficient to *always* compose the multiple policies as Pyretic [9] does.

As discussed above, there exist a few challenges in the application layer. First, since the security policies are generally considered more important than the policies produced by non-security modules, distinguishing security modules from non-security modules is vital in composing secure policies. In addition, commodity SDN switches typically support only a few thousands of rules [12], hence we should also strive to provide mechanisms with respect to an efficient policy composition.

Resolution Strategy. Our resolution approach globally examines all modules along with their rules to identify overlapping rules and generate disjointed matching space for removing intra-module and inter-module dependencies. To eliminate these dependencies, we first sort the rules in each module by their priorities and insert all modules into a global segmentation table. Derived from the approach discussed in [8], our policy segmentation mechanism generates a set of disjointed matching space, called *segment*. For example, r_1 and r_2 in FW policy are partially dependent with each other. Thus, we obtain three disjointed segments: $s_a = r_1 - r_2$, $s_b = r_2 - r_1$, and $s_c = r_1 \cap r_2$. Each segment maintains overlapping rules, which indicate the existence of intra-module or inter-module dependencies.

Regarding intra-module dependencies, not all overlapping rules from the same module in a segment are effective, since only one of those rules with the highest priority will be applicable to process matching packets. Therefore, to remove intra-module dependencies, we only need to consider the *effective* rule for policy composition. However, inter-module dependencies between security and non-security modules may cause insecure and inefficient policy composition as discussed above. To address such an issue, we distinguish security modules from non-security modules using a separator (:), which indicates that its left-hand side refers security modules with higher priorities while non-security modules are located on the right-hand side with lower priorities. At the same time, to achieve an efficient policy composition, our resolution only enables to composing *allow* rules from security modules with other rules from non-security modules since it is unnecessary to perform policy composition once a rule from security modules denies the matching space. For instance, the composition sequence, $LB \gg FW$, is not valid in our scheme since the separator (:) would distinguish security modules and non-security modules, i.e., $FW : LB$. In addition, our mechanism does not compose r_1 in FW policy with r_4 in LB policy. Because r_1 is a *deny* rule, our mechanism simply generates a *deny* flow entry without considering overlapping rules from non-security modules.

2.3   Policy Management in SDN Control Layer

Inter-application Dependency. The root cause for inter-application dependencies is that multiple SDN applications may attempt to enforce their policies over the same network flow. Suppose that APP 2 in Figure 1 composes LB, Route and Monitor modules sequentially, $LB \gg Route \gg Monitor$. However, APP 3 composes the same modules in the opposite order, $Monitor \gg Route \gg LB$. Incoming packets matching the source IP address 10.0.1.1 and the destination IP address 1.2.10.11 will be managed by two different applications, since both r_4 in LB policy and r_8 in Monitor policy can handle these packets. The APP 2 first applies r_4 in LB policy to modify the source IP address of matched packets to 10.2.2.2 and then applies r_6 in Route policy to forward them to port 2. Note that there is no matching rule in Monitor policy. On the other hand, the APP 3 first enforces r_8 in Monitor policy to count the packets of the same flow and then drops the matched packets because there is no matching rule in Route policy.

Resolution Strategy. In our resolution approach, we consider two situations: (i) different applications are allowed to jointly manage the same flow and (ii) applications are mutually exclusive. For the former case, we may allow inter-application dependencies and apply composition operators to combine multiple policies from different applications. With respect to the latter case, we eliminate inter-application dependencies by assigning different priorities to conflicting applications. Then, the application with the highest priority overrides the applications with the lower priorities when the flows are processed. For example, an application that employs security modules may have a higher priority to take the precedence over other normal applications. Different conflict resolution strategies proposed by our previous work [8] are also applied to resolve inter-application dependencies caused by conflicting applications.

2.4 Policy Management in SDN Data Layer

Intra-table Dependency. The flow paths of distinct flows managed by different SDN applications may overlap each other in the flow tables, introducing intra-table dependencies. For example, suppose that there exist two traffic flows processed by different applications as shown in Figure 1. One application, App 1, generates a policy for a flow Flow 1, which matches packets whose source and destination IP addresses are 10.2.2.2 and 1.2.3.4 respectively and forwards the packets to the port 2. On the other hand, another application App 2 manages a different flow Flow 2, but the generated policy modifies the source IP address of matched packets to 10.2.2.2 and forwards the packets to the port 2. Even though incoming packets of two flows might be different, outgoing packets for those flows may overlap with each other. Thus, this situation may cause a potential loss of flow control for an application if there exists an intra-table dependency between the flow paths.

Resolution Strategy. Our resolution approach for this layer is to remove intra-table dependencies through *flow isolation*. Inspired by the approach discussed in [7], which leverages tags to differentiate packets belonging to different versions of policies for enabling consistent network updates, we also utilize tags to eliminate the dependencies in a flow table. Using this strategy, a new flow policy is preprocessed by adding a tag to distinguish the matching pattern with other policies. The rule of the flow policy in the ingress switch will take additional action on the packets to label them with the same tag. When the packets leave the network, the corresponding rule of the flow policy in the egress switch will remove the tag from the packets.

3   Implementation and Evaluation

We have implemented our framework on top of an open SDN controller, Floodlight [1]. Our proof-of-concept implementation captures every flow rule created by applications and produces a set of segments, which are able to remove intra-module and inter-module dependencies. Also, our resolution strategy component obtains a global view of network from the Floodlight controller and utilizes various resolution strategies for SDN control layer and data layer.

Our experiments were performed with Floodlight v0.90 and Mininet v2.1.0 [3]. We obtained a *real-world* network configuration from Stanford backbone network [2], which has 26 switches with corresponding ACL rules. We removed redundant ACL rules, converted them to a FW policy, and in turn obtained 1, 206 FW rules in total.

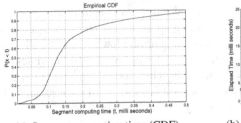
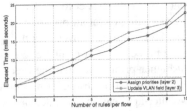

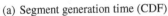

(a) Segment generation time (CDF)   (b) Elapsed time for resolution strategies

Fig. 3. Experimental results of our approach

At the same time, we generated 8,908 Floodlight-recognizable flow rules by parsing original network rules in Stanford network configuration. Because these real network rules perform both routing and load-balancing tasks, we assume that these rules are generated by two modules, *Route* and *LB* modules.

To measure overheads caused by our policy segmentation mechanism, we installed all network rules into the simulated network and measured the update operation of policy segmentation. Our experiments show that 456 segments out of 688 FW rules were produced by the policy segmentation mechanism and 8,273 segments out of 8,908 network rules were generated. As shown in Figure 3(a), 75% of updates were completed within 0.2 milliseconds and most of cases (98%) were computed in less than 0.5 milliseconds.

We also evaluated the performance of two resolution strategies: (i) assigning priorities to eliminate inter-application dependencies in the SDN control layer and (ii) updating VLAN fields (flow-tagging) to eliminate intra-table dependencies in the SDN data layer. Both resolution strategies update a set of flow rules which define corresponding flows. First, we measured elapsed time for assigning priorities of rules. As shown in Figure 3(b), the elapsed time grows in accordance with the increased number of rules per each flow. Similarly, we checked the elapsed time for updating VLAN fields for isolating conflicting flows. The elapsed time increases with the increased number of rules per each flow, as expected. However, it generally took more time, since our mechanism needs to figure out ingress and egress switches in examining flows, adding and striping VLAN tags from the packets.

4   Related Work

Modular network programming has recently received considerable attention in SDN community. For instance, Pyretic [9] enables a program to combine different policies generated by different modules together using policy composition operators. However, due to the lack of policy dependency detection mechanism in Pyretic, it is obviously inefficient to *always* compose the multiple policies and install them into the network switches. FRESCO [11] deals with security application development framework using modular programming for SDN, but it cannot directly handle dependencies between modules in SDN applications either. Several policy composition mechanisms such as [4,5] support *pair-wise* composition for access control policies and could be potentially utilized to deal with intra-module dependencies in SDN. In contrast, our framework addresses *various* dependencies including intra-module, inter-module, inter-application, and intra-table dependencies in SDN.

5 Conclusion

We have articulated numerous problematic issues and security challenges in SDN policy management and proposed a novel framework to facilitate a layered policy management approach with respect to three layers in the SDN architecture. Our experimental results with the proof-of-concept prototype showed that our resolution is efficient and only introduces manageable performance overheads to the networks. For the future work, we will extend our framework to support dynamic policy updates. In addition, we would expand our solution to support comprehensive SDN policy management considering heterogeneous and distributed controllers.

References

1. Floodlight: Open SDN Controller, http://www.projectfloodlight.org
2. Header Space Library, https://bitbucket.org/peymank/hassel-public
3. Mininet: An Instant Virtual Network on Your Laptop, http://mininet.org
4. Bandara, A.K., Lupu, E.C., Russo, A.: Using event calculus to formalise policy specification and analysis. In: Proceedings of the 4th IEEE International Workshop on Policies for Distributed Systems and Networks, pp. 26–39. IEEE (2003)
5. Bonatti, P., De Capitani di Vimercati, S., Samarati, P.: An algebra for composing access control policies. ACM Transactions on Information and System Security (TISSEC) 5(1), 1–35 (2002)
6. ONF Market Education Committee, et al.: Software-defined networking: The new norm for networks. ONF White Paper. Open Networking Foundation, Palo Alto (2012)
7. Fayazbakhsh, S.K., Chiang, L., Sekar, V., Yu, M., Mogul, J.C.: Enforcing network-wide policies in the presence of dynamic middlebox actions using flowtags. In: 11th USENIX Symposium on Networked Systems Design and Implementation (NSDI 2014), pp. 543–546. USENIX Association (2014)
8. Hu, H., Ahn, G.-J., Kulkarni, K.: Detecting and resolving firewall policy anomalies. IEEE Transactions on Dependable and Secure Computing 9(3), 318–331 (2012)
9. Monsanto, C., Reich, J., Foster, N., Rexford, J., Walker, D.: Composing software-defined networks. In: Proceedings of the 10th USENIX Conference on Networked Systems Design and Implementation, pp. 1–14. USENIX Association (2013)
10. Porras, P., Shin, S., Yegneswaran, V., Fong, M., Tyson, M., Gu, G.: A security enforcement kernel for openflow networks. In: Proceedings of the First Workshop on Hot Topics in Software Defined Networks, pp. 121–126. ACM (2012)
11. Shin, S., Porras, P., Yegneswaran, V., Fong, M., Gu, G., Tyson, M.: Fresco: Modular composable security services for software-defined networks. In: Proceedings of Network and Distributed Security Symposium (2013)
12. Stephens, B., Cox, A., Felter, W., Dixon, C., Carter, J.: Past: Scalable ethernet for data centers. In: Proceedings of the 8th International Conference on Emerging Networking Experiments and Technologies (CoNEXT 2012), pp. 49–60. ACM (2012)

On Minimizing the Size of Encrypted Databases

Giovanni Di Crescenzo and David Shallcross

Applied Communication Sciences, Basking Ridge, NJ, USA
{gdicrescenzo,dshallcross}@appcomsci.com

Abstract. Motivated by applications to maintaining confidentiality and efficiency of encrypted data access in cloud computing, we uncovered an inherent confidentiality weakness in databases outsourced to cloud servers, even when encrypted. To address this weakness, we formulated a new privacy notion for outsourced databases and (variants of) a classical record length optimization problem, whose solutions achieve the new privacy notion. Our algorithmic investigation resulted in a number of exact and approximate algorithms, for arbitrary input distributions, and in the presence of record additions and deletions. Previous work only analyzed an unconstrained variant of our optimization problem for specific input distributions, with no attention to running time or database updates.

1 Introduction

As the cloud computing paradigm is entering many of today's distributed computing applications, the research community is investigating a host of associated problems in many areas, including privacy, security, and algorithmic efficiency. One central cloud computing capability consists of outsourcing data to servers in the cloud, in a way that delegates the management of the data to the cloud servers while allowing efficient data access from authorized clients. In a typical instantiation of this capability, the data owner publishes a searchable database in the cloud and clients make their ordinary database queries directly to the cloud server. Because of confidentiality requirements on the data, and of the often unknown location of cloud servers as well as unknown entities who closely manage them, the data owner typically chooses to publish an encrypted version of the database, which can be later queried using privacy-preserving database retrieval protocols, and subject to compliance to specific query-based access policies. Unfortunately, encryption alone does not suffice to protect data confidentiality in these contexts, as encryption is known to hide all partial information but the length of the encrypted data. Accordingly, a cloud server with side channel information about the length of individual database records can derive confidential information about the content of the encrypted database. (As an example from the finance industry, if stock fund prospectuses are longer than single stock prospectuses, a cloud server can detect the relative density of stock funds and/or single stocks in the database, even if encrypted).

Our Contribution. Our approach to overcome these shortcomings consists of a suitable combination of padding short database records and splitting long database records so to normalize all records to have the same length, while still guaranteeing efficient access to them from clients. This approach calls for a new privacy model and a new optimization problem. In our privacy model, we require that the outsourced encrypted database

V. Atluri and G. Pernul (Eds.): DBSec 2014, LNCS 8566, pp. 364–372, 2014.

at most leaks a symmetric function of the original record lengths. Our optimization problem (a variant of a classical record length problem, studied in the statistical and computer memory management literature) is defined as follows: an encrypted database with a large number n of records of different sizes $s_1, \ldots, s_n \leq s_{max}$, needs to be normalized, via padding (e.g., adding a fixed string of a determined length) or splitting (e.g., dividing the record into 2 or more pieces and possibly padding again on the last piece) into a database with a potentially larger number n' of records, all having the same size σ. Padding obviously increases the database size, but so does splitting, as each record contains an a-bit searchable header, which has to be replicated on all pieces resulting from the record split. We want to find the (exactly or approximately) optimal σ so that the total size of the database (increased due to padding and splitting) is minimized under a constraint that bounds the increase in the maximum (or average) search time for a given record. For a cleaner problem formulation, applicable to any possible search strategy, we model this constraint by imposing an upper bound on the number of pieces derived from a split of any given record (or of all records, respectively).

Our exact algorithms perform $O(n \cdot s_{max})$ or $O(n + s_{max} \log s_{max})$ arithmetic operations (for both the unconstrained and the two constrained versions of our problem), which is super-polynomial in the input length (being linear in s_{max}). Our approximation algorithms can find c-approximate, for $c \sim 2$, solutions with $O(n)$ arithmetic operations (for both the unconstrained and the two constrained versions of our problem), and a $(1 + \epsilon)$-approximate solution with $O(n * \text{polylog}(s_{max}))$ arithmetic operations (for both the unconstrained and one constrained version of our problem). The latter algorithm can be shown to maintain a $(1 + \epsilon)$-approximated solution by only requiring $O(1)$ amortized arithmetic operations over a sequence of record additions and deletions, for any $\epsilon > 0$ and under very general parameter settings. (Descriptions of this result and our formal privacy model, and almost all proofs are omitted due to space restrictions.)

Related Work. In the model of databases outsourced to cloud servers, there is a significant amount of work on data encryption (seemingly originated in [7]), and some amount of work on privacy-preserving database retrieval protocols (see, e.g., [1]), and query-based access policy compliance (see, e.g. [2]). Minimizing the record length is an old problem considered in contexts like statistics and memory management, and that does not appear to have been investigated with an algorithmic viewpoint. An unconstrained version of our problem was introduced by [10], who showed that when record lengths follow some classes of continuous probability distributions, the optimal choice of target record length is a quantity close to our result for arbitrary distributions. In [9], the author analyzed this problem in terms of the characteristic function of the distribution of the record length, and gave solutions for the cases of the uniform, exponential, and geometric distributions. In [4] and [3], the authors considered several different target record sizes, and presented solutions based on dynamic programming and non-linear optimization techniques. In [8], the author considers a similar problem in an extended model (somehow merging multiple records into one), which does not preserve some of the database search functionalities. None of these works focused on minimizing the running time required to produce a solution for an arbitrary distribution of a discrete set of record lengths. We are also not aware of any work considering constrained versions of this problem or the case of dynamic databases.

2   Definitions, Privacy and Algorithmic Models

Preliminary Definitions. A *database* is an indexed sequence of records that can be modified, added, and removed over time. We denote as n the current number of records in the database. For $i \in \{1, \ldots, n\}$, the i-th database record can be seen as composed of two parts: the *header*, whose size $a \geq 1$ is constant across all records, and the *payload*, whose size $s_i \geq 1$ is variable. We denote as s_{max} the maximum integer among $s_1, \ldots, s_n$. We define a *fixed record length database* as a database where all record lengths are equal.

Privacy Model. We consider the following *Private Database Outsourcing* (PDO) problem: a data owner, on input a database, wants to outsource some version of the database to a cloud server so that the server only learns minimal information about the database content, and yet can engage in database retrieval protocols with one or more clients, as well as policy compliance protocols ensuring that clients' queries are authorized. In this paper we only deal with the database outsourcing part of the PDO problem, but note that our approach integrates well with privacy-preserving database retrieval solutions (e.g., from [1]) and privacy-preserving policy compliance solutions (e.g., from [2]). Encryption is a natural candidate tool to keep the outsourced database private from the server, who can still later run database retrieval and policy compliance protocols using techniques based on computing over encrypted data. Although in the cryptographic literature leakage of the length of an encrypted plaintext is usually considered a very minimal privacy violation (both the formal definitions of encryption [6] and of 2-party and multi-party private function evaluation protocols [11,5] admit leakage of plaintext/input lengths), leaking the lengths $s_1, \ldots, s_n$ of all database records may well be an unacceptable privacy loss. We then ask the natural privacy question of what could/should be kept private in any solution to the PDO problem. In a similar question on the encryption of multiple different-length messages, solutions used in practice include either (a) padding each message to its next block length, which leaks a close upper bound of all length values; or (b) padding all messages to a common block length, which, although not the most efficient solution, has more satisfactory privacy as it only leaks an upper bound of all length values. Both (a) and (b) leak the exact number of encrypted messages.

(Informal) Privacy requirement: In formulating our privacy model, we attempt to capture the satisfactory privacy properties of the solution approach in (b), and at the same time generalize it to allow for a richer set of solutions to the PDO problem. Specifically, we require any solution to the PDO problem to leak at most:

1. the output of a function that is *symmetric*[1] over the record lengths $s_1, \ldots, s_n$;
2. an upper bound on the number n of database records.

A formal description of this requirement can be provided in the simulation-based privacy framework and is omitted due to space restrictions.

Algorithmic Model. To transform any database into a fixed record length one, we only use two types of operations: (1) *padding* a payload; i.e., concatenating the payload with a predefined string (e.g., a 1 followed by an all 0's string), and (2) σ-*splitting* a record into multiple smaller records, where each new record has a copy of the same a-bit

---

[1] A function f is *symmetric* if it satisfies $f(x_1, \ldots, x_n) = f(x_{\rho(1)}, \ldots, x_{\rho(n)})$ for any input $(x_1, \ldots, x_n)$ and any permutation ρ over $\{1, \ldots, n\}$.

header and a distinct σ-bit piece of the original record's payload, where the last record may be padded so to have a σ-bit payload as well. Note that while the total length of the i-th record is $a + s_i$ in the original database, this length becomes $a + \sigma$ in the fixed record length database, for some σ that can be chosen from a set of allowed values P. In particular, we can consider, without loss of generality, $P = \{1, \ldots, s_{max}\}$, in which case for *any* $\sigma \in P$, any above defined database can be transformed into a fixed record length database via the following sequence of padding and σ-splitting operations, as follows: each record with payload shorter than σ can be padded and each s_i-bit record with payload longer than σ can be split into $\lceil s_i/\sigma \rceil$ records, the last one being padded. Then, we can compute the size of the fixed record length database as function

$$f(\sigma) = \sum_{i \in [n]} \left\lceil \frac{s_i}{\sigma} \right\rceil (\sigma + a), \tag{1}$$

where the input σ is taken from the set P which will usually be $\{1, \ldots, s_{max}\}$ or a subset of that, although in our analysis we will often abuse notation to consider σ taken from the set of real numbers. We then define our problem of interest as the problem of minimizing the Encrypted Database Size (EDS), as captured by the function f defined in Formula 1, and coming into two main variants, depending on the constraints that we pose on the number of splitting operations. In the first variant, denoted as maxEDS, there is a maximum number of pieces into which we may split any record payload. In the second variant, denoted as avgEDS, there is a maximum total number of pieces into which we may split all of the record payloads. Formal definition follows.

Definition 1. [EDS] Given $n + 1$ positive integers $a, s_1, \ldots, s_n$, find the integer σ from set $P = \{1, \ldots, s_{max}\}$ that minimizes $f(\sigma)$.

Definition 2. [maxEDS] Given $n + 2$ positive integers $a, s_1, \ldots, s_n, c_{max}$, find the integer σ from set $P = \{1, \ldots, s_{max}\}$ that minimizes $f(\sigma)$ subject to the constraints $\lceil s_i/\sigma \rceil \leq c_{max}$, for $i = 1, \ldots, n$.

Definition 3. [avgEDS] Given $n + 2$ positive integers $a, s_1, \ldots, s_n$ and c_{avg}, find the integer σ from set $P = \{1, \ldots, s_{max}\}$ that minimizes $f(\sigma)$ subject to the constraint $\sum_{i=1}^{n} \lceil s_i/\sigma \rceil \leq c_{avg}$.

We investigate algorithms that solve these problems either exactly (i.e., returning any σ^* that minimizes $f(\sigma)$), or δ-approximately (i.e., returning a σ such that $f(\sigma) \leq \delta f(\sigma^*)$), or δ-approximately even across a sequence of record additions and deletions. We will not try the approach of naturally extending f so that it is defined over all real numbers, and finding an analytical expression for a σ that exactly minimizes f as f is not convex, and is discontinuous at many points. To meet our privacy requirement we will only design algorithms $\mathcal{A}$ which return a value σ that is a symmetric function of the values $s_1, \ldots, s_n$. For the exact algorithms, this can be easily verified since these algorithms return the value σ that minimizes the function f defined in Formula 1, and f is a symmetric function of $s_1, \ldots, s_n$. For the approximate algorithms, this is verified by direct inspection that the formula used in each of these algorithms is also a symmetric function of $s_1, \ldots, s_n$.

3 Exact Algorithms

We discuss two exact algorithms: a naive algorithm that runs in time $O(n\sigma_{max})$ and an improved algorithm that runs in time $O(n + \sigma_{max} \log \sigma_{max})$.

A First Exact Algorithm. On input $a, s_1, \ldots, s_n$, define algorithm $\mathcal{A}_{0,1}$ for the EDS problem as follows: for each value σ from P, evaluate $f(\sigma)$ using Formula (1); finally, select the value σ that minimizes $f(\sigma)$. This algorithm finds an optimal solution for EDS in $O(n|P|) = O(ns_{max})$ arithmetic operations. By further checking that the constraint is satisfied, this algorithm is directly extended to find an optimal solution for maxEDS and avgEDS in the same asymptotic running time.

A Second Exact Algorithm. As a potential improvement, we consider algorithm $\mathcal{A}_{0,2}$ that precomputes two sets of values related to the multiplicities of the payload sizes, and uses an alternative expression for $f(\sigma)$ that is faster to compute, given the precomputed values. Specifically, the precomputed values consist of the multiplicities of the payload sizes $m_v = |\{i \in N : s_i = v\}|$, and the related values $m_v^+ = |\{i \in N : s_i \geq v\}|$, defined for all $v \in P$. We note the following

Fact 1. For each $v = 1, \ldots, s_{max}$, it holds that $m_v^+ = m_{v+1}^+ + m_v$.

The alternative expression for $f(\sigma)$ is the following:

$$f(\sigma) = \sum_{h=1}^{\lceil s_{max}/\sigma \rceil} \sum_{i:\lceil s_i/\sigma \rceil = h} \left\lceil \frac{s_i}{\sigma} \right\rceil (\sigma + a) \qquad (2)$$

$$= \sum_{h=1}^{\lceil s_{max}/\sigma \rceil} h \left(m_{1+\sigma(h-1)}^+ - m_{1+\sigma h}^+ \right) (\sigma + a) \qquad (3)$$

Based on these definitions, we define algorithm $\mathcal{A}_{0,2}$ for the EDS problem, as follows:

Algorithm $\mathcal{A}_{0,2}$: On input $a, s_1, \ldots, s_n$, do the following:

1. Calculate s_{max}
2. Calculate m_v, for each v from 1 to s_{max}.
3. Calculate m_v^+, for each v from s_{max} down to 1, using recurrence relation in Fact 1.
4. Calculate $f(\sigma)$, for each σ in P, using Formula (3).
5. Return the value σ_f^* that minimizes f.

For the running time, we observe that steps 1, 2 and 3 can be run in time $O(n)$, step 4 in time $O(s_{max} \log s_{max})$ (that is, $O(s_{max}/\sigma)$, for $\sigma = 1, \ldots, s_{max}$), and step 5 in time $O(s_{max})$. This algorithm is directly extended to find an optimal solution for maxEDS by further checking that the constraint is satisfied, which can be done in time $O(n)$. Checking that the constraint for avgEDS is satisfied can be done in time $O(s_{max} \log s_{max})$ by observing that the left hand side of the constraint can be rewritten similarly as in Formula (3). Thus, algorithm $\mathcal{A}_{0,2}$ can be extended to work for maxEDS and avgEDS by keeping the same asymptotic running time. We obtain the following

Theorem 1. For each of the problems EDS, maxEDS and avgEDS, we can construct an algorithm that exactly solves the problem in $O(\min\{ns_{max}, n + s_{max} \log s_{max}\})$ arithmetic operations.

The running time in Theorem 1 is not polynomial in the input length (as it is linear in s_{max}) and can be too expensive in practical large databases (e.g., when $n \geq 10^9$ and $s_{max} \geq 10MB$). Thus, we turn our attention to finding approximation algorithms with faster running times (possibly, linear in n and polylogarithmic in s_{max}). As both the algorithm's running time and the quality of the approximation are of interest, we study algorithms that attempt to minimize one metric while achieving satisfactory performance on the other one. Specifically, we study algorithms with constant approximation factor and very fast running time (i.e., $O(n)$) in Section 4, and algorithms with very small (i.e., $(1 + \epsilon)$, for any $\epsilon > 0$) approximation factor and any running time improving over $\mathcal{A}_{0,1}$ and $\mathcal{A}_{0,2}$ in Section 5.

4 Faster Algorithms with O(1) Approximation Factor

In this section we study algorithms for maxEDS and avgEDS that attempt to minimize their running time while achieving a constant approximation factor. When compared with the exact algorithms in Section 3, the algorithms in this section achieve a smaller running time (only linear in n and with no dependency on s_{max}) at the cost of achieving approximation factor 2 or slightly greater than 2. We start with a definition useful for both algorithms; we define function g over the set of real numbers, as follows:

$$g(\sigma) = \sum_{i=1}^{n} \left(\frac{s_i}{\sigma} + 1 \right)(\sigma + a), \tag{4}$$

Then, our first algorithm, for problem maxEDS, and its properties are as follows.

Algorithm $\mathcal{A}_1^{max}$: On input $a, s_1, \ldots, s_n, c_{max}$, compute $\bar{s} = \sum_{i=1}^{n} s_i/n$ and then $\sigma_g^* = \sqrt{a\bar{s}}$, and then return σ, computed as the value among $\lfloor \sigma_g^* \rfloor, \lceil \sigma_g^* \rceil, \lceil s_{max}/c_{max} \rceil$ that is at least $\lceil s_{max}/c_{max} \rceil$ and results in the smaller value for $f(\sigma)$.

Theorem 2. $\mathcal{A}_1^{max}$ 2-approximately solves the maxEDS problem in $O(n)$ arithmetic operations.

An algorithm $\mathcal{A}_1$ for problem EDS with the same running time and approximation factor can be obtained by directly simplifying $\mathcal{A}_1^{max}$. We cannot directly adapt these techniques to avgEDS, as a value for σ satisfying the equality in constraint $\sum_{i=1}^{n} \lceil s_i/\sigma \rceil \leq c_{avg}$ may be hard to find, due to the n rounding operations. Instead, we minimize the approximating function g subject to an even tighter constraint, and bound the additional error produced. We now define an algorithm for avgEDS and state its properties.

Algorithm $\mathcal{A}_1^{avg}$: On input $a, s_1, \ldots, s_n, c_{avg}$, compute the quantities $\beta = c_{avg}/n$ and $\bar{s} = \sum_{i=1}^{n} s_i/n$. Then check whether $\lfloor \sqrt{a\bar{s}} \rfloor \geq \bar{s}/(\beta - 1)$. If yes, set s_g^* the value among $\lfloor \sqrt{a\bar{s}} \rfloor$ and $\lceil \sqrt{a\bar{s}} \rceil$ that has a lower value of function g, as defined in Formula 4. If not, set $s_g^* = \lceil \bar{s}/(\beta - 1) \rceil$. Finally, return s_g^*.

Theorem 3. $\mathcal{A}_1^{avg}$ $(2 + 1/\bar{s} + 1/(\beta(\beta - 1)))$-approximately solves the avgEDS problem in $O(n)$ arithmetic operations, where $\beta = c_{avg}/n$.

5 Fast Algorithms with $(1 + \epsilon)$ Approximation Factor

We show an algorithm for maxEDS (and thus EDS) that achieves $(1+\epsilon)$ approximation factor, for any $\epsilon > 0$, and running time asymptotically smaller than the exact algorithms described in Section 4. Our algorithm extends the technique used in Section 4 where we approximated function f by a convex function g. Here, we approximate function f with several functions g_k, for any integer $k > 0$. First, for any integers $k > 0$ and any real number $x > 0$, we define $w(k, x)$ as $\lceil x \rceil$ if $x \leq k - 1$ or $1 + x$ if $x > k - 1$. Then, for any integer $k > 0$, we define an approximation function g_k to f as

$$g_k(\sigma) = \sum_{i \in N} w\left(k, \frac{s_i}{\sigma}\right)(\sigma + a)$$

Note that for $k = 1$, function g_1 is the same as function g defined in Section 4, where we have showed that g can be computed in time $O(n)$. For $k > 1$, we can still evaluate function g_k more efficiently than f, using some auxiliary variables and a suitable piece-wise decomposition and rewriting of g_k. A first set of definitions relevant to this goal include the previously defined quantities m_v, m_v^+ and some new quantities $b_v, c_{h,v}$, defined as follows, for each $v = 1, \ldots, s_{max}$, and each integer $h > 0$:

1. $b_v = \sum_{s_i \geq v} s_i$; and
2. $c_{h,v} = |\{i \in N : \lceil s_i/v \rceil = h\}|$.

To reduce the number of candidate σ values from P from which we plan to evaluate $g_k(\sigma)$, for any integer k and any $j = 0, \ldots, q$, where q is the max value such that $(1 + \epsilon)^q * \lceil s_{max}/c_{max} \rceil \leq s_{max}$, we define the quantities:

1. $\tau_0 = \lceil s_{max}/c_{max} \rceil$, $\tau_j = \lceil (1 + \epsilon) * \tau_{j-1} \rceil$;
2. $M_j = |\{i \in N : 1 + \tau_j(k - 1) \leq s_i < \tau_{j+1}(k - 1)\}|$; and
3. $B_j = \sum_{s_i \geq 1 + \tau_j(k-1)}^{\tau_{j+1}(k-1)} s_i$.

By applying the definitions of $m_v, M_j, b_v, B_j, c_{h,\sigma}, m_v^+$, we derive the following

Fact 3. For each $j = 0, \ldots, q$ and each integer $h > 0$, it holds that
1. $m_{1+\tau_j(k-1)}^+ = m_{\tau_{j+1}(k-1)}^+ + M_j$
2. $b_{1+\tau_j(k-1)}^+ = b_{\tau_{j+1}(k-1)}^+ + B_j$
3. $c_{h,\tau_j} = m_{1+\tau_j(h-1)}^+ - m_{1+\tau_j h}^+$

We can then evaluate $g_k(\sigma)$, for all $\sigma = \tau_0, \tau_1, \ldots, \tau_q$, as

$$g_k(\sigma) = \sum_{h=1}^{k-1} \sum_{i:\lceil s_i/\sigma \rceil = h} \left\lceil \frac{s_i}{\sigma} \right\rceil (\sigma + a) + \sum_{i:s_i/\sigma > k-1} \left(1 + \frac{s_i}{\sigma}\right)(\sigma + a) \quad (5)$$

$$= \left(\sum_{h=1}^{k-1} c_{h,\sigma} h\right)(\sigma + a) + \left(m_{1+\sigma(k-1)}^+ + b_{1+\sigma(k-1)}^+ \frac{1}{\sigma}\right)(\sigma + a) \quad (6)$$

Based on the above, we can now construct our algorithm $\mathcal{A}_2^{max}$, by setting $k = \lceil 1/\epsilon \rceil$, quickly computing g_k based on Formula 6 and Fact 3, approximating f with g_k, and minimizing g_k subject to the constraint $\lceil s_{max}/\sigma \rceil \leq c_{max}$ and σ varying over the multiplicative grid of $\tau_0, \ldots, \tau_q$.

Algorithm $\mathcal{A}_2^{max}$: On input $a, s_1, \ldots, s_n, c_{max}, \epsilon$, do the following:

1. Calculate s_{max} and set $k = \lceil 1/\epsilon \rceil$.
2. Calculate all M_j, for $j = 0, \ldots, q$ by scanning all s_i's only once and, for each s_i, using binary search to find the associated M_j.
3. Calculate all B_j, for $j = 0, \ldots, q$ by scanning all s_i's only once and, for each s_i, using binary search to find the associated B_j.
4. Calculate $m^+_{1+\tau_j(k-1)}$, for $j = 0, \ldots, q$, using recurrence relation in Fact 3, item 1.
5. Calculate $b_{1+\tau_j(k-1)}$, for $j = 0, \ldots, q$, using recurrence relation in Fact 3, item 2.
6. Calculate c_{h,τ_j}, for $j = 0, \ldots, q$, and $h = 1, \ldots, k-1$, using recurrence relation in Fact 3, item 3.
7. Choose the value $\sigma^*_{g,k}$ that minimizes g_k, by examining every value of σ from $\{\tau_0, \tau_1, \ldots, \tau_q\}$ and using Formula (6) to evaluate $g_k(\sigma)$.

Theorem 4. For any $\epsilon > 0$, $\mathcal{A}_2^{max}$ $(1 + \epsilon)$-approximately solves the maxEDS problem in $O(n \log(\log(c_{max})/\epsilon) + \log c_{max}/\epsilon^2)$ arithmetic operations.

Acknowledgement. We thank Euthimios Panagos for interesting discussions. This work was supported by the Intelligence Advanced Research Projects Activity (IARPA) via Department of Interior National Business Center (DoI/NBC) contract number D13PC00003. The U.S. Government is authorized to reproduce and distribute reprints for Governmental purposes notwithstanding any copyright annotation hereon. Disclaimer: The views and conclusions contained herein are those of the authors and should not be interpreted as necessarily representing the official policies or endorsements, either expressed or implied, of IARPA, DoI/NBC, or the U.S. Government.

References

1. Di Crescenzo, G., Cook, D., McIntosh, A., Panagos, E.: Practical private information retrieval from a time-varying, multi-attribute, and multiple-occurrence database. In: Atluri, V., Pernul, G. (eds.) DBSec 2014. LNCS, vol. 8566, pp. 337–352. Springer, Heidelberg (2014)
2. Di Crescenzo, G., Feigenbaum, J., Gupta, D., Panagos, E., Perry, J., Wright, R.: Practical and Privacy-Preserving Policy Compliance for Outsourced Data. In: Proc. of 2nd WAHC Workshop (2014)
3. Erickson, R.E., Halfin, S., Luss, H.: Optimal Sizing of Records when Divided Messages Can Be Stored in Records of Different Sizes. Operations Research 30, 29–39 (1982)
4. Erickson, R.E., Luss, H.: Optimal Sizing of records Used to Store Messages of Various Lengths. Management Science 26, 796–809 (1980)
5. Goldreich, O., Micali, S., Wigderson, A.: How to Play any Mental Game or A Completeness Theorem for Protocols with Honest Majority. In: Proc. of ACM STOC 1987, pp. 218–229 (1987)
6. Goldwasser, S., Micali, S.: Probabilistic Encryption. J. Comput. Syst. Sci. 28(2), 270–299 (1984)

7. Hacigümüs, H., Iyer, B.R., Li, C., Mehrotra, S.: Executing SQL over encrypted data in the database-service-provider model. In: Proc. of SIGMOD Conference 2002, pp. 216–227 (2002)
8. Luss, H.: An Extended Model for the Optimal Sizing of Records. Journal of Operation Research Society 34, 1099–1105 (1983)
9. Sipala, P.: Optimum Cell Size for the Storage of Messages. IEEE Transactions on Software Engineering SE-7, 132–134 (1981)
10. Wolman, E.: A Fixed Optimum Cell-Size for Records of Various Lengths. Journal of the ACM 12, 53–70 (1965)
11. Yao, A.C.: How to Generate and Exchange Secrets. In: Proc. of IEEE FOCS 1986, pp. 162–167 (1986)

Efficient and Enhanced Solutions for Content Sharing in DRM Systems

Michal Davidson[1], Ehud Gudes[2], and Tamir Tassa[1]

[1] The Open University, Ra'anana, 43100, Israel
michalsaraw@gmail.com, tamirta@openu.ac.il
[2] Ben-Gurion University, Beer-Sheva, 84105, Israel
ehud@cs.bgu.ac.il

Abstract. We present a solution to the problem of content sharing in digital rights management (DRM) systems. Users in DRM systems purchase content from content providers and then wish to distribute it between their own devices or to other users. The goal is to allow the sharing of such content, with the control of the content provider, while ensuring that it complies with the content's usage rules. While most of the previous studies on content sharing in DRM systems assume the existence of authorized domains, ours does not make that assumption. The solutions that we present here are based on Certified Sharing Requests which are used when devices request from the content provider authorization to share content with other devices. Our solutions enhance the usability of DRM, from both the users' and content provider's perspective, by supporting on-the-fly sharing, sharing and re-sharing of controlled content, and a pay-per-share business model.

Keywords: digital rights management, content sharing, authorized domain, proxy re-encryption.

1 Introduction

The usage of Digital Rights Management (DRM) in the digital media industry is controversial, since it limits the use of legally purchased content, and it does not allow certain scenarios that were previously possible. One of the main controversies with DRM systems is with regard to content sharing. When physical or DRM-free content is purchased it can be shared, copied, and re-sold. On the other hand, in DRM systems, the content provider (CP) wants to control such content sharing, and ideally would like to get paid whenever such content is further shared with other users.

Most current solutions for content sharing propose and expand upon the use of an "Authorized Domain" — a group of devices which can freely share content between themselves [1]. However, such solutions have two main drawbacks: they do not support "on the fly" sharing, namely, sharing between devices that do not belong to the same domain; and they do not offer means to control which content can be shared between two devices.

V. Atluri and G. Pernul (Eds.): DBSec 2014, LNCS 8566, pp. 373–381, 2014.
© IFIP International Federation for Information Processing 2014

In this paper we propose solutions for content sharing that do not rely upon authorized domains. A recent scheme that solves the content sharing problem without assuming authorized domains was proposed by Ma et al. [2]. Their scheme uses a proxy re-encryption method [3] which allows re-encryption of a message without decrypting it first. Although this method is elegant and secure (see its detailed description in the next section), it involves a considerable overhead in terms of storage, and it relies on the complex cryptographic primitive of bilinear pairing. Moreover, the implementation of the pairing in [2] dictates using the El-Gamal public key cryptosystem and prevents using other public key methods like the prevalent RSA cryptosystem. Finally, the solution in [2] does not support re-sharing of purchased content with other users, or a flexible payment scheme.

Here we address the above two problems and present a simpler scheme for controlled sharing in DRM systems. Our scheme is called the *Certified Sharing Request (CSR) Scheme*. It supports "on the fly" sharing, re-sharing to any pre-set depth, verification of content-dependent sharing privileges, CP knowledge of sharing, and a pay-per-share business model. We achieve those functional objectives while ensuring common security and privacy properties.

2   Background and Related Work

2.1   Definitions

Digital Rights Management ("DRM") is a method for controlling the viewing and distribution of digital content. A DRM system consists of the following entities:

- Content (C) - a purchasable item of digital content. The content is distributed in an encrypted format, using a symmetric encryption, and can only be decrypted using the corresponding content key.
- Content License (CL)- a record that includes the content key and a set of usage rules. Content licenses are typically encrypted using public key encryption.
- Content Provider (CP) - The entity that owns the content items and wishes to control the distribution of the content to its client devices.
- Device (will be denoted by A, B, A_0, A_1 etč.) - a tamper proof computer processing unit that is capable of parsing and decrypting the encrypted content and the encrypted content licenses. Each device holds a secret key and a corresponding certificate, which is signed by a Certificate Authority. We assume that the device's secret key, as well as the content keys which the device extracts from content licenses, are securely stored and processed in a trusted hardware device (so called Trusted Computing Base, or TCB) and cannot be accessed by a third party.

2.2   Related Work and Content Sharing with Proxy Re-encryption

Most literature on the topic of content sharing within DRM systems focuses on the use of the Authorized Domain model [1]. This is the classic DRM solution for content sharing, in which a group of authorized devices are defined as belonging to a joint domain, and devices within the same domain can freely share content between them.

The studies [4,5] suggest improvements in the authorized domain model. Other studies do not assume that model: Sadeghi et al. [6] provide a secure platform on open systems which allows the usage of dynamic licenses; Lee et al. [7] propose a system for content sharing which relies on time-based rights.

A recent work on DRM and content sharing [2] uses the method of proxy re-encryption [3]. The method in [3] allows users who received a message that was encrypted with their public key to re-encrypt it for other users without decrypting it first. They describe two types of probabilistic public key encryption functions — *first* and *second level encryptions*. If (sk_A, pk_A) denotes the private and public key pair of user A, then $E_\ell(m, pk_A)$, $\ell = 1, 2$, denote the first and second level encryptions of the plaintext m for user A. User A may decrypt any ciphertext in $E_\ell(m, pk_A)$ using his private key sk_A. In addition, he may re-encrypt $E_2(m, pk_A)$ into $E_1(m, pk_B)$ without decrypting it first. Their method uses bilinear pairings that are based on the Tate pairing [8]. We now proceed to describe the content sharing solution of [2].

Purchasing Content. When device A requests from the CP to purchase content C, the CP sends to A a message $x \in E_1(m, pk_A)$, where $m = CL$ is the content license of the requested content. In addition, the CP generates a random key pair (sk_R, pk_R) and sends to A a message $y \in E_2(m, pk_R)$. Finally, it adds to its records a new record that holds the identifiers of A and C, the generated random key pair, and a counter of the number of times in which A shared C so far. After the purchasing protocol is completed, A uses the message x to recover the content license CL, with which it can decrypt the encrypted content.

Sharing Content. When device A wishes to share the purchased content C with another device B, it sends a corresponding request to the CP. The CP checks the details of the two devices A and B, and the number of times in which A had already shared that particular content. If that sharing request is approved, the CP computes a re-encryption key, rk, using B's public key pk_B and the random private key sk_R that was generated when A purchased that content, and sends it to A. A uses rk together with the message y which it received upon purchasing that content in order to compute a ciphertext $z \in E_2(m, pk_B)$, by means of bilinear pairing. Device A then sends z together with the encrypted content to device B. B proceeds to recover the content license m and decrypt the content.

There are several disadvantages to this solution: (a) Payment for sharing content can only be performed by the device A who is sharing the content; a better business model would be for the device B to pay to the CP for the shared content. (b) This model requires that the CP stores a record for each device and each purchased content, where each record stores the corresponding counter and a pair of cryptographic keys. (c) The method is limited to only one level of sharing; it does not allow device B to re-share the content with another device. (d) The method relies upon the complex and costly bilinear pairing function. (e) The usage of bilinear pairings in [2] is based on El-Gamal public key cryptography and, thus, prevents using other public key cryptosystems, such as RSA.

3   Certified Sharing Requests (CSR) and the CSR Scheme

Here we present our solution for content purchasing, sharing and re-sharing. We describe how a given device A_0 can purchase content C from the CP; how A_0 may share C with another device A_1; how A_1 can re-share C with A_2; and, in general, how to perform re-sharing of any depth.

While in the proxy re-encryption solution A_0 re-encrypts the content licence for A_1, in our solution the CP encrypts the content license for A_1. We chose to transfer the task of encrypting the content license from A_0 to the CP for the following reasons: (a) The CP must be involved in any such sharing or re-sharing operation since it needs to verify that the sharing or re-sharing is consistent with the usage rules for the content C. Hence the CP can also encrypt the content license for the new device. (b) In [2], the process of re-encryption can be performed only once per content and device, and thus does not support re-sharing. In our scheme, the CP can perform a direct encryption rather than re-encryption, hence re-sharing of any depth is possible.

Our solution is based on Certified Sharing Requests (CSRs). The CSRs include: information on the content C, the certificates of the devices that are involved in the sharing and re-sharing operations, and payment information. The CSRs are signed by all involved devices. The mechanism of CSRs is flexible enough to support interoperability between DRM systems; namely, a device in one DRM system can share content with a device that belongs to a different DRM system, under the above assumptions. This will allow content providers to charge devices for "pay per sharing", regardless of the DRM system to which they belong.

3.1   Purchasing Content

Here we describe the process that takes place when a device, A_0, wishes to purchase a certain content, C. At the completion of this process, A_0 receives from the CP three items: (a) the content C, encrypted by a symmetric encryption using the content key k_C; (b) the content license (which includes k_C), encrypted by A_0's public key; and (c) a corresponding sharing license, denoted SL, which will be used only when A_0 chooses to share C with other devices. Note that in the entire paper the content license and the content itself can be decrypted only by the TCB, so no key in the clear (i.e., non-encrypted key) can be sent out by the device.

When A_0 wishes to purchase a content C, the following protocol is executed:

1. A_0 sends to the CP a message with A_0's certificate and C's ID.
2. The CP verifies A_0's certificate, and that it is not revoked, then encrypts the content license $m = $ CL of C with A_0's public key, creates a corresponding sharing license SL, and certifies it by signing it. The signed sharing license will be denoted by $[SL, Sig_{CP}]$. The CP then sends to A_0 the encrypted content, the encrypted content license, and the signed sharing license.
3. The CP creates and stores a record of the form (A_0, C, ST_{C,A_0}), where ST_{C,A_0} is a counter of the number of times in which A_0 shared the content C with other devices; it is initialized to zero.
4. A_0 also creates a counter ST_C for the number of times that it shared the content C with other devices.

The sharing license SL which the purchasing device A_0 receives upon purchasing the content C will be used when A_0 wishes to share that content with another device A_1. The SL will contain the following fields: (1) C (the ID of the purchased content); (2) GDI (the Global Device ID of A_0); (3) MSL (Maximum Sharing Level), denoting the depth of permitted sharing for C; and (4) NoS (Number of Sharings), bounding the total number of devices that can receive the shared content from A_0 by means of sharing or re-sharing.

3.2   Sharing Content

When A_0 wishes to share C with A_1, the following protocol is executed.

1. A_0 sends to A_1 the message $[SL, Sig_{CP}, COD]$ where $[SL, Sig_{CP}]$ is the certified sharing license that A_0 received from the CP when it purchased C, and COD (Charge Original Device) is a field that indicates which device will be charged for the content sharing: $COD = 0$ means that A_0 will be charged, while $COD = 1$ means that A_1 will be charged.
2. A_1 adds to the received message its certificate $Cert_{A_1}$ and a payment information field EPI. EPI includes the information needed to charge A_1 for performing this sharing, if $COD = 1$; otherwise, if $COD = 0$, EPI is empty.
3. A_1 sends to A_0 the message $[SL, Sig_{CP}, COD, Cert_{A_1}, EPI, Sig_{A_1}]$, where the last field is A_1's signature on the preceding fields in the message.
4. A_0 verifies that the internal counter ST_C which it maintains for the content C is smaller than NoS (the value that appears in SL), and that A_1 did not alter the value COD. If those verifications passed successfully then A_0 increments ST_C and signs the sharing request. The result is called a CSR (Certified Sharing Request):

$$CSR_1 := [SL, Sig_{CP}, COD, Cert_{A_1}, EPI, Sig_{A_1}, Sig_{A_0}].$$

Here, Sig_{A_0} is the signature of A_0 on all preceding fields in CSR_1.
5. A_0 sends CSR_1 to the CP.

6. The CP performs the following verifications: (a) the three signatures in CSR_1; (b) neither of the devices A_0, A_1 is revoked; (c) the MSL field, as appears in SL, is at least 1; and (d) it retrieves the record (A_0, C, ST_{C,A_0}) and checks that $ST_{C,A_0} < NoS$ (and if so, it increments the value of ST_{C,A_0}). If all verifications were successful, the CP encrypts the content license with A_1's public key and sends it to A_1 (either via A_0 or directly).
7. A_0 sends to A_1 the encrypted content. (Recall that A_0 already has the encrypted content, since it received it from the CP upon purchasing it.)
8. A_1 decrypts the content license using his private key in order to recover the content key. It then proceeds to decrypt the content using that key.

Note that the device A_0 has to verify the internal counter ST_C in Step 4 in the protocol above in order to refrain from unnecessary communications vis-a-vis the CP. The CP repeats the same check (Step 6d) since it does not trust A_0, but, as explained above, the check by A_0 in Step 4 is still necessary for communication overhead considerations. We note that if the check in the device is performed in the TCB, it can prevent Denial of Service attacks.

3.3   Re-sharing Content

Assume that a specific content C was already shared by the following chain of devices, $A_0, A_1, \ldots, A_{i-1}$; i.e., A_0 purchased that content from the CP, and then it shared it with A_1, who continued to share it with A_2, and so forth. Below we describe how A_{i-1} can re-share the content with a new device A_i. Before doing so, we comment that if the field COD equals 0, then, as before, it means that A_0 will pay for that re-share; however, if $COD = 1$ then the recipient of the content in the re-sharing operation (i.e., A_i in this case) will be charged for that operation.

The re-sharing protocol proceeds as follows:

1. Device A_{i-1}, that already possesses $[SL, Sig_{CP}, COD, Cert_{A_1}, \ldots, Cert_{A_{i-1}}]$ from the protocol that took place when it obtained the shared content, sends this sharing request to A_i.
2. A_i adds to the sharing request its certificate $Cert_{A_i}$ and the payment information field EPI (where $COD = 1$) or an empty EPI (where $COD = 0$).
3. A_i sends to A_{i-1} the sharing request

$$[SL, Sig_{CP}, COD, Cert_{A_1}, \ldots, Cert_{A_{i-1}}, Cert_{A_i}, EPI, Sig_{A_i}],$$

   where the last field is A_i's signature on the preceding fields in the message.
4. The message is sent up the chain of devices, where device A_j adds its own signature on the message that it received from A_{j+1}, and then sends it to A_{j-1}, $j = i - 1, \ldots, 1$.
5. A_0 verifies that ST_C is smaller than NoS, and that A_i did not alter the value COD. If those verifications passed successfully then A_0 increments ST_C and signs the sharing request. The resulting CSR is:

$$CSR_i := [SL, Sig_{CP}, COD, Cert_{A_1}, \ldots, Cert_{A_i}, EPI, Sig_{A_i}, \ldots, Sig_{A_0}].$$

6. A_0 sends CSR_i to the CP.
7. The CP performs the following verifications: (a) it verifies all $i+2$ signatures that appear in CSR_i; (b) none of the devices $A_0, \ldots, A_i$ is revoked; (c) the MSL field, as appears in SL, is at least i; and (d) it retrieves the record (A_0, C, ST_{C,A_0}) and checks that $ST_{C,A_0} < NoS$ (and if so, it increments the value of ST_{C,A_0}).
8. If all verifications were successful, the CP encrypts the content license with A_i's public key and sends it to A_i (either via A_0 or directly).
9. A_{i-1} sends to A_i the encrypted content. (Recall that A_{i-1} already has the encrypted content, since A_{i-2} shared it with him.)
10. A_i decrypts the content license using his private key in order to recover the content key. It then proceeds to decrypt the content using that key.

3.4   The Partial Trust Scenario

Due to space limitations, we focused in this paper on a scenario of non-trust, where devices that are direct clients of the CP are not granted any trust regarding the right to authorize a sharing request. The CP does not delegate to A_0 any verification tasks; it performs all necessary checks before sending out the content license encrypted for the new device. The disadvantage in such a non-trust scenario is greater storage and performance overhead. In the full version of this paper we present a relaxed scenario of partial trust, in which the CP has a partial trust in its direct client devices. In particular, device A_0 is trusted to do most of the verification which is currently done by the CP in the full-trust scenario. Therefore, in such a model, the storage and computational costs for the CP are reduced significantly.

3.5   Advantages and Disadvantages of the CSR Scheme

The CSR scheme supports re-sharing, where the depth and number of re-sharings can be set upfront and controlled. Payment can be made by either the device which originally purchased the content from the CP or from the device which is the recipient in the re-sharing act, what allows a more flexible pay-per-share business model. Compared to the proxy re-encryption scheme, the CP has to store a smaller database that holds only the counter per device per content, without the need to store a pair of cryptographic keys. In the partial trust scenario the amount of data that needs to be stored by the CP is further reduced, since the CP has to store just one counter per device (and not per device per content). Finally, the CSR scheme does not rely upon the complex and costly bilinear pairing function.

When comparing the security of the proxy-reencryption and the CSR scheme, we see that in both schemes public key encryption is used to protect the content license which contains the content key. In addition, the sharing requests in the CSR scheme are always signed, by the tamper-proof TCB, so that they are authenticated and cannot be repudiated. This is an advantage over the proxy re-encryption solution which does not use signatures, and thus is vulnerable to both man-in-the-middle attacks, and Denial of Service (DOS) attacks. Both solutions require each device to have a trusted computing base (TCB). The TCB of A_0 is not required by the proxy re-encryption solution for content sharing, since the re-encryption can be performed on the device itself without exposing either the content key or the device's secret key. In the CSR scheme, on the other hand, any action that involves signatures is a TCB operation. Hence, both schemes depend on a TCB, but in the CSR scheme the overhead on the TCB is greater due to the use of signatures. The conclusion is that the security of both schemes is comparable, but the CSR scheme is advantageous in terms of protecting sensitive information on the CP, in providing authentication and non-repudiation to sharing requests, and in reducing the risk of DOS and man-in-the middle attacks.

4   Conclusions and Future Work

We proposed a scheme for content sharing in a DRM system. Content sharing is performed using a Certified Sharing Request (CSR). In contrast to most related work on content sharing in DRM systems, our approach does not rely on the Authorized Domain model. The CSR model improves upon the limitations of the Authorized Domain model by supporting "on-the-fly" sharing, controlled content sharing and re-sharing, and a pay-per-share business model. We propose versions of our CSR scheme both for the fully secure non-trust scenario and for the partial trust scenario with improved performance.

In the future, we would like to enhance the CSR scheme by supporting privacy preservation, i.e. allowing content sharing where the content provider receives payment and sends a content license while remaining oblivious of the identity of the user who purchased that content. We intend to investigate the application of proxy re-encryption in order to support privacy preservation within the CSR scheme. We may also refine the payment model, and define in more depth the rules whereby the content provider should halt sharing in the partial trust scenario.

References

1. Popescu, B.C., Crispo, B., Tanenbaum, A.S., Kamperman, F.: A DRM security architecture for home networks. In: Digital Rights Management Workshop, pp. 1–10 (2004)
2. Ma, G., Pei, Q., Jiang, X., Wang, Y.: A proxy re-encryption based sharing model for DRM. Int'l J. of Digital Content Tech. and its Applications 5(11), 385 (2011)
3. Ateniese, G., Fu, K., Green, M., Hohenberger, S.: Improved proxy re-encryption schemes with applications to secure distributed storage. ACM Trans. Inf. Syst. Secur. 9(1), 1–30 (2006)
4. Abbadi, I.M.: Digital rights management using a master control device. In: Cervesato, I. (ed.) ASIAN 2007. LNCS, vol. 4846, pp. 126–141. Springer, Heidelberg (2007)

5. Sheppard, N.P., Safavi-Naini, R.: Sharing digital rights with domain licensing. In: The ACM Workshop on Multimedia Content Protection and Security, pp. 3–12 (2006)
6. Sadeghi, A.-R., Wolf, M., Stüble, C., Asokan, N., Ekberg, J.-E.: Enabling fairer digital rights management with trusted computing. In: Garay, J.A., Lenstra, A.K., Mambo, M., Peralta, R. (eds.) ISC 2007. LNCS, vol. 4779, pp. 53–70. Springer, Heidelberg (2007)
7. Lee, S., Kim, J., Hong, S.J.: Redistributing time-based rights between consumer devices for content sharing in DRM system. Int. J. Inf. Sec. 8(4), 263–273 (2009)
8. Galbraith, S.D., Harrison, K., Soldera, D.: Implementing the tate pairing. In: Fieker, C., Kohel, D.R. (eds.) ANTS 2002. LNCS, vol. 2369, pp. 324–337. Springer, Heidelberg (2002)

A Scalable and Efficient Privacy Preserving Global Itemset Support Approximation Using Bloom Filters

Vikas G. Ashok[1] and Ravi Mukkamala[2]

[1] State University of New York, Stony Brook, NY 11794, USA
vganjiguntea@cs.stonybrook.edu
[2] Old Dominion University, Norfolk, VA 23529, USA
mukka@cs.odu.edu

Abstract. Several secure distributed data mining methods have been proposed in the literature that are based on privacy preserving set operation mechanisms. However, they are limited in the scalability of both the size and the number of data owners (sources). Most of these techniques are primarily designed to work with two data owners and extensions to handle multiple owners are either expensive or infeasible. In addition, for large datasets, they incur substantial communication/computation overhead due to the use of cryptographic techniques. In this paper, we propose a scalable privacy-preserving protocol that approximates global itemset support, without employing any cryptographic mechanism. We also present some emperical results to demonstrate the effectiveness of our approach.

Keywords: Privacy Preserving Set Union Protocol, Privacy Preserving Data Mining, Secure Multiparty Computation.

1 Introduction

With the increasing need for global data mining, mining of data dispersed among a wide variety of data owners, several schemes have been developed in literature. In addition, the ever increasing awareness for preserving privacy of individuals and organizations has prompted the development of several privacy-preserving global data mining schemes. In this paper, we focus our attention on secure global set operation algorithms. Current techniques in this area are primarily based on data perturbation and secure multiparty computation (SMC) [1–3].

In the case of data perturbation based techniques, each data owner deliberately distorts its private data before sharing it with a third party data miner. The onus now is on the data miner to use special techniques to reconstruct the original distribution of the received perturbed data for data mining purposes. In the SMC approach of [2], data owners securely perform global data mining without revealing individual private data. While data perturbation techniques (e.g. [4]) trade utility for privacy and suffer from security problems, SMC

V. Atluri and G. Pernul (Eds.): DBSec 2014, LNCS 8566, pp. 382–389, 2014.

techniques (e.g. [3]) are in general expensive in terms of computation and communication overhead since they may depend on encryption mechanisms.

The goal of our work is to present an efficient scalable and privacy preserving protocol for secure set union computation that does not rely on any cryptographic techniques and requires minimum cooperation between the participating data sites. In our approach, we strategically decompose a single bloom filter representing an itemset at each data source into several *partial* bloom filters that can be shared with other sites without violating privacy. Our cooperative protocol ensures that the final result obtained from operations on these *partial* bloom filters is the same as that obtained from a naive protocol employing the original undecomposed bloom filters without any privacy concerns. We also show that our protocol performs better than some of the well known approaches with respect to the overall communication cost. We present a brief discussion of the related work next.

2 Background

A standard Bloom filter [5] uses an m bit array to represent a set S where all m bits are initially set to 0. Every element $x \in S$ is hashed using k independent uniform hash functions $h_1(), \ldots, h_k()$ each with the range $\{1, \ldots, m\}$ and the corresponding bits $h_i(x)$ in the array are set to 1. Any membership query can therefore be addressed by simply hashing the query element y using the same k hash functions and checking if the corresponding bits in the Bloom filter array are set to 1.

It has been shown in [9] that the number z of 0 bits in a Bloom filter for a set S is strongly concentrated around its expectation $m(1 - 1/m)^{k|S|}$. Therefore, given z, m and k, we can approximate the size of S using (1).

$$|S| = \frac{\ln(z/m)}{k \ln(1 - 1/m)} \tag{1}$$

The secure computation performed by previous work (e.g. [7,8]) typically refer to the cooperative determination of set intersection/union cardinality for itemsets distributed across several sites. To the best of our knowledge, all existing approaches (e.g. [7,8]) rely on some encryption mechanism for their effective operation, thereby making them either unscalable or cost intensive. Our approach overcomes these deficiencies by employing Bloom filters.

3 Problem Statement

We assume that there are $n \geq 2$ data sites which independently collect similar data for a sample of individuals belonging to some population $\mathcal{P}$. Each site (or data owner) $S_i, 1 \leq i \leq n$, has data for a sample $\mathcal{D}_i$ drawn from population $\mathcal{P}$. Each transaction in $\mathcal{D}_i$ is assumed to have a unique identifier TID (e.g., SSN, driver's license number, etc.). Overlaps between samples at different sites may exist; the data corresponding to the same individual may exist at multiple sites. The goal is to determine the overall global support of an itemset, without violating privacy of individual private data. In other words, for a given itemset X and a site S_i, if $L_i(X)$ denotes the set of TIDs of transactions in $\mathcal{D}_i$ that contain X, the goal is to preserve individual privacy while estimating the global support $(s_g(X))$ of X given by $|\bigcup_{1 \leq i \leq n} L_i(X)|$.

With respect to privacy, we assume an *Honest-but-Curious* (HBC) adversary model [10]. Informally, in the HBC model, the participating parties correctly observe the protocol but they may utilize any information exchanged in the intermediate stages of the protocol to learn certain private details about individuals. Therefore, the privacy requirement in this model states that any party should not be able to learn anything more than what can be deduced from the final output of the multiparty computation.

4   Privacy Preserving Global Itemset Support Computation Protocol

This protocol involves direct communication among the sites (data owners) without any third party. The main idea behind the protocol is based on the following observation: determining global support $s_g(X) = |\bigcup_{1 \leq i \leq n} L_i(X)|$ for an itemset X is approximately equivalent to determining the number of elements hashed into the global Bloom filter $BF_G(X)$ using (1), where the set of hashed elements in BF_G equals $\bigcup_{1 \leq i \leq n} L_i(X)$. Therefore, the task boils down to computing $BF_G(X)$ in a privacy preserving manner. The protocol is shown in Algorithm 1. It involves two phases, decomposition and reconstruction, described below.

4.1   Decomposition

In the decomposition phase, each site S_i generates n Bloom filters BF_j^i, $1 \leq j \leq n$, one for each of the n sites, which are individually incomprehensible/incomplete but collectively represent $L_i(X)$. Therefore, each of these component Bloom filters can be *safely* shared with another participating site without any concern of privacy violation. To generate these BF_j^i, $1 \leq j \leq n$, we propose a *partial Bloom filter construction* technique that leverages the services of *GenerateLocalKeys* routine presented in Algorithm 1.

In this technique, given an itemset X, a site S_i uses only subsets of publicly known k hash functions to generate any Bloom filters for $L_i(X)$. Both the size and composition of these subset of hash functions are private to S_i. In our protocol, since we generate n component Bloom filters, we need n such subsets of hash functions. In addition, each hash function has to appear in at least one of these subsets so that the Bloom filters collectively represent $L_i(X)$.

The *GenerateLocalKeys* function (Algorithm 1) produces n random subsets (Keys) of **indices** of k Bloom filter hash functions such that each of the k indices appear in at least one subset or Key. As seen in Algorithm 1, in the initialization phase (lines 22–26 in Algorithm 1), n keys are initialized with random subsets

---

Algorithm 1. Protocol for global support approximation of itemset X

Input: $n \geq 2$, $L_i(X)$ for $1 \leq i \leq n$, m, X, and $H = h_1, \ldots, h_k$ such that $k > n$.

Output: Global support $s_g(X)$ and global Bloom filter $BF_G(X)$.

1: **for all** Sites S_i, $1 \leq i \leq n$ **do**

                                                     ▷ Phase 1: Decomposition

2:     $Keys \leftarrow GenerateLocalKeys(k, n)$

3:     **for** $j = 1$ *to* n **do**

4:         $BF_j^i \leftarrow CreateBloomFilter(Keys[j], L_i(X))$

5:         Send BF_j^i to site S_j

6:     **end for**

                                                  ▷ Phase 2: Reconstruction

7:     initialize temporary variable BF_i' to 0.

8:     **for** $j = 1$ *to* n **do**

9:         Receive BF_i^j from site S_j.

10:        $BF_i' \leftarrow BF_i' \vee BF_i^j$

11:     **end for**

12:     Send BF_i' to all sites.

                                          ▷ Merge intermediate results

13:     Initialize $BF_G(X) \leftarrow BF_i'$.

14:     **for** $j = 1$ *to* n **do**

15:        Receive BF_j' from site S_j.

16:        $BF_G(X) \leftarrow BF_G(X) \vee BF_j'$

17:     **end for**

18:     $s_g(X) =$ Approximate size of $BF_G(X)$ using equation 1.

19: **end for**

20: **procedure** GENERATELOCALKEYS(k, n)

     Private: random subset length parameters a, b.

21:     Create a set $K \leftarrow \{1, 2, \ldots, k\}$

     Initialize: Create n random subsets of K, each of random size r.

22:     **for** $i = 1$ to n **do**

23:        $r = RandomNumber(a, b), 1 \leq a < b < k$

24:        $K' = RandomSubset(K, r)$

25:        $Keys[i] \leftarrow K'$

26:     **end for**

     Finalize: Ensure that all hash functions in HS are considered.

27:     **for** $hf = 1$ to k **do**

28:        $r' = RandomNumber[1, n]$

29:        $Keys[r'] = Keys[r'] \cup \{hf\}$

30:     **end for**

31:     return $Keys$

32: **end procedure**

33: **procedure** CREATEBLOOMFILTER($Key, List$)

34:     Create set $H' \leftarrow \{h_j | j \in Key\}$

     Create BF by hashing $List$ using H'.

35:     Return BF

36: **end procedure**

---

of K, where K is the set of all Bloom filter hash function indices. The size of these initialized keys can be controlled using private parameters a and b. In the finalization phase (lines 27–30 in Algorithm 1), we ensure that each hash function index is present in at least one key. In other words, the k hash function indices are randomly distributed among the n keys just like throwing k balls into n bins assuming that each ball is equally likely to fall into any one of the n bins. The index subsets generated by *GenerateLocalKeys* function are then used by the *CreateBloomFilter* subroutine (Algorithm 1) to produce the *partial* Bloom filters.

At the end of the decomposition phase, partial bloom filter BF_j^i is sent to S_j, for every $1 \leq j \leq n$. This sharing is *safe* since the size and composition of $Keys[j]$ used in generating BF_j^i is unknown to S_j. Note that it is not a wise decision to share more than one *partial* Bloom filter with a single site as it is publicly known that these bloom filters collectively represent $L_i(X)$ and therefore may allow adversary to make stronger assumptions about the content of $L_i(X)$.

4.2   Reconstruction

The reconstruction phase is simple and based on the following insight - the global bloom filter BF_G is simply the bitwise 'or' of all the bloom filters generated by all the sites in the decomposition phase.

By the end of the decomposition phase, every site S_i receives BF_i^j, $1 \leq j \leq n$, at the beginning of the reconstruction phase. Therefore, as a first step, the protocol performs a bitwise 'or' of all received BF_i^j and broadcasts the corresponding intermediate result to all other sites. For example, S_1 performs $BF_1^1 \vee BF_1^2 \ldots \vee BF_1^n$ and sends the result of this operation to all sites. Once S_i receives all intermediate bloom filters from other sites, another round of Bitwise OR operation yields the global bloom filter BF_G. The global support $s_g(X)$ can then be obtained from BF_G using (1).

4.3   Privacy Analysis

The extent of privacy achieved by our protocol depends on the confidence with which a site S_i can predict the number and identities of hash functions used by another site S_j, $j \neq i$ for generating BF_i^j. This is because the knowledge of the number of hash functions can reveal the size of the input set through (1) and the knowledge of identities of used hash functions can reveal private data at any site. It is easy to notice that no meaningful information can be deduced from individual analysis of BF_j', $1 \leq j \leq n$, received during reconstruction phase as these bloom filters are composed of various *partial* chunks belonging to different sites. Therefore, we limit our focus to BF_i^j, $1 \leq j \leq n$, received at the beginning of reconstruction phase.

For a given bloom filter BF_i^j received by S_i from S_j, let T be a random variable indicating the number of hash functions used by S_j to generate BF_i^j. Also, let E_x denote the event that x hash function indices were placed in $Keys[i]$ after

Table 1. Commnication cost of various protocols. Notation: s - average size of input set of $TIDs$ and $|P|$ - domain size of input set $TIDs$

Protocol	Communication Cost(bits)
Commutative encryption (Vaidya [7])	$O(n(2n-2)s * EncryptionSize)$
Homomorphic encryption (Kissener [8])	$O(n^2 s \log_2 |P| * EncryptionSize)$
Proposed protocol	$2n(n-1)m$

initialization phase of $GenerateLocalKeys$ subroutine and let E'_y be the event that $Keys[i]$ is selected y times during finalization phase of $GenerateLocalKeys$ subroutine.

$\Pr\{T = t\}$ represents the probability that t hash functions were used in generating BF_i^j. Ideally, we expect this probability to be low for all possible values of t, or in other words the distribution of $\Pr\{T = t\}$ to be uniformly spread out. $\Pr\{T = t\}$ can be computed using the law of total probability as shown in equation (2).

$$\Pr\{T = t\} = \sum_{x=a}^{b} \sum_{y=0}^{k} \Pr\{E_x \cap E'_y\} \Pr\{T = t|(E_x \cap E'_y)\} \tag{2}$$

Since E and E' are mutually independent events, $\Pr\{E_x \cap E'_y\}$ is simply the product of $\Pr\{E_x\}$ and $\Pr\{E'_y\}$. Informally, $\Pr\{T = t|(E_x \cap E'_y)\}$ represents the probability of obtaining t distinct hash functions as a result of union between two random subsets of hash functions having sizes x and y respectively. Therefore, $\Pr\{T = t|(E_x \cap E'_y)\}$ has a non-zero value shown in (3), only when both $x, y \le t$ and $x + y \ge t$.

$$\Pr\{T = t|(E_x \cap E'_y)\} = \frac{\binom{k-x}{t-x}\binom{x}{y-(t-x)}}{\binom{k}{y}} \tag{3}$$

The probability of determining the identities of hash functions H used in generating BF_i^j can therefore be computed as $\frac{\Pr\{T=|H|\}}{\binom{k}{|H|}}$. These probabilities are typically small as shown in the experimental section. Next, we evaluate the cost of our protocol.

4.4 Cost Analysis

Table 1 compares the communication cost of our protocol with existing popular cryptography dependent approaches proposed in [7] and [8]. The communication cost in our approach is easy to derive since each site transmits $(n-1)m$ bits of information to other sites **twice** during the execution of the protocol. As seen in Table 1, our approach reduces the communication cost to a considerable extent since, in practice, $m << s * EncryptionSize$. In addition, the absence of encryption tends to lower the computation cost as well.

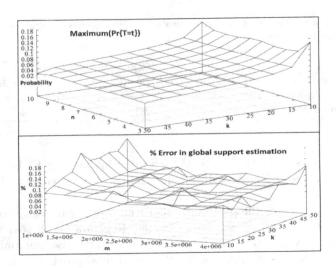

Fig. 1. (top:) Height of density function of T given n and k. (bottom:) Percentage error in global support approximation where actual support is $100,000$.

5   Empirical Results and Analysis

In this section, we study the impact of various protocol parameters on accuracy and privacy of the global frequent itemset mining. As explained earlier, while accuracy is dependent on correct estimation of global union cardinality using equation (1), privacy is dependent on the high confidence prediction of the number (T) and identity of hash functions constituting the keys generated privately using *GenerateLocalKeys*.

Let the height of a probability distribution of T given n and k be defined as the maximum value on the curve representing that distribution. Obviously, smaller the height, better the privacy. Figure 1(top) shows the heights of different probability curves of T obtained by varying the number of sites n and total hash functions k. It is observed that irrespective of n, the height is lowered when k is increased. However, k cannot be arbitrarily increased as it adds to both computation and communication overhead (since $m \propto k$).

We now look at the accuracy measure. In order to assess the impact of m and k on accuracy, we plot average percentage error in global support estimation for an itemset X in Figure 1(bottom) where actual global support $s_g'(X)$ is $100,000$. Specifically, for a given combination of m and k, we plot $\frac{Abs(s_g'(X)-s_g(X))}{s_g'(X)} \cdot s_g(X)$. $s_g(X)$ is computed by averaging results over $10,000$ runs. Each of the runs constitutes a simple experiment where we first insert $s_g'(X)$ random elements into a Bloom filter. We compute the number of 0s (z) in the Bloom filter, and then estimate the size of input set from z using (1). As observed in Figure 1(bottom), the global support approximation method is very robust as the maximum percentage error for this scenario is 0.18%. Also, for a few values of m (1.5, 2.5 million bits), the error is very low and independent of k.

In summary, the proposed method has mechanisms to control the accuracy and privacy of the resulting global frequent itemsets obtained through data mining across different data owners.

6   Conclusions and Future Work

In this paper, we looked at an efficient mechanism to approximate global frequent itemset support from data owned by several independent data owners. The primary objectives that inspired the protocol development were local data privacy, scalability, reduced communication and computational cost, and finally high accuracy. While the earlier schemes in literature had high accuracy and privacy, they were deficient in offering scalability and efficiency due to extensive use of cryptographic mechanisms. On the other hand, we employed bloom filters as a means to preserve privacy across data owners. We also carried out empirical analysis of the protocol and determined the relationship between the parameter values of the protocol and the resulting accuracy and privacy. In future, we plan to extend this work by building full-scale prototypes of the protocol to validate the results and gain a deeper understanding of the impact of the hash functions on the performance.

References

1. Liu, K., Kargupta, H., Ryan, J.: Random projection-based multiplicative data perturbation for privacy preserving distributed data mining. IEEE Trans. Knowledge and Data Engg. 18(1), 92–106 (2006)
2. Lindell, Y., Pinkas, B.: Privacy preserving data mining. In: Bellare, M. (ed.) CRYPTO 2000. LNCS, vol. 1880, pp. 36–54. Springer, Heidelberg (2000)
3. Kantarcioglu, M., Nix, R., Vaidya, J.: An efficient approximate protocol for privacy-preserving association rule mining. In: Theeramunkong, T., Kijsirikul, B., Cercone, N., Ho, T.-B. (eds.) PAKDD 2009. LNCS, vol. 5476, pp. 515–524. Springer, Heidelberg (2009)
4. Kargupta, H., Datta, S., Wang, Q., Sivakumar, K.: On the privacy preserving properties of random data perturbation techniques. In: Proceedings of the Third IEEE International Conference on Data Mining (ICDM 2003), November 19-22. IEEE Computer Society, Los Alamitos (2003)
5. Bloom, B.H.: Space/time Trade-offs in Hash coding with Allowable Errors. Communications of the ACM 13(7), 422–426 (1970)
6. Qiu, L., Li, Y., Wu, X.: Preserving privacy in association rule mining with Bloom filters. Journal of Intelligent Information Systems 29(3), 253–278 (2007)
7. Vaidya, J., Clifton, C.: Secure set intersection cardinality with application to association rule mining. Journal of Computer Security 13(4), 593–622 (2005)
8. Kissner, L., Song, D.: Privacy-preserving set operations. In: Shoup, V. (ed.) CRYPTO 2005. LNCS, vol. 3621, pp. 241–257. Springer, Heidelberg (2005)
9. Andrei, A., Mitzenmacher, M.: Network applications of Bloom filters: A survey. Internet Mathematics 1(4), 485–509 (2004)
10. Goldreich, O.: Foundations of Cryptography. Basic Applications, vol. 2. Cambridge University Press (2009)

Author Index